An Introduction to

BUSINESS and MANAGEMENT

An Introduction to
BUSINESS and MANAGEMENT

Edited by

Rossana Guttilla and
Christine Parkin Hughes

Sage

3rd Floor
HYLO
103–105 Bunhill Row
London, EC1Y 8LZ
UK

2455 Teller Road
Thousand Oaks
California 91320

10th Floor, Emaar Capital Tower
2 MG Road, Sikanderpur, Sector 26
Gurugram, Haryana – 122002
India

8 Marina View Suite 43-053
Asia Square Tower 1
Singapore 018960

Editor: Ruth Stitt
Assistant editor: Clara Landgren
Production editor: Martin Fox
Marketing manager: Elena Asplen
Cover design: Sheila Tong
Typeset by: C&M Digitals (P) Ltd, Chennai, India
Printed in the UK by Bell & Bain Ltd, Glasgow
BB00361777

Library of Congress Control Number: 2025944989

British Library Cataloguing in Publication data

A catalogue record for this book is available from the British Library

ISBN 978-1-03-623116-3
ISBN 978-1-03-623115-6 (pbk)

CONTENTS

ONLINE RESOURCES

Introduction to Business and Management is supported by a range of additional resources for lecturers to support teaching, which are available at: **https://study.sagepub.com/guttilla-parkinhughes**

FOR LECTURERS

- A comprehensive **Teaching Guide** with step-by-step guidance, ideas for tutorials and seminars, and case study teaching notes.
- **PowerPoint Decks**, which can be adapted and edited to suit your own teaching needs.
- A **Testbank** of multiple-choice questions to support assessment.
- A **Resource Pack**, which allows you to upload the testbank directly to your university's virtual learning management system.

Set up or use your instructor login to access these lecturer resources.

ABOUT THE EDITORS

Dr Rossana Guttilla is a Senior Lecturer in HRM and OB at the University of Exeter Business School, with over 20 years' experience in UK higher education. She has directed Business Management programmes at both the University of Exeter and the University of Plymouth, leading large, diverse cohorts and delivering high-impact modules in IHRM, general management, and graduate skills. Her academic interests include IHRM, curriculum design and skills development. She co-developed the University of Exeter's *Skills to Thrive* and currently serves as Induction and Transition Coordinator and Wellbeing Champion for the school. Rossana was the recipient of the 2023 *Course of the Year award* and a 2022 nomination for *Academic of the Year*. A Senior Fellow of the HEA, active member of BAM and book reviewer for Sage, CIPD and OU, she is committed to nurturing academic, personal, and professional growth through innovative and reflective learning – the core focus of this foundational text.

Professor Christine Parkin Hughes is a Senator at the University of Exeter. She is the *Director of Education and Student Experience* for the Management department, and the *Educational Director of the Exeter Centre for Leadership* (ExCL). Chris also leads the Organisational Behaviour & Human Resources Subject Department. Her research centres around sustainability in the workplace. Having begun her teaching career over 25 years ago, she is a multi-award-winning educator and Qualified Teacher (QTS), Senior Fellow of the Higher Education Academy (SFHEA), and a Certified Management and Business Educator (CMBE). Externally, Chris is an Examiner, Moderator and Validator, levels 1–8. She is also a Trustee and Member of the People and Nominations Committee for The Royal College of Occupational Therapists.

ABOUT THE CONTRIBUTORS

Abdulrahman Mahmoud is a Senior Lecturer and Director of Education at the University of Exeter Business School. He holds a PhD from Coventry University and is a Fellow of the Higher Education Academy. His teaching focuses on operations and business analytics.

Adam Smith is a business leader, consultant and educator within local and global high innovation environments. He has worked for 5 years as Senior Lecturer and Director with the University of Aberdeen Business School and has 20 years of C-suite experience across service, manufacturing and engineering industries.

Adrian Ball leads Workplace Learning at the University of Exeter, enhancing degree apprenticeships through its mentoring provision. With 30 years in financial services, he brings expertise in leadership, resilience, and coaching, inspired by his experience as an ultramarathon runner.

Ahmed ElKattan is a Lecturer in Business Analytics and Deputy Programme Director for the MSc Business Analytics, University of Exeter since 2024. Prior to this, he worked as a teaching fellow in marketing research and analytics at the University of Surrey, UK. He has over 10 years of experience in academia across different countries (UK, France, Spain, and Egypt). He is also a certified instructor in artificial intelligence (AI) and Python (HCIA-AI).

Alison Sydenham is a Senior Lecturer in Management and Programme Director for the Senior People Professional Apprenticeship at the University of Exeter. Her research focuses on the impact of workplace coaching on mental well-being.

Andreas Georgiou is a Lecturer in Sustainable Entrepreneurship at the University of Exeter Business School. His research explores the role of place and community in entrepreneurial phenomena, as well as the factors that contribute to sustainable and resilient cities and communities.

Beth Kewell is a Senior Lecturer at INDEX, Exeter, specialising in interpretive research at the intersection of innovation, STS, and risk. Her work explores digital technologies, blockchain, data ethics, and risk society through qualitative, epistemic, and philosophical lenses.

Bill Russell is a Senior Lecturer in Innovation at the University of Exeter Business School. After 25+ years working in the automotive, motorsport and publishing sectors he now teaches innovation to students and practitioners in organisations such as Amazon, JP Morgan, Panasonic and the Bank of England.

Chris Reedthomas is a Lecturer in Leadership and Management at the University of Exeter Business School. With over 25 years as a leadership coach, educator and organisational development consultant, Chris is committed to helping students connect academic learning with real world leadership and management challenges.

Clare Hearn is a Senior Lecturer in Leadership & Management at University of Exeter. She is passionate about supporting students to develop the strategic skills of analysis, creativity and ethical innovation to support their current and future organisational practice.

Colleen Smith is a Lecturer/Academic Mentor at the University of Exeter Business School, supporting students on the Degree Apprenticeship Management programmes. She has a background in corporate recovery and insolvency law having worked in the public and private sector.

David Chambers-White is a Senior Lecturer at the University of Exeter specialising in business law and management. He is passionate about teaching and life-long learning and about inspiring, supporting and helping to develop the next generation of business and legal professionals.

David Kolitz is a Senior Lecturer in the Business School at the University of Exeter. He was previously Associate Professor and Assistant Dean in the Faculty of Commerce, Law and Management at the University of the Witwatersrand. He is an experienced accounting academic and author with a special interest in accounting education.

David Walker is a Senior Lecturer in Computer Science at the University of Exeter with research interests on the interface between multi-objective optimisation, evolutionary computation, explainable AI, and hyper-heuristics. He is Director of Education and Student Experience for the Department of Computer Science.

Edvard Glücksman is Faculty Director of Education in Sustainability at the University of Exeter, specialising in the relationship between organisations and the environment. Drawing from his biosciences background, Edvard's teaching encourages development of evidence-based sustainability solutions using innovative, experiential methods.

Emma Sweeney is the Insessional and TESOL Academic Manager at the University of Exeter International Study Centre. She has more than 20 years' experience teaching intercultural communication and English for specific and academic purposes. Her passion is facilitating students to develop the confident interpersonal communication skills they need to thrive at university and beyond.

Emma Wood is Senior Lecturer in Marketing at the University of Exeter and Programme Director for the MSc Digital Marketing. Having come to education following 20 years working in marketing and environmental communications, Emma is passionate about supporting students to develop the skills they will need to face the challenging and rapidly changing workplace.

Erno Tornikoski is a Professor of Entrepreneurship at the MBSC in Saudi Arabia since February 2025. He was Professor of Entrepreneurship and the Director of the Centre for Entrepreneurship at the University of Exeter between March 2019 and October 2024.

Fernando Correia joined Exeter Business School in 2022 as Senior Lecturer in Sustainable Business. With over 20 years' experience, his academic and consultancy work spans sustainable tourism, low-carbon economies, leadership, and skills for sustainability across sectors and geographies.

Frank Donkor, Programme Director for MSc Operations Management at the University of Exeter, specialises in supply chain sustainability, operations management, leadership in supply chains, degree apprenticeships, and industry-academic collaboration in the pharmaceutical sector in both developed and developing countries. Frank uses both quantitative and qualitative research methods for his research.

Fujia Li is Senior Lecturer in Innovation and Entrepreneurship and Director of Strategic Education Portfolio for the Innovation, Technology, and Entrepreneurship (ITE) sub-department at University of Exeter. His research interests lie in entrepreneurship and responsible innovation. He leads inclusive curriculum design, pedagogical innovation, and scalable education strategies with interdisciplinary impact.

Hannah Collis is a Lecturer in Leadership and Organisational Behaviour at the University of Exeter. Her research explores individual differences at work, and how work environments and styles can impact employee outcomes. As an educator, she is passionate about encouraging personal development and adapting to demands.

Isbahna Naz is a Lecturer in Organisational Behaviour and Human Resource Management at the University of Exeter. She is passionate about equality, diversity and inclusion, and explores this in both her teaching and research.

Jackie Bagnall is a Senior Lecturer in Leadership and Management at the University of Exeter, working with experienced managers on improving their impact in the workplace. She has designed and led programmes that explore how responsible leadership is an essential part of business and society.

John Shanahan is an Academic Study Skills Adviser at the University of Exeter and an Associate Lecturer with the Open University. He delivers workshops on writing, critical reading, and time management, supporting student success across all levels of study.

Jude Fleming is a qualified, professionally chartered Academic Liaison Librarian supporting the University of Exeter Business School, assisting staff and students with effective searching and retrieving information to enhance teaching, learning and research.

Kamal M. Mustafa is Associate Professor in Sustainable Operations and Analytics and Deputy Head of Management at Exeter. He specialises in digital supply chains, sustainability, and capacity-building, with over 100 publications, £1M+ research income, and 24 PhD completions to date.

Katie Ledingham is a Senior Lecturer in Responsible Innovation at Exeter. An interdisciplinary social scientist, her research and teaching reimagine innovation for social and environmental impact. She recently published *Rethinking Innovation* (2024), a student textbook transforming innovation studies for systemic change.

Kellan Nguyen is a Lecturer and Programme Director of MSc in the Project Management at the University of Exeter Business School. Prior to joining Exeter, Kellan taught at Middlesex University and at IESEG School of Management in Lille France. His teaching expertise spans operations management, consultancy management, and project management.

Lee Snook is the Law Librarian at the University of Exeter. She supports the legal research and education activities of the Law School through the delivery of training and enquiry support services in digital and information literacy.

Levke Henningsen is a Lecturer in Leadership and Organisational Behaviour at the University of Exeter Business School. Her research and teaching interests include gender diversity and leadership in organisations, work-life balance, and discriminatory and uncivil behaviour at work.

Martin Darling has been teaching for over 20 years in a number of different contexts including Saudi Arabia and Finland. He is currently a tutor on the Academic Literacy and English (In-sessional) programme for University of Exeter International Study Centre.

Michelle Civile is a Senior Lecturer in Management at the University of Exeter. She previously held roles in human resources and career counselling and now specialises in work-based learning and impact-focused research.

Mihaela Bishop is a Senior Lecturer in Marketing and Programme Director for MSc Management at the University of Exeter. Passionate about educational innovation and sustainability, she explores creative assessments and researches waste reduction through collaborative, real-world learning and industry partnerships.

Nick Davies (CMgr MCMI) is a strategic leader and adjunct lecturer at the University of Exeter. His expertise spans efficiency programmes, transformational change and organisational innovation with a financial foundation across diverse educational and commercial environments.

Nicky Thomas is the Programme Director for the University of Exeter Business School's year-long placement programme. She is committed to empowering students to build the professional skills they need to succeed through their university experiences and beyond.

Olha Matviiets is a Lecturer in Economics and Induction & Transition Lead (Economics) at the University of Exeter. Her research focuses on economics education and teaching effectiveness. She is passionate about inclusive, engaging education and supporting students' academic transition and success through evidence-based teaching strategies.

Rachael Johnstone is Dean for Professional Education and Partnerships at Exeter and a national leader in Degree Apprenticeships. She is an educational intrapreneur who drives strategic employer collaborations, leads quality initiatives, and who champions innovation, workforce development and widening participation across professional education.

Sarah Tudor is an Associate Professor in Leadership at the University of Exeter; she brings a passion for inclusive education and mentoring to everything she does. As lead author of the Leadership Chapter, she draws on years of experience supporting others to grow and succeed. A recognised authority in degree apprenticeships, Sarah regularly presents at academic and professional conferences.

Shaun Grimshaw is a Senior Lecturer and Director of Education and Student Experience for the Department of Economics at the University of Exeter. Shaun is passionate about helping students develop key skills in economics that they can use to examine business or policy problems.

Shirley Atkinson is an Associate Professor in Business Analytics at University of Exeter Business School and leads the curriculum development for Data Science and AI. Her work spans Internet Privacy, online safety for children and software engineering pedagogy.

Sian Robinson is a Senior Lecturer in Human Resource Management at the University of Exeter and Programme Director for BSc Business and Management. She is a moderator for CIPD and has co-authored a textbook on Strategic Learning and Development Practice.

Stephen Hickman, Associate Professor, Director of Education (Sustainable Futures) at the University of Exeter and founding academic of the Business Schools Cornwall campus, specialises in transformative education. His expertise spans digital tech, sustainable business, change management, and experiential learning, fostering responsible leadership, resilience, and real-world impact.

Stephen Taylor is Associate Professor in HRM at Exeter University and a longstanding Chief Examiner and Chief Moderator for the CIPD. He previously taught at two universities in Manchester and prior to that worked as a practicing HR manager in the NHS and in the hospitality industry. He is the author, editor or co-author of over 20 books in the fields of people management and employment law.

Stuart So, MSc Business Analytics Programme Director at the University of Exeter, researches supply chain sustainability, renewable energy, AI/ML, and climate mitigation. With over 50 publications and awards, he teaches analytics, holds multiple professional certifications, and consults on decarbonisation and environmental management.

Sue Kinsey is a Senior Lecturer in Applied Management at the University of Exeter with over 20 years' academic experience and a background in HR at Lloyds Banking Group. Former roles include Associate Head for Teaching and Learning and Head of Business Management at Plymouth Business School. She is currently Director of EDI for the Department of Management.

Suman Saha is a labour governance expert at Exeter Business School. His interdisciplinary research informs ethical frameworks in global supply chains, working with corporations and policymakers – including the EU – on sustainability, labour rights, and corporate responsibility across international contexts.

Thaer Alhalabi is an Assistant Professor in Finance and Accounting at the University of Exeter Business School, also acting as the Director of the Accounting programmes of undergraduates. He has practical experience in the corporate field through holding a position of financial manager. His research covers a variety of topics related to Accounting, Financial Institutions and Corporate Finance. His work has been published in top academic journals.

Thomas Sisk is a Senior Lecturer in Finance and Programme Director at the University of Exeter Business School, with expertise in finance, sustainable finance, fintech, degree apprenticeships, and industry–academic collaboration in the financial services sector. Thomas also advises governmental organisations on educational policy.

Yan Huang is a Senior Lecturer in Finance and Programme Director at the University of Exeter. Her research focuses on asset pricing, M&A, and market efficiency. She previously held roles in academia and equity consultancy with several investment banks.

YOUR GUIDE TO USING THIS BOOK

Introduction to Business and Management has been developed with a number of learning features to help you succeed in your course.

Intended Learning Outcomes: At the start of each chapter, to help guide you on what the chapter will cover.

'Sustainable Development Goals' box: A 'Sustainable Development Goals' box in the Introduction shows you which SDGs are covered in each chapter.

Reflective Activities and Exercises: Providing Guided Reflective Prompts to reflect and discuss for each chapter.

Mini Case Studies and **Longer Case Studies:** To bring theory to life with questions that can be used in class discussion or as assessment, if needed.

'Students Like You Change the World' boxes: To show students how their learning can be applicable to the working context and how they can make a difference and have a positive impact on the world.

Further Reading: A list of articles and books at the end of each chapter, to help you build your bibliography for assignments.

End of Chapter Reflection: Highlighting what skills have been developed in the chapter.

PREFACE

Edvard Glücksman, Rossana Guttilla, Sue Kinsey, Christine Parkin Hughes, Suman Saha, and Nicky Thomas

THE PURPOSE OF THIS TEXT

This book is written for anyone interested in studying business and management. It offers the reader an insight into the multilayered world of responsible practice, provides an overview of key functional areas, and clarifies the expectations, development opportunities and career trajectories of a business and management education.

From many years of experience in academia, the editors know that students often start business and management studies without fully grasping the scope of the subject matter. They don't always realise that this field demands an understanding of diverse factors – from human behaviour and organisational culture to economics, technology, and global contexts – and that profit is not the only, or even the ultimate, aim of the discipline. Moreover, students may not realise the **knowledge**, **skills** and **behaviours** they will develop or how these will shape their personal and professional growth, helping them make a positive impact in the world.

If you are reading this book, you might be finishing your NVQ, National Diploma or A-levels, studying at a partner college, exploring a Degree Apprenticeship, or considering a career change after working in another field. You may be an international student planning to continue your studies at a UK university. Whatever your background, this book can be used as a 'primer', a basic introductory text to the world of business and management, with which to familiarise yourself before joining your programme of study. It will also serve as a companion text – a helpful accompanying handbook to refer to throughout your educational journey at university and beyond. It can be used as a reference point to dip into, whenever you wish to be reminded of theories and examples discussed in your modules, to inform your strategic thinking and planning. The final chapter on academic skills will serve you as a guide, as you negotiate the practical skills in academia, such as referencing or essay writing.

As such, the book is meant as a 'one-stop shop' for all those who might be considering developing the skills and competences needed for pursuing a career in any of the key functional areas of business management and be successful during their academic journey.

The editors have undertaken a review of a wide range of business management programmes across the UK, both from Russell and non-Russell group universities, and have identified the common essential topics, the pillars that most courses rely on, to build the foundation of a solid business and management education. In many HE institutions these topics are called 'modules' or 'units'. Each chapter is dedicated to one of the key topics, e.g. Leadership, Human Resource Management, Economics, **Finance** and Data Analytics.

The editors have asked teams of expert lecturers, who have extensive experience in designing and delivering these topics, to prepare chapters which provide an overview of the content constituting a typical Business and Management degree. They incorporate the skills to be developed, as well as presenting the reader with examples of key recent challenges, to stimulate reflection and strategic thinking. They also feature examples of former students' real-life workplace application and career direction, which might help current students realise the many possibilities and impact their learning might have in the world.

Most Business Schools not only focus on theoretical knowledge, they also aim to shape responsible **leaders** who can hone their strategic vision and thinking, manage resources sustainably, inspire teams, and adapt to sudden and constant change. Critical skills, from problem solving in data analytics to cross-cultural communication, that are highly sought by employers will also be at the forefront of the curriculum. Therefore, the focus of this book is not only on the content covered in a generic business and management degree, but also to raise awareness of some of the greatest challenges in the field and to prepare students to effectively deal with these in a responsible manner. Emphasis is placed on career readiness and on personal and professional development.

This book has been designed to introduce key concepts and skills and to support students in their development. To achieve this, some special features have been added, such as:

1. **A strong emphasis on developing both managerial and academic skills.** The managerial skills developed in each chapter are clearly mapped in a table. Also, Chapter 14 has been dedicated to academic skills development (for example, assessment, giving presentations, working in groups, various writing formats such as reports and essays, referencing etc.);
2. **A pronounced reflective element.** At the end of each section, students are encouraged to reflect on how this new knowledge builds on previous assumptions and how it has changed their perspectives (knowledge and skills) and ultimately, how it will inform their future managerial choices (impact/behaviours);
3. **Clear reference to employability** via case studies and examples;
4. **Sustainability.** The promotion of practices and behaviours which are aligned with the United Nations Sustainable Development Goals (UN SDGs) will be clearly signposted in every chapter;
5. **Accent placed on inclusivity.** Equality, diversity and inclusivity, and **decolonisation** of the management curriculum;
6. **Contemporary issues.** Students will explore modern challenges in management and global affairs, such as sustainability, technological disruption, and data-driven decision-making. They will also develop essential skills to navigate a **VUCA** (Volatile, Uncertain, Complex, and Ambiguous) world, adapting to post-pandemic changes and the impact of the Great Resignation.

The remainder of this Preface considers three core elements which are mapped throughout the text:

a **Knowledge, Skills, and Behaviours** – those that business and management degrees seek to develop in their students.
b **Sustainability** – the interdependence between 'professional' management (Laasch, 2021) and the attainment of the UN SDGs and how sustainable management should be at the forefront of teaching and learning.
c **Equality, Diversity and Inclusivity** – the importance of considering different perspectives of management which are ethical, inclusive, and representative of pluralist voices and diversity across the world.

KNOWLEDGE, SKILLS AND BEHAVIOURS

It is widely recognised that a university degree will enhance your career prospects and long-term financial stability. In 2024, the Office for National Statistics reported that 67% of working age graduates were in high-skilled employment, compared to 23.7% of non-graduates, with the average annual **graduate premium** £6,500 higher for graduates than non-graduates (ONS, 2024).

University is a significant investment of your time and money, so it is important to recognise and take advantage of the personal development opportunities that your studies and university experiences offer, in order to maximise your future career success (McGettigan, 2015).

The Importance of Knowledge, Skills, and Behaviours

University is not simply about acquiring knowledge, especially when information is so readily accessible. It involves developing the skills to effectively apply knowledge to practical and technical situations, adapting and thriving in the university environment to achieve meaningful educational outcomes, and preparing for future professional roles (Barnett and Coate, 2005).

Knowledge (Learning)

Knowledge is the theoretical understanding of a subject you develop through your educational experiences, the facts, information, and principles you will acquire. 'Learning' also includes your personal relationship with the intellectual field, your genuine understanding and engagement with publicly attested and ever-evolving ideas (Barnett and Coate, 2005).

Skills (Doing)

Skills represent your ability to perform tasks and apply knowledge effectively. They encompass both technical skills, such as essay writing or **data** manipulation in Excel, and interpersonal skills like communication, **critical thinking**, and teamwork. You can expect to develop skills throughout your programme by engaging in activities and gaining new experiences, both within your academic studies and through extracurricular involvement (Andrews and Higson, 2010).

Behaviours (Being)

As you enter a new university environment, it will be important to adapt and thrive by observing and reflecting the positive *behaviours* that influence how academics, staff, and students interact and conduct themselves. While defining such behaviours can be challenging, focusing on being respectful, ethical, compassionate, engaged, responsible, and collaborative will help you build a solid foundation for success (Eraut, 2010).

Recognising, Recording, and Reflecting on Skills

When applying for graduate roles or internships, you will need to demonstrate the relevant skills you have developed for that industry or business. Keeping track of your skills development will not only prepare you for the recruitment process but will also help you identify your strengths and areas for improvement as you advance through university (Moon, 2004; University of Exeter Business School, 2024).

How and where you record these experiences is up to you. You might prefer using a journal, an online document, or a university portfolio tool designed to support you. It is however important to dedicate regular time in your daily or weekly schedule to reflect and record your experiences. This will ensure your thoughts are fresh, that you build up a complete portfolio of evidence and importantly that the process effectively contributes to your own personal development (Di Stefano et al., 2014).

The STAR method is a well-regarded technique to analyse and articulate experiences. When used effectively the answers can be used to respond to situational job application or interview questions, for example 'Describe a time when you...' or 'Give an example of...' (Indeed, 2025a).

1. **Situation**: Describe the context or background.
2. **Task**: Explain the specific challenge or responsibility.
3. **Action**: Detail the steps you took.
4. **Result**: Share the outcome or impact. Be as specific as possible.

A concise reflective paragraph or response to an interview question can be written by merging the Situation and Task into an introduction about the project or problem, presenting the Actions as the main content, and concluding with the specific Results (Indeed, 2025b).

Reflecting on what you are doing is important because employers seek employees with a growth mindset, who take responsibility for their personal development, are resilient and adaptable. Incorporating reflection into your regular routine helps develop these essential skills, allowing you to learn from your university experiences and boosting your chances of academic and career success (Kolb, 1984).

Relevant Skills

The specific skills required for your first graduate role or internship will vary, so it is crucial to identify these requirements when applying and tailor your applications accordingly. As you accumulate evidence throughout your degree, focusing your analysis and documentation on relevant skill sets will be beneficial.

In this book we will refer to the University of Exeter Business School's 'Skills to Thrive', which aim to foster students' skills for:

- Confident communication
- Innovative problem-solving
- Proactive collaboration
- Digital fluency
- Resilient self-advocacy
- Critical thinking
- Global **engagement**

Through industry research, the University has identified these are essential skills to prepare you to succeed in your professional career after graduation, and hence why it is so valuable for you to focus on this aspect of your university experiences (University of Exeter Business School, 2024).

Developing Skills at University

During your university studies you will experience a variety of learning activities, which will range from simple actions like speaking to the person next to you in class or carrying out independent reading, through to group work, presentations, case studies, and role plays. Engaging in these activities, within the supportive university environment, will not only develop these important soft skills but will also transform your experiences into deeper understanding and knowledge (Kolb, 1984).

Your learning will not solely be through your academic modules. There will be opportunities for you to apply your management theory and skills in student roles of responsibility, perhaps as an ambassador, a mentor, or in a student committee leadership role. You may also be in a position to apply your knowledge and develop your skills in a professional environment, maybe through a formal work placement or shorter vacation internships (Andrews and Higson, 2010).

Skills and Behaviours Signposting

At the end of each chapter, you will find a section highlighting skills development opportunities related to the topic. Written by subject experts, each chapter offers a unique perspective on the skills essential for your growth. These opportunities are designed for you to explore during your time at university, in the workplace, or through extracurricular activities, supporting your development into a well-rounded manager.

The authors have also identified key behaviours they view as critical for success in their areas of management expertise. You are encouraged to reflect on these behaviours and skill-building opportunities, along with your classroom experiences and learning activities, to strengthen your skills profile and align them with your future career aspirations.

For an overview of the key skills you will be developing in each chapter see the tables in the Appendix.

SUSTAINABILITY

Sustainability sits at the heart of the University of Exeter's research and education. It is the long-term goal of the processes and pathways that characterise sustainable development (Jeroen, 2013). Sustainability drives our most impactful collaborations and informs our strategic and operational priorities. In management, sustainable solutions, by definition, incorporate equality, diversity and inclusion principles in their design. Alongside **digital literacy**, an understanding of key elements of sustainability will offer you a lens through which you can better understand industry skills gaps and associated employability opportunities which may shape your future career.

During your studies, you will incorporate sustainability paradigms wherever possible. You will learn to access, understand and critically reflect upon the primary scientific research, putting key concepts into practice and crafting solutions to our most pressing global challenges.

In the context of management, we can understand sustainability through the commonly paraphrased definition of sustainable development from the Brundtland Report, as *'meeting the needs of the present without compromising the ability of future generations to meet their own needs'* (United Nations, n.d.). This definition is broad but implies that managers and businesses need to think about the past, present, and future context of their operations; that is, they must take into account historical context, align with expectations of today's consumers, and anticipate the interests and rights of future generations (Blowfield, 2013).

A Planet in Crisis

In 2023, our planet experienced the warmest year ever recorded (Copernicus, 2024) and a number of extreme weather events were seen across the globe, such as tropical cyclone Freddy, the longest-lasting tropical cyclone on record (Scoccimarro et al., 2024). Elsewhere, including in Europe, South America and Australia, extreme heat was more intense and persevered longer, breaking records concurrently in both hemispheres and even during shoulder seasons (spring and autumn) across many locations (Perkins-Kirkpatrick et al., 2024).

The current climate and ecological crisis is one of the most pressing challenges that humanity has ever faced (Artmann 2023; Gabric 2023). It includes climate change, biodiversity loss and the depletion of finite natural resources (Steffen et al., 2015; Zeng et al., 2020). Global emissions of greenhouse gases, which drive global warming, continued to increase in

2023 and reached all-time highs after temporarily dipping during the COVID-19 global pandemic (Friedlingstein et al., 2022). As of 2023, only about six years of CO_2 emissions at current rates remained for humanity to have a 50% chance of limiting global warming to 1.5 °C, a critical threshold for avoiding the most severe global impacts (Lamboll et al., 2023). However, with 2024 now confirmed as the warmest year on record – about 1.55 °C above the pre-industrial average – this remaining window appears even more precarious (World Meteorological Organization [WMO], 2025).

At the same time, human activity such as deforestation, intensification of agriculture, pollution and exploitation of resources have driven rates of biodiversity loss on land and in the oceans to dramatically high levels (Díaz and Malhi, 2022). Biodiversity loss threatens the global economy and society at large, with the World Economic Forum estimating that over half of the global Gross Domestic Product is highly or moderately dependent on nature and its services (Russo, 2020).

Sustainable Development and Education

Our current understanding of sustainability in education emerges from decades of progressively more detailed, practical and evidence-based research. Since the 1970s, environmental education reflects the latest global charters, reports and frameworks, designed to explain the relationship between the growing human population and its environmental impact.

In 1975, the Belgrade Charter developed early educational guidelines around ecology, awareness of the natural world, protecting nature and the acquisition of skills to help address environmental challenges (UNESCO and UNEP, 1975). A year later, the Tbilisi Declaration developed these ideas further. The result of the first intergovernmental conference on environmental education, the Tbilisi Declaration (UNESCO and UNEP, 1977) put environmental protection at the core of a new wave of pedagogic content.

The 1987 Brundtland Report (WCED, 1987) paved the way for the development of a formalised integration of sustainability in educational curricula, called Education for Sustainable Development (ESD). The UN Sustainable Development Goals (UN SDGs), including SDG4 on teaching the knowledge and skills needed to promote sustainable development, subsequently inspired the Education for Sustainable Development Goals (UNESCO, 2017) programme, which continues to inform current methods.

Universities and Sustainability 'By Default'

Universities and other higher education institutions play a key role formulating the collective response to the global climate and ecological crisis. They host novel research, inform policy, drive cross-sector partnerships in innovation, and educate future leaders and policymakers (Dyke and Monbiot, 2024). They are also bastions of thought-leadership where opinions, perceptions and suggested actions may differ, yet everyone remains committed to creating a greener, healthier and fairer future.

For example, in management, researchers may vehemently disagree on how best to take action to solve our most pressing sustainability challenges. Some see the ongoing planetary crisis and associated sustainability frameworks as an opportunity for investment and further growth. From this perspective, aligning with emissions targets by switching from high-carbon (e.g. oil or coal) to low-carbon (e.g. solar or nuclear) energy sources would drive innovation in technology and infrastructure, fundamental aspects of economic growth. They seek incremental change within the conventional economic system. Others take the view that dramatically more profound changes are needed to mitigate against the worst risks that threaten our planet, questioning the very nature of economic growth and even its long-term desirability (Blowfield, 2013).

Despite these fundamentally different opinions about what actions to take, and how to take them, business leaders of tomorrow will play a critical role in tackling sustainability challenges. The 2007 Principles for Responsible Management Education (PRME) initiative represents a call to action based on seven Principles (PRME Principles, 2023) that management-related academic institutions should align with to enable current and future leaders to generate sustainable value for business and society at large (Haertle et al., 2017).

As you progress through your degree, you will learn about concepts that challenge the way you think about the world around you. These transformative experiences will help you develop a mindset that 'by default' aims to achieve sustainable outcomes, equipping you with the knowledge and skills needed to tackle the wicked, interrelated challenges that underpin the climate and environmental crisis, and its implications.

Growth Through Disorientation

Transformative experiences can be disorienting, as they challenge conventional thinking about the communities and wider nature around you (Mezirow, 1994). They aim to help you understand where you see yourself making impactful change. Indeed, it is these disorienting experiences that reinforce learning and offer you a chance to further develop your mindset and worldview, gaining new perspectives by overcoming adversity. This is an important part of your university experience, gained through practical work in the classroom, work placements and internships, and challenge-based groupwork, not least because it gives you valuable points of reference as you reflect upon your future career path.

Take, for example, the challenge-based Future17 programme, led by the University of Exeter in partnership with higher education experts Quacquarelli Symonds (QS) (Barr et al., 2025). Students from a global network of universities design and deliver solutions to challenges pitched by 'live' organisations based worldwide. Teams work remotely and independently across a global breadth of time zones and cultures, across disciplines, and with colleagues at all academic levels. Since early 2022, around a thousand students on five continents have graduated from Future17, and the programme continues to thrive as it incorporates additional universities and challenge partners. Reflecting on their experience, students often cite the disorientation created by the programme's unique structure, and the associated journey to overcome these moments of perceived 'adversity', as having equipped them with confidence and skills they subsequently used in job applications.

Towards an Employer-Informed Sustainability Curriculum

Employers increasingly value the interdisciplinary knowledge and practical skills associated with a curriculum anchored in sustainability 'by default'. Some universities (e.g. the University of Exeter), are fortunate to experience this demand for training first-hand across our suite of professional education offerings, where training opportunities for employees at leading businesses and NGOs based around the world are provided.

For example, the Exeter open masterclass in circular economy, delivered in partnership with the Ellen MacArthur Foundation, regularly convenes business representatives to learn from our experts about how they can harness circular economy practices to drive innovation for their respective companies. Other professional and executive education programmes are co-developed and bespoke to individual businesses, combining sustainability principles with innovative management research in leadership. These courses provide the latest climate and environmental science alongside the skills, confidence, and context for managers and their employees to develop innovative products and services that align with broader sustainability objectives.

Throughout your studies, you will receive similar training, including developing business cases and management frameworks for sustainable solutions, matching theory with practical skills, and critically reflecting on 'live' case studies. Like senior managers in industry, you, too, will learn how nature inspires innovation through biomimicry (e.g. the shape of a Japanese bullet train inspired by the beak of a kingfisher); how crucial thresholds, known as tipping points, can be harnessed to mitigate the negative impacts of climate change (e.g. positive tipping points); or how a greener, healthier and fairer world requires us to source more natural resources to drive low-emissions technology (e.g. responsible mining and circular economy).

For detailed listings of UN Sustainable Development Goals (SDGs) relevant to each chapter, please consult the Appendix.

EQUALITY, DIVERSITY AND INCLUSIVITY (EDI)

EDI (sometimes referred to as DEI) stands for Equality, Diversity, and Inclusion, an important set of ideas and practices which aim to ensure a fair and equitable environment in workplaces and other contexts, including places of study. EDI initiatives are essential to fostering positive work cultures where everyone can be successful. In the UK, the Chartered Institute of Personnel and Development suggest that EDI is about 'Promoting and delivering EDI in the workplace ... creating working environments and cultures where every individual can feel safe, experience a sense of belonging, and is empowered to achieve their full potential' (CIPD, 2024).

- **Equality** (sometimes amended to '**Equity**') is about ensuring equal access to opportunities and fair, just, and impartial treatment for all employees. Whilst both equality and equity aim to achieve fairer outcomes, equality focuses on giving everyone the same resources and opportunities, whereas equity recognises that people have different circumstances and therefore resources or support will be allocated accordingly.

- **Diversity** is about welcoming individuals from all backgrounds, identities and perspectives, including those who have been traditionally underrepresented. Specific consideration might be given to characteristics including race, ethnicity, gender, age, sexual orientation, and disability.
- **Inclusion** is about creating environments where any individual or group can feel welcomed, respected, supported, and valued, and about creating workplaces where everyone can contribute fully.

A successful EDI approach in organisations can help to eliminate discrimination, harassment and victimisation and to advance equality of opportunity for all. Recognising and addressing the disparities that exist within societies and organisations can help to eliminate systemic inequality, unconscious bias and privilege, which have acted as barriers to success for all. The removal of these barriers can also enhance organisational performance, and this is discussed in more detail below.

EDI and Intersectionality

EDI is multifaceted and incorporates a range of aspects such as race, gender, age, sexual orientation, religion, and disability. However, these aspects do not exist in isolation; instead, they intersect and interact in complex ways. The term **intersectionality** was coined by American academic Kimberlé Crenshaw in the late 1980's. People often have more than one characteristic that might be subject to discrimination, and the concept of intersectionality reminds us that race, class, gender and other personal characteristics 'intersect' with one another. Intersectionality means that individuals can experience discrimination or privilege in multiple, overlapping ways. Intersectionality challenges simplistic narratives and encourages a more nuanced understanding of identity and inequality. By recognising and addressing the multiple, intersecting forms of discrimination, organisations can work towards creating more inclusive and equitable environments for all.

Why Is EDI Important in Organisations?

EDI is essential in organisations because it strengthens performance, culture and fairness. When people feel respected, valued and able to contribute authentically, they are more engaged, innovative and productive. Diverse teams bring a wider range of perspectives and problem-solving approaches, improving decision-making and adaptability. Ensuring equity reduces barriers and creates fair opportunities for all, helping attract and retain talent, reduce turnover and maintain wellbeing. Below we will be discussing the 'legal' and the 'business' case, but remember, although there is proof that EDI drives better outcomes, fosters trust and belonging, and enables organisations to thrive in an increasingly diverse and interconnected world, first and foremost EDI is the right thing to do.

The Legal Case

Many countries will have Equality legislation which requires organisations to comply or face penalties. For example, in the UK, the Equality Act (2010) provides legal protection for nine protected characteristics: age, disability, gender reassignment, marriage and civil partnership, pregnancy and maternity, race, religion or belief, sex and sexual orientation. Whilst legal frameworks vary across different countries, there is evidence that the law does not always achieve its desired outcome. For example, while women living in the UK and EU benefit from legislative equality, there is often a gap between organisations' stated equality policies and their practices (Davis et al., 2016), and the gender pay gap which exists in many organisations in the UK suggests that the Equal Pay legislation in existence since 1970 has not addressed gender-based pay inequality.

The Business Case

There is substantial research to show that diversity can bring many other advantages to an organisation, including increased profitability and creativity, stronger governance, and better problem-solving abilities (Eswaran, 2019). A study undertaken by the Boston Consulting Group in 2018 found evidence that in both developing and developed economies, increasing the diversity of leadership teams can lead to more and better innovation as well as improved financial performance for organisations (Lorenzo et al., 2018).

Additionally, EDI contributes to a positive organisational culture, where employees feel valued and engaged, which can lead to higher levels of productivity and lower turnover rates, as well as attracting the best talent from a wider pool of candidates. Employees with diverse backgrounds bring their own perspectives, ideas, and experiences, helping to create organisations that are resilient and effective, and which outperform organisations that do not invest in diversity.

EDI Strategy, Policy and Practice

EDI works most effectively when it is embedded into the core values, practices, and policies of an organisation, rather than seen as an add-on. Sometimes referred to as 'mainstreaming', this approach ensures that an equality perspective is integrated into an organisation's day-to-day working across all functions. This can include setting clear goals, such as increasing the representation of underrepresented groups in leadership positions, and implementing measures to achieve these goals, such as mentorship programs for underrepresented groups. It also involves training and educating employees at all levels about unconscious biases and how their own behaviour can have an impact and the importance of inclusion. Of course, monitoring and evaluating the impact of these actions is critical to ensuring that the EDI initiatives are effective.

Global Perspectives on EDI

EDI is a global issue, but its implementation and challenges vary across different cultural and legal contexts. In some regions, the focus may be on gender equality, while in others, race, ethnicity, or LGBTQ+ rights may be more prominent. In light of recent political developments – such as

Executive Orders introduced under President Donald Trump that seek not only to roll back but also to actively challenge EDI initiatives – EDI (or DEI) has become increasingly politicised. This changing climate highlights how organisational commitments to equity and inclusion now operate within contested social and political spaces, as illustrated by recent state-level actions such as Florida's 2023 Executive Order banning DEI programs in public universities and Texas's 2023 directive restricting DEI offices in state institutions.

Understanding these differences is crucial for multinational organisations that operate across borders. They must navigate varying legal frameworks, cultural norms, and societal expectations to implement effective EDI initiatives. Global perspectives on EDI can also highlight the importance of context-specific strategies, recognising that a single approach or set of recommendations may not be effective. For instance, while affirmative action may be a legal requirement in one country, it might be seen as controversial in another.

The United Nations Sustainable Development Goals recognise that gender inequality is an issue of global concern. They say 'At the current rate, it will take an estimated 300 years to end child marriage, 286 years to close gaps in legal protection and remove discriminatory laws, 140 years for women to be represented equally in positions of power and leadership in the workplace, and 47 years to achieve equal representation in national parliaments'. SDG 5 therefore aims to 'Achieve gender equality and empower all women and girls […] as a necessary foundation for a peaceful, prosperous and sustainable world' (UN, 2023).

The Significance of EDI in the Study of Business and Management

The previous sections outline the potential benefits for organisations who engage meaningfully with EDI strategy, policy, and practice. Organisations that prioritise EDI are more likely to attract and retain top talent, enhance employee satisfaction, and foster innovation (Everett and Hill, 2025). Diverse teams bring varied perspectives, leading to better problem-solving, innovation, and decision-making. It's clear that understanding the role and impact of EDI is of relevance for effective leadership and management, and for understanding the design of good workplaces and organisational cultures.

However, EDI benefits and awareness extend beyond employee considerations: an inclusive culture not only benefits employees but can also strengthen the organisation's reputation and relationship with external **stakeholders**, including customers, partners, and the community. Organisations that reflect the diversity of their customer base can be better positioned to understand and meet the needs of those customers, potentially improving customer service and loyalty. EDI also plays a role in risk management by helping organisations navigate the legal and reputational risks associated with discrimination and exclusion. And in the context of supply chain management, organisations which actively broaden their supply 'pool', with a focus towards more diverse suppliers (such as those owned and led by women or ethnic minorities) rather than relying on more conventional sources, can ensure better value (Sweeney, 2024).

Given the significance of EDI, it's useful to consider its role in every aspect of your studies, and in your own experiences and interactions. An equality and inclusivity lens can be useful for evaluating your own learning, and for informing how you engage with others in work or study settings.

Managers as Leaders and Changemakers

Due to being practical and forward-looking in nature, Business Schools are ideally positioned to develop graduates who are equipped to tackle ambitious global objectives around ending poverty, protecting the planet and ensuring prosperity for all.

Managers are leaders. In this Preface, you will have learned about the importance of developing your management skillset. You will also have learned about the critical need to incorporate continuous improvement around EDI practices. As a guiding mindset and focal lens through which to view your successes and challenges, sustainability 'by default' sets you up to thrive as a manager and leader. Taken together, as PRME approaches its twentieth anniversary, there is no doubt that universities and their enthusiastic, engaged, and entrepreneurial graduates – in other words, you, in the near future – will continue to play an increasingly vital role in developing the solutions that shape our society of tomorrow.

Final Thought

One of the key messages of this book is that when opting for business education, students are not only investing in their future career; they are also becoming change agents, empowered to make meaningful changes in the world. The world needs responsible leaders who understand both profit and purpose. A business degree isn't just about learning – it's about becoming that leader. As a result, business graduates consistently rank among the most employable worldwide (THE, 2024).

For detailed listings of five EDI values – discovery, respect, excellence, inclusion, and community – and their application for each chapter, please consult the Appendix.

CONCLUSIONS

As we navigate an era of rapid change, businesses are increasingly expected to balance profitability with purpose. This book explores how sustainability, ethical leadership, and responsible management can shape the future of work while equipping you with the skills needed to thrive in a dynamic world. Through thought-provoking case studies and student vignettes, we highlight the real-world impact of business and management education.

Here are some key takeaways to keep in mind as you embark on the reading of this book:

- **Business as a Force for Good** – Future leaders have the power to drive positive change through sustainability, ethical decision-making, and responsible leadership.
- **Skills for a Changing World** – Success in business requires adaptability, creativity (amongst other skills that we will explore in this book), and a commitment to lifelong learning.
- **The Power of People** – Equality, diversity, and inclusion are not just values but essential ingredients for innovation and long-term success and will be embedded in every single chapter of this book.

- **Real-World Impact** – Case studies and student vignettes will highlight how business and management graduates are contributing to a more sustainable and just world.
- **Your Journey Starts Here** – This book equips you with the knowledge, skills, and inspiration to build a career that has the potential to make a meaningful difference.

STUDENTS LIKE YOU CHANGE THE WORLD

Anuar Umirzhanov, Business and Management Student – University of Exeter

During my time at the University of Exeter, I had the privilege of founding a sports clothing brand in Kazakhstan called Aurelius. In 2024, I led a highly successful marketing campaign that significantly boosted our brand's popularity, allowing us to stand out in a competitive market. The campaign was so effective that I managed to sell the brand for a strong valuation before starting my final year at Exeter.

Studying business at Exeter played a pivotal role in my entrepreneurial journey. The knowledge I gained – particularly in Human Resource Management, leadership, and marketing – allowed me to build and manage a strong team, fostering both collaboration and innovation. My academic foundation also helped me secure competitive internships in Investment Banking, the Ministry of Trade, and Private Equity across London, Europe, and Asia, reinforcing my ability to apply business principles in diverse professional settings.

Additionally, the leadership modules at Exeter taught me the importance of connecting with people and businesses, which led to some remarkable opportunities. I was honoured to be invited as a guest speaker by the Exeter Business and Finance Society, where I shared insights on my entrepreneurial experiences with fellow students. Through these connections, I was also invited to the House of Lords as a notable guest by Rupert Goodman DL, an experience that further enriched my understanding of leadership and networking.

REFERENCES

Andrews, J., and Higson, H. (2010) 'Graduate employability, "soft skills" versus "hard" business knowledge: A European study', *Higher Education in Europe*, 33. http://doi.org/10.1080/03797720802522627

Artmann, M. (2023) 'Human-nature resonance in times of social-ecological crisis – A relational account for sustainability transformation', *Ecosystems and People*, 19 (1). http://doi.org/10.1080/26395916.2023.2168760

Barnett, R., and Coate, K. (2005) *Engaging the Curriculum in Higher Education*. Open University Press.

Barr, S., Dally, I., Glücksman, E., Hilser, H., Oakley, R. A., Quine, T. A., and Winks, L. (2025) 'Transformative learning for sustainability: A case study of the Future17 Sustainable Development Goals Challenge program'. *International Journal of Sustainability in Higher Education*. https://doi.org/10.1108/IJSHE-08-2024-0549

Blowfield, M. (2013) *Business and Sustainability.* Oxford University Press.

CIPD (2024) *Equality, Diversity and Inclusion (EDI) in the Workplace.* CIPD Factsheet. https://www.cipd.org/uk/knowledge/factsheets/diversity-factsheet/ (accessed August 29, 2025).

Copernicus (2024) 'Copernicus: 2023 is the hottest year on record, with global temperatures close to the 1.5°C limit', *Copernicus*, January 9. https://climate.copernicus.eu/copernicus-2023-hottest-year-record (accessed October 24, 2025).

Crenshaw, K. (1989) 'Demarginalizing the intersection of race and sex: A Black feminist critique of antidiscrimination doctrine, feminist theory and antiracist politics', *University of Chicago Legal Forum*, 1: Article #8. https://chicagounbound.uchicago.edu/uclf/vol1989/iss1/8/ (accessed August 29, 2025)

Davis, P.J., Frolova, Y., and Callahan, W. (2016) 'Workplace diversity management in Australia', *Equality, Diversity and Inclusion: An International Journal*, 35 (2): 81–98. http://doi.org/10.1108/EDI-03-2015-0020

Díaz, S., and Malhi, Y. (2022) 'Biodiversity: Concepts, patterns, trends, and perspectives', *Annual Review of Environment and Resources*, 47 (1): 31–63.

Di Stefano, G., Gino, F., Pisano, G., and Staats, B. (2014) 'Learning by thinking: How reflection can spur progress along the learning curve,' Harvard Business School NOM Unit Working Paper No. 14-093. https://papers.ssrn.com/sol3/papers.cfm?abstract_id=2414478# (accessed August 29, 2025).

Dyke, J.G., and Monbiot, G. (2024) 'What is the role of universities at a time of climate and ecological crisis?', *Geo: Geography and Environment*, 11 (2): article #e00146.

Eraut, M. (2010) 'Informal learning in the workplace', *Studies in Continuing Education*, 26 (2): 247–73. http://doi.org/10.1080/158037042000225245

Eswaran, V. (2019) 'The business case for diversity in the workplace is now overwhelming', *World Economic Forum*, April 29. https://www.weforum.org/agenda/2019/04/business-case-for-diversity-in-the-workplace (accessed August 29, 2025).

Everett, S., and Hill, I. (eds) (2025) *Diversity, Equity and Inclusion for Business & Management*. CABS.

Friedlingstein, P., O'Sullivan, M., Jones, M.W., Andrew, R.M., Gregor, L., Hauck, J., [...] and Zheng, B. (2022) 'Global carbon budget 2022', *Earth System Science Data Discussions*, 14 (11): 4811–900. http://doi.org/10.5194/essd-14-4811-2022

Gabric, A.J. (2023) 'The climate change crisis: A review of its causes and possible responses', *Atmosphere*, 14 (7): article #1081.

Haertle, J., Parkes, C., Murray, A., and Hayes, R. (2017) 'PRME: Building a global movement on responsible management education', *The International Journal of Management Education*, 15 (2): 66–72.

Indeed (2025a) 'How to use the STAR interview response technique', *Indeed*, March 23. https://in.indeed.com/career-advice/interviewing/how-to-use-the-star-interview-response-technique (accessed August 29, 2025).

Indeed (2025b) 'A definitive guide to the PAR method (with examples)', *Indeed*, June 9. https://www.indeed.com/career-advice/interviewing/par-method?utm (accessed August 29, 2025).

Jeronen, E. (2013) 'Sustainability and sustainable development', in S.O. Idowu, N. Capaldi, L. Zu, and A.D. Gupta (eds), *Encyclopedia of Corporate Social Responsibility.* Springer. pp. 2370–8. http://doi.org/10.1007/978-3-642-28036-8_662

Kolb, D. (1984) *Experiential Learning: Experience as the Source of Learning and Development*. Prentice Hall.

Laasch, O. (2021). *Principles of Management: Practicing Ethics, Responsibility, Sustainability*. Sage.

Lamboll, R.D., Nicholls, Z.R., Smith, C.J., Kikstra, J.S., Byers, E., and Rogelj, J. (2023) 'Assessing the size and uncertainty of remaining carbon budgets', *Nature Climate Change*, 13 (12): 1360–7.

Lorenzo, R., Voigt, N., Tsusaka, M., Krentz, M., and Abouzahr, K. (2018) 'How diverse leadership teams boost innovation', *Boston Consulting Group*, January 23. https://www.bcg.com/publications/2018/how-diverse-leadership-teams-boost-innovation (accessed August 29, 2025).

McGettigan, A. (2015) 'The Treasury view of HE: Variable human capital investment' (*Political Economic Research Paper Series, 6*), Political Economy Research Centre, May 5. www.goldperc.uk/project_posts/perc-paper-the-treasury-view-of-higher-education-by-andrew-mcgettigan/ (accessed August 29, 2025).

Mezirow, J. (1994) 'Understanding transformation theory', *Adult Education Quarterly*, 44 (4): 222–32.

Moon, J. (2004) *A Handbook of Reflective and Experiential Learning Theory and Practice*. Routledge.

Office for National Statistics (ONS) (2024) 'Graduate labour market statistics – 2023', *Gov.uk Explore Education Statistics*, June 27. https://web.archive.org/web/20241231160604/https://explore-education-statistics.service.gov.uk/find-statistics/graduate-labour-markets (accessed August 29, 2025).

Office of the Governor of Florida (2023) Executive Order on Higher Education Reform. https://www.flgov.com (accessed December 19, 2025).

Office of the Governor of Texas (2023) Directive on Diversity, Equity, and Inclusion in Public Institutions. https://gov.texas.gov (accessed December 19, 2025).

Perkins-Kirkpatrick, S., Barriopedro, D., Jha, R., Wang, L., Mondal, A., Libonati, R., and Kornhuber, K. (2024) 'Extreme terrestrial heat in 2023', *Nature Reviews Earth & Environment*, 5: 244–6. http://doi.org/10.1038/s43017-024-00536-y

PRME Principles (2023) 'The seven principles', *PRME*. https://www.unprme.org/what-we-do/ (accessed August 29, 2025).

Russo, A. (2020) 'Half of world's GDP moderately or highly dependent on nature, says new report', *World Economic Forum (WEF)*, January 19. https://www.weforum.org/press/2020/01/half-of-world-s-gdp-moderately-or-highly-dependent-on-nature-says-new-report/ (accessed August 29, 2025).

Scoccimarro, E., Lanteri, P., and Cavicchia, L. (2024) 'Freddy: Breaking record for tropical cyclone precipitation?' *Environmental Research Letters*, 19 (6): article #064013.

Steffen, W., Richardson, K., Rockström, J., Cornell, S.E., Fetzer, I., Bennett, E.M., [...] and Sörlin, S. (2015) 'Planetary boundaries: Guiding human development on a changing planet', *Science*, 347 (6223): article #1259855. http://doi.org/10.1126/science.1259855

Sweeney, C. (2024) 'The importance of prioritizing DEI in supply chain management', *Charlotte Sweeney Associates*, April 3. https://charlottesweeney.com/thought-leadership-articles/2024/04/03/the-importance-of-prioritizing-dei-in-supply-chain-management/ (accessed August 29, 2025).

Times Higher Education (THE) (2024) 'Best universities for graduate jobs: Global Employability University Ranking 2025', *Times Higher Education*, November 14. https://www.timeshighereducation.com/student/best-universities/best-universities-graduate-jobs-global-university-employability-ranking (accessed December 16, 2025).

UN (2023) 'Sustainable development goals: 17 goals to transform our world', *United Nations Exhibits*. https://www.un.org/en/exhibits/page/sdgs-17-goals-transform-world (accessed August 29, 2025).

UNESCO. (2017) *Education for Sustainable Development Goals*. UNESCO. https://stairwaytosdg.eu/images/UNESCO_Education_for_Sustainable_Development_Goals_ENG.pdf (accessed August 29, 2025).

UNESCO and UNEP (1976) *The Belgrade Charter.* https://www.eusteps.eu/wp-content/uploads/2020/12/Belgrade-Charter.pdf (accessed August 29, 2025).

UNESCO and UNEP (1977). *The Tbilisi Declaration*. https://www.gdrc.org/uem/ee/Tbilisi-Declaration.pdf (accessed August 29, 2025).

United Nations (n.d.) 'Sustainability', *United Nations Academic Impact*. https://www.un.org/en/academic-impact/sustainability (accessed August 29, 2025).

University of Exeter Business School (2024) 'Prepare to succeed – Graduate skills to thrive & principles of professional practice', *University of Exeter*, July 17. https://business-school.exeter.ac.uk/study/prepare-to-succeed/ (accessed August 29, 2025).

WCED (1987) *Our Common Future* [Brundtland report]. Oxford: Oxford University Press.

World Meteorological Organization (WMO) (2025) 'WMO confirms 2024 as warmest year on record at about 1.55°C above pre-industrial level', *WMO*, January 10. https://wmo.int/news/media-centre/wmo-confirms-2024-warmest-year-record-about-155degc-above-pre-industrial-level (accessed October 24, 2025).

Zeng, Y., Maxwell, S., Runting, R.K., Venter, O., Watson, J.E.M., and Carrasco, L.R. (2020) 'Environmental destruction not avoided with the sustainable development goals', *Nature Sustainability,* 3 (10): 795–8. http://doi.org/10.1038/s41893-020-0555-0

1
WORLD OF BUSINESS

David Chambers-White, Stephen Hickman, and Colleen Smith

INTENDED LEARNING OUTCOMES

After reading this chapter, you should be able to:

1. Explore the historical context and evolution of the business landscape, influenced by economic, social, and technological factors.
2. Examine the impact of international trade, finance, and economic policies on global business operations.
3. Suggest how responsible leadership can help businesses integrate social justice and environmental sustainability into their practice.
4. Identify modern challenges facing businesses, from technological disruptions to regulatory changes and discover strategies for managing in a volatile, uncertain, complex, and ambiguous world.
5. Explain, summarise, and analyse how legal principles shape businesses and business decisions including: types of organisations; contract and negligence.

SUSTAINABLE DEVELOPMENT GOALS

In this chapter we address the following SDGs:

- SDG 1: No Poverty – Ethical business practices and fair wages help lift people out of poverty.
- SDG 2: Zero Hunger – Sustainable businesses could improve food security (e.g., **Corporate Social Responsibility [CSR]** programs funding regenerative farming).
- SDG 4: Quality Education – Companies investing in employee training and community education contribute to lifelong learning.
- SDG 5: Gender Equality – CSR policies promoting equal pay and leadership diversity advance workplace gender equality.
- SDG 7: Affordable and Clean Energy – Businesses investing in renewable energy support access to sustainable power (e.g., solar energy startups in rural communities).

- SDG 8: Decent Work and Economic Growth - Ethical labour practices ensure safe working conditions and fair wages (e.g., anti-exploitation policies in global supply chains).
- SDG 9: Industry, Innovation and Infrastructure - Business innovation drives sustainable infrastructure and technological advances (e.g., green building initiatives).
- SDG 12: Responsible Consumption and Production - Sustainable business models reduce waste and emissions (e.g., circular economy practices in manufacturing).
- SDG 13: Climate Action - Corporate carbon reduction commitments drive sustainability (e.g., net-zero targets in multinational companies).
- SDG 16: Peace, Justice, and Strong Institutions - Ethical governance and anti-corruption measures build fairer economies.
- SDG 17: Partnerships for the Goals - Cross-sector partnerships help achieve sustainability goals.

INTRODUCTION

Imagine standing at the threshold of tomorrow's business world – a vibrant arena where **sustainability** meets **innovation**, and global challenges await creative solutions. This chapter will assume you're already interested in the topic and that a thrilling and rewarding career in the dynamic world of business appeals to you. It uses case studies and reflection to help you to **critically analyse** business scenarios and develop your analytic skills.

THE EVOLVING BUSINESS ENVIRONMENT

This section answers the question: what is business and why is its study crucial in today's world? We'll explore its historical evolution and global reach, revealing its profound impact on societies and economies. Understanding business using a PESTLE framework will help us further to highlight the critical external factors that shape its operations and significance. It is important to study the history of business to learn how businesses have changed and adapted over time. This helps us understand how businesses work today and how to make better decisions for the future. By exploring the historical context, we can develop a sharper eye for identifying trends, anticipating future challenges, and crafting effective strategies for success. What is more, understanding past strategies, challenges, and innovations can provide you with profound insights into contemporary organisational dynamics and your own potential for strategic thinking.

In simple terms a *business organisation* is simply a group of people working together to achieve a common goal, usually to make money. Businesses exist to provide either goods or services to consumers and the public. These products are sold by either public or private sector businesses. It could be a small shop, a large **corporation**, or anything in between. All businesses, large or small, are affected by internal and external factors that influence business managers' decision-making.

Introductory texts and chapters about business and management often begin with how it is important to have some understanding of the business environment, contrasting factors directly controllable to the organisation (internal environment), with factors that are beyond its direct control (external environment). However, a business is best understood not as an isolated entity, but as a dynamic system that interacts with its environment. It is constantly adapting to changes in the market, technology, and society. Businesses must also be agile and responsive to legal changes to maintain compliance and avoid penalties. By recognising these interconnections, businesses can make informed decisions and thrive in a competitive landscape.

The business environment is highly complex. It has become ever more interconnected through technological modernisation and is seen in many instances as an international and growing market in an interdependent world system. This new, more dynamic global economy, also referred to as **globalisation,** continues to influence political and legal factors, and sometimes not in a sustainable way. The important matter of globalisation is discussed in more detail later in this chapter.

Historical Perspective on the Evolution of the Business Landscape

By studying the history of how businesses have evolved, we can see how closely connected business and management are to the past. When we can accurately determine what really happened in the past and identify the lessons relevant to today's businesses (Lawrence, 1984; Clark and Rowlinson, 2004), it can help managers make better decisions in the future.

It is worth noting that the development of business, from early **commerce** to the information era and today's global digital marketplace, is often told from an **imperialist perspective**. This narrative tends to overlook the voices and experiences of Indigenous communities and the Global South. This topic, often referred to in business and management education as **decolonisation**, will be explored in more detail later in the chapter.

REFLECTIVE ACTIVITY 1.1

Consider for example, the global coffee trade. Companies such as Nestlé and Starbucks profit the most, while farmers in coffee-growing regions receive minimal rewards for their labour. These practices reflect colonial-era patterns, where value is extracted from the South and concentrated in the North.

- How can businesses today address these imbalances and create fairer systems that respect and include the perspectives of all **stakeholders**?

The Building Blocks of Modern Business: Early Economic Exchanges

The foundations of commerce can be traced to two pivotal developments in human history: the establishment of trade networks and the invention of currency.

Long before the *Industrial Revolution* reshaped the business landscape, ancient civilisations had already laid the groundwork for global commerce. One of the most renowned examples are the Silk Roads, a vast network of trade routes that linked the flourishing empires of China and Rome (Whitfield, 2018). This intricate web of connections not only facilitated the exchange of goods but also ideas and cultural practices, setting the stage for future globalisation.

In these early stages of **commerce**, transactions in many settled societies were fundamentally governed by social relationships and credit systems (debts or 'IOUs'), alongside forms of gift exchange. Some form of direct barter (the spontaneous, spot exchange of goods without money) occurred too, particularly between strangers. However, the idea of a pure barter economy as the predecessor to money, as it was believed until recently, seems to be a myth: non-monetary societies relied instead on sophisticated commodity standards (like grain or livestock) primarily to track credit, debt, and value, rather than facilitating direct exchange (Graeber, 2011). The complexity of these non-monetary systems, including the need for a unit of account to track obligations, laid the groundwork for the development of money.

This foundational commerce gave way to several crucial milestones (Findlay and O'Rourke, 2007) that shaped modern trade and demonstrate a consistent, long-term development path:

- The Development of Coinage and Metal Standards which emerged to facilitate regional trade, taxation, and military payments, providing a portable, reliable medium of exchange and a dependable store of value.
- The Codification of Commercial Law (e.g., Roman Law, the Lex Mercatoria in the medieval period) which established rules for contracts, property, and dispute resolution, creating a secure environment for trade growth.
- The Establishment of Banking and Bills of Exchange – crucial advancements during the medieval and Renaissance periods that enabled long-distance trade, reduced the need to transport physical money, and laid the foundation for modern international finance.
- The Development of Double-Entry Bookkeeping – a crucial 13th-century accounting innovation that allowed businesses to manage increasingly complex capital structures and transactions accurately.
- The Rise of Mercantilism and Chartered Companies during the early modern period, introducing large, state-sponsored business organisations (like the Dutch and British East India Companies) with significant capital and global reach.

These successive trade systems and financial innovations paved the way for the rapid commercial developments that characterised the Industrial Revolution in the 18th and 19th centuries.

The Industrial Revolution and the Rise of Corporations (1800s)

The late 18th century marked the beginning of the Industrial Revolution in Britain, characterised by mechanisation and increased production efficiency. This period saw the improvement of the steam engine and the introduction of steam-powered railroads that revolutionised transportation and connected distant markets. By the mid-1800s, modern organisational structures, such as the **firm** and the corporation, began to emerge.

Figure 1.1 is an image of Trevithick's steam engine (patented 1802), a landmark invention of the Industrial Revolution. Steam power, harnessed by machines like this, fuelled the rapid growth of factories, mines, and transportation systems, ushering in a new era of industrial production and societal change.

Figure 1.1 Trevithick's steam engine

World Wars, Globalisation, and Technological Advances (1900s)

The 20th century was a period of immense upheaval and transformation, witnessing a series of profound economic and political events that reshaped the global landscape, including:

- World Wars disrupted and reshaped global trade
- The Great Depression led to significant economic reforms
- Post-World War Two saw the establishment of new international economic systems

- Anti-colonial movements, such as the campaign for the partition of India (1947) and international recognition for non-Western power
- The establishment of the People's Republic of China in 1949
- Telecommunications (telegraph, telephone, radio) accelerated globalisation
- The rise and fall of South American military dictatorships (1960s–1980s)
- Oil crises and stagflation in the 1970s reshaped economic thinking
- The 1980s brought neoliberalism and deregulation
- The 1990s heralded the Digital Age and Global Connectivity

The 20th century also saw the establishment of significant new regulatory regimes that shape business. For example, the refinement of labour laws, which began with the Labour Relations Act of 1935.

ACTIVITY 1.1

Choose an event: Select one of the listed events (World Wars, Great Depression, etc.).

Quick research: Spend 15 minutes researching your chosen event online and connect it to real-world consequences. Think about how this event affected the economy or business practices in a specific country or organisation - what changed, and why did it matter?

Write a microblog entry: Summarise your finding in a concise summary (under 280 characters). It should:

Clearly state the event.

Briefly explain its impact on society and businesses.

Be informative and engaging.

Reflect: Think about how your findings might be similar or different to someone else's.

IMPACT OF INTERNATIONAL TRADE, FINANCE, BANKING, AND ECONOMIC POLICIES ON GLOBAL BUSINESS OPERATIONS

Globalisation is about countries becoming more connected through trade, **culture**, and technology, leading to a more interconnected world.

Das (2011) explains how globalisation creates a complex web of global interconnections. Conventional wisdom suggests we now operate in a highly globalised world, where individuals and organisations grapple with balancing global sustainability, stakeholder interests, and ethical considerations against economic profit motives. Globalisation is a complex issue with different perspectives and is shaped by global trade and competition.

Notably, the internationalisation of business activities, markets, and trade predates the contemporary globalisation trend, having roots in much earlier periods of human history.

Early forms of finance and banking emerged in ancient civilizations like Mesopotamia and Egypt. The 17th century witnessed the establishment of the world's first central banks, such as the Bank of England, founded in 1694 (Encyclopaedia Britannica, 2025). The development of banking in the UK, particularly the innovation of paper money and the close relationship between banks and government finance, has been a defining characteristic of the London money market. This evolution contrasts with the development of banking systems in other world markets, each shaped by unique historical, cultural, and economic factors. These differences have played a crucial role in shaping the modern landscape of international trade and global business operations. An early example of international trade which illustrates several key business concepts is the Hanseatic League.

The Impact of International Trade

Early trade organisations included:

- Srivijaya was a maritime and commercial empire comprising a network of trading ports that controlled important sea routes between Indonesia, Malaysia, and Thailand from 600–1200 CE (Bank and Davies, 2002). Like their European counterparts, they dominated maritime trade in their region, just in spices and silks rather than European commodities. Srivijaya flourished between the 7th and 13th centuries and predated the Hanseatic League (Bang et al., 2020).
- The Hanseatic League, or Hansa, was a powerful alliance of north German merchants and townspeople that dominated North European trade during the medieval period. Active primarily around the Baltic Sea, the League brought immense political and economic power to its member states, shaping the economy of the Late Middle Ages and Early Modern Period. It is an important early example of globalisation.

Currency and International Trade

The Hanseatic League did not have a single currency. Instead, all of medieval Catholic Europe theoretically used the same money: the denarius or silver penny. This coin, known by different names in various languages (denier in French, dinero in Spanish, denaro in Italian, penny in English, penning in Dutch, and pfennig in German), was introduced by Charlemagne (a powerful Frankish king who ruled much of Western Europe from 768 to 814) around the year 800 AD as part of a major currency reform (Cefalo, 2014).

This early attempt at currency standardisation can be seen as a precursor to modern currency unions, such as the euro. The development of standardised currencies has played a crucial role in facilitating international trade and economic integration.

The Rise of International Trade and Globalisation

In the modern context, international trade has evolved to encompass complex global value chains, multinational corporations, and the internationalisation of markets. This globalised business environment is characterised by:

- **International Business:** Companies operating across national borders, adapting to diverse cultural, legal, and economic environments.
- **Global Value Chains:** The distribution of production processes across multiple countries to optimise efficiency and cost-effectiveness.
- **Types of International Firms:** Including multinational enterprises, born-global firms, and international joint ventures.
- **Market Internationalisation:** The increasing interconnectedness of national markets and the growth of global consumer segments.

Financial and Economic Shocks of Recent Years

The global financial landscape has experienced significant shocks in recent years, with one of the most notable being Brexit. Prior to the UK's referendum on June 23, 2016, much of the European Union's financial power was concentrated in the City of London. The decision to leave the EU initiated a seismic shift in the European financial sector.

Despite these challenges, the European Commission has maintained its commitment to the Capital Markets Union (CMU) action plan, even accelerating efforts to implement it. The CMU action plan aims to create a single market for **capital** across the EU. Its objectives include enhancing access to **finance** for European companies, particularly SMEs, increasing and diversifying sources of funding, and making capital markets more efficient. This initiative is crucial for fostering economic growth, job creation, and financial stability within the EU, especially in the post-Brexit landscape.

ACTIVITY 1.2

Conduct your own research comparing the European Union (EU) perspective and policies related to the UK's departure with the UK Government's perspective.

Tip: If searching the internet use questions such as:

- What are some common misconceptions about Brexit, and how do they differ from the evidence?
- What are the impacts of Brexit in the context of UK-EU relations and why does it represent more than just a political decision?

Avoid relying solely on news headlines or social media summaries. Cite at least one academic or government source (e.g., UK Parliament, European Commission, academic journals).

The Digital Age and Global Connectivity (2000s)

The mid to late 1990s and early 2000s marked the dawn of the internet age. The new millennium brought further change with the digitisation of business processes such as sales and **stock** management, which is explained in Chapters 7 and 8. The internet saw entrepreneurs pioneering the dot-com bubble (and its aftermath), whilst the integration of business systems between different organisational functions such as purchasing and finance, and the introduction of ideas such as just-in-time (JIT) management reshaped business activity in **supply** and demand management. You can explore the impact of the digital age such as the internet, e-commerce, social media, and globalisation on businesses and society by engaging with the resources available from the Initiative in the Digital Economy (INDEX) Research Centre at the University of Exeter (https://exeterindex.org/).

JIT management is a system that focuses on efficiency by only producing goods when they are needed and in the exact quantities required. It's like ordering groceries only when you're about to cook, instead of stocking up on everything at once. This helps businesses avoid waste and reduce costs.

However, looming at this time was the 2008 global financial crisis and resulting regulations for trade and industry. Coupled with this was a resurgence of internet business activity with the rise of e-commerce giants and **fintech**. Whilst the impact of the COVID-19 pandemic severely impaired both the global and local economy, the accelerating **digital transformation** of business is regarded as a positive consequence. A major event like a global pandemic clearly shows how different external factors can impact a business, both positively and negatively.

SHAPING FORCES: INTERNAL AND EXTERNAL FACTORS IN BUSINESS

Throughout this business history, several key themes and trends emerge:

1. Technological Advancements
2. Globalisation and Trade
3. Regulatory Changes
4. Social and Environmental Awareness
5. E-Commerce and Digital Transformation

MINI CASE STUDY 1.1

Large International Corporation: Puma

For a large international corporation like Puma, operating on global scale, both internal and external factors significantly influence its operations. Internal factors, such as its product

(Continued)

strategy, marketing campaigns, and supply chain logistics across multiple regions, are directly controllable. External factors like geopolitical tensions, consumer trends, and global economic shifts, which are beyond its immediate control, can have a substantial impact on its overall performance. However, its international presence provides resilience, but also exposes it to a wider range of risks associated with strategic decisions and long-term performance.

MINI CASE STUDY 1.2

Small and Medium-Sized Enterprise (SME): Finisterre

A UK-based SME like Finisterre focused on sustainable outdoor apparel, operates primarily within regional markets. Its internal decisions – such as product design, pricing, and customer engagement – are crucial to its identity and competitiveness. Finisterre is more susceptible to the influence of both internal and external factors such as competition from larger brands. While internal factors, such as its product offerings, pricing strategy, and customer service, are within its control, external factors like local economic conditions, competitor activities, and regulatory changes can have a disproportionate impact on its business. Unlike Puma, Finisterre may have fewer resources to buffer against these pressures, making agility and niche positioning essential to its survival and growth.

A simple yet effective framework for making smarter business decisions requires the assessment of these environmental aspects using six factors, namely political, economic, sociological, technological, legal, and environmental (PESTLE).

The PESTLE Framework: An Interconnected Reality

In today's interconnected marketplace, business is no longer merely about profit (commerce) but about creating value for society while navigating complex business and legal environments. Analytical frameworks such as PESTLE (Political, Economic, Sociological, Technological, Legal, Environmental factors) help managers and business analysts decode market forces, while SWOT analysis (Strengths, Weaknesses, Opportunities, Threats) sharpens an organisation's strategic thinking. Learning to apply such frameworks, combined with understanding the United Nations' Sustainable Development Goals (UN SDGs), can equip business graduates to drive positive change.

ACTIVITY 1.3

Find specific case studies by using academic databases like Google Scholar or JSTOR.

Tip: search for keywords like 'PESTLE analysis,' 'case study,' and the industry or company you're interested in.

For example, Ford used PESTLE analysis to identify external factors like changing consumer preferences and economic conditions:

Political factors: Political and environmental regulations significantly influence vehicle design and manufacturing decisions across global markets.

Economic factors: Economic conditions including recessions and inflation impact industry stability and consumer purchasing power.

Social factors: Consumer preferences, brand perceptions, and demographic shifts influence product development and marketing strategies.

Technological factors: AI, IoT, and autonomous systems and advancements reshape vehicle capabilities and manufacturing processes.

Legal factors: Labor laws, union relationships, and regulatory compliance shape workforce management and operational decisions.

Environmental factors: Growing pressure for sustainable practices and reduced emissions drives innovation in electric and low-emission vehicles. (SAP Community, 2023)

This helped them develop strategies like investing in electric vehicles and research and development to adapt to these changes.

The PESTLE framework focuses on six types of external business factors:

Political Factors

Political factors significantly shape the business environment through government policies, stability, and international relations. Key aspects include:

- Government types and stability
- Tax policies and trade regulations
- Labour laws and environmental regulations
- International trade agreements and geopolitical tensions

Political decisions can have far-reaching effects on other PESTLE factors. For instance, trade policies directly impact economic conditions, while environmental regulations influence technological innovation and social attitudes.

Economic Factors

Economic factors encompass both macro and microeconomic conditions:

- Economic growth rates and business cycles
- Inflation, interest rates, and exchange rates
- Unemployment levels and labour costs
- Income distribution and consumer spending patterns

Economic conditions are closely intertwined with political decisions, technological advancements, and social trends. For example, monetary policies affect inflation and interest rates, while technological disruptions can lead to structural changes in employment.

Sociological Factors

These include social and cultural factors reflecting the characteristics of the society in which businesses operate:

- Demographic trends and population dynamics
- Education levels and skills distribution
- Cultural norms and values
- Consumer attitudes and lifestyle changes

These factors significantly influence consumer behaviour, workforce composition, and corporate social responsibility expectations. They are often shaped by historical events, technological changes, and economic conditions.

Technological Factors

Several key technological factors significantly impact the business environment, including:

- Rate of technological change and innovation
- Research and development activities
- Automation and **artificial intelligence**
- Digital infrastructure and connectivity

The above technological advancements have become increasingly crucial in shaping the business landscape, as they often drive changes in other PESTLE factors. They can reshape industries, alter labour markets, influence social behaviours, and necessitate new regulations.

Legal Factors

Legal factors encompass the regulatory framework within which businesses operate (discussed later in this chapter and in Chapter 5):

- Business and corporate laws
- Consumer protection and safety regulations
- **Intellectual property** rights
- Employment laws and anti-discrimination legislation

Legal factors are closely tied to political rulings and social expectations. They often evolve in response to technological advancements, economic changes, and shifting social norms, and can impact business decisions.

Environmental Factors

Environmental considerations have gained prominence in recent years as businesses implement social and environmental initiatives in response to such matters as:

- Corporate social responsibility expectations
- Business ethics and transparency
- Environmental sustainability practices
- Fair trade and labour practices
- Equality, Diversity and Inclusion (EDI)

Environmental factors are increasingly influencing consumer choices, investor decisions, and regulatory frameworks. They reflect evolving ecological concerns and social values and often drive changes in legal and political landscapes.

Connecting PESTLE Factors

The PESTLE factors should not be viewed in isolation but as an interconnected web of influences. For instance:

- Political decisions shape economic conditions, which in turn influence social factors
- Technological advancements drive changes in all other factors
- Social expectations often lead to new legal requirements
- Economic conditions can influence political stability and technological innovation
- Environmental threats can lead to government interventions.

Understanding these interconnections is crucial for businesses to navigate the complex modern environment effectively.

ENVIRONMENTAL SUSTAINABILITY AND SOCIAL RESPONSIBILITY IN BUSINESS

The growing awareness of environmental challenges and social inequalities has led to increased emphasis on sustainable and responsible business practices. This shift is reflected in:

- The rise of **ESG (Environmental, Social, and Governance)** investment
- Increased consumer **demand** for sustainable products and ethical practices
- The integration of sustainability into core business strategies
- The development of sustainable **business models** such as the circular economy and shared value creation

These trends are reshaping the business landscape, influencing everything from product and service design to supply network management and corporate governance. In Business Schools this is resulting in an increasing focus on environmental sustainability and social responsibility, with business and management educators adopting frameworks such as Principles of Responsible Management Education (PRME) and mapping learning content onto UN Sustainable Development Goals (SDGs). An extended discussion can be found later in this chapter (see: Business in a Changing World).

The business environment is a complex, dynamic system shaped by the interplay of political, economic, sociological, technological, legal, and environmental factors. By understanding the historical context and the interrelated nature of these influences, businesses can better navigate challenges and seize opportunities. As we move towards a more sustainable future, the ability to balance economic goals with environmental and social responsibilities will be crucial. The next generation of business **leaders** must be prepared to reshape the business environment, and drive innovation and growth. At the same time there is the critical priority to address pressing global challenges such as climate change, biodiversity loss, and social deprivation. In addition to rise in ESG investments mentioned earlier, a key trend in the world of modern business is the increasing integration of ESG factors into regulatory frameworks.

However, while ESG is a crucial and rapidly evolving area, it's important to understand how these more recent regulatory developments are built upon the foundational legal principles that govern business operations as discussed later in this chapter.

Economic Policy

Economic policy plays a crucial role in shaping the global business environment. It encompasses various aspects, including:

- **Economic Capital:** The financial and physical assets that contribute to a nation's productive capacity.
- **Economic Crises:** Periods of significant decline in economic activity, often requiring policy interventions.
- **Economic Ethics:** The moral principles guiding economic decision-making and policy formulation.
- **Economic Systems and Subsystems:** The organisational structures and mechanisms through which economic activities are coordinated.
- **Economic Value vs. Sustainable Development:** The balance between economic growth and long-term environmental and social sustainability.

From a globalisation perspective, economic policy has been significantly influenced by the concept of laissez-faire (Tanzi, 2023), or 'let do/let go.' This principle precedes Adam Smith's idea of the 'invisible hand,' a term which suggests that free markets can efficiently allocate resources without government intervention.

The 'invisible hand' metaphor illustrates how, in a free market economy, self-interested individuals operate through a system of mutual interdependence.

MINI CASE STUDY 1.3

The Invisible Hand in Action: Building a Bicycle

Imagine you want to buy a new bicycle. You're not just buying a bicycle; you're participating in a vast, interconnected network of people and activities.

Think about the journey: How did the steel for the frame get mined? Who transported the rubber for the tyres? How were the gears manufactured? Who designed the bike, and who assembled it?

Consider the motivations: Each person involved - the miners, the factory workers, the designers, the delivery drivers - is working for their own reasons: to earn a living, to contribute their skills, to provide for their families.

This intricate process, where countless individuals pursue their own goals, ultimately results in the bicycle you want to buy. This is an example of the 'invisible hand,' an economic concept that suggests that individual actions, even when driven by self-interest, can benefit society.

Adam Smith introduced this concept in his 1759 book *The Theory of Moral Sentiments* and later in *An Inquiry Into the Nature and Causes of the Wealth of Nations* (1776). He argued that free exchanges create signals about which goods and services are valuable and how difficult they are to bring to market.

However, critics argue that the invisible hand does not always produce socially beneficial outcomes and can encourage greed, negative externalities, inequalities, and other harms. This perspective is at odds with the philosophy set out in the UN Sustainable Development Goals (SDGs), which emphasise balanced economic growth, social inclusion, and environmental protection.

To understand global business, we need to think about how companies operate in a world where everything is interconnected. This means considering how businesses interact with people and other companies in different countries. Laasch and Conaway (2015) suggest that successful businesses need to be 'globally responsible,' meaning they need to consider the impact of their actions on people and the environment. This is especially important today as businesses face challenges like climate change and social inequality. Furthermore, Visser (2012) highlights the difficult decisions that global business leaders must make when trying to be socially responsible, emphasising the need for careful consideration of their impact on society. In conclusion, economic policy, in the context of sustainable global trade, must strike a balance between free market principles and regulatory measures that ensure fair competition, protect vulnerable populations, and promote long-term sustainability.

BUSINESS AND MANAGEMENT IN A VUCA WORLD: NAVIGATING CHALLENGES AND SEIZING OPPORTUNITIES

In today's rapidly evolving global landscape, businesses of all sizes face an environment characterised by Volatility, Uncertainty, Complexity, and Ambiguity (VUCA). This framework, originally developed by the U.S. Army War College to describe the post-Cold War world, has become increasingly relevant in the business sphere (Stein, 2021). For undergraduate students aspiring to enter the world of business and management, understanding and navigating the VUCA landscape is crucial for identifying both employment opportunities and challenges.

Volatility: The New Normal in Markets

Volatility in markets has become a defining feature of the modern business environment. Rapid shifts in consumer preferences, technological advancements, and global events can cause sudden and significant changes in market conditions. This volatility creates pricing challenges for businesses, as they must constantly adjust their strategies to remain competitive and relevant.

However, volatility also presents opportunities for agile firms. Those able to quickly adapt to market shifts can capitalise on emerging trends before their competitors. For instance, companies that swiftly pivoted to e-commerce and digital services during the COVID-19 pandemic often saw substantial growth, while less adaptable businesses struggled.

To thrive in volatile markets, businesses must develop robust forecasting capabilities, maintain flexible operations, and cultivate a culture of rapid decision-making. This might involve implementing real-time **data analytics**, adopting agile project management methodologies, or creating cross-functional teams that can quickly respond to market changes.

Uncertainty: The Catalyst for Innovation

Uncertainty in regulations and consumer behaviour necessitates flexible strategies but also offers chances to innovate. Regulatory landscapes are constantly evolving, particularly in areas such as data privacy, environmental protection, and labour laws. This uncertainty can lead to governance disagreements as businesses attempt to ensure compliance while remaining competitive.

Similarly, shifts in consumer behaviour, accelerated by technological advancements and changing societal values, create uncertainty in market demand. However, this uncertainty also presents opportunities for innovation. Companies that can anticipate or quickly adapt to changing consumer preferences can gain a significant competitive advantage.

To navigate uncertainty, businesses should focus on **scenario planning**, maintain a diverse portfolio of products or services, and foster a routine of ongoing innovation (see Tidd and Bessant, 2020). This might involve creating project-oriented innovation teams, implementing co-creation design thinking methodologies (Hutchins, 2013), or partnering with startups to stay at the forefront of emerging trends.

Complexity: Managing Global Networks Sustainably

The complexity of global supply networks poses logistical risks but also enables diverse sourcing and market expansion when managed sustainably. As businesses increasingly operate on a global scale, they must navigate intricate webs of suppliers, distributors, and partners across different countries and cultures.

This complexity can lead to increased risks, such as supply chain disruptions, quality control issues, or reputational damage due to unethical practices in the supply chain. However, when managed effectively, this complexity can also provide significant benefits. It allows businesses to access a wider range of resources, tap into diverse talent pools, and expand into new markets.

To address the challenges of complexity, businesses should focus on developing robust risk management strategies, implementing advanced supply chain tracking technologies, and fostering strong relationships with partners across their network. Additionally, adopting sustainable and ethical practices throughout the supply chain can help mitigate risks and build long-term resilience.

A Holistic Approach to Marketing and Sustainability

In this complex environment, businesses need to adopt a more holistic approach to **marketing**. Rather than viewing consumers through the narrow lens of demographic segments or purchasing behaviours, companies should strive to understand consumers as real, complex individuals with diverse needs, values, and aspirations.

This approach aligns with the growing emphasis on sustainable business practices as outlined in the UN Sustainable Development Goals (SDGs). By truly understanding their consumers, businesses can better align their marketing activities and production practices with sustainability goals. This might involve developing products that address specific environmental or social challenges, adopting circular economy principles in production, or creating marketing campaigns that emphasise a company's commitment to sustainability.

Ambiguity: Navigating Technological Trends and Resource Management

Ambiguity in technology trends, particularly in areas such as artificial intelligence (AI), requires careful assessment of an organisation's capabilities before making strategic investment decisions. There are of course pros and cons, presented by the rapid pace of technological advancement where challenge is always accompanied by opportunity. Furthermore, ambiguity in technology trends requires careful investment but presents opportunities for early adopters to gain advantages.

For example, Tesla navigated market volatility to lead in electric vehicles. Amazon adapted to uncertain consumer behaviours during the pandemic. Apple managed complex global supply chains to maintain product delivery. Google thrived on ambiguous tech trends by diversifying into various emerging technologies. More recently, SAP has begun building AI into financial software applications, e.g. for supply chain management (https://learning.sap.com/products/supply-chain-management).

New technologies can dramatically improve efficiency, and afford greater prioritisation and decision-making capabilities, which could ultimately deliver new business models. These technologies, however, do also require significant investment and can disrupt existing operations. Similarly, ambiguity in resource management, including the shift towards flexible and remote working arrangements, presents both challenges and opportunities. While these changes can increase productivity and employee satisfaction, they also require new management approaches and robust infrastructure development.

To navigate this ambiguity, businesses should focus on developing a clear technology strategy aligned with their overall business goals. This might involve creating multi-discipline teams to assess new technologies, partnering with tech startups or research institutions, or implementing pilot programmes to test new technologies before full-scale adoption.

Integration of the VUCA Framework with PESTLE Factors

The analytical usefulness and applicability of the VUCA framework can be further contextualised when integrated with a PESTLE analysis (introduced earlier in this chapter) to anticipate trends in each PESTLE category (see Table 1.1).

Table 1.1 Tabulation of the VUCA framework with PESTLE analysis

	VUCA			
PESTLE	**Volatility**	**Uncertainty**	**Complexity**	**Ambiguity**
Political	Geopolitical volatility impact	Navigating uncertain landscapes	Complex international relations	Ambiguous policy and regulation
Economic	Market and economic fluctuations	Financial management uncertainty	Global economic system complexity	Ambiguous economic indicators
Sociological	Rapid consumer behaviour changes	Uncertain demographic shifts	Complex stakeholder relationships	Ambiguous cultural contexts
Technological	Disruptive tech market volatility	Uncertain tech advancements	Digital transformation complexity	Tech leveraging for integration challenges
Legal	Volatile regulatory environments	Uncertain compliance risks	Complex international frameworks	Ambiguous decisions about what is legally permissible
Environmental	Volatile environmental conditions	Uncertain climate change impacts	Complex environmental regulations	Ambiguous environmental challenges

Source: Authors

This contextualisation of the VUCA framework integrated with PESTLE analysis emphasises the interconnectedness of external factors and thus improves our understanding and navigation of the complex business environment.

Despite the challenges posed by the VUCA environment, there is reason for optimism about the resilience of the business community. Early adopters of innovative, 'business-unusual' models have the opportunity to create wealth, preserve the natural environment, and nurture **social capital**. These models offer alternatives to traditional business approaches that may be ill-equipped to tackle the myriad challenges facing society and our planet.

Managing in a VUCA world requires creating systemic change. This involves rethinking traditional business models, embracing sustainability as a core business principle, and fostering a culture of continuous innovation and adaptation. By doing so, businesses can not only navigate the challenges of the VUCA environment but also contribute to solving some of the world's most pressing problems.

For undergraduate students entering the business world, understanding and embracing the VUCA framework offers a valuable perspective on the challenges and opportunities that lie ahead. By developing the **skills** and mindset needed to thrive in this environment, they can become the business leaders of tomorrow, driving innovation, sustainability, and positive change in an increasingly complex and interconnected world.

BUSINESS IN A CHANGING WORLD: TACKLING SOCIAL AND ENVIRONMENTAL CHALLENGES

In the context of sustainability and social responsibility, it is essential for undergraduate students to understand the interconnectedness of these concepts within the business environment. Sustainability refers to the necessity to meet the needs of the present without compromising the ability of future generations to meet their own needs. This principle, highlighted in the Brundtland report (WCED, 1987), emphasises the necessity for development that does not undermine the life-support systems of our planet or perpetuate issues of inequality and deprivation.

Another related idea or concept is Generation Flux, which refers to people who thrive in the rapidly shifting era in which we live, as well as the kinds of people best positioned to take advantage (Safian, 2012). Businesses operate in a chaotic and rapidly changing environment, influenced by factors such as climate change, resource scarcity, and socio-economic disparities. The notion of Generation Flux illustrates the unpredictability of business contexts, where competitive advantages may shift overnight, requiring managers to adapt swiftly. For instance, the complex energy crisis encompasses significant challenges, including air pollution, the depletion of fossil fuels, and biodiversity loss. These crises necessitate proactive management strategies that consider both environmental impact and social equity.

The implications for companies are profound. Businesses must recognise that their operational choices directly affect resource use and social well-being. For example, the production of food requires significant energy – where high fossil fuel inputs can lead to increased environmental degradation. Furthermore, the top wealthiest segments of the population disproportionately consume resources, accounting for 70-80% of global energy use, which raises ethical questions about equity and sustainability. More information about the changing nature of the planet and the effect on energy security can be found on sites such as the National Aeronautics and Space Administration (NASA) (2022).

Embedding social responsibility into business strategy in what has been termed 'The Age of Responsibility' by Visser (2011) is not only an ethical imperative but also a strategic advantage. Thus, understanding sustainability and social responsibility is critical for future business leaders as they navigate the complexities of modern markets and strive to create positive impacts on society and the environment.

Responsible Leadership in a Changing World

In a rapidly evolving global landscape, the concept of responsible leadership has emerged as a cornerstone of modern business. At its heart, responsible leadership is about balancing profit-making with ethical considerations, social responsibility, and environmental sustainability. This approach ensures that businesses contribute positively to society while addressing some of the most pressing global challenges of our time.

Two interconnected themes lie at the core of responsible leadership. The first theme focuses on social justice, encompassing **equality, diversity, and inclusion (EDI)** to challenge unjust systems and empower underrepresented groups.

MINI CASE STUDY 1.4

Patagonia

Patagonia, a global outdoor clothing and gear company, actively works to avoid marginalisation linked to colonial legacies by engaging directly with Indigenous communities in conservation efforts. The company's product line – including jackets, backpacks, and technical outdoor wear – is designed with sustainability in mind, using recycled materials and promoting product durability through its Worn Wear program, which encourages repair and reuse. Patagonia also leads in Fair Trade Certified™ production, ensuring that workers in its global supply chain receive fair wages, work in safe conditions, and have access to community development funds that they democratically control. These funds have supported initiatives such as childcare centers, healthcare access, and education in countries like Sri Lanka and India. Actively working with communities harmed by past practices, to understand their perspectives and needs, helps address inequalities and promotes respect for diverse voices. In business and management education this is referred to as decolonisation.

Source

Savage, W. (2024) 'Protecting the rights of workers who make our products'. Patagonia. https://eu.patagonia.com/gb/en/stories/protecting-the-rights-of-workers-who-make-our-products/story-157223.html (accessed September 1, 2025).

REFLECTIVE ACTIVITY 1.2

Decolonisation is more than a buzzword or a once-a-year topic during Black History Month. Dar et al. (2020), in their article 'The business school is racist: Act up!', call for collective action to dismantle the racial power structures embedded in education, including Business Schools. They highlight the urgent need for institutions to move beyond surface-level gestures and address systemic inequalities. This call-to-action challenges us to reflect on how these ideas are applied within education. Honest, open discussions are a starting point, but conversations that lead to lasting, visible change in, for example, Business Schools involves recognising widespread inequalities and taking active steps to create fairer, more inclusive organisations and societies.

Can you share an experience where you felt marginalised or excluded? How did that shape your understanding of inclusivity and fairness in your learning or working environment?

The second theme centres on environmental sustainability, urging businesses to adopt practices that minimise harm to the planet, conserve resources, and support long-term ecological health.

Modern businesses also face contemporary challenges that intersect with these themes, such as technological advancements, regulatory shifts, and global inequalities. Leaders must navigate these complexities thoughtfully, ensuring that their organisations adapt to change while upholding ethical and sustainable practices.

Historical Milestones in Responsible Leadership

The journey towards responsible leadership can be traced back to pivotal frameworks and initiatives, each building on the last to shape the global discourse on business ethics and sustainability. A landmark moment came with the Brundtland Report (WCED, 1987), which introduced the widely accepted definition of sustainable development: meeting present needs in a way that preserves resources and opportunities for future generations. The report was critical in raising awareness within the business and management community about the interconnectedness of environmental, social, and economic sustainability.

Titled 'Our Common Future', the Brundtland Report was published in 1987 and introduced the concept of sustainable development, a concept further advanced by subsequent frameworks such as the Earth Charter, UN Global Compact, PRME, GRLI, and the broad set of global objectives, the Sustainable Development Goals (SDGs).

The SDGs build on decades of work by countries and the UN, including the UN Department of Economic and Social Affairs. More information about the SDGs universal agenda, comprising 17 goals and 169 targets, can be found on the up-to-date UN SDG website (https://sdgs.un.org/goals).

By understanding these frameworks and their historical development, business and management students can gain insights into the responsibilities of modern leaders. This section explores how responsible leadership integrates social justice and environmental sustainability to navigate contemporary challenges, helping you identify the skills needed to analyse these topics and apply them to real-world situations, thereby helping you prepare for the changing demands of the modern workplace.

Table 1.2 Timeline of Key Milestones

Year	Framework	Key Focus
1987	**Brundtland Report**	Commissioned by the United Nations. Defines sustainable development and raises awareness of sustainability in business.
2000	**Earth Charter**	Promotes respect for all life, sustainability, and social and economic justice.
2000	**United Nations Global Compact**	Encourages businesses to adopt sustainable and socially responsible policies.
2004	**Globally Responsible Leadership Initiative (GRLI)**	Advocates for leadership rooted in ethics and global sustainability.
2007	**Principles for Responsible Management Education (PRME)**	Embeds sustainability principles into business and management education.
2015	**Sustainable Development Goals (SDGs)**	Defines 17 global goals for sustainable development across all sectors.

Note: For more information on each of these frameworks, please see: Brundtland Report - https://www.brundtland.co.za/other-publication/brundtland-report-1987-our-common-future/; Earth Charter - https://earthcharter.org/; United Nations Global Compact - https://unglobalcompact.org/; GRLI - https://grli.org/; PRME Principles - https://www.unprme.org/about/; UN SDG - https://sdgs.un.org/goals.

ACTIVITY 1.4

- Look into the background, purpose, and principles of two of the sustainability management frameworks in Table 1.2.
- Identify when and why each framework was developed and the key issues they address.
- Consider how these frameworks influence businesses and leaders.

SOCIAL JUSTICE IN BUSINESS: EDI (EQUALITY, DIVERSITY, AND INCLUSION)

EDI stands for equality, diversity, and inclusion – concepts that focus on creating fair, respectful, and welcoming spaces for everyone. Equality is about treating people fairly and ensuring everyone has access to the same opportunities. Diversity recognises the value of different backgrounds, cultures, and perspectives, while inclusion is about building environments where everyone feels respected and supported to thrive.

EDI is essential for graduate employability because modern employers prioritise diverse and inclusive workplaces. Candidates who understand EDI are better prepared to thrive in inclusive environments, work effectively with diverse teams, and align with legal and ethical standards. This makes them valuable in today's global and innovative job market.

Global Justice and Equity: Expanding the Conversation Beyond EDI

In today's interconnected world, the pursuit of justice in business and management extends far beyond equality, diversity, and inclusion (EDI) alone. While EDI remains essential for fostering fairness and representation within organisations, it is equally important to confront the legacies of colonisation and imperialism that continue to shape global systems of trade, labour, and power. These historical forces have left lasting inequalities that disproportionately affect marginalised communities, particularly in the Global South.

The concept of Global Justice and Equity expands on EDI by addressing these deeper, global issues. It encourages a critical examination of how businesses operate within international markets shaped by colonial histories and imperialist structures, while also emphasising the importance of decolonisation – a process of addressing and challenging these systems to allow for the inclusion of diverse perspectives and ideas. Practical work on decolonising business education, such as the *British Academy of Management Guide to Decolonising the Business School Curriculum* (2024), highlights steps for critically reflecting on and restructuring curricula, teaching practices, and organisational norms to foreground equity and diverse ways of knowing in business contexts.

By understanding these interconnected issues, students can better appreciate the broader responsibilities of businesses in the modern world. Discussions of Global Justice and Equity equip future leaders with the tools to critically evaluate how organisations impact people, communities, and environments. This **knowledge** prepares graduates to actively engage in shaping ethical and inclusive workplaces, while recognising their role in promoting fairness and justice on a global scale.

CASE STUDY 1.1

Exploring Colonialism and Imperialism Through the Works of Akala

Akala is a well-known figure in the UK, a hip-pop artist, social entrepreneur, author and public speaker. He is an outspoken critic on (the growing) inequality in the UK, focusing on inequality, class and race (2018).

Questions

1. Watch a short video of Akala discussing his views on inequality, colonialism, and the lasting impact of imperialism. You can find videos on platforms like YouTube.
2. Reflect on Akala's key points about colonialism and imperialism.
3. How do these ideas connect to business practices today, especially in areas like diversity, ethical decision-making, and global operations?
4. Summarise how Akala's insights contribute to understanding the legacy of colonialism and its influence on modern business. Include thoughts on how these ideas affect issues such as class disparities, racial inequalities, and corporate responsibility.

ENVIRONMENTAL SUSTAINABILITY IN PRACTICE

Earlier in this section the Sustainable Development Goals (SDGs) were introduced. In this next section the need for companies to recognise their impact on these goals and adopt practices that contribute to sustainability and EDI are discussed.

Climate Change and COP

The importance of climate change is a recurring theme in today's society, especially when discussing air pollution and climate impacts from fossil fuel use. The COP (Conference of the Parties), which meets annually, is the main decision-making body of the United Nations Framework Convention on Climate Change (UNFCCC), which aims to address the global challenge of climate change.

International climate agreements such as the **Paris Agreement**, which emerged from COP discussions, highlight the critical importance of the topic. The urgency of the situation is underscored by the need to limit global warming to below 2 degrees Celsius, aligning with the goals set during COP meetings. The ongoing COP discussions emphasise the necessity for nations and businesses to collaborate on mitigation strategies and transition towards renewable energy sources.

Biodiversity and Energy Insecurity

A complex emergency for the earth and humanity concerns biodiversity loss intertwined with energy security that can be directly linked to SDG 7 (Affordable and Clean Energy) and SDG 14 (Life Below Water). The discussions at COP conferences highlight how urgent action is required to protect ecosystems and reduce reliance on fossil fuels, which are major contributors to climate change and biodiversity loss.

Corporate Responsibility and Legislation

The implications for companies can also be contextualised within the framework of the SDGs, emphasising corporate responsibility in achieving these goals. Companies are encouraged to integrate sustainability into their core strategies, which would align with the global agenda set forth by the SDGs and the commitments made during COP conferences.

By integrating these contemporary frameworks, business leaders can enhance the relevance of the discussion on sustainability and position it within the broader global efforts to address critical challenges facing humanity today.

Responding to Modern Challenges

This section concludes by connecting these challenges and opportunities back to social justice and environmental sustainability, to show how managers and leaders must adapt a more comprehensive approach to the business environment.

In the contemporary business landscape, sustainable management has emerged as a critical imperative for organisations seeking to balance economic performance with environmental and social responsibilities. This approach requires a comprehensive strategy that fundamentally reimagines business purpose and operational frameworks.

At its core, sustainability demands a strategic realignment that transforms traditional business models, moving environmental and social considerations from peripheral concerns to central organisational objectives. This transformation necessitates a sophisticated approach to financial risk management, where ecological challenges are quantified and integrated into comprehensive economic models that extend beyond conventional financial metrics.

Increasing stakeholder expectations drive this evolution, with investors, consumers, and regulators demanding greater transparency, accountability, and demonstrable commitment to responsible business practices. These pressures catalyse technological innovation, compelling organisations to develop creative solutions that address environmental challenges through circular economy principles and green technologies.

Such profound organisational transformation requires extensive human capital development – building leadership capabilities, workforce skills, and inclusive organisational cultures that naturally embed sustainable thinking. These cultural shifts are simultaneously supported by adaptive regulatory strategies that anticipate and respond to evolving environmental standards and legal frameworks.

By adopting a sustainable approach, businesses can move beyond simply meeting legal requirements. They can create genuine value for their customers, employees, and the environment, making sustainability a key factor in their success and ability to adapt to the challenges of a changing world.

REFLECTIVE ACTIVITY 1.3

Imagine you're explaining 'being green' to a friend who doesn't study business.

- How would you describe what it means for a company to be environmentally and socially responsible?

BUSINESS LAW IN ACTION: HOW LEGAL PRINCIPLES SHAPE BUSINESSES AND BUSINESS DECISIONS

Understanding the basics of law in action is a vital skill for business graduates. Before navigating the complexities of sustainability and social responsibility business graduates need to acknowledge that aspects of law have a significant impact on how businesses operate. Without a firm grasp of fundamental legal principles, business and management students risk making decisions that expose their future companies to crippling lawsuits, regulatory penalties, and reputational damage, potentially jeopardising the entire enterprise.

Two important areas to consider are how a business is formed and the importance of operating it in such a way that legal obligations are met under contract and negligence. Employment law is another area that businesses must be aware of (see Chapter 5).

Laws will differ depending on the country and jurisdiction. This section will be referring to the laws of England and Wales.

Business Organisations

Anybody who is setting up a business has options as to how they structure that business. Clear roles, responsibilities and obligations are set out in the Companies Act 2006. Most will do so as a sole trader (self employed) and will be responsible for everything that happens within the business. Where two or more people are setting up a business then a partnership may well be the better option; again, in this situation the partners remain personally liable for any debts incurred by that business. Setting up and registering the business as a limited liability company has the advantage of limiting liability for those members of the company.

Sole Trader

Any person may start a business and trade under their own name and operate as a sole trader. In the UK, you must register for self-assessment with HMRC (the UK tax authority) if you earn more than £1000 in a tax year. As a sole trader they have control of the business and over what happens within the business. It also means that they have unlimited liability both legally and financially and have a responsibility for the same; because of this it can often be a risky move to operate as a sole trader as they could be made bankrupt by creditors of the business. The business will come to an end on the death of the sole trader.

Partnerships

Where two or more people have a business together and do so with the intention of making a profit then this becomes a partnership. Section 1 subsection 1 [S1(1)] of the Partnership Act 1890 defines a partnership as 'the relation which subsists between persons carrying on a business in common'. Very often the formalities of the partnership will be outlined in a written agreement – a partnership deed – which will state, amongst other things, the nature and purpose of the partnership; the business name; capital invested and how the profits are to be shared. Whilst it is good practice to have a written agreement, as stated above, a partnership can be implied simply by two or more people running a business and sharing the profits.

The partnership can trade under the names of the partners or under a business name; if it is the latter then any name must adhere to the regulations set out in the Companies Act 2006.

The Partnership (Unrestricted Size) No 17 Regulation 2001 removed the rule that a commercial partnership could have no more than 20 partners. This rule has never existed for professional partnerships such as solicitors and accountants, whose professional bodies do not allow them to incorporate the business.

All partners have a relationship with each other and owe a duty of good faith including the need to be transparent with each other over any issue or information that relates to, and affects, the partnership; the need to declare any personal benefit received in carrying out partnership business and not to act in competition of the partnership without the agreement of the other partners.

A partnership is not a legal person and because of this the partners are not protected by limited liability and will be personally liable for any debts and/or other legal obligations. Whilst legal action can be taken against a partnership in its own name, the partners remain personally liable for any legal outcomes based on that cause of action. Partners are agents of the business when carrying out business for the partnership and therefore the action of one will have significance for the other partners in terms of any liability under contract and also in tort.

Section 5 of the Partnership Act 1890 states that a contract made by one partner will be binding on all the other partners; however this is only where the contract is made by the partnership in the usual course of its business.

Section 10 of the Partnership Act 1890 states that the partnership is only liable for another partner's tort if: the tort occurred during the ordinary course of the firm's business or the other partners authorised the tort.

Limited Liability Partnerships

The Limited Liability Partnership Act 2000 allows for a partnership to be registered and incorporated and as such they are more like a registered company with the advantage that the liability of the partners (members) is limited to their investment.

Companies

There are several types of companies. The two main types of limited liability companies are public and private companies. They are often referred to as 'legal entities' as once they are incorporated, they acquire their own separate legal existence and are legally independent. The owner of a limited company will have 'limited liability,' meaning personal responsibility for the company's debts is usually limited to the amount of capital (or money) invested when the company was started. The legal principle that marks the beginning of the concept separating a business owner from its incorporated business is drawn from the decision in the case of Salomon v Salomon (1897). Legally all incorporated companies are required to have the words Limited or Ltd after the company name and public companies must have Public Limited Company or PLC.

Private Limited Companies

Private limited companies are the most common form of limited company. They are private companies because, although they issue shares within the company, they cannot sell them to the public through the London Stock Exchange. In comparison, a Public Limited Company (PLC) can sell its shares to the public via the Stock Exchange, which is the primary reason for establishing a PLC.

The process of setting up a limited company requires registration of the company and its proposed name at Companies House. The primary documents that are required to be submitted to the registrar of companies to obtain a certificate of registration are the articles of association and the memorandum of association. The articles of association define the internal rules and regulations of the company, for instance the powers of directors and the allocation of share capital. Historically, the memorandum of association focused on the external regulation of the company, for example its purpose or objectives. However, since the Companies Act 2006, much of the information previously found in the memorandum has been incorporated into the articles, making it most the important company document. At present, a private limited company only requires one director. It is the director who is appointed by the shareholders to manage the day-to-day affairs of the company.

Public Limited Companies

A Public Limited Company (PLC) is similar to a private limited company, but with the significant difference that a PLC can sell its shares on the London Stock Exchange. Establishing a PLC requires a few additional legal steps, including raising £50,000 in share capital. Typically, capital would be raised by advertising in newspapers or online, announcing the creation of the PLC and detailing its purpose and objectives. Once the required £50,000 has been raised, a trading certificate is obtained, and trading can commence.

Similar to a private limited company, a PLC must prepare articles of association and a memorandum of association and obtain a trading certificate. A PLC, however, requires at least two directors and must appoint a qualified company secretary. The company secretary ensures that the company adheres to all its obligations under the Companies Act 2006. The primary purpose of a PLC is to access the larger pool of capital available through the sale of shares on the London Stock Exchange.

Community Interest Companies

Community Interest Companies (CICs) are limited companies designed to benefit the communities they serve, with a primary focus on community welfare rather than private profit. A CIC functions like any other company, possessing all the typical features of a limited company, including being a distinct legal identity, the capacity to enter contracts and own assets in its own name, and the ability to be flexible in its borrowing and fundraising. This separate legal identity ensures that a CIC survives despite changes in ownership or management. Directors of a CIC can be either paid or unpaid and have the same rights and responsibilities as directors of any other company. A CIC must be either a company limited by guarantee, or a company limited by shares. Once incorporated, a company limited by guarantee cannot be converted to a company limited by shares, or vice versa. Historically, companies limited by guarantee have been the traditional choice for entities operating without the intent to distribute profits to members.

Established by the Companies (Audit Investigations and Community Enterprise) Act 2004, CIC's are governed by the Companies Act 2006 and the Community Interest Company Regulations 2005 (secondary legislation). CICs are expected to establish themselves with a clear social purpose that the public understand, and cannot be operated solely for the financial gain of a particular group, for political purposes, or for the benefit of its employees, directors, members, or a single organisation. CICs must demonstrate to the Regulator that their activities are or will be conducted for the benefit of the community, a requirement known as the 'community interest test', and must continue to meet this test throughout their existence. The test will not be met if the CIC engages in certain political activities or if a reasonable person might perceive that its activities are solely for the benefit of a specific group of members or employees of a particular organisation.

If you would like to know more about setting up a business, a good resource is https://www.gov.uk/set-up-business.

REFLECTIVE ACTIVITY 1.4

Consider the following:

- What do you think are the advantages and disadvantages of the different types of business organisation?
- What do you have to consider if you are thinking of setting up a business?

Contract

A contract is an agreement between two or more people. Usually this will be a written agreement, although it is possible to make a verbal contract. An issue with the latter is that, should something go wrong, it can be very difficult to prove in a court of law. Only someone who has legal capacity (18 years old or over) is able to enter into a legally binding contract. For a contract to be legally binding on the parties, a number of elements must exist: there must be an offer, an acceptance of that offer, and an intention to create legal relations; there must also be consideration.

Offer

For an offer to be binding it must be clearly communicated and the terms stated; there will also need to be an intention to be legally bound. The communication of an offer can be written or spoken, but it can also be by conduct such as choosing an item of clothing and taking it to the checkout. Most offers will be bilateral whereby a promise is made in return for a promise, for example to supply goods. A unilateral offer is one where a promise is made subject to the completion of a task such as a reward for the return of a lost pet or item; it is also one that is made to the general public and anyone who would be able to fulfil the terms of that offer, as held in the case of Carlill v Carbolic Smoke Ball Co (1893 CA) which concerned a flu remedy in the form of a 'smoke ball' and an offer of £100 to any buyer who found it did not work. Advertisements are not usually treated by the courts as constituting an offer and are seen as an 'invitation to treat', inviting a party to make an offer regarding, for example, a display of goods in a shop window – Fisher v Bell (1960). An offer can cease to exist in a number of ways including: by death of one of the parties; a rejection or counter offer of the original offer; and if it is not accepted within a specified time or within a reasonable time.

Acceptance

To be legally binding, the acceptance must agree to all terms of the offer and it must be unconditional. The acceptance will also need to be communicated to the person making the offer. There are a number of rules on communication: it must be made by an authorised person and it can also be made by conduct although this needs to be unambiguous as held in the case of Inland Revenue Commissioners v Fry (2001). Acceptance can also be effectively communicated verbally and if not face to face then the courts have held that acceptance by telephone is acceptable and have extended this principle to include communication by telex in the case of Entores Ltd v Miles Far East Corp (1955 CA). In this and similar situations the courts will apply the guidelines of the 'reasonable expectations of honest men' and will no doubt continue to do so concerning other methods of communication such as emails. The postal acceptance rule is an exception to the usual communication rule and established that a contract is binding once a letter of acceptance is posted as in the case Adams v Lindsell (1818).

Consideration

Consideration was defined in the case of Currie v Misa (1875). Each party must give something in return for that which is gained from the other party; it must be sufficient, and it must be of economic value and can be a thing or a service. It can also be a promise, for example, a promise is made not to sue in the event of a car crash providing the person who caused the damage pays to repair the damage. Although exceptions exist, consideration cannot be for something that happened in the past.

Intention to Be Legally Bound

Where there is no intention to be legally bound or to create legal relations, the courts will not consider that the agreement is a contract. Social and domestic agreements between friends or family member are generally presumed not to have that intention while business/commercial agreements are presumed to have the intention to be legally bound.

Terms

The terms of a contract describe the duties and obligation of each party within the agreement. Express terms are generally clear, are specific and are usually put in writing. Implied terms are things that are so obvious that they do not need to be written down. Terms may be implied through: common law; the usual course of business dealings; trade custom and business; and through statute such as the Sale of Goods Act 1979 (as amended by the Sales and Supply of Goods Act 1994) and the Consumer Rights Act 2015.

What Happens When a Term Is Broken?

Where a term of a contract has been broken, damages would be available automatically for such a breach. Damages are designed to compensate the innocent party for any losses suffered because of that breach. It is important to note however that damages can be limited in three ways: by causation; by remoteness; and by mitigation. In addition to the automatic damages, the court has discretion to order other remedies such as specific performance, whereby one party is ordered to perform their contractual obligations and injunctions which are designed to stop or prevent a course of action.

If you would like to know more about contract law, a good resource is Quinn et al.'s *Contract Law* (2025).

REFLECTIVE ACTIVITY 1.5

- Choose two countries and carry out research to identify whether contract principles are the same as those discussed above.
- What might an international company, trading in the UK but based in Asia, have to consider?
- Do you feel that we still need the postal rule for acceptance or is it now outdated with modern technology and social media?

TORT LAW AND ITS RELATIONSHIP WITH THE BUSINESS WORLD

Torts are civil wrongs that are distinct from contract law, and which are crucial for business. The owner and/or business could be held liable for tort claims resulting from negligent actions taken by the owner or those performed by the business at the owner's direction. Essentially, a tort is a civil offence that typically occurs when one person wrongs another, without constituting a criminal offence.

Negligence

The tort of negligence involves situations where an individual owes a duty of care to another person or a group. This duty of care is breached when a wrongful act results in injury, loss, or damage to the person or their property. Notably, negligence can also occur through an omission, where someone fails to act despite having a duty to do so. The primary purpose of tort law is to compensate the injured party by requiring the negligent person to pay damages.

The tort of negligence can be divided into two categories: negligent physical acts that cause harm to others, and negligent statements that others (including businesses) rely on, leading to financial loss.

Negligent Physical Acts

Negligent physical acts (or omissions) are central to the development of the 'modern' law of negligence. Donoghue v Stevenson (1932) AC 562 is the landmark case in negligence law that marks the beginning of this modern approach. It is important to note that this case is the foundation of what we now refer to as the modern law of negligence. The key issue the court needed to determine was whether a product manufacturer has a 'duty of care' to ensure that the end user is not harmed by the product they create. The court ultimately ruled that manufacturers do have such a duty of care to their customers.

In his judgement, Lord Atkin's notable speech emphasised the 'neighbour' principle. He clarified that by 'neighbour,' he meant anyone whom we should reasonably consider might be affected by our actions or inactions in the course of our daily lives. In modern terms, this applies to various activities such as driving a car or riding a bike. Essentially, it covers almost anything you do where your careless or negligent actions (or inactions) could potentially cause harm or loss to someone nearby who is in 'close proximity' and this refers to both physical and legal closeness Bourhill v Young (1943) AC 92. When Lord Atkin uses the term 'reasonable,' he is referring to the reasonable man test, often called the 'Man on the Clapham Omnibus' test. This test represents the perspective of an ordinary person in everyday situations.

Duty of Care

Each case must demonstrate that a duty of care existed, that there was a breach of this duty, and that the breach caused injury before any legal action can proceed. To establish liability, factual causation must be proven. This requires demonstrating a connection between the act or omission and the resulting loss or damage, commonly referred to as the 'chain of causation.' The key question is whether the negligent act or omission was a necessary condition for the harm to occur. If the harm would have occurred regardless of the defendant's carelessness, there is no factual causation. This is commonly referred to as the 'But For' Test: 'But for the carelessness (breach), would the claimant have avoided harm?' If the answer is 'yes', factual causation is established. This principle is illustrated in the case of Barnett v Chelsea and Kensington Hospital Management Committee (1969) 1 QB 428.

We do not owe a duty of care to everyone; each situation must be evaluated on its own merits. Employers have a duty of care to ensure the safety of their employees. Similarly, professionals and professional firms, such as solicitors, banks, surveyors, and accountants, owe a duty of care to their clients, ensuring that the services provided are not negligently performed. This extends to the area of negligent misstatements: Hedley Byrne & Co Ltd v Heller and Partners Ltd (1964) AC 465 HL.

The Significance of Donoghue v Stevenson (1932)

Donoghue's case set out the original test to determine whether a duty of care exists, requiring the answer to each of the following questions to be 'yes' for a negligent claim to succeed:

1 Is a duty of care owed?
2 Has this duty of care been breached?
3 Has damage been caused directly as a result of the breach?

In Caparo Industries v Dickman (1990) the court developed a more modern approach to determining whether a duty of care exists in new cases. This approach is known as the Caparo test, applying a further criterion of whether it is 'fair, just, and reasonable' to impose a duty of care. This last criterion was introduced because the court recognised that there could be situations where imposing a duty of care might be unfair.

Once all three criteria have been met, the court will award damages to place the person in the position that they would have been in had the tort never been committed. Damages are categorised into two types: general and special damages.

If you would like to know more about tort law, a good resource is Quinn's *Elliott & Quinn's Tort Law* (2019).

REFLECTIVE ACTIVITY 1.6

Consider the following:

- What significance do the principles of tort have on businesses and business relations?
- Consider the legal rights that you are likely to have when you enter into a contract based on negligent advice and information given to you by your company bank.
- What reasonable steps would you take to protect your company from being sued by a customer for any harm suffered on your premises?

CHAPTER SUMMARY

This chapter investigated the historical evolution of finance and banking, the role of international trade organisations, and the interconnected nature of PESTLE and VUCA frameworks in business operations.

- Particular attention was given to environmental sustainability and social responsibility, introducing crucial concepts like Equality, Diversity, and Inclusion (EDI) and sustainability management frameworks including SDGs.
- The chapter examined how historical factors such as colonialism have influenced modern business practices, while addressing contemporary challenges like climate change and energy security. Throughout, we emphasised the growing importance of balancing economic performance with environmental and social responsibilities.
- We also explored the legal frameworks governing different business structures – from sole traders to incorporated companies – and the critical importance of understanding contract law and negligence.

STUDENTS LIKE YOU CHANGE THE WORLD

Sean Kelly

Figure 1.2 Sean Kelly

Following a career flitting between St Petersburg, Moscow and Marbella, Sean decided to return home after circumstances in Russia changed. Now working in a large multi-national organisation, he decided to further develop his career by enrolling on the Chartered Management Degree Apprenticeship and hasn't looked back.

Learning about different aspects of business and leadership and management has helped him refocus, given him renewed confidence and opened doors. Sean feels as though he is bettering himself, broadening his horizons and it has taught him how to be a better manager; 'it's not teaching you how to manage, it's about teaching you to lead'.

Sean Kelly's journey proves the transformative power of education. After his travels, he returned home uncertain of his future - until a degree apprenticeship helped him redefine his path. Now, armed with leadership skills and renewed confidence, Sean is shaping the future at his current organisation, mentoring others, and proving that management learning can create lasting impact.

END OF CHAPTER REFLECTION

Have a look at the skills you should have developed in this unit (find more details in the Key Skills Table in the Appendix on pp. 497–98).

1. Which of the skills listed do you think you have developed the most?
2. Can you give two examples on why you feel you have now developed these skills/developed them further?
3. How will you use these new/refined skills in the future (give two examples of the impact of your development on your future behaviour)?

FURTHER READING

Creighton, S. (2022) 'Taiichi Ohno: Hero of the Toyota Production System', *Life QI blog*, June 23. https://blog.lifeqisystem.com/taiichi-ohno

To make processes more efficient, Taiichi Ohno, from Toyota, identified '7 types of waste'. These are things that do not contribute anything useful and that he thought were important to eliminate.

David, N. and Burns, J. (2019) *Business in Context: An Introduction to Business and its Environment*. Cengage Learning.

A useful introductory textbook on business and management offering insights about key activities and contemporary challenges.

Laasch, O. and Conaway, R.N. (2015) *Principles of Responsible Management: Global Sustainability, Responsibility, and Ethics*. Cengage Learning.

A recommended text on the principles and theories of sustainable business management.

Kelly, P. and Ashwin, A. (2013) *The Business Environment*. Cengage Learning.

An accessible text for those new to business and management which usefully reviews the external environment in which organisations operate.

Bates, P. (2021) *Getting Started in Business Law*. Goodfellow.

A useful guide for those who are new to business and/or are looking to start their own business.

Macintyre, E. (2018) *Business Law*. Pearson.

An excellent source for information on all areas of law that affect businesses.

McKendrick (2023) *Contract Law* (Hart Law Masters, 15th edition). Hart.

A very useful guide to contract law with cases and materials.

Finch, E.E. and Fafinski, S. (2021) *Tort Law* (8th edition). Pearson.

A very useful guide to tort law with cases and materials.

REFERENCES

Adams, A., Caplan, E., and Lockwood, G. (2023) *Law for Business Students* (12th edition). Pearson.

Akala (2018) 'The great British contradiction', *RSA Journal*, 164 (2): 18–21.

Bank, J.H., and Davies, G. (2002) *History of Money: From Ancient Times to the Present Day*. University of Wales.

Bang, P. F., Bayly, C. A., and Scheidel, W. (eds.) (2020) *The Oxford World History of Empire: Volume Two: The History of Empires*. Oxford University Press.

British Academy of Management (2024) 'The BAM guide to decolonising the business school curriculum'. https://www.bam.ac.uk/knowledge-hub/decolonising-the-business-school-curriculum.html (accessed October 15, 2026).

Cefalo, A. (2014) 'Inventing the penny: Charlemagne's lost effort at a standard currency', *The Writer-ly World of Andrea Cefalo*, 23 October. https://andreacefalo.com/2014/10/23/inventing-the-penny-charlemagnes-lost-effort-at-a-standard-currency/ (accessed September 1, 2025).

Dar, S., Liu, H., Martinez Dy, A., and Brewis, D.N. (2021) 'The business school is racist: Act up!', *Organization*, 28 (4): 695–706.

Das, D.K. (2011) *Conceptual Globalism and Globalisation: An Initiation* (CSGR Working Paper No. 275). University of Warwck, Centre for the Study of Globalisation and Regionalisation. https://warwick.ac.uk/fac/soc/pais/research/csgr/papers/workingpapers/2011/27511.pdf (accessed September 1, 2025)

Encyclopaedia Britannica (2025) Bank of England. https://www.britannica.com/money/Bank-of-England (accessed September 1, 2025)

Finch, E. and Fafinski, S. (2021) *Tort Law* (8th edition). Pearson.

Findlay, R., and O'Rourke, K.H. (2007) *Power and Plenty: Trade, War, and the World Economy in the Second Millennium*. Princeton University Press.

Graeber, D. (2011) Debt: *The First 5,000 Years*. Melville House.

Hutchins, G. (2013) *The Nature of Business: Redesign for Resilience*. New Society.

Laasch, O., and Conaway, R.N. (2015) *Principles of Responsible Management: Global Sustainability, Responsibility, and Ethics*. Cengage Learning.

NASA (2022). 'Why does climate change matter? We asked a NASA scientist', *NASA*. https://archive.org/details/nasa_tv-Why_Does_Climate_Change_Matter_We_Asked_a_NASA_Scientist (accessed October 30, 2025).

Quinn, F. (2019) *Elliott and Quinn's Tort Law* (12th edition). Pearson.

Quinn, F., Elliott, C., and Aksamit, T. (2025). *Contract Law* (13th edition). Pearson.

Safian, R. (2012) 'This is generation flux: Meet the pioneers of the new (and chaotic) frontier of business', *Fast Company*. https://www.fastcompany.com/1802732/generation-flux-meet-pioneers-new-and-chaotic-frontier-business (accessed November 21, 2025)

SAP Community (2023) 'Strategic insights through PESTEL analysis: Case studies and best practices', *SAP Community*. https://community.sap.com/t5/technology-blog-posts-by-members/strategic-insights-through-pestel-analysis-case-studies-and-best-practices/ba-p/13552745 (accessed October 15, 2025).

Stein, S. (2021) 'Reimagining global citizenship education for a volatile, uncertain, complex, and ambiguous (VUCA) world', *Globalisation, Societies and Education*, 19 (4): 482–95.

Tanzi, V. (2023) 'Laissez faire and the Industrial Revolution', in *Monitoring the State or the Market: From Laissez Faire to Market Fundamentalism* (pp. 17 -24). Cambridge University Press.

Tidd, J., and Bessant, J. (2020) *Managing innovation: Integrating technological, market and organizational change* (7th edition). John Wiley & Sons.

Visser, W. (2011) *The Age of Responsibility: CSR 2.0 and the New DNA of Business*. John Wiley & Sons.

WCED (1987) *Our Common Future* [Brundtland report]. Oxford University Press.

Whitfield, S. (2018). *Silk, Slaves, and Stupas: Material Culture of the Silk Road*. University of California Press.

Williams, H. (2015) *Small Business Handbook* (3rd edition). Lawpack.

2
STRATEGIC MANAGEMENT

Chris Reedthomas

INTENDED LEARNING OUTCOMES

After reading this chapter, you should be able to:

1. Define management and understand the variety of management activities
2. Understand how management thinking has changed over the last 100 years
3. Understand how to apply the POLC cycle and some activities associated with each function
4. Understand why managing strategically is important to business success
5. Reflect on aspects of your management capability

SUSTAINABLE DEVELOPMENT GOALS

In this chapter we address the following SDGs:

- SDG 1: No Poverty - Providing economic benefits to countries to help address poverty.
- SDG 4: Quality Education - Investing in education and training to build a skilled workforce.
- SDG 5: Gender Equality - Reducing inequality by fostering inclusive policies and practices.
- SDG 8: Decent Work and Economic Growth: Providing meaningful work and fair pay to create a more equitable workforce.
- SDG 9: Industry, Innovation, and Infrastructure - Driving innovation through research, development, and sustainable practices.
- SDG 10: Reduced Inequalities - Promoting social and economic inclusion through fair policies.
- SDG 12: Responsible Consumption and Production - Encouraging sustainable business practices and responsible resource use.
- SDG 13: Climate Action: Developing clean technologies and sustainable solutions to combat climate change.
- SDG 16: Peace, Justice, and Strong Institutions - Promoting ethical management and leadership through transparent governance and social justice.
- SDG 17: Partnerships for the Goals - Engaging stakeholders from all parts of society to develop collaboration and community engagement.

- General SDG Alignment: Monitoring and reporting key metrics on progress towards the SDGs to ensure accountability and continuous improvement.

Effective and ethical management within organisations is a key factor in delivering many of the UN Sustainable Development Goals (UN SDGs). Managers have a key role to play in embedding the SDGs into core business functions to ensure businesses are contributing meaningfully to global challenges and fostering a sustainable future.

INTRODUCTION

This chapter will provide a brief overview of the history of management and discuss the relevance of the subject matter to today's world. There will also be some consideration of how a 'one size fits all' does not exist and how principles of management vary across countries and depend on contextual factors.

Why Is Management Important?

Management can be seen as a universal process that occurs in all social and economic activities. It is a key part of any business and, without effective management, organisations of any type will struggle to use resources effectively and meet objectives. Management has a long history, dating back to the beginning of human civilisation. Any activity that requires co-ordination also requires some management ability. In early recorded history, it is clear that the Egyptians used management techniques such as planning, organising, controlling and record keeping. The Chinese, Romans and Greeks also used these principles, along with job descriptions, specialisation and delegation (Wilson and Thomson, 2006).

Management is a core function in any business and the quality and the performance of managers is key to ensuring the success and sustainability of organisations.

What Is Management?

There are many, many definitions of management. Almost all of these allude to co-ordination, or control, over resources to achieve a goal. It is about getting work done to achieve organisational objectives. Managers create and co-ordinate the systems for delivering work, rather than completing the work themselves (Daft, 2014).

Drucker (1963) explains that management is essentially the process through which a group's goals and purposes are identified, clarified, and put into action.

These perspectives reflect a predominantly Western philosophy, but there is a rich diversity of management philosophies across different **cultures**, which can provide valuable lessons and insights for global businesses. Western management philosophy tends to emphasise individual performance and competition, efficiency and short-term shareholder benefits. These ideas have been spread by Western business education, but many cultures are rejecting these notions in favour of integrating cultural values with contemporary business principles, often drawing on traditional values and teachings and incorporating more collective, collaborative, long-term approaches. These will be considered in more detail in the next section.

ACTIVITY 2.1

Conduct some research of your own and find some alternative definitions of management. Consider other cultures and explore their approach:

- How are these similar and how are they different?
- Can you see any consistent themes?

Changes in Thinking About Management

Management is in transition (Laasch, 2024). There has been a growing dissatisfaction with management practice around the world and this has been going on for some time. Parker (2018: 51) discusses how management evolved and became reduced to 'dull grey administration', recently replaced by '**leadership**' as a more attractive alternative. So, we are in a state of flux, a shift from **Old World management** paradigms (seeing businesses as machines) to **New World management** principles (seeing businesses as gardens). This shift is rooted in changing ideas about how organisations function and what they value. Taylor's early 20th-century 'machine' metaphor, originating in his *Principles of Scientific Management* (Taylor, 1911) reflected his view of organisations as systems of control and efficiency, where each worker functioned as a precise part of a larger mechanism. The newer 'garden' metaphor shifts this logic, seeing organisations as living systems that thrive through growth, adaptability, and human creativity rather than rigid control.

A SHORT HISTORY OF MANAGEMENT

Western notions of management developed to ensure consistency and quality. Early management thinking focused on developing scientific principles for managing people and things. An example of the application of scientific thinking were Frederick Taylor's Time studies (Taylor, 1911), which established time taken to achieve a standardised task. These times became the basis for performance of the task. Much of this way of thinking was about reducing cost, increasing profit and efficiency, streamlining processes, and increasing competitiveness, and they often ignored the well-being of workers.

Management became essential following the Industrial Revolution, when workers moved into factories to produce goods at scale. The factories were based on division of tasks and did not require the skilled craftsperson of the past. The semi-skilled labour force, often rural farmworkers, required supervision and with many people engaged in production, co-ordination of activities became essential. As organisations grew and became more complex, management became more and more important and, in time, management came to be seen as a profession.

Many of these factories were unpleasant places to work, often dangerous and brutal. Employers had a huge amount of control and dissent was not tolerated. Local blacklisting meant workers who caused trouble were not able to find work and there was no welfare system back then, just the workhouse.

One of the legacies of the Great War in Europe was a heightened concern for workers' welfare. This growing attention developed alongside the rise of scientific management, reflecting an effort to balance efficiency-driven managerial practices with an increased awareness of employees' well-being. Edward Cadbury, founder of Cadbury's chocolate, brought together employers to consider changes to the management philosophy of the time, known as *Cadbury Conferences*. Around the same time Benjamin Rowntree organised the Rowntree Lecture Series, which brought together people from different levels of the organisation – such as directors, managers, supervisors, and shop-floor staff – to discuss and address the challenges facing industry. (Maclean et al., 2022). This approach helped change British management philosophy to a more scientific and humanistic style. In some ways, this was the start of what we now know as Human Resource Management (see also Chapter 5).

Management was still seen through a scientific lens, often referred to as the machine metaphor. In this, the organisation is seen as a machine, predictable, efficient, and robust. Each part of the organisation performs its task, and each part is essential to the operation of the whole machine. Controlling inputs or processes leads to predictable outputs. If one part of the machine is not functioning properly, it needs to be repaired or replaced.

The profession of management has changed and is becoming increasingly concerned with broader aspects of organisations, rather than simply production. Laasch (2024) suggests professions are occupations serving society and the world, and professional business management should be no exception. This means managers should be working to agreed codes of practice and conduct and should be accountable to society, not just the business.

REFLECTIVE ACTIVITY 2.1

Think about your experience of the modern world.

- Where can you still see scientific management principles applied?
- Can you identify examples of the garden metaphor?
- What other ways of describing organisations can you think of?

NON-WESTERN MANAGEMENT PHILOSOPHIES

The following section introduces a number of non-Western management philosophies, including Bharativa management, Ubuntu management and Confucian management.

Bharatiya Management

This philosophy arose from the recognition that although India has been guided by theories and techniques from the Industrial Revolution, these **models** do not always work well in the Indian context. The perspective integrates traditional Indian values and teachings with innovative modern management practices to create a unique organisational culture. The approach emphasises the development of long-term relationships, flexibility and social responsibility (Cappelli, 2010).

Bharatiya management is based on several key principles, drawn from Indian spiritual wisdom. These include:

Spiritual and ethical practice (Dharma) – ethics and moral values provide the basis for decision-making, rather than shareholder returns.

Servant leadership – workers are seen as key **stakeholders** and not simply resources. There is a focus on development and spiritual well-being.

Innovation with limited resources (Jugaad) – this is a flexible approach to problem-solving which focuses on the creation of innovative solutions with limited resources.

Inclusivity (Vasudhaiva Kutumbakam) – this can be translated as 'The World Is One Family'. Businesses need to focus on their social responsibilities, **sustainability** and inclusivity.

MINI CASE STUDY 2.1

Examples of Organisations Embracing Bharatiya

This case study looks at two different organisations integrating Bharatiya principles in different ways.

Tata Group

The Tata Group embraces the concept of Bharatiya (Sudhakar, 2021), blending this with Western management approaches. In line with Bharatiya principles, where management is seen as a moral and holistic practice that balances material success with social duty and collective wellbeing, Tata prioritises employee welfare and sustainable development to maintain a strong and positive relationship with its workforce. There is a focus on supporting social initiatives and creating sustainable value that reflects long-term thinking as they help transform the Indian economy. Tata supports CSR activities in four main areas: Health, Environment, Education and Skill Development and Women Empowerment (Tata Group, 2024).

(Continued)

Infosys

Infosys is a leader in digital services and consulting, operating in more than 50 countries around the world with more than 300,000 employees. The purpose of Infosys is 'To amplify human potential and create the next opportunity for people, businesses and communities' (Infosys, 2025). Their **ESG** roadmap reflects many of the principles of Bharatiya and focuses on an inclusive workplace, community strategies to leverage technology and balancing stakeholder expectations and a sustainable future through continuous engagement (Infosys, 2024).

Ubuntu Management

The Ubuntu management philosophy is also based on the understanding that traditional Western notions of management do not work well in other cultures. Ubuntu philosophy originates from Bantu-speaking communities across sub-Saharan Africa and represents a worldview that emphasizes communal values such as interconnectedness, mutual respect, and shared responsibility (Mangaliso, 2001). The philosophy gained international prominence following South Africa's transition to democracy in the 1990s, when leaders such as Nelson Mandela and Desmond Tutu advocated for Ubuntu principles to be integrated into national reconstruction efforts. At its core, Ubuntu embodies what Mangaliso (2001: 24) describes as 'humaneness – a pervasive spirit of caring and community, harmony and hospitality, respect and responsiveness that individuals and groups display for one another.' Mbigi (2005) explores the non-individualistic character of sub-Saharan Africa and suggests 'Although African cultures display awesome diversity, they also show remarkable similarities. Community is the cornerstone in African thought and life' (Mbigi, 2005: 75). While the term 'Ubuntu' is most-commonly associated with Southern Africa, equivalent concepts exist across the continent, including 'umunthu' in Malawi and Zambia, 'unhu' in Zimbabwe, and 'obuntu' in Uganda and Kenya.

To address the imbalance between what African managers have been taught about management by Western educational institutions and their lived experience of communal social systems, Lutz (2009) suggests the first step is in recognising the **firm** as a community and not a collection of individuals.

Like Bharatiya, the Ubuntu management philosophy is based on a number of key principles (Hampden-Turner and Trompenaars, 1995; Mangaliso, 2001). These include:

Human centred leadership – the focus is on people first, profit second. Ubuntu management views organisations as a community and success is seen as a collective rather than individual achievement. Leaders are expected to act with compassion and humility.

Ethical and moral responsibility – businesses embrace honesty, fairness and integrity in decision-making.

Consensus-based decision-making – employees contribute to strategic decision-making and leaders make decisions based on collective agreement.

Trust – relationships are built on trust and interpersonal connections between stakeholders including employees, customers and society.

MINI CASE STUDY 2.2

Examples of Organisations Embracing Ubuntu Management

This case study looks at two different organisations embracing Ubuntu management.

Nelson Mandela Foundation

The Nelson Mandela Foundation is a non-profit organisation doing memory, dialogue and legacy work, founded by Nelson Mandela in 1999. The vision for the Foundation is *'Our vision is a just society, one which learns from its past and listens to all its voices.'* Their principles are to promote ethical leadership and social justice, and Ubuntu is a key part of this, as it was to Mandela. He promoted Ubuntu as the foundation for reconciliation in post-apartheid South Africa and the Truth and Reconciliation Commission embodies Ubuntu with its focus on healing rather than revenge.

South African Breweries (SAB)

SAB is a leading brewery operating seven breweries across South Africa. The values of Ubuntu are embedded into the corporate culture through community initiatives and leadership. There is a people first approach with an emphasis on the collective, not the individual. This is reflected in their principles which are built on ownership, informality, candour, transparency and meritocracy (SAB, 2025). The SAB Foundation is involved with the creation of sustainable businesses, supporting job creation, building communities and helping address social issues.

Confucian Management

Well over half of private enterprises in China (some data from a Chinese industry federation actually report numbers as high as 80%) are family owned (Xie and Yuan, 2025) and will be heavily influenced by the Confucian philosophy in their management practices and governance (Li et al., 2021). Based on the teachings of Confucius, the philosophy emphasises hierarchy and respect for authority, virtue and integrity in leadership and harmony in the workplace. Business success is based on the quality of relationships, trust and loyalty, rather than formal contracts. The philosophy has influenced businesses across East Asia.

The key principles of Confucian management include (Ip, 2009):

Hierarchy and respect (Li) – Li can be seen as being about rituals and traditions, respect for authority and hierarchy, and this is embedded in Confucian philosophy. Employees show respect for their leaders and, in turn, leaders show benevolence and ethical behaviour.

Moral Leadership (Ren) – benevolence and humanity are foundations of Confucian thought and suggest leaders should act with integrity and fairness. Leaders should make decisions based on ethics.

Harmony and Consensus (He) – collaboration and teamwork are encouraged, and conflict is minimised through diplomatic behaviour.

Relationships and Networking (Guanxi) – long term success is built on strong personal and business relationships, not rigid contracts. This leads to trust and loyalty.

MINI CASE STUDY 2.3

Examples of Organisations Embracing Confucian Management

This case looks at two companies embracing Confucian philosophy.

Huawei

Huawei is one of China's largest technology companies and it operates in many technology sectors including telecommunications, consumer goods, IT infrastructure and smart devices. It employs over 200,00 people in 170 different countries.

Huawei embraces Confucian philosophy. It has a strict hierarchy, and respect for leadership as a core value. This is balanced by benevolence from senior managers, exemplified through mentoring and collective leadership based on common values, focused responsibility and democratic centralised authority (Huawei, 2025). There is a strong sense of community, supported by employee **stock** ownership.

However, the highly disciplined corporate structure can lead to long hours and an 'overtime culture'. This intense work culture has been associated with high staff turnover.

Samsung

Samsung is one of South Korea's largest conglomerates, operating a highly diversified portfolio. Confucian philosophy is embedded in their mission, values and principles that are based on respect (for customers, employees and shareholders), harmony, dignity, relationship building and collective growth (Samsung, 2025).

There is a hierarchical structure with respect for seniority based on formality and respect. Ethical responsibility is also emphasised in Samsung's culture and Samsung has an aim to be one of the most ethical companies in the world.

This culture does have a downside, and the expectation of loyalty can result in difficulties for employees to push back against excessive hours. The rigid hierarchy can make it difficult for younger workers to challenge leaders, and increased bureaucracy can slow decision-making.

Systems Thinking

The *machine* or *garden* metaphors work quite well to describe the function of management, but they do not really address the complexity of organisations. In the 1940s a new way of looking at social structures, which includes organisations, began to emerge (Von Bertalanffy, 1950). In this view, organisations are regarded as systems and systems are made of small, highly interrelated subsystems which interact with one another. The output of one system becomes the input for another. Often these relationships are reciprocal. So, changes to one subsystem can affect other connected subsystems, often in unpredictable ways.

This gives rise to complex webs of interactions in which cause and effect become unpredictable.

Imagine an organisation with the usual departments – e.g. **finance**, human resource management (HRM), sales, **marketing**, production. The marketing subsystem hits on a novel way to promote a product, sales increase dramatically, but production cannot keep up with **demand**. Delays to shipping orders and a drop in quality (as production is ramped up) result in increasing customer complaints and a decline in reputation. Sales drop. Production now outstrips demand. Marketing has to change strategy. Revenue drops, human resources (HR) ban overtime and make redundancies, talent leaves. A vicious cycle ensues, and the organisation is out of control.

These effects are often only clear in hindsight and managers are left wondering why their solutions did not work. This reflects organisations as **complex systems**.

Peter Senge defines systems thinking as: ‘a framework for seeing interrelationships rather than things, for seeing patterns rather than static snapshots. It is a set of general principles spanning fields as diverse as physical and social sciences, engineering and management’ (Senge, 1997: 68–9).

Systems can be open or closed.

Closed systems are isolated from the environment and people or things tend to stay within the system. Closed social systems may include social media systems, such as Facebook. Our smartphones act as a sort of ecosystem and one can think of Apple’s iOS as being a closed system – Apple has full control over the software (OS and apps) and the hardware. Google’s Android OS could be seen as an open system as it can be run on different hardware and there is no control over the apps that can be installed. The Apple iOS is becoming a more open system as it is forced to allow sideloading (installation of apps from outside the App Store) in order to comply with the EU’s Digital Markets Act (DMA) (Apple, 2024).

Open systems interact with their environment so include most organisations, countries, societies etc. The environment is one component of a system, which establishes the resources it can access and relationships with other systems.

An essential component of open systems, and one of the most interesting, is feedback. Feedback is information from outputs that can be applied to the input, to change the nature of transformation of resources. What this means is the interrelationship is reciprocal. This gives rise to the view of organisations as **Complex Adaptive Systems** (CAS) and this leads us into the sometimes-strange world of complexity theory and organisations. Complex adaptive systems are found all around us, in our societies, organisations and social systems (Miller and Page, 2007).

Holland (1992) defines a CAS as: 'a dynamic network of agents acting in parallel, constantly reacting to what other agents are doing, which in turn influences behaviour and the network as a whole' (p. 68).

CAS show a number of characteristic properties:

- a large number of elements that interact dynamically
- any element in the system is affected by and affects several other systems
- non-linear interactions, so small changes can have large effects
- openness, so it may be difficult to define system boundaries
- a constant flow of energy to maintain the organisation of the system
- a history whereby the past helps to shape present behaviour
- elements in the system are not aware of the behaviour of the system as a whole and respond only to what is available or known locally (Health Foundation, 2010)

From a management perspective, individual employees are those agents, acting in networks, influencing and, in turn, being influenced by each other. These characteristics make the behaviour of the system inherently unpredictable in which cause and effect is hard to determine and order is an emergent phenomenon. Whilst this may sound like a big problem for managers, understanding organisations as systems, and people as the individual agents, gives us a guide to how we can direct organisations and prepare for unexpected consequences. Many authors suggest CAS cannot be controlled, in the way traditional management would like to, but they can be directed. Some of the ways managers can do this is to encourage employees to be autonomous whilst setting clear objectives, delegation of responsibility and authority, building a diverse workforce and ensuring feedback loops operate effectively (Palmberg, 2009).

Systems thinking is itself evolving with an increasing emphasis on complexity thinking. The complexity view reflects the nature of organisations as many managers see them in practice – unpredictable, non-linear (cause and effect are hard to determine) and often paradoxical. Understanding this and being open to 'nudging' systems can help managers in this increasingly VUCA (volatile, uncertain, complex and ambiguous) environment (Bennett and Lemoine, 2014).

WHAT DO MANAGERS DO?

REFLECTIVE ACTIVITY 2.2

Take a few moments and think about your experience of managing or being managed. This can be formal management roles at work or school, or it could be informal management, where you were trying to get something done. Write some brief notes in response to this question - what do managers do?

You have probably come up with things like

- Organising people
- Making to do lists
- Planning activities
- Co-ordinating activities
- Controlling people and activities
- Monitoring progress
- Checking performance against objectives

Your list probably looks similar to the definitions above, and the ideas put forward by Fayol and others still provide a basic framework for modern management practice. Fayol suggested that management consisted of five core elements: forecasting and planning, organising, commanding, coordinating, and controlling (Fayol, 1949). He defined management as: 'to forecast and plan, to command, to co-ordinate and to control' (Fayol, 1949: 5).

This framework is still very prevalent today and is usually represented as the **POLC cycle (Planning, Organising, Leading, and Controlling)**. This is shown in Figure 2.1 as a cycle, as there is an order, but some managers may not be involved in all parts, and it may not run sequentially all the time!

Figure 2.1 The POLC cycle

- **Planning** – setting objectives and then devising actions to achieve that objective. This is a fundamental organisational process and operates at all levels of an organisation. Objectives are set within the context of the internal and external business environments. Planning is also cyclical in nature and involves setting objectives, identifying possible actions to take, deciding on the best action, implementing the action and evaluating effectiveness.

- **Organising** – operates at many levels within an organisation. Indeed, organisational design – how we should structure our business for success – is a fundamental organising process. Organising extends through functions, departments, teams, and to individual job design, skill requirements and competence.
- **Leading** – in this model, leadership is seen as a subset of management. This is quite controversial and for a more detailed discussion of leadership, read Chapter 4. In brief, the difference between leadership and management is still a hotly debated subject. Management can be seen as controlling the production of outputs, whereas leadership can be seen as inspiring people to perform. So managers 'do things right' and leaders 'do the right things'. What is clear is that to be effective in modern organisations, we need to be able to act as leaders *and* managers. Here, managers need to be able to exercise leadership, which is usually seen as motivating and inspiring action in others through social influence.
- **Controlling** – standards of work, quality and performance. Control is needed to ensure quality standards are met. We all want to know quality standards are being met as we board an aircraft or are wheeled into an operating theatre!

The POLC model has been criticised as it is often seen as an ideal. Mintzberg (1989: 9) suggests, 'If you ask managers what they do, they will most likely tell you that they plan, organise, coordinate, and control. Then watch what they do. Don't be surprised if you can't relate what you see to those four words'. Lamond (2004) suggests Mintzberg and Fayol are both right, they are just giving different perspectives and taken together this gives a more integrated base for management research.

THE POLC CYCLE

This section will look in more detail at the POLC cycle and consider some aspects of what managers do in each of the phases.

Planning

Planning is a key role for managers in most organisations, large or small. Managers will spend time deciding where the organisation needs to go and how it will get there. This may be formal or informal, but all other management activities follow from this fundamental process. This section will consider some core aspects of the planning process.

Planning can take place at different management levels. Indeed, one factor that defines seniority in management is the time span and scope of planning activities. The higher the level of planning, the longer the timescale and the more complex and uncertain the outcomes. Company directors may be looking at where the whole organisation is going over a time scale of ten or more years. Senior managers will develop plans for how these high-level objectives can be met by divisions or departments and lower-level managers will be planning local and short-term delivery of objectives (see Figure 2.2).

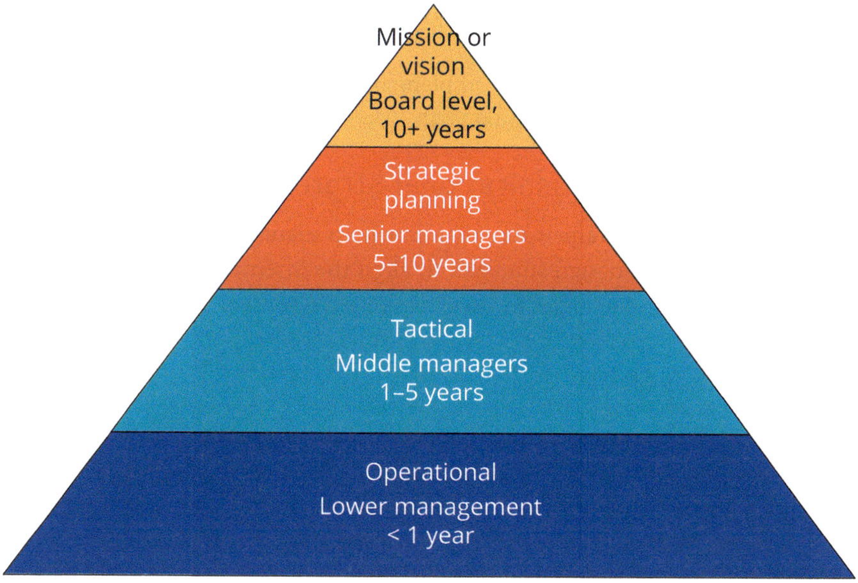

Figure 2.2 Levels of planning and decision-making

There is a clear connection between levels so that activity across the organisation is focused on delivering the mission or vision. Individuals and teams should be able to describe a clear link from their day-to-day activities to the overall departmental and organisational goals. Sometimes a preoccupation with operational issues can cause senior managers to lose sight of the big strategic goals as they wrestle with short term, monthly or quarterly targets. This can lead to underperformance at many levels.

Organisational Strategy

At the top of the triangle in Figure 2.2 lies organisational strategy. Strategy is a key element of management and defines the long-term direction and the goals of the organisation. Strategy reflects the vision and mission of the organisation, which in turn, are based on the core values and purpose of the organisation.

An effective strategy helps an organisation address current challenges but also helps anticipate future trends, opportunities and threats. In this way, strategy provides a road map for organisational adaptability in a changing world.

Components of Organisational Strategy

1. **Vision and Mission**: The vision articulates the long-term aspirations, while the mission defines the purpose and core values of the organisation.
2. **Goals and Objectives**: Clear, measurable targets that guide the organisation's efforts.
3. **Resource Allocation**: Efficient distribution of human, financial, and technological resources to achieve objectives.

4 **Competitive Advantage**: Identification and development of unique capabilities that set the organisation apart.
5 **Strategic Planning**: Formulation, implementation, and evaluation of strategies to ensure alignment with organisational goals.

Theoretical Models in Organisational Strategy

There are many theoretical frameworks that can help managers analyse the internal and external environments and design strategies to align the internal structure and processes to meet the requirements of challenges in the external environment.

Porter's Five Forces Model

Possibly one of the most commonly used models was developed by Michael Porter in 1979. Although this was originally developed as an economic model, it has proved popular in helping organisations understand their environment and shape strategies. The model can be used to analyse the competitive forces that shape industries and affect profitability. The five forces are:

- **Threat of New Entrants**: The ease with which new competitors can enter the market. Barriers might include cost, access to resources or regulatory approval.
- **Bargaining Power of Suppliers**: The influence suppliers have on pricing and quality. Supply chain management is a key element of strategy.
- **Bargaining Power of Customers**: The power customers have to influence prices.
- **Threat of Substitute Products or Services**: The ease with which customers can switch to alternative products or suppliers.
- **Industry Rivalry**: The intensity of competition among existing players. (After Porter, 1979)

Understanding how these forces affect the organisation can help managers devise strategies to reduce threats and maximise opportunities for growth.

SWOT Analysis

Another widely used tool is SWOT analysis. SWOT stands for Strengths, Weaknesses, Opportunities and Threats. SWOT can be used to review the current situation in an organisation, allowing managers to anticipate internal and external factors to support strategy. The strengths and weaknesses are internal factors and opportunities and threats are the external factors. Understanding these factors can help managers maximise strengths, address weaknesses, exploit opportunities and minimise threats.

PESTLE Analysis

PESTLE analysis (Political, Economic, Sociological, Technological, Legal and Environmental) examines the macro-environmental factors affecting an organisation. Each factor provides insights into external influences, enabling organisations to align their strategies with broader trends and conditions. This can involve techniques such as **scenario planning**, where organisations look many years into the future, extrapolating trends to try and guide strategic thinking. Shell, the global petrochemical company, has pioneered scenario planning and published its scenarios for the future (Shell, n.d.). The scenarios are not predictions, they are simply what seem plausible results of different action paths, given current trends. (Chapter 1 considers PESTLE analysis in more detail.)

Balanced Scorecard

Developed by Robert Kaplan and David Norton (2005) the Balanced Scorecard provides a comprehensive framework for performance measurement and strategy implementation. It evaluates an organisation's performance across four perspectives:

- **Financial**: Profitability and revenue growth.
- **Customer**: Customer satisfaction and retention.
- **Internal Processes**: Efficiency and quality of operations.
- **Learning and Growth**: Employee development and **innovation**.

Resource-Based View (RBV)

The Resource-Based View of the firm emerged in the later part of the 20th century. It focuses on an organisation's internal resources and capabilities as the foundation for competitive advantage. According to the RBV, resources must be:

- **Valuable**: Contribute to efficiency and effectiveness.
- **Rare**: Not readily available or commonly held by competitors.
- **Inimitable**: Difficult to replicate.
- **Non-Substitutable**: Cannot be replaced by alternative resources.

An example of RBV is Toyota's lean manufacturing system. Its focus on efficiency and quality has enabled it to achieve sustained competitive advantage in the automotive industry.

The Planning Process

Kaplan and Norton (2008) put forward a 'closed loop planning management system' linking strategy and operations. This has five stages and is a typical planning cycle:

Step 1: Devise the strategy. Integration of analysis (of market, stakeholders, economy, competition etc.), mission and values, competencies and processes to form a strategy statement.

Step 2: Translate the strategy. The statement can then be broken down into smaller steps, with objectives, goals and measures.

Step 3: Operationalise. Develop actions to deliver the objective and identify resources required. Develop sub-plans like HRM planning and sales planning.

Step 4: Monitor. Review progress on a regular basis and monitor against agreed measures of success.

Step 5: Adapt. Adapt the strategy to keep it on track to deliver objectives and be prepared to look again at strategy in the light of changing assumptions.

This classic planning process is rooted in the Old World Management. The reality of delivering a plan like this in the real world involves constant adjustment of the plan to meet organisational needs. The system view suggests the need for plans to be deeply interconnected and ensure changing one functional plan does not adversely influence another function. Managers need to look out for the law of unintended consequences. This may be evidenced in performance management. Setting targets can lead to unethical behaviour as individuals seek to meet their goals.

Because complex adaptive systems are continuously and dynamically changing in response to changes in the environment, strategic planning that focuses on logical cause and effect steps may not be sufficient. The focus needs to shift to managing the relationships among internal and external groups, increasing connections, managing uncertainty and dealing with **emergence**.

CASE STUDY 2.1

Unintended Consequences

In a complex system, cause and effect are hard to determine, so change can be difficult to achieve. The system can become resilient to change programmes, particularly top-down traditional change. When change happens, it is **emergent**. It arises from the complex interactions of the many individuals and groups. Sometimes, what emerges is not what was expected, and these can be described as unintended consequences. Unintended consequences can be functional or dysfunctional (Harris and Ogbonna, 2002) and they seem to be an inevitable part of most change efforts in complex systems. Meissener and Mello (2022) analysed the unintended consequences of UN sanctions and found there was often a negative impact of sanctions on the general population. The sanctions on Haiti between 1993 and 1994 resulted in severe health problems due to malnutrition. Similarly sanctions on Iraq (2003) and Iran (2006) resulted in a lack of clean drinking water and food which led to disease and death. Other unintended consequences included increased domestic production to cope with shortages and the strengthening of trade relations with non-sanctioned countries.

Whilst sanctions are designed to punish nation states, international development projects are designed to benefit the general population in nation states. Yet, here too, there are unintended consequences. Davidson et al. (2022) looked at unintended consequences from interventions in **fragile and conflict-affected situations (FCAS).** They found the most common unintended consequences were aggravation of the conflict and unintended support for one side or another. They also found assessments of the intervention were only from the donor side and suggest alternative viewpoints need to be analysed.

A good example of unintended consequences in the developed world comes from a study of target setting in the NHS in the UK (Quinn et al., 2023). The NHS is a huge, complex adaptive system. Braithwaite (2018) suggests no other industry offers such a wide and complex landscape – with intricate funding structures, numerous interconnected elements, diverse clients with varying needs, and an array of options and interventions tailored to each individual.

The NHS in the UK sets many targets for performance in hospital trusts and other elements of the health system. In 2012 the NHS introduced a new target for NHS hospital trusts to reduce waiting times. The new target stated that 92% of patients should be seen within an 18-week window – the '18-week referral to treatment standard'.

This states that 92% of patients waiting for treatment (notwithstanding those who, for good reasons, cannot be seen within the 18-week period) should have been waiting 18 weeks or less. If a hospital trust feels achieving this is unlikely, there will be little change in behaviour. For hospitals close to the targets, there could be an incentive to prioritise patients who are close to the 18-week window, rather than patients already beyond 18 weeks, or have been waiting less than 18 weeks, irrespective of clinical need. If a hospital trust is motivated by meeting the target, rather than by clinical need, this will show up as a spike of trusts where the threshold is only just met. This is known as a discontinuity and there are many examples from all walks of life.

Sanctions for failing to meet the standard varied during the study but could include increased external monitoring and financial penalties. The financial penalties could be up to 2.5% of healthcare income.

The **data** did show a threshold effect which was most pronounced in 2016/17, after which the sanctions became non-financial. This showed a large spike in the number of trusts exactly meeting the 92% target threshold for the 18-week referral, followed by a drop after the target had been reached. It is interesting to note that the effect disappeared in 2020/21 and 2021/22 as hospitals struggled with the COVID-19 pandemic and the majority of trusts were unable to meet the target.

Quinn et al. (2023: 719) conclude that: 'While targets may improve hospital trust performance in healthcare systems, our data suggest that this comes at a cost and that hospitals may target specific patients rather than implementing systematic change, which can help all patients and respect clinical judgement.'

Questions

1. How can the inclusion of multiple perspectives (e.g., donor vs. recipient in international aid) improve the design and implementation of interventions in fragile contexts?
2. What strategies could be used to minimise dysfunctional unintended consequences when designing interventions in complex systems?
3. In what ways might well-intentioned interventions – like development aid or performance targets – reinforce existing inequalities or power imbalances?

Organising

Once strategy has been decided and plans made, the manager's role is to organise efforts to deliver the plan. This is another aspect of managing that operates at many different levels, the differentiator being the scope and timescale of the organisational effort.

Organising is the process of assigning tasks and allocating resources to achieve strategic goals. Strategy defines *what* the organisation, and managers, need to do and organising defines *how* the strategy will be delivered. The way the organisation is structured is a key part of this process and includes how formal tasks are assigned to departments, teams and individuals. It will also define the reporting relationships, lines of authority and span of managerial control.

The formal task allocation and reporting relationships is often represented as an **organisation chart**, a visual representation of the structure. This will show the chain of command, the formal line of authority, responsibility and communication that defines who each employee reports to in the organisation.

Organisational Design and Structure

Organisational design (OD) is the process whereby senior management match organisational strategy to internal and external demands and identify the structure needed to meet the strategy.

The CIPD (Chartered Institute of Personnel and Development) defines organisational design as:

> Organisation design, or re-design, focuses on aligning the shape and structure of an organisation with its strategy. It involves:
>
> - reviewing what an organisation wants and needs
> - analysing the gap between where it is and where it wants to be
> - designing organisational practices that bridge that gap.
>
> (CIPD, 2023)

There are many models to help managers with OD but many of them are still rooted in the stable, the predictable, linear models of organisations. These models include the *McKinsey 7 S model, the Weisbord 6 boxes* and the *Burke-Litwin Model*, all well-known and frequently used models. Discussing these models in depth is beyond the scope of this chapter, see below for a summary of their key contributions:

- The McKinsey 7 S model was developed by Robert Waterman, Tom Peters, and Julien Phillips in 1980 (Waterman et al., 1980). This is still a useful tool to understand the complexity of organisations. It focuses on the coordination and interrelatedness of seven elements – Structure, Strategy, Shared Values, Style, Skills, Systems and Staff.
- Marvin Weisbord (1976) suggests that organisations need to understand six factors, namely:
  - **Purposes** – our mission and goal
  - **Structure** – how does the work get divided up? Does the current structure (departments, units, hierarchy) clearly support the achievement of purposes?
  - **Relationships** – are the relationships between individuals, groups, and necessary technologies effective and collaborative?
  - **Rewards** – what are the incentives for delivering goals?

  - **Leadership** – who is monitoring all of this? Is the leadership ensuring the fit between the other five boxes?
  - **Helpful Mechanisms** – have we adequate coordinating technologies and processes? Are the formal systems (planning, budgeting, information technology) truly helping us coordinate our activities across the organisation? (After Weisbord, 1976)
- The Burke Litwin model (Burke and Litwin, 1992) is used to understand drivers of change. It emphasises the external environment as the most important driver of change and focuses on identifying the implications of these drivers internally.

Naomi Stanford suggests many organisations need a more dynamic approach to OD. She defines OD as: 'Organization design is arranging how to do the work necessary to effectively and efficiently achieve a business purpose and strategy while delivering high-quality customer and employee experience' (Stanford, 2018: 7).

This definition clearly shows that OD is not just about structure, but about the integration of the strategy, the processes for delivering strategy, the work itself and the people delivering the work. This is something many organisations miss as they fiddle with the organisation chart, thinking that will solve their problems.

Complexity thinking suggests seeing organisations as a web of interconnected and coordinated elements, rather than boxes, is a better way of viewing OD and structure as it allows organisations to adapt to changing circumstances more effectively. This reflects the nature of organisations as open systems, as discussed earlier.

Organising Teams

In most organisations teams are the fundamental building block for delivering objectives and it is usually a manager's job to set teams up for success.

Katzenbach and Smith (2015) proposed that teams outperform individuals acting alone and felt that, despite teams existing for hundreds of years, the potential impact of teams on organisational performance is under-exploited. This may be explained by misunderstandings about what makes teams perform and a reluctance to recognise group accountability. Their model of team basics blends Accountability, Commitment and **Skills** to help develop high performing teams.

Accountability – within teams, accountability is mutual, not just individual. So, in effective teams, individuals are accountable for each other's performance. These are underpinned by trust and commitment to a common purpose.

Commitment – teams will only be effective when they are working towards a common purpose (mutually agreed goals) with a common approach (an agreed way of working together).

Skills – teams require an appropriate mix of skills in order to be effective. Skills include technical skills, problem-solving and decision-making skills and interpersonal skills.

CASE STUDY 2.2

Creating a High Performing Team at Mercedes-AMG Petronas

Formula 1 (F1) began in 1950 with the British Grand Prix at Silverstone. It is now a global motorsport event, with 24 races around the world visiting 21 countries. It is owned by Liberty Media. The 'Formula' refers to the set of rules that govern all aspects of the car - engine size, engine components, car design and many more elements.

Mercedes entered Formula 1 in the 1950s but dropped out only to re-enter in the 2010 season. Since then, they have won seven consecutive Drivers' World Championships and a record eight consecutive Constructors Championships. Teams can have around 1000 people working in them, in a huge variety of roles. It is a demanding environment, and performance is delivered through technical excellence and teamwork.

As Mercedes-AMG Petronas put it:

> Best Team wins. Best driver wins. In that order.
>
> (Mercedes-AMG Petronas, 2024)

The team is organised like many other businesses with a Board and a Management Team covering all the areas you would expect in a business, for example, technical, communications, HR and people, and finance.

Mercedes has a very strong ethos of performance based on trust. They recognise the need for people to be accountable, they need to learn from failure and demonstrate integrity. This can only happen with high levels of psychological safety, when employees feel able to trust others and voice their opinions. Edmondson (1999: 354) defines psychological safety as: 'a shared belief amongst individuals as to whether it is safe to engage in interpersonal risk-taking in the workplace'.

Trust is essential in building psychological safety and has two components, *cognitive trust* and *affective trust*.

Cognitive trust is the trust we have in someone's competence; their ability to do the job effectively to the highest standard.

Affective trust is the trust we have in someone to care about us rather than caring about themselves. It is also the integrity of another person, the trust we have that they will do what they say they will do.

For teams to perform to a high level, trust and psychological safety are essential. Teams need a high degree of interdependence, relying on each other through mutual support. To achieve high performance, there can be no functional silos, as in many organisations.

In Mercedes-AMG there is a tightly woven network of relationships between the functional areas, which include design, engineering, mechanics, testing, racing, marketing, finance and logistics. The network becomes even more complex through close collaboration with many external partners. These separate disciplines become further inter-related through a growing number of complicated collaborations with partners outside their own organisations. It is how these pieces are brought together through visionary leadership and effective teamwork that creates a culture of trust, continual learning and psychological safety (Pasternak, 2024).

Questions

1. How do cognitive and affective trust contribute differently to team dynamics at Mercedes-AMG Petronas?
2. What challenges might arise from the high level of interdependence across functions and external partners in a high performing team?
3. How can a culture of continual learning and failure-based improvement help maintain competitive advantage?

REFLECTIVE ACTIVITY 2.3

Think about a team you have been a member of. This may be a social group or a work group, at university or in a work setting.

- How much did you *trust* other team members to perform their role effectively?
- Did you feel able to make mistakes or speak your mind safely?
- Did you understand a clear shared mission and goals?

Leading

Whilst good management is important in delivering organisational outcomes, managers need to be leaders too. Management and leadership are based on different skillsets and attributes that are complementary. To be effective in organisations, individuals need to be able to demonstrate both sets.

Much has been written about the differences between managers and leaders. Leadership is often seen as being about creativity and change and management about stability and order. One cannot replace the other. Good managers help the organisation deliver its current services or products whereas leadership is essential for organisations to adapt to the future.

Thinking about leadership success has changed significantly over the last 100 years. This section is an overview of how thinking has changed. (For more detail on leadership models and theories, see Chapter 4.)

Early models focused on the personal characteristics, the traits, that leaders possessed. This approach is problematic as there was no agreement on a consistent set of traits that might define good leadership. Much the same could be said for the skills approach to understanding leadership. Rather than being based on innate characteristics, this approach was based on the **knowledge** and skill required for leadership. This included technical skills, decision-making and problem-solving skills and interpersonal skills.

It was clear that understanding personality characteristics and the capabilities of leaders did not explain leadership. During the mid-part of the 20th century the behavioural approach emerged, based on what leaders do and how they act. Many behavioural models emerged, many based on the balance between task-focused **behaviours** and people-focused behaviours. This led to the development of situational leadership models, which emphasised different types of leadership were required in different situations. This was the first leadership thinking that included recognition of the role of followers and the need to consider follower motivation in order to balance giving direction with giving support.

In the 1980s the transformational leadership approach emerged. This approach attracted a huge amount of interest and is still a much-studied theory. Transformational leadership acknowledges the crucial role of followers and focuses on the relationship between leaders and followers in achieving organisational goals.

These views of leadership as a social influence process have continued with the development of many different perspectives including servant leadership, authentic leadership, adaptive leadership and ethical or moral leadership.

Ethical Leadership

One of the more recent perspectives on leadership is ethical leadership, which is concerned with the role leaders have in building a more caring, sustainable society. The focus here is on what leaders do and who they are (Northouse, 2021), their behaviour and their moral integrity. Leaders have an ethical responsibility to followers, whether inside or outside an organisation, and this includes external stakeholders such as customers, communities and society. As leaders exercise considerable influence in directing followers towards goals, they have a special responsibility towards others.

CASE STUDY 2.3

The Dark Side of Leadership

Leadership, as a social influence process, can be enacted by people at any level in an organisation, not just people in designated 'leadership' roles. However, if leadership becomes divorced from ethics, leadership motives can be directed towards goals that are not consistent with ethical practices. The lack of responsible leadership, also referred to as the **dark side of leadership**, toxic leadership or destructive leadership, in which leadership goals are for personal gain rather than societal good, has caused many scandals over the last few years.

Cross Selling Scandal at Wells Fargo

Wells Fargo is one of the biggest and most successful banks in the USA. It emerged largely unscathed from the banking collapse in 2008 and became the third largest bank in the US. This success was built on a combination of building deep customer relations and an active sales culture. The vision and values of the company were reflected in the following statement:

> Our vision has nothing to do with transactions, pushing products, or getting bigger for the sake of bigness. It's about building lifelong relationships one customer at a time. ... We strive to be recognized by our stakeholders as setting the standard among the world's great companies for integrity and principled performance. This is more than just doing the right thing. We also have to do it in the right way. (as cited in Tayan, 2019)

However, within the company a toxic culture of sales pressure was evident. Wells Fargo's success was built on cross-selling where customers were encouraged to have multiple Wells Fargo products, including mortgages, credit cards, checking accounts, insurance and more. Low level employees were under pressure to sell more and more products, even if this was not what customers wanted. Branch managers were assigned daily quotas and any shortfall was added to the next day's quota. Financial incentives were offered to employees, alongside alleged threats of losing their jobs if quotas were not met (Tayan, 2019).

In 2013, the *Los Angeles Times* investigated and found that some 30 employees were dismissed for opening new accounts and issuing debit or credit cards without customer knowledge, in some cases by forging signatures (Reckard, 2013). By 2016 the extent of the scandal was clearer, and Wells Fargo was fined $185 million after admitting more than 2 million customer accounts had been opened without customer consent. In 2020 Wells Fargo was fined more than $3 billion (US Department of Justice, 2020).

The company refused to admit any wrongdoing and blamed low-level employees. More than 5300 employees lost their jobs for breaking company rules. A US Senate hearing was particularly scathing about the bonuses received by senior directors during this period and the fact that no directors or senior executives lost their jobs (S.Hrg. 114-510).

Despite claiming to be cleaning up its act, the bank has been in violation of other customer protection laws. In 2018, Wells Fargo was fined $1 billion for widespread consumer law violations (Helmore, 2018). In 2022, the bank agreed to pay over $3 billion over a range of illegal fees and interest payments (Roush, 2022).

Carrie Tolstedt, the former head of Wells Fargo retail banking, pleaded guilty to obstruction charges but avoided jail, with a three-year probation order, a fine of $100,000, six months home confinement and 120 hours of community service (Morrow, 2023).

No-one has been imprisoned for any of these actions, and it is unlikely anyone will be.

(Continued)

Questions

1. In what ways does this case exemplify the concept of the 'dark side of leadership'?
2. How could ethical leadership have changed the outcome of this situation? What specific actions could senior leaders have taken?
3. Should corporate leaders face stronger personal consequences for unethical behaviour within their organisations? Why or why not?

Controlling

Using the POLC framework, the final key role of managers is controlling. Once the planning and organising has taken place, and staff are sufficiently motivated, managers need to ensure the outcomes are delivered to the correct standard. As people are involved at almost every step of production in an organisation, control often involves making sure employees are doing what they are supposed to do. Individual goals and organisational goals do not always align, and failures of management control can have a severe impact on the organisation.

There are many aspects to management control and many activities and processes which need to be controlled. It is often one of the aspects of managing that new managers find hardest to get right. How do I exercise control without demotivating or disengaging people?

REFLECTIVE ACTIVITY 2.4

Control Spans Many Areas of Organisations

- Identify some areas in which you think managers need to exercise control.
- Write these areas down.
- Identify any systems or processes managers might use to exercise control in these areas.
- What are the implications of too much or too little control being exercised?

Your list may include things like:

- Work processes
- Financial control
- HR systems
- Quality systems
- Production
- Operations
- Employee behaviour

The basic process of management control involves a number of steps (see Figure 2.3). This is a feedback process that operates to bring performance to the correct standard.

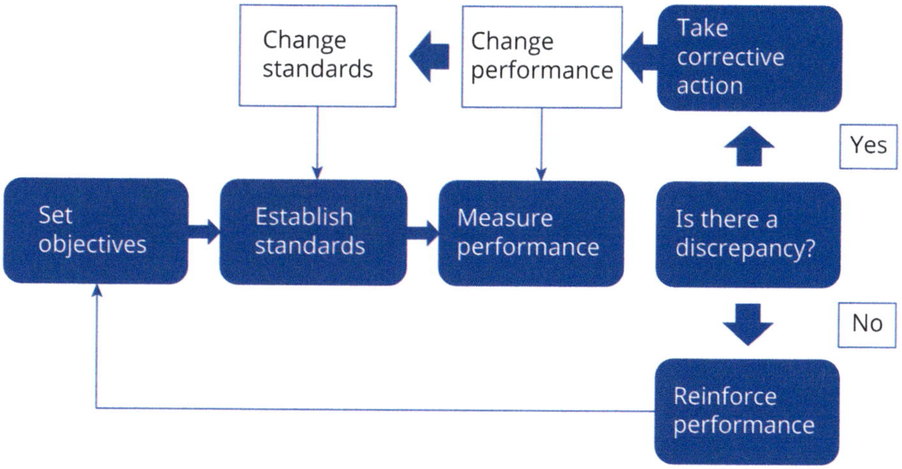

Figure 2.3 Basic process of management control

Setting objectives – Objectives for departments, teams and individuals cascade down from the organisation's strategy. Managers will translate this strategy into meaningful objectives for individuals, usually through some form of performance review process.

Establish standards of performance – These goals will contain **standards of performance** against which managers can compare **actual performance**. Standards need to be clearly defined and will often refer to things that can be measured, such as *Quality, Quantity, Time* or *Cost*.

Measure actual performance – Most managers will receive regular reports updating them on performance against standards. These may include financial data, production data, sales data, delivery times and many, many more. Managers will compare the actual performance against the targets.

Is there a discrepancy? – If targets are being met, no remedial action is required and performance can be reinforced. If there is a discrepancy between desired performance and actual performance, remedial action is required. This may take the form of changing performance or adjusting the standards. Performance change may be achieved through individual performance or may require the need for changes to processes.

This is a useful way of looking at control and it applies in many cases. However, as already discussed, social structures such as large companies are complex systems and sometimes control needs to accommodate this. The following example discusses how the logical and rational processes involved in health and safety monitoring sometimes fail due to the complexity of the interactions of the parts of the system.

CASE STUDY 2.4

Managing Safety - A Case Study in the Power Industry

Many organisations in the power industry are **high reliability organisations (HROs)**. These organisations operate in situations with the potential for large scale harm, but operate safety policies that keep this harm from occurring and so accident rates are kept low. This case study looks at organisations carrying out maintenance work in traditional power generation facilities, such as nuclear, gas and coal fired power stations and considers the manager's role in achieving safety.

Typically, a power plant will have multiple generators, so that one can be taken offline for maintenance while the plant continues to generate electricity. The generator maintenance period is known as an outage and may last from a few weeks to several months. Before the outage, a schedule of work will be produced detailing all the maintenance activities that need to take place.

Managers play several roles in preventing accidents and one is the use of safety management systems. One key element of an effective safety management system is the **Permit to Work**. This is a good example of a control process. Before any work is carried out, a Permit to Work must be issued. This identifies exactly what works need to be done and when it needs to be done. The permit will also indicate the safety checks have been done to ensure the work can be carried out safely. Those carrying out the work must sign the permit, to show they understand the nature of the work and the risks involved. Managers have a key role to play at all steps in the process, and will be exercising control of the system, processes and people involved.

The issue of a Permit to Work, however, does not make a job safe. There are many human factors involved, and managers need to understand the complexity of these factors. The historical view of managing safety was the 'Bad Apple Theory'. This idea suggests accidents are caused by a few misfits; workers prone to make errors. This has been debunked and more recently a systems approach has been advocated that focuses on the relationships and roles of people within the systems. The New View of human error (Dekker, 2017) asks *what* caused the accident, not *who*, and sees human error as a *symptom* not the *cause*.

There are two sources of accidents in organisations, **latent errors** and **active failures**.

Latent errors are pre-existing conditions in an organisation such as systems, poor equipment design, job distractions, fatigue, stress, working hours and culture that may be dormant for many years. These don't directly cause accidents, but they make the active failures more likely. Managers have a key role in identifying latent errors through robust risk assessment.

Active failures are the things workers do that are unsafe, which directly and immediately cause an accident. These may be things like pushing the wrong button.

Managers are involved at all levels in identifying latent errors and preventing active failures. They need to actively control the systems and process as well as worker behaviours in order to keep people safe.

CASE STUDY 2.5

Issues at the Power Plant

This is a fictional account based on real incidents. See if you can spot the latent errors and active failure in this case study.

An outage at a UK power plant was nearing completion. All of the scheduled work was complete and most of the workers had left the site, looking forward to a break before the next project. Two technicians were asked to stay behind and complete some emergent work - work that was not in the schedule of work but had emerged as a result of work carried out. This was a simple job replacing a length of pipe and would take just a few hours and the technicians reluctantly agreed. One technician was very experienced but was known to 'bend the rules'. The other was a newly qualified apprentice, on their first job. The pipe in question was in the roof, about 10m off the ground and, when in use, contained highly toxic fire retardant under high pressure.

They walked with the Supervising Engineer to the job site. On arrival they were told to 'prep the job while I go to get the permit.' (Permits are issued by the Senior Authorised Person (SAP) and work cannot start until all have seen the permit.) On arrival at the SAPs office, the Supervisor was told there was no permit and the SAP would need to inspect the site and make sure it was fully isolated and there was no pressure in the pipe.

On arrival at the site the SAP found the technicians had built a scaffold (they were not qualified scaffolders but there were no scaffolders on site) and were busy unbolting the flange connecting the pipes and separated them, prior to replacing the defective pipe. Neither technician was secured by a harness for working at height, as the equipment store was locked.

The SAP immediately halted the work as there was no permit and no isolation safety checks had been carried out. The pipe could still have been under pressure. The technicians were told to leave the site and a 'near miss' investigation started. In this case, no one was injured, but the outcome could have been different if the pipe had been opened under pressure. When being interviewed, neither technician could explain why they had carried on without a permit.

Questions

1. Can you identify the active failure?
2. Can you identify some latent errors that may have contributed to this near miss?
3. What would be your action as the manager in charge, the SAP?

MANAGING IN THE FUTURE

It's increasingly clear that we are facing some serious, existential threats over the next few decades. A poly-crisis comprising climate change, social justice and unrest, conflict and war and environmental decline. If we are to meet these challenges, organisations, institutions and the underlying economic systems must change. It is also clear that managers have a key role to play in implementing these changes, through planning, organising, leading and controlling the response.

If you take one thing from this chapter, we hope it is an understanding of the underlying complexity of the social systems and structures that underpin our organisations. It is no longer sufficient to think of organisations as machines with linear, predictable processes; 'if we do this, then we get that'. Organisations are complex adaptive systems, existing on the edge of chaos. This is the space between rigid, stable and stagnated systems and the unpredictable randomness of chaos. We are learning more and more about how to manage this complexity, not through controlling in the traditional sense, by guiding individuals and groups to collective action.

For decades we have been talking about discussing solutions to the climate change, the depletion of natural resources, and the increasing levels of species extinction around the world. We're not going to reach the target set in the **Paris Accord** without strong action. And this must be led by a new generation of managers in organisations and institutions of all sizes, all around the world.

Concepts such as the circular economy are imperative if we are to manage these crises. This will take a new approach to management, one that is led through values, not through efficiency. Drucker (1963: 54) said: 'There is surely nothing quite so useless as doing with great efficiency what should not be done at all.'

In a consumer-driven world, we need to switch to a focus on what's really important to us, the things that are intrinsic to being human. Social inclusion, fairness, justice, equality are all essential in a New World. Managers need to embrace new principles from emerging ways of thinking about our world.

- The **UN Sustainable Development Goals** seek to provide 'a shared blueprint for peace and prosperity for people and the planet, now and into the future' (United Nations, 2024).
- **Doughnut economics** is 'a compass for human prosperity in the 21st century, with the aim of meeting the needs of all people within the means of the living planet' (Doughnut Economics Action Lab, 2024).
- The **Circular Economy** is a system that addresses the linear consumption cycle prevalent now – the *take – make – waste* system. The circular economy, in contrast, 'is a system where materials never become waste and nature is regenerated. In a circular economy, products and materials are kept in circulation through processes like maintenance, reuse, refurbishment, remanufacture, recycling, and composting' (Ellen MacArthur Foundation, 2024).

CHAPTER SUMMARY

- This chapter has explored several elements of management, based on the POLC cycle.
- These elements of planning, organising, leading and controlling are essential to the successful operation of any organisation.

- As you read through this book, you will see how management underpins all the chapters, from Finance to HRM and from Logistics to Marketing.
- Without good managers and good management, none of these functions will work.
- The chapter has reviewed the development of management thinking and looked at how management thinking continues to develop. The view of organisations as complex adaptive systems changes the way managers perform.
- Recognising that managing in complex systems is difficult, messy and uncertain can free managers to innovate and adapt to changing situations.
- Management is also essential in delivering solutions to global social issues through the effective delivery of the UN SDGs.

STUDENTS LIKE YOU CHANGE THE WORLD

Sean Tilson – BSc Business and Management student

I found that studying business and management provides a robust foundation for entering the world of work. The generalist nature of the degree means you can gain exposure to the various business functions, resulting in a comprehensive overview of how a business operates in the real world. With the nature of optional modules, you can delve deeper into a subject that interests you; I tailored my modules to be more entrepreneurial and leadership-oriented as I enjoyed the creative aspects of these modules. I also valued the emphasis on soft skills such as communication (e.g. presenting, managing and negotiating), as I see the transferability to my everyday life. Enrolling in a business and management degree has enabled me to apply classroom theory to my companies, societies, and social enterprises. For example, in 2024, I travelled to India for two months, where I worked in a slum community on various livelihood projects, with my primary goal to scale charity operations to deepen their impact. Upon returning home, I created a social enterprise with 14 volunteers and have increased the income of marginalised artisans threefold using principles and systems taught to me in the degree. It has also given me connections and confidence that will last a lifetime. I enjoyed the focus on sustainability and circularity and feel better able to build and create an enterprise that lasts for generations to come, a personal ambition of mine. The degree embeds a culture of treating everything like an experiment and not being afraid to fail; I feel optimistic about leaving university and am excited to embark on the next chapter of my life.

Figure 2.4 Sean Tilson

END OF CHAPTER REFLECTION

Have a look at the skills you should have developed in this unit (find more details in the Key Skills Table in the Appendix on p. 498).

1 Which of the skills listed do you think you have developed the most?
2 Can you give two examples on why you feel you have now developed these skills/developed them further?
3 How will you use these new/refined skills in the future (give two examples of the impact of your development on your future behaviour)?

FURTHER READING

Daft, R.L. (2014) *New Era of Management* (11th International edition). South-Western.

There are many books covering aspects of management. Richard Daft has written several books on management and *New Era of Management* is a good introductory text. It effectively introduces fundamental management principles while integrating contemporary challenges and global trends, making core concepts relevant to today's evolving workplace.

Laasch, O. (2024) *Principles of Business and Management: Practicing Ethics, Responsibility, Sustainability* (3rd edition). Sage.

To find out more about **ethical and sustainable leadership** see *Principles of Business and Management: Practicing Ethics, Responsibility, Sustainability*. The text is an excellent resource because it provides a comprehensive, practically oriented framework that integrates ethics, responsibility, and sustainability into all fundamental management topics, positioning them not as add-ons but as the core of 'professional' management.

Dekker, S. (2017) *The Field Guide to Understanding 'Human Error'*. CRC Press.

There are many books about the nature of **risk and risk management.** Dekker's *The Field Guide to Understanding 'Human Error'* is a good primer as it shifts the focus from blaming individuals for errors ('Bad Apple Theory') to understanding human error as a symptom of deeper, systemic organisational vulnerabilities, which is the true target of proactive risk mitigation.

Reason, J. (1990) *Human Error.* Cambridge University Press.

Reason's *Human Error* is a 'must read' for those interested in safety in systems. The 'Swiss Cheese Model' discussed here teaches that accidents result not from one mistake, but from multiple system weaknesses lining up, fundamentally changing how organisations approach safety.

Miller, J.H. and Page, S.E. (2007) *Complex Adaptive Systems: An Introduction to Computational Models of Social Life* (Princeton Studies in Complexity, Vol. 14). Princeton University Press.

Miller and Page give a comprehensive overview of the principles of **Complex Adaptive Systems**. The book is very effective in demonstrating how global behaviours emerge from local interactions among agents in social life.

Gleick, J. (2008) *Chaos: Making a New Science*. Penguin.

This is a seminal, highly readable narrative that makes the complex, counter-intuitive concepts of **Chaos Theory** (such as the butterfly effect and fractals) accessible by framing them through the exciting stories of the diverse scientists who developed the field.

REFERENCES

Apple (2024) 'Installing apps through alternative app distribution in the European Union', *Apple*, August 1. https://support.apple.com/en-gb/117767 (accessed September 3, 2025).

Bennett, N. and Lemoine, G.J. (2014) 'What a difference a word makes: Understanding threats to performance in a VUCA world', *Business Horizons*, 57 (3): 311–17.

Braithwaite, J. (2018) 'Changing how we think about healthcare improvement', *BMJ*, 361: article #k2014. https://doi.org/10.1136/bmj.k2014

Burke, W.W. and Litwin, G.H. (1992) 'A causal model of organizational performance and change', *Journal of Management*, 18 (3): 523–45.

Cappelli, P. (2010) *The India Way: How India's Top Business Leaders are Revolutionizing Management*. Harvard Business Press.

Chartered Institute of Personnel and Development (CIPD) (2023) 'Organisation design', *CIPD Factsheets*. https://www.cipd.org/uk/knowledge/factsheets/organisational-development-design-factsheet (accessed September 3, 2025).

Daft, R.L. (2014) *New Era of Management* (11th International edition). South-Western.

Davidson, A.A., Young, M.D., Leake, J. E. and O'Connor, P. (2022) 'Aid and forgetting the enemy: A systematic review of the unintended consequences of international development in fragile and conflict-affected situations', *Evaluation and Program Planning*, 92, 102099. https://doi.org/10.1016/j.evalprogplan.2022.102099

Dekker, S. (2017) *The Field Guide to Understanding 'Human Error'*. CRC Press.

Doughnut Economics Action Lab (2024) 'About Doughnut Economics', Doughnut *Economics Action Lab*. https://doughnuteconomics.org/about-doughnut-economics (accessed September 3, 2025).

Drucker, P. F. (1963) 'Managing for business effectiveness', *Harvard Business Review*, 41 (3): 53–60.

Drucker, P. F. (2007). *The Practice of Management*. Butterworth-Heinemann.

Edmondson, A. (1999) 'Psychological safety and learning behavior in work teams', *Administrative Science Quarterly*, 44 (2): 350–83. doi.org/10.2307/2666999

Ellen MacArthur Foundation (2024) 'Circular economy introduction', *Ellen MacArthur Foundation*. https://www.ellenmacarthurfoundation.org/topics/circular-economy-introduction/overview (accessed September 3, 2025).

Fayol, H. (1949) *General and Industrial Management*. Pitman.

Gleick, J. (2008) *Chaos: Making a New Science*. Penguin.

Hampden-Turner, C. and Trompenaars, F. (1995) *The Seven Cultures of Capitalism: Value Systems for Creating Wealth in the United States, Japan, Germany, France, Britain, Sweden, and the Netherlands*. Doubleday.

Harris, L.C. and Ogbonna, E. (2002) 'The unintended consequences of culture interventions: A study of unexpected outcomes', *British Journal of Management*, 13 (1): 31–49. doi.org/10.1111/1467-8551.00221

Health Foundation (2010) *Evidence Scan: Complex Adaptive Systems*. London.

Helmore, E. (2018) 'Wells Fargo to pay $1bn in largest fine levied against a bank under Trump', *The Guardian*, April 20. https://www.theguardian.com/business/2018/apr/20/wells-fargo-fine-financial-products-trump-administration (accessed September 3, 2025).

Holland, J.H. (1992) *Adaptation in Natural and Artificial Systems: An Introductory Analysis with Applications to Biology, Control, and Artificial Intelligence*. MIT Press.

Huawei (2025) 'Corporate governance', *Huawei*. https://www.huawei.com/en/corporate-governance/corporate-governance (accessed September 3, 2025).

Infosys (2024) *Next Up: The Next Opportunity to Grow Sustainably – ESG Report 2023-24*. https://www.infosys.com/sustainability/documents/infosys-esg-report-2023-24.pdf (accessed September 3, 2025).

Infosys (2025) 'About us', *Infosys*. https://www.infosys.com/about.html (accessed September 3, 2025).

Ip, P.K. (2009). 'Is Confucianism good for business ethics in China?', *Journal of Business Ethics*, 88 (3): 463–76.

Kaplan, R.S. and Norton, D.P. (2005) 'The balanced scorecard: Measures that drive performance', *Harvard Business Review*, 70: 71–9.

Kaplan, R.S. and Norton, D.P. (2008) Mastering the management system, *Harvard Business Review*, 86 (1): 62–77.

Katzenbach, J.R. and Smith, D.K. (2015) *The Wisdom of Teams: Creating the High-Performance Organization*. Harvard Business Review Press.

Laasch, O. (2024) *Principles of Business & Management: Practicing Ethics, Responsibility, Sustainability* (3rd edition). Sage.

Lamond, D. (2004) 'A matter of style: reconciling Henri and Henry', *Management Decision*, 42 (2): 330–56.

Li, X., Li, C., Wang, Z., Jiao, W. and Pang, Y. (2021) 'The effect of corporate philanthropy on corporate performance of Chinese family firms: The moderating role of religious atmosphere', *Emerging Markets Review*, *49*, 100757.

Lutz, D.W. (2009) 'African Ubuntu philosophy and global management', *Journal of Business Ethics*, 84 (Supplement 3): 313–28.

Maclean, M., Shaw, G., and Harvey, C. (2022) 'Business as service? Human Relations and the British interwar management movement', *Human Relations*, 75 (8): 1585–614. doi.org/10.1177/00187267211070771

Mangaliso, M. P. (2001) 'Building competitive advantage from Ubuntu: Management lessons from South Africa', *Academy of Management Perspectives*, *15*(3): 23–33.

Mbigi, L. (2005) *Spirit of African leadership*. Knowres.

Meissner, K.L. and Mello, P.A. (2022) 'The unintended consequences of UN sanctions: A qualitative comparative analysis', *Contemporary Security Policy*, 43 (2): 243–73. doi.org/10.1080/13523260.2022.2059226

Mercedes-AMG Petronas (2024) 'Our team', Mercedes AMG. https://www.mercedesamgf1.com/team (accessed September 3, 2025).

Miller, J.H. and Page, S.E. (2007) *Complex Adaptive Systems: An Introduction to Computational Models of Social Life* (Princeton Studies in Complexity, Vol. 14). Princeton University Press.

Mintzberg, H. (1989) *Mintzberg on Management: Inside Our Strange World of Organizations*. Free Press.

Morrow, A. (2023) 'Former Wells Fargo executive avoids prison time for her role in fake-accounts fraud', *CNN Business*, September 15. https://edition.cnn.com/2023/09/15/business/wells-fargo-exec-charged-accounts-scandal/index.html (accessed September 3, 2025).

Northouse, P.G. (2021) *Leadership: Theory and Practice*. Sage.

Palmberg, K. (2009) *Complex Adaptive Systems: Properties and Approaches*. Luleå University of Technology. https://www.diva-portal.org/smash/record.jsf?pid=diva2%3A997968&dswid=9728 (accessed September 3, 2025).

Parker, M. (2018) *Shut Down the Business School*. University of Chicago Press.

Pasternak, K. (2024) 'Leadership lessons from Formula 1 motor racing', *Leader to Leader*, 111: 20–7. doi.org/https://doi.org/10.1002/ltl.20784

Porter, M.E. (1979) 'How competitive forces shape strategy', *Harvard Business Review*, March. https://hbr.org/1979/03/how-competitive-forces-shape-strategy (accessed September 3, 2025).

Quinn, L., Bird, P., Remsing, S., Reeves, K., and Lilford, R. (2023) 'Unintended consequences of the 18-week referral to treatment standard in NHS England: A threshold analysis', *BMJ Quality & Safety*, 32 (12): 712–20. doi.org/10.1136/bmjqs-2023-015949

Reason, J. (1990) *Human Error*. Cambridge University Press.

Reckard, S. (2013) 'Wells Fargo accuses workers of opening fake accounts to meet goals', *Los Angeles Times*, October 3. https://www.latimes.com/business/la-xpm-2013-oct-03-la-fi-1004-wells-fargo-firings-20131004-story.html (accessed September 3, 2025).

Roush, T. (2022) 'Wells Fargo ordered to pay customers $3.7 billion for causing "financial harm"', *Forbes*, December 20. https://www.forbes.com/sites/tylerroush/2022/12/20/wells-fargo-ordered-to-pay-customers-37-billion-for-causing-financial-harm/?sh=6fc95e7568f4 (accessed September 3, 2025).

SAB Board (2025) 'Our Principles', *SAB*. https://www.sab.co.za/about-us/our-principles (accessed September 3, 2025).

Samsung (2025) 'Company info', *Samsung*. https://www.samsung.com/uk/about-us/company-info/ (accessed September 3, 2025).

Senge, P.M. (1997) 'The fifth discipline', *Measuring Business Excellence*, 1 (3): 46–51.

Shell (n.d.) 'What are the previous Shell Scenarios', *shell.com*. https://www.shell.com/news-and-insights/scenarios/what-are-the-previous-shell-scenarios.html (accessed September 3, 2025).

S.Hrg. 114-510 (2016) *An Examination of Wells Fargo's Unauthorized Accounts and the Regulatory Response*, US Government Publishing Office... https://www.congress.gov/event/114th-congress/senate-event/LC51974/text (accessed September 3, 2025).

Stanford, N. (2018) *Organization Design: The Practitioner's Guide*. Routledge.

Sudhakar, G.P. (2021) 'Bharatiya management: the new paradigm for Indian managers', *International Journal of Indian Culture and Business Management*, 23 (3): 324–42.

Tata Group (2024) *Annual Report on CSR Activities*. https://www.tata.com/content/dam/tata/pdf/fy24/Tata-Sons-Combined-CSR-Report-FY24.pdf (accessed September 3, 2025).

Tayan, B. (2019) *The Wells Fargo Cross-Selling Scandal* (Rock Center for Corporate Governance at Stanford University Closer Look Series: Topics, Issues and Controversies in Corporate Governance No. CGRP-62 Version 2), Stanford University Graduate School of Business Research Paper No. 17 (1). https://ssrn.com/abstract=2879102 (accessed September 3, 2025).

Taylor, F. (1911) *Principles of Scientific Management*. Harper & Brothers.

United Nations (2024) 'The 17 Goals', *sdgs.un.org*. https://sdgs.un.org/goals (accessed September 3, 2025).

US Department of Justice (2020) 'Wells Fargo agrees to pay $3 billion to resolve criminal and civil investigations into sales practices involving the opening of millions of accounts without customer authorization', justice.gov, February 21. https://www.justice.gov/opa/pr/wells-fargo-agrees-pay-3-billion-resolve-criminal-and-civil-investigations-sales-practices (accessed September 3, 2025).

Von Bertalanffy, L. (1950) 'An outline of general system theory', *British Journal for the Philosophy of Science*, *1*(2): 114–29.

Waterman, R.H., Peters, T.J., and Phillips, R.H. (1980) 'Structure is not organization', *Business Horizons*, 23: 14–26.

Weisbord, M. (1976) 'Organizational diagnosis: Six places to look for trouble with or without a theory', *Group and Organization Management*, 1 (4): 430–47. doi.org/10.1177/105960117600100405

Wilson, J.F. and Thomson, A.W. (2006) *The Making of Modern Management: British Management in Historical Perspective*. Oxford University Press.

Xie, J. and Yuan, S. (2025). The cultural origins of family firms. *Journal of Comparative Economics*, *53* (1): 1–24.

3
ORGANISATIONAL BEHAVIOUR

Hannah Collis, Isbahna Naz, and Levke Henningsen

INTENDED LEARNING OUTCOMES

After reading this chapter, you should be able to:

1. Explain how and why organisational behaviour is important to business and understand how organisational behaviour can help us to build a better workplace.
2. Understand what we mean by a better workplace, for both employees and employers.
3. Describe and apply theoretical models that help to design work in a way which improves employee behaviour and outcomes.
4. Consider how new ways of working are presenting unique challenges that will shape the future study of organisational behaviour, and the research in this field.

SUSTAINABLE DEVELOPMENT GOALS

In this chapter, we address the following SDGs:

- SDG 3: Good Health and Well-being - Looking at promoting healthier work environments with greater focus on work-life balance.
- SDG 5: Gender Equality - Exploring leadership diversity, inclusive workplace cultures, and policies to reduce gender bias.
- SDG 8: Decent Work and Economic Growth - Covering motivation theories, employee engagement, and ethical leadership can improve job satisfaction and productivity, contributing to sustainable economic growth.
- SDG 9: Industry, Innovation and Infrastructure - Highlighting the role of organisational culture and change management in fostering innovation and adaptability can enhance business resilience and competitiveness.
- SDG 10: Reduced Inequalities - Examining diversity and inclusion strategies in organisations can help reduce workplace discrimination and create equal opportunities for all employees.
- SDG 16: Peace, Justice and Strong Institutions - Enhancing ethical and open organisational cultures, facilitating diversity within decision-making to have a peaceful and inclusive workplace.

INTRODUCTION

In this chapter, we will introduce core topics on the micro (i.e., personality, identity, perception, motivation), meso (i.e., interpersonal relationships and group dynamics), and macro level (i.e., organisational **culture** and change) before we introduce contemporary issues in OB research that lay the foundation for creating healthier, happier and better-performing organisations in which employees can thrive.

What Is Organisational Behaviour (OB) and Why Should We Study It?

Within the field of OB, researchers aim to explore how individuals, groups, and organisational (and even cultural and national) structures influence behaviours within organisations. The overarching goal of these efforts is to apply this **knowledge** to enhance organisations' effectiveness (Robbins and Judge, 2024). From an OB perspective, organisations can thus only be as effective as the people working in them (Robbins and Judge, 2024).

But how can OB help us to build a better workplace, or, to put it differently, what can be done from an OB perspective to make organisations more effective? To answer these questions, some of the dependent variables that are commonly assessed in OB research, such as job satisfaction, job performance, employee well-being, motivation but also turnover intentions or 'negative' deviant behaviour at work, are of particular importance (Ashkanasy and Dorris, 2017). The goal of OB research is to create a workplace where employees are healthy, productive, motivated, and satisfied with their jobs and organisations, while at the same time show fewer 'negative behaviours like organisational withdrawal to enhance organisational effectiveness that can be measured in profits, sales, or return of investment' (Ashkanasy and Dorris, 2017).

You might now ask yourself: But how do we know how to increase employees' job satisfaction, how can we build trust and positive interactions between members of work teams, or how do we build a culture that has a positive effect on the behaviours and interactions in our organisations? One way to enhance your competencies as a (future) people manager is to gain a comprehensive knowledge of the theories, theoretical **models** and empirical evidence of OB research and apply your knowledge to the practice. OB research provides managers with insights into what drives performance and helps them implement practices that promote a positive, effective work environment.

In recent years, OB has evolved significantly to meet the demands of today's workplace changes and increasing **globalisation**. For example, technology has transformed work practices, increasing remote work options (e.g., Gibson and Gibbs, 2006), whilst creating challenges with an aging workforce (e.g., Pit et al., 2021). Consequently, OB research focuses on helping employees develop technological and interpersonal skills while at the same time providing managers with tools for addressing complex workplace issues such as work-life balance, cultural differences in global teams, or workforce diversity.

By now, you might have realised that the study of Organisational Behaviour has some overlap with related fields such as Human Resource Management (see Chapter 5). However, while each of these disciplines deal with workforce management, they are distinct fields. OB is primarily concerned with understanding and predicting behaviour in organisations, focusing on sociological and psychological aspects (Robbins and Judge, 2022), while HRM focuses on aligning workforce capabilities with organisational goals (Dessler, 2020). It deals with practical functions related to managing employees such as recruitment, training, compensation, and employee relations.

There are three interrelated levels of OB research:

1 the individual (micro) level
2 the group (meso) level
3 the organisational (macro) level (Ashkanasy and Dorris, 2017).

MICRO APPROACHES TO ORGANISATIONAL BEHAVIOUR

Key study topics on the micro level refer to individual differences in organisations and the effects on performance, such as differences in employees' personality, motivation, values, emotions, perceptions or decision-making skills.

Personality

Understanding individual differences is key to predicting how employees will behave in different situations. One substantial individual difference that is studied within OB is personality, which is defined as characteristic patterns of effect, behaviour, and thoughts (Funder, 2001). While there are several models of personality, the most widely used is the Five Factor Model (Goldberg, 1992), which may also be called the 'Big Five' personality factors (Digman, 1997). This model suggests that personality can be categorised into five 'traits':

- Extraversion
- Conscientiousness
- Agreeableness
- Openness
- Emotional Stability

This 'trait' approach argues that personality is a continuum – think of getting a score on a trait from 1–100. This means that everyone has a unique profile of personality. However, when people typically score high or low in any trait, we can predict a range of employee outcomes.

Extraversion

Extraversion is defined as an individual's levels of sociability, assertiveness, energy, and excitement-seeking (Goldberg, 1992). Employees higher in Extraversion are generally more talkative, likely to emerge as **leaders**, and can excel in roles relating to teamwork, collaboration or social interaction, such as customer service. In comparison, individuals with lower levels of Extraversion tend to perform better with individual tasks requiring little interpersonal interaction. Extraversion is also closely linked to other employee outcomes, with higher levels of Extraversion linked to greater job satisfaction, **engagement**, and well-being.

Conscientiousness

Conscientiousness is the personality trait most closely linked with work performance, as this trait encompasses characteristics such as organisation, being goal driven, diligence, and attention to detail (Goldberg, 1992). As such, research has consistently linked higher Conscientiousness with work performance across many different types of job roles. In relation to other work outcomes, lower Conscientiousness is associated with **counter-productive work behaviours** while higher Conscientiousness is associated with **organisational citizenship behaviours**, job satisfaction and faster promotions.

Agreeableness

Agreeableness is associated with interpersonal relationships, and captures characteristics such as friendliness, empathy, and (lack of) argumentativeness (Goldberg, 1992). Individuals high in this trait value getting along with people and having harmonious relationships, meaning they are excellent in roles that require teamworking and supporting each other. In contrast, job roles that require a level of criticism and argumentativeness (such as lawyers) would be best suited to individuals lower in this trait.

Openness

Openness is the creative trait, with higher Openness associated with creative thought and problem solving, appreciation of art/environment, and intellectual curiosity (Goldberg, 1992). While research has found less evidence that links this trait to specific employee outcomes, employees who are higher in Openness typically suit roles that allow creative freedom or flexibility or are focused on tackling difficult problems.

Emotional Stability

Emotional Stability, previously called Neuroticism, relates to anxiety, depression, and emotional volatility. Individuals who show more stability generally perform better in most job roles and can foster stronger relationships with colleagues (Goldberg, 1992). Employees low in Emotional Stability often struggle with receiving feedback or criticism, question their own abilities and can be unable to perform under pressure. This trait is further associated with low levels of well-being and job satisfaction.

Psychometric Assessments

To capture personality, employers may use psychometric assessments (questionnaires which typically ask you to agree/disagree with statements about your own behaviours or attitudes). Employers are encouraged to use these as an employee development tool, rather than a recruitment tool, as personality has been shown to change throughout the lifespan, particularly within young adults.

REFLECTIVE ACTIVITY 3.1

Looking at the above personality traits

- Can you identify which ones you would be higher or lower in?
- What sort of jobs would be suited for your personality profile?

Personal and Protected Characteristics

Within organisations, individuals bring with them a range of identities and characteristics that shape their experiences. Understanding these characteristics in organisations is essential for promoting inclusion, ensuring fair treatment and upholding the rights of all people. This section explores what these characteristics are, why they matter and how they impact the work experience of different individuals in organisations.

Gender

Gender in organisations is an area of study that examines how socially shared gender roles (i.e., culturally shared beliefs about how women and men behave or should behave in societies; Eagly et al., 2000) and gender stereotypes (i.e., culturally shared expectations of women's and men's psychological characteristics; Best and Williams, 2001) affect workplace dynamics, including support and power structures, leadership **emergence** and effectiveness, and access to workplace resources. Research in this area explores various issues and their gendered effects on careers, such as the glass ceiling effect (e.g., Ryan et al., 2016), pay disparities (e.g., Sterling et al., 2020), gender biases and self-selection processes (e.g., Henningsen et al., 2022). It further considers the impact of organisational policies and culture on gender equality, such as flexible working arrangements, and equality, diversity, and inclusion (EDI) initiatives. Research in this area provides implications for developing evidence-based policies and strategies that promote fairer and more inclusive workplaces, enabling organisations to unlock the full potential of their workforce.

Age

Age diversity in organisations is another crucial factor that may influence workplace dynamics, productivity, and team cohesion, with important implications for employee well-being and organisational performance. The presence of multiple generations in the workforce often reflects diverse perspectives, abilities, **skills**, and communications styles that can enhance creativity, collaboration, and knowledge transfer when managed effectively (e.g., Frosch, 2011). However, age-related stereotypes, such as assumptions about younger employees' lack of experience or older employees' resistance to change and insufficient technological skills, can lead to misunderstandings and discrimination (e.g., Kunze et al., 2013). Organisations that proactively address age-related stereotypes and implement inclusive practices, such as training and the management of age-diverse teams, can experience improved employee **engagement**, health, and productivity (e.g., Truxillo et al., 2014).

Race and Religion

In the UK, protected characteristics under the Equality Act 2010 include race (colour, nationality, ethnic or national origins) and religion or belief which safeguard individuals from discrimination based on ethnic and religious backgrounds. This law protects against unfair treatment in employment, education, and public services, ensuring individuals are not disadvantaged due to their ethnic origins or religious practices. For example, employers must accommodate religious observances when reasonable and cannot discriminate based on ethnic attire. By upholding these protections, the Equality Act promotes an inclusive work society, ensuring respect for diversity and equal opportunities for individuals from varied backgrounds (UK Government, 2010).

Neurodiversity

Neurodiversity draws together a range of neurological and cognitive differences and diagnoses, such as autism, ADHD, and dyslexia, which all focus on individuals having different ways of thinking. This population has been overlooked historically, which has resulted in individuals not being supported to reach their potential, omitting key talent pools from the business, and significantly damaging employee wellbeing (e.g., CIPD, 2024). To harness strengths of neurodiverse thinking, organisations must create supportive environments, such as flexible workspaces, clear communication, and tailored training programmes. The extent to which neurodiversity impacts an individuals' ability to work varies across employees and diagnoses, with no two neurodiverse employees requiring the same support. Therefore, organisations should provide individual-focused accommodations, making sure they benefit the specific employee's needs. Being open and actively supporting neurodiverse employees increases positive organisational culture for both neurodiverse and neurotypical employees (see Case Study 3.1), and enhances employee well-being, performance, and job satisfaction.

CASE STUDY 3.1

Embracing Neurodiversity at Work

A company that has not only valued neurodiversity, but actively encouraged neurodiverse applicants and employees is SAP. SAP is a multinational software company, specialising in resource management and planning, headquartered in Germany with offices around the world.

SAP has always valued different backgrounds and experiences. In relation to neurodiversity, the company had previously been involved in offering temporary opportunities to individuals from a range of neurodiverse backgrounds, in an effort to increase their participation in the workforce. As a company, they recognised that neurodiverse individuals were underrepresented and underemployed - often due to a lack of work experiences early in their career. Yet, their contribution was also extremely valuable:

> When neurodiverse perspectives are missing from the workforce, there is a lost opportunity for innovation and creativity. (SAP, 2024)

In 2013 SAP announced their Autism at Work programme, which focused on reducing entry barriers for individuals with Autism. Initially, this started by recruiting autistic individuals for specific roles, such as software testers, programmers and data quality assurance specialists in India and the USA, but this has since evolved to cover 16 different countries and 28 different job roles.

One of the ways SAP supported potential employees with Autism is during the recruitment process. Rather than having to complete psychometric assessments and many interviews, applicants were instead required to complete week-long work sample assessments, where you have to complete the job tasks that would be required in the actual role. This allowed applicants who have Autism the time and space to demonstrate their abilities, whilst also learning the job role. Additionally, these applicants were offered job coaches, to help both before and during interviews, particularly supporting their ability to discuss and sell their skillset.

When SAP launched the Autism at Work programme in 2013, they set the goal of having 1% of their workforce as part of this programme by 2020. Unfortunately, the company was unable to meet this goal, which would have accounted for 650 people worldwide. However, SAP has stated that it has offered over 800 opportunities, often to students with Autism diagnoses, to support them in their studies, and as such, has not provided as many permanent, full-time opportunities.

Despite this, as of 2024 SAP has 240+ colleagues in this programme and it is widely considered to be a success. Of note, in 2019 SAP awarded its most prestigious employee award to Nico Neumann, who had been hired in 2016 through the Autism at Work programme (this award had previously been given to teams). Additionally, in September 2024 SAP launched the Autism Inclusion Company of the Year award with Disability:IN, to recognise the efforts of other organisations in the UK and abroad.

In conclusion, SAP claims to be the first global company to develop a programme specifically focused on individuals with autism. SAP has made significant strides in improving the experiences for embracing neurodiversity in the workplace, having expanded its support to individuals with other diagnoses. The efforts and awards demonstrate how simple, and effective, it can be to harness the skills of everyone in society, not just neurotypical individuals.

Questions

1. How did SAP's Autism at Work programme align with its broader strategic goals, and what competitive advantages might result from embracing neurodiversity in this way?
2. Evaluate SAP's decision to redesign its recruitment process for neurodiverse candidates. What business considerations should be taken into account when altering traditional hiring practices?
3. Considering SAP did not meet its initial goal of 1% workforce inclusion by 2020, how should companies measure the success of diversity initiatives beyond numerical targets?

(Continued)

Sources

https://www.sap.com/resources/the-win-win-potential-of-hiring-neurodiverse-workers
https://www.linkedin.com/pulse/saps-9-year-neurodiversity-journey-50-years-making-jos-%C3%A9-velasco/
https://news.sap.com/uk/2024/10/sap-expands-commitment-to-neurodiversity-awareness/
https://www.sap.com/assetdetail/2022/12/7ac5e873-537e-0010-bca6-c68f7e60039b.html
https://www.sap.com/discover/autism-inclusion/index.html

Identity

Identity plays a crucial role in shaping how individuals understand themselves and interact with others. It includes both self-identity – how a person perceives their own unique qualities – and social identity, which is shaped by group affiliations such as ethnicity, gender, religion, or professional roles. Many of these identity markers are recognised as protected characteristics under equality legislation, highlighting the importance of treating all individuals with fairness and respect. This section examines the concepts of self and social identity, drawing on Social Identity Theory (Tajfel and Turner, 1979) to explain the impact of group membership. It also explores how perception can be influenced by biases, stereotypes, and cognitive effects such as the halo and horn effects. Understanding these concepts is essential for fostering inclusive, respectful, and equitable environments in society and the workplace.

Self-Identity

Understanding self-identity and social identity is an essential component to understanding how individuals perceive themselves and how they relate to or interact with others within a society. Self-identity is often considered synonymous to one's personal identity. Self-identity is how an individual perceives themselves, based on their own unique qualities, physical features, personal beliefs, and goals. For example, an individual may identify themselves based on the following personal or protected characteristics:

- **Gender**: A person may identify themselves as male, female or non-binary.
- **Age:** A person might identify with a specific age group, such as young adult, middle-aged, or older adult.
- **Ethnicity:** Someone might identify with a specific ethnic group like South-East Asian, Hispanic, Irish, or Chinese.
- **Religion or Belief:** An individual could identify as Christian, Muslim, Jewish, Buddhist, atheist, or having another belief system.
- **Sexual Orientation:** Someone could identify as heterosexual, homosexual, bisexual, or another sexual orientation.
- **Disability:** An individual might identify as having a physical or mental disability.

It's crucial to respect everyone's identity and avoid discrimination or prejudice based on these factors. Self-identity may evolve over time as individuals integrate new experiences and self-reflection into their sense of who they are.

REFLECTIVE ACTIVITY 3.2

Think about how you identify, and what characteristics are important to you.

- What experiences do you think will shape your identity in the future?

Social Identity Theory

In contrast to self-identity, Social Identity Theory (SIT), developed by Henri Tajfel and John Turner (1986), emphasises the significance of group membership in shaping self-identity (Tajfel, 1974; Tajfel and Turner, 1979). According to SIT, individuals categorise themselves and others into social groups based on characteristics such as nationality, ethnicity, or shared interests, creating 'in-groups' (groups to which they belong) and 'out-groups' (groups to which they do not belong). Group membership provides individuals with a source of pride, social support, and self-esteem, contributing positively to their self-identity. SIT illustrates how employees use group membership as a means of understanding and positioning themselves within organisational hierarchies. Within a corporate setting, employees may align their identities with specific departments, teams, or professional affiliations, such as **finance**, **marketing**, or human resources. For instance, a marketing team that receives recognition for a successful campaign may experience a heightened sense of pride and self-worth. This sense of accomplishment reinforces their group affiliation and boosts individual self-esteem by association. In summary, both self-identity and social identity contribute to an individual's sense of self, with self-identity emphasising personal uniqueness and SIT highlighting the role of group membership.

Perception and Biases

While individual and group identification can foster a positive organisational culture (as discussed earlier in this chapter) by promoting loyalty and companionship, it may also lead to biases, stereotype or favouritism.

Biases

Biases can be systematic tendencies to favour certain perspectives of individuals or groups over others, often resulting in unfair judgement or decision-making. Biases can be conscious or unconscious, and they influence how we perceive a situation or individual.

Stereotype

A stereotype is a belief or assumption about the characteristics, behaviours, or attributes of a particular group or category of people. Stereotypes can be positive or negative, but they often lead to prejudiced attitudes and may not accurately represent individual differences within a group.

Favouritism

Favouritism is the practice of giving preferential treatment or biased support to certain individuals or groups, often based on personal feelings, relationships, or affiliations. In the workplace, favouritism can undermine fairness by creating an unequal environment where certain people are privileged over others without objective justification.

In-group favouritism can result in biases and competition between departments, where members perceive themselves as superior to those in other departments, potentially leading to communication barriers or **organisational silos** (Hogg and Terry, 2000). For example, individuals in a marketing department of a company may view their customer interpersonal expertise as more essential than other departments in the company, resulting in an 'us versus them' mentality that can hinder collaboration and lead to conflict. This may lead to *perceptual biases*, where members of each department view their own group's contributions as more valuable while downplaying the skills and roles of other departments. Such biases can lead to misunderstandings and reduced respect across teams, as each group selectively focuses on the positive attributes of their own members and the perceived weaknesses of others. Over time, these perceptions reinforce stereotypes, making it difficult to bridge the communication gap and foster an inclusive work environment. In summary, perception and its associated biases – ranging from in-group favouritism to perceptual biases – significantly impact workplace interactions. While identification with a group can build a strong organisational culture, unchecked biases can lead to conflict, hinder communication, and undermine collaboration across departments. Recognising and addressing these perceptual biases is essential for promoting a more inclusive and cohesive work environment. Among these biases, the halo/horn effect play notable roles in shaping how we see our colleagues and their actions.

The Halo and Horn effects

The halo effect and horn effect are two common perceptual biases that affect how we judge people based on initial impressions or a single trait.

Halo

The *halo effect* occurs when one positive characteristic (such as punctuality or friendliness) leads us to form an overall favourable impression of a person, often resulting in the assumption that they excel in other unrelated areas. For example, an employee who is consistently on time might be perceived as more reliable or competent in their work overall, even if there is no direct evidence of their proficiency. This positive bias can result in overlooked weaknesses as the initial positive impression highlights our perception of the individual.

Horn

The *horn effect,* on the other hand, occurs when one negative characteristic (such as a single mistake or perceived shortcoming) causes us to form an overall unfavourable impression. For instance, if an employee makes an error during a presentation, they might be viewed as incompetent or careless, even if they have a history of strong performance. This bias leads to a fixation on negative attributes, causing us to discount positive qualities or achievements.

Both the halo and horn effects can lead to unfair biases and assessments in the workplace, as they prevent us from accurately evaluating people's skills and contributions. These biases contribute to organisational silos and can prevent constructive feedback, as people may be reluctant to critique those they have a favourable view of (halo effect) or may overemphasise shortcomings in those they view unfavourably (horn effect).

Motivation Theories

Motivation is a final key driver of employee performance but varies across individuals. The concept of motivation itself is to be moved to do something, that you are energised and driven to achieve an outcome (Ryan and Deci, 2000). Understanding what motivates people can lead to better management practices and employee outcomes. There are two main approaches for understanding motivation: content theories and process theories.

Content Theories of Motivation

These theories identify specific factors that drive motivation, for example having specific goals or attainment of resources. There are two main theories within this category that are discussed below:

- Maslow's Hierarchy of Needs Theory; and
- Herzberg's Two-Factor Theory.

However, it is important to acknowledge that many of these theories have been developed within Western contexts. As a result, they may not always fully capture the motivational and organisational dynamics of non-Western cultures (e.g., Van der Wal, 2015). Few studies are available which focus on classical motivational theories in non-Western countries and consider how local cultures, norms, and values affect people's motivation (e.g., Mdhlalose, 2024).

Maslow's Hierarchy of Needs

This theory suggests that human needs are arranged like a hierarchy, often depicted as a pyramid. Maslow (1943) claims you can't reach the top of the hierarchy (i.e., personal growth) without first fulfilling the needs at the lower levels (i.e., food and water), so individuals may move back and forth across levels depending on life circumstances. Five levels of needs are outlined:

1. **Basic Physiological Needs** = food, water, shelter
2. **Safety Needs** = personal, health and financial security
3. **Love and Belongingness Needs** = social and emotional connections
4. **Esteem Needs** = self-worth, respect from others
5. **Self-Actualisation Needs** = personal growth, realising potential, meaningful activities

Within the work environment, Levels 1–3 should be provided based on the provision of decent work and wages. Typically, managers will focus on Esteem and Self-Actualisation Needs as a way to motivate employees, for example by providing opportunities for development and gaining a positive reputation from others.

However, other perspectives suggest that motivation is not necessarily always hierarchical. For example, Japanese management practices (e.g., 'Kaizen' as seen in Toyota) emphasise collective motivation through continuous improvement (e.g., Cheser, 1998).

Herzberg's Two-Factor Theory

This theory (Herzberg et al., 1957) outlines two types of factors influencing motivation: hygiene factors and motivating factors. *Hygiene factors* are things such as salary and working conditions and should be provided in order to prevent dissatisfaction. However, providing more of these factors will not lead to greater motivation. Instead, managers should provide *motivating factors,* which include things such as recognition, achievement, and responsibility, which create drive for individuals to perform their best.

Process Theories of Motivation

These theories focus on understanding the cognitive and psychological processes that influence how an individual would be motivated to behave in a specific way. Again, there are several theories that describe different processes, and we will introduce two examples below: Vroom's Expectancy Theory and Goal Setting Theory.

Vroom's Expectancy Theory (1964)

This theory posits that an individual's motivation is based on the expectation that effort will result in performance, and performance will result in the desired outcomes. It is often presented using the following formula (Vroom's Expectancy Theory, 1964):

> Expectancy (Effort) × Instrumentality (Performance) × Valence (Rewards) = Motivation

Within the workplace, this approach is commonly used to motivate employee performance, especially by using rewards such as promotion or bonuses. More generally, it is the premise of contracts (e.g., employer pays an employee for a specific work output) and acts as a foundation for many other work attitudes both employers and employees hold.

Goal Setting Theory

Goal Setting Theory describes the process of goal setting as important within employee motivation. However, for goals to be successful motivators, Locke and Latham (1990) propose the following principles:

1 **Specificity:** goals need to be well-defined, clear, and specific
2 **Challenge:** goals that are challenging but possible are the most motivating
3 **Feedback:** regular feedback on progress enhances motivation

Overall, the best work-related goals are aligned with the values and goals of an individual and so should be developed keeping in mind the individuals' skills and areas for personal development.

REFLECTIVE ACTIVITY 3.3

Often in business, people believe that money is the biggest motivator: the more you pay someone, the more invested and driven they are to complete their work. But that isn't entirely the case. Money does motivate employees up to a point, however after this point (which is determined by the individual employee's attitudes to money), adding more money has no impact on their motivation.

- What motivates you?
- Why do you want to come to university and study Business and Management?

The above section has outlined a number of ways in which the study of organisational behaviour focuses on the 'micro' level, aiming to understand how an individual's unique characteristics, behaviours, attitudes, personality, and patterns of thinking can impact their performance at work. The core factor of almost any form of work is people, and so understanding what drives different people, how we can facilitate better work outcomes, and match the best people to different roles, is vital for any form of effective work. However, we need to remember that individuals doing any form of work do not operate in a vacuum – they need to interact with other people. Therefore, whilst understanding people is essential for promoting high quality work, we need to also consider broader relationships, and what happens when people come together. The following section will explore this: the 'meso' level.

MESO APPROACHES TO ORGANISATIONAL BEHAVIOUR - INTERPERSONAL RELATIONSHIPS AND GROUP DYNAMICS

The meso level of OB research relates to groups and teams and explores topics that include managing team performance, team communication, team conflict, leadership styles, as well as power dynamics.

The Nature of Groups and Teams

Working together in groups or teams is an essential criterion in shaping an individual's behaviour and performance in a workplace. Such collaboration between individuals can lead to effective problem-solving, innovative solutions, and fostering a rich exchange of ideas. Therefore, understanding the distinction between groups and teams, as well as the dynamics of group development, is vital for organisations aiming to leverage such collective effort. Groups and teams both consist of individuals working together, but their structures, purposes, and processes may differ. Groups and teams are often used interchangeably, but they represent different dynamics and organisational purposes.

Groups

According to Schein (1988), a group is where a number of individuals engage in mutual interaction, are aware of one another's existence, and perceive themselves as belonging to a collective entity. The individuals in the group may or may not work together cohesively toward a common goal. Their interaction can range from casual to structured. For instance, there may be a single leader of the group, or the decisions may be shared between multiple group members.

On the other hand, teams are a subset of groups characterised by a higher degree of interdependence and collaboration. Teams work towards shared objectives, and success is measured collectively. Members are interdependent, with specific roles contributing to the team's overarching goals. They may also have shared and rotating leadership, instead of one solo leader.

The distinction between these entities matters in organisational settings because teams are often designed for complex tasks requiring coordinated efforts, while groups may be better suited for broader purposes.

Types of Groups

Groups can be categorised based on their purpose and structure, which helps organisations align group functions with strategic goals.

Formal Groups

Created by the organisation to fulfil specific objectives. These groups operate with defined roles, tasks, and hierarchies. The primary characteristic of a formal group is the specific tasks it was designed to accomplish. Management sets the goals and outlines the rules, relationships, and expected behaviours within the group. They may be a combination of the following subcategories:

Command Groups

Comprised of individuals reporting to a specific manager or supervisor. For example, a marketing team within the department will have a head of the department to whom they would have to report. While individual members may have specific tasks, the group often shares broader goals aligned with the department or organisation. Members typically interact regularly, either in person or virtually, to coordinate tasks, share information, and seek guidance from the supervisor. The supervisor has formal authority to assign tasks, make decisions, and evaluate performance.

Task Groups

Formed to complete a project or task, often with members from various departments. Unlike command groups, which are based on the organisational hierarchy, task groups are formed to address specific needs or challenges. Members may come from different departments or levels within the organisation, bringing diverse perspectives and skills. For example, a company may form a task group to develop a new product. This group would consist of members from various departments, such as engineering, marketing, and finance. They would work together to define the product, develop a marketing strategy, and create a financial plan. Once the product is launched, the task group would disband.

Informal Groups

These groups emerge naturally within the workplace, driven by social relationships or common interests. Informal groups frequently bring together individuals from diverse areas and levels of the organisation. As such, these groups are formed as part of a common interest and can be termed as interest groups.

Interest Groups

The group is formed by individuals with shared concerns, such as employees advocating for workplace improvements. The groups are formed to serve psychological safety and social needs between colleagues. They may not be related to a relevant task.

Members of informal groups may choose their own leader, who gains authority through the group's consent. This leader, often reflecting the group's shared attitudes and values, may be tasked with resolving conflicts, guiding the group toward its goals, and liaising with management or external parties.

By identifying these types of groups, organisations can strategically harness both formal and informal groups to create a collaborative work environment, addressing organisational challenges and opportunities.

Stages of Group Development

Effective group work between individuals will depend on understanding and navigating the dynamic interplay between group members. This dynamic process involves various factors such as communication, leadership, roles, and conflict resolution. The way a group develops can affect how close its members become. As groups go through different stages of development, they may experience difficulties and take time to become cohesive. For groups to run efficiently,

Tuckman (1965; Tuckman and Jensen, 1977) suggested five main successive stages towards group development:

- **Stage 1 Forming:** A newly formed project team meets for the first time. Members are cautious, introducing themselves, and trying to understand the project goals. The members may also set their own rules at this stage. There is uncertainty, dependency, and politeness between group members.
- **Stage 2 Storming:** In this stage, there might be differing ideas floating around between group members, which may lead to conflict, disagreement, and competition. Some members may try to dominate discussions, while others may feel marginalised. The storming stage is crucial for a group's development. If managed well, it can lead to constructive discussions about how the group should work together, resulting in improved structures and processes.
- **Stage 3 Norming:** At this point, members form ground rules, have communication protocols and shared goals. Members start to appreciate each other's strengths and weaknesses, and conflicts are resolved constructively.
- **Stage 4 Performing:** When groups have progressed successfully through the earlier stages, the members will start to work seamlessly together on the assigned task. They focus on achieving their goals and celebrate their successes.
- **Stage 5 Adjourning:** Once the members have worked together in all the earlier stages, they complete the final task and disband. Members may feel a sense of accomplishment and loss as they move on to new projects or roles.

Understanding Tuckman's theory can help individuals and teams:

- **Manage expectations:** Recognising the stages of group development can help individuals and teams anticipate challenges and set realistic goals.
- **Build effective relationships:** By understanding the importance of trust, respect, and open communication, individuals can foster positive group dynamics.
- **Resolve conflicts:** By identifying the root causes of a conflict, team members can address issues constructively and move forward.
- **Enhance productivity:** By focusing on collaboration, shared responsibility, and efficient decision-making, teams can achieve their goals more effectively.

By applying the principles of Tuckman's theory, individuals and teams can optimise their performance and create a positive and productive work environment.

Belbin's Team Roles

Team effectiveness is a complex interplay of various factors, including individual skills, shared goals, effective communication, and strong leadership. One key aspect that significantly influences a team's effectiveness is through the understanding and utilisation of different members' roles within the team. Meredith Belbin (1981) identified nine distinct team roles that contribute to a team's success.

- **Plant:** Creative minded, imaginative, and often unconventional thinker.
- **Resource investigator:** Extroverted, enthusiastic, and a good networker.
- **Coordinator:** Calm, confident, and a natural leader.
- **Shaper:** Challenging, dynamic, and driven to achieve goals.
- **Monitor-evaluator:** Critical, analytical, and strategic thinker.
- **Team worker:** Cooperative, diplomatic, and supportive.
- **Implementer:** Practical, disciplined, and efficient.
- **Completer finisher:** Perceptive, conscientious, and detail-oriented.
- **Specialist:** Thought-orientated, single-minded, dedicated.

Belbin's team roles model offers a valuable lens for understanding individual contributions within a team. Understanding one's natural team role helps individuals focus on their strengths and manage weaknesses. This not only improves efficiency but also minimises conflicts arising from overlapping responsibilities or mismatched expectations. Team members benefit by gaining self-awareness, understanding how they can best contribute to the group, and appreciating the diverse skills of their colleagues. Furthermore, the framework fosters better communication, as individuals become more accepting of different working styles. Leaders can also use Belbin's model to assign tasks more effectively, promote career development, and improve overall team dynamics. Ultimately, applying Belbin's knowledge creates a more harmonious and productive work environment, where individuals feel valued, and collective goals are achieved more efficiently.

Communication in Groups

Effective communication is the cornerstone of collaboration and productivity in groups. Whether formal or informal, communication allows team members to share information, resolve conflicts, and work cohesively. Information flows between group members through formal, informal, or digital communication channels.

Formal Communication Channels

Formal channels are structured and follow the organisation's established hierarchy or protocol. Examples include team meetings, official memos, and performance reports. These channels ensure that information is transmitted accurately and that it is aligned with organisational goals (Robbins and Judge, 2022).

Informal Communication Channels

Informal communication, also referred to as the 'grapevine,' occurs naturally among group members without structured rules. Conversations during breaks or casual exchanges of ideas often happen in these channels. While informal communication can enhance camaraderie, it may lead to **misinformation** if not managed effectively (Koch and Denner, 2022).

Digital Communication Channels

The digital era has revolutionised group communication by introducing tools such as email, instant messaging, and video conferencing. Digital communication channels can be both formal (e.g., email) and informal (e.g., instant messaging platforms such as Slack or Discord). Digital platforms allow for real-time collaboration across geographies (e.g., synchronous interactions via video call technologies) but also present challenges like misinterpretation of tone and miscommunication when there is an over-reliance on asynchronous communication, such as email or messaging platforms (Bolino et al., 2018). To maximise efficiency, groups must balance the use of digital tools with face-to-face or synchronous communication for clarity and engagement.

Even with well-established communication channels, barriers can still arise in group communication, preventing a smooth exchange of information. Common barriers include:

- **Selective Perception**
  - Individuals interpret messages through their own filters based on past experiences, biases, or emotions. Selective perception can distort a message's intent, especially in diverse groups with varying perspectives (Robbins and Judge, 2018).
- **Information Overload**
  - Modern workplaces expose teams to vast amounts of information, which can overwhelm members and hinder decision-making. When individuals focus on processing volume rather than depth, critical insights may be missed (Mullins, 2023).
- **Cultural Differences**
  - Cultural disparities in communication styles, language, and nonverbal behaviour can lead to misunderstandings. For example, members from high-context cultures may rely on implicit messages, while low-context cultures prefer explicit communication (Ting-Toomey and Chung, 2012).

Groupthink and Decision-Making

While cohesion benefits teams, excessive cohesiveness can lead to groupthink, which may hinder decision-making. Janis (1972) introduced groupthink to describe scenarios where teams prioritise agreement over rational analysis. Symptoms of groupthink can include:

- **Illusion of invulnerability:** Members feel overly optimistic, underestimating risks.
- **Suppression of dissent:** Members avoid expressing opposing views to maintain harmony.
- **Rationalisation:** The group dismisses alternative viewpoints without critical evaluation.
- **Pressure to conform:** Dissenters are directly or indirectly pressured to align with the majority.

Groupthink often leads to poor decision-making, as **critical thinking** and diverse perspectives are suppressed.

Overcoming Groupthink in Communication

To minimise groupthink, teams must foster open, transparent communication:

1. **Encourage Diverse Perspectives**
   Teams should invite input from members with different backgrounds or viewpoints. A diverse group composition reduces the likelihood of homogenous thinking and increases the pool of ideas (Robbins and Judge, 2018).
2. **Designate a Devil's Advocate**
   Assigning a team member to challenge ideas and question assumptions ensures that alternatives are considered without fear of conflict (Janis, 1972).
3. **Promote Psychological Safety**
   Leaders should create an environment where members feel safe expressing dissenting opinions. Constructive feedback should be encouraged and rewarded to counter the pressure to conform (Edmondson, 2018).
4. **Independent Evaluation**
   Teams can periodically break into smaller groups or seek feedback from external parties to counter biases and gain fresh perspectives.

This section has outlined several areas of research within the field of organisational behaviour that study the 'meso' level, which is the relationship between individuals within the context of work. As you can see from the discussions, this section has built upon our understanding of individual characteristics to apply them to group settings, highlighting how bringing together similar individuals may form well-functioning groups and teams, but can make them vulnerable to 'groupthink' and biases towards outgroup members. The research at this 'meso' level is focused on relationships between individuals, up to groups of individuals, but what happens when we want to understand what people or employees are like at a whole organisation level, or even shape these patterns of behaviour? The following section exploring 'macro' organisational behaviour research will shed light on these challenges.

MACRO APPROACHES TO ORGANISATIONAL BEHAVIOUR – ORGANISATIONAL CULTURE AND CHANGE

The third level of OB research refers to the level of the organisation and explores topics such as the organisational design, culture, or climate, and the effects on attitudes and behaviours in organisations.

Organisational culture is defined as the shared values, norms, and practices that guide employee behaviours, thoughts and feelings towards colleagues, customers, and the broader organisation. From a management perspective, it can be seen as a tool that binds employees together to work towards a common goal – sometimes seen as a motivating factor.

Levels of Organisational Culture

Seminal work by Edgar Schein (2010) identified different levels of organisational culture, which is structured based on how visible different aspects of culture is. He viewed culture as shared beliefs by members of an organisation, which are often unconscious and invisible to managers and outsiders. He proposed three levels:

1 **Artifacts –** the visible aspects of organisational culture. This could include the physical workplace, technology, and **branding**.
2 **Espoused Values –** the reasons why organisational members behave the way they do. This level includes aspects of culture such as traditions, shared assumptions, norms, and values.
3 **Underlying Assumptions –** the unconscious beliefs held by organisational members that influence how they think, feel and act. These assumptions are argued to be 'taken for granted' by organisations, as they can have little influence over them, and can take a long time to change.

Types of Organisational Cultures

There are many ways organisations can define their culture, often adopting bold statements in order to stand out. However, Quinn and Rohrbaugh (1983) developed the Competing Values Framework as a way of understanding and assessing organisational culture. The model is split across two axes: internal vs. external focus, and stability vs. flexibility, which results in four types of culture:

1 **Clan** – internal/flexible = family-like culture, valuing teamwork, trust, and a sense of belonging
2 **Adhocracy** – external/flexible = entrepreneurial and innovative culture, values creativity, agility, risk-taking and experimentation
3 **Market** – external/stable = competitive and result-driven, values productivity and results
4 **Hierarchy** – internal/stable = highly structured and controlled, values efficiency, consistency and predictability

There are pros and cons to each of these different types of culture, but the framework allows organisations to identify their culture, match leadership styles to their approach and address any weaknesses. Many of the buzzwords companies use to describe their culture can be allocated to one of these four categories.

Cultural Strength and Subcultures

To summarise the above, there are many different types of culture, which can be observed at different levels of the organisation and employees. However, one of the main ways in which organisational culture can impact employee behaviour, attitudes, and general outcomes is whether the culture is considered to be 'strong' or 'weak'.

A strong organisational culture is one that has clear and consistent values about how the business should operate, and how employees should behave. Behaviours are exhibited from senior management all the way to newcomers, with common goals that are motivating, empowering, and fulfilling. Employees often feel a strong sense of identity and pride in being part of an organisation with a strong culture, fostering loyalty and advocacy. When a culture is strong, we see higher levels of performance, engagement, job satisfaction, greater talent attraction and retention, and smoother change management (see the following section on Managing Organisational Change).

A weak organisational culture, on the other hand, is one that generally lacks cohesion. This can be across values, work environments, traditions, behaviours, or job levels – anything relating to ways of working. Within weak cultures there is often lower job satisfaction and engagement, predominantly as a result of inconsistent expectations around behaviours and performance targets, and a lack of organisational identity, making it difficult for employees to feel proud or invested in their work.

Managers play a pivotal role in shaping a robust organisational culture by embodying and promoting the company's core values and practices. To cultivate a positive culture, managers can lead by example, demonstrating behaviours that reflect organisational values. Open communication is essential, as it encourages transparency and ensures employees feel heard (Smithson, 2024). Recognising and rewarding positive behaviours reinforces desired actions, while promoting inclusivity and psychological safety fosters a sense of belonging. Additionally, investing in employee development shows a commitment to long-term success.

MINI CASE STUDY 3.1

Google

Google provides a prominent example of strong organisational culture. The company promotes **innovation**, openness, and employee well-being, encouraging employees to think creatively and share ideas freely (Smithson, 2024). However, organisational culture is dynamic, and recent reports suggest Google has restructured its diversity, equity, and inclusion (DEI) initiatives, sparking conversations about the long-term impact on the company's culture (Bhuiyan, 2025). This highlights the need for managers to continuously adapt and reinforce positive cultural values in response to evolving internal and external factors.

In summary, a strong organisational culture fosters alignment, engagement, and performance, while a weak culture can lead to fragmentation, disengagement, and inefficiency. Organisations should actively cultivate their culture to support their goals and enhance overall effectiveness, through identification and clarification of cultural values, norms and goals, and consistent application of behaviour throughout all levels of the organisation.

Ultimately, effective management of an organisational culture can bring a host of benefits to employees and strategic advantage to the organisation.

MANAGING ORGANISATIONAL CHANGE

Change is a constant in modern organisations, but managing it effectively is challenging. Organisational change is the process through which an organisation changes any part of itself, perhaps in response to market changes, to improve performance, or other internal/external pressures. There are several types of change that are typically observed:

1. **Strategic change** – altering the direction of the organisation, such as its mission or goals
2. **Structural change** – changing the hierarchy, reporting structures or departmental structure of an organisation
3. **Process change** – considering policies, procedures, and workflows
4. **Cultural change** – attempts to shift the underlying beliefs, values and behaviours which shape an organisation's identity

As such, organisational changes are typically substantial and can impact a number of **stakeholders** both within and outside of the organisation. Therefore, several theories have been proposed as ways in which organisations can effectively manage these changes. Here, we focus on two interrelated perspectives:

Lewin's Change Management Model

One of the earliest and simplest models of change management is Lewin's (1947) work, which proposed three stages: Unfreeze, Change, and Refreeze. These stages are considered to be cyclical, recognising that organisations are dynamic and can go through changes often.

- The **Unfreeze** stage is focused on breaking down the existing 'status quo' in preparations for the changes to be made. Actions at this stage can include raising awareness for why changes are required, providing a sense of urgency, and addressing areas of resistance.
- The **Change** stage is where the actual changes are implemented. This can be in relation to new processes, cultural values, new technology or reporting structures. Managers are encouraged to engage employees, provide training, share updates regularly and with clear communication pathways, and again manage resistance to change as effectively as possible.
- Finally, the **Refreeze** stage concerns the efforts required to establish the new way of working. It may involve recurring training, monitoring, implementation of supportive policies and procedures, and importantly celebrating the success of the changes to promote positivity and embed them into the organisation's culture.

Kotter's 8-Step Change Model

While Lewin's work was well regarded, it faced criticism that the actions and steps were very vague, and hard to implement by organisations. Therefore, Kotter (1996) expanded upon the above model, providing an 8-step framework for managing an organisational change.

1. **Create a sense of urgency** to motivate stakeholders and encourage engagement
2. **Form a powerful coalition**, bringing together the people who can actually make the changes happen
3. **Create a vision for change**, which is inspiring and demonstrates how the changes will benefit both the organisation and employees
4. **Communicate the vision**, sharing the new directions and changes with all stakeholders through a range of different channels to ensure understanding and buy-in
5. **Empower action**, remove obstacles to change, encourage innovativeness and risk-taking to speed the change along
6. **Create quick wins**, especially important at the start, demonstrating ways in which the change is resulting in positive outcomes to build and sustain buy-in and progress
7. **Build on the change**, following the quick wins to tackle and/or implement the bigger change initiatives
8. **Anchor changes in the organisational culture**, reinforcing the new behaviours, norms, values, and expectations

This model offers a more specific programme through which managers can effectively implement changes in a range of organisational settings. Both models recognise the cyclical nature of change and highlight that the change programme doesn't end when it is implemented, but needs to be actively sustained in order for the new culture to become established.

Resistance to Change

A key challenge raised within both of the above change management theories was being able to manage and prevent resistance to change. As humans, we tend to favour stability, so when an organisation proposes substantial changes that can impact daily behaviours, employees can exhibit a range of resistance behaviours, such as denial, refusal to support changes and undermining behaviours (Agócs, 1997). In many ways, human responses to change map to experiences of grief, moving through stages of denial, anger, bargaining, depression and then acceptance (e.g., Kubler-Ross, 1973; Zell, 2003). These behaviours are typically a result of experiences such as a lack of information, fear of the unknown, personal threat, and dealing with powerful stakeholders. However, there are many ways in which organisations can deal with, and prevent, resistance.

Education and communication are one of the easiest ways to respond to resistance when there is a general lack of understanding. This approach can increase commitment and bring different viewpoints together. Similarly, getting different stakeholders and employees involved in the change process can reduce fear and increase buy-in through utilising the skills of different stakeholders. In both of these cases, however, a downside is that they can take time, which is not often available if the change process has a deadline or is in response to a significant external pressure (such as global societal/economic events).

When dealing with stakeholders who may feel threatened or are being difficult to manage, options include using a method such as negotiation, or more unethical approaches such as manipulation and coercion. While these methods are very quick and inexpensive to implement, they raise ethical concerns and can result in future challenges such as resistance, lack of engagement or efforts to undermine the organisation in future.

By employing these strategies, organisations can effectively manage and mitigate resistance to change, fostering a more positive environment that embraces transformation. A proactive approach enhances employee engagement, builds trust, and ultimately leads to successful change implementation, rather than waiting and reacting to resistance which emerges during the change process.

Three Levels or One Whole?

This final 'macro' level section has summarised two core themes of organisational behaviour research when we are considering whole organisations and large groups of employees: organisational culture, and organisational change. Building upon the levels, from micro to macro, we can identify where individual differences can play a role in both relational and group level dynamics. For example, resistance to change is likely to be shaped by individual characteristics, and influential people can emerge based on personality, as well as their roles within teams. As such, while we have structured this chapter based on the three levels of micro to macro-based research, we encourage you to think about work-related challenges *holistically*. This means that you should consider not only each level when faced with a problem but try to understand how the levels may link together or affect each other.

CONTEMPORARY ISSUES IN ORGANISATIONAL BEHAVIOUR

This section explores contemporary issues in Organisational Behaviour (OB). The key challenges and developments that have gained increased attention in today's dynamic work environments include Equality, Diversity, and Inclusion (EDI), and the role of technology in shaping workplace interactions and practices.

Equality, Diversity, and Inclusion

Equality, diversity, and inclusion are central pillars in current contemporary organisations across the world, despite more recent political moves by governments to reduce focus on EDI initiatives (e.g. USA). These pillars reflect the organisation's commitment to creating workplaces that are fair, respectful, and accommodating of all individuals regardless of their age, gender, faith, sexual orientation, race, ethnicity, and other attributes.

Equality is understood as the context of ensuring fairness and justice in organisational practices, where discrimination and bias are addressed and removed. According to Barmes (2016), equality is the principle that individuals should have an equal opportunity to achieve success and advancement, regardless of their age, gender, beliefs, ethnicity, race or any other characteristics. This principle is foundational to fair treatment policies and anti-discrimination laws within an organisation.

Diversity, as per Cox (1993), refers to the different kind of people of social and cultural identities coming together in a work environment. Emphasising diversity in organisations is not only about numerical representation, where individuals of different ethnicity, race or gender are hired. It also acknowledges the unique perspectives and strengths that different individuals bring to organisations to make effective business decisions.

Inclusion, meanwhile, focuses on creating a sense of belonging. Roberson (2006: 217) defines inclusion as 'the degree to which an employee is accepted and treated as an insider by others in a work system'. Inclusion ensures that diversity efforts translate into meaningful engagement and equal participation. Henceforth, equality, diversity and inclusion are interrelated and important concepts to bring together people's unique differences and work in a collaborative work environment.

Importance of EDI in Organisational Behaviour

Incorporating EDI principles within organisations has become imperative as organisations operate in more and more globalised work settings. Most employees nowadays are keen to work in such globalised and multinational organisations, for which proper policies and strategies of EDI principles must be in place to welcome individuals to work in these environments. There are many factors that contribute to an organisation's success when EDI principles are incorporated, which may include the following principles.

1 EDI principles help enhance workplace culture and employee morale. When employees perceive fairness and respect, they feel committed, and their job satisfaction, commitment, and productivity increase (Shore et al., 2011). This positive organisational climate fosters a sense of psychological safety, encouraging employees to express their ideas and innovate without fear of discrimination or ridicule.
2 EDI contributes to better decision-making and problem-solving. Diverse teams bring a wider range of perspectives, enabling organisations to address challenges more effectively and respond to diverse customer needs. Research shows that companies with greater diversity are more likely to outperform competitors (Brahma et al., 2021).
3 EDI is a moral and legal imperative. Promoting equality and preventing discrimination are not only ethical responsibilities but also legal requirements in many jurisdictions. Non-compliance can result in reputational damage, employee turnover, and costly lawsuits.
4 Finally, EDI drives organisational resilience and adaptability in a globalised economy. A diverse workforce enhances an organisation's ability to operate across different cultural contexts, fostering innovation and adaptability in rapidly changing environments (Harrison and Klein, 2007).

CASE STUDY 3.2

Diversity and Teamwork in Google's Project Aristotle

Google's *Project Aristotle* is a landmark study in organisational behaviour that highlighted the value of team dynamics and the role of diverse teams in driving performance. Google's *Project Aristotle* study investigated over 180 diverse teams across multiple offices in different countries, which was conducted between 2012 and 2015. The project aimed to understand why some teams outperformed other teams, despite having access to similar resources and talent pools. The findings have had a significant impact on how organisations approach team composition and dynamics, particularly regarding diversity and inclusion. They found that there were five key factors that helped teams perform well:

Psychological Safety: An example from the study involved a Google team working on a project with tight deadlines. Initially, some team members hesitated to speak up during meetings because they feared their ideas might be dismissed. This created tension and limited collaboration. However, when the team leader implemented specific practices, like encouraging everyone to share their thoughts and emphasising that mistakes were learning opportunities, the atmosphere changed. This meant that team members later felt safe to speak up, share ideas, and make mistakes without being judged or punished. Eventually, their productivity improved, and they could complete the task.

Dependability: Another team studied by Google showed how dependability influenced performance. In this team, everyone reliably completed their tasks on time, which allowed the group to stay on schedule and maintain trust. When one team member fell behind due to personal challenges, other members stepped in to help, ensuring the project remained on track. This mutual understanding strengthened the team's cohesion and overall effectiveness.

Structure and Clarity: Teams perform better when roles are clear. For example, in one high-performing team at Google, each member knew exactly what was expected of them, including deadlines. Meetings were structured with clear agendas, so no time was wasted. This clarity allowed the team to stay focused and avoid confusion about responsibilities, leading to higher efficiency.

Meaning of Work: In another case, a Google team worked on developing new features for Gmail. For this team, the work had personal significance - several members had family members who used Gmail regularly, and they saw their efforts as directly improving the lives of people they cared about. This sense of purpose motivated the team to go above and beyond.

Impact of Work: Lastly, the impact of their work was evident in a team tasked with designing tools for small business owners. The team started to understand that their work was making a difference. They felt that they contributed to the company's goals but also had a positive effect on society. When they saw the value of their work, they felt more driven and engaged.

The study highlighted several dynamics at play, particularly psychological safety, where team members felt safe and valued. This sense of belonging motivated employees to contribute more effectively, resulting in strong group dynamics. Despite the diverse backgrounds of team members, effective leadership leveraged both their similarities and differences to drive success and foster a sense of personal satisfaction.

Questions

1 Why is psychological safety important in a team, and what can a team leader do to help people feel safe to share their ideas?
2 How do clear roles and being reliable help teams work better, especially when team members come from different backgrounds?
3 How can knowing that their work matters help team members stay motivated, and how can leaders make sure everyone feels this way?

Source

Poyton, B. (2024) 'Google's Project Aristotle: Building high-performing teams', *Psychological Safety*, March 28. https://psychsafety.co.uk/googles-project-aristotle/ (accessed September 8, 2025).

THE IMPACT OF TECHNOLOGY ON OB

The impact of technology on OB has been transformative, reshaping how individuals interact, communicate, and perform in the workplace. Key technological advancements in flexible work arrangements and virtual teams, artificial intelligence (AI), automation, and **data analytics** have brought both opportunities and challenges to OB (e.g., Wang et al., 2021), requiring careful management to enhance the potential of these technologies.

Remote Work and Virtual Teams

Whilst triggered by the COVID-19 pandemic, advancements in technology have facilitated a significant shift to newer ways of working, allowing employees to work from more places and in diverse ways (Aroles et al., 2021). However, managing teams of remote workers poses a challenge to managers, raising several issues.

- Firstly, around the **social impact**: how do you manage teams that are remote, and what effect does this have on organisational culture, a sense of belonging and team identity?
- Secondly, the question of **job performance**: do employees need to be visible to complete their job tasks effectively?
- Finally, from an **employee perspective**, do they have the space and means to be able to work from home effectively, without disrupting their work-life balance?

However, these technological advancements have significant positive impacts on the way we work, from enhanced global communication and connectivity (e.g., Autio et al., 2021) to greater job satisfaction (e.g., Winkelhaus et al., 2022) and performance (e.g., Zheng et al., 2024) when managed effectively. As such, it remains an ongoing challenge for OB researchers to understand the most effective way to support these new ways of working.

Automation and Artificial Intelligence

AI and automation have significantly influenced OB by altering workflows and creating new dynamics between employees and technology. AI systems can handle routine, repetitive tasks such as data entry, scheduling, and basic customer service, allowing employees to focus on higher-level work that requires creativity and strategic thinking (e.g. Campbell et al., 2025). This shift in job responsibilities impacts employee motivation and job satisfaction but can also raise concerns regarding job security (Chui et al., 2016). Furthermore, AI applications in recruitment and talent management have streamlined hiring processes by automating initial screenings and analysing candidate profiles, reducing human bias, and enhancing efficiency (e.g., Oman et al., 2024). However, relying solely on AI-driven assessments can perpetuate biases if algorithms are trained on skewed data and prompted to favour key characteristics or unfounded biases (Guo et al., 2024).

Automation has transformed operational efficiency across sectors, such as manufacturing and finance, requiring employees to adapt quickly to modern technologies (e.g., Autor, 2015). As machines handle repetitive tasks, employees are increasingly expected to engage in more complex, decision-making roles, which may enhance job satisfaction for those seeking meaningful work. However, this shift can also cause work-related stress for employees facing skill gaps. Training and development programmes play a significant role in helping employees adapt to changing roles, and organisations that foster reskilling practices are more likely to sustain employee performance and satisfaction.

The Role of Data Analytics in OB

Data analytics has redefined organisational decision-making processes and the evaluation of success, by providing data-driven insights into employee performance, engagement, and overall effectiveness. With real-time data collection and predictive analytics, managers can make better-informed decisions regarding team dynamics, employee development, and project management. For example, data analytics can identify patterns in employee engagement surveys, allowing leaders to proactively address factors affecting job satisfaction and turnover.

Moreover, data analytics supports personalisation within the workplace by tailoring development programmes and career trajectories based on employees' skills, preferences, and performance data. This customisation can lead to higher employee engagement and retention, as workers feel their individual growth is valued. However, the adoption of employee monitoring and data collection raises privacy and ethical concerns. While data can improve organisational outcomes, it is crucial for companies to maintain transparency with employees about how their information is used to build trust, underscoring the need for responsible practices (e.g., Gierlich-Joas et al., 2024).

Challenges for Organisational Behaviour

As organisations face rapid technological advances and shifts in workforce expectations, understanding OB will continue to be critical for navigating the challenges of the modern workplace. It is important to consider how OB will deal with new ways of working, such as the role of AI, the future of the workplace, and increased diversity. Individuals make an organisation, and so it is vital that we understand how employees work well, and thrive, for the business to survive.

CHAPTER SUMMARY

- This chapter has explored key aspects of OB, emphasising its importance for fostering effective leadership, teamwork, communication, and cultural change.
- Organisational behaviour is a core topic for understanding how employees behave, think, and feel within their work. It can be understood at a micro, meso, and macro level.
- The 'micro' level of OB explores the individual, exploring topics such as personality and identity, with a goal of understanding how and why an individual is unique.
- The 'meso' level of OB explores the relationships between employees, colleagues, and leaders, with an aim to understand how they can be effective and result in key organisational outcomes.
- The 'macro' level of OB examines organisational-level events, such as change, and broader relationships, in the form of culture.
- Personality can be used to predict employee behaviour and responses to job tasks, often assessed before and during employment as part of employee development programmes.
- Personal and protected characteristics cover broad themes but can shed light on how and why these characteristics can help or hinder employees at work. These are often linked to identity, which is formed from both personal and social categorisations.
- Understanding what motivates employees at work is key to increasing performance and employee satisfaction, and can be evaluated utilising both content and process theories.
- Groups and teams make up the vast majority of the workforce, and can produce high performance, job satisfaction, and engagement. However, poorly managed or structured groups can also result in conflicts, groupthink, and breakdowns in communication.
- Organisational culture relates to the shared norms and ways of working across the organisation, binding employees together. It is often 'taken for granted' and can result

in inconsistencies between publicly stated company values, and the ways in which the work is *actually* done.

- Organisations inevitably go through periods of change, but how they manage their employees during this process will determine how successful it is. Using a change process will help create a successful change and prevent employee resistance.
- EDI and technology present new challenges for the study and understanding of OB, but these are seen as exciting new ways to explore how changes to work can impact (either positively or negatively) the individuals who are employed within these companies.

STUDENTS LIKE YOU CHANGE THE WORLD

Max Booth, 2025 Graduate BSc Business & Management (with Industrial Placement), University of Exeter

Figure 3.1 Max Booth

My placement year as a workplace strategist provided an insightful lesson; transforming a workspace is fundamentally about transforming people. The core challenge was not the physical space, but the psychological transition required to implement an activity-based working system. From the employee perspective, this transition involved relinquishing their current workplace habits and embracing a new philosophy. Simply by observing behaviour in the office, it was clear that a shiny new floorplan would not be sufficient, significant buy-in and behavioural change was necessary for the programme to be successful.

The primary issue we faced was territoriality - a psychological need for ownership. Asking employees to use the space fluidly threatened this. This ingrained behaviour created a strong resistance to change, requiring a sensitive approach toward change management.

To address this, we created a vision. Painting a picture of a dynamic, collaborative environment that allowed employees to operate autonomously in a vibrant workplace. We continuously showcased positive outcomes and examples of successful implementations to create a shared understanding of our desired outcome.

Creating a vision was only the first step; we needed champions to bring it to life. To form our 'volunteer army', we enlisted senior leaders to leverage their influence within the organisation. Recruiting these individuals helped us to communicate our vision, build credibility, and overcome resistance by demonstrating visible support from key stakeholders.

This experience underscored the critical role of organisational behaviour principles in navigating real-world problems. It highlighted the importance of understanding human behaviour in the workplace, and how strategic interventions can create positive and lasting organisational change.

END OF CHAPTER REFLECTION

Have a look at the skills you should have developed in this unit (find more details in the Key Skills Table in the Appendix on p. 499).

1 Which of the skills listed do you think you have developed the most?
2 Can you give two examples on why you feel you have now developed these skills/developed them further?
3 How will you use these new/refined skills in the future (give two examples of the impact of your development on your future behaviour)?

FURTHER READING

Edmondson, A.C. (2018) *The Fearless Organization: Creating Psychological Safety in the Workplace for Learning, Innovation, and Growth*. Wiley.

This book delves into the importance of psychological safety in the workplace. Edmondson explores how a safe environment where individuals feel comfortable taking risks and learning from mistakes fosters innovation, creativity, and overall organisational performance.

Mullins, L.J. (2023) *Management and Organisational Behaviour*. Pearson.

This textbook provides a comprehensive overview of management theories and principles, that offer insights into organisational behaviour concepts, also on leadership and strategic management which are essential for understanding the fundamental concepts that underpin organisational dynamics.

Robbins, S.P. and Judge, T.A. (2024) *Organizational Behavior* (19th global edition). Pearson Education.

The book delves deeper into the intricacies of individual and group behaviour that are useful to get further insights on group dynamics. It also covers practical implications to how groups and teams work and strategies to improve overall organisational performance.

Schein, E.H. (2010) *Organisational Culture and Leadership* (Vol. 2). John Wiley & Sons.

This book is a cornerstone in understanding organisational culture. It explores the underlying assumptions, values, and beliefs that shape an organisation's behaviour and performance. Schein provides practical insights into diagnosing, changing, and leading organisational cultures.

Ting-Toomey, S. and Chung, L.C. (2012) *Understanding Intercultural Communication* (2nd edition). Oxford University Press.

This book is crucial for navigating the complexities of cross-cultural interactions. It examines the impact of cultural differences on communication styles, conflict resolution, and negotiation. This will help students understand the need for developing effective intercultural communication skills in diverse workforces.

REFERENCES

Agocs, C. (1997). 'Institutionalized resistance to organizational change: Denial, inaction and repression', *Journal of Business Ethics*, 16 (9): 917–931.

Aroles, J., Cecez-Kecmanovic, D., Dale, K., Kingma, S.F., and Mitev, N. (2021) 'New ways of working (NWW): Workplace transformation in the digital age', *Information and Organization*, 31 (4). doi.org/10.1016/j.infoandorg.2021.100378

Ashkanasy, N.M. and Dorris, A.B. (2017) 'Organizational behavior', in O. Braddick (ed.), *The Oxford Research Encyclopaedia of Psychology*. Oxford University Press. pp. 1-32.

Autio, E., Mudambi, R. and Yoo, Y. (2021). 'Digitalization and globalization in a turbulent world: Centrifugal and centripetal forces', *Global Strategy Journal*, 11 (1): 3–16.

Autor, D.H. (2015) 'Why are there still so many jobs? The history and future of workplace automation', *Journal of Economic Perspectives*, 29 (3): 3–30. doi.org/10.1257/jep.29.3.3

Barmes, L. (2016) *Bullying and Behavioural Conflict at Work: The Duality of Individual Rights*. Oxford University Press.

Belbin, R.M. (1981) *Management Teams: Why They Succeed or Fail*. Butterworth-Heinemann.

Best, D.L. and Williams, J.E. (2001) 'Gender and culture', in D. Matsumoto (ed.), *The Handbook of Culture and Psychology*. Oxford University Press. pp. 195–219.

Bhuiyan, J. (2025) 'Google defends scrapping AI pledges and DEI goals in all-staff meeting', *The Guardian*, February 12. https://www.theguardian.com/us-news/2025/feb/12/google-all-staff-meeting-ai-dei (accessed September 8, 2025).

Bolino, M.C., Klotz, A.C., and Turnley, W.H. (2018) 'The unintended consequences of organizational citizenship behaviors for employees, teams, and organizations', in P.M. Podsakoff, S.B. MacKenzie, and N.P. Podsakoff (eds), *The Oxford Handbook of Organizational Citizenship Behavior*. Oxford University Press. pp. 185–202. doi.org/10.1093/oxfordhb/9780190219000.013.11

Brahma, S., Nwafor, C. and Boateng, A. (2021) 'Board gender diversity and firm performance: The UK evidence', *International Journal of Finance & Economics, 26*(4): 5704–5719.

Campbell, C., Sands, S., Whittaker, L. and Mavrommatis, A. (2025) *The AI Intelligence Playbook: Decoding GenAI Capabilities for Strategic Advantage*. Business Horizons.

Cheser, R.N. (1998) 'The effect of Japanese Kaizen on employee motivation in U.S. manufacturing', *The International Journal of Organizational Analysis*, 6 (3): 197–217. doi.org/10.1108/eb028884

Chui, M., Manyika, J., and Miremadi, M. (2016) 'Where machines could replace humans - and where they can't (yet)', *McKinsey Quarterly*, July 8. https://www.mckinsey.com/capabilities/mckinsey-digital/our-insights/where-machines-could-replace-humans-and-where-they-cant-yet#/ (accessed September 8, 2025).

CIPD (2024) 'Neuroinclusion at work'. *CIPD*, February. https://www.cipd.org/uk/knowledge/guides/neuroinclusion-work/ (accessed September 8, 2025).

Cox, T. (1993) *Cultural Diversity in Organizations: Theory, Research, and Practice*. Berrett-Koehler.

Dessler, G. (2020) *Fundamentals of Human Resource Management*. Pearson.

Digman, J. M. (1997) 'Higher-order factors of the Big Five', *Journal of Personality and Social Psychology*, 73(6): 1246-1256. https://doi.org/10.1037/0022-3514.73.6.1246

Eagly, A.H., Wood, W., and Diekman, A.B. (2000) 'Social role theory of sex differences and similarities: A current appraisal', in T. Eckes and H.M. Trautner (eds), *The Developmental Social Psychology of Gender*. Erlbaum. pp. 123–74.

Edmondson, A. (1999) 'Psychological safety and learning behaviour in work teams', *Administrative Science Quarterly*, 44 (2), 350–83. doi.org/10.2307/2666999

Edmondson, A.C. (2018) *The Fearless Organization: Creating Psychological Safety in the Workplace for Learning, Innovation, and Growth*. Wiley.

Frosch, K.H. (2011) 'Workforce age and innovation: A literature survey', *International Journal of Management Reviews*, 13 (4): 414-30. doi.org/10.1111/j.1468-2370.2011.00298.x

Funder, D.C. (2001) *The Personality Puzzle* (2nd edition). W. W. Norton.

Gibson, C.B. and Gibbs, J.L. (2006) 'Unpacking the concept of virtuality: The effects of geographic dispersion, electronic dependence, dynamic structure, and national diversity on team innovation', *Administrative Science Quarterly*, 51 (3): 451–95. doi.org/10.2189/asqu.51.3.451

Gierlich-Joas, M., Baiyere, A., and Hess, T. (2024) 'Inverse transparency and the quest for empowerment through the design of digital workplace technologies', *Journal of the Association for Information Systems*, 25 (5): 1212–39. doi.org/10.17705/1jais.00879

Goldberg, L.R. (1992) 'The development of markers for the Big-Five factor structure', *Psychological Assessment*, 4 (1): 26–42.

Guo, H., Venkit, P. N., Jang, E., Srinath, M., Zhang, W., Mingole, B., ... and Yadav, A. (2024). 'Hey GPT, can you be more racist? Analysis from crowdsourced attempts to elicit biased content from generative AI', *preprint arXiv*: 2410.15467.

Harrison, D.A. and Klein, K.J. (2007) 'What's the difference? Diversity constructs as separation, variety, or disparity in organizations', *The Academy of Management Review*, 32 (4): 1199–228. doi.org/10.5465/amr.2007.26586096

Henningsen, L., Eagly, A.H., and Jonas, K. (2022) 'Where are the women deans? The importance of gender bias and self-selection processes for the deanship ambition of female and male professors', *Journal of Applied Social Psychology*, 52 (8): 602–22. doi.org/10.1111/jasp.12780

Herzberg, F., Mausner, B., Peterson, R.O., and Capwell, D.F. (1957) *Job Attitudes: Review of Research and Opinion*. Psychological Service of Pittsburgh.

Hogg, M.A. and Terry, D.J. (2000) 'Social identity and self-categorization processes in organizational contexts', *The Academy of Management Review*, 25 (1): 121–40. doi.org/10.2307/259266

Janis, I.L. (1972). *Victims of Groupthink: A Psychological Study of Foreign-Policy Decisions and Fiascos*. Houghton Mifflin.

Koch, T. and Denner, N. (2022) 'Informal communication in organizations: Work time wasted at the water-cooler or crucial exchange among co-workers?', *Corporate Communications: An International Journal*, 27(3): 494–508.

Kotter, J.P. (1996) *Leading Change*. Harvard Business School Press.

Kübler-Ross, E. (1973) *On Death and Dying*. Routledge.

Kunze, F., Boehm, S., and Bruch, H. (2013) 'Age, resistance to change, and job performance', *Journal of Managerial Psychology*, 28 (7/8): 741–760. doi.org/10.1108/JMP-06-2013-0194

Lewin, K. (1947) 'Frontiers in group dynamics: Concept, method and reality in social science; social equilibria and social change', *Human Relations*, 1: 5–41. doi.org/10.1177/001872674700100103

Locke, E.A. and Latham, G.P. (1990) *A Theory of Goal Setting and Task Performance*. Prentice Hall.

Maslow, A.H. (1943) 'A theory of human motivation', *Psychological Review*, 50: 370–96.

Mdhlalose, D.S. (2024) 'The applicability of contemporary, classical motivational theories and managerial methods in non-western countries', *International Journal of Management, Accounting and Economics*, 11 (5): 611–38. doi.org/10.5281/zenodo.11351766

Mullins, L.J. (2023). *Management and Organisational Behaviour*. Pearson.

Oman, Z.U., Siddiqua, A., and Noorain, R. (2024) 'Arteficial intelligence and its ability to reduce recruitment bias', *World Journal of Advanced Research and Reviews*, 24 (1): 551-64. doi.org/10.30574/wjarr.2024.24.1.3054

Pit, S., Fisk, M., Freihaut, W., Akintunde, F., Aloko, B., Berge, B., [...] and Yap, J.C.H. (2021) 'COVID-19 and the ageing workforce: Global perspectives on needs and solutions across 15 countries', *International Journal for Equity in Health*, 20 (221): 1-22. doi.org/10.1186/s12939-021-01552-w

Quinn, R.E., and Rohrbaugh, J. (1983) 'A spatial model of effectiveness criteria: Towards a competing values approach to organisational analysis', *Management Science*, 29 (3): 363-77. doi.org/10.1287/mnsc.29.3.363

Robbins, S.P., and Judge, T.A. (2022) *Essentials of Organizational Behavior* (15th edition). Pearson.

Robbins, S.P., and Judge, T.A. (2024) *Organizational Behavior* (19th global edition). Pearson Education.

Roberson, Q. M. (2006). 'Disentangling the meanings of diversity and inclusion in organizations', *Group & Organization Management*, 31 (2): 212-36. https://doi.org/10.1177/1059601104273064

Ryan, M. K., Haslam, S. A., Morgenroth, T., Rink, F., Stoker, J. and Peters, K. (2016). 'Getting on top of the glass cliff: Reviewing a decade of evidence, explanations, and impact', *The Leadership Quarterly*, 27(3): 446-55. https://doi.org/10.1016/j.leaqua.2015.10.008

Ryan, R. M., and Deci, E. L. (2000). 'Intrinsic and extrinsic motivations: Classic definitions and new directions', *Contemporary Educational Psychology*, 25 (1): 54-67. https://doi.org/10.1006/ceps.1999.1020

Schein, E. H. (1988). 'Organisational socialization and the profession of management', *MIT Sloan Management Review*, 30 (1): 53.

Schein, E.H. (2010). *Organisational Culture and Leadership* (Vol. 2). John Wiley & Sons.

Shore, L.M., Randel, A.E., Chung, B.G., Dean, M.A., Holcombe Ehrhart, K., and Singh, G. (2011). 'Inclusion and diversity in work groups: A review and model for future research', *Journal of Management*, 37 (4): 1262-89. https://doi.org/10.1177/0149206310385943

Smithson, N. (2024). 'Google's (Alphabet's) organisational culture and its traits', *Panmore Institute*. https://panmore.com/google-organizational-culture-characteristics-analysis (accessed September 10, 2025)

Sterling, A.D., Thompson, M.E., Wang, S., Kusimo, A., Gilmartin, S., and Sheppard, S. (2020). 'The confidence gap predicts the gender pay gap among STEM graduates', *The Proceedings of the National Academy of Sciences*, 117 (48): 30303-8. doi.org/10.1073/pnas.2010269117

Tajfel, H. (1974) 'Social identity and intergroup behaviour', *Social Science Information*, 13 (2): 65-93. doi.org/10.1177/053901847401300204

Tajfel, H. and Turner, J.C. (1979) 'An integrative theory of intergroup conflict', in W.G. Austin and S. Worchel (eds), *The Social Psychology of Intergroup Relations*. Brooks/Cole. pp. 33-47.

Tajfel, H. and Turner, J.C. (1986) 'The social identity theory of intergroup behavior', in S. Worchel and W.G. Austin (eds), *The Psychology of Intergroup Relations* (2nd edition). Nelson-Hall. pp. 7-24.

Ting-Toomey, S. and Chung, L.C. (2012) *Understanding Intercultural Communication* (2nd edition). Oxford University Press.

Truxillo, D., Cadiz, D., and Rineer, J. (2014) *The Aging Workforce: Implications for Human Resource Management*. Oxford University Press.

Tuckman, B.W. (1965) 'Developmental sequence in small groups', *Psychological Bulletin*, 63 (6): 384-99. doi.org/10.1037/h0022100

Tuckman, B.W. and Jensen, M.A.C. (1977) 'Stages of small-group development revisited', *Group and Organization Management*, 2 (4). doi.org/10.1177/105960117700200404

UK Government (2010) Equality Act 2010. https://www.legislation.gov.uk/ukpga/2010/15/contents (accessed September 7, 2025).

Van der Wal, Z. (2015) '"All quiet on the non-Western front?" A review of public service motivation scholarship in non-Western contexts', *Asia Pacific Journal of Public Administration*, 37 (2): 69–86. doi.org/10.1080/23276665.2015.1041223

Vroom, V.H. (1964). *Work and Motivation*. John Wiley & Sons.

Wang, B., Liu, Y., Qian, J., and Parker, S.K. (2020) 'Achieving effective remote working during the COVID-19 pandemic: A work design perspective', *Applied Psychology*, 70 (1): 16–59. doi.org/10.1111/apps.12290

Winkelhaus, S., Grosse, E. H. and Glock, C. H. (2022) 'Job satisfaction: An explorative study on work characteristics changes of employees in Intralogistics 4.0', *Journal of Business Logistics*, 43 (3): 343–67.

Zell, D. (2003) 'Organizational change as a process of death, dying, and rebirth', *The Journal of Applied Behavioral Science*, 39 (1): 73–96.

Zheng, Q., Jin, Y. and Xu, X. (2024) 'Artificial intelligence and job performance of healthcare providers in China', *Frontiers in Public Health*, *12*: 1398330.

4
LEADERSHIP

Sarah Tudor, Alison Sydenham, Jackie Bagnall, Michelle Civile, Adrian Ball, Fernando Correia, Clare Hearn, and Rachael Johnstone

INTENDED LEARNING OUTCOMES

After reading this chapter, you should be able to:

1 Consider what leadership is and how it is performed within a modern context.
2 Discuss a range of leadership styles and approaches.
3 Reflect on your own leadership preferences and how to develop these effectively.
4 Plan how you will improve and apply your leadership skills in future career choices.
5 Understand principles of ethical and sustainable management.

SUSTAINABLE DEVELOPMENT GOALS

In this chapter, the following SDGs will be addressed:

- SDG 4: Quality Education - Leadership development directly supports lifelong learning and skills development for effective professional growth.
- SDG 5: Gender Equality - Modern leadership contexts promote inclusive leadership practices that foster gender equity in leadership positions.
- SDG 8: Decent Work and Economic Growth - Ethical and responsible leadership promote sustainable economic growth and decent work environments.
- SDG 10: Reduced Inequalities - Inclusive leadership reduces workplace inequalities and promotes diversity and equal opportunity.
- SDG 12: Responsible Consumption and Production - Sustainable leadership brings about responsible organisational practices that consider environmental and social impacts.
- SDG 16: Peace, Justice and Strong Institutions - Ethical principles lead to accountable, inclusive organisational structures that promote just practices and decision-making.
- SDG 17: Partnerships for the Goals - Modern and collaborative leadership approaches aim to develop partnerships across sectors to achieve shared goals.

INTRODUCTION

This chapter will consider the most important aspects of **leadership** and how it relates to our global context. We will explore aspects of effective leadership as well as different approaches to leadership and how these interplay with the most pressing and most relevant issues in the modern world of business.

This chapter will lead you through an exploration of leadership in a modern context. You will consider how leadership differs to management and where the attributes for leadership and management overlap. You will consider leadership theories in different **cultures** and leadership approaches in today's business context. There will be an opportunity to reflect on leadership skills and competencies and which of these you consider vital to success. An overview of leadership styles will give you a concrete background from which you will then consider leadership in a global context, including the seismic shift in how we lead with a focus on inclusivity and well-being. You will then consider the role of mentoring and coaching in leadership, how to lead with an ethical focus and how to consider **sustainability** through a leadership lens. Finally, you will consider the future of leadership, and the impact of all this **knowledge** on leadership may help you shape your perspective and your future career.

An Introduction to Leadership

It is vital to consider leadership in the context of business and management, as every successful organisation is built on effective leadership. Leadership can be perceived as one person spearheading an organisation and driving it forward using a multitude of characteristics and styles, however, effective leadership can be fluid, everchanging and very often relies heavily on a group of people rather than on just one individual.

Effective and high performing leadership is often judged on the outputs which are being measured such as productivity, profit, and job satisfaction, but these are rarely down to the actions of one person but rather down to the culture they establish and the teams that they build around them.

REFLECTIVE ACTIVITY 4.1

- Think about when you have witnessed or experienced excellent or poor leadership and consider what made you feel it was either of those things?
- Was it how the leader spoke or how they influenced others?
- How they inspired action or inaction?
- Make a note of your reflections.

Defining Leadership and Its Importance in Business

What do you think of when you think of great leadership? Do you think of a sporting captain or manager shouting from the sidelines of an athletic competition, do you think of a world leader giving a great speech about how they think their country or the world should function, or do you think of someone more personal to you, someone who helped you, inspired you or gave you an example of great leadership in your own life?

All of these areas of leadership are legitimate examples of leadership across the globe and leadership in business is not significantly different. Great leadership in business is based on knowing your environment, knowing your vision and goals, and driving the business towards achieving those goals. How a leader chooses to try to accomplish those goals can be a significant differentiator between success and failure. In the context of business, 'Leadership is a set of mindsets and behaviours that aligns people in a collective direction, enables them to work together and accomplish shared goals, and helps them adjust to changing environments.' (McKinsey & Company, 2024).

Leadership is a fundamental factor in the success of any organisation and the style and approach to leadership that is selected within an organisation can significantly influence its culture and working practices. For many employees as well as for investors, the style of leadership can be a deciding factor in whether to join an organisation and how long they will stay within or align with that organisation.

Different sectors may also foster different leadership approaches, for example in the private sector where commercial targets and drivers may be paramount, it can be more challenging to adopt a more people-centred approach to leadership. In the public and in the third sector more emphasis may be placed on societal benefits and outcomes and therefore leadership which fosters a clear focus on these is required.

Great organisational leadership can inspire others within the organisation to engage with an organisational vision and to take responsibility for working towards achieving and delivering that vision. Leadership may also look different within different cultural and different national contexts, where politics and legislation will also influence which approach to leadership is adopted.

REFLECTIVE ACTIVITY 4.2

Stories of Leadership

When you think about leadership, what stories come to mind?

Now watch the following YouTube videos and think again: Does leadership have the same meaning across the world?

Simon Sinek on courage in leadership - https://www.youtube.com/watch?v=xGdb11YxUBQ

Young African leaders share stories of leadership - https://www.youtube.com/watch?v=sOod7pjzerM

The Difference Between Leadership and Management

Leadership differs from management in that great leadership inspires people to want to perform well, while effective management can be seen as a more operational function through which employees are directed and delegated to (see Figure 4.1).

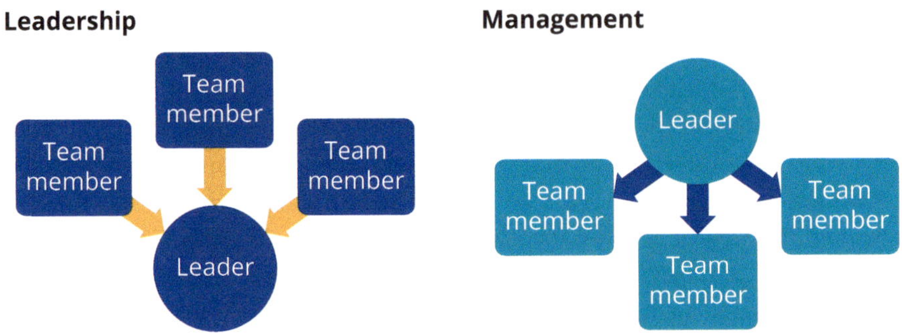

Figure 4.1 The difference between leadership and management communications

Source: Authors

Leadership can be depicted as an approach which identifies and builds the strengths of the team members and then coordinates the response and steers the direction of the progress that the team makes.

Management can be a more directive role, usually more operational, where the manager determines what tasks need to be completed and instructs the team members on what each of them should do to achieve the desired outcome.

A leadership role may be less focused on considering the functions of mechanics or their team, department, or business, and more concerned with getting the best out of their people and ensuring organisational effectiveness. This is often best achieved in tandem with highly effective management functions.

Although Leadership and Management can be defined as separate areas of theory, there is often an overlap in the **skills**, attributes and outputs of leaders vs. managers (see Figure 4.2).

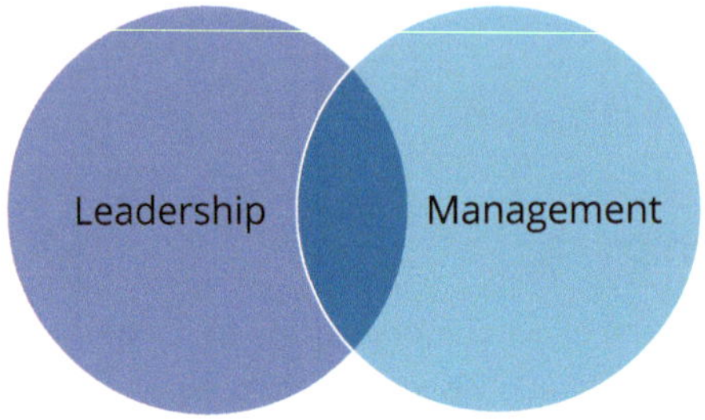

Figure 4.2 Overlap of leadership skills, attributes and outcomes with management skills, attributes and outcomes

Source: Author

REFLECTIVE ACTIVITY 4.3

Find out about Jacinda Ardern, former prime minister of New Zealand and Michael Jordan, former NBA basketball player (see Figures 4.3 and 4.4).

- Are they examples of great leaders or not? Why?

Figure 4.3 Jacinda Ardern

Figure 4.4 Michael Jordan

CORE LEADERSHIP THEORIES

The following section discusses a number of different leadership theories, including trait theory, situational and contingency theory and transformational and transactional theories.

Trait Theory

The trait theory of leadership (Stogdill, 1974; McCall and Lombardo, 1983) aims to identify the core traits which make an exceptional leader and to encourage leaders to aspire to develop those traits. Five commonly identified traits are neuroticism, openness, extroversion, agreeableness and conscientiousness. In trait theory there is a suggestion that the characteristics that are perceived to make great leaders are innate to a person's character and therefore that all successful leaders are born with these traits. However, theories on trait-based leadership have differed in the agreed set of attributes which make a successful leader and on whether these can be developed through experience or not.

The Blake and Mouton Managerial/Leadership Grid

The Blake and Mouton Managerial/Leadership grid (1964; see Figure 4.5) identified five kinds of leadership behaviour:

- **Country club:** This leadership style is a laid back approach, which has a high focus on people and a much lower focus on results.
- **Impoverished:** This leadership style is not invested in outcomes for people or in results.
- **Middle of the road:** This leadership style attempts to make compromises for both people and results.

- **Produce-or-perish:** This leadership style is highly focused on results, often at the expense of people.
- **Team orientated:** This leadership style has a high focus on both people and results. This is very difficult to achieve but can yield the best results.

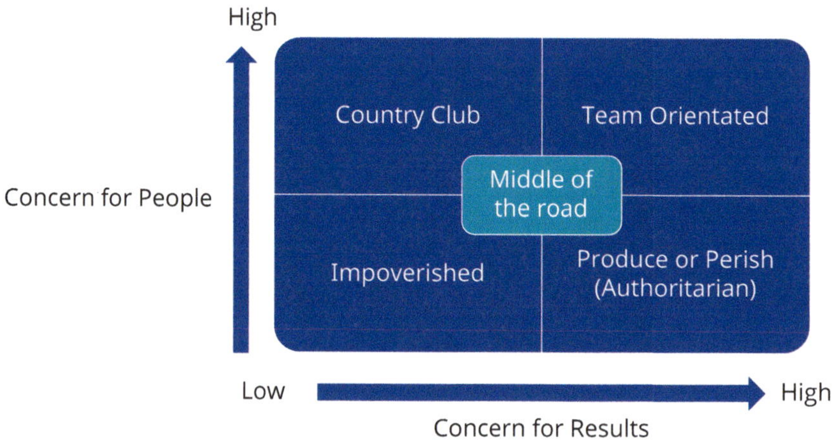

Figure 4.5 Behavioural theory - Blake and Mouton Managerial/Leadership Grid (1964)

Situational and Contingency Theories

Hersey and Blanchard's (1982) situational leadership theory suggests that leaders should adapt their approach and style according to the people they are leading, whether these are individuals or groups of people. Using the term 'situational' depicts the adaptability of the leader rather than referring to the situation in which they are leading.

Fiedler's (1967) contingency leadership model suggested that leaders have a strong bias to one of two leadership approaches; these are task-orientated leadership or relationship-orientated leadership. Fiedler discussed the strengths of both of these approaches, suggesting that neither is superior to the other, but that they are superior in certain situations and that an effective leader learns when to employ one or the other.

Ningen Ryoku

Ningen Ryoku (often translated as 'human skill') is the Japanese leadership approach which sets out to instil values of leadership, decisiveness, cooperativeness and adaptability in all employees (Padfield et al., 2012). This courageous approach to leadership is a central to the Japanese style of education and development of core and technical skills.

REFLECTIVE ACTIVITY 4.4

Worksheet 4.1 Leadership approaches

Leadership approach	Ranked in your opinion of which is the best approach to adopt for the benefit of an organisation	Ranked in terms of which you would prefer / be likely to adopt for your own leadership style
Country Club		
Impoverished		
Middle of the Road		
Produce or Perish		
Team Orientated		

Based on this ranking:

- Can you plot where you feel your natural leadership style currently sits?
- Reflect on why you think this is and whether you feel it will move as you gain further leadership experience.

Māori Leadership

Māori leadership is a relationship-focused approach which promotes harmony and connectedness throughout the workplace. This is a traditional vision of leadership but has been developed through a contemporary lens to enhance respectful approaches to work in modern New Zealand businesses.

Māori leadership can vary significantly from western leadership as it focuses on core values such as caring (manaakitanga), guardianship (kaitiakitanga) and relationship building (whanaungatanga), and traditionally the leader (or chief) is responsible for the wellbeing and protection of their people and achieves this through working with the community to make informed decisions that are best for the people (Food and Fibre CoVE, 2024). Te Rangikāheke described Māori leadership as dynamic and responsive to the tribal, political, and cultural needs of the time, while remaining founded in the Māori worldview (Matthews, 2011).

Transformational and Transactional Theories

Transformational leadership is a leadership style which aims to motivate and elevate employees in a way which inspires them to drive change in the organisation, which in turn drives success. This approach to leadership is focused on people and values, on the understanding that by investing in employees and by ensuring a safe, rewarding and trusting organisational culture, people will strive to perform at their best and therefore productivity and effectiveness will increase.

A transformational leader is an individual who demonstrates the values inherent in this style of leadership, which include optimism, **innovation**, empathy, and purpose, and who has the strength and skills to maintain enthusiasm throughout challenging periods. Transformational leadership is vision-led, with clear goals and supportive structures in place to enable everyone to fulfil their potential in alignment with those goals (MacGregor Burns, 1978) (see Figure 4.6).

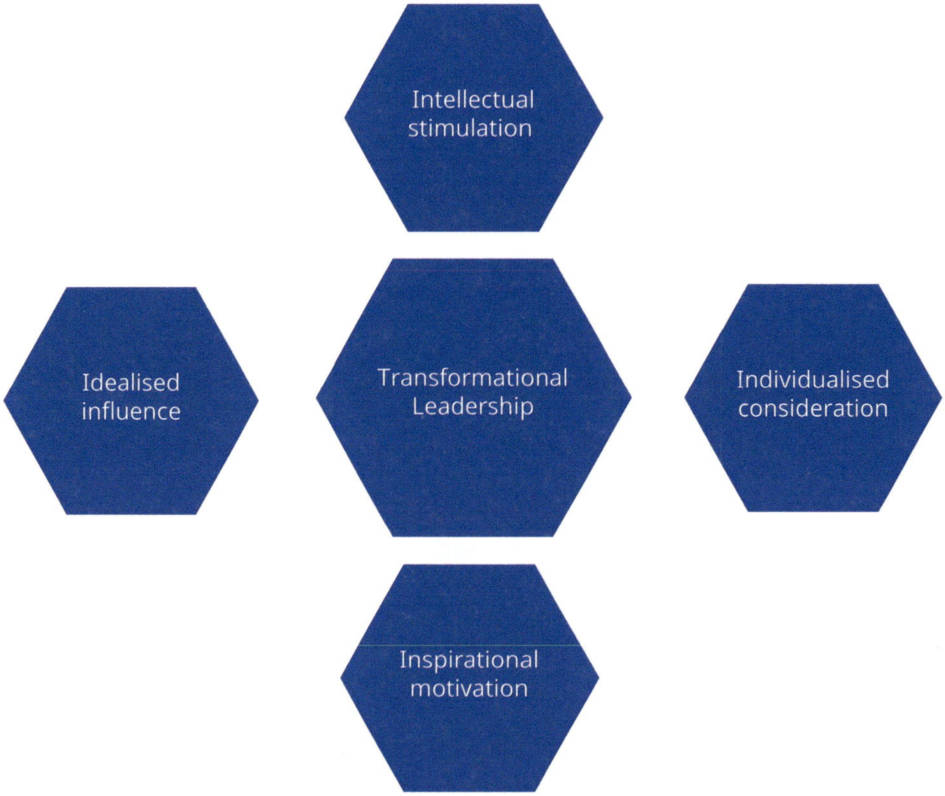

Figure 4.6 Transformational Leadership

Source: Author

Transactional leadership is a very different approach to transformational leadership and relies much more on structure, order and clear processes to ensure everyone understands their roles and the expectations of them to ensure all goals and objectives are met. There is more than a hint of hierarchical management in this leadership style as rewards are clearly linked to performance targets, which are closely monitored with punishments or rigid consequences in place if expectations are not met (Downton, 1973).

This approach can be a necessary tool in leaders' armoury if the organisation needs to meet short-term targets or is operating in a process-driven sector. It can lead to high levels of success and achievement, but this can sometimes be at the expense of flexibility, supportive policies and long-term career motivation.

CASE STUDY 4.1

University of Exeter: Leadership in Sustainability

Business leaders can identify 'tipping points' to lead their industries in the adoption of low-carbon technologies, according to a report by Gartner Inc. and the University of Exeter. A tipping point occurs when a small change sparks a transformation that is often rapid and irreversible. With the climate crisis accelerating – partly due to the threat from Earth system tipping points – positive socio-economic tipping points are now vital.

Professor Tim Lenton, from the University of Exeter, said: 'Business leaders can play a vital role in the switch to low-carbon technologies, helping to ensure the sustainable future upon which we all depend. Our report breaks down how tipping points work and how to influence them. The energy transition will happen rapidly, and in ways that may be difficult to predict. Understanding and harnessing the power of positive tipping points can allow business leaders to help drive that change, rather than simply reacting to it.'

Figure 4.7 Low Carbon Technologies (https://news.exeter.ac.uk/faculty-of-environment-science-and-economy/gartner-and-exeter-identify-tipping-point-opportunities-in-low-carbon-technologies-for-executive-leaders/)

Questions

The key question here will be: how will businesses adapt and respond to these tipping points?

1. Why do you think this is an important question for business leaders today?
2. Do you think it is a question for business leaders of all types of organisations?
3. What do you think business leaders might have to consider when deciding where this fits in their list of priorities?

Source

Morrison, A, (2024) 'Gartner and Exeter identify "tipping point" opportunities in low-carbon technologies for executive leaders'. University of Exeter News. https://news.exeter.ac.uk/faculty-of-environment-science-and-economy/gartner-and-exeter-identify-tipping-point-opportunities-in-low-carbon-technologies-for-executive-leaders/ (accessed September 9, 2025).

Contemporary Leadership Approaches and Considerations

The following section considers contemporary leadership approaches and considerations.

Inclusive Leadership

Inclusive leadership (Gallegos, 2014) means being able to support and lead a diverse range of individuals with compassion and authenticity. It is a style of leadership which has developed alongside the increased prominence of the EDI agenda within organisations, in line with changing individual, organisational and societal values. Traditional approaches to leadership, often referred to as heroic models of leadership, are less popular and less effective within modern western societal structures where mutual respect and empowerment of disadvantaged groups is more prevalent.

An inclusive leader is someone who invests in individuals without bias and who strives to support them through understanding, in an equitable way, to enable them to achieve their full potential. An inclusive leader can achieve this through effective listening, acceptance, self-awareness and empathy as well as using coaching skills to build their team's confidence and encourage their professional growth. This is often referred to as 'servant leadership' as the leader acts for the good of the whole team rather than selfishly. Further detail on self-awareness can be found in the 'Leader Development' section.

An inclusive style of leadership encourages diversity of thought, ideas, and perspectives with the aim of increasing innovation and success within an organisation as well as retaining high performing and talented team members.

Microaggressions

A microaggression is a subtle, everyday instance of racism, sexism, homophobia, transphobia and other forms of discrimination. Microaggressions can be intentional or unintentional statements, actions, or incidents which communicate some sort of negative bias towards minority groups. These often impact of the culture of an organisation and on the sense of belonging that individuals feel within an organisation. It is vital for an inclusive leader to address these and that the lack of awareness which often underpins these is addressed to create a more productive and harmonious working environment.

Intersectionality

It was Kimberlé Crenshaw (1989) who first coined the phrase '**intersectionality**' in her influential paper 'Demarginalizing the Intersection of Race and Sex: A Black Feminist Critique of Antidiscrimination Doctrine, Feminist Theory and Antiracist Politics' in which she explored multiplicity of identity and the implication of this for legislative approaches which often treat race, gender, and sexuality as mutually exclusive categories.

Digital Leadership

Being a digital leader demands a deep comprehension of current and developing technologies and the advantages such technology can offer the organisation under their guidance.

Additionally, the digital leader should understand these benefits and navigate legislative and ethical challenges to optimise the potential of technology and propel the organisation forward. A vital skill for a digital leader is recognising the cultural shifts required to adapt to rapid digital advancements across various job roles and functions within an organisation. Moreover, they must grasp transformational change management, which seeks to unlock the full potential of **digital transformation** while helping individuals adjust and thrive in a tech-driven modern business environment.

Digital leaders increasingly rely on various **data** types and insights for strategic decision-making. Consequently, they must understand the authenticity and origin of their data to support high-level decisions effectively.

Senior leadership teams are now responsible for carefully assessing the most appropriate digital solutions to tackle their business challenges, whether through digital twins in manufacturing or automated distribution centres. This assessment should guarantee cost-effectiveness and the potential to enhance efficiencies in business processes, manufacturing, or distribution while adding value, boosting sales, and increasing market share. A strategic evaluative approach, rather than a reactive embrace of emerging technology, is crucial for successful digital transformation and will always involve piloting and phased implementation of process and technology changes to prevent delays and confusion often associated with technology adoption.

When it comes to digital leadership, it's about more than just the benefits of complex software systems, AI, self-service, and individualised data representation. Equally important is the weight of responsibility that comes with considering how these tools could be misused for criminal or unethical activities. Responsible and ethical leadership demands this scrutiny, a crucial aspect of successful digital transformation. It's not just about the benefits, but also about the potential risks and the impact of every decision.

In a rapidly changing world, an agile digital leader must maintain an awareness of the organisational appetite for implementing digital innovations, and continuously adapt and learn. Balancing the complexity of transformation and disruption with efficiency and productivity is a constant challenge, and it requires a leader who is always ready to learn and adapt.

CASE STUDY 4.2

Vodafone – Sustainable Business

Vodafone have developed a sustainable approach to developing their business and the technology they use.

> We seek to connect everyone, regardless of who they are or where they live. We aim to close the digital divides, help our customers to benefit fully from digitalisation and support our communities, especially those in need, leaving no one behind.

(Continued)

Vodafone focuses on empowering people by working to close the digital divide, by improving network coverage and enhancing coverage for communities. They provide tailored support and services for small businesses across Europe and Africa and improve their digital readiness. They are addressing equity through inclusive policies and services for marginalised communities.

Questions

1. Do you agree that diversity makes an organisation stronger?
2. What do you think should be the priorities for businesses today in terms of contributing to global goals and why?
3. What do you think is meant by the 'digital divide'?

Source

Vodafone (n.d.) 'Empowering people'. https://www.vodafone.com/sustainable-business/empowering-people (accessed September 9, 2025).

LEADERSHIP SKILLS AND COMPETENCIES

We've already discussed some key theories and approaches to leadership. We know that in this ever changing and fast paced world, there is a need to help understand the key skills and competencies that modern leaders need.

Being given the title of leader does not always ensure that you will be a great one! There are five fundamental skills that stand out as essential for modern leaders:

- Communication
- Decision-making
- Emotional intelligence
- Adaptability
- Resilience

We'll explore each of those in turn during this chapter.

REFLECTIVE ACTIVITY 4.5

- Why do you think the five skills mentioned above are essential for modern leaders to consider?
- What current leaders in the news or on social media do you see using these skills?

The Importance of Good Communication in Leadership

Communication is the cornerstone for any leader. It's the way in which you speak to those that you lead to get messages across, give the direction of the organisation or maybe deliver difficult news. And communication isn't always about the way that you speak: modern leaders are scrutinised by the way that they speak, look, what they write and how they use social media in interacting with the people they lead. Technology is very much at the heart of communication since modern audiences receive messages to their devices immediately.

REFLECTIVE ACTIVITY 4.6

- Consider how Volodymyr Zelensky has used powerful communication skills to engage with the people of Ukraine.

Making Good Decisions

Good decision-making is crucial in leadership because it directly impacts the success, direction, and morale of teams of people, and, in turn, whole organisations. Leaders are responsible for setting the tone and direction for their teams, and every decision has an impact on both the day-to-day running and long-term achievements of the organisation. Leaders who make good decisions create clear guidance for their teams to achieve objectives, ensuring that resources are used effectively, risks are managed, and everyone achieves. Employees tend to have greater confidence in leaders who demonstrate sound judgment, which increases morale and **engagement**. A leader's ability to make well-informed, timely decisions can also prevent confusion and uncertainty, maintaining operational momentum and minimising disruptions.

Moreover, good decision-making is key to navigating change and overcoming challenges. In what sometimes is referred to as a VUCA world (Volatile, Uncertain, Challenging, Ambiguous), leaders who evaluate complex situations, consider diverse perspectives, and anticipate potential consequences are better equipped to guide their people and organisations through crises. Employees want to feel that their leaders consider them when making decisions as well as their customers and/or other **stakeholders**. Poor decision-making can result in missed opportunities, financial loss, and in some cases the failure of a business. Leaders must therefore create a culture of **critical thinking**, remain adaptable, and engage with all stakeholders to ensure their decisions support the long-term success of their organisation.

How Emotional Intelligence Is Essential for Modern Leadership

Emotional intelligence (EI) refers to the ability to recognise, understand, manage, and influence one's own emotions and the emotions of others. It is composed of several core components:

- Self-awareness
- Self-regulation
- Motivation
- Empathy
- Social skills

These are explored in Daniel Goleman's Emotional Intelligence Framework (Goleman, 1995). Leaders with high EI are attuned to their own emotional states, can regulate their reactions, and are skilled at navigating the social complexity of people and teams in the workplace.

Modern leaders are required to support collaboration, inspire teams, and navigate the challenges posed by change, all of which are benefited by strong interpersonal relationships. By demonstrating empathy and understanding, emotionally intelligent leaders can build trust and rapport with their teams, creating a more inclusive and supportive work culture.

Moreover, EI enhances a leader's capacity to handle stress, manage conflict, and make balanced decisions, especially in high-pressure situations. Leaders who possess emotional intelligence are better equipped to respond thoughtfully rather than react impulsively, maintaining stability during times of uncertainty.

As employees demand more focus from employers on well-being, flexibility, diversity, equality and inclusion, leaders need to connect with their teams on a deeper emotional level to inspire motivation and commitment. Emotional intelligence helps leaders address the unique challenges and needs of individuals, thereby boosting employee engagement and retention.

Adaptability in the Face of Change

Adaptability refers to the ability to adjust to new conditions, environments, or changes, both expected and unforeseen. In today's fast-paced, constantly evolving world, adaptability has become an essential trait for individuals and organisations alike. It involves being open to new ideas, willing to learn, and flexible in response to challenges, opportunities, and changing circumstances.

REFLECTIVE ACTIVITY 4.7

- Consider organisations or brands that have failed to adapt to changes in the world that they operate in, e.g. Nokia, Kodak, or Blockbuster.

REFLECTIVE ACTIVITY 4.8

Refer again to Case Study 4.2 - Vodafone

After reading the case study, take a moment to answer these questions:

- Do you think Vodafone have adapted well to societal shifts?
- How do you think they have done that?
- Do you think Vodafone have adapted because they feel it is the right thing to do? What other motivations might they have for adapting?

In a business or leadership context, adaptability is crucial for success. Leaders who are adaptable can effectively manage change, develop new strategies when necessary, and create a culture of innovation. They recognise that uncertainty is a constant, and rather than resisting change, they embrace it. This allows them to lead their teams through disruption and maintain organisational resilience, in turn building confidence in their ability as a leader.

For employees, adaptability means being willing to acquire new skills, adjust to different roles, or shift focus as business priorities evolve. In a volatile and complex work environment, individuals who can navigate these changes while maintaining performance are invaluable assets. Innovation is essential in business to consider the future and be prepared for it. If changes are unexpected, then they must adapt quickly. The worldwide COVID-19 pandemic of 2020 is an example of where some businesses couldn't innovate quickly, and others thrived. For example, the department store chain Debenhams entered an accelerated period of decline during the pandemic, when it became apparent that with outdated systems and platforms, they were unable to pivot and to compete effectively in the online retail space. The leadership of the organisation failed to adequately innovate and move with customer **demand** and trends. After 242 years of trading it ceased to exist on the high street.

Resilience

Finally, the last of our five key attributes in this section is resilience, which is a crucial attribute in modern leadership. Modern leadership challenges are characterised by rapid change, uncertainty and complex challenges. Leaders today face many disruptions, from technological advances and economic volatility to global incidents like pandemics and climate change. Resilience allows leaders to navigate these uncertainties effectively and emerge stronger for future leadership challenges that they may face.

Resilient leaders maintain a positive outlook while being adaptable and flexible in their approach. It is increasingly common that flexibility is essential as leaders may need to change strategies quickly to respond to new challenges. Resilience in a leadership context requires remaining calm under pressure, making sound decisions, and inspiring confidence in others, even when faced with setbacks. A leader who can be resilient and learn from failure and setbacks can learn for the future. Ultimately, this skill of not being put off by challenges can create an environment of innovation and **entrepreneurship** in teams, encouraging them to push boundaries and not fear making mistakes. By not creating a culture of fear or consequence, leaders enable an environment where individuals are more likely to innovate and collaborate, enhancing overall productivity.

In essence, resilience in modern leadership is not just about dealing with difficult and challenging times but thriving in the face of them, knowing when and how to deal with unplanned or unforeseen circumstances.

There will be other skills and competencies that you may read about, that you feel are more or less important than those discussed here. Much has been written about leadership and there is a wealth of resources that you can look to for guidance and support.

LEADERSHIP STYLES AND THEIR IMPACT

Effective leadership is a cornerstone of any successful team or organisation, shaping the dynamics, morale, and overall performance of its members. Leadership is all about guiding and inspiring people to work together to achieve goals (Kotter, 1999). The way a leader does this can vary a lot, and these different approaches are known as leadership styles. These styles are not just theoretical ideas; they have real effects on how a team or organisation works and how its members feel and perform. Here are some common leadership styles, their characteristics and impact on teams:

Autocratic Leadership

Autocratic leadership involves a leader making decisions unilaterally, without much input from team members. This style is characterised by individual control over all decisions with little or no input from group members.

The effect on teams of an autocratic leader is that decisions are made quickly which can be beneficial in emergencies or time-sensitive situations. Clear direction and expectations are set that can lead to high levels of productivity and efficiency. Adversely autocratic leadership can lead to low morale and high turnover due to lack of employee involvement. Creativity and innovation may be stifled as team members have limited input, and there is the potential for resentment and lack of motivation among team members.

The advantages for organisations to using autocratic leadership include streamlined processes with less room for dissent or confusion, which can be effective in crisis situations where decisions need to be made rapidly. Disadvantages include that long-term sustainability may be compromised due to lack of employee engagement and innovation. There is also a risk of dependency on the leader, which can be detrimental if the leader leaves or makes poor decisions.

Democratic Leadership

Democratic leadership involves team members in the decision-making process. While the leader still makes the final decision, team members have a voice and contribute their ideas.

The positives for implementing a democratic leadership style for teams include higher levels of job satisfaction and morale as employees feel valued and heard. It also encourages creativity and innovation by leveraging diverse perspectives and builds a sense of ownership and accountability among team members. Unlike adopting an autocratic leadership style, democratic leadership slows down decision-making due to the need for group consensus and increases the potential for conflicts or indecisiveness if there are strong opposing views.

Organisations with democratic leadership are often innovative and find effective solutions through collaborative efforts. Democratic leadership also leads to higher employee retention and engagement due to inclusive culture. However, some organisations may struggle with efficiency and speed in decision-making processes and this type of leadership style requires strong facilitation skills to manage diverse opinions and avoid conflict.

Democratic leaders ask for and value input from team members. This can make people feel appreciated and lead to creative solutions, but it can also slow down the decision-making process because it takes time to gather everyone's opinions.

Servant Leadership

Servant leadership focuses on the leader serving the needs of their team members. The leader prioritises the development, well-being, and growth of the team, and often leads by example.

Teams led by a leader with a servant leadership style will benefit from a supportive and collaborative team environment. These types of leaders will promote high levels of trust and loyalty among team members and encourage personal and professional growth, leading to a more skilled and competent team. Unfortunately, they can be perceived as lacking authority or decisiveness and risk of leader burnout due to high emotional investment in team members.

Having highly motivated and empowered employees is an advantage for any organisation with servant leaders building a strong organisational culture centred on mutual respect and support. Some employees may struggle in situations requiring quick and decisive action and organisations adopting this type of leadership style require a significant time investment in team development and individual coaching.

Servant leaders prioritise the needs of their team members and help them to develop and perform as highly as possible. This style can build strong, supportive relationships and a positive team culture but may be challenging if the leader needs to take firm control in critical situations.

Participative Leadership

Participative leadership is similar to democratic leadership but places a greater emphasis on collaborative decision-making. It involves team members actively participating in the decision-making process and contributing to the final outcome.

Advantages for teams of a participative leadership style are high levels of engagement and commitment from team members. Participative leaders leverage the collective knowledge and skills of the team, leading to well-rounded decisions, and encourage a strong sense of team cohesion and collaboration.

Some of the disadvantages for teams of a participative leadership style include a potential for frustration or conflict if team consensus is difficult to achieve, as decision-making can be time-consuming and less efficient.

Adopting a participative leadership style can lead to innovative and effective solutions through collaborative efforts for organisations as a whole and creates a positive organisational culture with high employee satisfaction and retention. Organisations may face challenges in fast-paced or high-pressure environments and participative leaders require strong facilitation and conflict resolution skills to manage diverse viewpoints.

Similar to democratic leadership, participative leadership involves team members in the decision-making process. However, it goes a step further by actively seeking and using their input to shape the direction of the organisation. This can lead to high job satisfaction and commitment, but can be time-consuming as it involves continuous consultation and feedback.

REFLECTIVE ACTIVITY 4.9

- Can you think of a leader who has used one of these styles?
- What do you feel they achieved as a leader?
- Do you think they achieved this due to their leadership style or in spite of it?

The impact of these leadership styles is significant. Good leadership can improve team cooperation, encourage new ideas, and drive success. On the other hand, a poor match between a leader's style and the team's needs can cause conflicts, lower motivation, and reduce productivity. Understanding these leadership styles and their effects is important for anyone looking to lead effectively and achieve long-term success in any organisation.

Each leadership style has its own strengths and weaknesses, and the effectiveness of a particular style can depend on the specific context, organisational culture, and team dynamics. Successful leaders often adapt their style to fit the needs of their team and the situation at hand (Goleman, 1995).

LEADERSHIP IN DIVERSE AND GLOBAL CONTEXTS

This section examines how leaders ensure that all workforce members feel included and motivated to perform well at work. It argues that commercial success depends on understanding the global environment within which the business operates and, importantly, understanding the drivers and motivations of the different humans that work within that global business environment.

Business comprises organisations employing a community of people we refer to as the *workforce*. This workforce includes people with diverse identities, including, but not limited to, gender, ability, ethnicity, sexual identity, socioeconomic background, age, learning style, personality, and education. These people with these multiple identities comprise the teams and departments that deliver business products and services. The success of a business relies on using all employees' knowledge and skills, which is vital in solving problems, making decisions, designing better products, and understanding the perspectives of current and potential customers. Therefore, a leader must understand how to engage and motivate these diverse identities, ensuring everyone feels valued, included, and part of their organisation. Ensuring that all people feel included requires intention; it requires deliberate action to ensure that the needs of all people in the workforce are understood and that leaders take the time to communicate and engage with people appropriately.

REFLECTIVE ACTIVITY 4.10

- Consider the identities outlined above; are there any others that you would include in a list; if asked to list diverse identities?

The Global Business Environment

In exploring how to lead in diverse and global contexts, we need to understand more about the broader business environment in which the business operates. The 21st century has seen rapid advances in **digital technology**, from the widespread adoption of online communications at the start of the century to **artificial intelligence** and complex **machine learning** capabilities at the time of writing.

In January 2016, Klaus Schwab, the Founder and Executive Chairman of the World Economic Forum, used the phrase '**Fourth Industrial Revolution**' to describe this enormous technological development. In his book of the same name, Schwab (2016) described how the fusion of physical, digital, and biological technologies is leading to unprecedented changes in the way we live, work, and interact with one another. Schwab's concept challenged business leaders to rethink traditional approaches to leadership, strategy, and operations. It required them to embrace something we have come to know as *digital transformation*. This transformation required businesses to foster a continuous learning and innovation culture and address ethical and societal implications; he argued that businesses can thrive in this new era and contribute to shaping a future that benefits everyone.

Indeed, these digital transformations, such as online meetings, online conferences, document sharing and platforms for collaborative activities have seen new opportunities emerge and enabled businesses and society to interact globally and at speed, leading to changing work patterns in many business sectors.

Changing Patterns of Work

In 2020, the global COVID-19 pandemic further accelerated the digital transformation that started at the turn of the 21st century, propelling the adoption and development of digital technologies by asking people to stay home and work remotely. The aftermath of the COVID-19 pandemic resulted in a considerable shift in how people work, with many people remaining online, working from a distance, and relying on digital infrastructures to perform their work.

In a time of rapid and unpredictable change, leaders must be increasingly adaptable, adept at navigating uncertainty, and skilled in managing complexity. These strategic skills ensure leaders' success in navigating the business landscape. However, they must also consider what it takes to engage, motivate, and lead the people who live and work in a society that endures such rapid technological change. This brings us to another essential aspect of understanding how to lead in diverse and international contexts: we must know what people need from their work to engage and motivate them.

Theories of Motivation and Employee Engagement

In the late 1980s, researchers Richard Ryan and Edward Deci examined employee performance to understand why some employees were more engaged and productive than others. They were interested in wellness and motivation, conducting experiments to test the factors that impacted a person's approach to completing various tasks. Their studies led to the *Self-Determination Theory* (2000), which challenged and overturned the dominant belief that the best way to get human beings to perform tasks is to reinforce their behaviour with rewards (**extrinsic motivation**). Instead, they argued that people perform better when they have an inner drive to complete the task to the best of their ability, finding it enjoyable or interesting (**intrinsic motivation**). For further discussion of motivation theories and employee engagement, see Chapter 3.

REFLECTIVE ACTIVITY 4.11

- Can you identify various types of reward that we would consider extrinsic?
- Do you have an enjoyable hobby or pastime that brings you intrinsic rewards?

They found that environments supporting *autonomy* (the sense of control over one's actions), *competence* (feeling capable and effective), and *relatedness* (feeling connected and included) lead to higher levels of intrinsic motivation and well-being. They argue these factors are crucial for employee engagement, motivation and wellness.

In 2009, Dan Pink developed these findings further when he proposed a theory on motivation that highlighted the importance of fostering autonomy, mastery, and purpose to create more engaged, productive, and satisfied individuals. These two theories provide valuable insights for leaders, as they both emphasise the need to create environments where employees flourish. Designing enjoyable and exciting work that enables employees to apply their skills and develop expertise for a clear purpose is fundamental to wellness and motivation.

If we combine the two theories, then autonomy, mastery (or competence), relatedness, and purpose are the four key motivating factors behind an engaged and productive workforce.

If we apply these theories to leading diverse teams, the leader's role is to carefully consider how these four factors affect everyone on their team.

Well-Being and Working Conditions

The findings from these studies gave employers a better understanding of what humans need from their work regarding motivation. However, since these theories emerged, evidence suggests that increased awareness of personal well-being among employees has meant that employees themselves are now demanding more from their workplaces. Various studies from academia, industry, and health bodies describe the proactive measures employees and employers must take to prioritise well-being. Again, the COVID-19 pandemic further exacerbated the focus on mental health, with many people struggling during and after the pandemic. This changing work environment, combined with the digital and psychological shifts happening across business and society, meant that leaders need to win the right to lead, not assume that they lead from the front, and have the right to make all decisions on behalf of the collective.

REFLECTIVE ACTIVITY 4.12

Refer again to Case Study 4.2 - Vodafone - and answer the following question.

- How well do you think Vodafone are leading their diverse workforce?

How to Lead in a Diverse and Global Context

Leaders must create an environment where employees feel secure and accepted. They must ensure that people are listened to, and their ideas acknowledged, that all employees have access to progression opportunities, and that salaries are fair and equal across similar job roles. As with all the theories we have covered, inclusive leadership fosters a sense of community and reduces feelings of isolation or exclusion.

Taking the time to understand both the social environment and the needs of the humans within those environments allows the leader to design and lead inclusive work environments.

LEADERSHIP DEVELOPMENT

This section will cover the fundamentals of leadership development, in terms of how we acquire the knowledge, skills, and abilities for use within a leadership role. In particular, this section will include the development of self-awareness for personal growth; mentoring and coaching; and continuous learning and adaptability.

Self-Awareness and Personal Growth

There are multiple definitions of self-awareness, and it is often confused with other terms such as self-consciousness and self-knowledge; nevertheless, it is considered an important aspect of leadership development and has been linked to improved team performance, effective and authentic leadership, creativity, humility, and self-improvement. Self-awareness is also one of the components of emotional intelligence (see 'How Emotional Intelligence Is Essential for Modern Leadership').

Self-awareness concerns our ability to understand ourselves (our strengths, weaknesses, motivations and values) and our impact on others. The distinction between self-awareness and that of *leader* self-awareness is the engagement in how we influence others. If we want to pursue a shared goal and thereby enact leadership, self-awareness becomes a key ability so that we might more effectively influence others in pursuit of our goal. It is this objective of influencing others (rather than simply being self-aware) that makes self-awareness for leadership distinct from general self-awareness.

How do we develop self-awareness for personal and professional growth? First and foremost, based on theories of adult development, there is an assumption that self-awareness can be developed. Popular ways of achieving this are through self-evaluation, introspection and reflection, and particularly with regard to leader self-awareness; reflective judgement (taking a step back in order to make a sound judgement). For instance, profiling tools such as MBTI (Myers-Briggs Type Indicator) (Myers and McCaulley, 1985), strengths-profilers, experiential learning (Kolb, 1984) (see section below), or motivational assessments may provide a focus against which we can evaluate our awareness of ourselves. We can develop our awareness further by comparing findings from these tools with feedback from others, alongside our own reflections, and in turn understand how this drives our behaviours and therefore our impact upon and influence on others. The approach to developing self-awareness is multi-faceted and continuous, but these tools provide a good starting point to recognising that you can develop your self-awareness and then being willing to learn and develop.

Self-awareness is considered by many a core proposition of coaching, which supports the development of desired behaviour change. The next section will consider both coaching and mentoring in this respect.

Mentoring and Coaching

The terms coaching and mentoring are often used interchangeably but are in fact distinct concepts each requiring different skills, although there is much overlap between them. What they have in common is the simplicity of a conversation one person has with another, and which is intended to provide a benefit to the person being coached or mentored. Coaching is a collaborative process between the coach and person being coached, the aim of which is to facilitate self-awareness and responsibility, in order that the person being coached can achieve something that they wouldn't without the aid of coaching. By comparison, mentoring concerns using one's own knowledge and wisdom to help another person develop high-quality thinking, ultimately leading to their own wisdom. Mentoring can take different forms such as workplace, youth, or academic mentoring as well as different structures such as reverse mentoring or peer mentoring. Similarly, coaching; can also take different forms including workplace coaching; executive coaching; life coaching; and solution-focused coaching.

Coaching supports an individual with personal growth and self-directed learning. Its purpose is ultimately to contribute to individual and organisational success, but this is achieved by enhancing behavioural change through self-awareness and learning. Mentoring, on the other hand, provides social learning, where the mentor supports the mentee to acquire new information, behaviours, or attitudes from the experience of the mentor. Neither coaching nor mentoring are structured to impart knowledge from the coach/mentor and instead are interested in the self-development of new knowledge as an outcome from the coaching and/or mentoring.

Self-awareness, coaching and mentoring have all been suggested as important tools to aid development of leaders and therefore are important for organisational and individual outcomes.

REFLECTIVE ACTIVITY 4.13

The following are some useful coaching questions. Try asking yourself them and then try asking a peer; what do you notice?

- What is most important to you whilst you are studying at university?
- If your time at university was to go just as you would like it to, what would it look like?
- What goal would you like to achieve by the end of your programme?
- What barriers might stop you from achieving your goal?
- What will help you when you get stuck?
- Why is going to university important to you?

Zimmerman's framework underscores the importance of **metacognition**, which is the awareness of one's learning processes and the capacity for self-direction. By employing self-regulated learning strategies, individuals can boost their motivation, achieve greater academic success, and cultivate lifelong learning habits (Zimmerman, 2002).

Metacognitive learning habits play in important role in the development of a growth mindset; a belief that abilities and intelligence can be developed through effort, learning, and persistence (Dweck, 2006; Duckworth et al., 2007). Unlike a fixed mindset, where individuals believe their talents are static, those with a growth mindset embrace challenges, learn from criticism, and view failures as opportunities for growth, thereby promoting resilience and enhancing enjoyment in their tasks. Cultivating a growth mindset can lead to greater achievement and personal development, encouraging the practice of reframing one's metacognitive responses to 'not yet' instead of 'no'.

Another widely used **model** relevant to continuous learning is Kolb's (1984) experiential learning cycle, which highlights the importance of hands-on experience, reflection, and the application of learned concepts to approach new experiences. Importantly, experiential learning is not merely 'learning through doing', but rather a cyclical process involving four equally important stages:

1. **Concrete experience:** Engaging in real events or situations.
2. **Reflective observation:** Reflecting on those experiences to gain insights.
3. **Abstract conceptualisation:** Formulating concepts and ideas based on reflections.
4. **Active experimentation:** Applying newly formed concepts in future situations.

Adaptability is often defined as the ability to adjust one's thoughts, behaviours, and strategies in response to changing circumstances and new information. Leaders exhibiting adaptability have been found to be better equipped to navigate uncertainty, inspire confidence in their teams, drive organisational change and self-report to be happier in their careers. Learning agility is when this adaptability is used to learn new skills. This concept encompasses not only the capacity to learn from experiences but also the skill to apply that knowledge effectively in diverse situations. Burke (2023) outlines that learning agility comprises several dimensions:

- **Cognitive agility** – the ability to think **critically** and strategically
- **Interpersonal agility** – the capacity to interact effectively with others
- **Change agility** – the capability to adapt to new environments

Further, he emphasises that self-awareness and feedback-seeking behaviours are essential for nurturing learning agility in individuals.

Self-awareness, personal growth, mentorship and coaching, continuous learning, and adaptability are important components for long-term leadership development. They create a holistic approach to leadership development, preparing leaders to meet future challenges as expectations and needs of organisations continue to evolve.

ETHICAL CONSIDERATIONS IN LEADERSHIP

The following section introduces ethics in the context of leadership in contemporary business. Leadership can be fraught with paradoxical challenges and opportunities arising from both the actual workplace and the global realities of climate change and ongoing exploitation of peoples and lands. It therefore involves making decisions that can have wide-reaching impacts. We also offer some guidance on how you might embrace this sometimes overwhelming responsibility.

What Is Ethics?

To explore ethical considerations for leadership, we first introduce ethics. There is little space here for the reflective, deliberate, and slow immersion into ethics, or moral philosophy, that we would urge every leader to undertake. Instead, we focus on key theories and approaches and offer some opportunities for slow reflection in your own time.

REFLECTIVE ACTIVITY 4.14

- What do you think ethics is?

It is perhaps easier to define what ethics is not. Ethics is not:

- Following the law
- Following your feelings
- Following your faith/religion
- Following society

Ethics is concerned with how we conduct ourselves in our relationships with other humans, with other species, and with Earth as an ecosystem supporting all life. Ethics is therefore about behaviours and the identification of which ones are right, and which are wrong, which are good, and which are bad.

In short, ethics informs our daily actions and therefore our decision-making. The purpose and importance of exploring ethics is to nurture practices that enable us to question and reflect on our thoughts and our values, to provide considered reasons for our decisions and to effectively challenge the actions of others.

Ethical Theories

Many codes and theories of ethics exist, developed over thousands of years by multiple societies and belief systems, making it a complex area of study. In the list overleaf, we present four of the most relevant Western ethical theories for contemporary leadership (for more information on each of these, please see Chakraborti, 2023).

REFLECTIVE ACTIVITY 4.15

- Do you think that some actions or behaviours are always morally wrong?

- **Deontology:** Relies on the following of rules and laws, or universal norms or principles, without exception. Deontologists would argue that some actions are and will always be categorically right or wrong, irrespective of context or the implications of the action.
- **Consequentialism:** Relies on the moral assessment of the consequences that actions/decisions may bring about. Consequentialists would argue that a decision should be made by conducting an analysis of whether the benefits resulting from the decision would outweigh the costs.
- **Pragmatism:** Considers that every situation is different, that we can never truly predict the impacts of our decisions and therefore that no rule or universal norm can or should always be applied. Pragmatists would argue that we need to develop the wisdom to identify multiple options and the courage to make the best decision and to act upon it.
- **Virtue Ethics:** Relies on the virtue or moral character of the decision-maker, which enables them to make morally good choices. Virtue theorists would argue that decision-making is informed by personal virtues which require cultivation, such as courage, moderation, kindness, honesty and 'phronesis' or practical wisdom, which is gained by experience and understanding of the world.

Frameworks for Ethical Decision-Making

There are multiple frameworks available to support ethical decision-making. These often take the form of a series of questions about the nature of dilemma or challenge, considering multiple angles and perspectives. Some frameworks invite extensive research, careful analysis and reflection. Some invite reflection on the past as well as on multiple possibilities and imagined futures.

A simple and popular framework is the Blanchard-Peale Framework (Blanchard and Peale, 2010) which consists of three questions:

- Is it legal?
- Is it fair?
- How does it make me feel?

A more complex framework is the Markkula Framework for Ethical Decision Making (Markkula Center for Applied Ethics, 2021), which consists of five steps:

- Identify the ethical issues
- Get the facts
- Evaluate alternative actions
- Choose an option for action and test it
- Implement your decision and reflect on the outcome

It is important to note that frameworks will not give you simple answers or firm solutions, but making use of them will help you practice deep thought about a dilemma or challenge and your approach to it as a leader.

Ethics in Business

Beyond the individual, within the broader business context, there exists an ever-evolving body of legislation, regulation and ethical codes of conduct, the sum of which point to an acknowledgement that people, and by extension organisations, do not always behave well when given the freedom to do so.

Since the 1970s, in countries characterised as post-industrialised, economically developed and democratic, ethical decision-making in business has been codified into a range of voluntary and legislated schemes designed to support and signify responsible business practice. In the following list, we present three of the most influential in current use.

- **Corporate Social Responsibility (CSR):** CSR is a form of voluntary ethical self-regulation in business, through which an organisation can acknowledge its responsibility for social, environmental, and economic performance by conducting a range of self-initiated activities and programmes of work. CSR gained increasing traction between the 1970s and 2010s, though it has suffered a loss of public trust due to exposure of false and inflated claims of good practice.
- **Environmental, Social, & Governance assessments (ESGs):** Environmental, Social, and Governance (ESG) assessments measure an organisation's impact and sustainability. Their development was driven in part by financial investors requiring accurate data on an organisation's performance against multiple targets, and in part by increased levels of regulation and reporting requirements on environmental impacts.
- **Sustainable Development Goals (SDGs):** The SDGs are a series of 17 goals promoting socially and environmentally responsible actions for a shared global prosperity. Organisations are increasingly adopting the SDGs as guiding principles informing their sustainable growth strategies.

REFLECTIVE ACTIVITY 4.16

Reflect on Case Study 4.1 about the University of Exeter.

https://news.exeter.ac.uk/faculty-of-environment-science-and-economy/gartner-and-exeter-identify-tipping-point-opportunities-in-low-carbon-technologies-for-executive-leaders/

Consider how the adoption of multiple SDGs presents an ethical dilemma, as when we address one goal, we likely do so at the cost of another.

- How would you prioritise the SD Goals?

Being Ethical

In addition to the use of frameworks and responsible business initiatives, we suggest that there are individual behaviours that can be honed over time to support ethical leadership, behaviours that enable the individual to 'take special responsibility for what's going on inside their own self, inside their own consciousness, lest the act of leadership create more harm than good' (Palmer, 1990).

- **Be curious** – the deeper your knowledge and understanding of the world around you, the more able you will be to understand the complex nature of dilemmas, to acknowledge their implications and to identify multiple solutions.
- **Practice ethical decision-making** – it is so easy to criticise the actions of leaders. Instead, consider what you might do in their place.
- **Talk less, listen more** – many voices have been silenced over many years. The more individual and collective perspectives and experiences you hear, the more able you are to understand the impacts of your actions and decisions on others.
- **Reflect** – your lived experience shapes who you are and therefore your decision-making. Regularly exploring your values, beliefs and behaviour patterns helps you to understand your ethical self.

These are practices to be held lightly – but to be held. Ultimately, this section is an invitation to consider how your decision-making can contribute to the existence of a diverse, just and sustainable future, where multiple worldviews and ways of being co-exist and flourish for the collective good.

LEADERSHIP AND SUSTAINABILITY

What is leadership for? Throughout this chapter you have already been exploring several relevant leadership questions and concepts, like what *is* leadership (and what it is not), what types and styles of leadership are there, are leaders born or made, and many other questions on what makes leadership effective, why, how, and so on. But let's take a moment to reflect on a more fundamental question. What is it all *for*? Surprisingly, such questions around the *purpose* of leadership, or *'leadership for what'* have tended to be overlooked, and have only recently started to receive some more explicit attention (e.g. see Kempster and Jackson, 2011, or Kempster et al. 2021).

Answering such questions is inextricably linked to the notion of sustainability and this section will explore some of those links. On the other hand, there is an emerging body of research on what distinguishes leaders working towards sustainability, so we will also summarise some of those insights. A better understanding of such factors should in principle help leaders to also better explore personal questions about their own purpose and their approach to their own leadership development.

A Failure of Leadership?

Sustainability inherently requires a broader, long-term perspective. The widely accepted Brundtland definition (WCED, 1987) has been a foundational guideline since its adoption by the UN over 30 years ago. This definition urges us to consider how our decisions impact future generations and diverse stakeholder groups, including those not yet born.

However, despite the adoption of this principle, global issues such as climate change, inequality, and biodiversity loss have worsened. UN Secretary-General António Guterres recently highlighted this failure, calling the lack of decisive action on climate change 'a damning indictment of failed global leadership' (UN, 2022).

Historically, leadership studies have focused on individual and organisational advancement, often through a commercial lens. While relevant, these approaches often prioritise short-term gains over long-term sustainability, overlooking the interconnectedness of organisations with their social and environmental contexts.

Returning to the Brundtland perspective, a true leader balances the immediate and future needs of society, environment, and organisation, aiming to create value for all. Eustachio et al. (2023: 7) extend this idea, describing a sustainability leader as someone who 'motivates and influences followers to overcome sustainability barriers, ensuring society meets current needs without compromising future generations.' Visser and Courtice (2020: 2) simplify it further: 'a sustainability leader inspires and supports action towards a better world.' This perspective brings us back to the question: 'What is leadership for?'

REFLECTIVE ACTIVITY 4.17

- What would be your own personal definition of a sustainability leader?
- Could you find any direct or indirect links to your own role (or future career aspirations)?

Are Sustainability-Focused Leaders Different?

Considering the previous discussion, clearly many of the characteristics of good leadership are also transferrable to sustainability-focused leadership. After all, we are still talking about ability to influence and motivate people towards common goals. Different leadership styles or approaches have been linked directly or indirectly to organisational sustainability efforts, including ethical leadership, **values-based** leadership, servant leadership, transformational leadership or responsible leadership, and indeed there are partial overlaps both within those and with leadership for sustainability. On the other hand, the latter can also encompass a variety of closely related leadership approaches like environmental, sustainable or sustainability leadership, which Boeske (2023) integrates under the notion of 'leadership towards sustainability'. But there are also some features that tend to distinguish sustainability-related leadership approaches from others, or that sustainability leaders exhibit in more marked ways. Several recent reviews have looked at such distinguishing factors (e.g. Shriberg, 2012; UN, 2020; Visser and Courtice, 2020; Murphy 2022; Boeske, 2023; Eustachio et al., 2023; and Sajjad et al., 2024), and below we summarise some of the key ones:

Sustainability-focused values and mindset: sustainability leaders demonstrate a range of moral and ethical values, beliefs and behaviours that are aligned with principles of environmental stewardship and justice, social and intergenerational equity, resource efficiency, nature conservation and caring for people and planet, amongst others. Informed by such values, they have different perspectives from other leaders on how their organisations should operate, pursuing solutions aligned with their sustainability principles.

Visioning and long-term orientation: sustainable leaders think long-term, set audacious goals, and have the ability to create a strong shared vision. This is normally an inspiring view of the future based on sustainable growth or even regeneration, rather than one of just 'impact minimisation' or 'doing less bad'. Their focus goes beyond short-term gains, but they understand the need to balance tensions and to meet short-term results that allow progress towards the vision.

Systems thinking: sustainability leaders understand the interconnectedness and interdependency of different systems at multiple levels, and the interplay of their own organisational system with the social-ecological systems it is part of. They are good at analysing, synthesising, and translating complex issues, finding creative ways to deal with uncertainty and paradoxes, and identifying options to drive change in the systems they operate in that can deliver sustainability benefits.

Multi-stakeholder orientation and inclusion: sustainability leaders actively seek multi-stakeholder inclusion and look to understand a wide range of views in the communities in which they operate and beyond. Their aim is to inform decisions and create solutions that can deliver long-term value for all, and where possible involve stakeholders directly on the definition of issues, implementation of actions, and sharing of benefits. They understand that complex challenges are better addressed through collaborations and that sustainable leadership is a shared responsibility built on trust.

Learning and innovation: with their aim to promote a positive impact on society and the environment, sustainable leaders are intentional about creating disruptive change. They are committed 'change agents', willing to challenge conventional approaches, ask why it cannot be done differently, and empower learning and innovation in organisations towards sustainable value. This includes being comfortable with not having all the answers, and willing to test novel solutions be it on processes, services or **business models**, or in our social and economic systems.

REFLECTIVE ACTIVITY 4.18

Reflect on Case Study 4.1 about the University of Exeter.

https://news.exeter.ac.uk/faculty-of-environment-science-and-economy/gartner-and-exeter-identify-tipping-point-opportunities-in-low-carbon-technologies-for-executive-leaders/

- How can sustainability leaders make tipping points happen?
- Can you think of any leaders that have sustainability leader characteristics?

Several other traits and characteristics are important for sustainability leaders, as they would be for most leaders (e.g. being enquiring and open-minded, empathetic, knowledgeable, have strong communication skills, and the ability to exercise judgment etc.). And clearly different people will have different degrees of the ability to or competence on the characteristics listed above. It is unlikely any leader excels equally at all of them. But they can provide a starting roadmap of areas of personal development, if your aim is to move towards a more purposeful and sustainability-oriented approach to leadership.

Looking Forward

In this section we argue that asking questions around the fundamental purpose of leadership (or 'leadership for what') will inevitably mean having to equally grapple with questions around long-term sustainability of the social and natural systems we are part of, and our role in influencing such systems towards a better place. Being intentional, proactive and effective in this will in turn mean adopting a more holistic approach to leadership that goes beyond the traditional focus on self and organisation alone, where much of leadership development and literature tended to focus. We have presented some of the factors that the literature identifies as key for sustainability-minded leaders, but ultimately it is your own personal leadership development journey that will help you determine what shared world you want to build, and what steps you should take towards it.

DEVELOPING LEADERSHIP SKILLS FOR EMPLOYABILITY

Developing and communicating key skills, experiences, and behaviours is important in today's labour market, with individuals holding more control and accountability for developing their careers to maintain a competitive advantage for opportunities. The following section brings attention to concepts related to planning, building and communicating one's leadership competencies to enhance employability in the labour market.

Planning

When considering your career development, it's beneficial to start with a clear goal that can guide and align your growth activities. A concept that underscores the idea of individual agency in career advancement is career capital. Career capital can be understood as the skills, behaviours, experiences, and interpersonal connections that support an individual's professional value and employability.

REFLECTIVE ACTIVITY 4.19

Consider

- what happens to career capital if any one of the four factors (i.e., either skills, behaviours, experiences or interpersonal connections) is lacking. How could this relate to career advancement?

Arthur et al.'s (1999) career capital framework encourages individuals to reflect on their leadership development by posing essential questions: 'Why?', 'How?', and 'Whom?'.

- **Why:** Why are types of career capital (whether that be individual or relational) strategic to your career trajectory?
- **How:** How will you gain this capital?
- **Whom:** Who are the stakeholders that could assist you?

By exploring these questions, leaders gain valuable insights into their motivations and aspirations, making it easier to navigate their career paths effectively. Importantly, building career capital involves not only gaining these assets but also understanding the motivations behind this pursuit, the strategies for acquiring them, and recognising the influential relationships that facilitate your development. Understanding your motivations for leadership is crucial for achieving meaningful professional growth.

In thinking about your caper capital and answering your 'why', conducting a gap analysis allows you to note areas of development. Conducting a gap analysis can bring clarity and agency to goals through breaking down larger (longer term) distal goals into smaller proximal (short term) goals, increasing overall performance, all while self-regulating motivation (Latham and Locke, 1991).

REFLECTIVE ACTIVITY 4.20

To perform a career gap analysis, consider these steps below as outlined in Figure 4.8.

1 Describe both your current roles (i.e., your study, work/volunteering, extra-curriculars) and the type of roles that would be ideal for you.

2 Define your motivation for considering/entering a new role: Clearly outline your rationale and motivation (i.e., what you care about, what you value and what you need).
3 Identify your career capital in your current role: This includes the skills, knowledge, and behaviours you have developed. It also includes the relationships that you utilise.
4 Identify the career capital you will need in your ideal role(s): Again, this includes the skills, knowledge, behaviours, and relationships. To broaden future options, this may include clusters of job roles and thinking about their shared qualities.
5 Assess Gaps: Compare your career capital between your current role(s) and the ideal role(s). After identifying gaps, create an action plan which you can monitor.

With that said, not every strategically driven career needs to have a set end goal in mind. It has been largely noted that chance plays an important part in leaders' and professionals' success, as well as making the most of the present moment opportunities. To capture these career paths Krumboltz and Levin (2010) suggested that planned happenstance is a useful career development model that encourages individuals to make the most of unexpected opportunities and experiences. This alternative model suggest that individuals can build their career from finding opportunities in unplanned events based on embracing the up and downs. This framework suggests that individuals can do this through three steps:

- **Clarifying career ideas:** this includes building self-awareness and following curiosity and interests.
- **Remove blocks:** wonder 'how I can' rather than 'I can't', and removing barriers that could present obstacles later.
- **Expect the unexpected:** be prepared for chance opportunities, which may include being flexible in timing and initial career ideas.

This framework is important because it provides leaders with a framework to build a strategic career without necessarily having a set end vision in mind.

Competencies

Identifying personal competencies is essential because it allows for targeted development efforts, enabling leaders to enhance specific skills that are critical for career development. A competency is a defined quality or characteristic that contributes to effective performance in a specific role or task (Lepak and Snell, 2002). Competencies can be categorised into several types, including knowledge, skills, and behaviours, while also including more hidden factors such as self-concept, traits and motivations. Thus, building knowledge, skills and behaviours should be done with attention to the self-concept, traits and motives that support these. Notably, there is considerable evidence that self-concept, trait and motives can be developed and are not fixed.

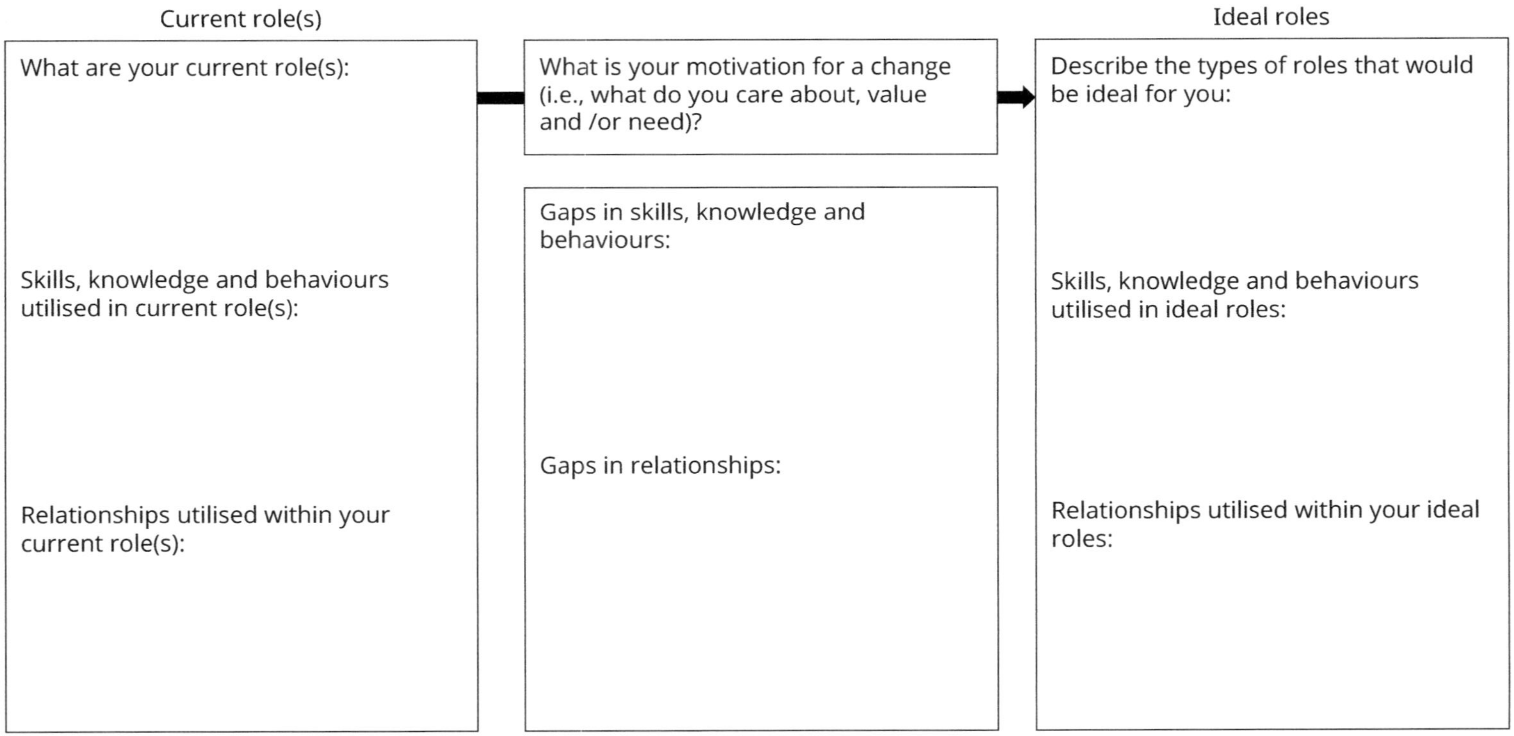

Figure 4.8 Career gap analysis career planning tool

Interpersonal Relationships

Importantly, interpersonal relationships are essential for supporting one's career development; these interpersonal relationships when related to one's career advancement and opportunities can be referred to as **social capital**. Social capital encompasses the value derived from social interactions and the trust and mutual understanding that develop within communities and organisations. Within the leadership development literature, it has been suggested that there is an important role in developing weak ties (i.e., casual or distant relationships) to bridge different social networks. Weak ties tend to connect individuals to diverse networks, leading to the dissemination of new information. They stand in contrast to strong ties who are often members of the same social circles, who may share similar knowledge and resources. Weak ties often connect disparate groups, facilitating access to information and opportunities outside one's immediate social circle (Latham and Seijts, 1999). This makes it particularly important for leaders to focus on activities related to networking, personal **branding** and joining diverse communities in their career development strategy.

Communicating

Finally, to leverage your leadership competencies, you must be able to communicate them. With that said, it is critical to note that within recruitment and selection practices, it is most common that these competencies are not measured, but 'signalled' to employers through past outcomes and generalisations that related competencies with transfer into a new environment. Therefore, providing details, bringing explicit attention to knowledge, skills, and behaviours gained and highlighting outcomes (i.e., business or personal) are useful for signalling employability.

In conclusion, developing and communicating key skills, experiences, and behaviours is increasingly vital in today's labour market, where individuals are empowered to take charge of their career paths. By understanding and strategically planning for career capital and building competencies, leaders can enhance their employability and adaptability in a constantly evolving environment.

CHAPTER SUMMARY

- This chapter has explored the diverse ways in which leaders can adapt their styles, from transformational and transactional leadership to situational and servant leadership, demonstrating the importance of flexibility and context in achieving organisational success.
- Leadership theories provide essential frameworks for understanding the behaviour, motivations, and influence of leaders.
- In an increasingly interconnected and globalised world, leading in a global context demands cultural intelligence, adaptability, and an appreciation for diverse

perspectives. Leaders must navigate complexities such as cultural diversity, communication barriers, and shifting global dynamics while fostering inclusivity and unity.

- The chapter has also emphasised the importance of well-being, mentoring, and coaching in leadership development. A leader's ability to support their team's mental, emotional, and professional growth fosters trust, loyalty, and long-term success. Mentoring and coaching serve as critical tools for both individual development and organisational resilience, enabling leaders to build sustainable pathways for growth.
- Ethics and sustainability remain at the heart of modern leadership. Ethical decision-making and a commitment to sustainable practices are no longer optional but essential for building credibility, trust, and long-term impact. Leaders must balance organisational goals with their responsibility to society and the environment.
- Leadership is an ongoing journey of learning and development. Career development in leadership involves continuous self-reflection, **upskilling**, and a commitment to growth.
- In essence, effective leadership is a balance of vision, adaptability, empathy, and responsibility. By integrating diverse leadership styles and approaches while prioritising global awareness, well-being, and ethical conduct, leaders can build stronger organisations and contribute to a more sustainable and equitable future.

STUDENTS LIKE YOU CHANGE THE WORLD

Figure 4.9 Gary Burnett (centre), Yasmine Zouari (left) and Alex Dakeyne (right)

Gary Burnett, Yasmine Zouari and Alex Dakeyne are Degree Apprentices who participated in the World Skills UK competition at the University of Exeter and who presented a prototype of an idea which they are now pitching to their senior leaders in their global organisation. Their idea is to introduce an initiative which re-purposes waste from within the organisation to support local community initiatives such as waste rubber being used for children's playgrounds. Their initiative is to track and share sustainable initiatives across the organisation and celebrate these through the internal communication channels as well as in the local press. They are leading this exciting initiative which has already received encouraging early feedback and could dramatically change the environmental impact of their operations.

END OF CHAPTER REFLECTION

Have a look at the skills you should have developed in this unit (find more details in the Key Skills Table in the Appendix on p. 500).

1 Which of the skills listed do you think you have developed the most?
2 Can you give two examples on why you feel you have now developed these skills/developed them further?
3 How will you use these new/refined skills in the future (give two examples of the impact of your development on your future behaviour)?

FURTHER READING

To learn more about leadership approaches in different cultures, consider these articles as a starting point.

Drucker, P.F. (1971) 'What we can learn from Japanese management', *Harvard Business Review,* March. www.hbr.org/1971/03/what-we-can-learn-from-japanese-management (accessed September 9, 2025).

This article provides early, detailed insights into how cultural values shape management and leadership practices in Japan, offering a comparative perspective that can inform cross-cultural analyses.

Matthews, N. (2011) 'Reflecting on Māori academic leadership', *MAI Review,* 3, Leadership Reflections. https://www.journal.mai.ac.nz/system/files/maireview/457-3371-1-PB.pdf (accessed September 9, 2025).

This text is important for understanding leadership because it highlights how cultural values and social context shape leadership practices, offering insights that are applicable across diverse organisational and cultural settings.

le Gentil, H. (2021) 'Leaders, stop trying to be heroes', *Harvard Business Review,* October 25. https://hbr.org/2021/10/leaders-stop-trying-to-be-heroes (accessed September 9, 2025).

It is tempting to approach leadership from a 'solution finder' perspective in today's VUCA world, but it is important to consider the value of 'heroic leadership', where it has a place and where it should be avoided. le Gentil's article challenges traditional 'hero-leader' models and emphasises how effective leadership today demands authenticity, collaboration, and human-centred connection rather than lone visionary control.

For further reading and insights on ethical leadership and its place in modern leadership, try this book:

Witzel, M. (2018). *The Ethical Leader: Why Doing the Right Thing Can Be the Key to Competitive Advantage*: Bloomsbury.

Witzel shows that ethical leadership is not just a moral imperative but a strategic advantage, demonstrating that doing the right thing can build trust, enhance reputation, and strengthen long-term organisational performance.

For more insights on sustainability leadership see:

Boeske, J. (2023) 'Leadership towards sustainability: A review of sustainable, sustainability, and environmental leadership', *Sustainability*, 15 (16): article #12626.

This article highlights that sustainable leadership integrates environmental, social, and economic considerations into decision-making, motivating followers to address sustainability challenges while balancing present needs with the well-being of future generations.

Eustachio, J.H.P.P., Caldana, A.C.F., and Leal Filho, W. (2023) 'Sustainability leadership: Conceptual foundations and research landscape', *Journal of Cleaner Production*, 415: article #137761.

This article discusses how leadership theory connects with sustainability and CSR and - identifying four main research clusters and 12 sub-clusters - offers a comprehensive landscape of how leadership practices can enable organisations to become more sustainability-oriented.

For further reading on leadership theory:

Dweck, C.S. (2006) *Mindset: The New Psychology of Success*. Random House.

Dweck illustrates that leadership effectiveness is strongly influenced by mindset, showing that leaders who embrace a growth mindset foster learning, resilience, and adaptability in themselves and their teams.

Sinek, S. (2014). *Leaders Eat Last: Why Some Teams Pull Together and Others Don't*. Portfolio.

Sinek demonstrates that effective leadership builds trust and collaboration by prioritising the well-being of team members, showing that leaders who create safe, supportive environments inspire loyalty and collective success.

Goleman, D. (2000) 'Leadership that get results', *Harvard Business Review*, March–April. https://hbr.org/2000/03/leadership-that-gets-results (accessed September 9, 2025).

'Leadership That Gets Results' teaches us that effective leadership involves flexibly switching among six distinct styles - each rooted in emotional-intelligence competencies - to shape organisational climate and drive performance.

REFERENCES

Arthur, M.B., Inkson, K., and Pringle, J.K. (1999) *The New Careers, Individual Action and Economic Change*. Sage.

Blake, R.R. and Mouton, J.S. (1964) *The Managerial Grid: Problems and Possibilities of Improving Production Through Participation of People*. University of Texas.

Blanchard, K.H. and Peale, N.V. (2010) *The Power of Ethical Management*. Vermilion.

Boeske, J. (2023) 'Leadership towards sustainability: A review of sustainable, sustainability, and environmental leadership', *Sustainability*, 15 (16): article #12626.

Burke, W.W. (2023) *Organization Change: Theory and Practice*. Sage.

Chakraborti, C. (2023) *Introduction to Ethics: Concepts, Theories, and Contemporary Issues*. Springer.

Crenshaw, K. (1989) 'Demarginalizing the intersection of race and sex: A Black feminist critique of antidiscrimination doctrine, feminist theory and antiracist politics', *University of Chicago Legal Forum*, 1: Article #8. https://chicagounbound.uchicago.edu/uclf/vol1989/iss1/8/ (accessed September 9, 2025).

Duckworth, A.L., Peterson, C., Matthews, M.D. and Kelly, D.R. (2007) 'Grit: Perseverance and passion for long-term goals', *Journal of Personality and Social Psychology*, 92 (6): 1087–1101.

Dweck, C.S. (2006) *Mindset: The New Psychology of Success*. Random House.

Eustachio, J.H.P.P., Caldana, A.C.F., and Leal Filho, W. (2023) 'Sustainability leadership: Conceptual foundations and research landscape', *Journal of Cleaner Production*, 415: article #137761.

Fiedler, F.E. (1967) *A Theory of Leadership Effectiveness*. McGraw-Hill.

Food and Fibre CoVE (2025) 'A literature review of Māori leadership'. https://mukatangata.workforceskills.nz/assets/Documents/Maori-Leadership-Literature-Review.pdf (accessed October 30, 2025).

Gallegos, P. V. (2014) 'The work of inclusive leadership: Fostering authentic relationships, modeling courage and humility', in B.M. Ferdman and B.R. Deane (eds.), *Diversity at Work*: The Practice of Inclusion. Jossey-Bass/Wiley. pp. 177–202.

Goleman, D. (1995) *Emotional Intelligence: Why It Can Matter More Than IQ*. Bantam Books.

Goleman, D. (2000) 'Leadership that gets results', *Harvard Business Review*, March-April. https://hbr.org/2000/03/leadership-that-gets-results (accessed September 9, 2025).

Hersey, P. and Blanchard, K.H. (1982) 'Leadership style: Attitudes and behaviors', *Training & Development Journal*, 36 (5): 50–2.

Kempster, S. and Jackson, B. (2021) 'Leadership for what, why, for whom and where? A responsibility perspective', *Journal of Change Management*, 21 (1): 45–65.

Kempster, S., Jackson, B., and Conroy, M. (2011) 'Leadership as purpose: Exploring the role of purpose in leadership practice', *Leadership*, 7 (3): 317–34.

Kolb, D. (1984) *Experiential Learning: Experience as the Source of Learning and Development*. Prentice Hall.

Kotter, J. (1999) *On What Leaders Really Do*. Harvard Business Press.

Krumboltz, J.D. and Levin, A.S. (2010) *Luck Is No Accident: Making the Most of Happenstance in Your Life and Career*. Impact.

Latham, G.P. and Locke, E.A. (1991) 'Self-regulation through goal setting', *Organizational Behavior and Human Decision Processes*, 50 (2): 212–47. doi.org/10.1016/0749-5978(91)90021-K

Latham, G.P. and Seijts, G.H. (1999) 'The effects of proximal and distal goals on performance on a moderately complex task', *Journal of Organizational Behavior: The International Journal of Industrial, Occupational and Organizational Psychology and Behavior*, 20 (4): 421–29. https://www.jstor.org/stable/3100381 (accessed September 9, 2025).

Lepak, D.P. and Snell, S.A. (2002) 'Examining the human resource architecture: The relationships among human capital, employment, and human resource configurations', *Journal of Management*, 28 (4): 517–43. doi.org/10.1177/014920630202800403

Markkula Center for Applied Ethics (2021) 'A framework for ethical decision making', *Santa Clara University*, November 8. https://www.scu.edu/ethics/ethics-resources/a-framework-for-ethical-decision-making/ (accessed September 9, 2025).

Matthews, N. (2011) 'Reflecting on Māori academic leadership', *MAI Review*, 3, Leadership Reflections. https://www.journal.mai.ac.nz/system/files/maireview/457-3371-1-PB.pdf (accessed September 9, 2025).

McCall Jr., M.W. and Lombardo, M.M. (1983) *Off the Track: Why and How Successful Executives Get Derailed* (Technical Report Number 21). Center for Creative Leadership.

McKinsey & Company (2024) 'What is leadership', *McKinsey*, September 10. https://www.mckinsey.com/featured-insights/mckinsey-explainers/what-is-leadership (accessed September 9, 2025).

Murphy, C. (2022) *Sustainable Leadership: Lessons of Vision, Courage, and Grit from the CEOs Who Dared to Build a Better World*. John Wiley & Sons.

Myers, I.B. and McCaulley, M.H. (1985) *Manual: A Guide to the Development and Use of the Myers-Briggs Type Indicator*. Consulting Psychologists Press.

Nealon, M. (2021) *The Pandemic as an Accelerant: How COVID-19 Advanced our Mental Health Priorities*. United Nations, September 16. https://www.un.org/en/un-chronicle/pandemic-accelerant-how-covid-19-advanced-our-mental-health-priorities (accessed September 9, 2025).

Palmer, P.J. (1990) *Leading from Within*. Servant Leadership School.

Pink, D.H. (2009). *Drive: The Surprising Truth About What Motivates Us*. Riverhead.

Padfield, R., Papargyropoulou, E., Baharun, S., Noor, M.J.M.M. and Kinoshita, C. (2012) '"Ningen Ryoku": The Japanese way in inculcating human skill into engineering education', *Procedia – Social and Behavioral Sciences*, 56: 369–376. 10.1016/j.sbspro.2012.09.665.

Riggio, R.E., Chaleff, I., and Lipman-Blumen, J. (eds.) (2008) *The Art of Followership: How Great Followers Create Great Leaders and Organizations*. Jossey-Bass.

Ryan, R.M. and Deci, E.L. (2000) 'Self-determination theory and the facilitation of intrinsic motivation, social development, and well-being', *American Psychologist*, 55 (1): 68–78. doi.org/10.1037/0003-066X.55.1.68

Sajjad, A. Eweje, G. and Raziq, M.M. (2024) 'Sustainability leadership: An integrative review and conceptual synthesis', *Business Strategy and the Environment*, *33* (4): 2849–67.

Schwab, K. (2016) *The Fourth Industrial Revolution*. Crown Business.

Shriberg, M. (2012) 'Sustainability leadership as 21st century leadership', in: *Environmental Leadership: A Reference Handbook* (vol. 2). Sage. pp. 469–80.

Stogdill, R.M. (1974). *Handbook of Leadership: A Survey of Theory and Research*. Free Press.

United Nations (2022) 'IPCC adaptation report "a damning indictment of failed global leadership on climate"', *United Nations*. https://news.un.org/en/story/2022/02/1112852 (accessed September 9, 2025).

Visser, W. and Courtice, P. (2020) 'Sustainability leadership: Linking theory and practice', *Effective Executive*, 23 (1): 26-39.

WCED (1987) *Our Common Future* [Brundtland Report]. Oxford University Press.

Zimmerman, B.J. (2002) 'Becoming a self-regulated learner: An overview', *Theory into Practice*, 41 (2): 64-70.

5
HUMAN RESOURCE MANAGEMENT

Sian Robinson and Stephen Taylor

INTENDED LEARNING OUTCOMES

After reading this chapter, you should be able to:

1. Explain what effective human resource management (HRM) functions achieve in organisations.
2. Distinguish between HRM and International HRM.
3. Understand and appreciate the major HRM challenges faced by contemporary employing organisations.
4. Set out the ways in which HRM is practiced in our case study organisation - IKEA.
5. Assess the arguments in favour of considering developing a career in HRM.

SUSTAINABLE DEVELOPMENT GOALS

In this chapter, the following SDGs will be addressed:

- SDG 3: Good Health and Well-being - Modern HRM functions increasingly address employee well-being, work-life balance, and psychological safety in the workplace.
- SDG 4: Quality Education - HRM functions and career development supports continuous professional development and skills enhancement within organisations.
- SDG 5: Gender Equality - Contemporary HRM challenges address gender equality in recruitment, promotion, and compensation practices.
- SDG 8: Decent Work and Economic Growth - Effective HRM functions directly contribute to creating fair employment opportunities, appropriate working conditions, and sustainable economic growth.
- SDG 10: Reduced Inequalities - International HRM perspectives and discrimination touch on managing diversity and inclusion and reducing workplace disparities.
- SDG 16: Peace, Justice and Strong Institutions - Contemporary HRM challenges include developing transparent, accountable organisational structures that uphold employee rights and ethical workplace practices.

INTRODUCTION

Human resource management (HRM) is focused on the effective management of the relationship organisations have with the people they employ. It also involves ensuring that these organisations are able to compete with other employers successfully in labour markets to recruit all the staff who are needed to carry out its various activities. While these activities are to some degree the responsibility of all managers, most organisations of any size have a dedicated team of people managers who specialise in HR and are often professionally qualified in this field of management activity.

In this chapter we will start by explaining what HR managers are looking to achieve and how they go about meeting their function's objectives. We go on to introduce some key, contemporary challenges that HR managers face. Throughout the chapter we will be illustrating key points using a case study focusing on aspects of human resource management in the retail chain IKEA. We end our chapter with a section making the case for considering a career in HRM.

CASE STUDY 5.1

IKEA

IKEA was founded by Ingvar Kamprad in 1943 in his home country of Sweden, initially selling goods like pens and wallets. They moved on to start selling furniture in 1948. The first store opening in Sweden in 1958. It has grown to have over 450 stores across 63 markets (IKEA, n.d.a). IKEA is recognised for their unique and cost-effective flat packaged products as well as their Swedish meatballs, but they are also known for their strong corporate culture and human resource management practices that are embedded within their values and their strategy.

Culture and Values

IKEA has a clear shared vision 'to create a better everyday life for the many people' (IKEA, n.d.b). To achieve this, they stand by a set of eight values that together create their overall company culture. The eight IKEA (n.d.b) key values are:

- **Togetherness** - they are strongest when everyone trusts each other, works towards the same goal and has fun together.
- **Caring for people and planet** - a focus on positive change and wanting to make a lasting impact now and for future generations.
- **Cost-consciousness** - allowing as many people as possible to have a functional and beautiful home without compromising on quality.
- **Simplicity** - having a simple and straightforward approach that is about staying true to themselves through informality and pragmatism rather than bureaucracy.

- **Renew and improve** – always looking for new and better ways of doing things and finding solutions to impossible challenges.
- **Different with a meaning** – wanting to be different to other organisations and thinking in unconventional ways, being happy to experiment and make mistakes for a good reason.
- **Give and take responsibility** – empowering people and developing individuals by giving them and allowing them to take responsibility, inspiring everyone to contribute to development through trust, positivity and a forward-looking approach.
- **Lead by example** – leadership is viewed as an action, not a position, and is therefore based on people's values and who will lead by example, bring their best selves and bring out the best in each other.

These values demonstrate the importance that IKEA places on working together as well as giving their teams roles that have meaning. Togetherness is at the front of this list as it is the most important factor for IKEA's culture, people working together, not just co-workers but also customers and suppliers. They also place importance on values-based promotions and empowering their staff. People are a key asset to IKEA, with the founder, Ingvar Kamprad, stating 'IKEA is not the work of one person alone. It is the result of many minds and many souls working together through many years of joy and hard work'.

The HRM Function at IKEA

IKEA has a human resources function named People and HR that sits under the People, Projects and Support team. The team 'support the IKEA business through people processes based on the IKEA values and a unique view on people' (IKEA Jobs, n.d.). The team supports over 230,000 co-workers in all aspects of their working life, with teams in recruitment, co-worker relations, leadership and competence.

A key part of the People and HR function is to ensure that their culture and values are at the centre of everything that the organisation does, supported through people processes. INGKA, the largest IKEA franchisee that operates the most stores, has three 'key movements' for their people strategy.

1. Firstly, people choose IKEA for what it stands for, and they are proud to be a part of the organisation with their values and vision, so they ensure that is at the heart of all of their people processes.
2. Secondly, they want to ensure they have engaged IKEA co-workers who have the customers at heart. This is developed through their culture of togetherness, enthusiasm and fun, and they are always on the lookout for people who share that positive mindset.
3. Finally, they want to ensure their people strategy is modern, lean, and agile to allow for growth and ensure that the business is fit for the future. This has led to a recent reassessment of the organisation and simplifying how it is led, how it works and is organised, and how they find new talent.

(Continued)

The Chief Human Resources Officer of INGKA Ulrika Biesèrt argues that the success of the company results directly from their approach to management, with people at the core of everything that they do (Forsdick, 2024).

Questions

1 Which of IKEA's core values stand out to you and why?
2 How do you think IKEA's people strategy impacts their employees?

Source

Forsdick, F. (2024) 'Ikea's CHRO on why culture is the company's "superpower"', *Raconteur*, April 12. https://www.raconteur.net/talent-culture/ikeas-chro-culture-companys-superpower (accessed September 10, 2025).

THE PURPOSE OF HUMAN RESOURCE MANAGEMENT

One of the reasons that working in HRM is so satisfying and interesting is the great variety of the activities that HR managers are involved in from day to day. This is partly due to the unpredictability of human personalities and the interpersonal relationships we have in our workplaces, but it is also due to the broad range of objectives that any HR function is looking to accomplish effectively. Some of our activities are 'hard' in nature and focused on the transactional aspects of the employment relationship. These include paying people accurately, dealing with employment contracts and enforcing rules. Others are 'soft', requiring high levels of emotional intelligence. These are focused on managing the 'relational' side of management, looking to motivate people, to negotiate agreements and to deal with problematic personal issues that are reducing organisational effectiveness. These varied types of HRM activity require different skill sets, and the two often need to be used in combination. When making redundancies, for example, HR managers are required to exercise excellent soft management skills, while also adhering to harder aspects such as the need to comply with government legislation.

The core objectives that a well-run HR function is looking to achieve are also quite diverse. They all add value for employing organisations, but involve a very wide range of different activities. There are six major objectives. Two that are really fundamental to any organisation's success (staffing and performance objectives), and five others that are increasingly becoming prominent: change; employee well-being; equality, diversity, and inclusion; corporate reputation; and administrative objectives (see Figure 5.1).

Staffing the Organisation

This is the most fundamental objective. If an organisation is not adequately staffed, none of the other objectives of the HR function can be met. Staffing is essentially about attracting and retaining people who are well-qualified to carry out their roles and capable of achieving a high level of performance. Effective recruitment processes are thus vital, particularly when an organisation is obliged to compete with others in competitive labour markets.

In the recent past, employee recruitment in the main involved placing advertisements in newspapers and trade journals when vacancies arose. Larger employers also engaged in large-scale graduate recruitment exercises each year, with the aim of recruiting a large cohort of new starters who were then trained and promoted up through the management ranks. These activities still happen, but recruitment activity almost always occurs online now, and it involves doing much more than advertising vacancies. Organisations now trawl social media looking to identify potential recruits so that they can be targeted directly. Headhunting agencies are often involved. There is also much more strategic activity as organisations look to build and sustain for themselves a positive reputation in the labour market. This involves developing compelling '**employee value propositions**' (EVPs) that potential recruits will find really attractive (e.g., good pay and benefits, career development opportunities, flexible working options, decent work-life balance, pleasant working environment, respectful managers, a collaborative corporate culture etc.). **Employer branding** exercises then follow, as slogans and appealing messaging are developed to 'sell' the compelling EVPs that have been developed.

Good branding and EVPs also help to retain good people. But they are often not enough in themselves. The actual lived experience of working for an organisation also needs to match the promises, and all kinds of interpersonal issues also need to be managed well. People are more likely to leave their managers than leave their jobs, demonstrating the importance of choosing the right people to lead teams and of timely management training for team leaders.

The staffing dimension of HRM also involves future workforce planning. This is sometimes referred to as making sure that the organisation always 'has the right people in the right jobs at the right time'. There is a need to assess how many people are going to be required in which roles and with which types of qualifications and experience in a year's time, in three years' time, and perhaps longer. This, too, is a strategic activity involving forecasting and then developing plans to ensure that staffing plans are met in practice via external recruitment and internal development of existing staff. There is also a financial aspect to this element of HR work as budgets for recruitment and training activity are negotiated with senior and financial managers.

REFLECTIVE ACTIVITY 5.1

Some argue that long-term workforce planning is no longer something that HR functions should prioritise because the business environment has become so volatile and unpredictable.

- What is your view?

Managing Performance

This is the second foundational HRM objective. Once staffing objectives have been met, we need to maximise the performance achieved by each person we employ. In this way maximum collective performance is achieved, helping the organisation to meet its commercial and other strategic objectives. There are two major aspects to the management of performance by an HR function, both of which require plenty of collaboration with team leaders and line managers if they are to be achieved consistently.

One involves looking to encourage excellent performance. Ideally any organisation wants to employ a team of highly qualified, highly motivated high achievers who are consistently out-performing expectations. This holy grail is, however, very difficult to reach. We can though move somewhere towards it by looking to ensure the following:

- selecting strong performers and making sure they are employed to do jobs that fit their **skills** and abilities
- investing in training and development so that people have the skills and experience to perform well
- rewarding outstanding performance
- noticing, appreciating, and thanking people when they perform well
- ensuring that people have sufficient work-life balance to perform well when they are at work
- providing people with future career development opportunities to aspire to when they perform well
- recruiting and developing cadres of senior **leaders** who are capable of inspiring high levels of performance

Ultimately what a well-run HRM function is looking to attain is a team of well-qualified, highly engaged people who support one another and go the extra mile on the part of their employer not because they feel obliged to do so, but because they want to. This is known as 'discretionary effort' because it involves working somewhat beyond legal, contractual obligations. It is hard to achieve this consistently, but it can be done with effective organisational leadership, great team leadership and a well-managed, supportive HRM infrastructure.

Equally challenging in a very different way is the need to manage poor performance effectively, efficiently, and lawfully. However elaborate and well-designed recruitment and selection practices are, it is inevitable that from time to time individuals will struggle to perform to an adequate level. It is often due to personal issues that have nothing to do with the workplace and that lead to unacceptable levels of absence, to lateness, a failure to complete tasks on time or inconsistent on-the-job performance. In these circumstances, which can be very difficult to handle well at a personal level, there is a need to monitor individual performance. Managers also need to communicate with people about where they are failing to perform and about organisational expectations in respect of performance. Training needs to be provided alongside positive encouragement, but ultimately when someone is unable or unwilling to perform their role to an adequate standard they will need to be 'managed out' of the organisation. This is another way of saying that they will need to be dismissed. This aspect of HR work is always highly unpleasant, particularly when an employee's only 'sin' is to be sick, or potentially terminally ill. But dismissals do need to be carried out from time to time, and it is the job of the HR manager to ensure that this happens thoughtfully and professionally, in a timely fashion, as well as in line with legal expectations. Typically this involves giving people formal warnings or looking to negotiate a financial settlement with them that involves immediate departure from the organisation.

Figure 5.1 Achieving HRM objectives

CASE STUDY 5.2

Staffing and Performance Management at IKEA

IKEA has specific strategies for both staffing and performance management that align with their culture and values, and people strategy.

Staffing

IKEA are very specific in the type of people that they want to attract to work for them. They align their recruitment with their organisational values, stating 'If you share our values, have a can-do attitude, and are interested in home furnishings, that's a good start'. They clearly exhibit their sense of humour when trying to attract the right new staff. As part of their job website Q&As about their interview dress code they highlight there is no need for ties or suits as they are interested in the person, not the clothes: 'We do however recommend that you wear clothes, no matter what you've heard about Swedish culture'. The CHRO, Ulrika Biesèrt, highlights that IKEA is very intentional in their recruitment, using a values-based strategy that will assess an individual's principles and how they align with the business rather than just their previous experience or the quality of their CV, and that if they don't share or feel engaged by the values of the organisation then they are not the right fit for IKEA (Forsdick, 2024).

Managing Performance

IKEA rewards performance in a number of ways: firstly they pay fair pay for all co-workers, paying a minimum of the National Living Wage. They also have the One IKEA bonus scheme. This bonus is based on rewarding everyone in a unit when specific business goals are met or exceeded. This is a group bonus scheme, as IKEA believe everything is achieved together. IKEA also provide a range of career development opportunities. As shown in IKEA's value of 'giving and taking responsibility' they want to support their employees to develop and become leaders; 88% of their leaders are recruited from within the organisation and they ensure all co-workers, both full-time and part-time, have the opportunity to progress if they wish to.

The IKEA 'In Any Direction' scheme gives co-workers the autonomy to choose how they grow their career and at what pace, allowing them to move across the business and between locations, either locally or globally. The IKEA value chain covers everything from the stores to distribution centres, as well as the creation of products in development centres, and the office hubs that run more central services. This means that co-workers can move into a role and a place that suits them. IKEA believe that they allow their co-workers to be the best they can be, whether they want to stay where they are or try something new. And that throughout holding an IKEA role they will be encouraged to learn and grow and be able to be promoted within the organisation. Finally, going back to their People Strategy, one of their main focuses is that they want engaged co-workers which they achieve through their culture of togetherness, enthusiasm and fun.

Questions

1 Would you want to apply to work for an organisation using a values-based staffing strategy?

2 How do you think that IKEA's approach to staffing and managing performance support creating an engaged workforce?

Source

Forsdick, F. (2024) 'Ikea's CHRO on why culture is the company's "superpower"', *Raconteur*, April 12. https://www.raconteur.net/talent-culture/ikeas-chro-culture-companys-superpower (accessed September 10, 2025).

Further HRM Objectives

In addition to ensuring good staffing and maximum performance, there is an increasing need to devote time to meeting (or helping to meet) other types of organisational objectives.

Change

A major example is the effective management of change. Many employing organisations are now obliged to function in much less stable and predictable business environments than used to be the case, not least because of the competitive pressures unleashed in the 21st century by **globalisation** and technological developments. This has required them to become much more agile and to embark on change management programmes much more frequently. Change has become almost continuous in some organisations as managers find that adapting swiftly and opportunistically to commercial pressures is necessary to ensure survival, let alone any kind of competitive advantage.

From an HRM perspective the upshot is that restructures as well as longer-term projects aimed at changing organisational cultures take place much more frequently. Achieving change of this kind, as is also true of **ergonomic change** and the introduction of new technologies, is always easy to do badly. We can easily force through change in such a way as to diminish morale, trigger the resignation of good performers, increase absence and reduce employee **engagement**. Doing it well, however, is tougher, but worth the effort as these highly undesirable side effects in people management can be avoided. HR managers thus need to be heavily involved in planning change thoughtfully, communicating about it thoroughly and effectively, and looking always to ensure that it creates positive opportunities for people wherever possible. Best of all, where it is possible, change management projects need to be planned with the active collaboration of the organisation's employees. That way it is not perceived as being something that managers are 'doing to us', but as something that we are all carrying through together. The old management mantra 'people support what they help to create' is apposite here. The best way of avoiding active or passive resistance to change is to make its genesis a collective affair that everyone affected has some part in planning.

Employee Well-Being

Another objective that is increasingly a priority for organisations is employee well-being. This is partly due to health and safety regulations and the potential legal risks now associated with people who become sick due to the stress they experience at work, but it also makes complete sense from a business perspective more generally. The healthier and happier your workforce is, the more likely you are to see it perform well and to improve its productivity. There are huge potential costs associated with staff absence and resignations triggered due to overwork or perceived bullying on the part of managers. Moreover, there are great benefits for people personally as well as in their capacity as team members if they feel fit and healthy both physically and mentally. Sometimes of course problems in people's home lives spill over into their working lives – bereavements, debt, chronic ill health, relationship breakdowns, child- and elder-care issues etc. There is little any organisation can do to prevent these things happening, but creating a supportive working environment and flexible working options while offering professional counselling services can go a long way to providing some amelioration. And it is in the employer's interests, as well as the employee's, that well-being is promoted and encouraged.

Equality, Diversity, and Inclusion

Equality, diversity, and inclusion objectives are another group that are much more prominent for HR managers than used to be the case. There is now an expectation that organisations will be proactive in these areas. It is expected not only by employees and potential employees, but also by customers. A failure to engage seriously with this agenda by, for example, paying men and women unequally, continually appointing people of one ethnicity to senior roles, or ignoring the needs of people with disabilities, can easily erode morale and levels of employee commitment. It can also in some circumstances lead to the development of a toxic reputation more generally that will then feed through into reduced commercial performance. Fairness and fair dealing really matter in an age of social media and it is in every organisation's interest to ensure that this is the perception that **stakeholders** have of them. Moreover, of course, there are major potential benefits for organisations that are equal, diverse and inclusive. People tend to be more highly motivated and proud to work for their employer, while the make-up of the team better reflects the organisation's wider customer base. Decision-making that is informed by diverse perspectives tends to be more effective too.

Corporate Reputation

Maintaining a positive corporate reputation more generally is also increasingly important, and HR managers have a role to play here, too. Not only is it necessary to ensure that HRM itself is carried out in an ethically sound manner, but there is also a need to contribute to the achievement of a high standard of business ethics in the organisation generally. The starting point is typically a published code of ethics that everyone in the organisation, including senior managers, is obliged to follow when at work. This then needs to be communicated effectively, updated regularly and to infuse all of the organisation's operations. From an HR point of view, this means complying with the code of ethics when recruiting people, promoting them, training them and managing their performance. There needs to be an ethical element included in all these activities if corporate reputations are to be built and enhanced over time.

Administration Objectives

Finally, there are administration objectives. These are not so compelling for most people (including HR managers), but they are important because they are necessary and unavoidable.

The HR function is usually responsible for running an organisation's payroll, ensuring that everyone is paid accurately and on time. It also needs to ensure that adequate records are kept in respect of training, sickness absence and holidays. It needs to issue contracts to new starters, write policy documents, deal with the documentation associated with resignations, and work through the many legal obligations that employers have in respect of maternity, paternity and parental rights. It is all time consuming and important, if not very exciting. AI can increasingly help us to complete these activities more efficiently, but there will always also be a need for human judgement and expertise. Some argue that these are non-value-adding activities that have no strategic significance. They therefore downplay their significance in HR work. This is a short-sighted perspective. If your organisation is able to achieve necessary administrative work more efficiently and more effectively than your competitors, you are, after all, in effect adding value. It is also important for the credibility of the HR function generally in an organisation that it is perceived as being administratively competent. If not, it will have limited influence and be unable to achieve all the other objectives we have outlined above.

REFLECTIVE ACTIVITY 5.2

- Which of these HRM objectives do you think will become more important in the future and why?
- Are there any that you think might become less significant?

CASE STUDY 5.3

Equality and Well-Being at IKEA

IKEA has a focus on both equality and well-being for its employees, seeing these as key approaches to ensure they are benefiting from their employees by supporting them well.

(Continued)

Equality, Diversity, and Inclusion

Equality, diversity, and inclusion are an important focus for IKEA. The company believes that being more diverse is a benefit to them as an organisation, allowing them to be more creative, innovative, and entrepreneurial. They understand that they need to have non-biased practices within recruitment but also have a continued dialogue about everyone's worth both inside and outside of the business. This is a reflection of Swedish labour institutions, with focus on equal pay, gender diversity and equality, no discrimination between regular and non-regular workers and providing a flexible working environment (Song, 2021). They have a commitment to reaching a 50/50 gender balance in all countries, levels of the organisation and positions across IKEA. In 2023, the INGKA group reached gender balance across their top leadership roles and is still working towards their commitment to this across the rest of the organisation. They have seven different areas of focus to increase equality:

- everyday inclusivity
- closing the gender gap
- multi-culturalism of ethnicity, race and nationality inclusion
- LGBTQ+ inclusion
- disability inclusion
- increasing accountability, leadership and competence
- **upskilling** and re-skilling refugees and local communities for a more equal world

Well-Being

IKEA believes that its key asset is its people, and as such they have ensured that well-being and caring for their co-workers is embedded in how the organisation works. This comes through its vision and values, as well as then ensuring that policies are in place to support this. The friendly workplace and IKEA culture are often what co-workers say they value the most about working for the organisation. Well-being is a central part of the IKEA ethos that has come from their home country of Sweden, such as the concept of Fika, where a coffee break is taken, and co-workers just talk to each other and not about business.

As part of their benefits package, IKEA provides access to health and well-being support for co-workers through medical and dental insurance, free healthy food, a well-being services network that is available 24 hours a day and a well-being hub that provides support on everything from exercise classes to tips for a healthy lifestyle. They also highlight that they offer flexible working options, but this is more aligned by offering part-time work to enable co-workers to have a flexible schedule that can be balanced with their life outside of work.

CHRO Ulrika Biesèrt (INGKA, 2023) argues that: 'Prioritising wellbeing at work isn't just the right thing to do, it's essential. A healthy workforce is key to a thriving workplace and business. Our approach is built on a foundation of blending global and local programmes. These programmes are designed to address three fundamental areas of wellbeing: mental, physical and financial, ensuring a holistic approach'. This focus by the franchise is shown to be working, with their Health and Wellbeing Index score increasing from 63% in 2021 to 73% in 2023 within their annual co-worker satisfaction survey.

Questions

1 Why is a focus on equality, diversity and inclusion, and well-being so important to IKEA?
2 How do you think these approaches impact their employees?

INTERNATIONAL HRM

Managing human resources in an international organisation involves looking to meet these same sets of objectives and carrying out these same types of activity, but there is a big difference. Achieving them effectively and efficiently in an international context is a great deal more complex and challenging. And the more countries an organisation employs people in, the greater the complexity. This is because however globalised an industry has become, it still has to manage people within the constraints of local, national workplace cultures and institutional frameworks. The way people are managed varies greatly around the world as a result and their expectations about how they will be managed vary accordingly.

Numerous studies conducted over many decades demonstrate that national workplace cultures are quite sticky and only change slowly (e.g., Hofstede, 1980, 2004; Hall and Hall, 1990; Basanez, 2016; Cheng and Groysberg, 2020). Employment law varies hugely around the world, as do national training and welfare systems, and the extent and nature of trade union membership. It is thus impossible, as convenient as it would be to do so, to construct a single global approach to HRM to operate in the same way across an international organisation's operations. Local cultural and institutional differences have to be respected. There can still be international HR strategies pursued and a single set of objectives set each year, but these have to be operationalised differently according to local needs. The mantra 'think global, act local' therefore has to be followed, and this often brings costs and challenges with it.

In addition, of course, when an organisation becomes global, there is a need to employ expatriate staff. Managers and people with professional expertise are required to work in overseas subsidiaries for periods of (typically) three to five years. They move abroad with their families for the purpose of maintaining control over global operations, spreading **knowledge** and developing their own career prospects. Expatriation is highly risky because people often find it difficult to live overseas for long periods. It is also costly and thus needs to be handled with great care. Expatriates need to be selected carefully, prepared well for their assignments and provided with a great deal of pre-departure training. Contact and support then has to be maintained right the way through until the repatriation process starts, and this too is associated with risks and costs. Bonache et al. (2020) provide an excellent introduction to this subject.

CONTEMPORARY CHALLENGES IN HRM

In addition to looking to achieve the diverse objectives discussed above, HR managers are always faced at different times with a range of particular, longer-term, strategic challenges.

Some of these arise from developments in the wider business environment that have an impact on organisations, while others are matters of wider social or economic concern that employing organisations may have a role in helping to improve. Many are complex and difficult to engage with, so it is difficult to give them full justice in a single, short introductory chapter. Here we briefly introduce some that current HR managers in the UK particularly are having to grapple with.

Skills Shortages

Difficulty in recruiting and retaining staff has been a major challenge for HR managers over recent years. Chronic skills shortages have afflicted many industries and show every sign of continuing to do so in the future. The same problem is affecting organisations across much of the world as unemployment levels have fallen along with birthrates in most industrial countries.

The causes of skills shortages are many and varied. Some are short-term, resulting for example from the boost in **demand** for goods and services that we saw after the COVID-19 pandemic as people went out and spent the savings they had built up. In some industries there has been a post-Brexit effect as the new immigration rules make it harder to source lower-skilled staff from overseas. Many older workers seem to have decided not to return to full-time work after being **furloughed** during the pandemic years, but to retire earlier instead or to work part-time. However, other causes are long-term and relate to the relatively low number of babies born in the UK during the 1990s in particular. Notably, these skills shortages are occurring at a time of significantly increased immigration from overseas, principally consisting of people who are of working age. So there are no easy public policy solutions available.

Skills shortages constitute by far the biggest contemporary challenge for HR managers who are, by consequence, obliged to spend a large proportion of their time looking to improve their organisation's capacity both to recruit and retain suitable employees, and particularly the high performers. The approach taken is often by necessity rather short-term because the priority is always to get the right people into posts now. Less attention thus tends to be given to addressing the problem in the long term.

Many employers are responding to this challenge, as is traditional, by increasing pay and are passing the costs on to their customers in the form of price rises. There is also focus on retaining individual staff members by making counter-offers when they secure alternative jobs. But simply raising pay is not ever going to be a long-term solution when all employers are fishing in the same pools for new recruits. There comes a point when it simply becomes unaffordable if an organisation is to remain competitive in terms of its pricing.

There is thus a need for creativity in reward policy. One approach is to employ fewer people to do the work, but to pay them better. This involves becoming more productive (see the following section) and is a sound, potential solution to the problem. However, it is often very difficult to achieve in practice without overworking people or investing a great deal of money in new technologies that may be imperfect or have a limited shelf life. So many employers are choosing instead to take what is known as a 'total reward' approach and to attract and retain staff by offering EVPs that contain much more that is valued than just pay.

People will trade higher pay for all manner of other elements, and employers need to be mindful of this. Flexible working opportunities can, for example, be offered. A small number of employers have recently been experimenting, for example, with a four-day working week – reducing hours of work while keeping pay at the same level. It may seem counter-intuitive, but many report that taking this step improves performance and productivity. Staff get done in four days what they previously did in five, while absence and staff turnover have plummeted. Allowing people to work from home on some days of the week is another approach that works because for many the removal of tedious and stressful commuting is something they are very happy to trade for limited increases in pay. More career development opportunities is another approach, but the one that works best of all is simply the creation of a very pleasant, respectful and engaging work environment.

If the economics of an industry preclude changing the way people are paid and rewarded, other alternative strategies can be pursued. An organisation can, for example, simply become smarter at recruiting people by investing in compelling employer branding or recruiting more staff overseas. There are major costs associated with this, but if it is a strategic priority for the organisation the case can be made. In some industries the approach taken has been to relocate entire operations to different regions and countries where labour supply is plentiful and more affordable.

Another approach involves recruiting people who do not have the skills or experience to perform roles, but to provide them with these via apprenticeship schemes and other training programmes. It is also possible to undertake what is known as 'a skills mix review' that essentially involves redesigning the allocation of tasks among teams of staff so that the higher-qualified people who are typically the hardest to recruit spend as close to 100% of their working hours as possible doing what only they can do. Managers remove from them duties that are more mundane – particularly administrative activities – and pass these on to lower paid staff who are usually easier to recruit. This has happened a great deal in the public sector in recent years as classroom assistants, for example, have been hired to work alongside fully qualified teachers, and Health Care Assistants to work with fully qualified registered nurses. Nurses in turn, as is also true of pharmacists, have then had duties traditionally performed by doctors passed to them, hence reducing demand for very highly trained and hard-to-recruit medical professionals.

REFLECTIVE ACTIVITY 5.3

- Are we right to assume that chronic skills shortages are going to persist in most industries for the foreseeable future?
- What might happen to change the situation?

Productivity

Low levels of productivity growth have been a major problem for the UK economy over the past 15 years. Gross domestic product (GDP) per head and GDP per worker have not really changed at all, while public sector productivity has actually fallen. There are huge regional variations, but taken as a whole the UK has performed poorly compared to major competitor countries such as Germany, France and the USA. This poor recent record compares unfavourably with the 30 years from 1980 to 2010 or so when productivity steadily improved year on year.

There are many different causes of this sluggish productivity. It is partly a failure to make full use of new technologies like superfast broadband and AI that can improve an organisation's productivity. It is partly a function of our failure to upskill the working population so that they have the higher-level technical and specialist skills necessary to build the more productive economic sectors faster. We have seen reduced national infrastructure investment and periods of business uncertainty developing thanks to recessions, leaving the EU, the COVID pandemic and the war in Ukraine that have all played some role in preventing investment in the achievement of greater productivity, making banks cautious about lending and entrepreneurs more risk averse. Some argue that population ageing is adversely affecting productivity, while others argue that we are simply over-taxed and over-regulated. There has also been a tendency on the part of UK employers to hire cheap workers rather than to invest in labour-saving technologies. It may thus be that low unemployment has been achieved off the back of poor productivity (Wolf, 2020).

You will see from this brief analysis that improving productivity is by no means a task that employing organisations and HR managers can be expected to achieve alone. There needs to be a lot of government action and support too. But HRM can and should play a role as so much of what we do in the function relates directly to labour productivity at the level of the organisation.

There are two major alternative strategies that can be pursued. These can usefully be labelled the 'high road' and the 'low road' to improved productivity. The latter is less desirable and can be damaging to an organisation over the long term. But it is a strategy that is nonetheless widely used to generate more profit via greater labour productivity. Essentially it involves greater intensification of work. Put simply, that means squeezing more work out of an employed workforce while maintaining or cutting labour costs. It works in the short term, but in an era of low unemployment and skills shortages, it can be very ineffective as a long-term strategy. This is because organisations that pursue low road strategies quickly run into major recruitment and retention problems while also suffering from high absence levels and relatively low levels of employee engagement. Governments are thus right to look to discourage the approach on the grounds that it leads to the creation of a 'low skill – low wage' economy that is bad for national productivity in the long term. A 'high skill – high wage' economy is what we aspire to, and that requires employers instead to take a high road strategy to productivity improvement.

What does that involve? It can be summed up as good practice HRM and consistently meeting all the function's objectives that we set out above more efficiently than competitors. The first step involves investing in extensive and accurate evaluation of HR activity in an organisation. There are many metrics that **finance** departments use, but which often have only a limited part to play in day-to-day HR management. Examples are the following:

- profit generated per employee
- sales per employee

- recruitment cost per new recruit
- labour costs as a proportion of total costs
- absence costs as a proportion of staff costs

These can be evaluated regularly alongside figures for absence rates, staff turnover rates, accident rates, overtime rates etc, and statistics gathered from staff satisfaction surveys on levels of staff motivation, engagement and understanding concerning what is expected of them.

Once such **data** is collected it can be used to set targets for improvement, to track progress over time and to make comparisons between different business units so that they can learn from one another.

The data permits HR managers to pinpoint the major areas of strengths and weakness and hence to focus efforts on the particular types of activity that will produce the best results in terms of productivity improvement. It may be that employee satisfaction rates are poor in some areas, for example, and that improving them will lead to higher levels of performance. The expression 'a happy team is a productive team' is a touch simplistic, but it nonetheless carries truth. It may, by contrast, be that absence rates are too high and that improvements could be made to employee well-being in order to improve them. Payment arrangements may simply not incentivise increased productivity, making a good case for making changes there. If employees are not rewarded for engaging in changed productivity-enhancing activity, there is less chance that they will do so. There are measures that can be taken to reorganise work so as to cut down on slack-time during the working day. This may involve monitoring people more effectively, but it can just as easily be achieved through more multi-skilling so that individuals can be deployed to work in the parts of a workplace that are busiest at different times of the day. Why not train people to do two or three different jobs? There is also potential in introducing more strengths-based performance management so that as far as possible team members are allocated the work to do that they most enjoy. We all tend to be more productive when working inside rather than outside our natural comfort zones. More generally taking the high road to greater productivity involves upskilling, particularly in respect of new technologies. No organisation can expect to reap the full cost-saving benefits of IT, robotics, AI or virtual reality, if its people are not fully trained to appreciate their potential and put these benefits into effect.

In truth there is not generally one big intervention that is needed to make individual organisations more productive. As is shown in Figure 5.2, the need is to work at the same time on a number of different fronts, achieving steady year-on-year improvements incrementally.

Technology

As is true of all professions, including all the major management specialisms, major ongoing challenges are continually being created as our technological capabilities improve. For the most part evolving technology makes it either more effective or more efficient to carry out core HR activities, but there are also important ethical issues raised and difficult judgements – in the form of cost-benefit analyses – to be made about which technologies should be invested in. Quality can also be adversely affected as efficiency improves, requiring managers to think carefully about the full long-term range of impacts that particular technologies are likely to have.

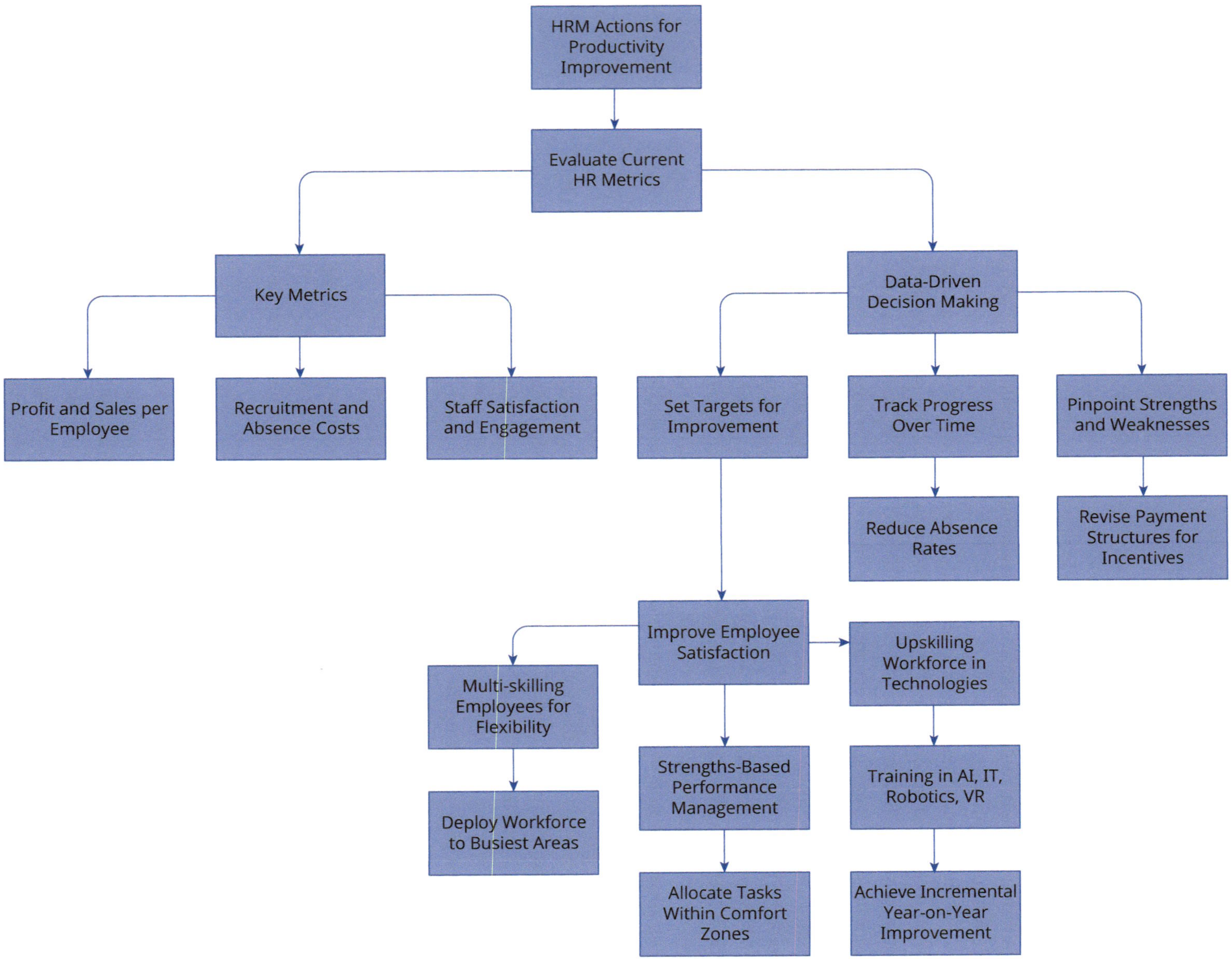

Figure 5.2 HRM and productivity improvement

Recruitment

One example we have already commented on is the field of recruitment and selection. IT is in some ways turning traditional recruitment processes on their heads. For many decades recruitment has almost always preceded selection. Advertisements of various kinds were published and people were then invited to apply for positions. The employer would receive many applications from appointable people, would draw up a shortlist, would interview candidates and make a decision about who to recruit. Increasingly this no longer happens. Instead, software is used to trawl social media in search of potential recruits. Shortlisting thus, in effect, comes first. The employer then seeks to open up a dialogue with 'ideal recruits' with a view to persuading them to come for an interview.

We are also seeing widespread use of 'applicant tracking software' that has the ability to carry out shortlisting much more quickly, and some producers argue, more effectively than HR officers. It trawls CVs and application forms for key words, manages and 'marks' online tests designed to select out weaker candidates, and carries out tasks such as collating the results of psychometric tests while also communicating these to candidates. Selection interviews are also commonly carried out nowadays by chatbots, the software not only judging people's suitability in terms of what they say, but how they say it and the facial expressions they display when doing so.

Training

We are seeing a similar revolution in the way in which training is carried out in organisations. It is a great deal cheaper potentially to train people online over time. We can remove the need for classroom-style activities and the need to employ trainers. The training can also be carried out much more flexibly at times and in ways that suit the trainee's preferences and commitments. Initial investment in online training packages, however, can be very costly, particularly when they include the gamification features that can radically improve engagement and effectiveness. There is also the potential for systems to test their own effectiveness with lots of tailored self-testing and evaluation.

Monitoring and Improving Performance

Another example is the use of online surveillance of employees as a means of monitoring and potentially improving performance. This is essentially about increasing management control, and so is inevitably controversial. But it is always going to be very tempting for managers to use technology as a means of observing and measuring what employees are doing while they are being paid to work. Staff may increasingly work from home, but that need not mean that they are free to use their time in ways they want to. Software can very easily be installed that monitors everything they do at a workstation and generates reports for managers setting out how productive they have been, how much work they have completed in specific time periods and whether or not they adhere to company protocols. For workers based in workplaces like warehouses and factories, managers can require that they have 'wearables' on their persons at all times – wristbands, necklaces etc. – that enable electronic monitoring. What all these surveillance technologies effectively do is carry out the supervisory duties that used to have to be done directly by managers physically observing staff at work. There is always a need to comply with data protection laws, but provided the monitoring is being carried out during working time and is not excessive, that will be the case. The management control aspects of the supervisor's job are thus now increasingly carried out remotely and automatically by machines.

These are just three illustrative examples. HR work is being affected in all kinds of ways by all manner of other technologies that can manipulate data and make predictions. Use of such **data analytics** can aid decision-making, ease the process of workforce planning and provide access in an easily digestible form to all manner of reports derived from trawls of '**Big Data**'. Decision-making in HR, and particularly longer-term strategic decision-making, are being enhanced considerably as a result.

Ethics

In each of these cases there are legitimate questions to be asked and answered about ethicality and fairness. Software producers always claim that their products are more reliable than humans at carrying out management tasks. Not only are they more efficient, but they are also allegedly less susceptible to unconscious bias and make more consistent judgements. Not everyone, by any means, is convinced, and there have been some well-publicised examples of algorithms actually making deeply unfair judgements that humans might not have (Dastin, 2018). Moreover, it is always important in HR to think in terms of what is perceived to be fair rather than what, objectively speaking, is actually fair. If employees and would-be employees form the view that a process is operating unfairly or unethically, managers should think very carefully about using it because of the potential negative impact it might have on an organisation's capacity to attract, retain, motivate and engage strong performers.

AI

Finally in this context, mention must be made of **artificial intelligence** (AI) and its potential to revolutionise aspects of HR work (see Chapter 12). The launch of the ChatGPT system in 2022 and its much improved version 4 in 2023 are just the most prominent examples of numerous AI applications that are now in development and coming onto the market. Collectively these represent an extraordinary revolution in the apparent capacity of machines to undertake tasks currently or previously carried out by humans, and HR work will be affected profoundly in many ways.

In the immediate future it will be more routine activities that will be most transformed by AI. These systems can generate lengthy contracts, for example, in a few seconds and can write reports at similar speed. All that is required is to give ChatGPT4 a load of data, and it will analyse it instantly while writing a report of the desired length that is beautifully written with an executive summary, justification for key points and well-argued recommendations. In a few years' time the idea that a human being should commit valuable time to writing a recruitment ad, or a job description, or any kind of policy document, or a training video, without a very heavy dose of AI involvement will seem extraordinary.

REFLECTIVE ACTIVITY 5.4

- How far do you agree with the view that we are about to enter an era in which AI and other technologies effectively destroy so many jobs that people will struggle to find enough work?
- What arguments can be made against this proposition?

EQUALITY, DIVERSITY, AND INCLUSION (EDI)

In a business context of globalisation and demographic changes, workplaces are becoming increasingly diverse. The UK has legislation, voluntary codes of practice, and various initiatives; however, discrimination persists. This ongoing inequality is highlighted by several of the Sustainable Development Goals; 5: Gender Equality and 10: Reduced Inequalities. Organisations need to develop equal opportunities and diversity and inclusion strategies to both attract and retain staff, as well as to meet their legal requirements. There are two main approaches to equality, diversity and inclusion: the equal opportunities approach and the management of diversity approach (Torrington et al., 2020).

Equal Opportunity

Equality is ensuring that every individual has an equal opportunity to make the most of their lives and their talents using legislation. The Equality Act 2010 is in place to legally protect people from discrimination in the workplace and wider society (UK Government, 2015). The law requires equal treatment in access to employment for nine protected characteristics:

- age
- gender reassignment
- being married or in a civil partnership
- being pregnant or on maternity leave
- disability
- race (including colour, nationality, ethnic or national origin)
- religion or belief
- sex
- sexual orientation

For human resources, equality aims to achieve sameness or equal treatment through the systems and processes of the organisation, such as hiring and pay. However, despite legal protection having been in place for many years, there are still many people who face inequality in the workplace. The assumption that fair procedures in line with the law will lead to fair outcomes is not reliable in practice. Historically, certain groups of people have experienced discrimination. Examples of this include workplace harassment, less favourable treatment or unfair disadvantage, unequal parental leave, gender and race pay gaps, hiring biases, and the glass ceiling and glass cliff faced by women in leadership.

There are many reasons why inequalities still exist in the workplace. Sometimes individuals are consciously biased against others, which is a traditional assumption for why discriminatory behaviours happen. However, there is also unconscious bias where individuals make judgments about people and situations without realising. This is influenced by many factors such as their background, culture and personal experiences. As they are often not aware of these views and their impacts it can be difficult to tackle unconscious biases in the workplace.

Stereotyping, the belief or expectation about people who are part of a group or social category, can lead to unfair assumptions about people or groups. This can impact human resource management processes such as hiring decisions and performance evaluations and it can create barriers to career progression. An example of a stereotype that could impact hiring is for industries that are viewed as male-dominated such as STEM (science, technology, engineering and mathematics) and therefore less likely to hire women into positions.

The twin concepts of otherness and belonging also help to provide an understanding of some of the more subtle aspects of bias in employment practices (Özbilgin and Woodward, 2004). Otherness is when individuals are viewed as different or outside of a majority group within a workplace. This is often based on characteristics such as ethnicity, gender, age or other dimensions of diversity. As being an 'other' they are treated differently. Belonging is the feeling of being accepted and included within a group. This is a feeling of connection and acceptance by peers and the organisation. Belonging to part of a group can bring positive bias, by preference being given to this group, and lead to othering of outsiders to the group.

Stigmatisation is the negative attitudes and beliefs (including stereotypes) that can lead to the unfair treatment of an individual or group based on specific characteristics, such as sexual orientation, gender or other protected characteristics. Stigma can create a hostile environment for individuals and groups and is not only unequal treatment but also hinders the promotion of both diversity and inclusion (Goffman, 1963). There are also increased disadvantages when **intersectionality** occurs. This is where multiple different social identities intersect with discrimination (Crenshaw, 1991). The more of these disadvantaged identities an individual has, the more disadvantaged they are.

An example of ongoing inequality in the workplace is the gender pay gap. Despite equal pay being part of the Equality Act 2010, there is still a pay gap that exists. The gender pay gap has been declining slowly over time; as of April 2025 the pay gap was at 12.8%, compared to 27.5% in 1997 (ONS, 2025). Although this is a significant closing of the gap, a gap still exists and there is still inequality in pay. This gap is also larger for certain demographics, there is a wider pay gap between high earners. An example of intersectional disadvantage is that women who are over 40, so meeting two characteristics of sex and age, are more disadvantaged with an even bigger pay gap.

Diversity

Diversity goes beyond a focus on meeting legislative requirements and recognises that valuing differences is an asset for an organisation. There has been a shifting focus to this perspective from equal opportunities as inequality remains despite legislation. Diversity is recognising that everyone is different and that these differences should be respected, valued and promoted, and this is not limited to the differences protected by equality law (CIPD, 2024).

There is evidence that more diverse organisations will have increased performance in certain areas such as financial performance, better attraction, development and retention of employees, better decision-making, and increased employee satisfaction (Hunt et al., 2018).

Inclusion

Inclusion is a critical part of the management of the diversity approach. It is the practice of valuing people's differences and ensuring that people are empowered and enabled to be themselves and achieve their full potential at work. In an inclusive workplace, everyone should feel as though they belong, the policies and practices are fair, and everyone is supported to work together effectively (CIPD, 2024). Inclusive work environments need to consider a range of different factors, such as accommodations for physical and neurodivergent needs via flexible working (e.g. hybrid/remote) and adjusted start/finish times; the design of the physical space e.g. step-free access, adjustable desks, lifts and accessible toilets; the leadership and culture of the organisation by focusing performance management on outputs rather than physical presence; and interpersonal relations through adapted communication, such as providing both written and verbal instructions. It is important to ensure that this is clear through the culture and values of the organisation, as it is about creating an inclusive working environment where difference is valued by all. Therefore, to meet the ongoing challenges of unequal treatment, organisations need to go beyond the legislative requirements of equality and focus on diversity and inclusion as core values, which in turn can support better organisational performance.

Sustainability

The economic environment is changing constantly and there is an ever-increasing need for organisations to be more ethical and sustainable, and to care for more than just their profits. Therefore, for human resource management, there is a growing focus on long-term **sustainability** for organisations, employees and society, with the term 'sustainable HRM' being coined and widely used.

This approach to human resource management is a challenge to the traditional approach of organisations only looking to maximise value for their shareholders. It instead supports meeting the needs of a wide range of stakeholders over the longer term. This changing focus to being held accountable by a wide range of stakeholders presents a key HRM challenge. This links to a wide range of sustainable development goals but in particular SDG 8: Decent Work and Economic Growth and SDG 12: Responsible Consumption and Production.

There are arguments on how best to define sustainable HRM, but there are two common features across most definitions.

- Firstly, a focus on the values of an organisation as well as its financial objectives and targets.
- Secondly, a commitment to using ethical decision-making to meet a business's purpose whilst ensuring the business is taking both social and environmental responsibility.

There is also a range of characteristics that cover the core aspects of what sustainable HRM constitutes (Stankevičiūtė and Savanevičienė, 2018):

- **Long-term orientation** – future planning for the availability of human resources, the needs of future employees, and eliminating a 'hire and fire' approach
- **Care of employees** – work-life balance and health and safety management
- **Care of environment** – using environment-related criteria to evaluate and reward performance and develop 'eco-careers'
- **Profitability** – profit-sharing programmes
- **Employee participation and social dialogue** – using a range of different types and forms of employee participation
- **Employee development** – use of job rotations, different training forms, transferring of experience and having a focus on future employability and skills
- **External partnership** – cooperating with education systems and having partnerships with all external stakeholders
- **Flexibility** – flexible work arrangements and job rotation
- **Compliance beyond labour regulations** – involving employee representatives in decision-making beyond statutory requirements and further financial and non-financial support for employees
- **Employee cooperation** – promoting teamwork and good relationships between managers and employees
- **Fairness and equality** – fostering diversity, relationships that are respectful and having fairness for pay and careers

Sustainable HRM can be broken down into four main different types (Aust et al., 2020):

- Socially Responsible HRM
- Green HRM
- Triple Bottom Line HRM
- Common Good HRM

Socially Responsible HRM

This focuses on the social impacts of human resource management that go beyond just what happens within an organisation. It focuses on the use of socially responsible practices and **behaviours** such as equality, diversity and inclusion, fair labour and good work, and health and well-being initiatives.

Green HRM

This has a more specific focus on environmental awareness. It uses human resource management practices to embed environmental or green values across the organisation and put environmentally friendly practices into place. This can include environmental awareness training and rewards for employees who meet green goals such as reducing their carbon footprint.

With both Socially Responsible and Green HRM it is argued that the organisation's economic benefits are still the main purpose of their implementation. Although there are other, wider benefits – social and environmental – these are secondary to the purpose of profitability and are used to serve the economic outcomes.

Triple Bottom Line HRM

This has a focus on all three purposes of HRM, economic, social and environmental. It has each as a main objective, rather than using social and environmental outcomes to lead to economic outcomes. All three elements are intertwined and therefore are shared values. HRM's impacts are measured on social and environmental goals, as well as economic.

Common Good HRM

This takes the approach that it is a fundamental need for organisations to resolve sustainability challenges. Therefore, sustainability is a core value and becomes of equal importance to the organisational needs and outcomes. This perspective moves beyond the organisation's economic outcomes and focuses on the social and environmental needs of the world, pushing the need to address the grand challenges of the current time. Therefore, the SDGs become a central focus for the organisational outcomes.

Although a more sustainable focus is unquestionably needed for human resource management and organisations more generally, this presents a significant challenge when organisations are not already focused on this. Shifting to a sustainable HRM strategy to revolve around grand challenges and SDGs is a process that can occur easily enough at face value, such as having a sustainability strategy. However, embedding this into the values and culture of an organisation is a more difficult task, especially as all stakeholders need to be on board. If this is not achieved sincerely it can also bring questions of 'greenwashing', where organisations promote their sustainability efforts and credentials as a **marketing** tactic but continue to use non-sustainable practices. Therefore, sustainable HRM needs to be adopted over time, with measures being put in place that are relevant to the organisation and its needs. It is also not always realistic for an organisation to forego its economic outcomes for the sake of sustainability, therefore choosing the right type of sustainable HRM will be an important choice for organisations in line with what is achievable to get all their stakeholders on board.

REFLECTIVE ACTIVITY 5.5

What could you do in your own working life to help increase the sustainability of employment practices?

CASE STUDY 5.4

Some Contemporary HRM Challenges for IKEA

Although IKEA is at the forefront of innovative and progressive approaches to HRM, this does not mean that they have not faced any challenges along the way. IKEA has utilised a range of different approaches to meet these challenges, which has helped to both reduce their impact and link with the company's focus on its culture and values.

Loss of Staff

Although historically IKEA lost fewer workers than others across the retail industry thanks in part to its values, a few years ago it found itself facing large losses of staff. In 2022 more than 62,000 employees were leaving a year who proved difficult to replace (Boyle, 2024). IKEA put in place a range of different strategies to try and solve the issue, increasing pay, giving frontline employees more flexibility, introducing better onboarding for new employees and making use of emerging technology to make roles easier for their co-workers. One example of offering frontline employees more flexibility was to give them more options with their shift timings, moving the shift scheduling tool online and offering part-time workers the option to take on additional hours working remotely. These initiatives led to a reduction in their voluntary attrition rate across most countries, with the INGKA group having a global reduction from 22.4% in August 2022 to 17.5% in April 2024.

Attracting New Staff

IKEA has previously struggled to attract younger staff; to aim to meet these needs they created an innovative technological employer branding campaign called 'Careers done differently', which uses the game Roblox to attract a new and younger generation of co-workers. As part of the scheme, they offered people the chance to become an employee in a virtual version of IKEA within the Roblox game. The new virtual co-workers would do everything from moving around flatpack furniture to serving meatballs, with four different co-worker roles. These include being a sales co-worker, an interior design co-worker, a sales team leader, and a food team leader. Although there were only ten paid roles to work in the virtual store who would each earn £13.15 per hour, IKEA had over 178,000 applications in the two-week application window. The game opened in June 2024 and alongside paid players, other gamers and IKEA fans can explore the virtual store and become co-workers too.

Darren Taylor, the Country People and Culture Manager for the UK and Ireland said; 'We are always looking for new ways to attract and inspire the next generation of co-workers to imagine a career at IKEA. "The Co-Worker" game is a fantastic way to give players a taste of our culture and insight into what makes the world of work at IKEA so special'. The game also shows the different progression routes that co-workers in IKEA can take, with no clear set route and having the ability to change roles or switch across departments. It pushes that IKEA is there to support co-workers to learn and grow.

Kelly O'Callaghan, the Recruitment & Sourcing Manager, stated that: 'At IKEA, co-workers can grow their careers in any direction they want – by reskilling and moving into a new department or by taking on more responsibilities and growing in leadership roles. "The Co-Worker" game aims to help more people experience what a career at IKEA could be like' (Kemp, 2024). This shows the **innovation** and different approaches that IKEA is willing to undertake to reach their potential new co-workers, in keeping with their values.

Technology

With the increasing impact of **generative AI** on retail, IKEA has been using this to enhance customer experience (Forsdick, 2024). However, rather than laying off employees whose roles have been replaced, instead IKEA has been retraining their workers, with call centre workers being retrained as remote interior designers. CHRO Ulrika Biesèrt again argues here that although they are automating processes, the emphasis is on retraining co-workers to enable them to work across multiple departments, which she argues will make their jobs more fun by adding variety but acknowledges that it requires an open mindset for learning from their co-workers.

Sustainability

IKEA is a forward-focused organisation that is actively facing the challenges that are happening within the world today and taking responsibility to help solve them. In particular, the company focuses on the challenges of unsustainable consumption, climate change and growing inequality. IKEA Global (2025) has created a *People and Planet Positive Strategy* that details their sustainability agenda for the entirety of their value chain.

To IKEA, sustainability means a better life for more people, linking back to their overall company vision, with a balance between environmental, social and economic factors. The commitments made are set for achievement in 2030 and are aligned with the UN Sustainable Development Goals. They are taking steps to create a more sustainable future by collaborating with their partners, co-workers and customers with a focus on three areas: healthy and sustainable living, circular economy and climate, and fairness and equality. For people practice in particular this means focusing on respecting human rights, providing work that is decent and meaningful, paying and promoting a living wage for all employees, focusing on vulnerable groups, and being an organisation that is more equal, diverse and inclusive. It is again clear that this links back to their overall organisation vision 'to create a better everyday life for the many people'.

For equality, diversity, and inclusion in the financial year ending 2023, IKEA took further steps to create a more inclusive people strategy. They launched EDI competence development training for management, developed a guide for assessment and goal setting for EDI to bring it in line with the overall business strategy, established an EDI franchisee network, and created co-worker resource communities to allow co-workers to contribute to a more inclusive IKEA business and workplace.

(Continued)

IKEA's strategy for sustainability is contributing to a range of SDGs, as reported in their Sustainability update. Their human resources strategy of 'fair and equal' focuses on the following SDGs:

SDG 1: No Poverty

SDG 4: Quality Education

SDG 5: Gender Equality

SDG 8: Decent Work and Economic Growth

SDG 10: Reduced Inequalities

SDG 16: Peace, Justice and Strong Institutions

SDG 17: Partnerships for the Goals

IKEA and People

It can be seen that IKEA views their people and how they work together as a key part of their organisation. Their strategy, right from their vision and values through to their more specific people strategy, is centred around doing better for people. IKEA is not afraid to change what they are doing to face challenges or to be ambitious in the face of changing world needs. Their people are an integral part of their business performance, with employees who embody their culture and values and provide great customer service for their customers.

Questions

1. Which of these contemporary HRM challenges for IKEA do you think is the most concerning for the organisation?
2. What strategies would you suggest they employ to help solve these challenges?

Sources

Forsdick, F. (2024) 'Ikea's CHRO on why culture is the company's "superpower"', *Raconteur*, April 12. https://www.raconteur.net/talent-culture/ikeas-chro-culture-companys-superpower (accessed September 10, 2025).

IKEA Global (2025) *IKEA Sustainability Strategy*. https://www.ikea.com/global/en/images/IKEA_Sustainability_Strategy_2025_2030_v3_251013_f76f0e6498.pdf (accessed September 10, 2025).

INGKA (n.d.) INGKA. www.ingka.com (accessed September 10, 2025).

WHY YOU SHOULD CONSIDER WORKING IN HRM

We are going to conclude our chapter by putting the case for considering a career in human resource management, a specialised field within HRM (e.g., recruitment, reward management, workforce planning), or an allied field like employment law or HR consultancy.

Our first major argument is rooted in the observation that people as a resource are, over time, becoming more critical to an organisation's operations. There has been a shift in the 21st century as the nature of the work we are employed to carry out has become increasingly knowledge-based. We are nowadays much more likely to be employed because we have expertise or experience in a specialist field than we are for our physical muscle power or willingness to carry out a physical task. There are, of course, still many manual jobs that people carry out, but they comprise an ever-smaller proportion of the total. Moreover, manual jobs are increasingly 'skilled' or 'semi-skilled' in nature, requiring some kind of specialist qualification or the completion of a specific apprenticeship. Kay (2024: 2) puts it succinctly when he argues that nowadays 'the workers are the means of production'.

A major consequence of this ongoing change is that recruiting, retaining, engaging and motivating people, whether or not they are directly employed by an organisation, is becoming an increasingly vital strategic imperative for employing organisations. When a company's activities are carried out by less highly skilled or unskilled labour, it is not hugely problematic when an individual employee leaves. It is neither costly, nor typically time consuming to find, employ and train up a suitable replacement. There is no dip in organisational performance, and customers probably don't even notice. However, the higher the skills of employees, and the more specialised the experience and qualifications that are required, the bigger the problems experienced when looking to replace leavers. This is particularly so when chronic skills shortages abound in the relevant labour market. So, more money needs to be spent on human resources and much more time invested in effective people management.

The HR function is thus, over time, like the human resources themselves, increasingly critical to organisation success and survival. This makes the practice of HRM more challenging but also means that HR specialists have a higher profile, are better paid and enjoy greater influence than they used to have. There is no sign whatsoever that this direction of travel is going to reverse in the future. Quite the opposite in fact.

The second argument relates to AI, advanced robotics and other emerging technologies, and the relative likelihood of professions being downsized in the future due to machines being more capable and more efficient at completing the major tasks that make up a job. Views vary greatly about how many current jobs are going to disappear in the next two or three decades as a result of this new industrial revolution. Authoritative surveys, however, consistently predict that the disruption in the field of HRM will be less than is the case in most other professions. Frey and Osborne's 2013 study focused on the US labour market is the most widely cited and respected of these studies. Their analysis concluded that out of 702 major professions, HRM is the fifth least likely to be readily automated in the future. As we saw above when discussing the use of AI in HR work, many HR jobs will be affected in all kinds of ways, and there will undoubtedly be opportunities for staff reductions. But it is also true that human judgement and inter-personal relationships are always going to be completely integral to the HR role. Good judgement, wisdom and emotional intelligence can be supported by highly intelligent machines, but they cannot replace these essentially human qualities. There is thus more of a limit as to how far HR can be automated than is the case for a good majority of other professions.

Finally, we would argue quite simply that HRM work is inherently interesting to carry out. It can be immensely challenging at times because there is always conflict in workplaces.

But it is just as often fun and deeply engaging work. It is also by its nature very varied, requiring many balls to be juggled and kept up in the air at the same time. Longer term project work is carried out side-by-side with shorter term troubleshooting in response to events. People are very varied and are highly unpredictable. No two days are the same for HR managers, making the effective practice of HR immensely satisfying and fulfilling.

REFLECTIVE ACTIVITY 5.6

- Which of these three arguments do you find most appealing and why?
- What arguments can you think of for *not* considering a career in HRM?

CHAPTER SUMMARY

- The two fundamental objectives of HRM activity are to ensure that the organisation is appropriately staffed and that the staff who are employed perform their roles to a high level.
- In addition, HR managers should always look to ensure that change is managed well, that the organisation meets its equality, diversity and inclusion objectives, that well-being is promoted, that the **corporation**'s wider reputation is protected and that HR administration is carried out effectively and efficiently.
- The objectives of HR work in international organisations are the same as in nationally-based organisations, but achieving them is more challenging due to cultural and institutional differences, and the need to employ expatriate staff.
- Major contemporary challenges in HRM include chronic skills shortages in many industries, a need to improve productivity, the introduction of HR technologies, a requirement to improve equality, diversity and inclusion, and the evolution of a sustainable HRM agenda.
- HR work represents a good career choice as it is a growing profession that can only be replicated by technologies to a limited extent as so much human judgement is required.

STUDENTS LIKE YOU CHANGE THE WORLD

A few years ago, Julie and Hannah met while studying Human Resource Management at university. They both did very well on their course and developed a particular interest in employment law. Both had some prior business experience, having worked in successful SMEs, and this led them to spot a gap in the market for consultancy services. They started their business, marketing not just their capacity to provide high quality and up-to-date advice on employment law, but also to provide more direct related services. They would work with clients carrying out disciplinary hearings and completing all the required associated documentation. They would sit alongside their clients to advise them during negotiations with trade unions, provide training and also offer a wider range of HR advice beyond the realm of employment law. It was not long before they had signed up a number of clients, mainly gained by a swiftly acquired word-of-mouth reputation. They began employing other people and established their own office premises. They chose their clients carefully, building long-term relationships with people they trusted and whose values matched their own. Their business has thrived now for over ten years.

END OF CHAPTER REFLECTION

Have a look at the skills you should have developed in this unit (find more details in the Key Skills Table in the Appendix on pp. 501–2).

1 Which of the skills listed do you think you have developed the most?
2 Can you give two examples on why you feel you have now developed these skills/developed them further?
3 How will you use these new/refined skills in the future (give two examples of the impact of your development on your future behaviour)?

FURTHER READING

The following are all recent editions of first-rate introductory HR textbooks which discuss in greater detail the topics and issues raised in this chapter.

Marchington, M., Wilkinson, A., Donnelly, R., and Kynighou, A. (2025) *Human Resource Management at Work: The Definitive Guide* (8th edition). Kogan Page.

This book provides a comprehensive, practical overview of HRM in the workplace, linking theory directly to contemporary organisational practice and emphasising the interplay between employees, line managers, and HR specialists.

Taylor, S. and Perkins, G. (2025) *Work and Employment in a Changing Business Environment* (2nd edition). Kogan Page.

This text explores how evolving economic, technological, and social factors are reshaping work and employment, highlighting the strategic challenges HRM faces in dynamic organisational contexts.

Torrington, D., Taylor, S., Hall, L. and Atkinson, C. (2025) *Human Resource Management* (12th edition). Pearson.

This book offers a structured, theory-driven approach to HRM, integrating core HR functions with analytical frameworks and decision-making tools to guide effective people management.

Wilkinson, A., Redman, T., and Dundon, T. (2021) *Contemporary Human Resource Management: Text and Cases* (6th edition). Pearson.

Combining case studies with conceptual insights, this text emphasises the practical and contemporary challenges of HRM, including industrial relations, diversity, and employee voice, giving students applied understanding.

Wilton, N. (2022) *An Introduction to Human Resource Management* (5th edition). Sage.

Wilton provides a clear, accessible introduction to HRM, focusing on foundational principles, policies, and processes, making it especially useful for those new to the field while contextualising HR practice in real organisations.

REFERENCES

Aust, I., Matthews, B., and Muller-Camen, M. (2020) 'Common good HRM: A paradigm shift in sustainable HRM?', *Human Resource Management Review*, 30 (3): article #100705. doi.org/10.1016/j.hrmr.2019.100705

Basanez, M. (2016) *A World of Three Cultures: Honour, Achievement and Joy.* Oxford University Press.

Bonache, J., Brewster, C., and Froese, F. (eds) (2020) *The Cambridge Companion to Global Mobility and the Management of Expatriates*. Cambridge University Press.

Boyle, M. (2024) 'Ikea lost $5,000 when each worker quit. So it began paying more', Bloomberg, June 11. https://www.bloomberg.com/news/features/2024-06-11/how-ikea-keeps-its-store-workers-from-quitting (accessed September 10, 2025).

Cheng, J.Y.-J. and Groysberg, B. (2020) 'How corporate cultures differ around the world', *Havard Business Review*, January 8. https://hbr.org/2020/01/how-corporate-cultures-differ-around-the-world (accessed September 10, 2025).

CIPD (2024) *Equality, Diversity and Inclusion (EDI) in the Workplace*. CIPD Factsheet. https://www.cipd.co.uk/knowledge/fundamentals/relations/diversity/factsheet (accessed September 10, 2025).

Crenshaw, K. (1991) 'Mapping the Margins: Intersectionality, Identity Politics, and Violence against Women of Color', *Stanford Law Review*, 43 (6): 1241–99. doi.org/10.2307/1229039

Dastin, J. (2018) 'Insight – Amazon scraps secret AI recruiting tool that showed bias against women', *Reuters*, October 11. https://www.reuters.com/article/world/insight-amazon-scraps-secret-ai-recruiting-tool-that-showed-bias-against-women-idUSKCN1MK0AG/ (accessed September 10, 2025).

Frey, C.B. and Osborne, M.A. (2013) 'The future of employment: How susceptible are jobs to computerisation?', *Technological Forecasting and Social Change*, 114 (1): 254–80. doi.org/10.1016/j.techfore.2016.08.019

Goffman, E. (1963) *Stigma: Notes on the Management of Spoiled Identity.* Prentice-Hall.

Hall, E. and Hall, M. (1990) *Understanding Cultural Differences*. Intercultural.

Hofstede, G. (1980) *Culture's Consequences: Software of the Mind*. Sage.

Hofstede, G. (2004) *Cultures and Organizations: Software of the Mind* (2nd edition). McGraw Hill.

Hunt, V., Yee, L., Prince, S., and Dixon-Fyle, S. (2018) *Delivering Through Diversity.* McKinsey & Company. https://www.mckinsey.com/capabilities/people-and-organizational-performance/our-insights/delivering-through-diversity (accessed September 10, 2025).

IKEA (n.d.a) 'The IKEA vision and values'. https://www.ikea.com/gb/en/this-is-ikea/ about-us/the-ikea-vision-and-values-pub9aa779d0/ (accessed December 17, 2025).

IKEA (n.d.b) 'How we work'. https://www.ikea.com/global/en/our-business/how-we-work/ (accessed December 17, 2025).

IKEA Jobs (n.d.) 'IKEA Jobs | See all job openings'. https://jobs.ikea.com/en (accessed December 17, 2025).

INGKA (2023) 'Ingka Group prioritizes co-worker everyday wellbeing'. https://www.ingka.com/newsroom/ingka-group-prioritizes-co-worker-everyday-wellbeing/ (accessed December 17, 2025).

Kay, J. (2024) *The Corporation in the 21st Century: Why (almost) Everything We Are Told About Business Is Wrong.* Profile.

Kemp, N. (2024) 'Ikea sets sights on youth appeal with Roblox jobs', *Creative Brief,* July 11. https://www.creativebrief.com/bite/hot-pick/ikea-sets-sights-youth-appeal-roblox-jobs (accessed September 10, 2025).

Office for National Statistics (ONS) (2025) 'Gender pay gap in the UK: 2025', *ONS*, October 23. https://www.ons.gov.uk/employmentandlabourmarket/peopleinwork/earningsandworkinghours/bulletins/genderpaygapintheuk/2025 (accessed December 19, 2025).

Özbilgin, M.F., & Woodward, D. (2004) '"Belonging" and "otherness": Sex equality in banking in Turkey and Britain', *Gender, Work, and Organization*, 11 (6): 668–88. http://doi.org/10.1111/j.1468-0432.2004.00254.x

Song, J.-W. (2021) 'How MNE subsidiaries transfer HRM practices in distant environments: A tale of two IKEA subsidiaries', *Journal of International Management*, 27 (2): article #100850. http://doi.org/10.1016/j.intman.2021.100850

Stankevičiūtė, Ž. and Savanevičienė, A. (2018) 'Designing sustainable HRM: The core characteristics of emerging field', *Sustainability,* 10 (12): article #4798. http://doi.org/10.3390/su10124798

Torrington, D., Hall, L., Taylor, S., and Atkinson, C. (2020) *Human Resource Management* (11th edition). Pearson.

UK Government (2015) 'Equality Act 2010: Guidance', *gov.uk*. https://www.gov.uk/guidance/equality-act-2010-guidance (accessed September 10, 2025).

Wolf, M. (2020) 'The UK's employment and productivity puzzle'. *Financial Times*, January 30. https://www.ft.com/content/a470b09a-4276-11ea-a43a-c4b328d9061c (accessed September 12, 2025).

6
MARKETING

Mihaela Bishop, Adam Smith, and Emma Wood

INTENDED LEARNING OUTCOMES

After reading this chapter, you should be able to:

1. Recognise, understand and evaluate the role of marketing in organisations.
2. Recognise and evaluate the importance of developing a detailed understanding of the customer journey to enhance the customer experience.
3. Evaluate how a range of relevant marketing strategies and frameworks might be deployed to secure organisational success.

SUSTAINABLE DEVELOPMENT GOALS

In this chapter, the following SDGs will be addressed:

- SDG 3: Good Health and Well-being - Ethical marketing promotes responsible advertising, e.g. in industries like healthcare and food, ensuring consumers make informed and healthy choices.
- SDG 4: Quality Education - Supporting educational initiatives though marketing sponsorships and partnerships. Collaborating with educational institutions.
- SDG 5: Gender Equality - Inclusive marketing strategies challenge stereotypes and ensure representation of diverse genders and identities, fostering equality in branding and advertising.
- SDG 8: Decent Work and Economic Growth - Marketing plays a key role in driving ethical and consumer-focused strategies.
- SDG 9: Industry, Innovation, and Infrastructure - Digital and innovative marketing approaches support business growth and the development of resilient, future-ready industries.
- SDG 10: Reduced Inequalities - Ethical marketing practices ensure accessibility and inclusivity, preventing discrimination and making products and services available to underserved communities.

INTRODUCTION

In this chapter, you will build a strong understanding of the basic principles that underpin effective **marketing** in modern organisations. There are three sections that outline the key **skills** and knowledge that every marketer needs in order to add value to their organisation:

1 Understanding the marketplace
2 Maximising **customer value**
3 Growing in dynamic markets

In today's environment where online communication is constantly available and open to everyone, some assume that marketing is easy and that anyone can effectively identify and reach new markets. However, this chapter will show why this is not the case. Marketing is a complex, evolving and challenging field and good, evidence-led marketing can add measurable value to an organisation.

What Is Marketing and Why Is It Important?

So, what is marketing? The American Marketing Association (AMA) definition emphasises the broad scope of marketing activities, including value creation and exchange, along with a focus on **stakeholders** beyond just customers. '**Marketing** is the activity, set of institutions, and processes for creating, communicating, delivering, and exchanging offerings that have value for customers, clients, partners, and society at large' (American Marketing Association, 2017).

Philip Kotler and Kevin Keller focus on marketing as both a scientific and creative process aimed at fulfilling needs profitably. Marketing can be viewed as the science and art of exploring, creating, and delivering value to satisfy the needs of a target market at a profit. The role of marketing is also to identify unfulfilled needs and desires within markets. Crucially, it also needs to define, measure and quantify the size of the identified market and the profit potential (Kotler and Keller, 2016).

The Chartered Institute of Marketing (CIM) define marketing as 'the management process responsible for identifying, anticipating, and satisfying customer requirements profitably' (CIM, 2023). This definition highlights the managerial aspects of marketing, with a strong focus on profitability. This is not an easy thing to do and it takes real skill to develop a marketing strategy that meets clearly defined objectives and adds value to an organisation in a cost-effective way.

Marketing also serves an essential function as the bridge between businesses and consumers, fulfilling economic and social functions that sustain both **commerce** and society. From a practical, utilitarian perspective, marketing creates value by identifying and meeting consumer needs, which enhances overall well-being (Kotler and Keller, 2016). It enables businesses to communicate the usefulness of their products and services, effectively adding value to both parties.

Philosophically, marketing reflects the broader idea of exchange in **social contract theory**, where businesses and consumers enter into mutually beneficial relationships

(Smith, 1776). Though **capitalism** is often associated with financial gain, in a modern capitalist system, marketing is not only about profit but also about fostering trust, reputation, and long-term customer loyalty (Aaker, 1996). Moreover, ethical marketing practices often play a key role in shaping consumer behaviour and promoting **sustainability**. This aligns with principles of Kantian ethics, where the duty and moral responsibility of both individuals and organisations is emphasised (Schlegelmilch, 1998).

Yet like many subjects in this book, there is often debate and misunderstanding around common terminology. Below you will find three common areas where using the correct terminology can help you to show your understanding of marketing.

B2B Versus B2C Marketing

B2B (Business-to-Business) and B2C (Business-to-Consumer) marketing are distinguished principally by their target audiences and strategies.

B2B marketing aims to provide products or services to other businesses. It emphasises rational decision-making, lengthy sales cycles, and relationship building because purchases are often high-value and include several stakeholders (Kotler and Keller, 2016). B2B marketing is primarily dependent on personal selling and specific product knowledge.

In contrast, *B2C marketing* centres on individual consumers. It focuses on emotional appeal, shorter decision-making processes, and mass communication tactics such as advertising and digital marketing to influence customer behaviour (Solomon et al., 2016). B2C marketing often focuses on increasing brand awareness and driving immediate purchases.

Branding Versus Marketing

Branding and marketing are two linked but distinct concepts.

- **Marketing** encompasses the activities, strategies, and processes involved in promoting and selling products or services in order to meet consumer wants and achieve organisational objectives (Kotler and Keller, 2016). It covers market research, product creation, pricing, distribution, and communication strategies.
- **Branding**, on the other hand, aims to create a distinct identity for a product, service, or the business. It involves shaping the perceptions, feelings, and experiences that individuals identify with a brand, which influence their loyalty and long-term value (Aaker, 1996). While marketing generates short-term revenue, branding creates long-lasting client relationships and uniqueness.

Customer Versus Consumer

In many circumstances, the words 'customer' and 'consumer' are used interchangeably. However, it is critical to fully understand the distinction because having an in-depth understanding of your target audience is one of the most fundamental elements for efficient marketing.

Understanding that your 'customer' is not always the 'consumer' of your product may help you in developing more engaging and effective marketing campaigns.

MINI CASE STUDY 6.1

Baby Food

An example of this is how the person purchasing baby food (the customer) is not the same as the person eating it (the consumer). In this scenario, your marketing efforts are more likely to be successful if you convince the customer rather than the consumer; after all, not many newborns buy their own food! In contrast, if you are a toy producer, you may focus on making the toy appealing and desirable to the youngster who will play with it (the consumer), rather than the family member who may purchase it (the customer). In this situation, you may use so-called 'pester power' - the ability of children to convince their parents - to secure the sale. However, like with all marketing, you must ensure that it is ethical, and additional care should be taken when intentionally targeting minors, both ethically and legally.

So even with just this cursory look at the definition of common marketing terms, we can see how complex and challenging good marketing practices can be. As the world of business changes, marketers can play a significant role in identifying new opportunities, better understanding marketplace needs and communicating the value that organisations can bring. This makes it an exciting and rewarding career choice for anyone looking to play an active role in the modern business world.

A Timeline of Marketing

Perhaps surprisingly though, marketing as a management discipline and a career choice is a relatively new subject (see Figure 6.1). It emerged out of the field of economics but as commerce developed and the marketplace changed from a small, physical, local market to an industrialised, highly competitive environment, 'marketing' became a commercial imperative.

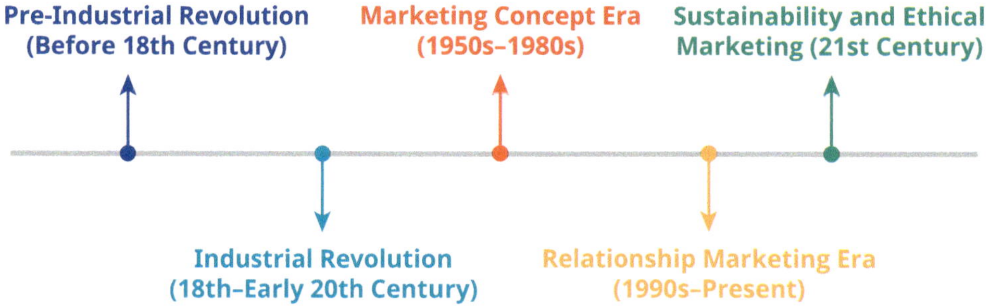

Figure 6.1 Marketing timeline

Pre-Industrial Revolution (Before 18th Century)

Bartering and Trading: Marketing activities were informal, based on direct exchange of goods and services. Markets were small, local, and personal.

Industrial Revolution (18th-Early 20th Century)

Mass Production: The shift to mechanised production increased **supply**, creating a need for more organised marketing efforts to distribute goods widely.

Sales-Oriented Era (1920s–1940s): Focus on aggressive sales tactics to move products in saturated markets. The 'hard sell' dominated this period.

Marketing Concept Era (1950s–1980s)

Consumer-Centric Approach: The **emergence** of the marketing concept, focusing on identifying and meeting customer needs rather than simply selling products.

Market Segmentation and Targeting: Marketing strategies began to focus on distinct customer groups.

Relationship Marketing Era (1990s–Present)

Customer Relationship Management (CRM): Focus on building long-term relationships and loyalty with customers, supported by technology.

Digital Marketing Emergence: Rise of the internet transformed marketing, emphasising personalisation, data-driven marketing and social media.

Sustainability and Ethical Marketing (21st Century)

Corporate Social Responsibility (CSR): Growing emphasis on ethical practices and sustainable marketing that balances profitability with social and environmental responsibility.

As you can see, marketing is an area that is often at the forefront of responding to ever-changing customer **demands** and dynamic market conditions. As professional marketers and marketing students, we need to do the same and must always be adaptable and committed to constantly learning new tools and new approaches.

REFLECTIVE ACTIVITY 6.1

- Did you already know the difference between the terms listed above?
- Take the opportunity to consider your existing understanding of the concepts. Think about how much you previously knew or understood about these ideas. Explain how you interpreted these terms previously and how your understanding has changed.
- From what you know so far, does marketing sound like an attractive career choice for you?

UNDERSTANDING THE MARKETPLACE

An effective modern marketer needs to deliver measurable impact in a cost-effective way and combine both data analysis skills and creativity. That's no easy task but the first step is to ensure that you understand your marketplace and customers better than anyone else.

In an increasingly customer-centric marketplace, companies must prioritise delivering superior value to customers through exceptional experiences and compelling **value propositions** – which essentially means the benefit offered by an organisation's products or services. This value proposition is not only about the quality or features of a product or service but also encompasses the entire experience customers have with a brand, from initial awareness to post-purchase interactions. By understanding and implementing these strategies, businesses can build lasting customer relationships, drive loyalty, and achieve sustainable growth.

Relationship marketing has become the priority for most modern organisations. Whilst some businesses – particularly those that rely on one large sale rather than repeat purchases – may be happy to have a more transactional relationship with their customers, most modern businesses recognise the value of customer loyalty and building a positive ongoing relationship. The differences between these two approaches are detailed in Table 6.1.

Table 6.1 Differences between relationship and transaction marketing

Area	Transaction marketing	Relationship marketing
Focus	Single sale	Customer retention
Orientation	Product features	Product benefits
Timescales	Short	Long
Customer service	Little emphasis	High emphasis
Customer commitment	Limited	High
Customer contact	Moderate	High
Concern for quality	Quality is the concern of the production department	Quality is the concern of all

Unlike traditional marketing, which frequently focuses on transactional interactions, market engagement aims to foster relationships based on trust, shared values, and ongoing communication. Understanding the needs, preferences, and **behaviours** of customers is essential for sustainable and positive market engagement. Businesses must have a customer-centric approach, with all marketing operations aimed at producing value for that customer. Businesses that promote engagement not only have greater opportunities to retain customers, but also convert them into brand advocates, resulting in improved word-of-mouth marketing and a stronger brand reputation. We'll look at brands and brand advocates in more detail when we consider Brand Differentiation.

Understanding Customer Value

Linked to value proposition, customer value is the customer's perception of the benefit that an organisation's product or service gives them, in comparison to its cost. *Perception* is an important word here, as it doesn't matter what value the organisation thinks it offers if the customer doesn't agree or doesn't see it. This is one reason why marketers must focus on the customer perspective and ensure that what the customers knows, thinks and feels is aligned with the organisation's goals.

Customer value is a key driver of client satisfaction, loyalty, and retention. Businesses that maximise customer value are more likely to attract new customers, keep current ones, and promote positive word-of-mouth. To effectively enhance customer value, businesses must first understand the customers' needs, preferences, and expectations. This requires a comprehensive understanding of the target audience, including demographic, psychographic, and behavioural insights. By leveraging customer **data** and analytics, businesses may obtain significant insights into consumer behaviour, preferences, and pain points, allowing them to adapt their products and services accordingly (see Figure 6.2).

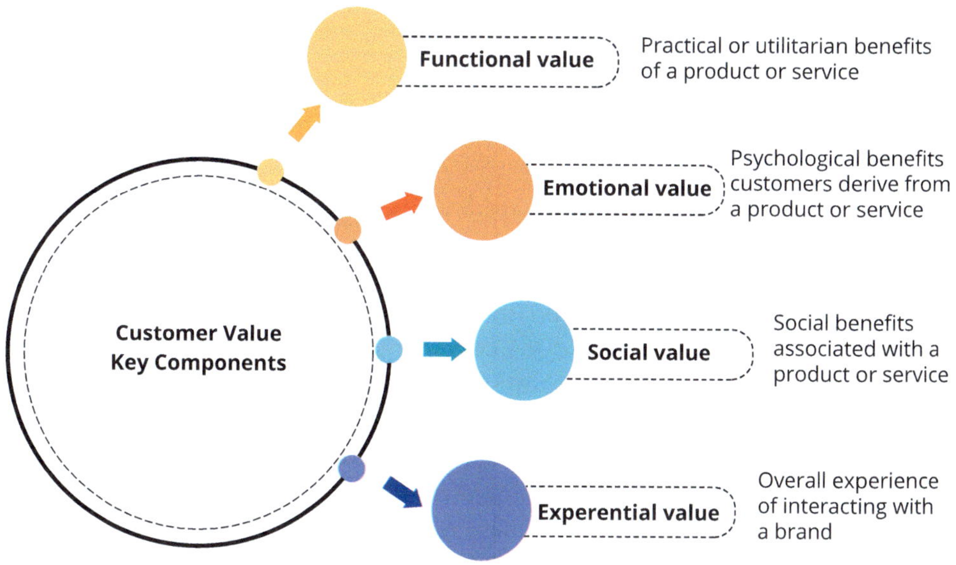

Figure 6.2 Customer value - key components

To gain an extensive understanding of the factors that influence their decisions, businesses must engage in:

- active listening,
- conducting ongoing research, and
- fostering honest communication.

By doing so, businesses can tailor their products or services to align closely with customer expectations, ensuring they meet current demands while also anticipating potential future desires. This comprehensive understanding enables businesses to create a more personalised and meaningful experience for customers, eventually developing lasting relationships and enhancing customer satisfaction.

MINI CASE STUDY 6.2

John Lewis Partnership

An example of an organisation that uses research to build a strong and detailed understanding of their consumers is the UK retailer John Lewis Partnership. Not only do they collate data via their loyalty card scheme, they also regularly undertake consumer testing and respond very effectively to online feedback. This has helped them to adapt to changing consumer trends, anticipate customer demands and position their organisation clearly in a highly competitive and challenging marketplace.

Customer Experience Management

Achieving a personalised and meaningful experience for customers is no easy task. Customer experience management (CEM) is responsible for managing and improving all consumer interactions with a brand throughout the customer journey. Every touchpoint, from the initial point of contact to post-purchase assistance, represents an opportunity to engage and create a positive experience.

To effectively manage the customer experience, businesses must first map the customer journey. Customer journey mapping (Bell et al., 2013) is an effective method for understanding and improving the customer experience. It involves visualising the entire customer journey, identifying critical touchpoints, and evaluating customer interactions at each level. By mapping out the customer journey, businesses can gain valuable insights into the customer's thoughts, emotions, and behaviours at each stage of the interaction. Additionally, gathering feedback and data from customers can provide valuable insights into areas that need improvement and help tailor strategies to better meet their needs.

The information gained through a detailed customer journey mapping exercise can then be used to tailor marketing strategies, streamline processes, and ultimately enhance the overall customer experience. This might include tasks such as offering additional customer support or creating a more consistent experience across digital and in-person channels.

MINI CASE STUDY 6.3

Accessibility

Journey mapping can also highlight accessibility issues, which may be making it harder for customers with disabilities to access your products and services. Simple steps, such as creating a website that can easily be accessed by screen readers, or choosing more distinctive and contrasting colours, can significantly improve the experience of these customers who may previously have struggled to access your content.

By focusing on these key areas, businesses can ensure that customers receive a seamless and enjoyable experience every step of the way. In today's competitive landscape, investing in understanding and improving the customer experience through journey mapping is essential for maintaining a strong brand reputation and driving business growth.

A strong understanding of the customer experience (CX) is a crucial component of maximising customer value – it considers all interactions a customer has with a brand along their journey, from awareness and consideration to purchase and post-purchase stages. A positive customer experience at each of these stages can result in improved satisfaction, loyalty, and advocacy, whereas a negative experience can drive customers away and damage a brand's image. A well-managed customer experience can lead to increased customer loyalty, positive word-of-mouth referrals, and ultimately, higher revenue for the brand (see Figure 6.3).

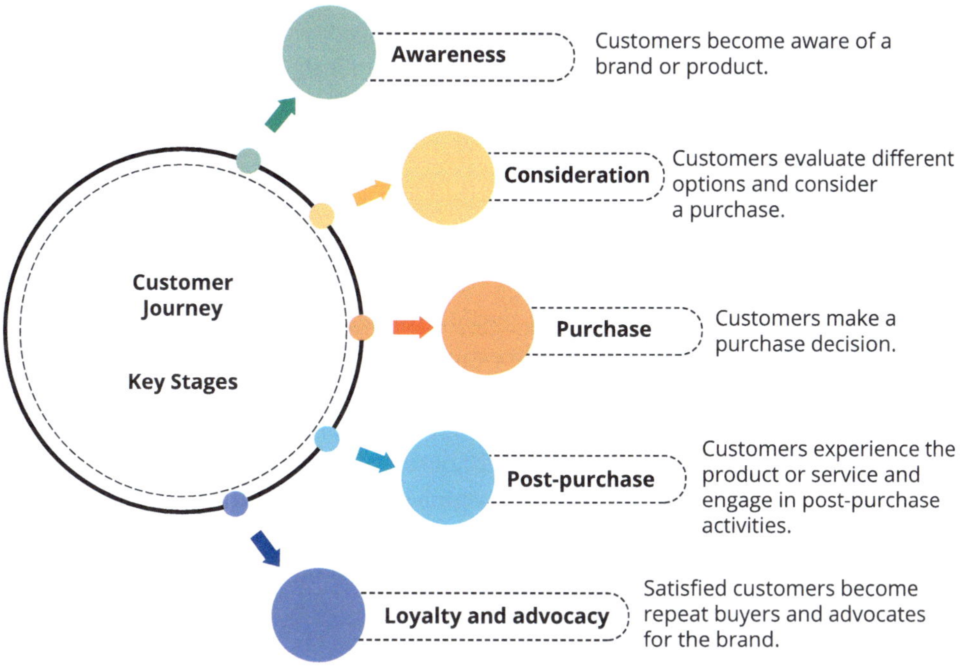

Figure 6.3 Customer journey – key stages

Some of the most useful strategies to enhance customer experience are detailed in Table 6.2.

Table 6.2 Strategies to enhance customer experience

Strategy	Description	Best practice
Personalisation	Tailoring experiences and communications to individual customer preferences and behaviours	Utilising **data analytics** and customer segmentation to enable targeted marketing
Omnichannel engagement	Providing a seamless experience across all channels, including online, offline, mobile, and social media	Integrating customer data and interactions across all touchpoints
Proactive customer support	Anticipating customer needs and providing proactive support, such as live chat, chatbots, and self-service options	Resolving issues quickly to enhance customer satisfaction
Customer feedback and continuous improvement	Actively seeking customer feedback through surveys, reviews, and social media	Using this feedback to improve products, services, and experiences

Crafting a Compelling Value Proposition

Given the importance of a strong, compelling value proposition, it's important to understand how organisations recognise, create, and communicate these. As we saw, a strong value proposition is critical to maximising customer value. It emphasises the distinct benefits and advantages of a product or service, explaining why customers should choose it over competitors. A good value proposition therefore addresses customers' requirements, desires, and pain points, to help the business to stand out in the marketplace.

Designing a strong value proposition requires an organisation to recognise the fundamental advantages of a product or service. This may not always be obvious. One classic example of this is the fast-food chain McDonalds, whose value is often linked to the speed of their service and convenience of their locations rather than their products specifically.

A common mistake that organisations make when trying to find their value proposition is to place too much attention on features that are actually not important to the customer. Rather than focusing on a new piece of technology or organisational strength, the first question should always be, 'what does the customer need' (see Figure 6.4).

A number of **models** exist to help organisations better understand the value they offer.

Finding the right 'value' demands an in-depth awareness of:

- customer wants and preferences, and
- an evaluation of competitors' products.

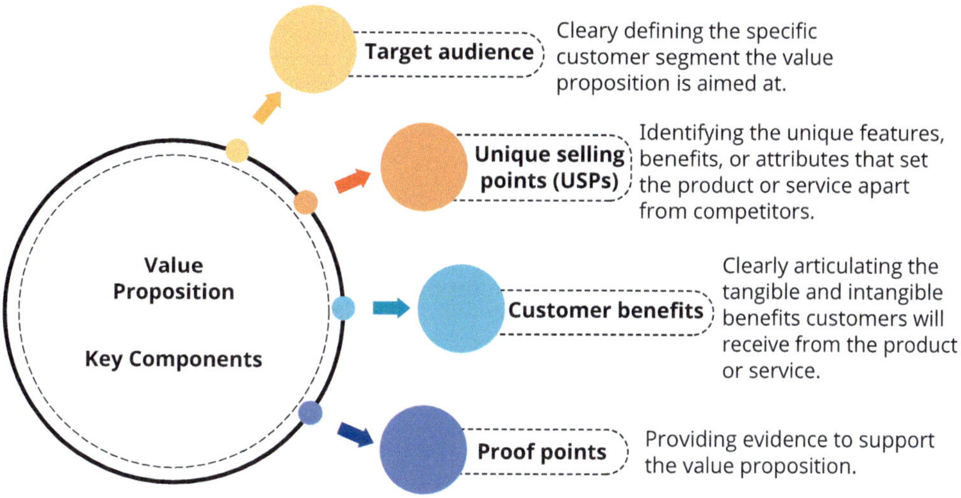

Figure 6.4 Value proposition - key components

Some of the strategies used by businesses who aim to deliver a compelling value proposition are described in Table 6.3.

Table 6.3 Strategies to develop a compelling value proposition

Strategy	Description	Best practice
Customer Centric Approach	Focusing on the needs and desires of the target audience, rather than the features of the product or service.	By understanding customer pain points and being clear about how their product or service addresses them, companies can build compelling propositions that are competitive in the marketplace and attractive to potential consumers.
Competitive Analysis	Analysing competitors' value propositions and identifying opportunities to differentiate.	Having a strong understanding of competitors' strengths and weaknesses helps to identify opportunities and gaps in the markets.
Clarity and Simplicity	Communicating the value proposition in a clear, concise, and compelling manner.	Businesses should avoid jargon and complex language and focus on the key benefits that matter most to customers.
Consistent Messaging	Ensuring consistent messaging across all marketing channels and customer touchpoints.	The value proposition should be reflected in all marketing communications, from advertising and website content to sales materials and customer support interactions.

Communicating Value

Once an organisation has identified their 'value', the next stage is to effectively communicate this. Generally, a compelling value proposition should be:

- clear,
- simple,
- customer-focused, and
- emphasise the precise benefits that are most important to customers.

We will look in more detail at effective communications when considering promotions and the **marketing communications mix**.

CASE STUDY 6.1

WaterAid - Transforming Lives Through Sustainable Water Solutions

Founded in 1981, WaterAid has cultivated a unique value proposition within the saturated non-profit industry by defining itself as more than only a water charity. The organisation's marketing strategy focuses on three fundamental value components:

- sustainable solutions
- community empowerment
- systemic change

Their core value proposition is conveyed through its 'water for good' branding, highlighting that its solutions foster enduring transformation rather than transient solutions. This is exemplified by their community ownership approach, wherein local communities are educated and empowered to sustain their own water infrastructure. This method guarantees sustainability while offering engaging narratives for donor involvement.

WaterAid distinguishes itself in the market by employing an integrated strategy to water, sanitation and hygiene (known as WASH). Instead of tackling these challenges separately, they promote their comprehensive strategy that integrates infrastructure development with behavioural change initiatives. This thorough technique appeals significantly to institutional funders and business partners desiring measurable long-term effect.

The organisation has utilised technology in its marketing initiatives effectively. Their digital campaigns frequently incorporate interactive components that enable donors to see their influence, while their use of mobile technology for project monitoring ensures transparency that attracts contemporary donors who seek accountability - as exemplified by the WaterAid Interactive Map project. WaterAid's marketing strategy highlights the cascading impacts of access to clean water. They clearly convey the influence of their work on education, gender equality, and economic growth. This comprehensive approach enables them to attract funders interested in various sustainable development goals, hence broadening their potential supporter base. The Deliver Life initiative significantly enhanced the comprehension and implementation of proper hygiene practices for thousands in Ethiopia, Malawi, and Rwanda.

WaterAid has established a robust brand symbolising knowledge and trustworthiness in the WASH industry via smart collaborations with companies and governments. Their explicit expression of technical proficiencies, coupled with emotive narrative, makes a persuasive argument for funding that distinguishes them from other water-centric organisations.

Questions

1. How does WaterAid's emphasis on sustainable solutions and community ownership enhance their marketing appeal compared to organisations focused solely on water infrastructure installation?
2. How does WaterAid's focus on broader development outcomes (education, gender equality, economic development) strengthen their value proposition?
3. What role does technology play in WaterAid's marketing strategy (wateraid.org), and how does it contribute to donor trust and engagement? Consider both their project implementation and communication approaches.

Source

WaterAid (n.d.) www.wateraid.org (accessed November 4, 2025).

Data-Driven Decision-Making

In today's modern business environment, one way to better understand customer needs and preferences is data. The dominance of online communication channels, e-commerce and social media means that many of our daily interactions are recorded. This means that there is often data readily available for organisations to analyse. It could be argued that success in the modern marketing environment relies substantially on effective data analysis and data-informed decision-making.

The wealth of data now available to marketers enables them to make better forecasts, personalise customer interactions, and allocate resources more efficiently. Data-driven market analysis underpins the understanding of intricate customer behaviours and market dynamics. By integrating several data sources into their market research, businesses can identify developing patterns in customer preferences, behaviours, and industry trends. This thorough perspective develops when examining customer transactions, social media engagements, website analytics, and conventional market research data. By leveraging this information, businesses may make better informed decisions and maintain a competitive advantage.

The analytical process can uncover significant insights using several methodologies.

- **Market segmentation** identifies specific customer categories and their characteristics.

- **Predictive analytics** reveals underlying patterns in consumer behaviour.
- **Machine learning approaches** augment this comprehension by identifying nuanced links throughout extensive datasets that may otherwise remain undetected.

These analytical tools explain consumer decision-making processes, market dynamics, and prospective future trends. Although analytical methods can provide significant insights, exclusive dependence on data analysis may neglect the value of qualitative research and human intuition in interpreting customer behaviour. The application of machine learning algorithms can raise ethical problems related to data privacy and bias in decision-making processes.

By systematically analysing these data, marketers can develop an insightful understanding of their target audience's wants and preferences. This knowledge underpins:

- the recognition of market possibilities,
- the identification of possible difficulties, and
- an awareness of the elements that drive customer choices.

The combination of several data sources offers a comprehensive perspective on market dynamics, enabling organisations to identify both existing trends and upcoming changes in consumer behaviour (see Figure 6.5).

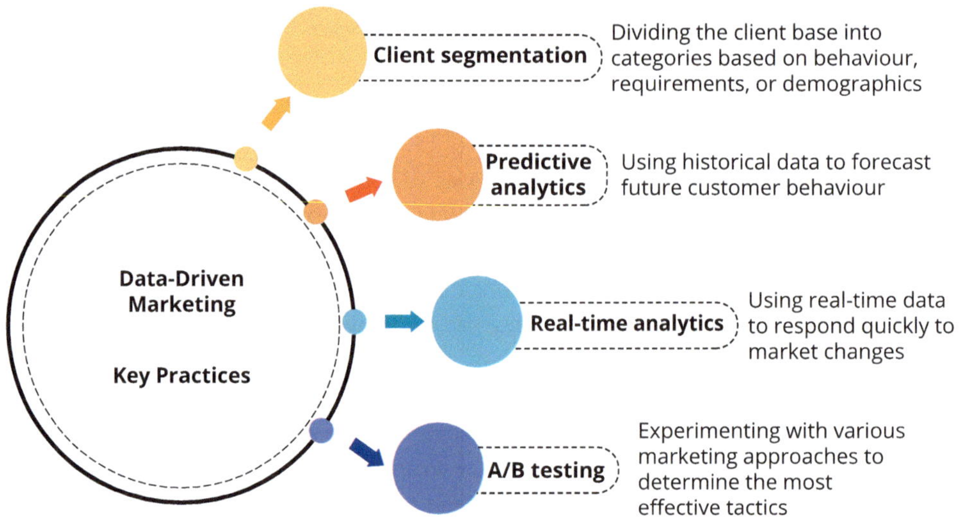

Figure 6.5 Data-driven marketing – key practices

Market Research

Technology provides us with many opportunities to collect data, but this should always be underpinned by a strategic approach to market research. **Market research** – essentially gathering and evaluating data – is an essential tool for analysing market dynamics, customer behaviour, and competitive forces. In a business environment where data is often plentiful, understanding whether data is useful can be the first and often most significant challenge.

A robust approach to market research should provide useful information that actively enables businesses to make informed decisions and respond to changing market situations. It is not merely 'interesting', it is informative, reliable and helpful in making or supporting business decisions. A structured and ethical approach to data collection, analysis, and interpretation will all be part of an effective market research strategy designed to detect trends, identify opportunities, and anticipate risks (see Figure 6.6).

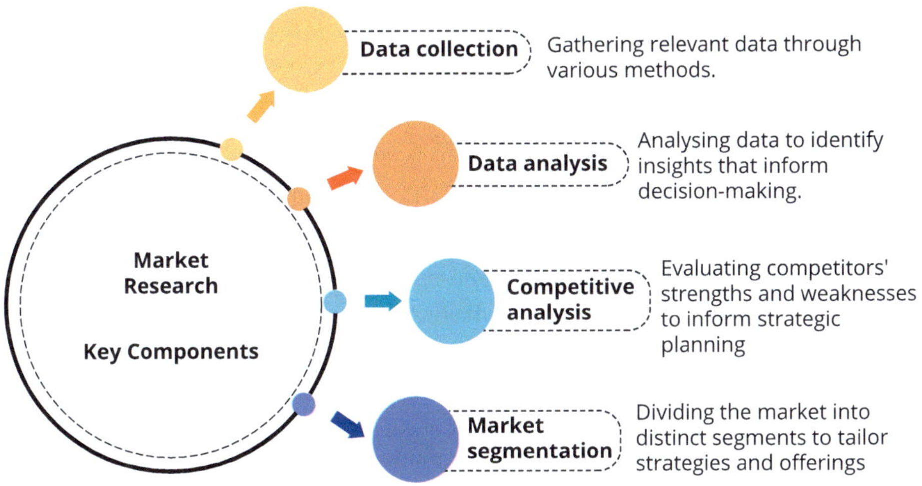

Figure 6.6 Market research – key components

Market research can be divided into two types: primary research and secondary research.

- **Primary research** entails collecting fresh information directly from sources such as surveys, interviews, and focus groups.
- **Secondary research** is reviewing existing data from sources such as industry publications, social media analysis, market studies, and competition analysis.

Some of the strategies for effective market research are highlighted below:

- Customer surveys: Conducting surveys to gather feedback on customer needs, preferences, and satisfaction levels
- Focus groups: Organising focus groups to gain in depth insights into customer attitudes and perceptions
- Competitive benchmarking: Analysing competitors' strategies, performance, and market positioning to identify best practices and opportunities for differentiation
- Trend analysis: Monitoring industry trends and emerging technologies to anticipate future changes and adapt strategies accordingly

Alongside strategic and market research benefits, technology has also had a profound impact on marketing operations and how we communicate with customers. Data-driven marketing allows businesses not only to collect and analyse massive volumes of client data to understand their journey or their preferences, it also enables highly personalised and targeted marketing campaigns (Chaffey and Ellis-Chadwick, 2022). Social media platforms have also transformed client connection, moving away from one-way communication and towards real-time, interactive involvement (Kaplan and Haenlein, 2010). We'll cover this more in the section on Content Marketing.

Technology has even changed how we obtain products and services, providing customers with more convenience and choice while also allowing businesses to experiment with new **business models** such as subscription services and direct-to-consumer (DTC) tactics (Batra and Keller, 2016).

Technology is now a feature of the entire customer journey and can have a beneficial impact at each point in the customer experience:

- CRM integration: Implementing a robust CRM system to manage customer data, track interactions, and automate marketing and sales processes
- AI and machine learning: Utilizing AI and machine learning to analyse customer data, predict behaviours, and personalise marketing efforts
- Data-driven decision-making: Using data analytics to gain insights into customer behaviour, preferences, and trends, and making informed decisions to enhance customer value
- Digital tools and platforms: Leveraging digital tools and platforms, such as chatbots, mobile apps, and social media, to engage with customers and enhance the overall experience

Key Performance Indicators

Data is also a key component when judging the success of marketing activities. *Key performance indicators* (KPIs), in other words an ongoing measure of performance against set targets, are a key feature of most marketing departments. They are essential for determining the effectiveness of marketing strategies and campaigns. Setting and monitoring KPIs allows **firms** to evaluate the efficiency of their marketing activities, identify areas for improvement, and make data-driven decisions to improve performance.

A variety of KPIs are commonly used to assess marketing performance, including customer acquisition, conversion rates, **customer retention**, and return on investment (ROI).

Some of the most common marketing KPIs:

- **Customer Acquisition Cost (CAC):** the total cost of acquiring a new customer, including marketing and sales expenses.
- **Customer Lifetime Value (CLV):** the total revenue a business can expect from a customer over the duration of their relationship.

- **Conversion Rate:** the percentage of visitors to a website or landing page who complete a desired action, such as making a purchase or signing up for a newsletter.
- **Return on Marketing Investment (ROMI):** the revenue generated from marketing activities relative to the cost of those activities.
- **Net Promoter Score (NPS):** a measure of customer satisfaction and loyalty based on the likelihood of customers recommending the brand to others.

Making sure that you are tracking the right KPIs is an important consideration. They need to be relevant and important, but that will be different in every organisation. When choosing, the priority should therefore be on isolating a limited number of KPIs that are closely aligned with the organisation's business objectives, not simply measuring what everyone else measures, or relying on data that is easily available.

MAXIMISING CUSTOMER VALUE

In today's competitive and ever-changing economy, just contacting customers is no longer enough for organisations seeking success. To stand out, companies must interact with their consumers in ways that are relevant, memorable, and mutually beneficial. Engaging the market is more than just marketing products or services; it requires creating value-driven interactions that engage customers on a deeper level, inspiring loyalty and encouraging advocacy.

The Marketing Mix

A common approach to optimising market performance is to consider the **marketing mix**, also known as the four Ps:

- Product
- Place
- Price
- Promotion

This term was first established in the 1940s by Professor Neil Borden (Borden, 1964) but remains a key principle, even today. Though constantly reinvented and adapted, this framework highlights how, by carefully considering each of the Ps, organisations are better positioned to match customer needs, differentiate themselves from competition, and increase sales.

Product

To remain competitive, businesses must constantly evaluate and improve their products to keep up with consumer feedback and **market developments**. Collecting customer data may indicate that specific product features have fallen out of demand. Consequently, businesses may adjust their products to sustain their market position. It is essential for businesses to develop and change their product offerings in order to meet changing customer demands or to penetrate new markets. For example, a company that initially provided just one version of its product may choose to add limited editions that would appeal to customers seeking exclusive versions. By expanding their services, companies could reach a broader audience and possibly enhance long-term revenue, a strategy that helps in maintaining current consumers while attracting new ones, therefore promoting growth and sustainability in a competitive environment.

Price

When considering price, businesses may often choose to implement dynamic pricing techniques and modify prices according to demand, competition and consumer price sensitivity. For example, pricing sunscreen at its highest in summer when demand is higher or increasing prices in locations with fewer competitors. This adaptability also enables the business to respond promptly to changes, optimising profitability and maintaining a competitive edge. In addition, by constantly evaluating and modifying pricing tactics, the company can improve its understanding of customer behaviour and make informed choices to boost sales and expand market share.

Many companies will also offer a range of pricing options within their product ranges, designed to appeal to different types of customers. For example, the latest laptop with multiple, innovative features will be priced high to appeal to 'early adopters'. These consumers desire the latest models and technology and are less sensitive to price. Yet many technology companies also recognise the value of customers who prefer a more cost-effective, proven option and will ensure that there is also a model for these customers within their range. This combination of product **innovation** with dynamic pricing strategies can enable companies to adjust to changing market conditions to secure both high margins and market share. However, caution must be taken not to alienate customers through aggressive or unfair pricing tactics, which might be viewed by customers as unethical or profiteering. Such an impression, once formed amongst your customer base, could have long-term repercussions that may damage your long-term brand loyalty.

Place

In the marketing mix, 'place' refers to channels and the locations where your customers buy your product, both in store and online. To remain relevant in the marketplace, businesses must consistently evaluate and adjust their distribution strategy, adopting innovation and exploring new possibilities. Companies may strategically position themselves for sustained growth and profitability in the constantly changing environment. This may include considering new markets or channels, such as e-commerce or direct-to-consumer (D2C) methods. This way, they can reach a wider demographic and engage new client segments, and in turn, increase brand recognition and market share.

Again, employing data analytics to monitor client behaviour and preferences can help businesses ensure that their items are effectively stocked in optimal places and accessible through several channels, including online platforms, physical stores, and third-party retailers.

Through optimising distribution networks, companies may enhance customer satisfaction and loyalty, consequently boosting sales and revenue growth. This strategy enables businesses to stay ahead of competition and adjust to evolving market trends, therefore reinforcing their position as market leaders.

Promotion

It may be surprising for some to learn that 'promotion' is just one of the elements of the marketing mix, as advertising campaigns, social media and sales promotions are often the first thought when considering marketing activities. Promotion is indeed an important part, but cannot be considered in isolation. After all, there's no point in creating effective promotional campaigns for your product if customers can't actually order them, if the price is too high, or the product itself poorly designed. This again would be a short-term approach that may potentially damage your long-term brand loyalty.

Naturally, a focused promotional strategy can result in more efficient marketing efforts, more consumer loyalty, and eventually, improved revenue. Particularly important in modern markets is finding the right combination of traditional and digital marketing methods for your specific marketplace. In many cases, a so-called multi-channel promotional strategy, which enables customers to repeatedly be exposed to your brand across different channels and media, can be an effective way to gain customers in a highly competitive and 'noisy' marketplace. This may involve using multiple channels of the marketing communications mix, similar in wording but not to be confused with the overall marketing mix (4Ps). The *marketing communications mix* are the techniques and medium often used as part of a communications campaign, such as social media, advertising, and public relations. Here again, investing in data analytics solutions could offer critical insights into customer behaviour and communication preferences, enabling companies to customise their promotional activities for optimal effectiveness.

Extending the Traditional Marketing Mix

The unique challenges of service marketing, where intangibility and simultaneous production/consumption require careful management of human interactions, tangible cues and operational procedures to effectively deliver and communicate value to customers, necessitated the extension of the traditional marketing mix to include People, Physical Evidence, and Process. This extended framework was first proposed by Booms and Bitner in 1981, marking a significant evolution in marketing theory that recognised the distinct characteristics of services compared to physical products.

People

The people component of the extended marketing mix includes all individuals involved in the delivery of services and customer interactions, including front-line employees, support teams and management. These human interactions have a profound impact on customer experience and brand perception. Skilled, motivated staff who exemplify brand values can foster great customer experiences while building relationships that last. They frequently represent the company and are crucial in influencing customer perceptions and interactions with the brand. Indeed, interactions between personnel and consumers can create enduring impressions – this aspect is why businesses should prioritise training and development, not only for those who interact with customers directly but also for the 'behind-the-scenes' employees whose contributions influence service quality. Research shows that internal culture, recruitment strategies, training programmes and various employment engagement efforts are essential for ensuring staff provide consistent, high-quality service (Sadeli, 2012; Kumar and Pansari, 2014).

Physical Evidence

Physical evidence includes all tangible components that customers experience while engaging with a service or brand – this might include the design and ambiance of retail environments, office designs, staff outfits, business cards, packaging, and digital interfaces. All of these physical components influence the entire perception and experience clients have with a service or brand. A thoughtfully created store environment featuring comfortable seating and appealing aesthetics can foster a sense of welcome and relaxation among customers, so augmenting their overall happiness. Conversely, outdated or unattractive physical evidence can create an adverse impression and discourage consumer return. These physical cues also function as visible evidence of service quality and brand values. For example, a luxury hotel's sophisticated lobby, immaculate uniforms, and premium room amenities collectively reinforce its premium status. In the digital domain, website design, application interfaces and virtual touchpoints serve as essential physical evidence. Ultimately, investing in physical proof boosts service quality perception and differentiates a business from its competitors in a saturated market.

Process

Processes include all procedures, systems and operations that help with service delivery and customer engagement. Examples of such processes include appointment scheduling, payment processing and complaint management. Successfully developed procedures provide consistent service quality, whereas inadequate processes could frustrate customers regardless of other marketing factors. For example, a well-structured online appointment scheduling system can optimise the booking process for customers, resulting in enhanced satisfaction and repeat patronage. On the other hand, a poorly executed complaint management process can lead to delayed solutions and adverse customer experiences. Organisations must consistently assess, adapt and improve their processes to eliminate difficulties, minimise waiting times and improve customer experience (Grewal et al., 2009), both for customer-facing processes and 'back-end' operations that provide service delivery.

Digital transformation has rendered process optimisation increasingly vital, as customers anticipate seamless interactions across various channels and touchpoints. For example, investing in technology and automation enables companies to optimise their complaint management processes and enhance efficiency. Johnson et al. (2021) outline how organisations could employ data analytics and customer input to identify areas for improvement and make informed, data-driven decisions to improve their services.

Content Marketing

Let's look at 'promotions' in more detail and the increasing importance of content creation within that. **Content marketing** is a strategic approach to engaging customers by creating and sharing valuable, relevant, and consistent content. The objective is to attract and keep a well-defined audience, resulting in profitable consumer action. Content marketing is not about selling directly to customers, but rather about delivering helpful content that expands their understanding, deals with their pain points, or entertains them. You might think that this is a very obvious approach but it is in fact relatively new for most organisations. Previously, most brands relied heavily on what is referred to as 'interruption' marketing. This means that they would find the audience they wanted to target, find out what they were doing and 'interrupt' them with sales messages. The classic example is TV advertising, where an audience's viewing of their chosen programme was, quite literally, interrupted by adverts at regular intervals. However, many organisations can no longer rely on this traditional form of advertising to secure success and are therefore recognising the value of developing content that is, in itself, of value to their target audience.

Understanding what material connects with your target audience is essential for successful content marketing. This might include blog articles, videos, and infographics, as well as podcasts, webinars, and interactive tools. The aim is that it is useful, entertaining or engaging enough to capture your audience's attention and leave them with a positive impression of your organisation. To maximise reach and engagement, content should be delivered across several platforms, including the company's website, social media channels, and email newsletters.

Some effective content marketing techniques that a company may consider:

- Educational blog posts: Provide informative articles that address typical consumer concerns
- Video content: Engage customers with stories, lessons, and behind-the-scenes glimpses
- Social media material: By using networks such as Instagram and Facebook to distribute bite-sized material
- E-books and white papers: To provide in-depth analysis and research, establishing the brand as a thought leader
- Influencers: Partnering with popular and trusted social media influencers to provide brand endorsements

Social media platforms provide businesses with a distinctive chance to interact directly with their customers in real time. Unlike traditional marketing methods, social media encourages two-way communication, allowing firms to interact with customers, solicit feedback, and create a community. Effective social media interaction requires more than simply posting promotional content. It involves actively listening to customers, reacting to their comments and questions, and engaging in brand-relevant interactions. Social media can also be used to distribute user-generated content, hold contests or surveys, and offer customer service.

Common social media engagement strategies include:

- **interactive posts** (using polls, quizzes, and questions to engage the audience),
- **live streaming** (hosting live sessions to interact with followers and provide real-time content),
- **community management** (building and nurturing online communities based on shared interests), and
- **influencer partnerships** (collaborating with influencers to increase reach and credibility).

The real marketing skill is however to understand your potential customer better than any of your competitors and develop the kind of content that they want, in the format and channels that they like.

AIDA

For many years, marketers have recognised the complexities involved in targeting potential customers with content. In fact, AIDA, one of the most famous marketing models, was reputedly invented in the 1890s (Strong, 1925). Though well over 100 years old, AIDA – which stands for Awareness, Interest, Desire, and Action, still provides a useful framework when trying to understand customer behaviour, and how people choose which products to buy (Strong, 1925). Your first task as a marketer is therefore to grab the attention of your intended audience, then you have to offer them something of interest to make them want to find out more. Then you have to convince them that your product or service is right for them, that they need it and must have it and then – perhaps the most difficult stage – get them to act on this and actually buy.

As you may notice, this is a very structured, logical approach. AIDA is one of the very many models that sit within the Hierarchy of Effects approach to consumer behaviour. These models all share the assumption that humans behave rationally and move from step to step in a linear way. Many would argue that this isn't, and never really was, the case (Vakratsas and Ambler, 1999). Whether this is entirely true or not, AIDA can be a useful tool to help marketers consider how different types of messages and even different channels may be better suited to different stages of the customer journey. For example, there's little point promoting a free delivery offer to people who have never even heard of your product. Similarly, why waste time offering lots of additional advice and information to customers who are already willing and poised to buy? This highlights the need to develop a range of communication channels and messages to suit all of your audience, whether they be potential customers who have never bought from you or loyal, repeat customers.

Community Development

If you're successful in consistently finding the right balance of communications and offering content of value to your audience, you may be in a position to build your own brand community. Community development involves creating a network of customers and followers who have a shared interest or affinity for the business. This is no easy task and very few brands achieve this. Those that do will successfully strengthen their relationships with customers by instilling a sense of belonging in them, resulting in a loyal customer base that is highly engaged and emotionally invested.

Communities can be formed both online and offline. Online communities can be social networking groups, forums, or branded communities housed on a company's website. Offline, marketers can engage customers by hosting events, workshops, or local social events. In both cases, the key to successful community building is to give a platform for customers to communicate with one another and with the business, share their experiences, and collaborate.

Creative Innovation

Content marketing, particularly content aimed at building long-term engaged audiences and communities, thrives on creative innovation. Successful content marketing transcends conventional blog posts and social media updates by including many forms and innovative storytelling techniques. Interactive infographics, podcast series, augmented reality experiences, and user-generated content campaigns can transform standard brand messaging into compelling storylines that engage viewers. An example of this is a clothing manufacturer developing an interactive infographic that enables visitors to combine various outfit configurations – this not only highlights the brand's offerings but also delivers an engaging and interactive experience for users.

Creative thinking in content marketing involves finding unique angles for common topics. Instead of following conventional formulas, marketers may investigate counterintuitive ideas, combine various content forms, or include surprising aspects that challenge customer assumptions. This could involve integrating instructional material with entertainment, transforming complex information into visual narratives, or developing immersive storytelling experiences that foster audience engagement. In reality, the potential for generating captivating material that connects with audiences is limitless.

Creativity also emerges as strategies for content distribution. Rather than depending exclusively on traditional channels, creative marketers explore unconventional platforms and collaborative opportunities. This may involve collaborating with atypical influencers, producing platform-specific material that leverages the distinct characteristics of each medium, or designing multimedia narrative initiatives which develop across several platforms. By employing innovative strategies and exploring innovative techniques, marketers can capture their audience's attention in compelling and engaging ways. Embracing innovation in content distribution enables companies to distinguish themselves in a saturated market and engage customers in greater detail. Ultimately, these unique techniques can enhance brand recognition, loyalty, and conversions.

Crucially, effective creative content marketing demands a deep understanding of customer preferences and willingness to explore innovative strategies. Success frequently comes from integrating known components with new combinations that engage attention without alienating the target audience.

REFLECTIVE ACTIVITY 6.2

Think about your own consumption of online content.

- Do you follow any brands on social media?
- Do you have ad blockers in place or do you find ads interesting or helpful?
- Do you trust recommendations from online content creators, even if this is paid/sponsored content?
- How creative do you think you are? If you'd like to test yourself, visit https://www.datcreativity.com/

Product Management

Understanding where a product is in its lifecycle is an important first step when managing ongoing success. Products at the start of their life often go through an 'early adoption' phase, where sales may be limited but the product appeals primarily to trend setters and those customers who are particularly attracted to innovative new products. Successful products will then often grow their appeal to a mass market audience, where sales reach a peak. At later stages of the **product lifecycle,** the marketer's task is to try to maintain strong sales or even manage the eventual decline of a product. Each stage requires a very different marketing strategy and tactics to meet the very different needs and motivations of potential customers and consumers (Moore, 2014).

This lifecycle can be relatively short for some products, such as mobile phones where products have to be developed and updated very quickly. Customers in this **competitive marketplace** actively want new technology and new features, so older models quicky lose their appeal and the price often reduces. In other cases, this product lifecycle can be very long and brands such as the soap Lifebuoy, which is over 130 years old (Hubberstey, n.d.), can successfully retain a strong share of markets throughout the world.

Ansoff's Matrix

The marketing model 'Ansoff's matrix' (Ansoff, 1965) outlines the common strategic approach to product management, incorporating **product development** and **diversification**.

New product development involves businesses reviewing their products regularly, to ensure that they are developing new products that meet changing customer needs. This strategy involves an in-depth understanding of customer preferences, market trends, and competition dynamics that may require a high investment in market research. Successful product creation can result in improved sales, customer loyalty, and market share, so the benefits of such an investment are clear.

Product diversification entails venturing into new markets or product categories that are different from the company's current offers. Diversification can be related (joining a market comparable to the present one) or unrelated (into a whole new market). It is important to recognise that diversification provides significant growth opportunities, but it also carries greater risks and involves careful planning and implementation (see Figure 6.7).

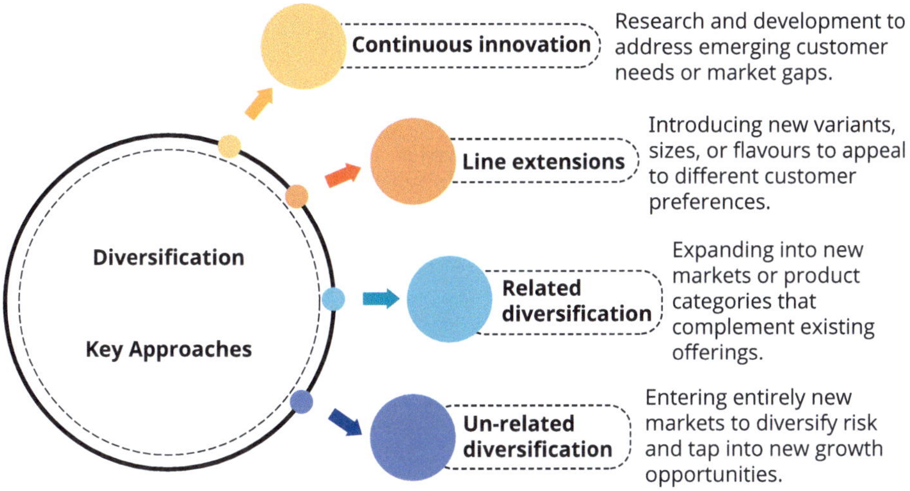

Figure 6.7 Diversification – key approaches

Market Share

Expanding market share is critical for sustaining growth, especially in mature industries where competition is intense. Companies can gain market share by employing **market penetration** and development strategies.

Market penetration aims to boost sales of existing products or services in the current market. This can be achieved through aggressive marketing efforts, promotional offers, increased product visibility, and better distribution networks. The goal is to attract prospective customers within the present market while encouraging repeat purchases.

Market development involves entering new markets with existing items. Geographic growth, targeting new consumer demographics, and experimenting with new sales channels are all possible components of this strategy. Market expansion requires extensive market research to identify growth prospects as well as understand the distinct demands and preferences of new customer segments.

For some effective strategies for expanding market share see Table 6.4.

Table 6.4 Strategies for expanding market share

Strategy	Description	Example
Aggressive marketing	Increasing marketing efforts through advertising, promotions, and sales campaigns to attract new customers	A very common tactic in gaming and apps, where audiences are repeatedly targeted with paid ads
Channel expansion	Expanding distribution channels to increase product availability and reach more customers	Often utilised as part of a maturing product lifecycle, for example where previously online brands expand through high-street retail partners
Geographic expansion	Entering new geographic markets, both domestically and internationally, to access new customer bases	E-commerce has enabled even small brands to identify and exploit new, global markets
Add new market segments	Targeting underserved or emerging customer segments with tailored products and marketing strategies	A strategic approach to growth that requires a strong understanding of the different needs of your consumer segments

MINI CASE STUDY 6.4

Student Perspective

Starting out in product management for an FMCG International company such as Unilever P&G is often an entry point into marketing for graduates who are looking to gain experience in a fast-paced consumer goods industry. Companies such as Unilever have multiple brands in the same product range and as a Product Manager, you will be responsible for ensuring that your brand or brands are clearly positioned and successful. This will often involve attending industry events and becoming an expert on current trends, as well as managing marketing campaigns and promotions.

FMCG companies operate in a fast-paced environment that offers extensive training and opportunities for career growth, making them attractive options for young professionals. Working in product management at a large FMCG company can provide valuable skills in market research, product development, and strategic planning that can be applied to future roles in marketing or general management.

GROWING IN DYNAMIC MARKETS

Sustaining market growth is critical for businesses that aim to thrive in competitive and dynamic environments. After establishing a market presence, the next challenge for companies is maintaining and expanding their market position, share, and revenue over the long term. This requires a strategic approach that focuses on:

- strengthening **brand equity**,
- exploring new market opportunities,
- optimizing customer retention, and
- driving continuous innovation.

Market dynamics are continually shifting whether through technological advancements, changes in consumer behaviour, economic fluctuations or competitive pressures. While engaging customers is a fundamental aspect of marketing, continuously improving marketing strategies and operations ensures that a business remains agile, efficient, and effective in reaching its goals. Optimization involves:

- refining marketing tactics,
- leveraging data and analytics,
- adopting new technologies, and
- improving processes to maximise return on investment (ROI) and drive sustainable growth.

This section will explore the strategies and practices necessary for companies to adapt to market changes, with a particular focus on building loyalty and operating efficiently. By understanding these strategies, businesses can refine their marketing approaches, reduce costs, and achieve better outcomes.

Customer Loyalty

Customer retention and loyalty are crucial for sustaining growth, as it's usually the case that acquiring new customers is more expensive than retaining existing ones. In some cases, business may not even recoup the income spent on acquiring a new customer until the second or third purchase. For most organisations, where there is an opportunity to take advantage of repeat business from customers, their focus is on building long-term relationships through exceptional service, personalised experiences and often loyalty programmes. Strategies for enchancing customer retention and loyalty are laid out in Table 6.5.

Loyalty Programmes

Customer loyalty programmes are a simple and effective tool for retaining customers and encouraging repeat purchases. Loyalty programmes range from a simple points-based discounts approach to more sophisticated tiered membership programmes offering exclusive offers, unique experiences or exclusive content to more loyal customers. These programmes reward customers for their continued patronage and, when done well, can also foster a sense of belonging and appreciation.

Table 6.5 Strategies for enhancing customer retention and loyalty

Strategy	Description	Example
Personalised communication	Engaging customers with personalised messages, offers, and recommendations based on their preferences and behaviour	Emails are often a great way to personalise communication with targeted discounts and product recommendations
Loyalty programmes	Implementing effective loyalty programmes that reward repeat purchases and encourage customer advocacy	Brands such as Tesco and Starbucks have led the way with their loyalty schemes
Customer feedback and improvement	Actively seeking customer feedback and using it to improve products, services, and customer experiences	Platforms such as Feefo and Trustpilot can prove to be a valuable source of feedback for organisations of all sizes
Proactive customer support	Providing responsive and proactive customer support to address issues and build trust	Apple's 'Genius Bar' has become a key feature of the company's commitment to outstanding customer care

The success of a loyalty programme depends on its perceived value to the customer. It should offer meaningful rewards that align with customer preferences and incentivise behaviours that benefit both the customer and the business. Moreover, loyalty programmes should be both easy to understand and use. Designing overly complex reward programmes or setting rigid limitations on how and when offers can be redeemed risks being counter-productive and may actually alienate or even anger customers, rather than incentivising them.

Marketing Automation

However, customer loyalty and retention are about more than just loyalty schemes. The focus for organisations should be on building positive ongoing relationships with customers and simple tools such as newsletters, emails and social media can help maintain contact and create ongoing conversations. Marketing automation can be particularly helpful here as technology has been invaluable to marketers by helping them to involve software and technology to automate repetitive marketing tasks, such as email marketing and social media posts. Automation not only saves time but also improves efficiency and accuracy, allowing marketers to focus on more strategic activities.

Figure 6.8 illustrates key benefits of marketing automation.

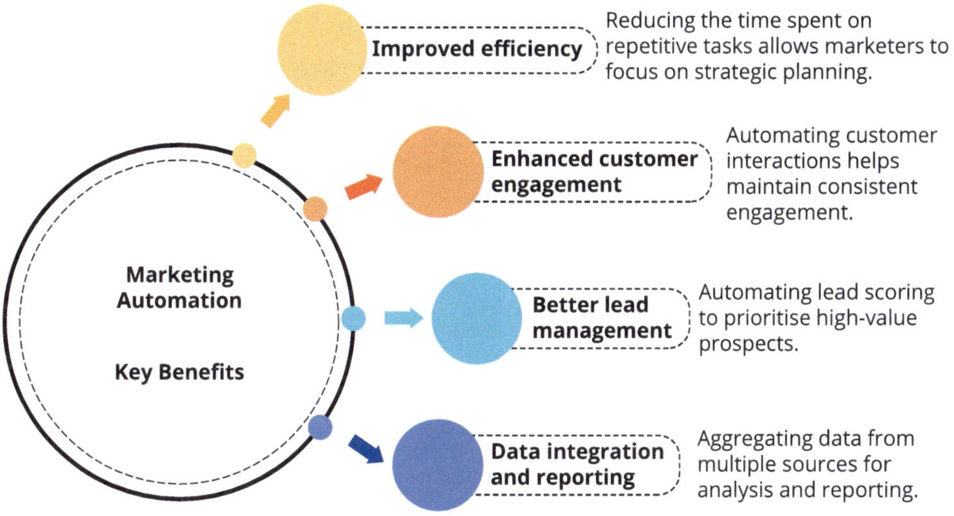

Figure 6.8 Marketing automation – key benefits

CASE STUDY 6.2

Brew Tea Co – Effective Email Marketing for Small Businesses

The Brew Tea Co is a small business based in Manchester specialising in high quality, whole leaf tea. Having started in 2012, Brew Tea has effectively utilised the Shopify website platform and plug-ins to grow its online presence.

The Brew Tea Co has a distinctive colour scheme and friendly, personal tone that is evident across all their marketing material, particularly their email communication. The simple email automation plug-in utilised by Brew Tea Co effectively leads the customer through the relationship journey in a structured and considered way.

The sample automated communications schedule below, taken from the author's own inbox, illustrates this simple yet highly effective approach.

First Order Confirmation

The warm, friendly tone utilised to great effect on the website, is carefully carried through in all communication. Through the careful use of a distinctive brand voice, a simple delivery update becomes an opportunity to build excitement and reinforce the brand's commitment to customer satisfaction.

(Continued)

Building Engagement

Encouraging first time customers to sign up for newsletters and loyalty schemes is an excellent step in building an ongoing relationship. Brew Tea use this to great effect with early encouragement to joining the Brew Tea community via their newsletter and 'Brew Coin' loyalty scheme.

Stimulate Repeat Purchase

A detailed understanding of customer types and purchasing patterns helps Brew Tea Co to send timely and relevant communications. Their engaging re-stock reminder, titled 'You must be running low...' utilises existing customer purchasing patterns to inform and effectively predict the needs of new customers.

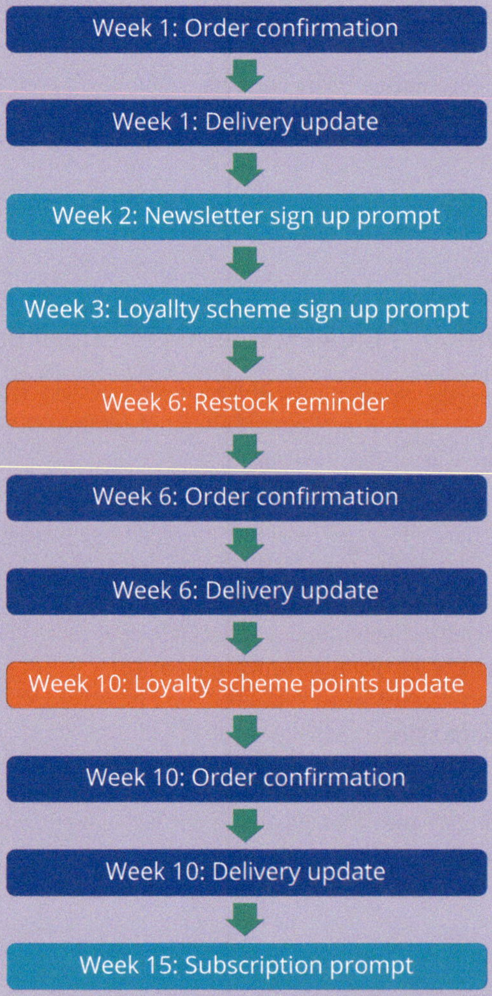

Figure 6.9 Brew Tea Co's approach to building customer loyalty

Secure Loyalty

Loyalty schemes such as the 'Brew Coin' programme provide a regular opportunity to contact customers with email communication designed to both build engagement and stimulate purchases. However, is only once a degree of loyalty has been secured through repeat purchases and engagement that Brew Tea Co promotes high-commitment activities, such as their subscription service. This enables the company to demonstrate the quality of their product and the value of an ongoing relationship with the brand before approaching customers with high-commitment sales messages.

Brew Tea Co's approach to building customer loyalty demonstrates that every company, no matter what its size, can capitalise on the benefits of a well thought out, strategic email automation process.

Questions

1. How does the Brew Tea Co avoid their emails being seen as 'email spam' and instead make their communication relevant and useful?
2. How might existing customer data be used to improve the relevance and timeliness of email communications?
3. Consider your own contact with brands you regularly buy from. Have you signed up to their newsletter or do you follow them on social media?

Source

Brew Tea Company (n.d.) https://www.brewteacompany.co.uk/ (accessed November 4, 2025).

Brand Differentiation

Maintaining and enhancing a strong market position is fundamental to sustaining growth. A strong market position enables a company to differentiate itself from competitors and often to command a premium price. This desire to build and maintain a distinctive presence in the marketplace is at the heart of branding and brand differentiation.

Branding refers to the process of creating a unique identity, image, and perception in the minds of its customers. In many ways, it can be considered as the process to create the story of a company, its vision and how it wants to be seen by its audience. As you might imagine, this doesn't happen overnight, and building a strong brand takes investment, time, and a strong understanding of your customers. After all, you are essentially trying to secure space in your customer's mind to make sure that you are their preferred, even automatic choice.

Many, when thinking of brands, will default to the logo. Whilst a recognisable logo is important, a successful brand is about much more than a logo, strapline or colour. Though elements such as these are referred to as 'tangible' brand elements, branding also incorporates more 'intangible' elements. These are often related to the value that a brand offers to its customers that may not be easy to isolate or categorise. This could be elements such as the vision, voice, or personality that a brand represents.

In 1996, the researcher Kapferer attempted to define the elements of a brand's identity via the Brand Identity Prism Model (Kapferer, 1992). He identified six key elements:

- physique
- personality
- **culture**
- relationship
- self-image
- reflection

He argued that successful brands understand the importance of each element and bring them together into a concise and clear brand positioning.

Figure 6.10 provides a simple summary of the common approaches to defining and understanding branding.

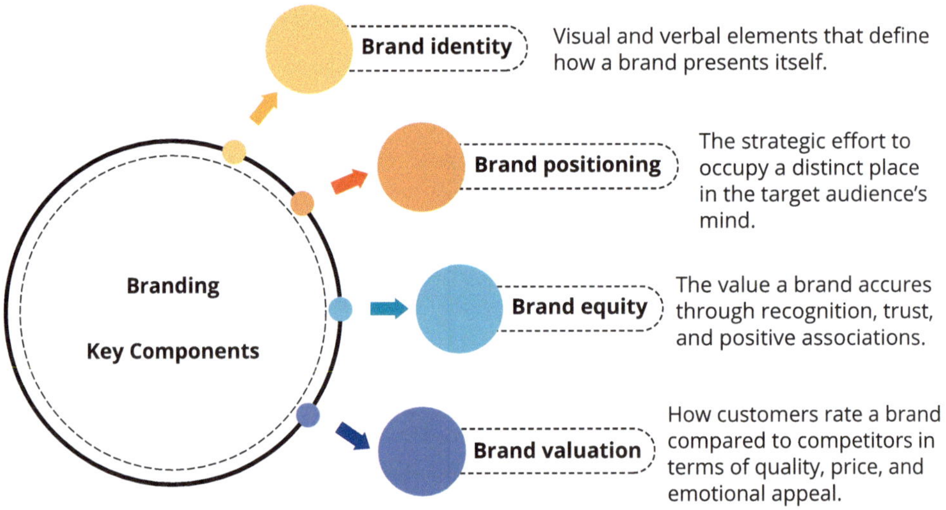

Figure 6.10 Branding – key components

Brand Equity

Let's now look at brand equity in more detail. Brand equity refers to the value a brand adds to a product or service beyond its functional benefits. It is built on customer perceptions, experiences, and associations with the brand. Again, this may not always be easy to recognise or quantify but can, over time, be a valuable asset to organisations. David Aaker has been referred to as the Father of Modern Branding and his book *Building Strong Brands* remains a core text for anyone seeking to better understand brands and how to build brand equity (Aaker, 1995).

It's important to remember that brands do not happen by accident. It takes a strong understanding of the value offered to customers and careful strategic positioning to differentiate your product from competitors'. Similarly, brands do not survive without constant investment. This often means investing in innovation to ensure your product remains relevant and continuously reinforcing brand values through consistent messaging, marketing campaigns and positive customer interactions.

REFLECTIVE ACTIVITY 6.3

Think about a brand you interact with regularly - perhaps your favourite coffee shop, a clothing label you trust, or even a tech product you use daily. Now, consider:

- What makes this brand stand out to you?
- How do you feel when you engage with this brand?

Write down your thoughts, focusing on how this brand's identity and values resonate with you.

Adapting to Market Changes

Staying relevant in markets characterised by fast-paced changes and intense competition can be a key challenge for many organisations. Continuing to offer the products and services that customers need is, after all, essential for sustaining long-term success. It involves aligning a company's products, services, and strategies with the evolving needs of the marketplace.

Changes in the market can be driven by multiple different factors. This could include new or growing competition from other organisations, regulatory changes, financial pressures or new technologies or ways of working. Responding effectively to these changes often requires businesses to be adaptable and agile. Those that take a strategic approach and successfully adapt will usually be better placed to capture new market opportunities, enhance their offerings and strengthen their market position.

Changing cultural values, historical contexts and societal norms can also drive marketing changes and adaptations. Businesses must recognise that consumer preferences, communication styles, and purchasing behaviours are shaped by local traditions, beliefs, and economic conditions. For instance, while digital marketing in North America often emphasises individualism and personal choice, marketing in many African and Asian countries incorporates themes of community, family, and collective well-being. Similarly, product adaptations are often essential to meet the needs of global audiences. This is particularly common in the food and hospitality industry: for example, fast-food chains like KFC offer vegetarian options in India to align with dietary practices. By understanding and respecting these cultural nuances, marketers can develop strategies that resonate with local audiences, ensuring both relevance and success in diverse global markets.

Figure 6.11 illustrates the key benefits of adapting to market changes.

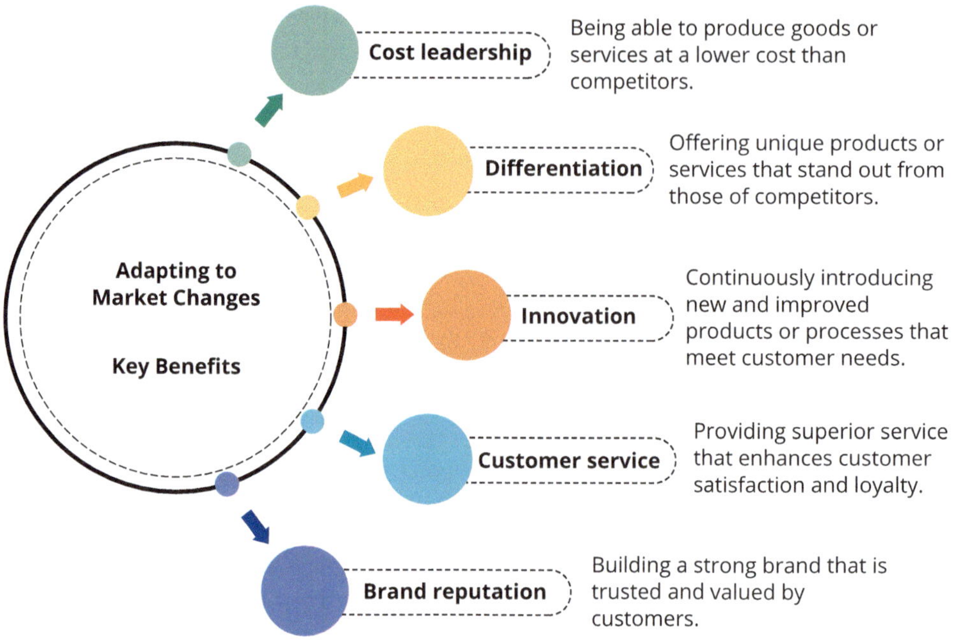

Figure 6.11 Adapting to market change – key benefits

Adapting to market changes is a critical capability for businesses seeking to thrive in a dynamic environment. By leveraging market research to gain insights into evolving trends and customer needs and fostering a culture of innovation to drive adaptation and growth, companies can remain resilient and seize new opportunities.

MINI CASE STUDY 6.5

Successful Market Adaptation

Examining real-world case studies of companies that have successfully adapted to market changes can provide valuable insights and lessons. These case studies illustrate how businesses have leveraged market research and innovation to navigate shifts in the market environment and achieve sustainable growth:

Netflix: Successfully transitioned from a DVD rental service to a leading streaming platform and content producer by leveraging market research and technological innovation.

Apple: Continuously adapts to market changes through product innovation, design thinking, and strategic foresight to maintain its competitive edge in the technology sector.

Unilever's Glow & Lovely: Formerly known as Fair & Lovely, this brand shift showcases how marketing strategies must evolve to align with cultural changes. Previously, fairness creams were marketed in India with a Eurocentric beauty ideal. However, due to increased awareness around colourism and postcolonial identity, Unilever rebranded the product to focus on skin health and confidence rather than fairness. This shift acknowledges the growing demand for inclusive and culturally sensitive branding moving away from Western beauty standards imposed through colonial history.

Amazon: Expanded from an online bookstore to a global e-commerce and **cloud computing** leader by adopting a customer-centric approach, embracing innovation and leveraging data analytics.

There are unfortunately also many examples of businesses that have failed to respond effectively to changing market conditions. They may dismiss technology that will transform their markets, their **leadership** teams may be reluctant to change or they may fail to invest in product development. In some cases, it may be multiple failings and the organisation may have missed multiple opportunities to adapt and secure their ongoing success.

REFLECTIVE ACTIVITY 6.4

Research the following brands that failed or lost significant market share to understand what happened:

- Kodak, Blockbuster, MySpace, Xiang Hu Bao
- What do you think caused their decline?
- What could they have done differently?
- What opportunities did they miss to adapt?

Strategies to Remain Relevant

Given the importance of effectively responding to market conditions, let's look in more detail at some of the strategies that might help businesses to stay relevant.

Trend Analysis

The first step in any process of adaptation is to be alert to change. Market research, such as customer satisfaction surveys, competitor research and trend analysis can help organisations to recognise risks and opportunities early on. Trend analysis enables companies to stay informed about external industry trends, technological advancements and economic shifts that may impact customer behaviour and preferences.

When considering '**Big Data**' and the wealth of data now available to many organisations, the task can seem overwhelming. However, the effective analysis and evaluation of large datasets can help organisations to gain valuable insights into customer behaviour, market trends and campaign performance.

In fact, failing to keep pace with technology and the changing needs of consumers driven by rapidly evolving technology remains a key threat for many organisations. Yet alongside this threat, technology can also present opportunities. Marketing automation has simplified what used to be time-consuming tasks; programmatic marketing enables the cost-effective targeting of segments and AI can present many opportunities to reduce the cost and workload associated with content creation.

Strategic Partnerships

Strategic Partnerships may also present organisations with the opportunity to combine expertise and share costs. This can be a cost-effective way of responding to market challenges but can also add value directly to customers by offering them access to additional products and services. Strategic partnerships with other companies, distributors, or technology providers can help businesses enter new markets or strengthen their position in existing ones. Mergers and acquisitions (M&A) provide opportunities to quickly gain market share, access new technologies or enter new geographic regions. Similarly, franchising allows businesses to expand rapidly by leveraging the resources and capabilities of their franchise partners. By expanding into new markets, businesses can access new customer bases, increase revenue, and enhance their market position.

Agility

Adopting an agile approach to marketing also offers organisations the opportunity to react quickly to market challenges. This may involve altering pricing strategies or revising product offerings. Quickly shifting marketing tactics can be an effective way of responding to customer need. For example, following your audience onto the latest social media platform and building an early presence there can ensure you have the 'first-mover-advantage'. Or switching your campaign messaging to focus on value-for-money when your consumers are facing difficult financial times can help position your organisation as a supportive and ethical partner.

Innovation

Innovation is a key driver of adaptation and growth, enabling companies to respond to market changes and create new value propositions. Innovation can take various forms, including:

- **incremental innovation** (improving existing products or processes),
- **disruptive innovation** (creating new markets or value networks), and
- **radical innovation** (introducing groundbreaking technologies or concepts).

To foster innovation encourages creativity, experimentation and risk-taking. This is not always a comfortable or welcome option for organisations, particularly when individual leader or boards are 'risk-averse'. This is often the case for larger businesses, which is why market innovation may often be led by smaller, more dynamic and responsive start-ups. These organisations can offer future marketers an exciting and rewarding opportunity to create entirely new marketplaces or challenge existing, highly developed market leaders.

Consumer Expectations

Consumer expectations often play a significant role in marketing and how businesses engage with their consumers. Once such example is the move towards personalisation. Personalisation is now a common feature of many organisations and their marketing campaigns. Customers today expect experiences that are tailored to their unique preferences and needs, not generic products or spam email campaigns. Personalisation strategies can range from simple tactics, such as addressing customers by their first name in emails, to more sophisticated approaches like recommending products based on past purchases or browsing behaviour. It can even involve creating dynamic apps and websites that automatically adjust to anticipate customer needs, based on real-time data.

To implement effective personalisation strategies, businesses usually rely on customer data. This includes using data analytics and **artificial intelligence (AI)** tools to gain insights into customer behaviour, preferences and purchase history. By capturing and understanding these insights, businesses can create highly targeted marketing campaigns that resonate with individual customers. Done well, personalisation can feel more like a trusted recommendation from a friend or trusted authority, rather than commercially driven marketing content.

CASE STUDY 6.3

Xiaomi's Adaptation to Market Demand

Xiaomi, a Chinese tech company founded in 2010, has become a global leader in consumer electronics by leveraging its adaptability to market demands. Initially, Xiaomi's strategy revolved around offering high-quality smartphones at competitive prices, directly challenging industry giants such as Apple and Samsung. This approach attracted tech-savvy consumers looking for value without compromising on performance. However, Xiaomi's sustained success has hinged on its ability to evolve, diversify, and address changing consumer preferences and market conditions.

Early Adaptation: From Flash Sales to E-Commerce and Diversification

In its formative years, Xiaomi employed a 'flash sale' model that limited product availability, creating a sense of exclusivity and urgency. While this strategy initially boosted demand, it also drew criticism for frustrating customers with insufficient stock. Recognising the limitations of this model, Xiaomi quickly pivoted to a more sustainable approach. In 2015, the company signed an exclusive partnership with the e-commerce company Flipkart and embraced e-commerce as its primary distribution channel, enabling better access for customers while maintaining cost efficiency.

(Continued)

Simultaneously, Xiaomi diversified its product offerings beyond smartphones. The company capitalised on the burgeoning interest in smart home devices, wearables, and **Internet of Things (IoT)** products. By entering these markets, Xiaomi positioned itself as a leader in connected technology. Its focus on affordability without sacrificing quality appealed to a wide audience, especially in price-sensitive regions. Products like Mi Band wearable, launched in 2014, and the Mi Smart Home Kit, launched in 2015, became staples of Xiaomi's expanding portfolio. This diversification not only mitigated the risks associated with a maturing smartphone market but also allowed Xiaomi to tap into the rapid growth of smart and connected devices.

International Expansion and Localisation

As the Chinese smartphone market became saturated, Xiaomi turned its attention to international markets. They established international headquarters in Singapore in 2014, swiftly followed with entry into the Indian market that same year. After an unsuccessful attempt at the Brazilian market in 2015, Xiaomi started their initial expansion into the EU in 2016. The company's expansion played a pivotal role in sustaining growth and meeting regional consumer needs. For example, in India, a market dominated by budget-conscious consumers, Xiaomi introduced affordable smartphones with features tailored to local preferences. Dual SIM support, long-lasting battery life, and language customization became defining characteristics of its offerings.

Xiaomi's localisation efforts extended beyond product features to include marketing strategies, partnerships, and supply chain adaptations. The company collaborated with local retailers and distributors to strengthen its market presence while continuing to prioritise e-commerce. In India, Xiaomi quickly became a leading smartphone brand, solidifying its reputation as a consumer-first company. Its success in these regions underscored the importance of understanding and responding to unique market dynamics.

The Smart Home Ecosystem and Future Trends

Another cornerstone of Xiaomi's strategy has been its focus on building an integrated smart home ecosystem. Recognising the growing trend of home automation and connected devices, Xiaomi developed a wide range of IoT-enabled products that seamlessly integrate with its Mi Home platform - now known as Xiaomi Home - launched in 2015. This now includes a growing range of products from water and air purifiers to WIFI repeaters and robotic vacuum cleaners. This ecosystem approach not only appealed to tech-savvy consumers but also fostered customer loyalty by encouraging users to invest in multiple Xiaomi products.

Xiaomi's investments in cutting-edge technologies like 5G and artificial intelligence further reinforced its forward-looking strategy. By staying ahead of emerging trends, the company ensured that its product offerings remained relevant and competitive. For instance, its early adoption of 5G technology in 2020 positioned Xiaomi as a leader in future-ready devices, appealing to consumers eager to embrace the next wave of innovation.

Xiaomi's ability to adapt quickly to market demand has been integral to its rise in the highly competitive tech industry. The company's diversification into consumer electronics, expansion into international markets with localised strategies, and development of a smart home ecosystem have enabled it to stay ahead of competitors and align with evolving consumer preferences. By combining affordability, quality, and innovation, Xiaomi has cemented its position as a global leader in consumer technology. Its journey offers valuable lessons in agility, customer-centricity, and the importance of anticipating future trends.

Questions

1 How did Xiaomi's shift from focusing solely on smartphones to diversifying into other consumer electronics contribute to its success in adapting to market demand?
2 What role did Xiaomi's expansion into international markets, such as India and Southeast Asia, play in the company's ability to stay competitive and meet local consumer needs?
3 In what ways has Xiaomi's strategy of building an integrated smart home ecosystem helped it align with the growing trend of connected devices and future technology demands?

Sources

Bardakçı, E, (2024) 'Xiaomi enters global market with new appliance launch', *XiaomiTime*. https://xiaomitime.com/xiaomi-enters-global-market-with-new-appliance-launch-24733/ (accessed November 17, 2025).

Chen, X. (2023) 'Research on international marketing strategy of Xiaomi Smart Home', *Academic Journal of Business & Management*, 5 (22): 133–37.

Martin, S. (2021) 'Xiaomi is now the world's largest smartphone manufacturer: Here's how it got there', *Kr-Europe*. https://www.kr-europe.com/xiaomi-is-now-the-worlds-largest-smartphone-manufacturer-heres-how-it-got-there/ (accessed November 17, 2025).

Panigrahi, A. (2019) 'Marketing Xiaomi', *International Journal of Management, technology & Social Sciences (IJMTS)*, 4 (2): 46–52. https://www.srinivaspublication.com/wp-content/ uploads/2019/10/4.MarketingXiaomi_FullPaper.pdf (accessed November 17, 2025).

PR Newswire (2024) 'Grow with Xiaomi: Building a sustainable open ecosystem for apps, services and content'. https://www.prnewswire.com/news-releases/grow-with-xiaomi-building-a-sustainable-open-ecosystem-for-apps-services-and-contents-302318172.html (accessed November 17, 2025).

Trivedi, N. (2024) 'Xiaomi reveals plans for sustainable open ecosystem for apps, connected TV and ads in India', *India Today*. https://www.indiatoday.in/technology/ news/story/xiaomi-reveals-plans-for-sustainable-open-ecosystem-for-apps-connected-tv-and-ads-in-india-2652792-2024-12-20 (accessed November 17, 2025).

Xiaomi Corporation (2019) 'Annual report 2019'. https://cnbj1.fds.api.xiaomi.com/company/announcement/en-us/2019_AR_E.pdf (accessed November 17, 2025).

Xiaomi Corporation (2020) 'Annual report 2020'. https://xiaomi.gcs-web.com/system/files-encrypted/nasdaq_kms/assets/2021/07/20/12-08-39/annual_report_2020_e.pdf (accessed November 17, 2025).

CHAPTER SUMMARY

- This chapter considered the history of marketing as well as emerging technologies to provide an insight into the changing role of marketing. Throughout, the importance of understanding the customer and the marketplace shines through.
- Customers remain at the heart of effective marketing and good marketers know these customers better than anyone else, either inside the organisation or in competitor companies.
- Good marketers also recognise the value of new technology and new channels in helping them to better meet the changing needs of their customers.
- Good marketers also recognise that marketing takes skill, planning and strategic thinking, and acknowledge the worth of trusted marketing frameworks.
- By applying these tools critically and creatively, modern marketers can develop effective, evidence-led strategies that add real value to organisations.

STUDENTS LIKE YOU CHANGE THE WORLD

Students who studied marketing have played a pivotal role in shaping the world by driving innovation, creating global brands, and transforming how businesses connect with consumers. Through their understanding of market trends, consumer behaviour, and digital tools, they have crafted campaigns that resonate with diverse audiences and bring attention to important causes. These marketing professionals have been instrumental in revolutionising industries, from technology to sustainability, by developing strategies that not only increase sales but also promote social responsibility and environmental awareness. By leveraging creativity, data analytics, and emerging technologies, they have influenced how we experience products, services and even ideas, ultimately changing the way businesses engage with society. Their work has empowered companies to adapt to the evolving digital landscape, leaving a lasting impact on culture, economy and the way we communicate globally.

Indra Nooyi, MBA in Marketing and Finance (IIM Calcutta) and Public and Private Management from Yale, former CEO of PepsiCo, revolutionised the company's branding and launched health-conscious product lines, creating long-lasting global marketing strategies.

Howard Schultz, Bachelor's degree in Communication/marketing, CEO of Starbucks, redefined the coffee experience globally, using marketing to create a 'third place' between home and work.

END OF CHAPTER REFLECTION

Have a look at the skills you should have developed in this unit (find more details in the Key Skills Table in the Appendix on p. 501).

1 Which of the skills listed do you think you have developed the most?
2 Can you give two examples on why you feel you have now developed these skills/developed them further?
3 How will you use these new/refined skills in the future (give two examples of the impact of your development on your future behaviour)?

FURTHER READING

Kotler, P. and Armstrong, G. (2010) *Principles of Marketing*. Pearson Education India.

A classic, comprehensive guide that covers fundamental marketing principles, frameworks, and real-world applications.

Godin, S. (2018) *This is Marketing: You Can't be Seen Until you Learn to See*. Penguin.

This book offers fresh insights into the modern marketing landscape, emphasising value creation and connection.

Trout, J. and Ries, A. (2000) *Positioning: The Battle for Your Mind*. McGraw-Hill.

This is a must-read on how to position a product or brand in the minds of consumers.

Cialdini, R.B. (2021) *Influence: The Psychology of Persuasion*. Harper Collins.

This book illustrates the principles of persuasion and how they affect consumer decisions.

Kim, W.C. and Mauborgne, R. (2014) *Blue Ocean Strategy, Expanded Edition: How to Create Uncontested Market Space and Make the Competition Irrelevant*. Harvard Business Review Press.

This title deals with creating new markets rather than competing in crowded spaces.

Ries, E. (2011) *The Lean Startup: How Today's Entrepreneurs Use Continuous Innovation to Create Radically Successful Businesses*. Crown Business.

This is focused on startups, and offers insights into marketing experimentation and iterative strategies.

REFERENCES

Aaker, D.A. (1996) *Building Strong Brands*. Free Press.

American Marketing Association (2017) 'Definitions of marketing'. https://www.ama.org/the-definition-of-marketing-what-is-marketing/ (accessed September 12, 2025).

Ansoff, I. (1965) *Corporate Strategy*. McGraw-Hill.

Batra, R., and Keller, K. L. (2016) 'Integrating marketing communications: New findings, new lessons, and new ideas', *Journal of Marketing*, 80 (6): 122–45.

Bell, C., Zemke, R., and Bush, J. (2013) *Managing Knock Your Socks Off Service*. Amacom.

Booms, B. and Bitner. M.J. (1981) 'Marketing strategies and organizational structures for service firms', in J.H. Donnelly and W.R. George (eds), *Marketing of Services*. American Marketing Association. pp. 47–51.

Borden, N.H. (1964) 'The concept of the marketing mix', *Journal of Advertising Research*, 4: 2–7.

Chaffey, D., and Ellis-Chadwick, F. (2022) *Digital Marketing*. Pearson.

Chartered Institute of Marketing (CIM) (2023) 'What is marketing', CIM, March 14. https://www.cim.co.uk/content-hub/quick-read/what-is-marketing/ (accessed September 12, 2025).

Grewal, D., Levy, M., and Kumar, V. (2009) 'Customer experience management in retailing: An organizing framework', *Journal of Retailing*, 85 (1): 1–14.

Hubberstey, N. (n.d) 'Lifebuoy turns 130'. Unilever. https://www.archives-unilever.com/discover/stories/lifebuoy-turns-130 (accessed December 19, 2025).

Johnson, D.S., Sihi, D., and Muzellec, L. (2021) 'Implementing big data analytics in marketing departments: Mixing organic and administered approaches to increase data-driven decision making', *Informatics*, 8 (4): 66.

Kapferer, J.N. (1992) *Strategic Brand Management*. Kogan Page.

Kaplan, A. M. and Haenlein, M. (2010) 'Users of the world, unite! The challenges and opportunities of social media', *Business Horizons*, 53 (1): 59–68.

Kotler, P. and Keller, K. L. (2016) *Marketing Management* (15th edition). Pearson.

Kumar, V. and Pansari, A. (2014) 'The construct, measurement, and impact of employee engagement: A marketing perspective', *Customer Needs and Solutions*, 1: 52–67.

Moore, G. A. (2014) *Crossing the Chasm: Marketing and Selling High-Tech Products to Mainstream Customers* (3rd edition). HarperBusiness.

Sadeli, J. (2012) 'The influence of leadership, talent management, organizational culture and organizational support on employee engagement', *International Research Journal of Business Studies*, 5 (3): 1–21.

Schlegelmilch, B.B. (1998) *Marketing Ethics: An International Perspective*. International Thomson Business.

Smith, A. (1776) *The Wealth of Nations*. W. Strahan and T. Cadeli.

Solomon, M.R., Marshall, G.W., and Stuart, E.W. (2016) *Marketing: Real People, Real Choices* (8th edition). Pearson.

Strong, E.K. (1925) *The Psychology of Selling and Advertising*. McGraw-Hill.

Vakratsas, D. and Ambler, T. (1999) 'How advertising works: What do we really know?', *Journal of Marketing*, 63 (1): 26–43.

7
OPERATIONS AND SUPPLY CHAIN MANAGEMENT

Kamal M. Mustafa, Abdulrahman Mahmoud, Frank Donkor, Ahmed ElKattan, Kellan Nguyen, and Stuart So

INTENDED LEARNING OUTCOMES

After reading this chapter, you should be able to:

1. Understand the fundamental concepts of operations and supply chain management (O&SCM) discipline and their strategic importance in achieving business objectives.
2. Analyse and design efficient production and service processes, incorporating principles of quality management, demand planning, and inventory control.
3. Explore the impact of technology, innovation, and sustainability on modern operations and supply chain practices, and how these factors contribute to operational excellence.
4. Apply performance measurement techniques to enhance the effectiveness and efficiency of operations and supply chains.

SUSTAINABLE DEVELOPMENT GOALS

In this chapter, we address the following SDGs:

- SDG 8: Decent Work and Economic Growth - The domain of O&SCM discipline is crucial in fostering economic development through increased efficiency, higher productivity, and competitiveness in businesses. By streamlining and optimising their operational processes and enhancing their delivery systems, businesses tend to create sufficient jobs while promoting sustainable economic growth.
- SDG 9: Industry, Innovation, and Infrastructure - The chapter discusses how technology and innovation are applied in O&SCM. Efficiently utilising new manufacturing procedures, distribution systems, and supply chain mechanisms are instrumental in enhancing strong physical structures while also encouraging equitable reuse of resources on a wide scale.

- SDG 11: Sustainable Cities and Communities - Optimising logistics and transportation to reduce environmental impact in urban areas. Supporting local suppliers and businesses to strengthen community economies. Implementing sustainable practices in operations to contribute to the development of sustainable cities.
- SDG 12: Responsible Consumption and Production - SDG 12 is directly related to areas such as quality management, inventory control and sustainable operations. These practices ensure responsible production, minimise waste, and promote efficient use of resources, leading to more sustainable consumption patterns.
- SDG 13: Climate Action - This chapter discusses how sustainability in O&SCM, including efforts to reduce carbon footprints in supply chains, aligns with SDG 13. By integrating environmentally friendly practices in operations, organisations can mitigate their impact on climate change and contribute to global climate action.
- SDG 17: Partnerships for the Goals - Effective SCM often requires alliance across different organisations, sectors, and borders. This aligns with SDG 17, which emphasises the importance of partnerships in attaining sustainable growth. Building strong, cooperative relationships within the supply chain can help address global challenges and drive collective progress toward the SDGs.

These SDGs highlight how effective O&SCM practices can contribute to sustainable development, not only improving business outcomes but also supporting broader global goals.

INTRODUCTION

The chapter is organised around several interrelated themes, with each theme building on the previous to create a comprehensive understanding of the field. We commence by exploring the strategic role of operations within an organisation. Understanding how operations strategy aligns with broader business objectives is vital for deploying resources and achieving competitive advantage. The chapter then delves into the fundamentals of process design and analysis. By examining how processes are structured and optimised, students will gain insights into how to enhance efficiency and productivity in both manufacturing and service environments. With a solid grounding in operations, we shift focus to the broader supply chain. This section covers the key components of SCM, including sourcing, production, logistics, and distribution, highlighting their interconnections and their impact on overall business performance. The chapter introduces quality management, forecasting, and **demand** planning. These topics are critical for ensuring that products meet customer expectations and production processes are aligned with market demand. Following this, we examine production planning, inventory management, and supply chain logistics. These areas are crucial for maintaining operational efficiency, reducing costs, and ensuring timely delivery of products to customers. The chapter also addresses the role of technology and **innovation** in transforming O&SCM. We explore how emerging technologies and sustainable practices are reshaping the field, driving improvements in efficiency, accuracy, and environmental impact. Finally, we cover practical aspects such as facility layout and performance measurement. These topics are essential for implementing and maintaining effective operations and supply chain systems. This chapter provides a general understanding of O&SCM discipline, ensuring that students are not only familiar with the fundamental concepts but also capable of applying them in real-world scenarios. With a foundational understanding of O&SCM, we can now examine how strategy guides these functions. Let's explore the role of operations strategy in shaping effective processes and decision-making.

What Is Operations and Supply Chain Management

O&SCM is a vital area of study that directly impacts the efficiency, productivity, and overall success of organisations (Stevenson et al., 2014). O&SCM are closely linked disciplines, in which operations management (OM) focuses on efficiently overseeing, designing, and controlling manufacturing and production processes (products and services) within an organisation, i.e., internally focused, whereas SCM extends this focus to include the flow of goods, services, and information from raw materials to final product delivery across various organisations, i.e., externally focused (Slack et al., 2009). Effective OM ensures optimal internal processes, while robust SCM integrates these processes with external partners to enhance overall efficiency, deliver orders on time, reduce costs, and improve customer satisfaction. Together, they both aim to streamline production, reduce waste and cost, and deliver value (Sanders, 2020).

In OM, the goal is to ensure that this process is executed efficiently, resulting in an output that exceeds the combined value of the inputs. Therefore, the primary role of operations is to create *value*. The transformation process can be seen as a series of activities along a *value chain*, stretching from supplier to customer. While extending the latter analogy, SCM concentrates on the input and output sides of the transformation processes. However, as the transformation process increasingly involves suppliers located worldwide, supply chain managers must also consider the timeliness, quality, and legal compliance of their operations. Figure 7.1 illustrates O&SCM as a transformation process, i.e., input to transformation process to output.

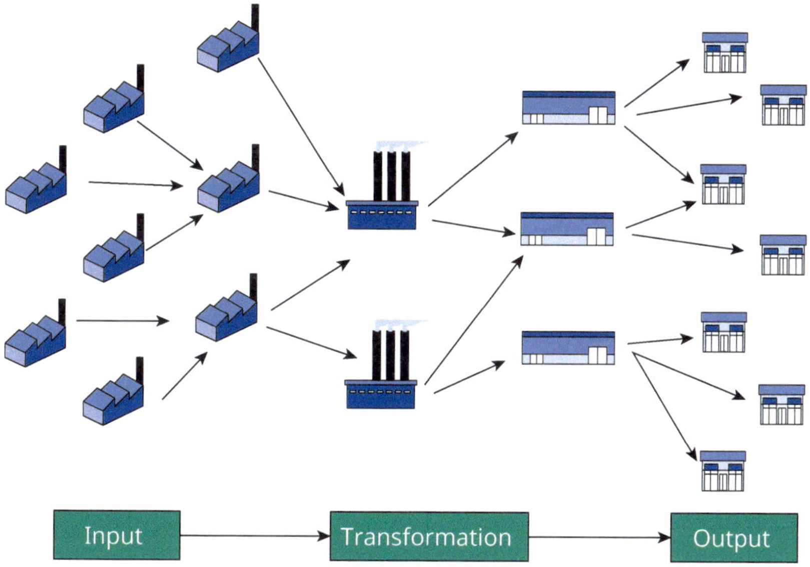

Figure 7.1 O&SCM

Source: Russell and Taylor, 2019: 9

Why Is O&SCM Important?

O&SCM are critical as they ensure the efficient production and delivery of goods and services, driving organisational success. *Operations* focus on optimising processes, resource utilisation, and quality, while *supply chain management* ensures seamless coordination among suppliers, manufacturers, and distributors. Together, they reduce costs, enhance customer satisfaction, improve competitiveness, and create sustainable value by aligning business strategy with market demands. Their importance has grown with **globalisation**, **digital transformation**, and the need for agility and resilience in today's dynamic business environment.

MINI CASE STUDY 7.1

Employability Pathways in Operations and Supply Chain Management

For Business School students preparing to enter the job market in the O&SCM field, the skills and knowledge outlined in this chapter offer critical pathways to various employability opportunities in roles like supply chain planners, operations support managers, and supply chain analysts. The demand for professionals in these roles is growing as businesses seek efficient ways to manage their supply chains, adapt to technological changes, and respond to global challenges like **sustainability** and supply chain disruptions. For instance:

- **Amazon** relies on cutting-edge technology such as robotics and AI to optimise its supply chain operations, ensuring rapid delivery and reducing costs.
- Similarly, **Unilever** has committed to making its supply chain more sustainable by achieving a net-zero carbon footprint by 2039, demonstrating the need for professionals skilled in sustainability and green logistics.
- **Walmart** also uses **data analytics** to improve demand forecasting and inventory management, in order to reduce excess stock and waste.

These companies showcase how modern supply chain roles require expertise in technology, innovation, and sustainability to drive operational efficiency and business growth. The learning outcomes of this chapter will equip students with a comprehensive understanding of the O&SCM discipline. Additionally, mastering technologies like AI, **IoT**, and data analytics, as explored in the chapter, will provide a competitive advantage in roles like supply chain analysts, where forecasting, demand planning, and data-driven decision-making are critical. Furthermore, understanding the role of sustainability in O&SCM, as emphasised in this chapter, will differentiate you from competitors.

After graduating, students can leverage their skills and knowledge to secure a position, e.g., as a *supply chain analyst* at a multinational company. In this role, you can apply your analytical skills to monitor and improve supply chain performance, ensuring that the company's operations are both efficient and sustainable. Your ability to manage projects will help you to coordinate with suppliers, logistics providers, and internal teams to streamline processes and reduce costs. Your communication skills will enable you to effectively present your analysis and recommendations to senior management, contributing to strategic decisions.

This vignette illustrates the tangible employability pathways available to business students specialising in O&SCM. By building and applying key graduate skills, students can transition smoothly from academic study to impactful careers in the dynamic field of O&SCM.

Questions

1. What key skills and knowledge areas can provide a competitive advantage for graduates entering roles in O&SCM?
2. Consider you are applying for a supply chain analyst position. How would you demonstrate your readiness for the role using the skills mentioned in the case study?

Operations Strategy

Operations strategy is a core component of any organisation's overall business strategy that helps foresee how it will grow and meet its set targets in the long term. However, in setting these long-term organisational targets, the term *strategy* comes into play which helps the organisation to critically set out its long-term plan/aspirations/targets. In simple terms, strategy is a collection of decisions and actions that drives the long-term direction of an organisation (Brown et al., 2018). Strategy shapes the broader direction of an organisation but also extends to its business and functional levels. Integrating organisational strategy into business units and daily activities ensures the practical implementation of the overall plan.

Operations strategy is the 'total pattern of decisions and actions which set the role, objectives and activities of the operation so that they contribute to and support the organisation's business strategy' (Slack et al., 2013: 70). This means that the strategy for the operations consists of more than one decision which collectively state clearly what the day-to-day activities/actions of the function aims to achieve and how well these aims are aligned with the business and organisation in general.

Organisational Strategy

Organisational strategy depicts a strategy designed to cover the entire organisation. Strategy at this level outlines what the whole organisation stands for and what the long-term goals are which can easily be seen in the mission and vision statements (Barnes, 2018). With cases where the organisation comprises of more than one business unit, strategy at the organisational level indicates what each unit aims to achieve, what they each stand for, and how resources will be distributed and managed in each of these units.

Business Strategy

In order to help meet the overall organisational strategy, specific business units within the organisation set their own aims and objectives to help define the business, and detail how the business competes with and differentiates itself from others in the industry. Note that the aim and objectives of each business unit must be well integrated and linked to meeting those of the organisational strategy.

Functional Strategy

At the functional level, strategies outlined in the form of objectives for each function or department (e.g., operations, accounting, etc.) must be created as well. It is important that these functional strategies are well aligned with those of the business strategy and organisational strategy. Some examples of questions that must be considered when setting a strategy at the functional level are:

- in what ways does the function contribute to the business
- what resources will be used
- how will it be used or operationalised

Perspectives of Operations Strategy

Despite the numerous definitions of operations strategy, there are four key pointers that runs through all of the definitions, which are known as the perspectives of operations strategy. These four perspectives (*top-down, bottom-up, operations-focused, market-focused*) collectively detail how a **firm's** operations strategy is developed.

Top-Down

The operations strategy is developed mainly based on tasks which contribute to meeting the strategic goals of the business and organisation. This shows that with the top-down approach, the operations strategy strongly supports the business strategy. For example, if a business aims to differentiate itself by offering high quality and sustainable products or services, the operations strategy will consist of tasks which keenly support fewer or no product or service defects whilst providing the exact needs of consumers under ethical and sustainable conditions.

Bottom-Up

This basically takes the opposite of the top-down approach. Thus, the operations function can gather series of decision patterns from the day-to-day activities or experiences which later feed into the designing of the operations strategy.

Operations-Focused

The specific type of product and/or services a business offers to its customers is made possible based on the capacity, processes, and resources available to the business. For example, a business can only offer high-quality and bespoke products when the business has the capacity and resources to do so. Based on this ideology, when the operations-focused approach is used, the operations strategy is developed to consist of tasks that are within the power (e.g., capacity, specific processes, and resources) of the business to operationalise.

Market-Focused

The focus is placed on the demands and requirements of the market (customers). For example, when operating in a market where the **marketing** department identifies that customers are more willing to buy products that are of high quality, delivered over a short lead time and produced under sustainable conditions, then the key operational objectives that should underpin the operations strategy are quality, speed and sustainability.

International Operations Strategy

Many organisations operate globally across multiple countries, making it essential to incorporate an international perspective when developing an operations strategy. An effective international operations strategy should enable the organisation to meet the specific needs of each market it serves efficiently and effectively, by utilising the four key perspectives:

Top-down: Aligning operations with the organisation's overall goals and objectives in the international market.

Bottom-up: Shaping and developing the strategy based on day-to-day experiences and feedback from each specific market.

Market-focused: Steering the strategy by directly responding to the unique demands of each market.

Operations-focused: Leveraging the organisation's resources and capacity collectively across different markets.

While organisations have various options and decisions to consider when crafting their international operations strategy to gain a competitive edge, one crucial aspect that has gained significant attention is *global sourcing* – a term used to describe the act of subcontracting a firm's activity to a supplier or provider mostly located in a faraway country (Johnsen et al., 2018).

PROCESS DESIGN AND ANALYSIS

After establishing the significance of operations strategy, we look at designing and analysing processes to ensure that operations are optimised for efficiency and quality. Companies follow specific processes to operationalise their strategies. The 'process' of a firm comes in the form of an arrangement of resources and activities purposed to transform inputs into outputs to meet customers' exact needs (Slack et al., 2013). The design of these processes, ensuring they are well-coordinated, integrated, and analysed across the entire organisation, is crucial for the successful implementation of operations, business, and organisational strategies.

Objectives of Process Design

Before a firm initiates its process design, it is essential to clearly define and understand the design objectives, typically guided by the metrics of volume and variety (Barnes, 2018) and the five operations performance objectives: *speed*, *cost*, *dependability*, *quality*, and *flexibility*. The process design must be closely aligned with the firm's product or service design, as these processes are directly responsible for producing the firm's offerings. For example, most of Amazon's fulfilment centres are equipped with robots; these robots are used to store and pick up ordered items in the quickest way (mostly in seconds). These items are further transported to customers making use of well-trained drivers, and distribution systems or maps integrated with **artificial intelligence** (AI) to fulfil customer orders within the shortest possible time.

Process Types

To understand the various process types, it is important to establish that all design processes fall within the volume-variety scale. Thus, the positioning of the design process on the volume-variety scale influences the classification and characteristics of the process. Although numerous terminologies have been used to classify the various process types, there are some popular or common ones typically used in the manufacturing and services sectors (Figure 7.2).

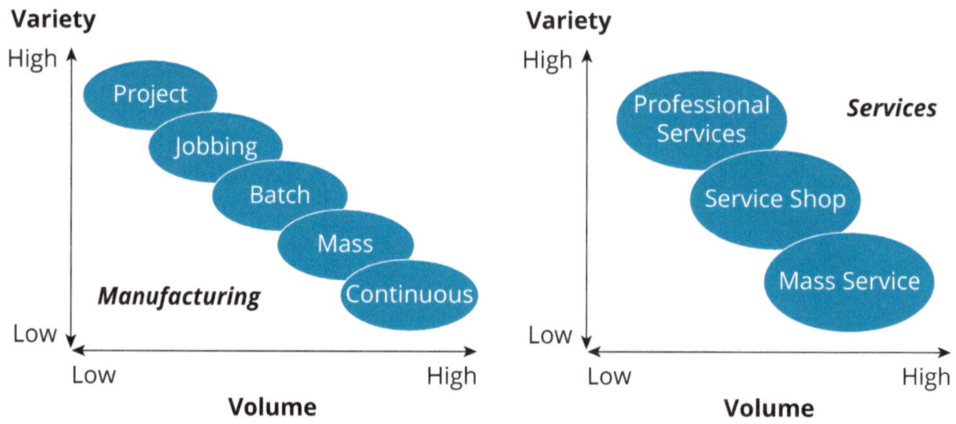

Figure 7.2 Types of process design

Source: Adapted from Barnes, 2018; Slack et al., 2013

Project

The term project depicts the process used to produce highly customised, unique, and one-off products. These products mostly have a long production timescale, and specified start and finish times. The various activities engaged during the project process are also sophisticated, detailed, and consist of the production of many items that are put together to produce the final product (Slack et al., 2013). An example of a project is a building or bridge construction.

Jobbing

The jobbing process describes the process used to produce a one-off or a small collection of items following a customer requirement. Although the jobbing process is characterised by high levels of variety and low volume, the main distinction between project and jobbing is that with the latter, resources used for each item are shared among other items too. An example of jobbing is having a manufacturer build specialised furniture to the exact needs of customers.

Batch

The batch process produces a collection of items at a time. Thus, when a batch (a collection of an item) has been produced, the various activities carried out as a result of the process are repetitive in nature. The main difference between jobbing and batch is that the latter has less variety and more volume as two or more items constitute a batch. Example is the production of a batch of specific clothes or food.

Mass

The mass process in comparison to a batch is characterised by producing products of high volume and low variety. An example of the mass process is that of a car assembly plant or manufacturing plant, where slightly different types of cars are produced in large quantities. Within the same manufacturing plant, there are instances where the company mass produces a specific car part which is then used for a variety of types of cars.

Continuous

The continuous process type has the highest volume and low variety characteristics as compared to all the other process types. Products from the continuous process are mostly produced in a continuum whilst the production line is inflexible and very costly to set up. An example of this is the generation of electricity.

Services

In services, customers are known to go through the actual process when the services have been rendered (Johnsen et al., 2018). Hence, customers get what we call 'experience' in the purchase process of a service. An example of a service is having a patient receive medical treatment in a hospital. The three main process types are professional services, service shops, and mass services.

Professional

The professional service is characterised by a high level of human contact with customers whilst the services rendered through the process are highly customised to meet the specific needs of customers. Services rendered through the professional service are of a high variety and low volume whilst being human-oriented rather than machine-oriented (Slack and Brandon-Jones, 2018). Examples include business consultants, lawyers, physicians, etc.

Service Shops

The service shop is characterised by medium levels of volume and variety. In some cases, within the service shop, both the professional service and mass services are integrated and used. An example of such a service shop is the retail bank. Thus, within the bank, mass services may be used for high volume banking activities such as depositing and withdrawal of money.

Mass

The mass service process type is the exact opposite of the professional services. Thus, mass service is characterised by high levels of volume and low variety. The high volumes are operationalised mostly in the form of high transactions for customers but with just a few contacts with these customers, whilst the services rendered are less customised for each customer. Examples include grocery stores, where customers select pre-stocked items without interaction with staff, and fast-food joints, where customers quickly receive standardised meals etc.

Product-Process Matrix

Every process design sits in a particular position within the volume-variety scale. Based on the position of the specific process design on this scale, the corresponding product design characteristics of the process design can be identified. The representation of the corresponding characteristics of a specific process design based on the volume-variety scale of a product is what is generally referred to as the product-process matrix (Barnes, 2018). It is essential for the process design to align closely with the characteristics of the products, achieving what is signified as a 'best fit' – see Figure 7.3.

Process Mapping

It is important for operations managers to determine and design the activities that will make up the overall design. The design of these activities is to be done in detail whilst

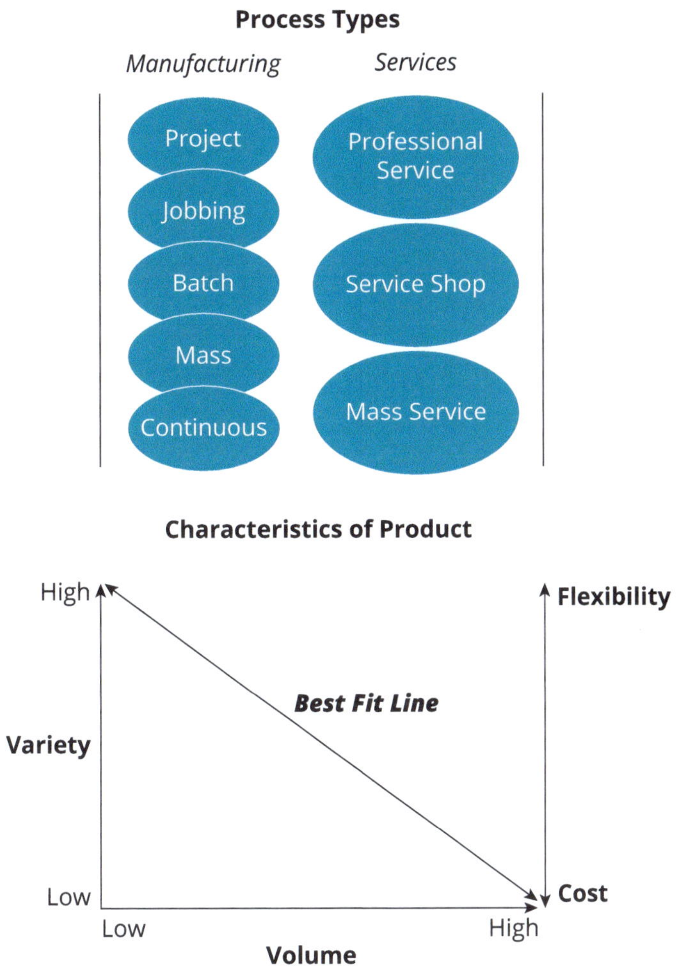

Figure 7.3 Best fit line using product-product matrix

Source: Hayes and Wheelwright, 1984

deciding on the specific sequence in which the activities will be arranged to meet the overall aim of the process design (Barnes, 2018). This detailed concept can simply be represented using universal symbols through the 'process mapping approach. Below are two process map examples:

Figure 7.4 illustrates the stages a patient goes through upon arrival at Hospital A (using symbols from system analysis).

Figure 7.5 illustrates the activities a product goes through upon arrival at a warehouse until it is shipped out for delivery to a customer (with scientific management symbols).

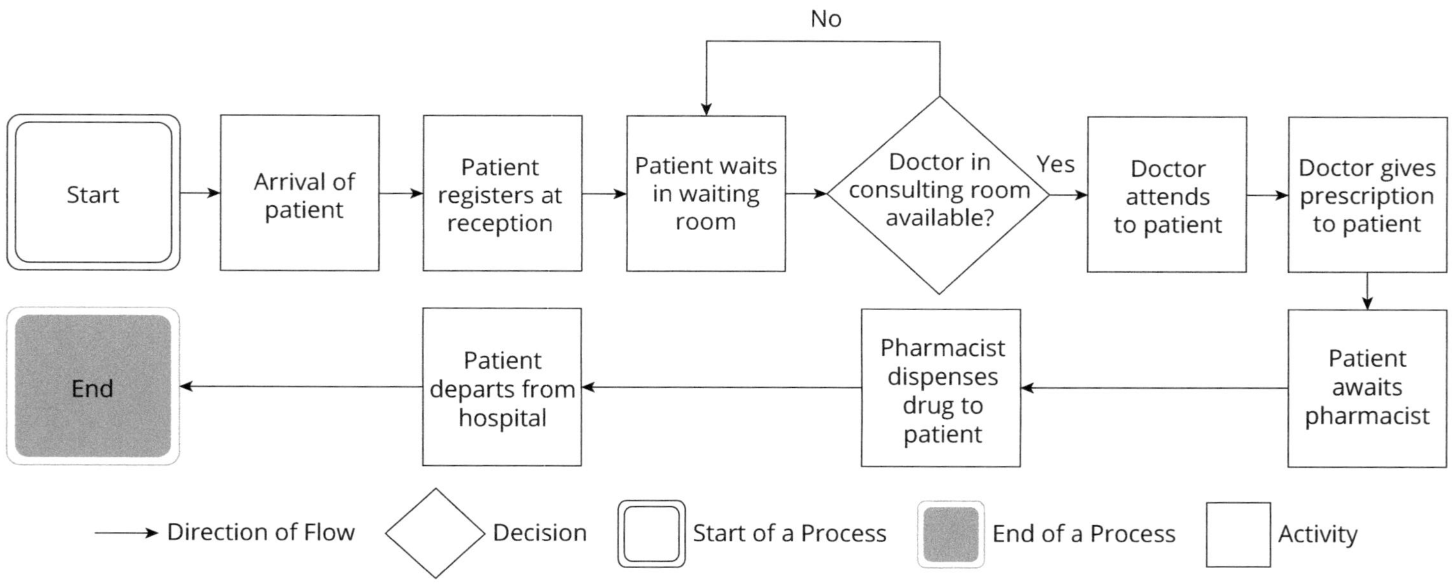

Figure 7.4 Process map for a patient receiving medical treatment at Hospital A

Source: Authors

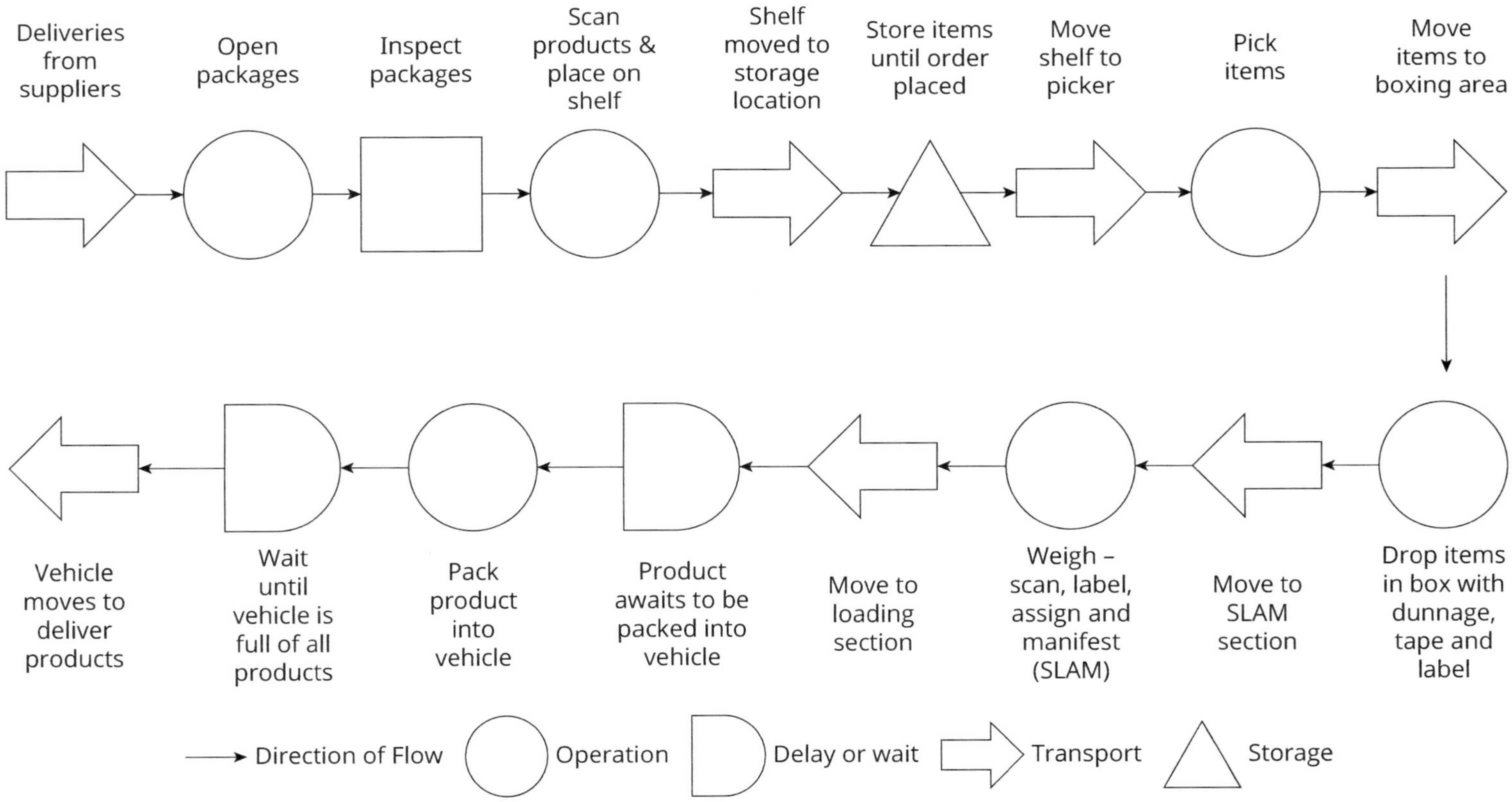

Figure 7.5 Process map of a product at a warehouse

Source: Authors

SUPPLY CHAIN MANAGEMENT FUNDAMENTALS

This section extends the discussion from operations to the broader supply chain, covering essential principles for coordinating suppliers, manufacturers, and distributors. The efficiency of an operation's product or service delivery to customers is fundamentally shaped by the effective management of its global supply chains. In essence, the supply chain – from local to global – is a network of activities that deliver a finished product or service to the customer, whereas SCM is a vital business function that coordinates and manages all the activities of the supply chain including linking suppliers, transporters, distributors, internal departments, third-party companies, and information systems (Reid and Sanders, 2019). Figure 7.6 illustrates a basic example of the supply chain process.

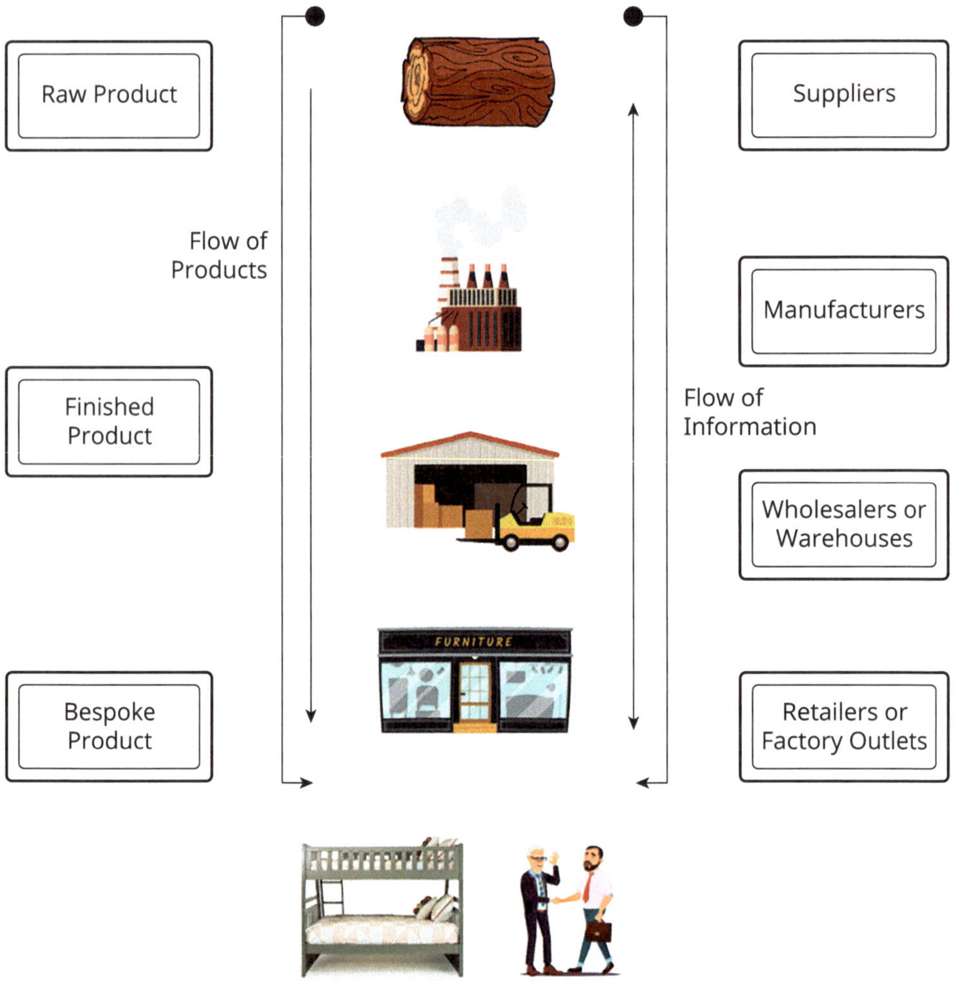

Figure 7.6 Basic supply chain

Source: Authors

Global supply chains are characteristically distinct from supply networks, which encompasses all the interconnected operations that collaborate to deliver products and services to the final consumer. This broader concept includes multiple supply chains across the globe, each representing a specific pathway of production and distribution. In large supply networks, there can be hundreds of supply chains, each involving a unique combination of suppliers, manufacturers, distributors, and retailers. These chains often overlap and intersect, with multiple supply chains passing through a single operation at various stages of the production and distribution process. As a result, managing a supply network requires a holistic approach that considers the complexities and interdependencies of all the operations involved. This interconnectedness highlights the importance of optimising not just individual supply chains but the entire supply network to ensure efficient and effective delivery to the end customer.

Contemporary SCM involves not only overseeing the physical flow of products and services but also managing the critical flow of information both upstream (from customers back to suppliers) and downstream (from suppliers to customers). Managing these information flows is essential for synchronising supply and demand, optimising inventory levels, and maintaining the overall efficiency and effectiveness of the supply chain. This indicates that there are three fundamental components of a company's supply chain structure: *external suppliers* encompass the farmer, cardboard container manufacturer, label company, plastic container manufacturer, paper mill, chemical processing plant, lumber company, and chemical extraction plant; *internal functions* involve processing raw product into consumable products and packaging these products for distribution to retail grocery outlets; and *external distributors* then transport the finished products from the manufacturer to retail grocers, where they are ultimately sold to customers. By effectively managing the flow of materials, information, and resources, SCM ensures that each stage of the process is seamlessly integrated, leading to a more responsive and resilient supply chain.

REFLECTIVE ACTIVITY 7.1

This reflective activity presents an ethical dilemma in SCM. Think about a situation where a company discovers that one of its key suppliers is engaged in unethical practices, such as labour exploitation or environmental degradation. The supplier is critical to the company's operations and finding a replacement could be costly and time-consuming. Using this prompt, you can reflect on the following proposed questions:

- What are the potential ethical dilemmas faced by the company in this situation?
- How should the company balance its business interests with its ethical responsibilities?
- What strategies could the company employ to address these issues while maintaining its supply chain integrity?

This reflection will help you consider the complexities involved in making ethical decisions in O&SCM, particularly when business and moral considerations conflict.

FORECASTING AND DEMAND PLANNING

An important part of SCM is forecasting. There are different quantitative and qualitative forecasting methods, as well as the key principles and practices of demand planning, which provide an understanding of how these processes are intertwined to support overall supply chain performance.

Forecasting

Forecasting – a key business function – is the process of predicting or estimating future events in a straightforward manner. It has an impact on the long-term planning of the business including facilities, capacities, locations, and layout, etc. Different types of forecasting methods are set out below (Reid and Sanders, 2019).

They are broadly classified into two main categories based on the nature of the **data** available and the approach used to make predictions. Qualitative forecasting methods use non-numerical data including consumer surveys and expert opinions, whereas quantitative forecasting methods rely on numerical data and statistical techniques.

Qualitative Forecast

There are several methods to record human judgment. Two often used methodologies are market research and the Delphi method.

Market Research

Market research involves systematically gathering and analysing data about consumers' preferences, behaviour, and attitudes to inform business decisions. In the context of forecasting, market research is particularly useful for qualitative forecasting, where it provides insights that are not easily captured by quantitative methods. Key methods include surveys, focus groups, and observations. For example, a company launching a new product might conduct surveys and focus groups to refine product features before the actual release. The insights gathered can then be used to forecast demand more accurately.

Delphi Method

The Delphi method is a structured communication technique used in forecasting, which relies on a panel of experts who provide predictions independently. The process involves several rounds of questioning, where experts offer their opinions on the matter at hand. After each round, the responses are aggregated and shared with the group, and experts are given the opportunity to revise their forecasts based on the anonymised feedback. This iterative process continues until a consensus is reached or the predictions converge.

Quantitative Forecast

There are two main methodologies used in quantitative analysis: causal methods and time-series methods.

Causal Model

The causal quantitative **model** serves to establish the interrelationship among several variables and their mutual impact. It represents the most advanced approach to forecasting. The causal model of forecasting has two primary strategies.

Regression analysis refers to the statistical methods employed to demonstrates the causal relationship between variables. Based on the number of variables, we formulate two categories of linear regression equations:

Simple Linear Regression

A *simple linear regression* is a statistical analysis that involves only two variables. Given two variables, x and y, two basic regression equations may be derived as:

$(x - \bar{x}) = b_{xy}(y - \bar{Y})$ when x depends upon y

$(y - \bar{Y}) = b_{yx}(x - \bar{x})$ when y depends upon x

where,

$$\bar{x} = \frac{\sum x}{n}, \bar{y} = \frac{\sum y}{n}$$

Multiple Regression Analysis

A *multiple regression analysis* is the quantification of the correlation between a single dependent variable and two or more independent variables. The multiple regression equation of y on x1 and x2 in the order least square approach can be derived as follows by considering y as the dependent variable and x1 and x2 as the two independent variables where ε is the error term.

$$y = a + b_1x_1 + b_2x_2 + \varepsilon$$

Econometric modelling uses statistical methods to quantify relationships between economic variables. Seasonal models, a subset of econometric modelling, account for patterns that repeat over specific periods, helping to predict and adjust for seasonal fluctuations in data.

Seasonal variation refers to the variance in time series caused by seasonal factors such as weather, climate, festivals, and occasions. The seasonal index must be calculated in order to quantify the seasonal fluctuations in the time series, and we demonstrate the measurement using the *simple average seasonal index.*

Simple average seasonal index – The seasonal index involves calculating the ratio between the average of separate seasons and the average of the average. The method comprises the following steps:

Step I: Calculate the seasonal total

Step II: Calculate the seasonal average

Step III: Obtain the average of averages (i.e., grand average)

$$\text{Grand average} = \frac{\text{Sum of seasonal averages}}{\text{Number of averages}}$$

Step IV: Calculate the seasonal index for each season

$$\text{Seasonal Index} = \frac{\text{Average of individual season}}{\text{Grand average}} \times 100$$

Time Series Models

A time series is a structured collection of statistical data organised in chronological order, based on the time they occurred. There are three common approaches in time series models.

The naïve approach is the simplest technique of forecasting when the predicted value of one period is equivalent to the actual value of the most recent period (the one immediately before). The model is highly cost-effective and efficient for objective forecasting. A naïve approach is unable to track down all historical data. The predicted value of the naïve analysis may not be accurate. Hence, the *moving average method* is used to compute the moving average value using a specified number of periods. There are two methods to calculate the moving average value:

A *simple moving average* (SMA) value can be calculated as follows:

$$SMA = \frac{Sum\ of\ value\ for\ chosen\ periods}{Chosen\ number\ periods}$$

In the field of technical analysis of financial data, a *weighted moving average* (WMA) refers to a statistical measure where the weights of securities decline in an arithmetic proportion. The moving average value is calculated as follows:

$$WMA = \frac{\Sigma DW}{\Sigma W}$$

Where:

- W = weight or proportion of demand
- D = demand of specific periods

Exponential smoothing is the updated version of the weighted moving average technique. In this approach, a singular weight denoted as alpha (i.e., α) is employed instead of multiple weights representing different time periods:

$$\hat{y}_{t+1} = \hat{y}_t + a(y_t - \hat{y}_t)$$
$$\alpha$$

Where:

- y_t = actual value for current period t
- $\hat{y}_t$ = forecasted value for current period t
- $\hat{y}_{t+1}$ = forecasted value for next period t+1
- α = weight or smoothing factor = $\frac{2}{n+1}$ (if not given)

Demand Planning

Demand planning provides essential demand data for both mid-term master planning and short-term production and distribution planning. It integrates forecasting with inventory management, production planning, and supply chain operations to ensure efficient demand fulfilment (Kilger and Wagner, 2014). Herein, it is important to introduce two inventory management concepts – Economic Order Quantity and Safety Stock – these are vital in managing inventory levels, controlling costs, and addressing ambiguities in supply chain operations.

- **The Economic Order Quantity (EOQ)** model is used in demand planning, optimising the order quantity to minimise the total costs of inventory management.

$$EOQ = \sqrt{\frac{2\ DS}{H}}$$

Where:

D = Annual demand

S = Ordering cost per order

H = Holding cost per unit per year

- **Safety Stock** is crucial for managing demand variability and ensuring a desired service level. It accounts for uncertainties in demand and lead time. For single-stage inventory systems, the safety stock (ss) is calculated as:

$$ss = Z\sqrt{Lx\sigma_d^2 + D^2 x\sigma_L^2}$$

Where:

Z = Z-score for the desired service level

L = Lead time

σ_d = Standard deviation of demand

σ_L= Standard deviation of lead time

Forecasting predicts future demand using historical data, while demand planning uses these forecasts to align supply with demand. Accurate forecasting enhances supply chain efficiency, reduces uncertainty, and ensures customer satisfaction. By integrating forecasting and demand planning, businesses can enhance supply chain efficiency, reduce uncertainty, and ensure that customer needs are met in a timely and cost-effective manner.

PRODUCTION PLANNING AND CONTROL

Production planning and control (PPC) is a vital function of O&SCM that helps manufacturers work smarter, thereby ensuring that the product manufacturing processes are executed efficiently and effectively. In essence, all the planning and control activities provide the systems, procedures and decisions which bring together different aspects of supply and demand (Slack et al., 2007). PPC involves three main steps – planning (scheduling), routing (coordinating operations), and managing (controlling) the flow of materials and work-in-progress to meet production targets and customer demands, optimise resources, and minimise costs (Kiran, 2019).

Key Stages of PPC

PPC is fundamental for ensuring that manufacturing processes run smoothly and efficiently. There are three key stages in PPC: planning (scheduling), routing (coordinating operations) and managing (controlling). Let's explore each of these stages in more detail with examples:

- **Planning (Scheduling)** is the process of planning when and how production activities will occur. It involves determining the timing and sequence of tasks, allocating resources (such as labour, machinery, and materials), and setting deadlines to ensure that production meets customer demand in a timely manner. For example, imagine a car manufacturing plant that produces multiple models of vehicles. Scheduling in this context would involve planning the sequence of production for each car model based on customer orders, available materials, and workforce availability.
- **Routing (Coordinating Operations)** is the process of determining the path or route that materials and work-in-progress will follow through the production process. It involves specifying the sequence of operations, identifying the machines and workstations required at each stage, and ensuring that materials move efficiently from one stage to the next. For example, in a textile factory producing garments, routing would involve planning the sequence in which fabric is cut, sewn, dyed, and finished.
- **Managing (Controlling)** is about monitoring and adjusting the production process to ensure that it stays on track with the schedule and routing plan. This involves tracking the progress of work-in-progress, managing resources, and making real-time adjustments to address any issues or disruptions. For example, consider a pharmaceutical company manufacturing a new batch of medication. The control phase would involve monitoring the production process to ensure that each stage (mixing, forming, packaging) is completed according to the plan.

REFLECTIVE ACTIVITY 7.2

This reflective activity presents a sustainability challenge in operations. Consider a manufacturing company that has traditionally relied on processes that are energy-intensive and generate significant waste. The company is now facing pressure to adopt more sustainable practices. Using this prompt, you can reflect on the following proposed questions:

- What challenges might the company encounter in transitioning to more sustainable operations?
- How can the company integrate sustainability into its operations strategy without compromising efficiency or profitability?
- What role do technological innovations play in overcoming these sustainability challenges?

Through this reflection, you will be able to explore the practical challenges of implementing sustainable practices in O&SCM, as well as the potential benefits of such a transition.

Types of Production Systems

In any business that produces goods or services, production activities must align with market demands, as reflected by the steady flow of customer orders (Kiran, 2019). The production system serves as the strategic framework to achieve this goal. PPC has the following four different types of production systems:

- **Job Shop Production** involves the creation of unique products tailored to specific customer requirements. Each product is made to order, and the process typically involves small-scale production or the manufacture of a single item. Examples include custom-made furniture, specialised machinery, and tailored clothing.
- **Batch Production** is a system where products are manufactured in groups or batches. Each batch undergoes one stage of the production process before moving on to the next stage. This method is common in industries where the demand for products varies, and level of standardisation is possible, but flexibility is still needed to produce different products in a series. Examples include the production of baked goods, pharmaceuticals, and clothing.
- **Mass Production** is a flow or continuous production, involves the large-scale manufacturing of standardised products. This system is highly efficient, designed to produce high volumes of goods at a low cost. It is characterised by the use of assembly lines where products move continuously through various stages of production. Examples include automobile manufacturing, consumer electronics, and household appliances.
- **Continuous Production** is a subset of mass production, where the manufacturing process is uninterrupted, and production runs 24/7. This system is typically used for products that are in constant demand and require high levels of consistency and uniformity. Examples include the production of chemicals, steel, paper, and oil refining.

Types of Production Techniques

Production control techniques are essential tools or systems and methodologies used to monitor, manage, and optimise the production process to ensure that manufacturing operations are efficient, cost-effective, and aligned with business objectives. These techniques help to minimise waste, reduce production times, maintain quality, and ensure the timely delivery of products. The following techniques are widely discussed and used in industry:

- **Just-in-Time (JIT)** refers to acquiring the right quantity of goods at the right place and the right time – these goods arrive just-in-time – this is where the terminology JIT came from (Reid and Sanders, 2019). The core focus behind the JIT philosophy is about elimination of waste and improving process efficiency – this is achieved by ensuring zero inventory throughout the whole supply chain.
- **Lean Production** is a methodology that focuses on maximising value for the customer while minimising waste. Womack et al. (1990) define lean production as 'use less of everything – half the human effort in the factory, half the manufacturing space, half the investment in tools, half the engineering working hours to develop a new product in half the time'.
- **Six Sigma** is a data-driven methodology that provides businesses with the required statistical tools and techniques to enhance the capability of their business functions and improving quality by reducing defects and variability in production processes (Yang et al., 2003). More so, the primary goal of process improvement is to enhance performance while reducing variability.

INVENTORY MANAGEMENT

Inventory management ensures that materials and supplies are available for manufacturing or service operations. Inventory management involves creating inventory replenishment policies to guide production scheduling, which are crucial for maintaining balance.

Basic Inventory Types

Organisations typically manage four types of inventories to support various functions (Reid and Sanders, 2019):

- **Raw Material** inventory consists of purchased but not yet processed items or extracted material. For example, gold is a raw material that is transformed into jewellery.
- **Work-in-Process** inventory includes raw materials that have started the transformation process but are not yet completed. After the product is completed, it becomes finished goods – the bicycles, dining sets, coffee tables, and cars that the company sells to its customers.
- **Maintenance/Repair/Operating (MRO)** inventory consists of supplies required to maintain machinery and keep processes running smoothly. Examples of MRO are hand tools, lubricants, and cleaning supplies.
- **Finished Goods** (or distribution) inventory comprises products that have been completed and are ready for delivery to customers.

Inventory-Related Costs

The following are four inventory-related costs that need to be considered (Reid and Sanders, 2019):

- **Item Costs** include the price paid for an item and any additional expenses, such as transportation, insurance, duties, or taxes. For an item made by the company, the cost includes direct labor, materials, and factory overhead.

- **Holding Costs** are variable costs incurred from carrying inventory over time. Holding costs include storage-related expenses such as insurance fees, additional staffing, and interest payments. As inventory increases, holding costs also increase.
- **Ordering Costs** are fixed costs incurred when placing an order. Ordering costs include the administrative work involved in preparing, releasing, and receiving orders, as well as the physical handling of the goods. These costs remain constant regardless of the number of items or the quantity ordered.
- **Shortage Costs** occur when customer demand surpasses the available inventory. For example, if a customer orders a high-end kayak from a company's website and it's out of stock, one of two things will happen. Either the customer agrees to wait until the kayak is back in stock (a backorder), or then buys it from another company, resulting in a lost sale for the business.

Managing Inventory in Manufacturing vs Service Organisations

Manufacturing firms manage inventory in several distinct ways. *Anticipation inventory* is built based on future demand, promotional programmes, plant shutdowns, and holidays. *Safety Stock inventory* is maintained as a buffer to protect against variations in demand and unexpected events. *Lot-size inventory* arises when a company purchases or produces more than is immediately needed, and the surplus units are held in inventory and used as customers place orders. In reality, extensive tangible inventory is required in wholesale and retail services. Successful wholesaling, retailing, and food service operations require excellent inventory control and accurate records.

SUPPLY CHAIN LOGISTICS AND DISTRIBUTION

Supply chain logistics and distribution are critical components of O&SCM. They encompass the processes and systems involved in moving goods from the point of origin to the point of consumption, i.e., from upstream to downstream. Effective and efficient logistics and distribution management ensure that products are delivered to the right place, at the right time, in the right quantity and quality, and at the right price.

Supply Chain Logistics

Logistics involves managing the physical and information flows related to the storage and movement of raw materials through to the final distribution of finished products. It focuses on planning and controlling these flows within organisations, ensuring that the right materials reach the right place at the right time, while optimising performance metrics like cost efficiency. It includes several activities:

- **Transportation** (e.g., Amazon depends on a high-level but complex transportation network – both ground and air freight – to deliver products and/or services to customers on time).
- **Warehousing** (e.g., Walmart controls a massive network of distribution centres strategically positioned across the United States).

- **Inventory Management** (e.g., Toyota employs a JIT inventory system, which minimises inventory levels by synchronising closely with suppliers to deliver resources as and when they are needed in the production process).
- **Order Fulfilment** (e.g., Zappos, a US based online shoe and clothing retailer, aspires to deliver orders rapidly and ahead of schedule).
- **Packaging** (e.g., Apple utilises simple, recyclable packaging material for its products in order to reduce environmental impact).

Role of Distribution in SCM

Distribution in SCM encompasses the processes involved in transferring a product from the manufacturer to the end consumer (Christopher, 2016). This includes managing the various channels through which products travel, such as wholesalers, retailers, and direct-to-consumer sales. Effective and efficient distribution is fundamental for fulfilling customer expectations, maintaining product quality, and decreasing expenses. This is possible through selecting the right *distribution channel*, e.g., Coca-Cola uses a widespread distribution network that includes bottling partners, wholesalers, and retailers to reach customers worldwide, facilitating the availability of their products across the globe. In contrast UPS uses advanced routing software and alternative delivery methods, such as using e-bikes, to improve the efficiency and sustainability of *last-mile delivery* in urban areas.

FACILITY LAYOUT AND LOCATION

Facility layout and location decisions significantly impact operational efficiency, cost structure, and ability to meet customer demands. Layout design involves arranging physical resources within a facility to optimise workflow and productivity, whereas location decisions involve selecting the best geographical sites for facilities based on factors like proximity to suppliers and customers, transportation costs, and labour availability (Greasley, 2009). In this section, we explore the importance of facility layout and location, the types of layouts, factors influencing location decisions, and real-world examples to illustrate these concepts.

Facility Layout

Facility layout can be outlined based on four types with each possessing distinct characteristics – *product, process, fixed position,* and *hybrid* (Greasley, 2009).

- **Product Layouts**, also known as line layouts, are layouts that arrange resources in a straight-line fashion to promote efficient production, i.e., equipment and workstations are arranged in a sequence that aligns with the steps in the production process (Reid and Sanders, 2002). This type of layout is common in companies that have mass production environments, i.e., with continuous processing systems, where one, few or large volumes of standardised products are made. Figure 7.7 illustrates an example of the product facility layout.

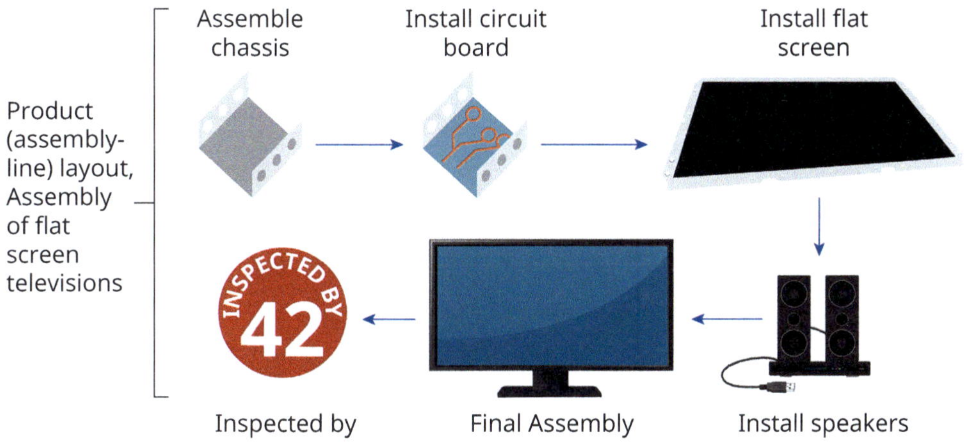

Figure 7.7 Example - Product facility layout

Source: Frazier, 2015

- **Process Layouts**, also known as functional layouts, are layouts in which resources which have similar types of processes or functions are grouped together. This layout is typically used in facilities where customised products are made or where production volumes are low. Figure 7.8 illustrates a classic example of production operations of kitchen cabinets, in which the assembly line is organised so that each station performs a specific task i.e., receiving, and storing raw material, foundry, rough machine, fabrication, painting, and finally packaging and shipping.

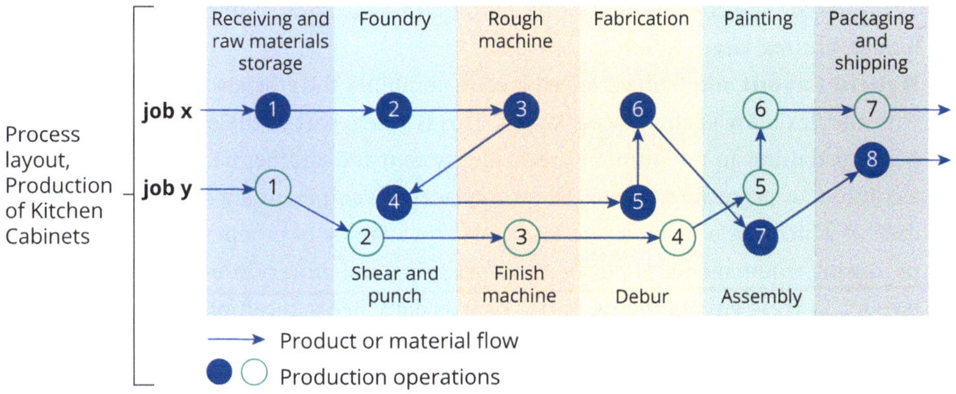

Figure 7.8 Example - Process facility layout

Source: Frazier, 2015

- **Fixed Position Layout** (see Figure 7.9) is used when the product is very large in size and cannot be moved, hence the transformation process takes places at the location of the product creation. All the equipment, labour needs and resources

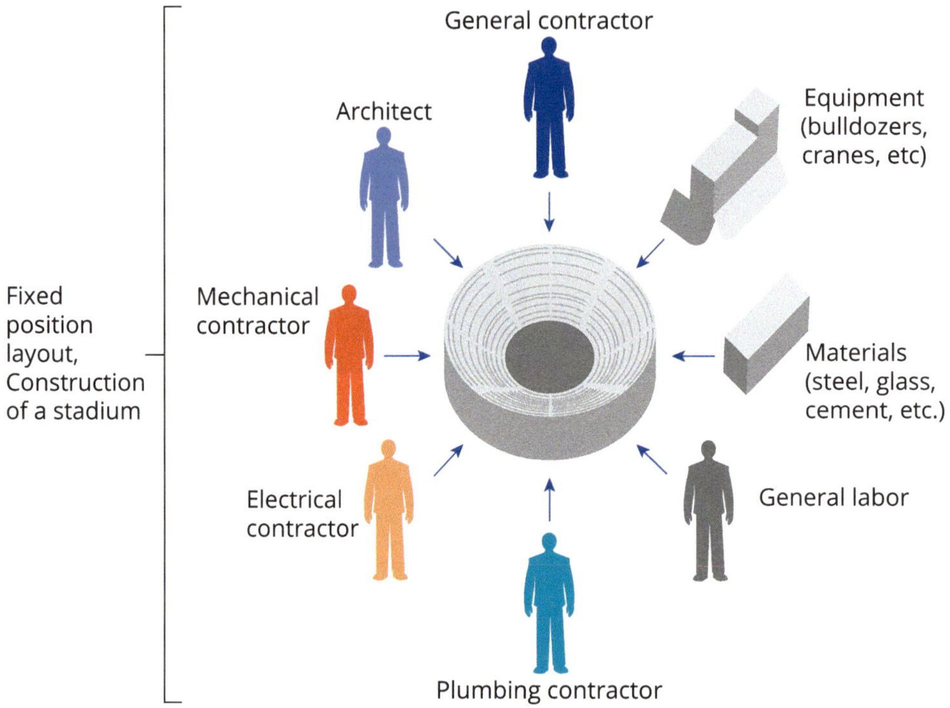

Figure 7.9 Example - Fixed position facility layout

Source: Frazier, 2015

required for product creation are brought to the site where the product is located. Examples are the construction of bridges, buildings, dams, ship building or manufacturing large aircraft.

- **Hybrid Layout**, also known as cell layout, combines the efficiency of a product layout with the flexibility of the process layout. This is where part of the operation is performed using an intermittent processing system and another part is performed using a continuous processing system. The workplaces or equipment are organised in cells, each of which can perform a set of processes on a family of products with similar processing requirements. For example, retail stores and grocery stores use hybrid layouts. In these environments, goods such as dairy items, meat, or produce are stored based on their function.

Facility Location

Determining an optimal geographic location for a company's facility is a strategic decision that impacts its operational effectiveness, access to workforce and supplies, transportation and infrastructure, cost of land and utilities, competitive advantage, and ability to serve its customers promptly and efficiently. For example, when Toyota decided to build its assembly plant in Georgetown, Kentucky, factors such as proximity to suppliers of automotive parts in the US market, access to major transportation routes within the surroundings of the location, access to skilled workforce, and state tax incentives were crucial in the decision-making process (Reid and Sanders, 2002).

QUALITY MANAGEMENT

One of the key perspectives from which quality is defined is from a consistent conformance perspective. Thus, quality in its basic form is known as meeting customers' exact needs through consistent conformance (Slack et al., 2013). This approach can reduce errors in customer orders to the barest minimum or preferably avoid them completely. This also suggests that for quality to be met, it is important to understand quality from the customer's point of view, mainly by understanding customers' exact needs and expectations. This raises the significance of integrating the activities of operations to match that of the customer's view of quality. Managing the concept of quality to ensure that the required operational processes are effectively executed throughout the entire organisation to meet the needs of customers is known as quality management (Isaksson et al., 2023).

Specification Conformance

The concept, conforming to specification, mainly refers to producing a product or service which follows the originally and methodologically designed specifications. To achieve conformity to specification, a number of researchers have proposed a series of steps to be followed (e.g., Barnes, 2018). A summary of these steps follows:

- You need to first define the features of quality in your organisational setting or context.
- Based on the outlined features, clearly indicate how each of these features can be monitored and measured.
- Clearly indicate the threshold points for each of the quality features.
- Now you can monitor and control the features with respect to the thresholds.
- Identify quality gaps and rectify them accordingly.
- Engage in consistent quality improvement by improving on the activities.

Measuring Quality

There are two main perspectives on operationalising the measurement of quality. These are the operations and financial perspectives.

- **Operations:** Measuring quality entails conforming to the product or service specification. Examples of questions organisations use to measure product or service conformance are 'Our company offers high-performance products that meet customer needs', 'We produce products with consistent specification and low to no defects', and 'We offer reliable products to our customers'.
- **Financial:** The amount of monetary value used to ensure that services and products offered to customers meet the customers' and product specifications will

have a concurrent effect on the monetary gain that is generated after selling the product or service. Thus, most organisations strive to achieve a strong positive correlation between 'the level of monetary investment in a product or service to meet the needs of customers', and 'the amount of revenue generated after offering these products/services to customers'.

Total Quality Management (TQM)

TQM is about quality development, maintaining quality, monitoring and improving quality in all areas and levels of an organisation (Isaksson, 2003). In TQM, quality needs should not be centred on only one specific section of the company's operation, but rather all activities within or across the organisation. More so, organisations should have quality as their top priority and improve quality continuously. In achieving quality under the TQM philosophy, it is key to have all persons **(stakeholders)** within or across the organisation well integrated or involved, whilst finding the most cost-efficient way of inculcating quality into everyday organisational activities. This also indicates that to efficiently operationalise TQM, the cost aspect of TQM needs to be considered. This has been detailed below:

- **Cost Model of TQM** – Understanding and assessing the costs of quality control and improvement is crucial, as these costs impact an organisation's financial performance. This section focuses on the initial costs companies should consider, categorised into four main types (Slack et al., 2013):
    - **Prevention cost:** This describes a cost firm incurs to prevent errors from occurring in the first place. An example could be continuously improving upon the firm's process and product design to prevent or significantly reduce the possibility of having product or service errors.
    - **Appraisal cost:** This mainly captures the cost of assessing the presence of failures when products or services are being rendered and after they have been produced or delivered to the customer. An example is checking the inputs used in production, the production process and the final product.
    - **Cost due to internal failure:** The cost involved in rectifying the occurrence of internal quality errors within an organisation. An example is reproducing faulty products or reoffering an initially faulty service.
    - **Cost due to external failure:** This describes the cost involved when errors in a product or service leaves the shores of the organisation and reaches that of the external customer. Examples of such failures could cost the company by losing it customers due to customer dissatisfaction.

Based on the above, it is clear that there is a strong correlation between (1) the amount spent to rectify quality failures or improve quality and the corresponding benefit this generates; (2) the time that an error occurs, and the cost involved in rectifying this failure at every stage of the supply chain. Thus, when higher efforts are made to improve quality, this comes along with a higher investment cost as well, however, the cost of failure reduces drastically as fewer failures will occur.

Additionally, expending effort, especially at the initial stages of producing a product or service, results in reducing the cost occurred in rectifying quality failures. For example, when companies invest more in preventing errors even before production kicks off, the possibility of having a higher number of quality issues also reduces drastically. However, when less effort is made and the failure gets to the external customer, a higher cost is involved in rectifying such failures.

International Organisation for Standardisation (ISO) 9000 Series

To effectively implement TQM on a continuous, daily basis, several standardised quality management systems are available. One of the most prominent is the ISO 9000 series, which encompasses:

1. a range of quality standards designed to ensure the implementation of best practices; and
2. a set of procedures to guide the development of quality management systems.

These standards and procedures are applicable to both manufacturing and service organisations, helping them to define, develop, and implement globally accepted quality practices in their daily operations and the final products or services they deliver.

TECHNOLOGY AND INNOVATION IN OPERATIONS & SCM

Technology and innovation are pivotal in transforming O&SCM practices, driving efficiencies, reducing costs, improving quality, and enabling businesses to respond swiftly to market changes. Scholars and practitioners advocate that technology and innovation serve as catalysts for operational excellence in modern businesses, thereby enabling companies to streamline processes, enhance decision-making, optimise supply chains, and offer better products and services to customers.

In the context of O&SCM, technology refers to the tools, systems, and platforms that support operations. The key technologies adopted are:

- AI and ML
- IoT
- **Blockchain**
- **Big Data** Analysis

Artificial Intelligence (AI) and Machine Learning (ML)

AI and ML algorithms help in enabling systems to learn from data and make informed decisions with limited human input. For example, UPS uses AI and ML in its ORION (On-Road Integrated Optimisation and Navigation) system to optimise delivery routes and minimise travel distances. This helps to reduce fuel consumption and hence creates less CO2 emissions as well as reducing delivery times. With the application of ORION, UPS estimates that for every mile reduced across its delivery network, the company saves around $50 million each year, thus showing the financial savings and implications attributable to AI and ML in O&SCM.

CASE STUDY 7.1

Ocado

Ocado is a leading online grocery retailer in the UK, recognised for its innovative use of AI and cutting-edge technologies. The company is pursuing several projects to leverage new technologies, driven by rising labour costs and advances in cost-effective solutions. Ocado is also developing robots designed to handle both heavy and delicate products, reducing worker injuries and efficiently managing a range of goods including fruits, vegetables, and eggs. They are further collaborating with global prestigious institutions for humanoid robots to assist maintenance engineers such as moving tools and materials and offering advice on troubleshooting. However, this rapid growth has brought significant challenges for Ocado, particularly in managing their global supply chain. As Ocado sources products from multiple countries and sells them worldwide, it faces complexities related to logistics, inventory management, supplier relationships, and sustainability. The following are some of the challenges reported:

- **Inventory Management**: Balancing stock levels across different regions to prevent stockouts and overstocking.
- **Logistics Optimisation**: Reducing transportation costs and carbon emissions while ensuring timely delivery of products to customers worldwide.
- **Supplier Management**: Ensuring that all suppliers adhere to Ocado's sustainability standards, while also being able to meet demand.
- **Technology Integration**: Leveraging technology to improve supply chain visibility, forecasting accuracy, and overall efficiency.

Case Study Task

Ocado's supply chain team must develop a strategy that addresses these challenges while supporting the company's growth and sustainability goals. This strategy should include recommendations for inventory management, logistics, supplier relationships, and the integration of new technologies. The company is also considering implementing more advanced forecasting tools to better predict demand and optimise stock levels globally. Students can respond to the following questions to help Ocado develop solutions to their challenges.

Questions

1 How could technology help Ocado improve inventory management and logistics across its supply chain?

2 In what ways could Ocado use technology to manage its suppliers more effectively?
3 How could technology help Ocado address environmental issues in its supply chain?

Source

Ocado Group (n.d) About Us. https://www.ocadogroup.com/about-us (accessed November 10, 2025).

Internet of Things (IoT)

This refers to the use of devices for collecting and exchanging data, and in this context, for O&SCM to monitor and track assets, inventory, and environmental conditions in real-time. DHL has implemented IoT-enabled smart sensors in its logistics network to monitor the condition of sensitive shipments, providing real-time data on location, temperature, and humidity (DHL, 2015). Another application of IoT in O&SCM is predictive maintenance. For example, Siemens uses IoT to reduce the likelihood of unexpected breakdowns and minimise downtime, by scheduling maintenance activities proactively.

Blockchain

Blockchain can be deployed to validate the source of products, authenticate the validity of transactions, and certify agreement with regulatory rules. De Beers deployed its TracrTM blockchain platform to trace the origin of diamonds from mine to consumer, ensuring that they are conflict-free and ethically sourced (De Beers, n.d.). Subsequently, Walmart in collaboration with IBMs Food Trust has implemented blockchain technology to enhance traceability and transparency in its food supply chain – i.e., tracing the journey of the food from farm to fork.

Big Data Analytics

Walmart utilises Big Data analytics (BDA) to optimise its inventory management. By analysing customer buying patterns, weather forecasts, and social media trends, Walmart is able to predict demand more accurately, ensuring that popular products are stocked in the right locations at the right times. Furthermore, through collecting and analysing thousands of sensor data embedded in aircraft components, Boeing utilises BDA to enhance predictive maintenance and improve supply chain efficiency. Elements of BDA can be noted across other technologies and innovations mentioned in this section as more data helps in improving decision-making accuracy.

On the other hand, innovation involves the development and implementation of new ideas, rethinking processes, or products that improve business performance, and **value propositions** to create more efficient, sustainable, and customer-centric operations. Some of the innovative practices in O&SCM include *Lean Manufacturing*, e.g., Toyota Production System (TPS), which emphasises JIT production, quality control, and respect for workers (Monden, 2011); *Agile Supply Chains* e.g., Amazon's agile supply chain is characterised by its customer-centric approach, advanced technology, flexible fulfilment network, fast delivery options, close supplier collaboration, and continuous improvement efforts; and *Circular Economy Supply Chains*, e.g., IKEA is adopting circular economy principles by designing products that can be easily disassembled and recycled, including returning used furniture for recycling or resale, reducing the environmental impact of its operations (Stahel, 2019). Technology and innovation are integral to the evolution of O&SCM. From automation and AI to blockchain and Big Data analytics, these advancements are transforming how companies operate, making them more efficient, responsive, and sustainable.

CASE STUDY 7.2

Tata Motors

Tata Motors, one of India's leading automobile manufacturers led by late Ratan Tata, has made substantial developments in sustainable transportation domain. They have invested heavily in electric vehicle (EV) technology in the past few years. One of their eco-friendly cars, the Tata Nexon EV, gained widespread recognition in emerging markets. In addition to producing EVs, Tata Motors has integrated sustainability across its supply chain by adopting green manufacturing practices, using recycled materials, and reducing carbon emissions in its production facilities. This approach aligns with Tata's long-term vision of making a greener, more energy-efficient automotive sector while addressing the growing demand for sustainable mobility solutions in non-Western markets.

Question

1 What similar type of project activities can be identified for this project to ensure it is successful and sustainable in the future?

Source

Tata Motors (n.d.) 'Welcome to Tata Motors'. https://www.tatamotors.com/ (accessed November 10, 2025).

SUSTAINABILITY AND OPERATIONS & SCM

The growing global demand for products and consumption has forced industrial output and supply chains to operate under increasing pressure and complexity, leading to adverse effects on the environment, society, and ethical standards. Sustainability has become a central concern in O&SCM as companies recognise the need to balance economic success with environmental stewardship, ethical considerations, and social responsibility. Some of the leading drivers of sustainability are environmental concerns, social responsibility, economic viability, and ethical supply chains.

Environmental Concerns

Continuous variations in ecological systems and their global impact, the decline in natural resources due to overconsumption, and increasing population demands are major issues that companies must resolve through sustainable operations. Instead of traditional linear 'take-make-dispose' models, firms are adopting circular economy practices – such as closed-loop recycling, product remanufacturing, and sustainable procurement – alongside water conservation and carbon emission reductions. These strategies allow organisations to optimise resource productivity without compromising the ability of future generations to meet their own needs.

Social Responsibility

Environmental, philanthropic, ethical, and economic are four major types of social responsibilities that businesses must consider through sustainable practices, i.e., reducing carbon emissions, enhancing welfare of the society by donating resources, conducting business with ethical practices, and promoting fair trade and supporting small local businesses to ensure wider economic sustainability.

Economic Viability

By implementing sustainable practices, organisations can reduce their operational overheads through energy savings, reducing wastage, and optimising resources. Enhanced efficiency often leads to simplified business processes and better use of resources, which can further cut costs. A strong commitment to sustainability often lead consumers to favouring certain businesses and their associated brands, resulting in increased customer loyalty and appealing potential clients.

Ethical Supply Chains and Modern Slavery Mitigation

Global frameworks like the OECD *Due Diligence Guidance for Responsible Business Conduct* (2018) and the UN *Guiding Principles on Business and Human Rights* (UNHR, 2011) provide clear guidelines for organisations on ethical and sustainable supply chains. These frameworks help in assessing risks on environmental damage, human rights violations, and modern slavery mitigation, thus making businesses conduct due diligence within their supply chains.

Businesses need to be strategic by adopting practices such as *sustainable sourcing*, e.g., Unilever is committed to 100% procurement of resources from suppliers that adhere to sustainable farming practices, resulting in protecting biodiversity and reducing deforestation, and *green manufacturing*, e.g., Interface, a global manufacturer of commercial flooring, has implemented green manufacturing processes that include using recycled materials in their products and reducing greenhouse gas emissions from their operations. Modern slavery, on the other hand, continues to be a challenge, particularly in industries with complex supply chains such as textiles, mining, and agriculture. Businesses are obliged to ensure that their suppliers and operations comply with ethical labour standards, as outlined in the UK Modern Slavery Act (UK Government, 2015), and other similar legislations across the world. While the SDGs provide a broader sustainable and ethical framework, the International Labour Organisation (ILO) conventions (2025) set a minimum standard for labour practices, which many countries incorporate into their national laws. Overall, sustainability is a strategic approach that is no longer a peripheral concern in O&SCM, but a central component of modern business strategy.

CASE STUDY 7.3

Paris Olympic Games

The Paris 2024 Olympic Games aimed to deliver a world-class sporting event while ensuring quality, adhering to a strict timeline, and managing costs effectively. Paris 2024 Olympic Games prioritised the use of existing venues, including the Stade de France, Roland-Garros, and the Paris La Défense Arena, to minimise new construction. Renovations and upgrades were made to these venues to ensure they meet the Games' requirements. At the same time, the Paris 2024 Olympic Games built 'The Village', transitioning from an industrial site to a sustainable urban neighbourhood, incorporating low-carbon materials, geothermal heating, and wastewater treatment.

Questions

1. What do you think are the core objectives, scope, innovation, and complexity of these two projects?
2. What key lessons can be drawn from their comparison?
3. Try comparing the projected post-Games use of the Olympic Village with its actual development and legacy outcomes.

Source

Paris 2024 Organising Committee (2024) Paris 2024 Sustainability & Legacy Pre-Games Report Summary. https://alaturidevoi.ro/wp-content/uploads/2024/08/Paris2024-240605-Sustainability-report-summary.pdf (accessed November 10, 2025).

PERFORMANCE MEASUREMENT AND IMPROVEMENT

The chapter concludes with performance measurement, binding together all sections by providing tools to assess and enhance efficiency across O&SCM processes. The section highlights five essential performance measures – *Quality*, *Speed*, *Dependability*, *Flexibility*, and *Cost* – that are crucial for any operation to satisfy customers and boost competitiveness. Without these measures, it becomes challenging to effectively control operations or assess performance over time. Designing an effective performance measurement system requires striking a balance between simplicity and comprehensiveness, ensuring alignment with the operation's overall strategy.

Five Operational Performance Measures

As an operations manager, it is important to evaluate five operational performance measures:

- **Quality (Doing things right):** Quality means consistent conformance to customer's expectations.
- **Speed (Doing things fast):** Speed is the elapsed time between ordered products and services and their delivery.
- **Dependability (Doing things on time):** Dependability means one operation's performance depends on how reliable the other operations are in delivering material or information on time.
- **Flexibility (Doing things flexibly):** Flexibility is the operations' ability to change quickly to adapt to customers' requirements.
- **Cost (Doing things cheaply):** Cost is a global major operational objective. *High-Quality, Speedy, Dependable* and *Flexible* operations introduce cost reductions.

Detailed Measures of Quality, Speed, Dependability, Flexibility, and Cost

The above five measures are the composites of smaller measures. For example, Cost covers many smaller measures such as transaction cost, labour productivity or machine efficiency. Each of those smaller measures individually gives a perspective on the overall cost performance of a specific operation. Taken together, they provide a complete picture of what is going on within your organisation. Table 7.1 provides more examples of detailed measures of quality, speed, dependability, flexibility, and cost.

Table 7.1 Examples of Measures - Quality, Speed, Dependability, Flexibility and Cost

Composite Measure	Quality	Speed	Dependability	Flexibility	Cost
Individual Measures Examples	• Customer complaints • Scrap level • Defects	• Delivery time • Service time • Customer query time	• Lateness • Spare parts delivery • Minimum stock	• Customisation • Time to market • Product ranges	• Labour productivity • Transation cost • Machine efficiency

Source: Authors

CHAPTER SUMMARY

- This chapter explored the key operations performance measures that are essential for effective OM. These measures help organisations meet customer expectations and maintain competitiveness. Managers must evaluate and adapt their strategies to balance these performance dimensions, considering both internal efficiency and external customer satisfaction.

- The chapter laid out the strategic importance of aligning operations with business goals, followed by a deep dive into process design, quality management, and inventory control – all essential elements for ensuring efficiency and effectiveness in operations.
- The discussion of SCM fundamentals emphasised the connection of sourcing, logistics, and distribution, laying out their critical role in achieving organisational success.
- We also examined the transformative impact of technology and innovation, as well as the growing importance of sustainability in modern supply chains.
- Finally, the chapter provided insights into performance measurement, equipping you with the tools to continuously improve and manage operations effectively.

STUDENTS LIKE YOU CHANGE THE WORLD

Connor Fletcher (BSc Business and Management) is a Future Leader Graduate at DHL Supply Chain in the Healthcare sector. Connor is responsible for managing two warehouse contracts: Ascencia Diabetes Care (ADC) UK and Union Chimique Belge (UCB) UK.

ADC

ADC, which is a world-renowned company, is known to mainly focus on improving the health and lives of persons with diabetes. With more than 80 years of history and locations in over 100 countries, ADC specialises in glucose monitoring systems. For ADC's UK warehouse project through DHL, Connor's role involves project delivery, ensuring that wholesalers, pharmacies, hospitals, and patient orders are effectively and efficiently fulfilled. With over 900 monthly orders, Connor is working with the customer (ADC UK) on Monthly Business Reviews to continuously improve operations to better serve the communities.

UCB

UCB is a global biopharma company focused on creating valuable solutions that improve the lives of people living with neurological and autoimmune conditions. Over the past 20 years, UCB UK has conducted 172 clinical trials over 464 trial sites involving 5,100 UK patients, securing a total of £168m investment across all clinical trials. Connor's role in the warehouse project was to manage project delivery and manage the temperature-controlled warehousing for over 20 active studies, manage the customer relationship, and complete sustainability reporting into the impact DHL has on UCB's carbon emissions, which helps the UCB Sustainability Advisory Board to make recommendations targeted at improving their sustainability performance.

Connor's role at DHL is largely focused on contributing to the UK healthcare sector, operationalised through driving forward new ideas for sustainability improvement and positively impacting communities across the UK.

END OF CHAPTER REFLECTION

Have a look at the skills you should have developed in this unit (find more details in the Key Skills Table in the Appendix on p. 502).

1 Which of the skills listed do you think you have developed the most?
2 Can you give two examples on why you feel you have now developed these skills/developed them further?
3 How will you use these new/refined skills in the future (give two examples of the impact of your development on your future behaviour)?

FURTHER READING

Heizer, J., Render, B., and Munson, C. (2020) *Operations Management: Sustainability and Supply Chain Management*. Pearson.

This is a foundational textbook widely used to understand core concepts such as process design, capacity planning, quality control, and lean systems. It also provides real-world case studies, quantitative problem-solving techniques, and a strong balance between theory and practice.

Sunil, C. (2013) *Supply Chain Management: Strategy, Planning, and Operation* (5th edition). Pearson India.

This book helps in understanding the strategic role of supply chains in business performance and introduces frameworks for designing and managing supply chains.

Christopher, M. (2016) *Logistics and Supply Chain Management*. Pearson UK.

This book focuses on the integration of logistics and supply chain strategies to create competitive advantage, and also emphasises **customer value**, agility, and sustainability, some key themes in contemporary supply chain thinking.

Simchi-Levi, D., Kaminsky, P., and Simchi-Levi, E. (1999) *Designing and Managing the Supply Chain: Concepts, Strategies, and Cases*. McGraw-Hill.

This book blends theory with practical tools and techniques and is highly useful for those interested in the quantitative and analytical side of supply chain management.

Ivanov, D., Tsipoulanidis, A., and Schönberger, J. (eds) (2021) *Global Supply Chain and Operations Management*. Springer.

This book offers a comprehensive and structured introduction to both supply chain and operations management, making it ideal for students at undergraduate and postgraduate levels.

REFERENCES

Barnes, D. (2018) *Operations Management: An International Perspective*. Bloomsbury.
Brown, S., Bessant, J., and Jia, F. (2018) *Strategic Operations Management*. Routledge.

Christopher, M. (2016) *Logistics and Supply Chain Management*. Pearson UK.

De Beers (n.d.) 'TRACR', *De Beers Group*. https://web.archive.org/web/20230601024043/https://www.debeersgroup.com/media/company-news/2022/de-beers-group-introduces-worlds-first-blockchain-backed-diamond-source-platform-at-scale (accessed September 15, 2025).

DHL (2015). *Internet of Things in Logistics*. DHL Customer Solutions and Innovations. https://www.ncl.ac.uk/media/wwwnclacuk/pressoffice/files/pressreleaseslegacy/DHLTrendReport_Internet_of_things.pdf (accessed September 12, 2025).

Frazier, G. (2015). *Operations Management* (9th edition). Thomson.

Greasley, A. (2009) *Operations Management* (2nd edition). John Wiley & Sons.

Hayes, R.H. and Wheelwright, S.C. (1984) *Restoring Our Competitive Edge: Competing Through Manufacturing*. John Wiley & Sons.

International Labour Organization. (2025) *Conventions, Protocols and Recommendations*. https://www.ilo.org/ (accessed November 12, 2025).

Isaksson, R. (2006) 'Total quality management for sustainable development: Process based system models', *Business Process Management Journal*, 12 (5): 632–45.

Isaksson, R., Ramanathan, S. and Rosvall, M. (2023) 'The sustainability opportunity study (SOS) – diagnosing by operationalising and sensemaking of sustainability using Total Quality Management', *The TQM Journal*, 35 (5): 1329–47.

Johnsen, T., Howard, M., and Miemczyk, J. (2018) *Purchasing and Supply Chain Management: A Sustainability Perspective*. Routledge.

Kilger, C. and Wagner, M. (2014) 'Demand planning', in H. Stadtler, C. Kilger and H. Meyr (eds), *Supply Chain Management and Advanced Planning: Concepts, Models, Software, and Case Studies*. Springer. pp. 125–54

Kiran, D.R. (2019) *Production Planning and Control: A Comprehensive Approach*. Butterworth-Heinemann.

Monden, Y. (2011) *Toyota Production System: An Integrated Approach to Just-In-Time*. Springer.

OECD (2018) *Due Diligence Guidance for Responsible Business Conduct*. OECD. https://www.oecd.org/en/publications/oecd-due-diligence-guidance-for-responsible-business-conduct_15f5f4b3-en.html (accessed September 12, 2025).

Reid, R.D. and Sanders, N.R. (2019) *Operations Management: An Integrated Approach*. John Wiley & Sons.

Russell, R.S. and Taylor, B.W. (2019) *Operations and Supply Chain Management*. John Wiley & Sons.

Sanders, N. R. (2020) *Supply Chain Management: A Global Perspective*. Wiley.

Slack, N. and Brandon-Jones, A. (2018) *Essentials of Operations Management*. Pearson UK.

Slack, N. and Lewis, M. (2002) *Operations Strategy*. Pearson Education.

Slack, N., Chambers, S., and Brandon-Jones, A. (2007) *Operations Management* (5th edition). FT Prentice Hall.

Slack, N., Chambers, S., and Johnston, R. (2009). *Operations Management* (6th edition). Financial Times Prentice Hall.

Slack, N., Brandon-Jones, A., and Johnston, R. (2013) *Operations Management* (7th edition). Pearson Education.

Stahel, W.R. (2019). *The Circular Economy: A User's Guide*. Routledge.

Stevenson, W., Hojati, M., and Cao, J. (2014) *Operations Management*. McGraw-Hill Education.

UK Government (2015) 'Modern Slavery Act 2015', *legislation.gov.uk*. https://www.legislation.gov.uk/ukpga/2015/30/contents (accessed September 12, 2025).

UNHR (2011) *Guiding Principles on Business and Human Rights*, United Nations. https://www.ohchr.org/sites/default/files/Documents/Publications/GuidingPrinciplesBusinessHR_EN.pdf (accessed September 12, 2025).

Womack, J.P., Jones, D.T., and Ross, D. (1990) *The Machine That Changed the World*. Rawson.

Yang, K., Basem, S., and El-Haik, B. (2003). *Design for Six Sigma*. McGraw-Hill.

8
ENTREPRENEURSHIP AND INNOVATION

Fujia Li, Erno Tornikoski, Andreas Georgiou,
Bill Russell, and Katie Ledingham

INTENDED LEARNING OUTCOMES

After reading this chapter, you should be able to:

1 Identify the skills, mindset and capabilities of entrepreneurial individuals.
2 Establish the sustainable value creation process and the role of place and community in entrepreneurship.
3 Confirm the innovation imperative - and the central role of the innovation management process.
4 Reflect on the impact of innovation and how we can innovate for good.

SUSTAINABLE DEVELOPMENT GOALS

In this chapter, we address/relate to the following SDGs:

- SDG 5: Gender Equality - Encouraging inclusive entrepreneurship ensures that women and underrepresented groups have equal opportunities to innovate and lead businesses.
- SDG 7: Affordable and Clean Energy - Innovation in clean energy technologies drives sustainable business models that improve energy access and efficiency.
- SDG 8: Decent Work and Economic Growth - Creating job opportunities and sustainable economic growth through entrepreneurship and innovation.
- SDG 11: Sustainable Cities and Communities - Entrepreneurship can create sustainable urban solutions by addressing housing, mobility, and infrastructure challenges.
- SDG 12: Responsible Consumption and Production - Sustainable business models encourage circular economy practices, reducing waste and promoting ethical production.
- SDG 17: Partnerships for the Goals - Collaborating with other entrepreneurs, businesses, and organisations to achieve shared goals.

INTRODUCTION

In this chapter you will learn both about what it takes to act entrepreneurially and foster innovation in organisations, creating social, environmental, and financial value. In addition, while the innovation imperative drives forward progress, it can also have a 'dark side'. Consequently, we will consider how the innovation process can build more just, equitable and sustainable societies. We analyse how **innovation** and **entrepreneurship** happens at different levels, considering: individuals, organisations, and business ecosystems. This chapter walks you through the different elements necessary for success when acting entrepreneurially and creating innovative organisations.

The Connection Between Entrepreneurship and Innovation

Entrepreneurship and innovation are words that seem to belong together, like yin and yang. Both drive economic growth, job creation, and the development of competitive advantage. Entrepreneurs working in startups, scaleups, and large organisations launch new products, services, and **business models** that can create social and environmental impact and disrupt markets through responding to evolving customer needs. Innovation also addresses societal challenges through developing solutions increasing health, **sustainability**, and education, thus improving the quality of life within society. However, while 83% of companies rank innovation as a top-three priority, only 3% feel prepared for this 'innovation imperative' (Manly et al., 2024). And even those that feel ready to innovate might not survive to reap the benefits. According to recent U.S. Bureau of Labor Statistics (2024), around 1 out of 5 new U.S. businesses fail within one year of establishment, with only around half of them still operating after five years. A similar situation occurs in other parts of the world, with 2.8 million enterprise terminations recorded in the European Union in a single year (Eurostat, 2024).

Understanding the interconnected themes of innovation and entrepreneurship is based on a **model** of growth developed by the Austrian economist and Finance Minister Joseph Schumpeter, which centres on three main ideas:

1. Innovation and the diffusion of **knowledge** are at the centre of the growth process, with each new innovator 'standing on the shoulders of giants' who preceded them.
2. Innovation relies on incentives and the protection of property rights, with growth relying on decisions to invest – especially in research and development (R&D) and building new organisations – by entrepreneurs motivated by potential profits.
3. Creative destruction sees new innovations (products and services) eclipsing former innovations, making them obsolete.

Through studying innovation, we can plot the evolution of new industries and see how societies adapt to challenges. The term highlights the creative and entrepreneurial spirit that drives forward continuous improvement and radical change, making understanding how innovation happens a key element in the story of human progress. Entrepreneurs and innovators both focus on opportunities for change. However, while entrepreneurship and innovation often overlap, they are not the same phenomenon – innovation is the process through which change happens, and the entrepreneurial mindset drives human activity forward to create value.

Entrepreneurship is particularly concerned with the individual and collective characteristics and activities that drive the innovation process forwards because innovation requires vision, passion, collaboration and influencing skills, decision-making and resilience – and lots of hard work – to turn good ideas into a reality that creates value. At different stages of the innovation journey, entrepreneurship drives the process forwards in all kinds of settings including early-stage ventures, large **firms** like Netflix, as well as socially driven organisations such as UNICEF.

The successful pursuit of innovation, in turn, involves a process that can be organised and managed, and which focuses on the creation of new offerings that include products, services, brands, processes, new **marketing** methods, and new ways of managing an organisation, e.g. supply chain innovation or the delivery of social services. The development of new technology or combinations of technologies to create new benefits are associated with innovation.

It is important to note that innovation and entrepreneurship operate at different levels.

Individuals

When most individuals try to start new projects or come up with new ideas, it is difficult not to be overwhelmed at some point – however experienced they are. Innovation and entrepreneurship are about much more than the first, creative, and solution-focused steps to solve a problem, important though this *invention* stage is. Entrepreneurship is about taking action, and making projects happen in a variety of contexts. The focus is on psychology and personal drive, managing risk and the ability to connect an idea with a market or sector that is willing to pay or fund it, as well as the role of place and community in supporting the process.

Organisations

Once the development and management of an opportunity has outgrown what can be achieved by an individual – however talented and driven – things get more complicated. As more people, processes, technology, relationships, and knowledge become involved inside an organisation, it is essential to establish a system to manage the processes and routines needed to develop, launch and sustain products and services over time.

Business Ecosystems

Increasingly researchers and practitioners use the notion of business, entrepreneurial, or innovation ecosystems to understand how different elements (e.g., individuals, managers, customers, technologies, organisations, regulators, regions, universities, networks, funders etc.) successfully create value through the innovation process. To understand success in innovation, it is essential to understand the business ecosystem and overall environmental context surrounding a development opportunity, considering the impact of potential solutions on the planet.

Entrepreneurship

Entrepreneurship begins with individuals – people who spot opportunities, take initiative, and turn creative ideas into reality. But who exactly are these entrepreneurial individuals, and what sets them apart from others? In the following section, we explore the characteristics, mindsets, and actions that enable entrepreneurs to successfully create lasting value for society.

The Entrepreneurial Individual

At its core, entrepreneurship is all about the capacity to take decisive action, transforming innovative ideas into viable new economic activities. These activities generate not only economic value but also social and environmental benefits that extend beyond the individual, impacting communities and the world at large. Through entrepreneurship, you harness creativity and resourcefulness to address challenges and opportunities, fostering sustainable development and contributing to the greater good.

When entrepreneurial individuals create 'new economic activities', it refers to the visible outcomes of entrepreneurship, which can manifest in different entities such as:

- a non-governmental organisation (e.g. Doctors Without Borders, World Wildlife Fund, Oxfam International);
- a cooperative (e.g. Ocean Spray, The Associated Press, Groupe Credit Agricole);
- an association (e.g. Federation of Small Businesses, European Association for Artificial Intelligence); or
- a public organisation (e.g. public healthcare, transportation, school).

However, entrepreneurship is not limited to the creation of new entities from scratch; it can also occur within existing organisations through internal ventures (i.e. **intrapreneurship**). This includes establishing new business units, diversifying products, services, or markets, developing new revenue streams (e.g. offering the possibility to rent a product rather than buying it, or offering additional services related to an existing product), and creating new social and environmental value. Thus, entrepreneurship encompasses a broad range of activities, including but not limited to intrapreneurship and social entrepreneurship. Furthermore, it is important to specify that entrepreneurship focuses on creating 'viable' new economic activities, rather than one-off transactions or events. This involves establishing economic activities that are sustainable over time, with their survival and prosperity depending on a clear value-capturing logic, whether for-profit, non-profit, or a combination of both.

Action, Mindset, and Competence in Value Creation

What makes entrepreneurial individuals successful in their endeavours? Figure 8.1 presents a general framework which encapsulates the key factors usually involved in entrepreneurship and innovation to explain success.

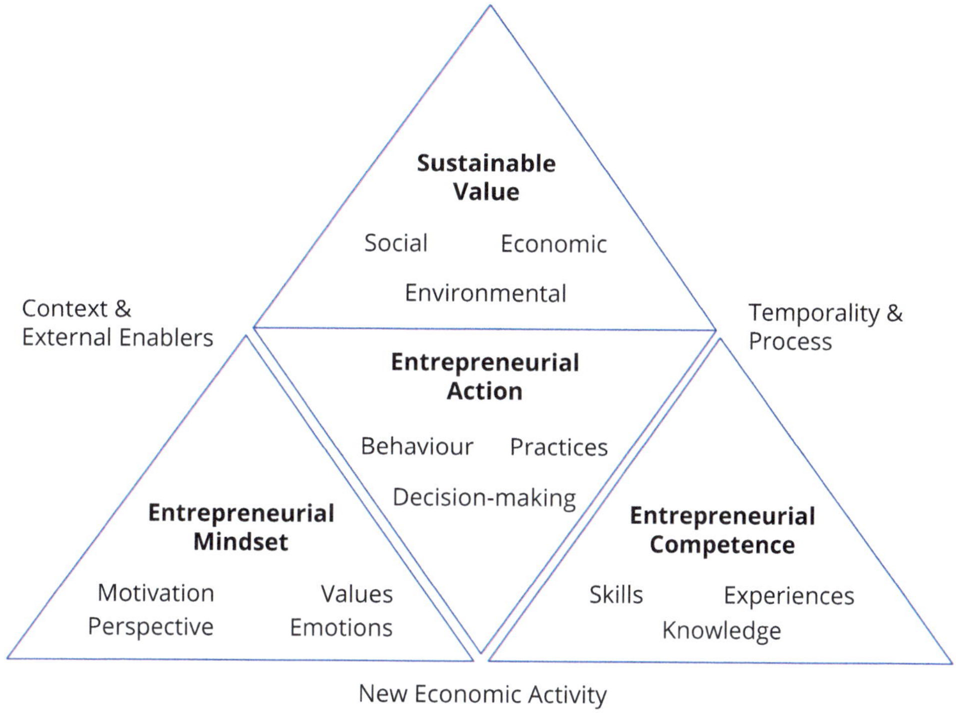

Figure 8.1 Core factors of entrepreneurship and innovation

Source: Authors

At the core of entrepreneurship and innovation lies *action* – it's about doing, making decisions, organising, and making things happen. A concept that captures this action-oriented and processual perspective is the verb 'entrepreneuring,' described as 'a fertile concept for understanding the processual aspect of entrepreneurship' (Steyaert, 2007: 453). Entrepreneurial individuals can rely on two different decision-making logics when taking action, namely effectuation and causation (Sarasvathy, 2008). When using effectual reasoning, entrepreneurs engage in entrepreneurial projects that are based on their available means and are doable now. Whereas, in causal reasoning, entrepreneurs first choose the most attractive opportunity and then spend time to gather/acquire the needed means to continue pursuing the attractive (big, risky) opportunity.

Furthermore, a key driver of entrepreneurial action is the *mindset* an individual possesses. Entrepreneurial individuals are motivated to make things happen due to their internal dispositions, such as passion, values, emotions, and perspective. Successful entrepreneurs also learn to overcome natural biases and misconceptions to develop accurate perspectives and knowledge (Gilovich et al., 2002). *Competence* is, in turn, what enables entrepreneurial action, encompassing a combination of **skills**, knowledge, and experiences necessary for entrepreneurial success. These skills include not only traditional technical skills related to entrepreneurship, such as opportunity identification, communication, and organisation, but also social skills, like emotional intelligence, empathy and **leadership** qualities, and behavioural skills, such as coaching and mentoring.

Finally, in Figure 8.1, entrepreneurship and innovation are viewed as a means to promote sustainable **value creation**. Every entrepreneurial project has the potential to address significant societal challenges, whether economic, social, or environmental. While not all projects will simultaneously target all three aspects of sustainable value creation, they should still strive to maximise their impact in each area. One often-cited example of pursuing sustainable value creation is Patagonia, which is 'in business to save our home planet' (Sonsev, 2021). Patagonia not only tries to limit its environmental impact by maximising the use of organic and recycled materials but also repairs damaged clothes and requires strong environmental protection standards from all supply chain partners.

To conclude, entrepreneurial individuals act as agents of change at the individual, firm, and ecosystem levels. The above framework underscores the importance of entrepreneurial agency in individuals, fostering independence, courage, initiative, and the ability to turn ideas into action. Through entrepreneurship, individuals are empowered to take control of their careers while generating value for broader communities and the world. Madam C. J. Walker, Sara Blakely, Sir Richard Branson, Peggy Cherng, among others, are individuals who demonstrate control over their lives despite adversities, and started small and ended up creating value and wealth over the years. In similar fashion, Virgin Group, Alibaba Group, Apple, Charity:Water, and Google are global operators, which were started by individuals with resilience, execution intelligence, customer-focus, and a desire to make a difference.

REFLECTIVE ACTIVITY 8.1

How often have you taken action or done something to improve the situation where you found yourself in which you felt annoyed, frustrated, and/or disappointed, or that something was missing? All these instances signal the presence of potential opportunity for entrepreneurial action.

INTRAPRENEURSHIP: FOSTERING INNOVATION WITHIN ORGANISATIONS

So, you might be wondering: now that I have learnt so much about the entrepreneurial individual, what if I don't want to be an entrepreneur, is there still any value in learning entrepreneurship? To answer this question, we turn to another concept – intrapreneurship.

In today's dynamic and competitive business environment, innovation is no longer solely the domain of start-ups and entrepreneurs. Established organisations are increasingly recognising the importance of fostering a culture of innovation within their structures. This concept, known as intrapreneurship, involves employees acting as entrepreneurs within a company, developing new products, services, or processes that can drive the business forward (Urbano et al., 2013). Intrapreneurship represents a vital strategy for organisations seeking to remain competitive, adapt to changing market conditions, and leverage the creative potential of their workforce (Elert and Stenkula, 2020).

The concept of intrapreneurship is rooted in the belief that employees at all levels of an organisation possess valuable insights and ideas that, if harnessed correctly, can lead to substantial advancements. By encouraging intrapreneurship, companies can tap into this latent potential, driving innovation from within rather than relying solely on external sources or top-down directives (Hornsby et al., 2002).

Unlike traditional entrepreneurship, which typically involves starting a new venture, intrapreneurship focuses on internal innovation. Employees, referred to as intrapreneurs, are encouraged to take ownership of projects and lead initiatives that could potentially result in significant business growth. This approach empowers individuals within the organisation to act with the autonomy and creativity typically associated with entrepreneurs, while still benefiting from the resources and stability of a larger entity (Kuratko et al., 2014).

Intrapreneurs are often given the freedom to experiment, iterate, and refine their ideas in a low-risk environment. This iterative process is essential for developing innovative solutions that may not emerge through traditional channels (Covin and Miles, 1999). Furthermore, because intrapreneurs operate within the structure of an established organisation, they have access to resources such as funding, expertise, and infrastructure that might not be as easily available to an independent entrepreneur. This combination of support and autonomy enables intrapreneurs to explore ambitious projects that could have a transformative impact on the company.

However, fostering a successful intrapreneurial culture is not without its challenges. For intrapreneurship to thrive, organisations must create an environment that supports risk-taking and tolerates failure. Traditional corporate structures, which often prioritise stability and efficiency, can be at odds with the experimental nature of intrapreneurship. Therefore, companies must be willing to adapt their management practices to encourage intrapreneurs to take calculated risks and explore unconventional ideas. This might involve redefining success metrics, offering incentives for innovation, and providing a safety net for projects that do not succeed (Ireland et al., 2009).

Another critical factor in promoting intrapreneurship is leadership (see Chapter 4 for more on leadership). Senior management must play an active role in championing intrapreneurial initiatives, setting a tone that values creativity and innovation. Leaders should also provide mentorship and guidance to intrapreneurs, helping them navigate the complexities of the organisation while allowing them the freedom to pursue their ideas (Hornsby et al., 2002). Moreover, leaders must be willing to allocate resources, including time and funding, to support intrapreneurial projects. This commitment signals to employees that the organisation is serious about innovation and is willing to invest in its people to achieve it (Gawke et al., 2017).

Organisational culture is equally important in cultivating intrapreneurship (see Chapter 3 for more on organisational behaviour). A culture that encourages open communication, collaboration, and knowledge-sharing is more likely to produce successful intrapreneurs.

In such environments, employees feel empowered to share their ideas and collaborate with colleagues across different departments, leading to cross-pollination of ideas and the development of more robust solutions (Ireland et al., 2009). Additionally, a culture that celebrates success and learns from failure helps to sustain the momentum of intrapreneurial efforts.

Case studies of successful intrapreneurial ventures highlight the potential impact of this approach. For example, Google's renowned '20% time' policy, which allows employees to spend 20% of their work time on projects of their own choosing, has led to the creation of products such as Gmail and Google News (AlignToday, 2024). Similarly, 3M's encouragement of intrapreneurship has resulted in the development of the iconic Post-It Note (AlignToday, 2024). These examples demonstrate how intrapreneurship can lead to breakthrough innovations that drive significant business growth and redefine industries.

However, it is important to recognise that not all intrapreneurial initiatives will succeed. The very nature of innovation involves a degree of uncertainty, and individuals as well as organisations must be prepared for the possibility that some projects will not achieve their intended outcomes. Rather than viewing these instances as failures, companies and employees should see them as valuable learning experiences that can inform future efforts.

REFLECTIVE ACTIVITY 8.2

Given the examples of success in intrapreneurship (e.g., Google's '20% time' and 3M's Post-It Note):

- What lessons do you take away about balancing creativity, collaboration, and organisational alignment?
- Looking ahead, how can you prepare yourself to be a successful intrapreneur in your future career?

In conclusion, intrapreneurship represents a powerful strategy for organisations seeking to foster innovation from within. As the business landscape continues to evolve, intrapreneurship will likely play an increasingly important role in shaping the future of successful companies. Especially for aspiring business professionals, understanding and embracing the principles of intrapreneurship will be crucial as you prepare to enter or continue to evolve in a world where innovation and adaptability are key drivers of success.

SUSTAINABLE VALUE CREATION PROCESS

Rather than adhering to a narrow economic focus, entrepreneurship can promote the broadest possible scope of value creation by generating social and environmental benefits. The primary areas of social, environmental, and economic value are underpinned by the UN SDGs and the UN Declaration of Human Rights as a minimum standard. Ideally, entrepreneurship and innovation should not only aim to mitigate or eliminate negative impacts but also to contribute positively to each aspect.

Creating value, which can be defined as 'the capacity of a good, service, or activity to satisfy a need or provide a benefit to a person or legal entity' (Haksever et al., 2004: 292), is not a straightforward process. First, value can mean different things to different **stakeholders**. For instance, renewable energy projects at the Isthmus of Tehuantepec, Mexico, have been considered by many a promising initiative towards achieving the SDGs and especially SDG#7 (Affordable and Clean Energy). However, a study by Ramirez (2021) reported that Isthmus community members were never adequately informed and equally involved in the process to propose what value they would like to be generated from such a project.

Entrepreneurs also face a dilemma, sometimes having to decide whether to satisfy the demands of local or global stakeholders (Seelos et al., 2011). This raises the question of who matters, and, relatedly, who defines what value means. In some cases, entrepreneurs and enterprises might initiate consultation processes before major projects or even actively co-produce solutions with stakeholders, so that they face less resistance. If you want to find out more about such engagement, you might find interesting the study by Arenas, Murphy and Jáuregui (2020), which delves into the fascinating context of Peruvian highlands and the mining industry.

A few decades ago, entrepreneurs could simply focus on creating economic value, following Friedman's (1970) doctrine that 'the social responsibility of business is to increase its profits'. One might also argue, very reasonably, that this made their life easier, as they could focus on one objective instead of multiple. Nevertheless, transformative changes in our society, the exceedance of several planetary boundaries and the empowerment of non-shareholder stakeholders suggests that entrepreneurs have to start creating multiple forms of value. If we look at the sustainability reports of Fortune 500 companies, we will note how much big companies currently emphasise their social and environmental orientation. In some instances, companies might report this to simply gain legitimacy and reputation but not follow through in practice, continuing with 'business as usual'.

Even when entrepreneurs genuinely aim to create simultaneously social, environmental, and economic value, this can prove challenging in practice as some of their employees and managers might not be able to synthesise different types of value. For instance, they might come from backgrounds that are more related to one type of value (e.g., financial analysts are more familiar with creating economic value) and could disagree with the mindset of their colleagues. One of the classic strategies for handling this complexity is 'segregating' different mindsets. For example, social and environmental value is usually created through the corporate social responsibility/sustainability department.

The challenge of creating multiple forms of value is sometimes resolved by developing new forms of enterprises that combine or balance different priorities. 'Hybrid' organisations, such as those created by social entrepreneurs (i.e., entrepreneurs prioritising social value creation), overcome the inertia and the narrow economic focus of mainstream business. Microfinance organisations, for instance, aim to achieve both increased access to financial services by disadvantaged individuals and to generate profits; in other words, they create both social and economic value. To be successful, social entrepreneurs usually need to hire individuals with little or no experience of creating value of any kind to avoid tendencies towards specific types of value, and focus on operational excellence (Battilana and Dorado, 2010). They also introduce goals, principles, structures, training, and incentives that fit into the mix of the values they aim to create.

Combining or balancing different forms of value is not always possible. This is where compromise might be necessary (Mitzinneck and Besharov, 2019). Thinking again of value creation as a process, collective social entrepreneurs, such as co-operatives, might have to initiate projects today that focus on economic value and commit that in the future they will invest in projects that create mainly environmental value or, let's say, social value. This is called 'temporal compromise'. Alternatively, they might offer project options and allow co-operative members to invest in or work for those that better align with their own values. This is known as 'structural compromise'. Finally, 'collaborative compromise' involves developing commonly agreed criteria on the minimum threshold of social, environmental, and economic value that each project should create to be eligible for selection.

All in all, sustainable value creation involves creating social, environmental, and economic value in a process of defining, prioritising and negotiating stakeholder needs and demands over time and understanding what value means in a specific context, project, product, and service. Entrepreneurs and enterprises follow multiple strategies to achieve this, develop novel structures and processes that combine effectively these values, and compromise when trade-offs are inevitable.

THE ROLE OF PLACE AND COMMUNITY IN ENTREPRENEURSHIP

Entrepreneurship does not occur in a vacuum. Entrepreneurs live, work, and operate their enterprises within local contexts, which play an important role. In fact, thinking about entrepreneurship without the place where it resides is like thinking about a soccer field without the lines. These lines in sports define the rules, the objectives, and the social relationships around the game. These 'lines' in entrepreneurship are the place and community where value is generated and entrepreneurial individuals reside. The following two sub-sections are devoted to this important topic.

Local Communities and Entrepreneurship

Have you ever wondered why Nike was founded and flourished in Oregon? Oregon has long been established as the 'Track Town USA', with many Olympic trials held there. The local 'running culture' was endorsed and reinforced by the local community, with residents actively volunteering for running events, participating in amateur running groups and forming a unique collective identity (Howard-Grenville et al., 2013). In turn, this proved to be fertile grounds for Nike, which benefitted from the emerging running-related expertise and local support and resources.

REFLECTIVE ACTIVITY 8.3

Nike leveraged the running culture at Oregon to become the successful multi-national company we all know.

- Can you think of any other big company in your country/locality doing something similar?

Place and community can play various roles in entrepreneurship. The most obvious one, as the above example illustrates, is that they provide the context in which some entrepreneurial opportunities and activities are supported, while others prove to be less accepted (Georgiou and Arenas, 2023). On the one hand, place and community can provide resources, valuable networks and skilled personnel, as well as tacit knowledge, to emerging enterprises. They might also make some economic activities part of their social and cultural fabric. As a result, suppliers and related businesses identify this emerging hotspot, relocate, and create an economic cluster. This leads to a virtuous cycle, with new skills, expertise and resources developed or devoted to the cluster, boosting entrepreneurship at the local level. In addition, place and community support idea generation, with entrepreneurs identifying local problems or market gaps and coming up with innovative solutions, and provide context-specific ways of decision-making, which sometimes might influence how enterprises are governed. Entrepreneurs also use place and community in their story-telling (Kimmitt et al., 2024), showing how they connect with, serve and are significant public figures.

On the other hand, place and community can inhibit entrepreneurship. Often enough, residents have protested, boycotted and, more broadly, hindered economic activities that do not comply to local standards. To illustrate this, if enterprises are oriented solely towards financial goals, instead of community goals, they might not get enough support to initiate activities (Almandoz, 2012). Relatedly, if enterprises are associated with non-local actors (e.g., national or international firms), this might lead to resistance and the development of new local enterprises against this trend. Beyond this, entrepreneurship in local contexts might end up reproducing the local status quo. For instance, we have seen in some contexts that women might be less likely to become entrepreneurs (Dimitriadis et al., 2017).

Community members can also contribute to entrepreneurship as beneficiaries, supporters, and partners (Bacq et al., 2022). Community members usually receive some of the benefits that entrepreneurship can bring in a place, such as vital products and services, jobs, community outreach initiatives, innovative and environmentally friendly technologies, and more advanced infrastructure. Taking more active roles, residents might engage in some form of collaboration with entrepreneurs. Becoming supporters, they might provide **capital**, information, volunteering services and co-create solutions. Engaging further and for longer periods of time with entrepreneurs and their enterprises, community members might become official partners. For example, Community Development Corporations in the United States include several community members as board members.

Place and community can also be the basis of enterprise, leading to what has been called 'place-based' and 'community-based' enterprises. Place-based enterprises are those 'with a local or place-based locus of ownership and control, embeddedness or rootedness in the physical, social, and human capital of a place, possessing a sense of place and a social mission' (Shrivastava and Kennelly, 2013: 90). They can be either for-profit or not-for-profit and might have multiple owners, insofar as they are based in place and oriented towards serving place and the local community. Such enterprises cannot simply relocate to different places, as their viability is directly associated with the prosperity of a place. As a result, they are keener to engage in socially and environmentally sustainable initiatives. For instance, consider the famous wine region of Bordeaux, where wines have protected designation of origin. Bordeaux wine-producing entrepreneurs operating in the area are heavily dependent on this place for natural resources and their own **branding**. It comes as no surprise, thus, that very recently place-based enterprises came together to develop a new approach to corporate social responsibility.

Objectives of the 'Bordeaux Cultivons Demain' are:

1 Ensuring the livelihood of the Bordeaux region
2 Making the wine sector attractive to employees
3 Cultivating dialogue and transparency with stakeholders and consumers
4 Preserving the environment

Among a large variety of place-based enterprises, **community-based enterprises (CBEs)** represent a distinctive case. What is unique here is that a significant majority of people living in the same place engage together in some form of economic activity. Imagine having to co-ordinate with hundreds or thousands of your fellow residents, each having different interests, preferences and mindsets. In the case of CBEs, the driving force is **culture**, as all residents, or the majority of them, share and hold some common values and/or history in high regard. For example, they might want to maintain or revive the traditions of their ancestors, who used to create a place-based product and for which they have developed a unique craft. Or, in other cases, they might want to protect the only pub in their village, acknowledging that this is a space where they share meaningful memories and where they could still preserve a sense of community.

CBEs are usually triggered by economic or social stress (Peredo and Chrisman, 2006). As the abovementioned example of the community pub reveals, many places face crises and lack of resources, while the interest of the market and political forces in the residing communities diminishes. As resources are removed from the community and residing enterprises cease operations, individuals realise that their quality of life is threatened, and they step up and work together to preserve their collective interests. It is important to note that developing CBEs is not necessarily the first time that residents step up, as evidence suggests that previous collective action, such as political mobilisation, might provide fertile grounds, routines and roles to support the operation of a CBE. Importantly, CBEs tend to flourish in communities of moderate size, big enough to gather a sufficient amount of resources and generate novel ideas, but small enough to allow for cohesion.

Turning to some key characteristics of CBEs, they usually build upon available community skills. More often than not, there is already a stock of expertise around producing specific goods, passed from generation to generation. This expertise is usually transmitted during the formative years of younger generations, making it almost natural for the youngsters to continue working on the same goods as adults. In other cases, many community members have already worked in an industry flourishing nearby, before understanding that they can organise together to develop a sustainable business. Speaking of sustainability, CBEs do not only focus on economic goals; in fact, they also aim to achieve social, cultural, and environmental objectives and their financial soundness is considered as a vehicle to further focus on the other objectives.

CASE STUDY 8.1

Indigenous People and Community-Based Entrepreneurship in Canada

Indigenous community-based entrepreneurship provides an apt example of sustainable value creation. Indigenous people bring to the table a unique set of skills, competences and mindset. They genuinely care for the place and the community they operate in, and 'see their own fortunes as linked with the health and welfare of a particular place' (Shrivastava and Kennelly, 2013: 90). They also employ an effectuation logic (Sarasvathy, 2008); in other words, they focus on who they are, what they know and can do, what means they have and what they can afford to lose, among others. This approach ensures that they do not embrace an extractivist approach.

This case focuses on entrepreneurship in British Columbia. Indigenous communities there understand the world as interconnected, with individuals having to maintain balance, care, and respect, reciprocate, be generous, and treat economic development as 'becoming whole' (Murphy et al., 2020: 9). A few years ago, one such community collaborated with a local university for a research project to assess which entrepreneurial opportunities are worth pursuing and whether such opportunities promote sustainable value creation and adhere to Indigenous values, knowledge and principles.

After assessing the key means the community brings to the table, they started creating a consensus on what is important to them in terms of well-being. Collaborating with the university, they co-created a system that includes selecting indicators of economic, community, cultural, and environmental well-being, putting relative weights in each dimension (e.g., 25% weight for each dimension) and subjectively assessing the expected impact of potential entrepreneurial projects on each indicator. This enabled comparing entrepreneurial projects holistically and in terms of each dimension of well-being, both at their initiation and over time.

As a result, they disregarded projects such as the construction of hotels and casinos and, instead, opted for community-based enterprises related to 'eco-tourism, shellfish farming and different aspects of the forestry industry' (Murphy et al., 2020: 11). Such entrepreneurial processes and mindsets

(Continued)

have enabled Indigenous communities in British Columbia to participate in partnerships, attract conservation finance (Kopecky, 2024) and overcome systemic barriers (Small Business BC, n.d.).

Questions

1. What distinguishes the entrepreneurial process the British Columbia indigenous communities followed from that of other entrepreneurs you might know?
2. Could you think of any communities that have followed or could follow the example of those in British Columbia? What are the (potential) differences to this case?
3. What relative weights would you put to economic, community, cultural and environmental well-being as a potential entrepreneur in the future? Think of different scenarios and what the resulting enterprises would look like.

Sources

Kopecky, A. (2024) 'Great Bear Sea's blueprint for doing business with nature', *Corporate Knights*, October 23. https://www.corporateknights.com/natural-capital/great-bear-sea-conservation-finance

Murphy, M., Danis, W.M. and Mack, J. (2020) 'From principles to action: Community-based entrepreneurship in the Toquaht Nation', *Journal of Business Venturing*, 35 (6). doi.org/10.1016/j.jbusvent.2020.106051

Sarasvathy, S.D. (2008) *Effectuation: Elements of Entrepreneurial Expertise*. Edward Elgar.

Shrivastava, P. and Kennelly, J.J. (2013) 'Sustainability and place-based enterprise', *Organization & Environment*, 26 (1): 83–101.

Small Business BC (n.d) 'A rich history of Indigenous entrepreneurship in BC', *SBBC*. https://web.archive.org/web/20241104084311/https://smallbusinessbc.ca/article/a-rich-history-of-indigenous-entrepreneurship-in-bc/ (accessed December 17, 2025).

CHALLENGING CONVENTIONAL WISDOM IN ENTREPRENEURSHIP DEVELOPMENT

While the previous section introduced the concept of place-based or community-based entrepreneurship, it centred on the idea that places and local communities provide crucial contexts for entrepreneurial activity. In this view, entrepreneurship plays a vital role in sustaining and developing communities, fostering innovation, creating jobs, and balancing the interplay between farming, land use, community growth, and economic development, particularly in rural areas (Atterton et al., 2011). However, an important question arises: when should local entrepreneurship be cultivated by individuals and collectives? Does a vibrant entrepreneurial ecosystem in a local community, such as a village or region, necessarily mean that everything else is also thriving? This section offers a new perspective: entrepreneurship should be promoted in any community if it supports the development of **community resilience**. Consequently, not all forms of entrepreneurial activity are beneficial in every context.

Community Resilience

Resilience is crucial because a resilient community is better equipped to absorb and recover from social, environmental, and economic shocks. For a local community to thrive despite the challenges it faces, it must prioritise building resilience. The concept of resilience is relevant across various fields. It has also been integrated into development and humanitarian aid programmes. The UN, for instance, views resilience as a critical tool for navigating a rapidly changing world increasingly characterised by shocks such as natural and human-induced hazards, climate change, violent conflict, pandemics, financial crises, food price fluctuations, poverty, inequality, discrimination, extremism, ecosystem degradation, and weak institutions (UN SDG, 2021). These shocks can compound and interconnect, posing significant threats to both human life and the environment.

Community Capitals

To understand what makes a community resilient and how to determine when to develop initiatives that enhance community resilience, we can consider the concept of *community capitals*. Community capitals comprise seven dimensions:

- human
- social
- political
- cultural
- built
- natural
- economic/financial (Emery and Flora, 2006)

These dimensions collectively define the strength and character of a community. Human capital refers to the people living within the community; **social capital** concerns the connections and interactions among community members; natural capital encompasses land and natural resources; and so forth. In essence, for a community to be resilient, it must develop and nurture all seven dimensions of community capital. Today, community capital has become an invaluable tool for understanding the strategic aspects of development planning that influence societal impact and foster resilient community development (Emery and Flora, 2006).

Developing community resilience is challenging when focusing solely on economic **capital**. For example, economic capital alone cannot address the lack of health services in a community, as this also requires investment in other forms of community capital, such as human capital. Similarly, while the introduction of a new manufacturing plant might boost economic capital, it could come at the expense of natural capital, like parks or forests, which are essential for fostering social capital and connections among community members. To build resilience against social, environmental, and economic shocks, a community must carefully assess which dimensions of community capital are lacking and then direct the development of local activities, including entrepreneurship, to address these gaps. Likewise, individuals interested in entrepreneurial activities should understand the different dimensions of community capital to design their projects in a way that contributes not only to economic capital but also ensures the balanced development of the other dimensions of community capital in the local community.

INNOVATION

We have established that value creation integrates social and environmental components, and that place and community have a major impact on how entrepreneurship happens. We have also considered the role of individuals, growing firms and collectives within increasingly interconnected entrepreneurial ecosystems. As you build your understanding of the interconnected themes of innovation and entrepreneurship, we need to explore further how change happens at the business and wider societal levels.

The Innovation Imperative

Everyone is talking about innovation. Whether it is politicians, the leaders of major **corporations**, public sector managers or individuals seeking to change the world with their new start up, it seems that one of the words that is deployed to provide hope and purpose is the word *innovation*. A recent survey by Boston Consulting Group (BCG) found that 83% of companies ranked innovation as a top-three priority for organisations (Manly et al., 2024).

The same survey evaluates how 'ready' companies are to innovate – with only 3% reporting that they feel prepared for what we can describe as the '*innovation imperative*'.

The Difference Between 'Invention' and 'Innovation'

A regular dictionary definition of innovation is 'change'; the word has its root in the Latin words *in* and *novare,* which translate as: 'to make something new'. With so many public sector, humanitarian and commercial organisations prioritising innovation due to a perception of the need to change – often enabled by technology – a big challenge is knowing how to ramp up innovation. A major problem for many organisations at the start of their innovation journey is the confusion between having good ideas – which can broadly be described as invention, and innovation, which we can define as: 'the successful exploitation of new ideas' (Bessant and Tidd, 2024).

To make sense of innovation, it is important to connect the invention and ideas aspects of innovation with a practical and tangible focus on creating and delivering value to individuals, organisations, and society more widely. It is widely recognised that innovation needs to be seen as a process that can be managed and organised, whether in a research lab, a huge enterprise like Microsoft, Samsung or Huawei, or in an organisation focused on socially centred work such as Save the Children (Dodgson et al., 2014; Poole and Van de Ven, 2021).

ZOOMING OUT: THE INNOVATION IMPERATIVE AT THE GLOBAL LEVEL

The world has never spent more money on research and development (R&D) into new ideas and opportunities. In 2022 a staggering $2.475 trillion was spent globally on R&D into finding new knowledge and ways of doing things – more money than the size of the world's 15th biggest economy, Spain (CIA, 2024; Statista, 2024a, 2024d). Allowing for inflation, this investment in R&D is three times more than in 2002.

The Innovation Imperative, as indicated by investment in R&D, is not consistent. The US spends almost $680 billion a year, over $100 billion more than the next biggest funder of R&D, China (Statista, 2024a). Some outlier countries prioritise investment in R&D, with South Korea spending over 4.5% of GDP on R&D – a much higher proportion than other major innovation-centred countries such as Switzerland or Germany (Statista, 2024b).

Major companies spend big on R&D, with Amazon investing $88.5 billion annually, followed by Alphabet, the holding company of Google ($49.6 billion), and Meta ($43 billion), the holding company of Facebook and WhatsApp (Statista, 2024c). In certain industries the innovation imperative is much greater than others – particularly when the potential growth and profits on offer are significant. The health industries including pharmaceuticals spend at the highest level, with over 13.5% of revenues focused on R&D (Statista, 2024b).

How Is Success in Innovation Measured?

Organisations prioritising the management of innovation have two main measures of success (OECD, 2023):

- An increase in the number, relevance and quality of new and improved products – which might be physical or service oriented in nature. First developed by leading research and development company 3M, the Vitality Index is often used to measure the effectiveness of an organisation's innovation efforts and calculates how much of an entity's revenue is generated by its newest products. The simple idea is that the more revenue that comes from new products (as compared to pre-existing), the more innovative the firm is (Cooper, 2013; Löfsten, 2014).
- New business (including management) processes – improving how an organisation functions, often with a focus on efficiency and productivity. Organisations can be seen as being made up of the various routines and processes that enable them to be productive. The better an organisation is at developing new processes – from new production lines to better project management techniques – then the more innovative it is (Garud et al., 2013; Repenning et al., 2018).

An additional way that organisations can measure innovation success is through registering patents. However, for most firms involved in research and development, the ultimate goal is the launch of new products, and so the Vitality Index is often seen as being a better indicator of innovativeness.

How Do We Manage for Innovation Success?

The organisations that make a success of managing innovation put the innovation process at the heart of everything that they do. The process is now so well understood that there is even an international standard that has been developed to guide how organisations manage innovation (ISO 56000, 2025).

Figure 8.2 below summarises how the innovation process flows and illustrates the key stages involved in making change happen. The model prioritises the role of knowledge, and emphasises how innovators need to seek, share, and deploy knowledge through continuous learning. Since 2000, the management of innovation has seen the rise of mobile communication, social platforms, cloud computing and the early development of machine learning. With knowledge and learning as key elements within the innovation process, innovators are increasingly deploying AI, GenAI, and agentic AI to transform how they work and the offerings they develop – with digital excellence underpinning innovation work from agriculture to net zero projects.

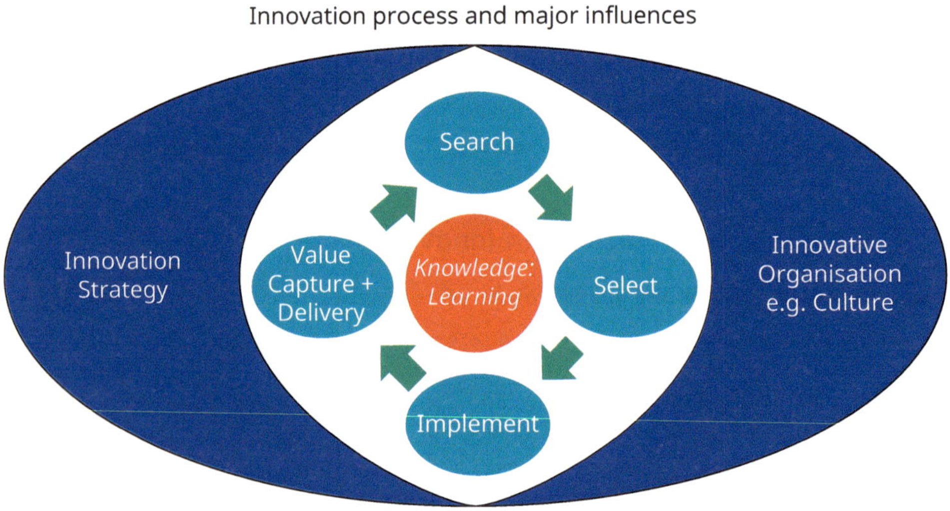

Figure 8.2 Innovation process and major influences

Source: Authors

Search

An important first step in the innovation process is the identification of new ideas and opportunities. This is often seen as the 'invention' or scanning phase and can involve ideas for new and improved products and services. The opportunities can extend to new processes (e.g. increasing quality, efficiency, and lowering cost through using new technologies), new ways of seeing the world (e.g. the rise of veganism or sustainability), new business models (e.g. Airbnb), or repositioning existing products for changing markets (e.g. caffeine in Red Bull drinks).

Select

Innovation is about much more than coming up with new ideas and processes. It is important to decide which of the opportunities to focus on – because even if you are working for

Amazon or Apple, time and resources are not available to follow up every interesting idea. Choices might be based on what the enterprise is good at, or the priorities of the organisation (e.g. healthcare professionals trying to reduce obesity).

Implement

Transforming the idea into something new, and launching it internally or externally – or changing a major business process to achieve savings – is not easy. Moving from the potential of an idea to a new product or a more efficient process is not about a single step. It involves acquiring the knowledge to create the innovation, project management under conditions of uncertainty (often involving problem solving over an extended time period), and the launch of the innovation to internal or external markets.

Value Capture

When it comes to launching new products, for example, the organisation needs to generate sales, sustain and grow the market, and persuade customers to adopt (buy and use) the innovation while making sure that the innovator captures value (sales and profit) – while keeping within budget limits.

Managing these four stages over time is complex and requires everyone involved to learn new and better ways to manage the innovation process (Ballé et al., 2016).

How to Support the Innovation Process for Incremental and More Radical Innovation?

Managing the four core stages of the innovation process in Figure 8.2 requires support from the organisations and individuals and teams that work in them, and increasingly from the networks or ecosystems of other organisations (suppliers, digital platforms, customers, regulators etc.) that are also involved in making a product or service a success (Jacobides, 2022).

When the media focuses on innovation, the emphasis is often on big technological breakthroughs such as AI, or the impact of emerging business models, e.g. the development of Uber. In established organisations there is a need to manage incremental (do better) innovation in existing activity areas alongside more radical (do different) innovations that are focused on the future. A major challenge is how to manage incremental and radical innovation at the same time. This requires organisational ambidexterity (Nagji and Tuff, 2012; Girod et al., 2023).

With the management of innovation recognised as a top three priority in 83% of firms, and the top priority in 35% of firms (Manly et al., 2024), it is clear that a major focus for organisations is to enable – over time – the successful management of innovation-centred activities considering the core (current) business and the next (future) business. There are two priority areas of activity that have a disproportionate impact on managing innovation successfully:

- Developing, communicating and implementing an *innovation strategy*
- Facilitating the culture, organisational design and routines that create an *innovative organisation*

Innovation Strategy

In most areas of social and commercial activity, the world is moving fast, triggered by new digital and scientific technologies and priorities driven by sustainability and ethics (e.g. equality, diversity, and inclusion). To plan activities in a changing world, organisations need an innovation strategy designed to bring together the firm-specific knowledge to respond to constantly changing external environments (Tidd and Bessant, 2025). The innovation strategy needs to identify and develop the specific knowledge needed for success, along with the capabilities to exploit the rapidly changing set of knowledge for future success.

Unclear or overly broad strategies have been identified as the biggest challenge limiting innovation/R&D/**product development**. The effective communication of a clear innovation strategy guiding current and future activities is an imperative for success (Sull et al., 2018).

Innovative Organisation

Studies examining why some organisations are successful when managing innovation, and why the majority are less effective, emphasise the importance of culture. Tellis (2013) asks why successful companies stumble and fall and identified 'The incumbent's curse' that is driven by three cultural traits: a focus on the present instead of the future; protecting (currently) successful products against the threat of innovation; and an aversion to risk.

The successful management of innovation is about much more than processes, tools and techniques (Tidd and Bessant, 2025), and demands that:

- At the **personal level**, different leadership approaches impact the ability to identify, assess and advance new opportunities and ideas.
- At the **collective level**, teams, larger work groups and processes all contribute to successful innovation outcomes.
- At the **wider context or climate level**, a variety of factors can accelerate or limit innovation and entrepreneurship.

The Dimensions and Imperative of Innovation: Who and What Is Involved

Informed by over 100 years of research, we know a great deal about what it takes to manage innovation successfully. The theme is driven by a very practical objective – to deliver value to individuals, groups of people, or organisations.

The successful management of innovation involves both incremental (do better – efficiency focused) activity *and* more radical (do different) projects that change whole industries, e.g. the development of streamed entertainment by Netflix. Innovation matters to individuals at any stage of their career – wherever they are working. It matters to organisations (it is often their top priority), cities, regions, countries and whole ecosystems. Without the innovation process – with entrepreneurial people at its centre – ideas will not be transformed into value for individuals, society and hopefully a better and safer planet.

Innovation for More Just, Equitable, and Sustainable Societies

Innovation can play a catalysing role in creating just, equitable, and sustainable societies. Through harnessing technology, increasing inclusivity, and addressing systemic inequalities, innovation has the potential to have a positive impact on previously marginalised communities and to widen global resilience.

Diversity and Inclusion

The past decade has seen an increasing focus on the importance of achieving levels of equality, diversity, and inclusion (EDI) in the workplace, so that the representation of different elements of society reflects age, gender, sexual orientation, and cultural and economic dimensions. While there has been progress on some of these elements, there is much to do (Terjesen and Sealy, 2016; Ingram, 2021).

The Impact of Diversity and Inclusion on Innovation Outcomes

While the ethical arguments for achieving greater diversity for more just, equitable, and sustainable societies receive significant attention, it is also important to build the argument for higher levels of EDI based on improved organisational performance, particularly focused on how greater diversity increases levels of innovation and is consistent with UN SDG 5: Gender Equality.

The Benefits of Diversity

The business case for inclusion and diversity is strong, because the evidence indicates that diverse companies are more likely to outperform other organisations in their sectors that are less diverse, considering gender and ethnic diversity (Hunt et al., 2023). There is an increasingly clear connection between the level of diversity at the most senior – board level – and diversity in the teams that work for the most senior staff in the organisation (Novacek et al., 2023).

The Diversity Dimensions That Boost Innovation

While much of the attention when considering the connection between diversity and innovation focuses on the impact of gender and country of origin, there are other dimensions that have a big impact.

A study found that the inclusion of staff who had worked in a variety of different industries, rather than continuing to build experience consistently within a sector, boosted innovation outcomes more than any other factor. An additional major diversity element that positively impacts innovation is when individuals have worked within multiple disciplines, e.g. IT, sales and human resources, as they develop their careers. Diversity of work and sector experience can make a big difference to innovation performance through introducing different perspectives (Lorenzo et al., 2017).

How Do Diverse Teams Support Innovation?

In a Spanish study, it was established that teams with greater gender diversity introduced more radical new innovations than those with less gender diversity. A London study found that businesses run by culturally diverse leadership teams were more likely to develop new products than those with homogenous leadership teams. Research indicates that more diverse teams focus more on facts than when teams are from similar backgrounds. Diverse teams also process facts more carefully, to make sure that assumptions are not made about the facts being analysed (Rock and Grant, 2016).

Making Good Use of Differences in How People Approach Change

People with different psychological dimensions approach innovation focused activity in a variety of ways, e.g. introverts collaborate and manage their work in different ways to extroverts (Cain, 2013). These differences extend to how people process knowledge. For example, when facing new situations, do individuals prefer to consolidate and deploy existing knowledge, or do they prefer to generate new knowledge? And when it comes to taking a perspective when developing options for change, do individuals prefer to deploy their own expertise? Or do they prefer to orchestrate and mix in the ideas of others with their own expertise when working in teams? Research has found that teams with higher cognitive diversity in terms of both processing knowledge and taking advantage of wider rather than narrower perspectives solve problems more effectively (Reynolds and Lewis, 2017).

Diversity Creates Wider Knowledge Sets and Better Innovation Outcomes

Greater diversity at the individual level increases the social and technical resources available for innovation-centred work. In a world where it is rare for individuals and organisations to win the innovation game on their own, higher levels of innovation tend to flow from diverse inter-organisational networks which are increasingly described as business ecosystems. It is often through working with people who are different from you that opportunities for creativity and value creation are generated (Burt, 2000).

Looking at the Evidence: Immigration Increases Diversity and Performance

Individuals with more diverse experiences and knowledge add disproportionally to team performance, as their skills complement those of others. Looking at the example of immigrants, they bring alternative contacts, knowledge and experiences into teams, making other colleagues more productive. A recent National Bureau of Economic Research (NBER) research project assessed this through looking at what happens to researchers when a colleague dies. The loss of an immigrant researcher took down the productivity of co-workers (measured in patents) by almost twice the level of the loss of a native worker (Bernstein et al., 2021).

In the case of the US, immigrants make up 14% of the population, 16% of inventors and directly produce over 23% of innovation, measured by patents, patent citations and the economic value of those patents. In addition, immigrants make their native-born collaborators more productive, supporting the assessment that they contribute a persuasive 36% of total innovation (Bernstein et al., 2021).

Steering Innovation to Do Good

Innovation has contributed to a world that is wealthier and healthier than for many in the past. Many of us now live longer, have more opportunities, and enjoy more experiences. Despite this, our planet is in crisis. There is growing recognition that current modes of organising and innovating may not only be insufficient to meet the deep, existential crises that we face today, but can also be directly implicated in contributing to irreversible planetary damage.

We do not have to look far to find a plethora of examples of innovation which, despite good intentions, have contributed to a diverse array of societal and environmental harms. Take the example of low carbon energy transitions in Europe, including solar energy, smart meters and electric vehicles. Whilst being celebrated by many governing institutions as a key part of more sustainable futures, these are innovations which nevertheless have 'sobering and troubling' connections to a range of negative impacts including environmental degradation, economic dislocation and poverty in different parts of the world (Sovacool et al., 2021: 10). Toxic e-waste dumping grounds in Ghana are being filled with smart meter and battery waste from the United Kingdom, and winemakers in France have been dispossessed and marginalised by nuclear suppliers (Sovacool et al., 2021). Even innovations heralded as being clean and green are by no means clean and green for everyone – there are always 'winners' and 'losers' (Sovacool et al., 2021) in innovation trajectories. It is amidst growing awareness of the harmful impacts and implications of contemporary innovation, that there is a clear imperative to do and develop innovations in ways that centre responsibility and care for all – for both people and planet.

As the celebratory zeal accompanying innovation is called into question, there has been a proliferation in innovation approaches, processes and governance frames that seek to tackle these issues head on (Fobel, 2019). Included in these approaches are 'responsible' innovation, 'sustainable' innovation, 'inclusive' and 'social' innovation and we can introduce their characteristics and dynamics as follows.

Responsible Innovation (RI)

RI is an innovation approach that has tended to focus on responsibility, particularly in relation to new technologies such as synthetic biology, **artificial intelligence**, and nanotechnology. It emerged partly in the wake of the 2008 global financial crisis that involved complex financial technologies (Owen and Pansera, 2019). Proponents of RI, including the

European Commission, the UK Engineering and Physical Sciences Research Council (ESPRC) and innovation theorists and practitioners, recognised that because many innovations are concerned with the generation of novelty (Owen et al., 2013) – and because they also become entangled and embedded within thick social worlds in ways which may involve them being repurposed – this can generate unintended consequences. RI was subsequently developed to help:

a delimit the unanticipated consequences of innovation, and
b better align innovation with societal values, helping RI to do more than simply avoiding harm (Voegtlin and Scherer, 2017)

To reach its goals, RI utilises different tools and methods to bring together diverse people and knowledge to better anticipate consequences before they arise. Participatory processes are designed to enable diverse publics to have a say over what types of innovations are developed and deployed in the world, under what conditions, and when.

One early approach to operationalising RI is the AREA framework that was co-developed with the UK Engineering and Physical Sciences Research Council (now encapsulated under UK Research and Innovation – a non-departmental governmental body that directs research and innovation funding). The fundamentals of the AREA framework are shown below (adapted from UKRI, 2023):

- **Anticipate:** What are the impacts, intended or otherwise, that might arise (economic, social, and environmental)? What are the possible impacts and implications that may otherwise remain uncovered and little discussed?
- **Reflect:** What are the motivations? What uncertainties, areas of ignorance, assumptions, and dilemmas might be involved?
- **Engage:** How to open up these visions, impacts, and questioning to broader deliberate, dialogue, engagement, and debate in an inclusive way?
- **Act:** Use these processes to influence the direction and trajectory of the research and innovation process itself.

Sustainable Innovation

Whilst exhibiting synergies with responsible innovation, sustainable innovation is a term that is typically used to refer to innovation that prioritises healthier environmental and planetary futures. Sustainable innovation encapsulates a diversity of activities that range from the development of less polluting technologies and products, through to the development of more environmentally friendly supply chain networks as well as more broadly business model innovation (Adams et al., 2016). Business model innovation refers to significant changes in how a business operates. Examples of sustainable business model innovation include developments in sharing or re-use economies which challenge mainstream production, ownership, and consumption regimes.

CASE STUDY 8.2

Gene Drive Technology – Responsible and Sustainable Innovation in Practice?

Gene drive is an innovative approach to genetic engineering that may play an important role in addressing a number of contemporary sustainability challenges. Using the latest genetic engineering technology, it enables specific genetic traits to be 'driven' through species populations (such as sterility and sex-biasing). Traditional hereditary processes mean that there is a 50% chance that a gene may be inherited by its offspring, but with gene drive this is increased to nearly 100%. Gene drive can be used to reduce (or eliminate) populations of pests and invasive species and to 'drive' traits through the population that make them less harmful. As climate change contributes to a resurgence in the transmission of vector borne diseases, a high-profile application area is the development of gene drive mosquitoes for malaria control (NASEM, 2016; Royal Society, 2018). Malaria is the leading cause of death in Uganda and Mali and this is where the release of gene drive mosquitoes may take place within a number of years (Hartley et al., 2023).

Gene drive is a contentious technology - its development has been accompanied by a commitment to responsible and equitable practice (Hartley et al., 2019). This is particularly important amidst the backdrop of mistrust and neo-colonial technology transfer, where Western technologies and health initiatives have historically been parachuted into the Global South in ways that have caused harm, and without due regard for local cultural contexts. In conjunction with the principles of the AREA framework, there is evidence of communities being engaged in a way that enables them to steer how the technology is being developed and appraised. There is also a commitment amongst technology developers to equip communities with the power to reject the technology (Ledingham and Hartley, 2021). These are key cornerstones of a responsible innovation approach. Importantly, technology partners in the Global North are seeking to enhance the scientific and regulatory capacity of countries in the Global South to develop and deploy the technology on their own terms (Hartley et al., 2021).

At the same time, however, pressing questions have been raised surrounding the meaningfulness and depth of responsible innovation in practice in this case (Hartley et al., 2021). For example, there has been no or limited capacity building in relation to social scientific expertise in the Global South or public engagement initiatives that may help to facilitate a more widespread questioning appraisal of this development on the ground. There is also a growing recognition that the principles of the AREA framework need reconfiguring in Global South contexts where cultures of deliberation operate in different ways (Wakunuma et al., 2021).

Questions

1. Why do you think a responsible innovation approach might be important in this case?
2. Can you think of any ways that gene drive technology developers might engage with communities in robust and power-sharing ways?

(Continued)

3 Why and how do you think responsible innovation might be reconceptualised from a Global South perspective?

Sources

Hartley, S., Kokotovich, A., Devos, Y., and Mumford, J. (2023) 'Engagement on risk assessment for gene drive mosquitoes by EFSA and Target Malaria', *Environmental Science and Policy*, *142*: 183–93.

Hartley, S., Ledingham, K., Owen, R., and Leonelli, S. (2021) 'Experimenting with co-development: A qualitative study of gene drive research for malaria control in Mali', *Social Science & Medicine* 276: article #113850.

Hartley, S., Thizy, D., Ledingham, K., Coulibaly, M., Diabaté, A., Dicko, B. [...] and Paré Toé, L. (2019) 'Knowledge engagement in gene drive research for malaria control', *PLoS Neglected Tropical Diseases*, 13 (4): article #0007233. https://doi.org/10.1371/journal.pntd.0007233

Ledingham, K. and Hartley, S. (2021) 'Transformation and slippage in co-production ambitions for global technology development: The case of gene drive', *Environmental Science and Policy*, 116: 78–85.

National Academies of Sciences, Engineering, and Medicine (NASEM) (2016) *Gene Drives on the Horizon, Advancing Science, Navigating Uncertainty, and Aligning Research with Public Values*. National Academies Press. https://www.ncbi.nlm.nih.gov/books/NBK379277/ (accessed September 15, 2025).

Royal Society. (2018) *Gene Drive Research: Why It Matters*. The Royal Society. https://royalsociety.org/-/media/policy/publications/2018/08-11-18-gene-drive-statement.pdf (accessed September 15, 2025).

Wakunuma, K., Castro, F.D., Jiya, T., Inigo, E.A., Blok, V., and Bryce, V. (2021) 'Reconceptualising responsible research and innovation from a Global South perspective', *Journal of Responsible Innovation*, 8 (2): 267–91. http://doi.org/10.1080/23299460.2021.1944736

Inclusive Innovation

At the start of this section, we noted that many of us, thanks to innovation, now live longer and have more experiences. But we also noted that this is not the case for all of us – that innovation has left many behind. Inclusive innovation can be distinguished from sustainable and responsible innovation by its focus on working towards greater inclusivity. For Heeks et al. (2014), mainstream innovation is an innovation of inequality because it has disproportionately improved the welfare of higher-income consumers over marginalised ones, formal producers over informal ones, and has focused on economic over social development needs. Inclusive innovation subsequently encapsulates a range of innovation activity that includes efforts and initiatives by multinational companies and other organisations to develop frugal (low-cost functional) products that meet neglected and unmet needs. However, social exclusion is a complex, multidimensional issue that goes beyond material deprivation. Inclusion cannot be redressed simply by the development of new and cheaper products – it requires systems-based change and new perspectives on what innovation entails. As Papaioannou (2014) stresses, innovation should do more than simply meet basic needs; it must enhance the capacity of individuals and communities to pursue the kinds of lives they value and desire.

Social Innovation

Social innovation is typically associated with the development of new business ventures with social goals – prominent examples include enterprises that channel profits towards specific social issues – these enterprises might be community owned and provide employment opportunities geared towards local needs and contexts. Social innovation can also be described as being about the reassembling of social relations and processes – it includes movement building, awareness raising and the creation of new connections and infrastructures that enable publics and innovation funders and policy makers to come together in new ways to co-create change in their communities.

The ongoing development and evolution of these innovation approaches is a key area for innovation studies today – particularly amidst still prevalent instances of innovations contributing to harm.

Towards Transformative Innovation

We have learnt so far in this chapter that innovation has become regarded as something that is inherently good but we have also learnt that innovation has a 'dark side' (Coad et al., 2020). Whether it's plastics in the ocean or new platforms that facilitate the spread of dis/**misinformation**, we do not have to look far to find examples of the less desirable impacts of innovation in the world. It is in response to growing awareness of these issues that we have seen the development of innovation approaches that can be put into practice to achieve kinder as well as more equitable and sustainable futures. Building on these initiatives is an intensifying commitment to work towards transformation and to 'rethink' innovation (Ledingham et al., 2024) in ways that broaden its scope, ontology and accompanying governance frameworks, so that it is better able to contribute to systems change. Schot and Steinmeuller (2018) identify the emergence of *Transformative Innovation Policy* (TIP) as an important step in this direction – one that reflects a commitment to centrally directing innovation towards the UN SDGs. But what does this mean and what might this look like in practice?

TIP challenges traditional ideas about what innovation looks like, how innovation gets done and who is involved. Innovation has historically been equated with technology and a key idea of our time is that advanced technology can redress social, environmental and economic ills (Huesemann and Huesemann, 2011: xxiii). However, TIP recognises that focusing only on technology might fix symptoms but mask systemic issues that are often social and political in nature. Under TIP, innovation focuses not only on developing new technical efficiencies and capabilities but also on fostering creative capacities for listening, learning, empathy, collaboration, and connection across sectors and communities.

A key underpinning of transformative innovation is looking at the bigger picture and asking questions about power, politics, and who gets to participate – topics that have not historically been at the heart of innovation or business management scholarship. For example, we might ask: Are electric vehicles just replacing one problem with another? Or, do food banks only provide temporary relief without addressing the root causes of food poverty? This kind of thinking acknowledges that society's complex problems can't be solved by simple products or technologies alone. Instead, they require deeper cultural, systems-based change – a re-assembling of social relations, norms and practices.

In Case 8.3 below, we explore how reverse innovation – a subset of inclusive innovation – is evolving in more transformative ways. Initially, reverse innovation focused on a narrow definition of inclusivity, centred around product and technology development to address unmet needs. Increasingly, it is alert to the value of social and organisational forms of innovation and recognises that the complex challenges of the 21st century are best tackled through collaborative efforts that actively seek knowledge, creativity, and insights from across diverse cultures, geographies, and perspectives.

CASE STUDY 8.3

From Reverse Innovation Towards Global Innovation Flow

Reverse innovation first developed as a growth strategy utilised by multinationals experiencing stagnating growth in the Global North. In established economic theory, the Global North has traditionally been thought of as the locus of innovation R&D, with other countries recipients of technology transfer (Von Zedtwitz et al., 2015). The multinational corporation (MNC) General Electric, in accordance with this way of thinking, offered stripped down, simplified and cheaper versions of existing products for sale in low-income country contexts. Often, as these innovations were designed elsewhere (i.e., they were not designed in their intended place of use, or in conjunction with innovation end-users), they did not always meet local needs. MNCs subsequently started to think of the Global South as constituting a huge untapped, underserved market, with GE developing new organisational capacities that empowered employees in low-income country settings to develop their own ideas and products. By developing innovation capacity this way, innovations emerged that addressed unmet local needs and unexpectedly generated market benefits for MNCs. Significantly, many of the innovations developed in the Global South were successfully deployed in the Global North (reversing the traditional flow of innovation), often fulfilling a different role to the original use case. An oft-cited example of this is the portable ultrasound developed in China to better serve the needs of rural communities, which was then repurposed in the Global North, assisting at accident and emergency sites to detect fluid around the heart (Immelt et al., 2009). Yet, as Hart (2014) cautions, this poses the risk that 'corporations come to view the world's slums and rural villages primarily as laboratories for incubating innovations for the rich.'

More recently, reverse innovation has evolved into a broader framework called 'global innovation flows,' which focuses on multi-directional exchanges of knowledge and ideas across diverse publics and geographies. This approach moves beyond a narrow focus on profits, products and technology, emphasising true partnerships and equitability. For Binagwaho et al. (2013: 3–4) this means 'having local co-principal investigators and equal contributions to and representation on scientific articles' and recognising that 'not all "reverse innovations" stem from economic scarcity; scientists and program managers in poor countries are endowed with creativity and cultural resources just like their rich-country counterparts, and partners on both sides have lessons to share.' For example, non-technological innovations, such as the friendship bench in Zimbabwe, have gained attention for addressing challenges like mental health (Fernando et al., 2021). This intervention, which involves problem-solving therapy, has been adopted in the U.S. (Ngaruiya et al., 2021). As Syed et al. (2012: 2) explains, interventions in the Global South have become recognised as being 'indispensable to the management and treatment of diseases like schizophrenia, through de-stigmatizing practices like therapeutic optimism, extended support networks, and more holistic appraisals of the disorder.'

Questions

1. What are some of the ethical issues associated with reverse innovation in its earlier manifestation?
2. In what ways is global innovation flow different from reverse innovation?
3. Why does global innovation flow matter?

Sources

Binagwaho, A., Nutt, C.T., Mutabazi, V., Karema, C., Nsanzimana, S., Gasana, M., [...] and Farmer, P.E. (2013) 'Shared learning in an interconnected world: Innovations to advance global health equity', *Globalization and Health*, 9: article #37. http://doi.org/10.1186/1744-8603-9-37

Fernardo, S., Brown, T., Datta, K., Chidhanguro, D., Tavengwa, N., Chandna, J. [...] and Prendergast, A.J. (2021) 'The Friendship Bench as a brief psychological intervention with peer support in rural Zimbabwean women: A mixed methods pilot evaluation', *Global Mental Health*, 8: article #e31. http://doi.org/10.1017/gmh.2021.32

Hart, S.L. (2014) 'The dark side of reverse innovation', Aalto Global Impact, March 5. https://web.archive.org/web/20250321201402/https://aaltoglobalimpact.org/the-dark-side-of-reverse-innovation/ (accessed September 29, 2025).

Immelt, J.R., Govindarajan, V. and Trimble, C. (2009) 'How GE is disrupting itself', *Harvard Business Review*, 87 (10): 56–65.

Ngaruiya, C., Sobowale, K., and Annamalai, A. (2021) 'Reverse innovation in mental health: Review and recommendations', *Global Journal of Community Psychology Practice*, 12 (4): 1–10.

Syed, S.B., Dadwal, V., Rutter, P., Storr, J., Hightower, J.D., Gooden, R., Carlet, J., Nejad, S. B., Kelley, E.T., Donaldson, L., and Pittet, D. (2012) 'Developed-developing country partnerships: Benefits to developed countries?', *Globalization and Health*, 8 (17): 1–10. http://doi.org/10.1186/1744-8603-8-17

von Zedtwitz, M., Corsi, S., Søberg, P.V., and Frega, R. (2015) 'A typology of reverse innovation', *Journal of Product Innovation Management*, 32: 12–28. https://doi.org/10.1111/jpim.12181

In summary, this is an exciting time for innovation. Despite challenges like green washing, there is a growing effort to rethink and reshape innovation. Traditionally innovation has been about turning modern science and technology into marketable products. However, the rise of TIP is broadening this view. Now, innovation is seen not just as creating new technologies or products, but also as developing new capacities and processes that can lead to systemic change and work towards more caring futures for people and planet. This approach aims to tackle complex, multifaceted challenges in ways that single technologies or products cannot.

Reflection: When Entrepreneurship Meets Innovation?

The chapter has connected you with the main concepts underpinning how the entrepreneurial mindset builds the momentum that powers the innovation process forwards. So when is entrepreneurship particularly important? And how does it influence how the innovation process is managed as different types of organisations grow? Table 8.1 below summarises the interplay between innovation and entrepreneurship at different points in the growth and renewal cycles of:

- Profit-driven organisations
- Social value focused organisations (often mixing commercial and social purpose)
- Public sector funded organisations

Table 8.1 Entrepreneurship and innovation priorities in action

Main focus	Start up (1–9 people)	Scale up (10–250 people)	Large organisation (>250)	Large organisation: Major renewal (>250)
	Entrepreneurship	Innovation while sustaining entrepreneurial mindset	Innovation *and* intrapreneurship *and* partnering with entrepreneurial actors	Innovation *and* intrapreneurship for radical change
Profit-driven organisations	Entrepreneur(s) developing new market opportunity. Framing and making the opportunity happen Acquiring resources to solve a problem for customers	Process improvements to increase efficiency and quality Adding new offerings (products and services) or targeting new markets Coordinating activities and processes	Portfolio of incremental and radical innovation Efficient application of new technologies e.g. AI Buying/investing in smaller entrepreneurial players Looking to future, and beyond existing customers	Reducing bureaucracy and outmoded processes/ thinking Core business: Efficiency Beyond the core: Entrepreneurial leadership identifying new opportunities

Main focus	Start up (1–9 people)	Scale up (10–250 people)	Large organisation (>250)	Large organisation: Major renewal (>250)
Social value driven organisations	Social entrepreneur solving a social or environmental problem Framing and making the opportunity happen Acquiring resources to solve a problem for stakeholders	Improving ideas and bringing in partners and volunteers to mobilise solutions to problems Improving processes, coordinating projects and partners	Disseminating ideas widely with social entrepreneur networks Collaborating with public sector and other major partners Focus on delivery *and* new projects	Redesigning the system Acting as change agents Synthesising innovation approaches from both social and commercial sectors Application of well-established technologies
Public sector organisations	Projects driven by intrapreneurial staff to solve a pressing or new challenge that can be solved in a novel way – often in crisis situations	Process development to improve quality and efficiency Securing ongoing funding and staff Developing networks and knowledge Maintaining entrepreneurial *and* delivery mindset	Portfolio of incremental and radical innovation Efficient application of new technologies e.g. AI Removal of **organisational silos**	System redesign Application of processes and technology from private sector applications Increase risk appetite – using crises to try new approaches

Important Trends

No one wins the innovation race on their own. Increasingly the successful management of innovation demands high levels of collaboration that avoids silo thinking as well as practice within organisations and across business and technical/scientific ecosystems. This trend has boosted the importance of:

Boundary spanning and extrapreneurship: Boundary spanning is the process of bridging gaps across different disciplines, groups and organisations to increase collaboration and resource sharing. Boundary spanners play a big part in extrapreneurship, building the understanding and synergy that helps interdependent groups work together and achieve shared goals.

Systems thinking: For entrepreneurs needing to progress their part of the innovation puzzle, systems thinking is an approach to understanding complex, interconnected systems through analysing relationships, patterns, and interdependencies. Through understanding complex issues holistically, problem-solving and decision-making are improved.

At the lowest level, that of the individual entrepreneur and start-up, innovation and entrepreneurship also come together through prototypes, which are increasingly evaluated using the minimum viable product approach (Ries, 2011). When entrepreneurs work towards developing a new product, they create – as quickly and cheaply as possible – a version that requires the least amount of work, but that still provides some concrete manifestation through which they can test their ideas, learn and receive feedback. Developing this version doesn't mean offering half or parts of the product. This product needs to be complete, even if not perfect, and can be used immediately by the customer to offer some value. When developing this, it is worth considering whether, beyond viable, the product is also desirable and feasible. If a product is viable in economic terms, but still customers do not need and desire it or it is technically difficult to build it (or to produce it for a large number of customers), then it is more likely that it will fail in the long term. If all criteria are met, this leads to what has been called by many as the 'sweet spot' of innovation, but also to a product with higher chances of success.

CHAPTER SUMMARY

- First, the chapter looks at entrepreneurial individuals – those who turn creative ideas into reality, not just by starting new businesses but also by innovating within existing organisations (a concept known as intrapreneurship). It's all about taking action, managing risks, and making things happen.
- Next, the chapter discusses the sustainable value creation process. Here, the focus is on how entrepreneurship isn't just about making money but also about creating social and environmental benefits. The challenge lies in balancing these different types of value, but some businesses are designed to do just that, blending profit with purpose.
- The role of place and community in entrepreneurship is another key point. The chapter highlights how local environments can either support or hinder your entrepreneurial efforts. It also introduces the idea of community-based enterprises, which are businesses deeply connected to and serving their local communities.
- Moving on to the innovation imperative, the chapter explains why innovation is crucial for growth, not just for companies but also for entire economies. It's about constantly searching for new ideas and turning them into valuable products or services.
- The chapter also explores innovation for more just, equitable, and sustainable futures. It emphasises the need to innovate in ways that are responsible and inclusive, ensuring that new developments benefit everyone, not just a select few.
- Finally, the chapter encourages the rethinking of innovation. It suggests that we need to look at innovation through a broader lens, focusing not just on technological advancements but also on creating systems and cultures that drive positive change in society.

STUDENTS LIKE YOU CHANGE THE WORLD

Kalkidan Legesse

Kalkidan Legesse is a social entrepreneur committed to creating sustainable value and eco-friendly and socially inclusive businesses. During her degree in Politics, Philosophy, and Economics, Kalkidan received grant funding from the Student Start-up programme to establish Sancho's, a sustainable clothing marketplace.

Kalkidan is a trailblazer in her industry, redefining ethical and sustainable fashion by introducing innovative business models such as transparent pricing and 'pay what you can afford.' She also works to educate consumers about clothing lifecycle.

Figure 8.3 Kalkidan Legesse

Her latest venture Owni is an AI-powered fashion resale platform for brands and consumers. The company is supported by the SETsquared Exeter Business Acceleration team and has attracted investment from Google and VC firm Sustainable Ventures.

Kalkidan has attracted many plaudits for her achievements, including being selected as one of Vogue Business's 100 innovators, as one of Drapers 30 under 30, winning High Street Shop of 2020 and being the subject of half hour BBC One Documentary 'Fighting for Fashion' which profiled her business journey. Kalkidan recently returned to university to complete the Exeter MBA.

Source

University of Exeter (n.d.) 'The Exeter entrepreneur'. https://www.exeter.ac.uk/research/centres/entrepreneurship/studentstartups/ theexeterentrepreneur/ (accessed September 15, 2025).

END OF CHAPTER REFLECTION

Have a look at the skills you should have developed in this unit (find more details in the Key Skills Table in the Appendix on p. 503).

1 Which of the skills listed do you think you have developed the most?
2 Can you give two examples on why you feel you have now developed these skills/developed them further?
3 How will you use these new/refined skills in the future (give two examples of the impact of your development on your future behaviour)?

FURTHER READING

Bacq, S., Hertel, C., and Lumpkin, G.T. (2022) 'Communities at the nexus of entrepreneurship and societal impact: A cross-disciplinary literature review', *Journal of Business Venturing*, 37 (5). http://doi.org/10.1016/j.jbusvent.2022.106231

Expanding on the 'Role of Place and Community' section of this chapter this paper analyses the role of local communities in entrepreneurship and societal impact creation. It highlights that there are different types of communities within local contexts and reveals pathways towards more impactful and active communities.

Mitzinneck, B.C. and Besharov, M.L. (2019) 'Managing value tensions in collective social entrepreneurship: The role of temporal, structural, and collaborative compromise', *Journal of Business Ethics*, 159 (2): 381–400.

Expanding on the 'Sustainable Value Creation Process' section of this chapter, this paper focuses on value creation and the tensions that arise when an organisation needs to prioritise and choose among different entrepreneurial projects and shows ways of navigating such complexities.

Bessant, J. and Tidd, J. (2024) *Innovation and Entrepreneurship*. Wiley.

An easy to read introduction to the connected themes of innovation and entrepreneurship by two leading researchers in both disciplines.

Ledingham, K., Hartley, S. and Owen, R. (2024) *Rethinking Innovation: Alternative Approaches for People and Planet*. Palgrave Macmillan.

With innovation traditionally viewed as a tool for financial return and market growth, there is mounting pressure to rethink and reframe the theory and practice of innovation for the pressing sustainability and inequality challenges of our time. This textbook provides students with a research-informed dive into the emerging space of innovation for systems/transformative change.

REFERENCES

Adams, R., Jeanrenaud, S., Bessant, J., Denyer, D., and Overy, P. (2016) 'Sustainability-oriented innovation: A systematic review', *International Journal of Management Reviews*, 18 (2): 180–205. http://doi.org/10.1111/ijmr.12068

AlignToday (2024) 'Intrapreneurship: How to foster innovation from within', *Align Today*, September 10. https://www.aligntoday.com/blog/intrapreneurship (accessed December 17, 2025).

Almandoz, J. (2012) 'Arriving at the starting line: The impact of community and financial logics on new banking ventures', *Academy of Management Journal*, 55 (6): 1381–406.

Arenas, D., Murphy, M., and Jáuregui, K. (2020) 'Community influence capacity on firms: Lessons from the Peruvian highlands', *Organization Studies*, 41 (6): 737–65.

Atterton, J., Newbery, R., Bosworth, G., and Affleck, A. (2011) 'Rural enterprise and neo-endogenous development', in G. Agnete Alsos, S. Carter, E. Ljunggren, F. Welter (eds), *The Handbook of Research on Entrepreneurship in Agriculture and Rural Development*. Edward Elgar Publishing. pp. 256–280.

Bacq, S., Hertel, C., and Lumpkin, G. (2022) 'Communities at the nexus of entrepreneurship and societal impact: A cross-disciplinary literature review', *Journal of Business Venturing*, 37 (5): article #106231.

Ballé, M., Morgan, J., and Sobek, D. K. (2016) 'Why learning is central to sustained innovation', *MIT Sloan Management Review*, 57 (3), 63–71.

Battilana, J. and Dorado, S. (2010) 'Building sustainable hybrid organizations: The case of commercial microfinance organizations', *Academy of Management Journal*, 53 (6): 1419–40.

Bernstein, S., Diamond, R., Jiranaphawiboon, A., McQuade, T., and Pousada, B. (2021) 'The contribution of high-skilled immigrants to innovation in the United States', *NBER Working Paper w30797.* http://doi.org/10.2139/ssrn.4312044

Bessant, J., and Tidd, J. (2024) *Innovation and Entrepreneurship*. Wiley.

Burt, R.S. (2000) 'The network structure of social capital', *Research in Organizational Behavior*, 22: 345–423. http://doi.org/10.1016/S0191-3085(00)22009-1

Cain, S. (2013) *Quiet: The Power of Introverts in a World That Can't Stop Talking*. Penguin.

CIA (2024) 'The World Factbook', cia.gov. https://www.cia.gov/the-world-factbook/ (accessed September 15, 2025).

Coad, A., Nightingale, P., Stilgoe, J., and Vezzani, A. (2020) 'Editorial: The dark side of innovation', *Industry and Innovation*, 28 (1): 102–12. http://doi.org/10.1080/13662716.2020.1818555

Cooper, R.G. (2013) 'Where are all the breakthrough new products?: Using portfolio management to boost innovation', *Research-Technology Management*, 56 (5): 25–33. http://doi.org/10.5437/08956308X5605123

Covin, J.G. and Miles, M.P. (1999) 'Corporate entrepreneurship and the pursuit of competitive advantage', *Entrepreneurship Theory and Practice*, 23 (3): 47–63.

Dimitriadis, S., Lee, M., Ramarajan, L., and Battilana, J. (2017) 'Blurring the boundaries: The interplay of gender and local communities in the commercialization of social ventures', *Organization Science*, 28 (5): 819–39.

Dodgson, M., Gann, D.M., and Phillips, N. (2014) 'Perspectives on innovation management', in M. Dodgson, D.M. Gann, and N. Phillips (eds), *The Oxford Handbook of Innovation Management*. Oxford University Press. pp. 3–25.

Elert, N. and Stenkula, M. (2020) 'Intrapreneurship: Productive and non-productive', *Entrepreneurship Theory and Practice*, 46 (5): 1423–39. https://doi.org/10.1177/1042258720964181

Emery, M., and Flora, C. (2006) 'Spiraling-up: Mapping community transformation with community capitals framework', *Community Development*, 37 (1): 19–35.

Eurostat (2024) 'More businesses opened than dissolved in the EU in 2022', *Eurostat*, November 25. https://ec.europa.eu/eurostat/web/products-eurostat-news/w/ddn-20241025-2 (accessed September 15, 2025).

Fobel, P., Forgon, T., and Fobelová, M.K. (2019) 'Innovation management in good practice context', *Management Systems in Production Engineering*, 27 (2): 69–73. https://doi.org/10.1515/mspe-2019-0011

Friedman, M. (1970) 'A Friedman doctrine – The social responsibility of business is to increase its profits', *The New York Times*, September 13. https://www.nytimes.com/1970/09/13/archives/a-friedman-doctrine-the-social-responsibility-of-business-is-to.html (accessed September 15, 2025).

Garud, R., Tuertscher, P., and Van de Ven, A.H. (2013) 'Perspectives on innovation processes', *Academy of Management Annals*, 7 (1): 775–819. http://doi.org/10.1080/19416520.2013.791066

Gawke, J., Gorgievski, M.J., and Bakker, A.B. (2017) 'Employee intrapreneurship and work engagement: A latent change score approach', *Journal of Vocational Behavior,* 100: 88–100. http://doi.org/10.1016/j.jvb.2017.03.002

Georgiou, A. and Arenas, D. (2023) 'Community in organizational research: A review and an institutional logics perspective', *Organization Theory*, 4 (1): 1–22.

Gilovich, T., Griffin, D., and Kahneman, D. (eds.). (2002) *Heuristics and Biases: The Psychology of Intuitive Judgment*. Cambridge University Press.

Girod, S.J.G., Birkinshaw, J., and Prange, C. (2023) 'Business agility: Key themes and future directions', *California Management Review*, 65 (4): 5–21. http://doi.org/10.1177/00081256231186641

Haksever, C., Chaganti, R., and Cook, R.G. (2004) 'A model of value creation: Strategic view', *Journal of Business Ethics*, 49: 295–307.

Heeks, R., Foster, C., and Nugroho, Y. (2014) 'New models of inclusive innovation for development', *Innovation and Development*, 4 (2): 175–85. http://doi.org/10.1080/2157930X.2014.928982

Hornsby, J.S., Kuratko, D.F. and Zahra, S.A. (2002) 'Middle managers' perception of the internal environment for corporate entrepreneurship: Assessing a measurement scale', *Journal of Business Venturing*, 17 (3): 253–73.

Howard-Grenville, J., Metzger, M.L., and Meyer, A.D. (2013) 'Rekindling the flame: Processes of identity resurrection', *Academy of Management Journal*, 56 (1): 113–36.

Huessemann, M. and Huesemann, J. (2011) *Techno-fix: Why Technology Won't Save Us or the Environment*. New Society.

Hunt, V., Dixon-Fyle, S., Huber, C., Martinez Marquez, M. del M., Prince, S., and Thomas, A. (2023) 'Why diversity matters even more', *McKinsey Reports*. https://www.mckinsey.com/featured-insights/diversity-and-inclusion/diversity-matters-even-more-the-case-for-holistic-impact# (accessed September 15, 2025).

Ingram, P. (2021) 'The Forgotten Dimension of Diversity', *Harvard Business Review*, 99 (1): 58–67.

Ireland, R.D., Covin, J.G. and Kuratko, D.F. (2009) 'Conceptualizing corporate entrepreneurship strategy', *Entrepreneurship Theory and Practice*, 33 (1): 19–46.

International Organization for Standardization (ISO) (2025) ISO 56000. https://www.iso.org/standard/84436.html

Jacobides, M.G. (2022) 'How to compete when industries digitize and collide: An ecosystem development framework', *California Management Review*, 64 (3): 99–123. http://doi.org/10.1177/00081256221083352

Kimmitt, J., Kibler, E., Schildt, H., and Oinas, P. (2024) 'Place in entrepreneurial storytelling: A study of cultural entrepreneurship in a deprived context', *Journal of Management Studies*, 61 (3): 1036–73.

Kuratko, D.F., Hornsby, J.S. and Covin, J.G. (2014) 'Diagnosing a firm's internal environment for corporate entrepreneurship', *Business Horizons*, 57 (1): 37–47.

Ledingham, K., Hartley, S., and Owen, R. (2024) *Rethinking Innovation, Alternative Approaches for People and Planet*. Palgrave Macmillan.

Löfsten, H. (2014) 'Product innovation processes and the trade-off between product innovation performance and business performance', *European Journal of Innovation Management*, 17 (1): 61–84. https://doi.org/10.1108/EJIM-04-2013-0034

Lorenzo, R., Voigt, N., Schetelig, K., Zawadzki, A., Welpe, I.M., and Brosi, P. (2017) 'The mix that matters', *BCG,* April 26. https://www.bcg.com/publications/2017/people-organization-leadership-talent-innovation-through-diversity-mix-that-matters (accessed September 15, 2025).

Manly, B.J., Ringel, M., Macdougall, A., Harnoss, J., Wolke-Perten, J., Backler, W., Gjerstad, K., Kimura, R., and Viner, B. (2024) 'Innovation systems need a reboot', *BCG*, June 4. https://www.bcg.com/publications/2024/innovation-systems-need-a-reboot (accessed September 15, 2025).

McKnight, B., and Linnenluecke, M. K. (2016) 'How firm responses to natural disasters strengthen community resilience: A stakeholder-based perspective', *Organization & Environment*, 29 (3): 290–307.

Mitzinneck, B.C., and Besharov, M.L. (2019) 'Managing value tensions in collective social entrepreneurship: The role of temporal, structural, and collaborative compromise', *Journal of Business Ethics*, 159 (2): 381–400.

Murphy, M., Danis, W.M., and Mack, J. (2020) 'From principles to action: Community-based entrepreneurship in the Toquaht Nation', *Journal of Business Venturing*, 35 (6). http://doi.org/10.1016/j.jbusvent.2020.106051

Nagji, B. and Tuff, G. (2012) 'Managing your innovation portfolio', *Harvard Business Review*, 90 (5): 66–74.

Novacek, G., Yousif, N., Dartnell, A., Farsky, M., Bansal, S., May, G., and Zborowski, A. (2023) *Inclusion Isn't Just Nice. It's Necessary.* https://www.bcg.com/publications/2023/how-to-improve-inclusion-in-the-workplace (accessed September 15, 2025).

Owen, R. and Pansera, M. (2019) 'Responsible innovation and responsible research and innovation', in D. Simon, S. Kulhmann, J. Stamm, and W. Canzler (eds), *Handbook on Science and Public Policy*. Edward Elgar. pp. 26–48.

Owen, R., Stilgoe, J., Macnaghten, P., Gorman, M., Fisher, E., and Guston, D. (2013) 'A framework for responsible innovation', in R. Owen, J. Bessant and M. Heintz (eds), *Responsible Innovation: Managing the Responsible Emergence of Science and Innovation in Society*. John Wiley & Sons. pp. 27–50.

Papaioannou, T. (2014) 'How inclusive can innovation and development be in the twenty-first century?', *Innovation and Development*, 4 (2): 187-202. doi.org/10.1080/2157930x.2014.921355

Peredo, A.M., and Chrisman, J.J. (2006) 'Toward a theory of community-based enterprise', *Academy of Management Review*, 31 (2): 309–28.

Poole, M.S. and Van de Ven, A.H. (2021) 'The Life Cycle Process Model', in M.S. Poole and A.H. Van de Ven (eds), *The Oxford Handbook of Organizational Change and Innovation* (2nd edition). Oxford University Press. pp. 305–12.

Ramirez, J. (2021) 'Governance in energy democracy for Sustainable Development Goals: Challenges and opportunities for partnerships at the Isthmus of Tehuantepec', *Journal of International Business Policy*, 4 (1): 119–35.

Repenning, N.P., Kieffer, D., and Repenning, J. (2018) 'A new approach to designing work', *Sloan Management Review*, 59 (2): 29–38.

Reynolds, A. and Lewis, D. (2017) 'Teams solve problems faster when they're more cognitively diverse', *Harvard Business Review*, March 30. https://hbr.org/2017/03/teams-solve-problems-faster-when-theyre-more-cognitively-diverse (accessed September 15, 2025).

Ries, E. (2011) *The Lean Startup: How Today's Entrepreneurs Use Continuous Innovation to Create Radically Successful Businesses*. Currency.

Rock, D., and Grant, H. (2016). 'Why diverse teams are smarter', *Harvard Business Review Digital Articles*, November 4. https://hbr.org/2016/11/why-diverse-teams-are-smarter (accessed September 15, 2025).

Sarasvathy, S.D. (2008) *Effectuation: Elements of Entrepreneurial Expertise*. Edward Elgar.

Schot, J. and Steinmueller, E.W. (2018) 'Three frames for innovation policy: R&D, systems of innovation and transformative change', *Research Policy*, 47 (9): 1554–67. doi.org/10.1016/j.respol.2018.08.011

Seelos, C., Mair, J., Battilana, J., and Dacin, M.T. (2011) 'The embeddedness of social entrepreneurship: Understanding variation across local communities', in C. Marquis, M. Lounsbury, and R. Greenwood (eds), *Communities and Organizations*. Emerald. pp. 333–63.

Shrivastava, P. and Kennelly, J.J. (2013) 'Sustainability and place-based enterprise', *Organization & environment*, 26 (1): 83–101.

Sonsev, V. (2021) 'Patagonia's focus on its brand purpose is great for business', *Forbes*, December 10. https://www.forbes.com/sites/veronikasonsev/2019/11/27/patagonias-focus-on-its-brand-purpose-is-great-for-business/ (accessed September 15, 2025).

Sovacool, B.K., Turnheim, B., Hook, A., Brock, A. and Martiskainen, M. (2021) 'Dispossessed by decarbonisation: Reducing vulnerability, injustice, and inequality in the lived experience of low-carbon pathways', *World Development*, 137: article #105116. https://doi.org/10.1016/j.worlddev.2020.105116

Statista (2024a) 'Leading countries by gross research and development (R&D) expenditure worldwide in 2022', *Statista*. https://www.statista.com/statistics/732247/worldwide-research-and-development-gross-expenditure-top-countries/ (accessed September 15, 2025).

Statista (2024b) 'Percentage of spending on research and development of total revenue in 2023, bby industrial sector', *Statista*. https://www.statista.com/statistics/270324/expenditure-on-research-and-development-by-industry-sectors/ (accessed October 22, 2025).

Statista (2024c) 'Ranking of the companies with the highest spending on research and development worldwide in 2024', *Statista*. https://www.statista.com/statistics/265645/ranking-of-the-companies-with-the-highest-spending-on-research-and-development/ (accessed October 22, 2025).

Statista (2024d) 'Total global spending on research and development (R&D) from 1996 to 2022', *Statista*. https://www.statista.com/statistics/732247/worldwide-research-and-development-gross-expenditure-top-countries/ (accessed October 22, 2025).

Steyaert, C. (2007) '"Entrepreneuring" as a conceptual attractor? A review of process theories in 20 years of entrepreneurship studies', *Entrepreneurship & Regional Development*, 19 (6): 453–77. https://doi.org/10.1080/08985620701671759

Sull, D.N., Turconi, S., Sull, C., and Yoder, J. (2018) 'Turning strategy into results', *Sloan Management Review*, 59 (2): 97–107.

Tellis, G.J. (2013) *Unrelenting Innovation*. Jossey-Bass.

Terjesen, S. and Sealy, R. (2016) 'Board gender quotas: Exploring ethical tensions from a multi-theoretical perspective', *Business Ethics Quarterly*, 26 (1): 23–65. https://doi.org/10.1017/beq.2016.7

Tidd, J. and Bessant, J. (2021) *Managing Innovation: Integrating Technological, Market and Organizational Change* (7th edition). John Wiley & Sons.

UK Research and Innovation (UKRI) (2023) 'Framework for responsible research and innovation,' *ukri.org*, March 16. https://www.ukri.org/who-we-are/epsrc/our-policies-and-standards/framework-for-responsible-innovation/ (accessed September 15, 2025).

UN SDG (2021) *The Sustainable Development Goals Report 2021*. https://unstats.un.org/sdgs/report/2021/The-Sustainable-Development-Goals-Report-2021.pdf (accessed December 17, 2025).

Urbano, D., Álvarez, C., and Turró, A. (2013) 'Organizational resources and intrapreneurial activities: An international study', *Management Decision*, 51 (4): 854–70. https://doi.org/10.1108/00251741311326617

U.S. Bureau of Labor Statistics. (2024) 'Entrepreneurship and the U.S. economy', *Bureau of Labor Statistics*. https://www.bls.gov/bdm/entrepreneurship/entrepreneurship.htm (accessed September 15, 2025).

Voegtlin, C. and Scherer, A.G. (2017) 'Responsible innovation and the innovation of responsibility: Governing sustainable development in a globalized world', *Journal of Business Ethics*, 143: 227–43. https://doi.org/10.1007/s10551-015-2769-z

9
ACCOUNTING

David Kolitz and Thaer Alhalabi

INTENDED LEARNING OUTCOMES

By the end of this chapter, you will be able to:

1. Describe the value of information in the decision-making process for a business and identify the main fields of accounting activity.
2. Identify the main components of a set of financial statements and explain their purpose, including analysing basic transactions using the accounting equation.
3. Apply Cost-Volume-Profit (CVP) analysis to explore the effect of changing unit selling price, unit variable cost, or fixed cost.
4. Calculate the full cost of a unit of output using OAR (Overhead Absorption Rate) and ABC (Activity-Based Costing) overhead allocation systems.
5. Analyse and prepare budgets using both fixed and flexible approaches to support business planning and control.

SUSTAINABLE DEVELOPMENT GOALS

In this chapter, we address the following SDGs:

- SDG 4: Quality Education – Building financial literacy through both financial statement analysis and managerial accounting techniques for informed decision-making.
- SDG 5: Gender Equality – Promoting transparency through standardised financial reporting and equitable resource allocation via inclusive budgeting practices.
- SDG 8: Decent Work and Economic Growth – Teaching financial performance measurement and cost management techniques to support sustainable business operations and profitability.
- SDG 9: Industry, Innovation and Infrastructure – Using accurate financial reporting and Activity-Based Costing to support efficient resource allocation and business resilience.
- SDG 12: Responsible Consumption and Production – Applying accrual accounting principles and full costing methods to enable sustainable production and resource optimisation decisions.
- SDG 13: Climate Action – Incorporating environmental impacts into financial statements and budgeting frameworks for sustainable business planning.
- SDG 16: Peace, Justice and Strong Institutions – Teaching transparent financial reporting standards, stewardship accountability and ethical accounting practices for institutional governance.

INTRODUCTION

This chapter begins by exploring financial accounting fundamentals, where we learn how businesses record and report their financial position and performance for external users. These concepts provide the foundation for understanding management accounting, where we use financial information to make internal business decisions. From product costing to budgeting, each topic builds upon previous concepts, creating a comprehensive framework for accounting practice.

Historical Perspective

Accounting has a rich history dating back to ancient civilisations, but its modern foundations were laid in the late 15th century by the Italian mathematician and Franciscan friar, Luca Pacioli. Often referred to as the 'Father of Accounting,' Pacioli published 'Summa de Arithmetica, Geometria, Proportioni et Proportionalita' in 1494, which included the first comprehensive description of the double-entry bookkeeping system.

This method, where every debit has a corresponding credit, transformed the way financial records were kept, providing a more accurate and systematic approach to tracking business transactions. Pacioli's work not only documented existing accounting practices of Venetian merchants but also set the standards that are still foundational in accounting today. His principles ensured a clear, organised, and transparent financial reporting system, which was crucial for the growth of **commerce** and the eventual development of modern-day accounting practices.

Information and Decision-Making in Accounting

Generally, accounting focuses on identifying, recording, and reporting financial data essential for making economic decisions. Accounting aids these decisions by determining what information will help decision-makers, how it should be recognised and measured, and how it should be communicated. It provides information about an entity to users for decision-making purposes. So, who are the users of accounting information?

Users of accounting information can be broadly grouped as internal and external users. Both internal and external users need and use financial information about an entity for decision-making (see Figure 9.1).

- **Internal users** of accounting information are the management of a business entity. Management is responsible for all decisions relating to an entity's activities and has access to all the information it needs internally.
- **External users** of accounting information are primarily *investors* and *lenders* but may be defined more widely to include employees, customers, and regulators. External users do not have unlimited access to the information they need and cannot require an entity to provide information to meet their specific needs. Therefore, they must rely on information provided by management in the form of **financial reports**. Some of the information included in the financial reports is likely to meet certain of management's needs but management has the ability to access detailed financial information and does not need to rely solely on financial reports.

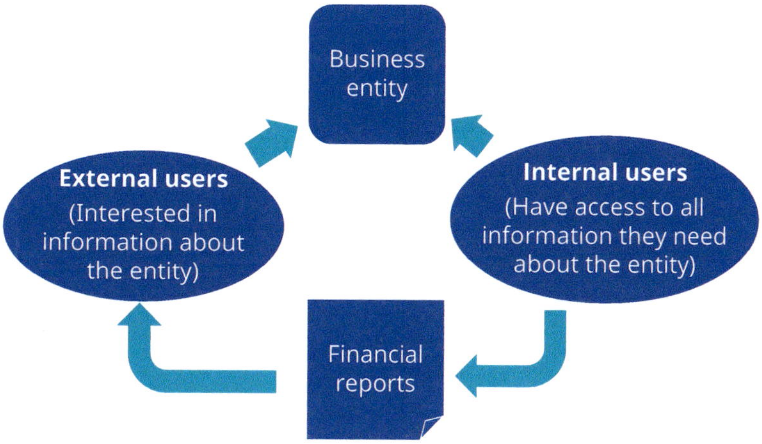

Figure 9.1 External and internal users

Financial statements also show the results of *management's stewardship* of the resources entrusted to it. In large companies, such as those listed on the London Stock Exchange, management and shareholders are different groups of people. The shareholders are the owners of the company and management manages the company on their behalf. The stewardship function refers to the relationship that exists between management and the shareholders, and the responsibility of management to the shareholders.

REFLECTIVE ACTIVITY 9.1

Imagine that you are an investor in a small private company.

- Will you have to rely on management to provide information about the company through a financial report?

The Business Cycle

Accounting is often called the language of business. Business owners, also known as investors, provide funding to the business, referred to as **equity**. Additional funds are obtained through borrowing from lenders, which are known as **liabilities**. These funds are used to acquire **assets**, the business's resources. Common examples include property, plants, equipment, inventory (goods for resale), and **cash** in the bank (see Figure 9.2).

The equity and liabilities are referred to as the *source of funds* that are used to acquire assets, the *use of the funds*. This leads to the important accounting concept of **duality**, meaning that the sum of the assets of a business entity is always equal to the sum of the liabilities and equity of the entity. This concept will be explored in further detail later in this chapter.

Management is responsible for utilising the resources to generate *income*, through, for example, the sale of goods to customers. During this process, *expenses*, such as the cost of the goods, rent, and salaries are incurred. The difference between income and expenses is termed profit, which increases the investors' equity.

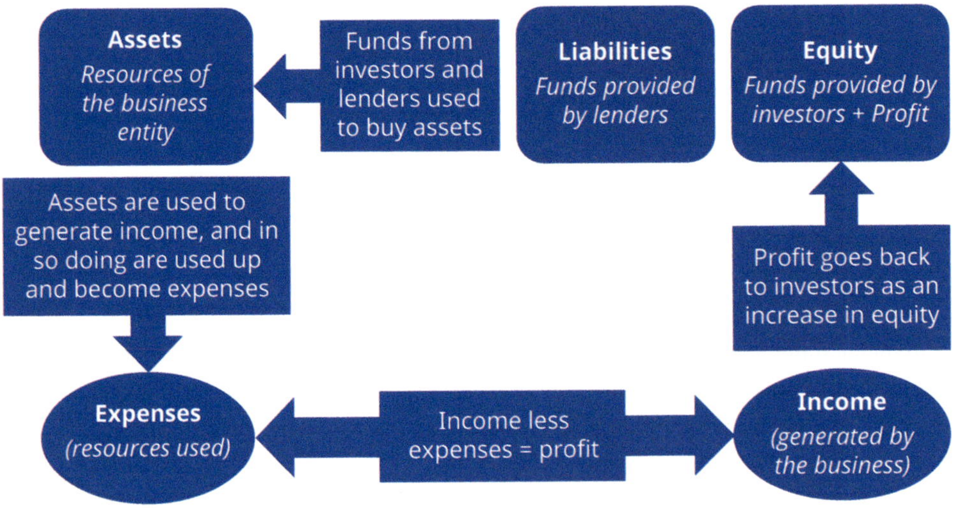

Figure 9.2 The business cycle

Fields of Accounting Activity

The fields of accounting activity can be classified according to the user group to whom it is directed.

- **Financial accounting:** is concerned with the reporting of information about business entities for external users. The information is provided through the financial statements. Such financial statements are prepared and presented at least annually.
- **Management accounting:** provides information to internal users, in other words, the management of an entity. Management accounting includes a great deal of information that is not reported outside the company.
- **Auditing:** All companies listed on the London Stock Exchange are required to appoint an auditor. The role of the auditor is to express an opinion on the fair presentation of the information and whether or not it has been prepared in accordance with accounting standards, known as International Financial Reporting Standards.
- **Taxation:** Accountants who specialise in taxation assist their clients in planning their affairs in order to minimise taxes payable. This is known as *tax avoidance*, which is legal. *Tax evasion*, on the other hand, is illegal. Taxes that you may be familiar with include income tax and Value Added Tax (VAT). (Auditing and taxation are not dealt with further in this text.)

FINANCIAL ACCOUNTING

This section addresses financial accounting as a field of accounting activity.

The Objective of Financial Reporting and the Entity Concept

The objective of financial reporting is to provide financial information that is useful to users for decision-making purposes. The information is provided through the financial statements.

It is important to understand that the financial statements are prepared from the perspective of the business and not from the perspective of the owners of the business. This is referred to as the **entity concept**. The importance and relevance of the entity concept is best understood by considering the situation of a sole proprietor, in other words, a one-person business. From a legal perspective, the owner of the sole proprietorship and the business are the same legal entity, but from an accounting perspective, the owner and the business are separate entities.

REFLECTIVE ACTIVITY 9.2

An individual starts a business as a sole proprietor and transfers £1,500,000 from his personal bank account to the bank account of the business.

- Who does the £1,500,000 belong to? To the individual (the owner) or the business?

Financial Statements

There are many well-known stock exchanges around the world, including the New York Stock Exchange in the United States, the London Stock Exchange in the United Kingdom, the Deutsche Börse Frankfurt in Germany and the Johannesburg Stock Exchange in South Africa. What would you do if you wish to buy shares in a company listed on a stock exchange? You will require information about the entity's financial position and its financial performance.

- Information about an entity's financial position is provided in the *statement of financial position* (also known as a balance sheet, detailing the *resources of the entity* and *claims against the entity*) at a particular point in time. It provides information about the assets, liabilities and equity of the business entity.
- Information about financial performance is provided in the *statement of profit or loss* (also known as an income statement) which measures of the *performance* and provides information about the income and expenses of an entity over a period of time.

These financial statements form part of the wider annual report produced by all companies, and are available online for all listed companies. There are five components of a set of financial statements and we will be focusing on the following two primary financial statements in this chapter: the balance sheet and the income statement. (The other components are the statement of cash flows, the statement of changes in equity and the notes to the financial statements.)

The Statement of Financial Position (Balance Sheet)

The statement of financial position is often described as a 'snapshot' of the financial position of an entity at one point in time. It shows the monetary value of the resources of the entity (known as *assets*) together with the obligations of the entity to lenders (known as *liabilities*) and the obligation of the entity to owners (known as *equity*).

Above, we referred to the concept of duality. The duality of accounting provides symmetry in the *statement of financial position* (and hence the alternative name, the balance sheet). Related to the concept of duality is the entity concept, which means that for accounting purposes, the business and its owners are separate accounting entities and the financial statements are thus always prepared from the perspective of the business entity.

There are three sections reported on the statement of financial position. These sections, known as *elements*, are the *assets*, *liabilities* and *equity*. These elements are all defined in a document called the *Conceptual Framework*, published by the International Accounting Standards Board (2018). It describes the objective of and the concepts for financial reporting.

Assets

An asset is defined as a present economic resource (a right that has the potential to produce economic benefits), controlled by the entity as a result of past events.

A business entity may sell goods to its customers *on credit*. Selling on credit means that the customer agrees to pay the business entity for the goods at a later date. Customers are known as the *accounts receivable* or *debtors* of the business entity. The right related to accounts receivable is the right to collect the amount owing from the customers. The economic resource, accounts receivable, is controlled by the entity through the legal contract of sale.

Are accounts receivable (or debtors) an asset of a business entity? To answer this question, we need to apply the definition of an asset.

- There is a *present economic resource,* being the *right* to collect the amount owing from the customers, that has the *potential* to produce economic benefits through the receipt of the cash.
- It is *controlled by the entity* through the legal contract of sale.
- As a *result of past events,* the sale and delivery of the goods to the customer.

Accounts receivable (or debtors) therefore do meet the definition of an asset.

Liabilities

A liability is defined as a present obligation of the entity to transfer an economic resource as a result of past events. Again, this is best understood with reference to an example.

A business entity may buy goods from its suppliers *on credit*. Buying on credit means that the entity agrees to pay the supplier for the goods at a later date. Suppliers are known as the *accounts payable* or *creditors* of the business entity. The present obligation related to accounts payable is a duty or responsibility to pay the supplier that the entity has no practical ability to avoid because of the legal contract. The economic resource that will be transferred in relation to accounts payable is the cash that will be used to pay the supplier.

Are accounts payable (or creditors) a liability of a business entity? To answer this question, we need to apply the definition of a liability.

- There is *a present obligation of the entity*, being the duty to pay the supplier that the entity has no practical ability to avoid because of the legal contract.
- To *transfer an economic resource*, the cash that will be paid to the supplier.
- As a *result of past events*, the obtaining of economic benefits from receiving delivery of the goods or services.

Accounts payable (or creditors) therefore do meet the definition of a liability.

Equity

Equity is defined as the residual interest in the assets of the entity after deducting its liabilities. It is also referred to as the net assets or net wealth of the entity.

The Non-Current/Current Distinction

When looking at financial statements, you will often see a distinction between current and non-current assets or liabilities. A detailed discussion of this distinction is beyond the scope of this chapter. For our purposes, current assets are realised in the short term (typically 12 months or less) meaning that they get sold or converted to cash within a short period of time.

Most businesses expect their customers to settle their accounts within 30, 60 or 90 days, thus accounts receivable is an example of a current asset. Compare accounts receivable to plants and machinery. This also meets the definition of an asset, however plants and machinery are expected to be used for several accounting periods to produce goods and services to sell to customers and thus are examples of a non-current asset.

The same logic applies to a liability. Accounts payable are typically settled within 12 months, thus accounts payable are an example of a current liability. Contrast this with a loan from a bank that gets repaid in five years. This is an example of a non-current liability.

Not all current assets and liabilities are realised or settled within 12 months. An asset realised or a liability settled during the normal operating cycle (but longer than 12 months) is also classified as current.

EXAMPLE 9.1

The Flat White is established as a coffee shop and the owners invest cash of £1,500,000. The business also borrows cash of £1,000,000 from lenders. The business therefore has cash of £2,500,000. The cash of £2,500,000 is an economic resource controlled by the entity (an asset); the £1,000,000 owed to the lenders is an obligation of the entity to a lender (a liability) and the £1,500,000 is an obligation of the entity to the owners (equity).

(Note that in a business context, cash and cash transactions include currency notes and coins, electronic funds transfer, as well as credit and debit card transactions.)

A simple statement of financial position can be prepared as follows:

Table 9.1 Statement of financial position

	£
Assets	
Cash	2,500,000
	2,500,000
Equity	
Capital	1,500,000
Liabilities	
Loan from lenders	1,000,000
	2,500,000

Applying the duality concept, the assets of £2,500,000 are equal to the sum of the equity of £1,500,000 and liabilities of £1,000,000. Using the entity concept, the £2,500,000 of assets belong to the business and not to the owners. Following on from that, the £1,000,000 of liabilities is an obligation of the business to lenders and the £1,500,000 of equity is the obligation of the business to the owners.

The Statement of Profit or Loss

The statement of profit or loss measures the performance of the business entity for a period of time. Income and expenses are reported in the statement of profit or loss. The *Conceptual Framework* also defines income and expenses. A full explanation of these definitions is beyond the scope of this chapter.

Income

Income is a measure of accomplishment. The *Conceptual Framework* simply tells us that an income is something that results in an increase in assets or a decrease in liabilities (i.e. something that is favourable).

Expenses

An expense is a measure of sacrifice. An expense is something that results in a decrease in assets or an increase in liabilities (i.e something that is unfavourable).

EXAMPLE 9.2

During the year ended 31 December 2024, The Flat White earns income of £250,000 and incurs expenses of £200,000. If the income of £250,000 comprises fees for services provided and the expenses of £200,000 comprise administrative expenses of £120,000 and distribution expenses of £80,000, a simple statement of profit or loss can be drawn up as follows:

Table 9.2 Statement of profit or loss for the year ended 31 December 2024

	£
Income	
Fees	250,000
Expenses	(200,000)
Administrative	120,000
Distribution	80,000
Profit for the period	50,000

Accrual Basis of Accounting

The accrual basis of accounting shows the effects of transactions when they *occur,* irrespective of when the cash is received or paid. This means that all transactions are recorded in the accounting records and reported in the financial statements of the periods to which they *relate.*

Remember that income is a measure of accomplishment. Focusing on when the cash is received in relation to when the activity giving rise to the accomplishment occurs, we have three possible scenarios:

Cash could be received by the business

- before the income is earned (that is, before the activity occurs)
- at same time as the income is earned (cash transaction)
- after the income is earned (that is, after the activity occurs)

However, only amounts that are *earned* in a period are recognised as income and included in the statement of profit or loss. The effect of cash received before income is earned is shown as a liability on the statement of financial position (as unearned income). Similarly, the effect of cash received after income is earned is shown as an asset on the statement of financial position (as accounts receivable).

Remember also that expenses are a measure of sacrifice. Focusing on when the cash is paid in relation to when the activity giving rise to the sacrifice occurs, we have three possible scenarios:

Cash could be paid by the business

- before the expense is incurred (that is, before the activity occurs)
- at the same time as expense is incurred (cash transaction)
- after the expense is incurred (that is, after the activity occurs)

However, only amounts that are *incurred* in a period are recognised as an expense and included in the statement of profit or loss. The effect of cash paid before an expense is incurred is shown as an asset on the statement of financial position (as a pre-paid expense). Similarly, the effect of cash paid after an expense is incurred is shown as a liability on the statement of financial position (as accounts payable or accrued expenses).

CASE STUDY 9.1

At the Bar

Benny Bar formed a legal practice on 1 February 2024, known as At the Bar. He invested cash of £10,000 into the business. During the three months ended 30 April 2024, the practice consults with 100 clients at a fee of £500 per consultation. The practice operates from rented premises and the landlord charges the practice rent of £5,000 per month.

Scenarios 1 and 2 below relate to the three-month period ended 30 April 2024 and are *unrelated*.

Scenario 1

1.1: The fee of £500 is received from 60 clients but 40 clients have not yet paid their accounts.

1.2: The practice pays £10,000 to the landlord in respect of rent for February and March, but the rent for April has not been paid.

Questions

1. State the amount of the cash received, cash paid and net cash flow for the period.
2. Prepare a statement of profit or loss for the three-month period ended 30 April 2024.
3. Prepare a statement of financial position at 30 April 2024.

Scenario 2

2.1: The fee of £500 is received from all 100 clients and the fee of £500 is also received in advance from a further 40 clients who chose to pay in advance for future consultations.

2.2: The practice pays £15,000 to the landlord in respect of rent for the February, March and April as well as £5,000 rent in advance for May.

Questions

1 State the amount of the cash received, cash paid and net cash flow for the period.
2 Prepare a statement of profit or loss for the three-month period ended 30 April 2024.
3 Prepare a statement of financial position at 30 April 2024.

Suggested Solutions

Scenario 1

Table 9.3 Operating cash flows

	Amount	£
Cash received		
Fees	(60 x £500)	30,000
Cash paid		
Rent	(£5,000 x 2 months)	(10,000)
Net operating cash flow		20,000

Table 9.4 Statement of profit or loss

	Amount	£
Income		
Fees	100 x £500	50,000
Expenses		
Rent	(£5,000 x 3 months)	(15,000)
Profit		35,000

Table 9.5 Statement of financial position

	Amount	£
Assets		
Fees receivable	(40 x £500)	20,000
Cash	(10,000 + 30,000 – 10,000; Investment + fees received – rent paid)	30,000
		50,000
Equity		
Capital	(Given)	10,000
Retained profit		35,000
Liabilities		
Rent payable	(£5,000 x 1 month; April rent not paid)	5,000
		50,000

(Continued)

Scenario 2

Table 9.6 Operating cash flows

	Amount	£
Cash received		
Fees	(100 x £500) + (40 x £500)	70,000
Cash paid		
Rent	(£5,000 x 4 months)	(20,000)
Net operating cash flow		50,000

Table 9.7 Statement of profit or loss

	Amount	£
Income		
Fees	(100 x £500)	50,000
Expenses		
Rent	(£5,000 x 3 months)	(15,000)
Profit		35,000

Table 9.8 Statement of financial position

	Amount	£
Assets		
Rent prepaid	(£5,000 x 1 month)	5,000
Cash	(10,000 + 70,000 – 20,000;	60,000
	Investment + fees received – rent paid	
		65,000
Equity		
Capital		10,000
Retained profit		35,000
Liabilities		
Unearned fees	(40 x £500; fees received in advance)	20,000
		65,000

Explanation

Considering the cash received and the earning of income in Scenario 1, the practice receives less than £50,000 in the current period, in this case £30,000, because some clients have not yet paid their accounts. In Scenario 2 the practice receives more than £50,000, in this case £70,000, as certain clients decide to pay in advance for future consultations.

In both of these cases, the statement of profit or loss still reflects £50,000 as income from fees as that is the amount which has been earned in the period from services provided. The recognition of income on the statement of profit or loss is a measure of *accomplishment* for the period and is not dependent on the cash received.

Considering the cash paid and the incurring of expenses, in *Scenario 1*, the practice does not pay the £10,000 in the current period and in *Scenario 2*, it pays £20,000 by paying the following month's rent in advance.

In both of these cases, the statement of profit or loss reflects £15,000 as rent expense as that is the amount which has been incurred in the period and which needs to be matched with the income earned. The recognition of expenses on the statement of profit or loss is a measure of *sacrifice* for the period and is not dependent on the cash paid.

Note carefully the story told by the statement of financial position. In Scenario 1, the business has assets of £50,000 (economic resources controlled by the business). The business has liabilities of £5,000 (obligation to pay rent to the landlord) and equity of £45,000 (obligation to the owner). The £45,000 obligation to the owner comprises £10,000 of the original capital invested and £35,000 of profit retained in the business).

Scenario 2 is similar, where the business has assets of £65,000 (economic resources controlled by the business). The business then has liabilities of £20,000 (obligation to provide legal services to the clients who have paid in advance) and equity of £45,000 (obligation to the owner). The £45,000 obligation to the owner comprises the same £10,000 of the original capital invested and £35,000 of profit retained in the business.

The Accounting Equation

As mentioned previously, a business entity is financed from two principal sources – *owner's funds* and *borrowed funds*. Owner's funds are sourced from the *owners*, also known as investors, and borrowed funds are sourced from *lenders*. All funding can be categorised into one of these two sources.

We can therefore develop an equation to measure the financial position of a business entity as follows:

- Assets = Funds provided by lenders and investors
- Assets = Borrowed funds and owner's funds
- Assets = Liabilities + owner's equity

The equation 'Assets = Liabilities + Owner's equity' (A = L + OE) is known as the *accounting equation*. This is a simple representation of the financial position of an entity, with the assets reflected on the left, and the liabilities and owner's equity on the right.

The accounting equation has two sides, which we can label the *left* side and the *right* side. Incorporating these labels, we can begin to develop an accounting equation worksheet that we can use to analyse transactions. Each transaction needs to be analysed to determine its effect on the accounting equation. The accounting equation must always be in balance.

CASE STUDY 9.2

Run for Life (1)

Tom is a keen runner and started a small business, Run for Life, that offers weekly running classes. The following transactions took place during the month ended 31 January 2024:

(Continued)

Table 9.9 Run for Life (1)

Date	Activity
02 January	Tom invested £1,200 cash as a capital contribution.
03 January	The business borrowed £200 from the bank.
04 January	Ten people signed up for a beginner's running group during January. The fee is £20 for the month and all ten people agreed to pay at the end of the month.
05 January	The business purchased ten reflective running belts at a cost of £70 from a local running shop. The running belts will be available to runners to use when attending a running class. Agreed to pay the running shop in the following month.
06 January	The business paid £40 for a bus-pass for Tom to travel to the running groups.
28 January	Received cash from nine of the ten people for the beginners running group.
29 January	Tom noted that the business had nine reflective running belts; one had been lost during the month.
30 January	The business distributed £60 to the owner.

Questions

1 Enter the above transactions in an accounting equation worksheet.

2 Prepare a statement of profit or loss and statement of charges in equity for Run for Life for the month ended 31 January 2024.

3 Prepare a statement of financial position for Run for Life at 31 January 2024.

Solution

Table 9.10 Accounting equation worksheet

	ASSETS			=	LIABILITIES		+	EQUITY			
Date	Supplies	Acc rec	Cash		Loan	Acc pay		Capital	Income	Expenses	Distributions
02/01			1,200					1,200			
03/01			200		200						
04/01		200							200		
05/01	70					70					
06/01			(40)							(40)	
28/01		(180)	180								
29/01	(7)									(7)	
30/01			(60)								(60)
Balance	63	20	1,480		200	70		1,200	200	(47)	(60)
	1,563			=	**270**		+	**1,293**			

Table 9.11 Explanation

Date	Activity
02	There is a £1,200 *increase in assets* (cash) on the *left side* of the equation and a £1,200 *increase in equity* (capital), on the *right side* of the equation. The equality of the accounting equation is maintained.
03	There is a £200 *increase in assets* (cash) on the *left side* of the equation and a £200 *increase in liabilities* (loan) on the *right side* of the equation.
04	There is a £200 *increase in assets (accounts receivable)* on the *left side* of the equation and a £200 *increase in equity (income)* on the *right side* of the equation. Note that income is increasing (fee income of £200 has been earned) and an *increase in income* leads to an *increase in equity.*
05	There is a £70 *increase in assets (supplies)* on the *left side* of the equation and a £70 *increase in liabilities (accounts payable)* on the *right side* of the equation. The running belts are recognised as an asset upon purchase and will be expensed when they are lost or become damaged.
06	There is a £40 *decrease in assets (cash)* on the *left side* of the equation and a £40 *decrease in owner's equity (expenses)* on the *right side* of the equation. Note, importantly, that although expenses are increasing (an expense for a bus-pass of £40 has been incurred), an *increase in expenses* leads to a *decrease in owner's equity.*
28	There is a £180 *increase in assets (cash)* on the *left side* of the equation and a £180 *decrease in assets (accounts receivable)* also on the *left side* of the equation. The equality of the accounting equation is maintained. Note that no income is recognised in this transaction; the income has been recognised as the running classes took place (transaction on the 4th).
29	There is a £7 *decrease in assets (supplies)* on the *left side* of the equation and a £7 *decrease in equity (expenses)* on the *right side* of the equation. Note, as in the transaction on the 6th, that although expenses are increasing (an expense for supplies used of £7 has been incurred), an *increase in expenses* leads to a *decrease in equity.*
30	There is a £60 *decrease in assets (cash)* on the *left side* of the equation and a £60 *decrease in equity (distributions)* on the *right side* of the equation. Note, importantly, and similar to expenses, that although distributions are increasing (a distribution of £60 has been made), an *increase in distributions* leads to a *decrease in owner's equity*

Table 9.12 Run for Life statement of profit or loss for the month ended 31 January 2024

	£
Income	
Fees	200
Expenses	
Travelling	(40)
Supplies used	(7)
Profit for the period	153

(Continued)

Explanation

- The statement of profit or loss is a measure of performance for the period.
- Applying the accrual basis of accounting, income represents the amount earned during the period (10 people participated in the running group), even though the cash received amounted to £180. The £20 owing to the business is reported as an asset, accounts receivable, on the statement of financial position.
- The expenses represent the amount incurred during the period.
- For the travelling expense, the amount incurred for travelling is equal to the amount of cash paid, so there is no corresponding amount on the statement of financial position.
- For the supplies used expense, this represents the cost of the one running belt that was lost during the month. The cost of the remaining nine running belts (9 x £7) is reported as an asset on the statement of financial position.
- Remembering that income increases equity and that expenses decrease equity, the excess of income over expenses, in other words, the profit, is reported as a component of equity called 'retained profit' on the statement of financial position.

Table 9.13 Run for Life statement of financial position at 31 January 2024

		£
ASSETS		
Current assets		
Supplies	(70 – 7)	63
Accounts receivable		20
Cash resources		1,480
		1,563
EQUITY AND LIABILITIES		
Equity		1,293
Capital		1,200
Retained profit	(Income 200 – Expenses 47 – Distributions 60)	93
Non-current liabilities		
Loan		200
Current liabilities		
Accounts payable		70
		1,570

Explanation

The statement of financial position is a measure of the financial position at a point in time, typically at the end of a period.

The assets are resources controlled by the business. The statement of financial position reports that at 31 January 2024, Run for Life has total assets of £1,563 - running belts that cost £63, customers/clients that owe £20 to the business (accounts receivable) and cash of £1,480.

The liabilities are obligations of the business to lenders. Run for Life owes £200 to the bank (a non-current liability that is payable more than 12 months after 31 January 2024) and it also owes £70 to the supplier of the running belts (a current liability, accounts payable).

Remembering the entity concept (the business and the owner are separate accounting entities), the equity of £1,293 is the amount that the business owes to the owner. It comprises £1,200 of the capital contributed by the owner plus £93 of retained profit. The retained profit is the profit retained in the business, in other words, the profit generated from business operations (income less expenses) less any amounts distributed from the business to the owner.

Note that the statement of financial position balances with reference to the accounting equation, 'Assets = Liabilities + Equity'. In this scenario, £1,563 = £270 + £1,293.

Double Entry Accounting

You learnt in the previous section that the equality of the accounting equation must be maintained for all transactions (see Figure 9.3).

Assets		=	Liabilities		+	Equity	
Left	Right		Left	Right		Left	Right
+	–		–	+		–	+

Figure 9.3 The accounting equation

You can see that assets are on the left side of the equation; liabilities and equity are on the right side. Further, each asset, liability or equity account can be split down the middle, with a left-side and a right-side.

In double-entry accounting, increases in assets are recorded on the *left-side* of asset accounts, for no reason other than that assets are typically shown on the left-hand side of the accounting equation. In contrast, increases in liabilities and equity are recorded on the *right-side* of those accounts in order to maintain the equality of the accounting equation. Conversely, decreases in assets are recorded on the *right-side* of asset accounts, and decreases in liabilities and equity are recorded on the *left-side* of the liability and equity accounts.

It is important to note here that equity is only affected by four types of transactions:

- **Capital contributions** from owners (which increase equity)
- **Income earned** by the business (which increases equity)
- **Expenses incurred** by the business (which decrease equity)
- **Distributions** to owners (which decrease equity)

We can thus expand the accounting equation as shown in Figure 9.4.

Assets		=	Liabilities		+	Equity											
						Capital			Income			Expenses			Distributions	
Left	Right		Left	Right		Left	Right		Left	Right		Left	Right		Left	Right
+	–		–	+		–	+		–	+		+	–		+	–
Dr	Cr		Dr	Cr		Dr	Cr		Dr	Cr		Dr	Cr		Dr	Cr

Figure 9.4 Expanded accounting equation

Furthermore, the left-hand side of any account (asset, liability or equity) is referred to as the *debit* side, abbreviated '*Dr*', and the right-hand side of any account (asset, liability or equity) is referred to as the *credit* side, abbreviated '*Cr*'. It is very important to understand debits and credits in an accounting context without trying to relate them to good and bad, or positive and negative.

Take a careful look at the components of equity – capital, income, expenses and distributions. You will see that capital and income follow the principles for increases and decreases as discussed above (increases in *capital* and *income* are recorded on the *right-side* of the respective accounts). However, take a careful look at the *expenses* and *distributions* accounts. Why are increases in expenses and distributions recorded on the *left-side* of the respective accounts?

The principle which governs the recording of movements in income and expense items is based on the *effect that the transaction has on equity*. As the contribution of capital and the earning of income both increase equity, increases in these accounts are recorded on the *right-side as credits* because increases in equity are also recorded on the *right-side*.

Conversely, as the incurring of expenses and distributions to owners both decrease equity, increases in these accounts are recorded on the *left-side as debits* because decreases in owner's equity are also recorded on the left side.

CASE STUDY 9.3

Run for Life (2)

The following transactions are the same as for Case Study 9.2, repeated here for ease of reference.

Tom is a keen runner and started a small business, Run for Life that offers weekly running classes. The following transactions took place during the month ended 31 January 2024:

Table 9.14 Run for Life (2)

Date	Activity
02 January	Tom invested £1,200 cash as a capital contribution.
03 January	The business borrowed £200 from the bank.
04 January	Ten people signed up for a beginners running group during January. The fee is £20 for the month and all ten people agreed to pay at the end of the month.
05 January	The business purchased ten reflective running belts at a cost of £70 from a local running shop. The running belts will be available to runners to use when attending a running class. Agreed to pay the running shop in the following month.

(Continued)

Table 9.14 (Continued)

Date	Activity
06 January	The business paid £40 for a bus-pass for Tom to travel to the running groups.
28 January	Received cash from nine of the ten people for the beginners running group.
29 January	Tom noted that the business had nine reflective running belts; one had been lost during the month.
30 January	The business distributed £60 to the owner.

Required

Enter the above transactions in an accounting equation worksheet, identifying the double entry (specifically the debit and the credit) for each transaction.

Table 9.15 Solution

	ASSETS						=	LIABILITIES				+	EQUITY							
	Supplies		Acc rec		Cash			Loan		Acc pay			Capital		Income		Expenses		Distributions	
	+	−	+	−	+	−		−	+	−	+		−	+	−	+	+	−	+	−
	L	R	L	R	L	R		L	R	L	R		L	R	L	R	L	R	L	R
Date	Dr	Cr	Dr	Cr	Dr	Cr		Dr	Cr	Dr	Cr		Dr	Cr	Dr	Cr	Dr	Cr	Dr	Cr
02/01					1,200									1,200						
03/01					200				200											
04/01			200													200				
05/01	70										70									
06/01						40											40			
28/01				180	180															
29/01		7															7			
30/01						60													60	
Bal	63		20		1,480				200		70			1,200		200	47		60	
	1,563						=	270				+	1,293							

Table 9.16 Explanation

Date	Activity
02	To increase an **asset** requires a left or debit entry, thus ***debit*** 'cash' with £1,200. To increase **equity** requires a right or credit entry, thus ***credit*** 'capital' with £1,200.
03	To increase an **asset** requires a left or debit entry, thus ***debit*** 'cash' with £200. To increase a **liability** requires a right or credit entry, thus ***credit*** 'loan' with £200.

Date	Activity
04	To increase an **asset** requires a left or debit entry, thus ***debit*** 'accounts receivable' with £200. To increase **income** requires a right or credit entry, thus ***credit*** 'income' with £200.
05	To increase an **asset** requires a left or debit entry, thus ***debit*** 'supplies' with £70. To increase a **liability** requires a right or credit entry, thus ***credit*** 'accounts payable' with £70.
06	To increase an **expense** requires a left or debit entry, thus ***debit*** 'expenses' with £40. To decrease an **asset** requires a right or credit entry, thus ***credit*** 'cash' with £40. Note here that the increase or debit to expenses leads to a decrease in equity.
28	To increase an **asset** requires a left or debit entry, thus ***debit*** 'cash' with £180. To decrease an **asset** requires a right or credit entry, thus ***credit*** 'accounts receivable' with £180.
29	To increase an **expense** requires a left or debit entry, thus ***debit*** 'expenses' with £7. To decrease an **asset** requires a right or credit entry, thus ***credit*** 'supplies' with £7. Note again that the increase or debit to expenses leads to a decrease in equity.
30	To increase **distributions** requires a left or debit entry, thus ***debit*** 'distributions' with £60. To decrease an **asset** requires a right or credit entry, thus ***credit*** 'cash' with £60. Note here that similar to expenses, the increase or debit to distributions leads to a decrease in equity.

You may be wondering what the difference is between the worksheet produced in Case Study 9.2 and the one produced in Case Study 9.3. They both look similar and both result in the same income and expenses for the income statement and the same assets, liabilities and equity for the statement of financial position.

In the worksheet in Case Study 9.2, each of the financial statement elements are shown as a single column with increases as positive numbers and decreases as negative numbers (in brackets). Compare this to the worksheet in Case Study 9.3, where each of the financial statement elements has a debit column (left side) and a credit column (right side). Increases and decreases are recorded using the principles of double-entry bookkeeping.

You also may ask whether the worksheet is necessary? It certainly is not, it is used here merely as a learning tool. The transactions can be recorded using a manual or computerised accounting system. The important point to remember is that irrespective of which system is used, the principles of double-entry bookkeeping are always applied.

Having established how businesses record and report financial information through the double-entry system and financial statements, we now turn to how this information can be used for internal decision-making. The concepts of assets, liabilities, equity, income, and expenses that we have explored will form the basis for understanding product costing, profitability analysis, and budgeting in management accounting.

MANAGERIAL ACCOUNTING

Having established how businesses record and report financial information for external users, we now explore how this information supports internal management decisions. Managerial accounting transforms financial data into actionable insights for planning, controlling, and decision-making within organisations. This section examines three interconnected aspects of managerial accounting: first, we learn how to determine the full cost of products using traditional and activity-based methods; next, we apply this cost information to analyse profitability and make short-term decisions through Cost-Volume-Profit analysis; finally, we integrate these costing and profitability insights into budgeting frameworks for planning and performance evaluation. Building on the financial accounting concepts of assets, liabilities, equity, income, and expenses, these managerial accounting tools work together to enable businesses to optimise resources, improve profitability, and achieve strategic objectives.

Historical Perspective

Managerial accounting evolved during the Industrial Revolution of the late 18th and early 19th centuries to meet the growing need for sophisticated cost control in complex businesses. Initially focused on financial reporting, it progressively developed essential tools for internal planning, controlling, and decision-making, with key concepts emerging such as product costing for understanding manufacturing expenses, Cost-Volume-Profit analysis for evaluating profitability, and budgeting for resource allocation. As businesses became more complex, the field adapted and now undergoes a significant **digital transformation** where **artificial intelligence** and **data analytics** enhance decision-making processes by providing real-time insights and predictive analyses. The field has also become more future-oriented, emphasising forward-looking strategies and risk management in an uncertain global economy, while incorporating diverse perspectives and promoting equitable resource allocation. This section introduces both historical and contemporary managerial accounting tools, bridging traditional methods with cutting-edge practices, enabling readers to apply these concepts effectively in real-world scenarios and drive business success in the digital era.

PRODUCT COSTING

Building on our understanding of how costs are recorded in financial accounting, we now explore how to classify and allocate these costs for better decision-making. Product costing is essential for effective financial management and strategic decision-making, involving the determination of full costs associated with producing goods or services. Clear costing methodologies support inclusive decision-making among diverse teams, leading to more comprehensive and innovative solutions. This section introduces key cost classifications, such as direct and indirect, manufacturing and non-manufacturing, and fixed and **variable costs**. It explores traditional absorption costing and Activity-Based Costing (ABC), emphasising their distinct advantages and accuracy impacts. Through practical examples, readers will learn to calculate product costs, allocate overheads, and understand the implications of cost information for business decisions. This foundational knowledge supports sustainable and responsible business practices, aligning with the United Nations SDGs.

Full Costing Principle

The full costing principle in managerial accounting is essential for understanding the true cost of producing a product or providing a service. It encompasses all costs involved, including direct costs like materials and labour, as well as indirect costs such as rent, utilities, and other overheads (Atrill and McLaney, 2022). By aggregating these expenses, businesses can accurately determine the total cost of production. This comprehensive approach enables businesses to set prices that cover all expenses, ensuring profitability and aiding in strategic decision-making. Understanding full costing is crucial for effective financial management and sustainable business practices. Indeed, when implementing full costing, organisations should consider accessibility features and cultural differences in their cost calculations, ensuring inclusive practices that benefit both the company and its diverse **stakeholders**.

Typology of Cost

Costs can be classified from different perspectives including their traceability (direct vs. indirect), their function (manufacturing vs. non-manufacturing), and their behaviour (fixed vs. variable):

- **Direct and indirect costs**
  - Direct costs are those directly related to a specific object, service, or location, such as direct labour and direct materials.
  - Indirect costs, or overhead costs, cannot be directly tied to a specific object or service and must be apportioned fairly. Examples include depreciation of machinery, insurance of factory premises, and rental of warehouse space.
- **Non-manufacturing (period) and manufacturing (product) costs**
  - Manufacturing (product) costs are costs that are incurred to create products intended for sale and include direct materials, direct labour, and manufacturing overhead.
  - Non-manufacturing (period) costs are costs that are not tied to production and include selling, general, and administrative expenses, marketing expenses, and rent for corporate offices.
- **Fixed and variable costs**
  - **Fixed costs** remain unchanged as output levels vary and are incurred regardless of output level, such as rent and insurance. However, fixed costs can become stepped costs if output increases beyond a specific threshold, necessitating additional resources.
  - **Variable costs** change with the amount of output produced and include costs for materials and labour. The unit cost of production is assumed to be constant, though in reality, bulk-buying discounts may lower the unit cost of materials.

REFLECTIVE ACTIVITY 9.3

1. Why do you think it's important for businesses to know the full cost of their products? Consider how knowing all the costs involved in making a product can help businesses in making good decisions.
2. What do you expect to learn about different types of costs, such as direct and indirect costs? Think about why it's useful to know the difference between these costs before diving into more detailed methods of costing.

Importance of Understanding Full Cost

Understanding the full cost of a cost object is crucial for several reasons (Atrill and McLaney, 2022):

1. **Pricing and Output Decisions:** Full-cost information enables managers to set appropriate prices for products or services, ensuring they cover all costs and achieve desired profitability.
2. **Exercising Control:** By analysing full-cost figures, managers can identify areas where costs are excessively high and explore opportunities for savings, enhancing overall cost control.
3. **Assessing Relative Efficiency:** Full costing helps compare the efficiency of different production methods or locations, aiding decisions on the most cost-effective approaches.
4. **Assessing Performance:** Calculating profit by comparing sales revenue with full costs helps evaluate past decisions and inform future strategies, such as whether to continue or discontinue a product or service.

In the remainder sections, we shall look at how to derive the full cost of a unit of output for a business providing a range of products or services using two methods of costing, the traditional (absorption) and ABC methods. When it comes to product costing, the issue we face is how to deal with indirect costs, which are called overhead costs, as they cannot be easily identified per unit (e.g., rent, insurance). With this in mind, the key difference between the traditional method and ABC lies in the way overhead costs are calculated for each unit produced.

Traditional Costing Methodology (Absorption Costing)

In the traditional method, overheads are applied to jobs using a predetermined rate, calculated by forecasting total manufacturing overhead at the beginning of the year and dividing it by a cost driver, such as budgeted machine hours or direct labour hours. Total manufacturing costs are absorbed into cost objects using one overhead absorption rate for the organisation. Historically, labour hours were used as the basis for absorption; it was appropriate when businesses were labour-intensive (Dyson and Franklin, 2020; Atrill and McLaney, 2022). Let's look at the following example and see how this method can be used in product costing.

EXAMPLE 9.3

TechPro Limited (1)

TechPro Limited manufactures engineering components, producing two products: Alpha and Gamma as shown in Table 9.17.

Table 9.17 Direct cost components

Cost	Alpha	Gamma
Materials	400,000	140,000
Labour	200,000	300,000
Direct cost	£600,000	£440,000

The total manufacturing overhead is £540,000, with specific costs allocated to light and heat, factory supervisor's salary, machinery insurance, and factory rental. Table 9.18 below shows the breakdown of the indirect costs. TechPro produces 30,000 units of Alpha and 20,000 units of Gamma, with each unit taking one hour in production, implying that Alpha requires 30,000 hours and Gamma requires 20,000 hours.

Table 9.18 Breakdown of indirect costs (overhead)

Overhead costs	Amount
Light and heat cost	£100,000
Factory supervisor's salary	£140,000
Machinery insurance costs	£40,000
Factory rental costs	£260,000
Total	£540,000

We know that the total overhead is £540,000 and we need to distribute such cost to each unit of output equally using the traditional method. We first need to calculate the rate for each unit, which is called overhead absorption rate (OAR) by dividing the total indirect cost by total basis (i.e., cost driver of such costs which is normally the total labour hours because the more labour hours worked, the more overhead costs) as follows.

$$OAR = \frac{Total\ Indirect\ Cost}{Total\ Basis}$$

OAR = 540,000/50,000 = £10.8

(Continued)

Note that the 50,000 hours (denominator) are the 30,000 hours of Alpha and 20,000 hours of Gamma. Now we know that each unit should be charged £10.8 as an indirect cost in addition to other direct costs (direct labour and material). Keeping this in mind, knowing that TechPro Limited produces 30,000 units of Alpha and 20,000 units of Gamma, we can estimate that the total indirect cost for Alpha and Gamma is as follows:

- Alpha: 30,000 units * £10.8 = £324,000
- Gamma: 20,000 units * £10.8 = £216,000

Now we can calculate the exact unit cost, including both direct and indirect costs as shown in Table 9.19

Table 9.19 Direct and indirect cost calculations

Cost component	Alpha	Gamma
Materials (given)	400,000	140,000
Labour (given)	200,000	300,000
Overhead cost (calculated above)	324,000	216,000
Total cost	£924,000	£656,000
Unit cost	£30.80	£32.80

Table 9.19 shows that the total cost for Alpha is £924,000 (£400,000 materials + £200,000 labour + allocated overhead costs £324,000). Knowing that TechPro Limited produces 30,000 units, we divide the total cost (£924,000) by the number of Alpha units (30,000), which gives us £30.8 which is the total cost per unit. In similar vein, the total cost of Gamma is £656,000 divided by the number of units produced (20,000), which gives us £32.8 per unit.

Activity-Based Costing (ABC)

ABC traces resource consumption and costs final outputs, assigning resources to activities and activities to cost objects based on consumption estimates using cost drivers. ABC not only provides more accurate costing but also promotes equitable resource allocation. Organisations can use ABC to evaluate and support diverse suppliers, potentially uncovering new markets and **innovations** while fostering inclusive business practices. Unlike traditional costing, which divides overheads equally, ABC uses multiple cost drivers to absorb fixed overheads, offering a more accurate picture of costs (Dyson and Franklin, 2020; Atrill and McLaney, 2022). To illustrate we continue with the TechPro Limited example (Example 9.3) using ABC.

EXAMPLE 9.4

TechPro Limited (2) with ABC

TechPro Limited's total manufacturing overhead of £540,000 is allocated to activities such as machining, production scheduling, and quality control. Costs are divided based on cost drivers like machine hours, production runs, and inspections. You are given Table 9.20 that shows the breakdown of the manufacturing overhead (Panel A) and the identification of activity cost drivers per cost object (Panel B).

Table 9.20 ABC cost allocation and activity drivers

Panel A: Allocating expenses to activities			
Activity	**Cost p.a.**	**Cost driver**	**Cost drivers p.a.**
Machining	300,000	Machine hours	160,000 hrs
Production scheduling	160,000	No. of production runs	500 runs
Quality control	80,000	No. of inspections	1,050 inspections
Total	£540,000		
Panel B: Identifying activity cost drivers per cost object			
Activity driver	**Alpha**	**Gamma**	**Totals**
Labour hours	20,000	30,000	50,000
Machine hours	120,000	40,000	160,000
Production run set ups	400	100	500
Number of inspections	800	250	1,050

We know that the total overhead is £540,000 and we need to distribute such cost to each unit equally using the ABC method. We first need to calculate the rate for each unit for each activity separately. In other words, we will have different rates (a rate for each activity), for both Alpha and Gamma. We divide the cost of each activity by its cost driver to find the rate for each unit for the referenced activity as shown in Table 9.21.

Table 9.21 Calculation of ABC rates

Activity	**Cost p.a.**	**Cost driver**	**Cost drivers p.a.**	**Rate**
Machining	300,000	Machine hours	160,000 hrs	300,000/160,000 = 1.875
Production scheduling	160,000	No. of production runs	500 runs	160,000/500 = 320
Quality control	80,000	No. of inspections	1,050 inspections	80,000/1,050 = 76.19

(Continued)

Once we calculate the rate of each activity, we then multiply each rate by the cost driver for each unit to calculate the total cost of each activity for both Alpha and Gamma as shown in Table 9.22.

Table 9.22 ABC overhead allocation by product type

Activity	Alpha	Gamma
Machining	1.875*120,000 = 225,000	1.875*40,000 = 75,000
Production scheduling	320*400 = 128,000	320*100 = 32,000
Quality control	76.19*800 = 60,952	76.19*250 = 19,048

Now we can calculate the cost per unit using ABC as shown in Table 9.23 below.

Table 9.23 Cost per unit using ABC

Costs	Calculation basis	Alpha	Gamma
Material	Given	400,000	140,000
Labour	Given	200,000	300,000
Machining	Use machine hours 120,000:40,000	225,000	75,000
Production scheduling	Use production runs 400:100	128,000	32,000
Quality control costs	Use inspections 800:250	60,952	19,048
Total manufacturing		£1,013,952	£566,048
Per unit		£33.80	£28.30

Table 9.23 shows that the total cost for Alpha is £1,013,952 (£400,000 materials + £200,000 labour + allocated overhead costs for machining costs £225,000 + allocated overhead costs for production scheduling costs £128,000 + allocated overhead costs for quality control costs £60,952). Knowing that TechPro Limited produces 30,000 units, we divide the total cost (£1,013,952) by the number of Alpha units (30,000) which gives us £33.8 which is the total cost per unit. In similar vein, the total cost of Gamma is £566,048 divided by the number of units produced (20,000) which gives us £28.3 per unit.

Let's now compare the cost per unit for each method used as shown in Table 9.24 below.

Table 9.24 Cost per unit for each method

Cost per unit	Alpha	Gamma
Traditional	30.8	32.8
ABC	33.8	28.3

Interestingly, we can see that when we use the traditional method the cost per unit for Gamma (£32.8) is greater than Alpha (£30.8), whereas when we use the ABC method Alpha's cost per unit (£33.8) is greater than Gamma's cost per unit (£28.3). This key difference would have a significant impact on the pricing accuracy for Alpha and Gamma. For example, let's assume that TechPro Limited decides to add a markup of 20% to the selling price (i.e., they want to add 20% over the cost of each unit to set the selling price for Alpha and Gamma). This can be done by multiplying the cost per unit by (1 + the markup) as shown in Table 9.25.

Table 9.25 Selling prices under traditional and ABC costing

Alpha	**Cost per unit**	**Markup**	**Selling price**
Traditional method	30.8	20%	30.8 * 1.20 = £36.96
ABC method	33.8	20%	33.8 * 1.20 = £40.56
Gamma			
Traditional method	32.8	20%	32.8 * 1.20 = £39.36
ABC method	28.3	20%	28.3 * 1.20 = £33.96

From Table 9.25, we can see that the selling price significantly differs when using each method separately. Specifically, when we use the traditional method, we find that the selling price for Alpha is understated since the price is £36.96, whereas the more accurate method, ABC, shows that the selling price should be £40.56. Similarly, by looking at Gamma, we find that the selling price under the traditional method is significantly overstated as the ABC method that the selling price should be £33.96.

As a university graduate entering the workforce, your **knowledge** of product costing can make a significant impact. By implementing ABC in your company, you can identify inefficiencies, reduce waste, and optimise resource allocation. This not only boosts profitability but also promotes sustainable business practices, aligning with the UN Sustainable Development Goals. Your ability to apply these principles can drive positive change, demonstrating how managerial accounting contributes to responsible and efficient production methods, benefiting both your organisation and society.

PROFITABILITY DECISIONS (SHORT-TERM DECISIONS)

While product costing helps us understand the full cost structure, Cost-Volume-Profit (CVP) analysis enables us to use this information for short-term decision-making. The cost classifications we learned in the previous section are fundamental to this analysis, particularly the distinction between fixed and variable costs. This section focuses on using management accounting information for decisions typically spanning weeks to a maximum of 12 months. During this time frame, some costs remain fixed, while others vary based on activity levels.

As we discussed earlier in this chapter, absorption costing determines the total cost of manufacturing specific units or valuing inventory by including both direct (labour, materials) and indirect costs, ensuring all costs are covered for profitability. However, when making short-term decisions, absorption costing may not be suitable as fixed costs often remain unaffected by specific decisions. This limitation leads us to marginal costing, which offers an alternative approach by focusing on the cost changes resulting from producing one additional unit. This method is particularly useful for managerial decision-making as it considers only direct costs tied to activities and additional units, excluding fixed or indirect costs from the decision-making process.

REFLECTIVE ACTIVITY 9.4

- How do you think understanding the behaviour of fixed and variable costs will help you in making short-term business decisions?
- Reflect on why it is important to distinguish between fixed and variable costs when planning business operations. Consider how knowing these costs can affect decisions related to pricing, budgeting, and managing resources effectively.
- What benefits do you expect from using CVP analysis in a real business scenario?
- Think about how CVP analysis can assist in determining the break-even point, setting sales targets, and evaluating the financial impact of different business strategies. Reflect on how this analysis can help you make informed decisions to achieve profitability and sustain business growth.

Marginal Costing Benefits

Marginal costing allows conducting CVP analysis that provides more useful information for decision-making than absorption costing in several situations, including:

- Break-even analysis
- Devising an optimum production plan where resources are limited
- Deciding whether to make a product or to buy it instead
- Accepting an order at a lower-than-normal selling price
- Closing down a branch or segment of the business

Separating Out Fixed and Variable Costs

For effective decision-making, it is crucial to separate fixed and variable costs within a Profit & Loss (P&L) account to highlight the key decision-making concept known as 'contribution'. However, many costs are mixed in nature, containing both fixed and variable elements. One technique to separate these costs is the 'Hi-Lo' method, which examines past activity and related costs and uses regression analysis to distinguish between fixed and variable components.

EXAMPLE 9.5

Sigma Limited: Hi-Lo Methodology

Consider the following example on activity levels and total costs for Sigma Limited over recent years in Table 9.26.

Table 9.26 Historical activity and cost data

Activity level (units)	Total cost
3,000	£16,500
5,000	£20,100
4,000	£18,200
8,000	£24,000
6,000	£21,900

Using the Hi-Lo method, we can separate the fixed and variable elements of Sigma Limited's cost structure to identify the variable cost per unit and the total fixed cost.

Hi-Lo Methodology Steps

1 Identify the high and low activity points and their related costs:
- High point: 8,000 units and £24,000
- Low point: 3,000 units and £16,500

2 Calculate the difference in cost at these two levels (this must be the variable cost):
- Difference in cost = £24,000 - £16,500 = £7,500
- Difference in units = 8,000 - 3,000 = 5,000

3 Calculate the variable cost per unit by dividing the difference in cost by the change in the number of units between the high and low points:
- Variable cost per unit = £7,500 / 5,000 = £1.50 per unit

4 Use this variable cost per unit to extract the fixed cost as the balancing figure at either the high or low point:
- At high point, total variable cost = £1.50 x 8,000 = £12,000, therefore fixed cost = £24,000 - £12,000 = £12,000
- At low point, total variable cost = £1.50 x 3,000 = £4,500, therefore fixed cost = £16,500 - £4,500 = £12,000

The Hi-Lo method provides a straightforward way to separate mixed costs into their fixed and variable components, which is essential for effective short-term decision-making in managerial accounting.

Introducing Cost-Volume-Profit (CVP) Analysis

CVP analysis examines the relationship between changes in activity and changes in total sales revenue, costs, and profit. It answers key questions such as:

- How many units of this product do we need to sell to break even?
- How many units do we need to sell to achieve our target profit?
- What additional sales volume is required to justify the additional costs of a new advertising campaign?
- What is our current margin of safety?

The Concept of Contribution

Contribution is a critical concept in CVP analysis and is calculated as:

- Sales Revenue – Variable Cost = Contribution (C)

Contribution represents the amount remaining after variable costs have been deducted from sales revenue, which then contributes towards fixed costs and profit (Dyson and Franklin, 2020; Atrill and McLaney, 2022). When analysing contribution margins, companies should consider diverse market segments and inclusive product ranges, which can lead to new growth opportunities and broader market reach. If the contribution is sufficient to cover fixed costs, any remaining balance is profit. If not, the entity incurs a loss.

For example:

- Sales: £100
- Less: Variable Costs: £40
- Contribution: £60

Contribution can be expressed in total or per unit and is vital for calculating the contribution margin, which is the ratio of contribution to sales.

1. Contribution = Revenue – Variable Costs
   - Contribution margin = Contribution/Revenue
2. Break-even point (BEP) in units = Fixed Costs / Contribution per unit
   - This indicates how many units must be sold before a profit is made.
   - Break-even calculations should account for diverse customer needs and market segments, potentially revealing new opportunities for sustainable growth while promoting inclusive business practices.
3. Volume to earn a target profit = (Fixed Costs + Target Profit) / Contribution per unit
   - This calculation determines the number of units needed to achieve a specific profit target.
4. Margin of safety = Expected sales – Break-even analysis
   - This measures how much sales can fall before a loss is incurred.

EXAMPLE 9.6

TechPro Limited (3)

Building on our analysis of TechPro Limited's costing structure from Example 9.3, let's examine how the company can use CVP analysis for short-term decisions. TechPro wants to determine the break-even point for their Alpha and Gamma products.

From our previous analysis, we know:

Table 9.27 Selling price and costs data

Selling price and costs	Alpha	Gamma
Unit cost (ABC method – see Table 9.24)	£33.80	£28.30
Selling price (with 20% markup)	£40.56	£33.96
Fixed costs (see Table 9.19)	£324,000	£216,000

Required

1 Calculate the contribution margin per unit for each product
2 Determine the break-even point in units for each product
3 Calculate the margin of safety (MoS) based on current production levels
4 Determine the number of units needed to achieve a target profit of £200,000 for each product

Solution

Table 9.28 Contribution per unit

Contribution per unit	Selling price - Variable cost per unit
Alpha	£40.56 – £33.80 = £6.76 per unit
Gamma	£33.96 – £28.30 = £5.66 per unit

Table 9.29 Break-even point (BEP) in units

Break-even point (BEP) in units	Fixed costs ÷ Contribution per unit
Alpha	£324,000 ÷ £6.76 = 47,929 units
Gamma	£216,000 ÷ £5.66 = 38,163 units

(Continued)

Table 9.30 Margin of safety (MoS)

MoS	Current production – Break-even point	Notes
Alpha	30,000 – 47,929 = –17,929 units	Alpha is operating below break-even point
Gamma	20,000 – 38,163 = –18,163 units	Gamma is also operating below break-even point

Note that both Alpha and Gamma operate below the break-even point. If we hypothetically assume that the current production is 50,000 units for Alpha and 35,000 units for Gamma, the margin of safety will be as follows:

Table 9.31 MoS for 50,000/35,000 units

MoS	Current production – Break-even point	Notes
Alpha	50,000 – 47,929 = 2,071 units	Alpha is operating above break-even point
Gamma	35,000 – 38,163 = –3,163 units	Gamma is operating below break-even point

Table 9.32 Units needed for a target profit of £200,000

Units needed for a target profit of £200,000	(Fixed costs + Target profit) ÷ Contribution per unit
Alpha	(£324,000 + £200,000) ÷ £6.76 = 77,157 units
Gamma	(£216,000 + £200,000) ÷ £5.66 = 73,498 units

Limitations of Break-Even Analysis

While break-even analysis is useful, it has limitations, such as:

- Variable costs may not be constant per unit due to factors like bulk-buying discounts or variable wages.
- Selling prices might fluctuate.
- Not all output produced is necessarily sold.
- Distinguishing between fixed and variable costs can be challenging.
- Fixed costs are only constant over a specific range of output.
- For **firms** producing multiple products, separating fixed costs becomes complex.

Applications of Cost-Volume-Profit Analysis

CVP analysis can be used to evaluate opportunities in underrepresented markets and assess ethical pricing strategies that consider diverse customer segments. Specifically, CVP analysis is useful in various decision-making scenarios, including (Atrill and McLaney, 2022):

- **Special orders**: Determining if a business should accept an order that requires full capacity.
- **Abandonment of a line of business**: Assessing whether to continue a line of business based on its contribution to fixed costs.
- **Existence of a limiting factor**: Optimising product mix when resources are limited.
- **In-house activity versus bought-in contract**: Comparing costs of producing in-house versus outsourcing.

Your mastery of CVP analysis and marginal costing equips you to make impactful decisions in real-world business contexts. By applying these techniques, you can enhance a company's profitability, efficiency, and **sustainability**. For instance, in your future role, you might use CVP analysis to determine the break-even point for a new product, ensuring its financial viability and resource efficiency. This practical application not only drives business success but also promotes responsible consumption and production, aligning with global sustainability goals. Your **skills** enable you to make a tangible difference in the workplace and beyond.

PLANNING AND PERFORMANCE - BUDGETING

Having understood how to determine costs and analyse profitability, we can now apply these concepts to planning and controlling business activities through budgeting. The financial statements we studied earlier serve as the foundation for budgetary planning. Budgeting is a cornerstone of managerial accounting, playing a critical role in the planning and performance evaluation processes within an organisation. This section delves into the theoretical foundations and practical applications of budgeting, highlighting its significance in achieving financial and operational objectives. By understanding the intricacies of various budgeting methods and their implications, managers can effectively coordinate resources, motivate employees, and steer the organisation toward its strategic goals. We will explore the benefits and challenges of budgeting, and differentiate between fixed and flexible budgets.

REFLECTIVE ACTIVITY 9.5

- Consider a time when you had to plan for a personal or group project. How did you estimate the resources (time, money, materials) you would need? What challenges did you face in sticking to your plan, and how did you address them?
- Think about the various purposes of budgeting discussed in this chapter. Which purpose do you find most challenging or potentially problematic in a real-world business scenario? Why? How would you mitigate these challenges in your role as a manager?

Budgeting Theory

A budget is a quantitative expression of a proposed plan of action by management for a future time period, serving as an aid for the coordination and implementation of the plan. Essentially, a budget is a financial and operational business plan for the short term, used to implement an organisation's objectives by setting financial targets. Companies typically prepare different budgets annually in advance of the financial year. The main budget, known as the master budget, comprises a budgeted profit and loss account, a budgeted balance sheet, and a budgeted cash flow statement. The master budget consolidates a company's lower-level budgets into one central document for ease of reference (Dyson and Franklin, 2020; Atrill and McLaney, 2022).

Types of Budgets

Budgets can be set for any resource that a business expects to use over future time periods. Budgets should incorporate metrics for addressing pay disparities and tracking progress on diversity initiatives, fostering an equitable business environment. Commonly used budgets include (Dyson and Franklin, 2020; Atrill and McLaney, 2022):

- **Cash Budget**: Also known as a cash flow forecast.
- **Sales Budget**: Shows the expected sales by volume or value.
- **Materials Budget**: Indicates the materials needed for production over future time periods.
- **Production Budget**: Details the units of production planned over future time periods.
- **Master Budget**: A full set of budgets usually summarised by a cash budget and forecast income statement and balance sheet.

The Interrelationship of Operating Budgets

Budgets are interconnected and do not operate in isolation. For example, a sales forecast leads to the preparation of other related budgets, such as production, materials, and cash budgets, based on the assumptions made in the sales budget (Atrill and McLaney, 2022).

Importance of Budgets and Forecasts

Despite actual results often differing from budgets and forecasts, the planning process remains crucial for several reasons (Atrill and McLaney, 2022):

- **Promotes Forward-Thinking**: Budgets encourage future planning, helping managers identify and address potential issues early, such as production capacity shortages.
- **Facilitates Coordination**: Budgets align departmental activities, ensuring purchasing matches production needs to prevent stoppages or excessive inventories.
- **Motivates Performance**: Specific budget targets motivate managers and staff, aligning their efforts with the business's strategic goals.

- **Provides Control**: Budgets allow comparison of **actual performance** against plans, highlighting variances and enabling corrective actions.
- **Enables Management by Exception**: Budget comparisons let senior managers focus on underperforming areas and help managers assess and improve their performance.
- **Authorises Spending**: Budgets allocate funds for specific activities, authorising spending up to a set limit.

Effective budgeting processes engage diverse stakeholders in planning and decision-making, leading to improved employee engagement and broader market reach while building organisational resilience.

Challenges of Budgeting and Forecasting

The budgeting process can be time-consuming and costly, often involving many personnel. Additionally, budgets may become outdated quickly as new events unfold. Budgeting can also act as a constraint, limiting flexibility and potentially stifling creativity. Furthermore, the practice of budgetary slack and padding, where expenses are overestimated and revenues underestimated, can lead to inefficiencies (Dyson and Franklin, 2020; Atrill and McLaney, 2022).

Budget Period

The main budget period is usually a calendar year, but it can vary depending on the product cycle (Dyson and Franklin, 2020; Atrill and McLaney, 2022). For instance, the fashion industry may use a budget period shorter than a year, while the construction industry may adopt a five-year period. Despite these variations, a calendar year is often convenient for aligning with financial accounting requirements.

Budget Preparation and Control

Budgetary control involves comparing budgeted results with actual outcomes, identifying significant variances, and taking corrective actions to align future results with the budget. This feedback process is a critical component of a broader organisational control system.

EXAMPLE 9.7

Sunny Bakes (1): Budget Preparation

Sunny Bakes, a small bakery specialising in custom cakes and pastries, has provided the following budgeted figures for the last quarter in Table 9.33. Review the data and analyse the business's financial performance.

(Continued)

Table 9.33 Previous quarter figures

Budget Item	Original Budget	Actual	Variance
Units Sold	1,000	800	–200
Revenue	£10,000	£7,800	–£2,200 Unfavourable
Material Costs	–£4,000	–£3,350	+£650 Favourable
Freelance Labour Costs	–£3,000	–£2,300	+£700 Favourable
Contribution	£3,000	£2,150	–£850 Unfavourable
Central Fixed Costs	–£1,000	–£1,100	–£100 Unfavourable
Profit	£2,000	£1,050	–£950 Unfavourable

From the above budget, we can calculate the variance, which is the difference between the actual and original budgets and identify whether the variance is favourable (good) or unfavourable (bad). For example, the variance in our revenues of £2,200 is unfavourable. That is, we estimate our revenues to be £10,000 but the actual revenues generated are £7,800. Therefore, the variance tells us that our actual revenues are £2,200 less than we estimated which is not a good indicator; therefore, it is unfavourable. For the material costs, on the other hand, we estimate the costs to be £4,000 but the actual material costs are £3,350. This is a good indicator because these are costs and we have incurred lower costs than the estimated costs. So the difference (£650) is favourable.

Flexing the Budget

The above example conducts the budgeting process and calculates the variance between the actual and estimated budgets. However, when we look at the difference between the items above, we can note that the number of units in the actual budget is different from the budgeted units. This would make our variance calculations unreliable because we are not comparing figures on an equivalent basis. Therefore, we need to allow for certain circumstances that might have taken place since the budgets were prepared such as changes in the number of units sold. Accountants call this flexing the budget. A flexible budget is an original budget that has been amended to take account of the actual level of activity (Dyson and Franklin, 2020; Atrill and McLaney, 2022).

Specifically, to understand discrepancies, managers may flex the budget to match actual production levels. Flexing involves revising the budget assuming a different volume of output. For example, if the budget was based on producing 1,000 units but only 800 were produced, the flexed budget recalculates the expected outcomes for 800 units. This helps identify where and why variances occurred.

EXAMPLE 9.8

Sunny Bakes (2): Flexed Budget

With the above in mind, if the actual activity level is 800 units, the variances can be calculated as shown in Table 9.34.

Table 9.34 Flexed budget

Budget Item	Original	Flexed	Actual	Flexed Budget Variance
Units	1,000	800	800	
Revenue	£10,000	£8,000	£7,800	–£200 Unfavourable
Material Costs	–£4,000	–£3,200	–£3,350	–£150 Unfavourable
Freelance Labour Costs	–£3,000	–£2,400	–£2,300	+£100 Favourable
Contribution	£3,000	£2,400	£2,150	–£250 Unfavourable
Central Fixed Costs	–£1,000	–£1,000	–£1,100	–£100 Unfavourable
Profit	£2,000	£1,400	£1,050	–£350 Unfavourable

Calculations for the flexed budget:

Revenue: (£10,000/1,000) * 800 = £8,000

Material costs: (£4,000/1,000) * 800 = £3,200

Freelance labour costs: (£3,000/1,000) * 800 = £2,400

Contribution: (£3,000/1,000) * 800 = £2,400

Alternatively, we can calculate the contribution by deducting revenues from the variable costs as follows:

£8,000 – £3,200 – £2,400 = £2,400

Central fixed costs: The fixed element of the budgeted cost will not need to be flexed since such costs are fixed. Therefore, the central fixed costs remain £1,000.

Finally, we calculate the profit manually (i.e., we do not follow the above procedure as we will have an error in calculation since the fixed costs are not flexed). Therefore, the calculation should be as follows:

Profit: £8,000 – £3,200 – £2,400 = £2,400 (contribution)

(Continued)

Then, we deduct the fixed costs from the contribution as follows:

£2,400 − £1,000 = £1,400

After that, we need to calculate the new variance, which is the variance between the flexed budget and the actual budget. This tells us where and why we have variances in our budget. For example, the new variance indicates that the freelance labour costs has a favourable variance whereas the rest have unfavourable variances. Such variances are more reliable than previous variances calculated between the actual and fixed budgets because they take into account the actual number of units sold so it is easier to identify any issues and solve them.

As you delve into the intricacies of budgeting, remember that these skills are not confined to theoretical exercises but are vital tools in the real world. Imagine leading a non-profit organisation that aims to combat climate change; your expertise in budgeting can ensure that every dollar is allocated effectively, maximising the impact of your initiatives. Or consider working in a tech start-up where flexible budgeting allows you to adapt quickly to market changes, driving innovation and sustainable growth. By mastering budgeting, you equip yourself to make informed decisions that contribute to economic stability, environmental sustainability, and social equity. Your knowledge and skills can drive meaningful change, fostering a better, more sustainable future for all.

CHAPTER SUMMARY

The accounting field supports business decision-making through two key branches. Financial accounting provides external stakeholders with standardised information through financial statements, using concepts like entity separation, accrual basis accounting, and the fundamental equation (Assets = Liabilities + Equity). Through double-entry bookkeeping, it ensures accurate reporting of an entity's financial position and performance.

Managerial accounting addresses internal planning and decision-making needs, now enhanced by AI and data analytics. Methods like ABC costing enable accurate cost allocation and pricing decisions by recognising diverse cost drivers. CVP analysis helps clarify relationships between costs, volume, and profit for short-term decisions, while budgeting frameworks facilitate planning and performance evaluation.

Understanding both branches and their applications enables organisations to navigate business challenges effectively, supporting objectives and contributing to long-term financial health and strategic success.

Summary of Introduction to Accounting Section

- Historical foundations: Modern accounting principles date back to Luca Pacioli's 1494 work on double-entry bookkeeping, ensuring systematic recording of transactions.

- Role of accounting: Accounting identifies, records, and reports financial data to support decision-making by internal (management) and external (investors, lenders) stakeholders.
- Internal vs. external users: Internal users (e.g., management) have complete access to financial data for decision-making, while external users rely on published financial statements.
- Stewardship and accountability: Management is responsible for the efficient use of resources and reporting to shareholders, highlighting the importance of the stewardship role in financial reporting.
- The business cycle and duality: Accounting reflects the business cycle: resources (assets) are funded by equity and liabilities, adhering to the duality concept (Assets = Liabilities + Equity).
- Key fields of accounting activity: Financial accounting focuses on external reporting, while management accounting serves internal decision-making. Auditing ensures compliance, and taxation aids legal tax planning.

Summary of Financial Accounting Section

- Two primary components of the financial statements:
    - **Statement of Financial Position** (balance sheet): Reflects assets, liabilities, and equity at a point in time.
    - **Statement of Profit or Loss** (income statement): Reports income and expenses over a period of time.
- Key elements of financial statements
    - **Assets:** Economic resources controlled due to past events (e.g., accounts receivable).
    - **Liabilities:** Present obligations requiring resource transfer (e.g., accounts payable).
    - **Equity:** Residual interest in assets after deducting liabilities (net assets).
    - **Income:** Amounts earned during the period.
    - **Expenses:** Amounts incurred during the period.
- Current vs. non-current distinction: Current assets (e.g., accounts receivable) are settled within 12 months, while non-current assets (e.g., equipment) provide long-term benefits.
- Accrual basis of accounting: Transactions are recorded when they occur, not when cash is received or paid. This ensures income and expenses are reported in the period to which they belong.
- The accounting equation
    - Assets = Liabilities + Equity.
    - This equation must balance in every transaction to maintain financial integrity.
- Double-entry accounting: Every transaction affects at least two accounts, ensuring the accounting equation remains balanced. Debits and credits are systematically recorded.

- Impact on equity: Equity changes through four types of transactions: capital contributions, income, expenses, and distributions to owners.
- Debits and credits: Increases in assets are recorded as debits, while increases in liabilities and equity are recorded as credits, following the double-entry framework.

Summary Points for Product Costing

- **Costs** are classified as *direct vs. indirect, manufacturing vs. non-manufacturing,* and *fixed vs. variable*, forming the foundation for effective product costing and decision-making.
- **Full costing** ensures all costs are included in calculations, supporting accurate pricing decisions and strategic planning for sustainable business operations.
- **Traditional costing** uses a single overhead rate, while ABC employs multiple cost drivers, with ABC typically providing more accurate cost allocation in complex operations.

Summary Points for Profitability Decisions (Short-Term Decisions)

- **CVP analysis** examines relationships between costs, volume, and profit to determine break-even points and target profits for short-term decisions.
- **Contribution (Sales Revenue – Variable Cost)** indicates how much each unit contributes to covering fixed costs and generating profit.
- Key benefits of CVP analysis include guiding decisions on special orders, business line abandonment, and make-or-buy scenarios, while considering limitations of constant cost assumptions.

Summary Points for Planning and Performance – Budgeting

- Budgeting coordinates business activities through various budget types (master, sales, production, materials, cash) to implement organisational objectives.
- The process promotes forward-thinking, coordinates departments, motivates performance, and provides control mechanisms, despite challenges of preparation time and inflexibility.
- Flexible budgeting adjusts for actual activity levels, enabling meaningful variance analysis and performance evaluation while adapting to changing business circumstances.

STUDENTS LIKE YOU CAN CHANGE THE WORLD

As you master both financial and managerial accounting concepts, you're equipped with powerful tools to drive positive change. Your understanding of financial statements enables transparent reporting that builds trust with diverse stakeholders, while your managerial accounting skills support resource optimisation and sustainable decision-making. By applying these complementary perspectives - from analysing cost structures to developing inclusive budgets that consider environmental and social impacts - you can help organisations balance profitability with purpose. Whether advocating for ethical financial practices, implementing cost-efficient production methods that reduce waste, or creating budgets that allocate resources equitably, your accounting knowledge empowers you to contribute meaningfully to organisational success while advancing economic stability, environmental sustainability, and social equity in your community and beyond.

END OF CHAPTER REFLECTION

Have a look at the skills you should have developed in this unit (find more details in the Key Skills Table in the Appendix on pp. 503-4).

1. Which of the skills listed do you think you have developed the most?
2. Can you give two examples on why you feel you have now developed these skills/developed them further?
3. How will you use these new/refined skills in the future (give two examples of the impact of your development on your future behaviour)?

FURTHER READING

Kolitz, D.L. (2023) *A Concepts-Based Introduction to Financial Accounting* (7th edition). Juta.

Accounting literature refers to the procedural and conceptual approaches in the teaching of an introductory accounting course. This book integrates these two approaches by teaching students to understand the why, before considering the how of accounting.

Frampton, P. and Robilliard, M. (2020) *The Joy of Accounting*. Wealthvox.

This book is written in a very informal and readable style, and visually shows how accounting works. This book is fun and rigorous at the same time. The book utilises a diagram that shows accounting on a single page.

Carey, M. and Knowles, C. (2020) *Accounting: A Smart Approach* (4th edition). Oxford University Press.

This book is designed specifically for business and management students, demonstrating business applications of concepts through the innovative running case study.

Bhimani, A. and Horngren, C.T. (2008) *Management and Cost Accounting* (Vol. 1). Pearson Education.

This book provides comprehensive coverage of both traditional and modern costing methods with excellent real-world examples from global companies. Particularly strong in ABC coverage and includes practical applications with detailed solutions to help reinforce learning.

Eldenburg, L.G., Wolcott, S.K., Chen, L.H. and Cook, G. (2016) *Cost Management: Measuring, Monitoring, and Motivating Performance*. John Wiley & Sons.

This book takes a strategic approach to cost management while emphasising behavioural aspects and contemporary issues including digital transformation. Excellent for understanding the practical applications of cost management in modern business environments.

Garrison, R.H., Noreen, E.W. and Brewer, P.C. (2021) *Managerial Accounting*. McGraw-Hill.

This book explains difficult accounting concepts in a simple way, especially Cost-Volume-Profit (CVP) analysis and business decision-making. The authors use easy-to-follow examples and real business cases to show how these tools help managers make better financial choices.

Bragg, S.M. (2014) *Budgeting: A Comprehensive Guide*. AccountingTools.

This practical guide breaks down budgeting concepts into simple, manageable steps, with particular focus on modern budgeting techniques and tools. The author uses straightforward examples to show how budgeting works in real businesses, making it especially useful for those new to financial planning.

Asogwa, I.E. and Etim, O.E. (2017) 'Traditional budgeting in today's business environment', *Journal of Applied Finance and Banking*, 7 (3): 111–20.

This journal article explores how traditional budgeting methods fit into modern business practices. The authors examine the strengths and limitations of conventional budgeting approaches, making it valuable for understanding whether traditional budgeting still works in today's fast-changing business world.

REFERENCES

Atrill, P. and McLaney, E.J. (2022) *Accounting and Finance for Non-Specialists* (12th edition). Pearson Education.

Dyson, J.R. and Franklin, E. (2020) *Accounting for Non-Accounting Students* (10th edition). Pearson Education.

The International Accounting Standards Board (2018) *Conceptual Framework for Financial Reporting*. www.ifrs.org/issued-standards/list-of-standards/conceptual-framework (accessed December 16, 2025).

Kolitz, D.L. (2023) *A Concepts-Based Introduction to Financial Accounting* (7th edition). Juta.

10
FINANCE

Nick Davies, Yan Huang, and Thomas Sisk

INTENDED LEARNING OUTCOMES

After reading this chapter, you should be able to:

1. Understand the fundamental concepts of finance and its role in the economy
2. Analyse and interpret financial instruments and markets
3. Evaluate the impact of sustainable finance and fintech within management
4. Consider financial analysis techniques in relation to real-world scenarios

SUSTAINABLE DEVELOPMENT GOALS

In this chapter, we address the following SDGs:

- SDG 1: No Poverty – Enabling access to banking for underserved populations through financial technology.
- SDG 4: Quality Education – Equipping individuals with financial literacy and accounting knowledge for informed economic decision-making.
- SDG 7: Affordable and Clean Energy – Mobilising capital for renewable energy projects.
- SDG 8: Decent Work and Economic Growth – Better financial decision-making supports economic growth and creates economic opportunities through financial inclusion.
- SDG 9: Industry, Innovation and Infrastructure – Enabling companies to raise capital for expansion and development.
- SDG 10: Reduced Inequalities – Financial inclusion and reducing economic inequalities.
- SDG 11: Sustainable Cities and Communities – Municipal bonds funding public infrastructure.
- SDG 12: Responsible Consumption and Production – Role of responsible investment practices.
- SDG 13: Climate Action – Managing climate-related risk through financial instruments/Green bonds and climate finance.

INTRODUCTION

This chapter on finance equips readers with the essential **knowledge** and tools to understand and navigate the world of financial decision-making. At its core, the chapter explores the critical concept of the time value of money, explaining how present and **future values** are crucial to comprehending investment decisions. The chapter covers various forms of investments, from equities and bonds to **derivatives** and alternative investments, clearly showing how **firms** and governments can raise *capital* through different financial products. We explore in detail how equities and bonds are priced and discuss key concepts of how investors are rewarded. Crucial to the investment process is understanding **risk**, and readers are presented with various types of risk and how these can be measured. Understanding risk is imperative to managing investment portfolios and ties in with using financial derivatives to manage investment risk. Beyond traditional financial instruments, the chapter explores other assets like cash, commodities, **cryptocurrencies**, and real estate. The chapter concludes with an examination of how financial technology (*fintech*) is transforming finance and how the financial sector contributes to promoting **sustainability** through innovative financial products and practices.

What Is Finance?

Finance is the management of money, investments, and resources over time. It encompasses how individuals, businesses, and governments raise, allocate, and use monetary resources. Finance extends beyond traditional banking and investments to include emerging areas like sustainable investing, financial technology, and digital currencies. Whether you're managing personal loans, considering investment apps, or thinking about future opportunities, finance impacts daily decisions and long-term planning. Understanding finance helps you navigate an increasingly complex financial landscape where traditional boundaries between banking, technology, and social impact are blurring.

Why Is It Important?

Finance is essential because it enables economic growth, **innovation**, and social progress. For individuals, financial literacy empowers better decision-making about savings, investments, and career choices. For businesses, finance facilitates growth, job creation, and the development of new products and services. The rise of sustainable finance and **fintech** is making financial services more accessible to previously underserved communities, supporting financial inclusion and economic equality. As climate change and social inequality become pressing global challenges, finance plays a crucial role in funding sustainable solutions and social enterprises. Understanding finance therefore isn't just about managing money – it's about understanding how financial decisions can create positive impact while generating returns, whether you're planning your own future or aspiring to shape the future of business.

Time Value of Money

Money today is worth more than the same amount in the future – this is called the time value of money. Throughout this section, we will follow Chetana, who is planning to save for her first home, and needs £15,000 for her deposit. Chetana has been offered £10,000 from her parents towards this, but they have given her two options:

- Receive £10,000 today
- Receive £11,000 in two years' time

Most people, including Chetana, would choose to receive money sooner rather than later. This preference exists because:

1 **Investment Opportunity:** Money available today can be invested to earn returns. If Chetana takes the £10,000 now and puts it in a savings account earning 6% interest annually, she could have more than £11,000 in two years.
2 **Inflation Impact:** Money typically buys less in the future due to rising prices. The house Chetana wants to buy might cost more in two years, so her deposit needs to grow just to maintain its purchasing power.
3 **Flexibility:** Having money now provides more choices. Chetana could start her house search sooner, invest the money differently, or use it for other opportunities that arise.

Understanding time value of money helps us make better financial decisions in many areas:

- Saving for future goals (like Chetana's house deposit)
- Evaluating loans and mortgages
- Planning for retirement
- Comparing investment opportunities

This understanding also supports sustainable economic development (connecting to UN Sustainable Development Goal 8 – Decent Work and Economic Growth). When people and businesses understand how to make better financial decisions, they can create more stable jobs and contribute to economic growth in their communities. For example, when Chetana eventually buys her house, her decision affects local estate agents, mortgage providers, and other local businesses. These principles also support inclusive economic development – when financial institutions assess the value of microloans or community development projects, understanding time value helps them structure affordable repayment terms that can benefit underserved communities and promote equal access to financial services. This is particularly important in regions where traditional banking services may be limited or where certain demographic groups have historically faced barriers to accessing capital.

Future Value, Present Value, and Net Present Value

These three concepts form the foundation of understanding the time value of money:

Future Value (FV)

This is what your money will be worth in the future after earning interest. Let us return to Chetana's example:

- If she takes the £10,000 today and invests it at 3% annual interest
- After one year: £10,300 (£10,000 + 3% interest)
- After two years: £10,609 (£10,300 + 3% interest)

This shows how money can grow over time through **compound interest** – earning interest not just on your initial amount, but also on previously earned interest.

Present Value (PV)

This works backwards – it tells you how much money you need today to reach a future goal. For Chetana, if she needs £15,000 for her house deposit in three years, and can earn 3% interest annually, she can calculate how much to save today.

In this case, she would need to save £13,727 today to reach her £15,000 goal in three years. This is her **present value** – the amount needed today to reach a future goal.

Net Present Value (NPV)

Net Present Value (NPV) builds on the concept of Present Value by considering both incoming and outgoing cash flows over time. NPV calculates the difference between the present value of cash inflows and the present value of cash outflows across all periods of an investment. A positive NPV indicates that the projected earnings exceed the anticipated costs (both in present value terms), suggesting a potentially profitable investment. A negative NPV indicates that the costs exceed the earnings. This makes NPV a crucial tool for evaluating investment opportunities and making capital budgeting decisions.

For example, if Chetana was considering buying a rental property, she would calculate the NPV by:

1. Identifying all cash flows (initial investment cost as a negative cash flow, followed by expected rental income as positive cash flows)
2. Converting each cash flow to its present value using an appropriate **discount rate**
3. Summing all these present values to determine if the investment has a positive or negative NPV

The formula to support this is as follows:

$$NPV = initial\ investment + \sum_{t=1}^{t=end\ of\ project} \frac{(Cash\ flows\ at\ year\ t)}{(1+r)^t}$$

Here, r is the discount rate, and t is time (years).

EXAMPLE 10.1

Real-World Applications

Let us see how Chetana might use these concepts in different scenarios:

Regular Savings Plans

Chetana decides to save £300 monthly towards her house deposit. Understanding time value of money helps her:

- Calculate how much her savings will grow
- Determine if she is saving enough to reach her goal
- Understand the impact of different interest rates

For example, saving £300 monthly for three years:

- At 2% annual interest = approximately £11,121
- At 3% annual interest = approximately £11,286
- At 4% annual interest = approximately £11,454

This shows how different interest rates affect her final savings.

Making Financial Decisions

Chetana can use these concepts to compare different financial choices:

1. Saving vs. Borrowing
    - Should she save for longer to build a bigger deposit?
    - Or should she borrow more and buy sooner?
    - Understanding time value helps compare these options
2. Different Investment Options
    - Regular savings account at 3%
    - Fixed-term deposit at 4% but money locked away
    - Investment fund with potential higher returns but more risk

Long-Term Planning

Time value of money becomes even more important for longer-term goals. While Chetana is focusing on her house deposit now, the same principles apply to:

- Retirement planning
- Children's education funds
- Long-term investment strategies

Key Takeaways

1. Money available now is typically worth more than the same amount in the future
2. The longer your time horizon, the more important these concepts become
3. Interest rates significantly impact your financial decisions
4. Regular saving benefits from compound interest over time
5. Understanding these concepts helps you make better financial decisions

These principles also support inclusive economic development – when financial institutions assess the value of microloans or community development projects, understanding time value helps them structure affordable repayment terms that can benefit underserved communities and promote equal access to financial services. This is particularly important in regions where traditional banking services may be limited or where certain demographic groups have historically faced barriers to accessing capital.

CASE STUDY 10.1

Renewable Energy Investment in Vietnam

TTC Energy has emerged as a leading renewable energy developer in Vietnam, with a substantial portfolio of solar and wind power projects across the country. In 2022, TTC Energy faced a crucial decision regarding its $500 million solar farm expansion project in Tay Ninh province. The company needed to choose between two investment options to meet Vietnam's growing energy demands while supporting the country's commitment to net-zero emissions by 2050.

Option A involved an immediate full-scale deployment requiring $500 million upfront but promising annual cash flows of $75 million for 10 years. Option B proposed a phased approach with an initial investment of $200 million, followed by $300 million in year three, with projected annual cash flows of $60 million for the first three years, increasing to $90 million for the remaining seven years.

With a cost of capital of 8%, TTC Energy's financial team needed to determine which option would create more value for the company. This decision was particularly significant as it would influence Vietnam's renewable energy landscape and impact the country's ability to meet its climate commitments.

Questions

1. Using NPV analysis, which option should TTC Energy choose?
2. What qualitative factors beyond NPV should TTC Energy consider?
3. How might this investment impact Vietnam's sustainable development goals?

Sources

Asian Development Bank (2015) *Viet Nam: Energy Sector Assessment, Strategy, and Road Map*. Asian Development Bank. https://www.adb.org/sites/default/files/institutional-document/178616/vie-energy-road-map.pdf (accessed September 17, 2025).

World Bank Group (2018) *Vietnam Maximising Finance for Development in the Energy Sector*. The World Bank. https://documents1.worldbank.org/curated/en/290361547820276005/pdf/133788-WP-OUO-9-Vietnam-Energy-MFD-Report-ENG-for-printing.pdf (accessed September 17, 2025).

World Bank Group (2022) *Vietnam Country Climate Development Report*. The World Bank. https://openknowledge.worldbank.org/entities/publication/29e72556-d255-5c50-a086-245c1ccc4704 (accessed September 17, 2025).

Answers

Option A: Initial investment of $500M with $75M annual cash flows for 10 years at 8%

NPV = -500 + 75x((1-(1.08)^(-10))/0.08) = $3.26M

Option B: Initial $200M + $300M in year 3, $60M for first 3 years, $90M for remaining 7 years

NPV = -200 - 300/1.08^3 + 60x((1-(1.08)^(-3))/0.08)+ (90x((1-(1.08)^(-7))/0.08))/((1.08)^3) = $88.44M

Option B offers higher NPV and should be chosen based on financial metrics.

ACTIVITY 10.1

1. Calculate the future value of £1,000 in 5 years at 4% interest.
2. Explain how this calculation demonstrates the role of finance in economic planning.
3. Identify three ways this concept impacts economic decision-making.

Time: 15 minutes

Answers for Activity

1. Future Value Calculation:
   - Initial amount: £1,000
   - Time: 5 years
   - Interest rate: 4%

(Continued)

- $FV = £1,000 \times (1 + 0.04)^5$
- $FV = £1,216.65$

2 How this demonstrates role of finance in economic planning:
   - Shows how money grows over time
   - Demonstrates importance of early investment
   - Illustrates compound interest effect

3 Three impacts on economic decision-making:
   - Influences saving vs. spending decisions
   - Affects investment timing choices
   - Impacts business capital budgeting decisions

REFLECTIVE ACTIVITY 10.1

Consider how financial concepts affect different economic stakeholders:

- How do interest rates impact household decisions?
- How do businesses use financial concepts for growth?
- What role does finance play in economic development?

EQUITIES AND EQUITY PRICING

When we talk about **equity**, things can seem a bit confusing. The term can be found on balance sheets of firms when subtracting a firm's total **liabilities** from the value of all its assets. Commonly, equities are also referred to as **stocks** and *shares*, or sometimes equity is used to express the value of a personal asset after subtracting any liabilities (think of the value of a house minus the outstanding mortgage). So, what exactly does this mean in the context of this chapter?

Equities represent ownership in a company. When an individual or institution purchases equity, they acquire a stake in the firm, granting them a claim on its assets and earnings. Firms sell equity to raise funds, which is essential for funding new projects, expanding operations, or paying off debt. Selling equity allows firms to access large amounts of capital without incurring debt, but it also dilutes ownership among existing shareholders. Equity markets also play a crucial role in supporting SDG 9 (Industry, Innovation and Infrastructure) by enabling companies to raise capital for expansion and development. Through public markets, innovative companies can access the funding needed to scale their operations, develop new technologies, and build sustainable infrastructure.

Shares can be held privately or listed publicly. If a firm meets regulatory and financial requirements, it can float its shares on a stock exchange, making them available for public trading. An **Initial Public Offering (IPO)** is the process by which a private company offers its shares to the public for the first time. During an IPO, investment banks play a crucial role as underwriters. They help the firm determine the initial share price, buy shares from the company, and sell them to the public, ensuring a successful market entry. Investment banks also provide advisory services, guiding the firm through regulatory requirements and market conditions (Ritter and Welch, 2002). Publicly listed shares offer advantages, such as increased capital access, liquidity, and enhanced corporate visibility. However, listing shares also comes with disadvantages, including the pressure of short-term performance, regulatory compliance costs, and the potential loss of control by original owners (Pagano et al., 1998). It is only when shares are publicly listed that companies can freely trade on organised secondary markets like the London Stock Exchange, NYSE and NASDAQ.

The pricing of shares in firms is influenced by various factors, including market conditions, company performance, and investor expectations. One key aspect is **dividends,** which are payments made to shareholders from a firm's net profits. The dividend yield, calculated as the annual dividend per share divided by the share price, indicates the return on investment from dividends alone.

The Dividend Discount Model (DDM), also known as the Gordon Growth model (GGM) is commonly used to value shares, particularly for firms with stable dividend payouts. The DDM posits that the value of a share is the present value of all future dividends, discounted back to their present value.

The formula is:

$$Po = \frac{D1}{r - g}$$

Where:

- Po is the current share price,
- D1 is the expected dividend in the next period,
- r is the required rate of return, and
- g is the growth rate of dividends (Gordon, 1959).

In essence the GGM calculates firms' intrinsic value based on a required rate of return for investors and a constant annual growth rate of dividends.

In addition to dividends, key financial ratios help investors evaluate stocks.

- The **Price-to-Earnings (P/E) ratio** compares a company's share price to its earnings per share – a high P/E might indicate investors expect strong future growth, while a low P/E could suggest undervaluation or underlying problems.
- The **Price-to-Book (P/B) ratio** compares market price to book value per share, helping investors understand if they are paying a premium above the company's accounting value.
- **Return on Equity (ROE)** measures how efficiently a company uses shareholders' investment to generate profits. Together, these metrics help investors to assess

whether a stock is fairly valued and how well the company performs compared to peers. This foundational analysis combines with broader economic factors like market conditions, interest rates, and industry trends that influence stock prices.

Revenue and profit growth are crucial in determining a firm's future earning potential, impacting both the DDM and financial ratios. Sustainable growth in these areas often leads to higher share prices, reflecting investor confidence in the firm's prospects (Damodaran, 2012). However, it needs to be noted that firms can either pay dividends to shareholders or retain earnings for reinvestment. Retaining earnings allows firms to fund growth opportunities, potentially leading to higher future profits and share prices, which can benefit shareholders more than immediate dividends (Ross et al., 2022).

Shares for public limited companies are traded in secondary markets, such as stock exchanges, where existing shares are bought and sold. Banks and brokers facilitate access for private and institutional investors, providing trading platforms, market analysis, and executing trades. Institutional investors, including pension funds, **mutual funds,** and **hedge funds**, are major players in these markets. They buy shares to diversify portfolios, generate returns, and meet long-term liabilities, such as pension payouts. These investors significantly influence market dynamics due to their large-scale transactions (Bodie et al., 2023). However, retail investors can also access stock markets directly through online brokerage accounts offered by firms like Hargreaves Lansdown, IG, AJ Bell or Robinhood and construct their own investment portfolios. Information on companies and shares is abundant and easily accessible. Retail investors can access information on websites like MarketWatch, Yahoo Finance or subscribe to the *Financial Times*. Also, social media platforms like LinkedIn and Reddit can be sources of information or an online space where other investors posit their take on markets and individual stocks.

ACTIVITY 10.2

Using financial **data** from the *Financial Times* or a similar financial source:

1. Compare three different financial instruments (e.g., stocks, bonds, ETFs)
2. Analyse their key metrics (P/E ratios, yields, etc.)
3. Interpret what these metrics suggest about market conditions

Time: 20 minutes

Answers for Activity

1. Sample Analysis (looking at companies in the technology sector)
   Apple Inc:
   - P/E Ratio: 28x
   - Dividend Yield: 0.5%
   - Market Cap: Large-cap

Microsoft:

- P/E Ratio: 32x
- Dividend Yield: 0.8%
- Market Cap: Large-cap

AMD:

- P/E Ratio: 45x
- Dividend Yield: None
- Market Cap: Mid-cap

2 Interpretation:

- Higher P/E for AMD suggests higher growth expectations
- Lower dividend yields typical for tech sector
- Different sizes indicate varying market maturity

REFLECTIVE ACTIVITY 10.2

Select a financial market event from the past month:

- What instruments were involved?
- How did markets interpret the event?
- What does this tell us about market behaviour?

BONDS AND BOND PRICING

While bonds are a major form of debt financing, they are part of a broader debt landscape. Debt instruments vary in their terms, security, and structure. Some of these terms will be well known to you, and some less so. *Bank loans* provide direct lending, often with customised terms and relationship-based monitoring. *Commercial paper* offers short-term, unsecured borrowing for **corporations** with strong credit ratings. *Syndicated loans* involve multiple lenders jointly providing funds, spreading risk and enabling larger loan amounts. *Asset-backed securities* represent debt secured by specific assets like mortgages or car loans. *Convertible debt* combines characteristics of both debt and equity, giving holders the option to convert to shares under certain conditions. Each form of debt serves different financing needs and comes with its own risk-return profile, making the debt market a diverse and crucial part of the financial system. Given their standardised nature and crucial role in both corporate and government financing, we will focus our attention primarily on bonds as a key debt instrument. Understanding bonds provides a foundation for analysing other debt instruments, as many of the principles of bond valuation and risk assessment apply across the debt market spectrum.

A *bond* represents a loan from an investor to a borrower with the agreement that the borrower will repay the principal amount at a set maturity date along with periodic interest payments. Selling bonds allows companies to raise capital without giving up any ownership or control of the company. Governments issue bonds to cover immediate expenses and pay back the money over time, with interest, from future revenues from public projects and services such as infrastructure. Bonds are a useful way to raise capital while spreading the repayment over a long period, providing flexibility for both companies and governments to manage their finances efficiently. Government bonds play a vital role in sustainable urban development (SDG 11) by financing essential infrastructure projects. For example, municipal bonds fund public transportation systems, affordable housing, and sustainable city planning. When governments issue infrastructure bonds, they can undertake large-scale community development projects while spreading the cost across generations who will benefit from these improvements.

A bond has several important features. The issuer is the entity borrowing money. The maturity date is when the issuer must repay the bondholder the **face value** of the bond. The **coupon rate** is the interest rate the issuer pays to bondholders. The coupon payment can be paid annually, semi-annually or at other intervals. A **zero-coupon bond** does not make regular interest payments (coupons) during its lifetime. Instead, investors buy these bonds at a price below their face value (at a discount) and receive the full face value when the bond matures. The return for investors comes from this difference between the purchase price and the face value.

For example:

- Face value (what you receive at maturity): £1,000
- Purchase price (what you pay today): £800
- Time to maturity: 5 years
- Your return comes from the £200 difference (£1,000 – £800)

This is different from regular bonds that make periodic interest payments throughout their life. With zero-coupon bonds, all the return comes from that single payment at maturity. The deeper the discount (the lower the purchase price compared to face value), the higher the implied interest rate or yield. Investors are drawn to bonds because they offer a more predictable income stream than stocks. However, interest rate risk which arises when changes in interest rates affect the market value of the bond and **credit risk** which is the possibility that the issuer may default in interest payments or the principal are important risk factors for bondholders. Bonds also come with specific legal and regulatory considerations, as well as contingency provisions like **call options**, which allow the issuer to repay the bond before its maturity date.

Bonds are traded in both primary and secondary markets. The primary market is where bonds are initially issued whereas the secondary market is where these bonds are subsequently bought and sold among investors.

In the primary market, issuers like corporations or governments raise capital by selling bonds directly to investors. There are two main methods of issuing bonds:

- public offerings; and
- private placements.

In a public offering, any member of the public can buy the bonds, usually through an investment bank or broker. On the other hand, a private placement involves selling bonds to a select group of investors or institutions, often bypassing the broader public market. Public offerings can take various forms. In an underwritten offering, an investment bank buys the entire bond issue from the issuer and takes on the risk of reselling it to the public. This method ensures the issuer receives the required funds upfront. An example of this would be Apple's multi-billion dollar bond issuance, which was underwritten by a group of banks such as Goldman Sachs, Barclays and J.P. Morgan. In contrast, a best-efforts offering sees the investment bank acting as a broker, attempting to sell the bonds but not guaranteeing that they will be sold. For governments, auctions are commonly used, especially for sovereign bonds. The UK debt management office (DMO) regularly sell **gilts** on behalf of His Majesty's Treasury. Investors bid based on the yield they are willing to accept. This mechanism helps discover the bond's fair price and to efficiently allocate securities. Once bonds are issued, they begin trading in the secondary market, which is primarily an over-the-counter (OTC) market. Here, bonds are bought and sold among institutional investors such as pension funds, insurance companies, and mutual funds. Unlike stocks, bonds are typically traded via dealer networks rather than centralised exchanges.

Bond pricing is an application of the time value of money to take account of cash flows of bonds. The price of a bond is the present value of all its future cash flows, which include periodic interest payments and the repayment of the bond's face value at maturity. These future cash flows are discounted back to the present using an appropriate *discount rate*, which reflects the market interest rate or the required return for that bond's risk level. The formula for calculating the price of a bond is

$$P = \sum_{t=1}^{n} \frac{C}{(1+r)^t} + \frac{Par}{(1+r)^n}$$

Where:

- P is the price of the bond,
- C is the coupon payment,
- Par is the face value (or par value) of the bond,
- r is the discount rate (or market interest rate),
- t is the time period
- n is the number of periods.

EXAMPLE 10.2

Suppose an investor is considering purchasing a £1,000 bond with a coupon rate of 5%, maturing in three years. The bond pays annual interest of £50 (£1,000 × 5%), and the discount rate is 4%. What is the price of the bond?

$$P = \frac{£50}{(1+0.04)} + \frac{£50}{(1+0.04)^2} + \frac{£50 + £1000}{(1+0.04)^3} = £1,027.99$$

Thus, the bond would be priced at £1,027.75. Since the price is higher than the bond's face value (£1,000), the bond is trading at premium because the market rate is lower than the coupon rate. If a bond is trading at discount, the market rate is higher than the coupon rate. If a bond is trading at par, the market rate is the same as the coupon rate.

If the market price of a bond is known, the same formula of bond price can be used to calculate its yield-to-maturity (YTM), which is the internal rate of return on the cash flows including coupon payments and the bond's face value. YTM represents the rate of return an investor can expect to earn if they hold onto the bond until it matures. YTM is calculated by equating the bond's market price to the present value of its future cash flows and solving for the discount rate.

$$P = \sum_{t=1}^{n} \frac{C}{(1+YTM)^t} + \frac{F}{(1+YTM)^n}$$

Where:

- P is the bond's current market price,
- C is the coupon payment,
- F is the face value,
- YTM is the **yield to maturity**, and
- n is the number of periods.

EXAMPLE 10.3

Suppose an investor buys a bond with a face value of £1,000, a coupon rate of 6%, and a maturity of three years. The bond makes annual coupon payments of £60. The current market price of the bond is £950, and the investor wants to calculate the YTM.

$$£950 = \frac{£60}{(1+\text{YTM})} + \frac{£60}{(1+\text{YTM})^2} + \frac{£60 + £1,000}{(1+\text{YTM})^3}$$

The YTM is 7.94%. This means that if the investor holds the bond to maturity, they can expect an annualised return of 7.94%, factoring in both the coupon payments and the capital gain from purchasing the bond at discount. The YTM is a valuable tool for comparing the potential returns of bonds with different prices, coupon rates, and maturities.

In summary, bonds provide a stable and predictable income stream for investors while offering companies and governments an efficient way to raise capital without sacrificing control or ownership. Bond pricing tools are useful to allow investors to determine the fair value of a bond by calculating the present value of future cash flows.

RISK

Risk refers to the uncertainty around potential outcomes associated with a decision or action. While often discussed in terms of potential losses, risk is also inseparable from opportunity – without taking calculated risks, innovation, entrepreneurship, and economic growth would be impossible. Companies like Tesla demonstrate how managed risk-taking in technologies or markets can lead to significant rewards. The key is not avoiding risk entirely, but understanding and managing it effectively to balance potential downsides with opportunities for growth and returns. The greater the uncertainty, the higher the risk.

Effective risk management is crucial for promoting financial stability and reducing poverty (SDG 1). When financial institutions properly assess and manage risks, they can better serve vulnerable populations by offering sustainable, affordable financial products like microloans and basic savings accounts. This responsible lending prevents over-indebtedness while ensuring access to credit. Additionally, strong risk management protects against systemic financial shocks that historically hit the poor hardest through job losses and economic instability. This understanding has shaped modern risk management practices, particularly in emerging markets where financial stability directly impacts poverty reduction efforts. The greater the uncertainty, the higher the risk. In the financial industry, risk management is about optimising returns while considering the risks involved and aligning them with an investor's risk tolerance.

Standard deviation, which was firstly introduced by Karl Pearson as a way to measure the spread or dispersion of data points around the mean, began to be applied as a measure of risk, particularly with the development of modern portfolio theory by Harry Markowitz in the 1950s (Markowitz, 1950). While Pearson initially introduced standard deviation as a general statistical tool, it was Markowitz who brought it into the financial world to measure the volatility of asset returns and portfolio risk. Standard deviation measures how much individual returns deviate from the average return, providing investors with a way to quantify the uncertainty and variability of potential investment outcomes. A higher standard deviation indicates greater dispersion, meaning the returns are more spread out, signifying higher risk. The variance calculates the average of the squared deviation from the mean and the standard deviation is the square root of the variance.

Sample variance:

$$S^2 = \frac{\sum_{i=1}^{n}\left(x_i - \bar{x}\right)^2}{n-1}$$

Where:

- s^2 = **sample variance**,
- x_i = each individual data point,
- $\bar{x}$ = sample mean,
- n = number of data points in the sample.

Sample standard deviation:

$$S = \sqrt{\frac{\sum_{i=1}^{n}\left(x_i - \bar{x}\right)^2}{n-1}}$$

If a stock has an average return of 8% with a standard deviation of 3%, it suggests that with 95% probability, the stock's returns will fall within the range of 2% to 14%.

While quantitative risk measures are important, they must be applied equitably. Risk assessment frameworks should be designed to avoid discriminatory practices and biases against underrepresented groups. This includes evaluating credit risk **models** for potential bias in lending decisions, ensuring risk metrics don't unfairly penalise businesses in underserved communities, and developing inclusive approaches to risk evaluation that consider diverse economic circumstances and **business models**. For example, some microfinance institutions have developed alternative risk assessment methods that better serve entrepreneurs from marginalised communities while still maintaining robust risk management standards.

Harry Markowitz further classified risk into two types: **systematic risk** and **unsystematic risk.** Systematic risk, also known as market risk or undiversifiable risk, is inherent to the market and cannot be diversified away. It is influenced by macroeconomic factors such as inflation, political stability and natural disaster. For example, the 2008 financial crisis led to a global economic downturn. All asset classes were negatively affected. Another example is the COVID-19 pandemic which made the stock market experience significant declines due to economic shutdowns, supply chain disruptions and uncertainty surrounding the virus. This type of risk is unavoidable and affects the entire market. Hence, it represents the baseline level of risk that investors must accept when participating in the markets. This risk can be measured by the **beta** model that was introduced as part of the Capital Asset Pricing Model (CAPM).

The beta model was developed by Jack Treynor (1962) and William Sharpe (1964) in the 1960s to explain the relationship between systematic risk and expected returns on assets, particularly stocks. Beta (β) quantifies how much an asset's price tends to move in response to movements in the whole market. The market has a beta of 1.0 and individual assets are measured against this benchmark. If beta is larger than 1, it means that the asset is more volatile than the market. Beta is calculated using regression analysis, where the returns of a stock are compared to the returns of the overall market over a period of time. The formula is:

$$\beta = \frac{Variance\ of\ the\ market's\ returns}{Covariance\ of\ stock's\ returns\ and\ market's\ returns}$$

Another component of the total risk defined by Markowitz is unsystematic risk, also known as specific or diversifiable risk. This risk is unique to a particular company or industry. It is caused by factors such as management decisions, labour strikes or regulatory changes.

An example of this is Toyota's recall of cars due to faulty airbags. This issue is specific to Toyota and did not impact the rest of the automobile industry. Another example is Steve Jobs's departure from Apple in 1985. The company's performance suffered significantly over the years that followed. This type of risk can be diversified in the portfolio across various industries and asset classes. For example, instead of investing all capital in one stock, an investor can spread the investment in different industries such as technology, healthcare and utilities. This **diversification** approach ('do not put all your eggs in one basket') ensures that poor performance in a single stock or sector will not have significant impact on the overall portfolio.

Another risk measure is *Value at Risk (VaR),* which provides a specific threshold for potential losses over a given period at a certain confidence level. For example, a 95% VaR of £1 million over one day means that there is a 5% chance that the portfolio could lose more than £1 million in one day. The concept of VaR emerged in the late 1980s and became popular in the 1990s after J.P. Morgan introduced the Risk Metrics system (Morgan, 1996). Since then, the Basel Committee on Banking Supervision have incorporated VaR into capital adequacy frameworks to ensure financial institutions have sufficient capital to withstand adverse market conditions. However, VaR has its limitations. It assumes the market returns follow a normal distribution. It fails to capture **tail risk** or extreme events that occur with low probability but cause significant impact. In the event of the collapse of Lehman Brothers, the VaR model failed to take the possibility of a severe downturn in the housing market and the financial contagion into account.

For **fixed-income instruments,** one major risk is credit risk which is the risk that a borrower will fail to meet their financial obligations, either by defaulting on interest payments or principals. When such risk is high, investors may require higher interest rates to compensate for the greater likelihood of default. Credit ratings, assigned by agencies like Moody's, S&P and Fitch, assess the creditworthiness of companies, sovereigns and financial products with metrics that cover various aspects including payment behaviour, outstanding debts and cash flow. These ratings range from high grade investment ratings to lower grade speculative or junk ratings. For instance, Apple has bonds rated AAA or AA+, which indicates low credit risk, due to its strong financial health. In 2019, Ford was downgraded to Ba1, which are considered as 'junk bonds', due to its weak earnings and cash generation. These ratings provide investors with a quick reference to the credit risk of a bond issuer. However, it is worth noting the issues with credit rating agencies. For instance, there is an inherent conflict of interest in their business model. The rating agencies are paid by the entities that they rate. Issuers might pressure the rating agencies to give them favourable ratings in order to keep their business. Moreover, there is also criticism on the complex and opaque methodologies used by the credit rating agencies.

REFLECTIVE ACTIVITY 10.3

Choose a current business situation:

- What financial analysis techniques would be most relevant?
- How would you apply these techniques?
- What real-world factors might affect your analysis?

DERIVATIVES

This section explores the world of *derivatives*. Financial derivatives are contracts whose value is derived from the performance of an underlying asset, index, or rate. Common types of derivatives include:

- **options,** which give the right but not the obligation to buy or sell an asset;
- **futures,** which are agreements to buy or sell an asset at a predetermined price in the future; and
- **swaps,** which involve exchanging cash flows between parties.

These instruments are used for hedging risk, speculation, and arbitrage in **financial markets** (Hull, 2021). Derivatives play an increasingly important role in addressing climate change (SDG 13). Weather derivatives help businesses manage climate-related risks, while carbon credit derivatives facilitate emissions trading markets. For example, agricultural companies use weather derivatives to protect against crop losses due to extreme weather events, while renewable energy producers use derivatives to hedge against fluctuating energy prices. These instruments are becoming crucial tools for managing climate transition risks and supporting sustainable business practices.

Institutional investors use financial derivatives, such as options, futures, and swaps, to manage risk and enhance portfolio performance. These instruments allow investors to hedge positions, reducing the potential impact of adverse price movements. For example, options provide the right to buy or sell an asset at a predetermined price, offering protection against unfavourable price changes. **Futures contracts** enable investors to lock in prices for future transactions, shielding them from market volatility. Swaps, particularly interest rate and currency swaps, allow investors to exchange cash flows, mitigating exposure to fluctuating interest rates or currency values (Hull, 2021).

Derivatives also provide leverage, enabling investors to control large positions with a relatively small capital outlay. This leverage can amplify gains but also increases the risk of significant losses. Speculation with derivatives involves betting on the future price movements of underlying assets. While this can yield substantial profits, it also poses considerable risk if the market moves against the investor.

A notable example of the risks associated with derivatives is the collapse of Long-Term Capital Management (LTCM) in 1998. LTCM, a hedge fund managed by renowned financial experts, used highly leveraged derivative positions to speculate on fixed-income instruments. When the Russian financial crisis triggered unexpected market movements, LTCM's positions rapidly deteriorated, leading to losses of billions of dollars and requiring a bailout organised by the Federal Reserve to prevent a broader financial crisis (Jorion, 2007).

Let us explore the concept of *options* a little more in-depth. Options are financial derivatives that grant the holder the right, but not the obligation, to buy or sell an underlying asset at a specified price **(strike price)** before or at the option's maturity date. There are two primary types of options: calls and puts. A *call option* gives the holder the right to buy the underlying asset, while a **put option** provides the right to sell it.

The payoff structure of these options varies based on the option type. A *call option* is valuable if the market price of the underlying asset exceeds the strike price at maturity, leading to a profit equal to the difference minus the premium paid. Conversely, a *put option* is profitable when the asset's market price falls below the strike price.

Figures 10.1–10.4 represent the pay-off structure of either type of option contract from the perspective of the holder (long) and the writer (short).

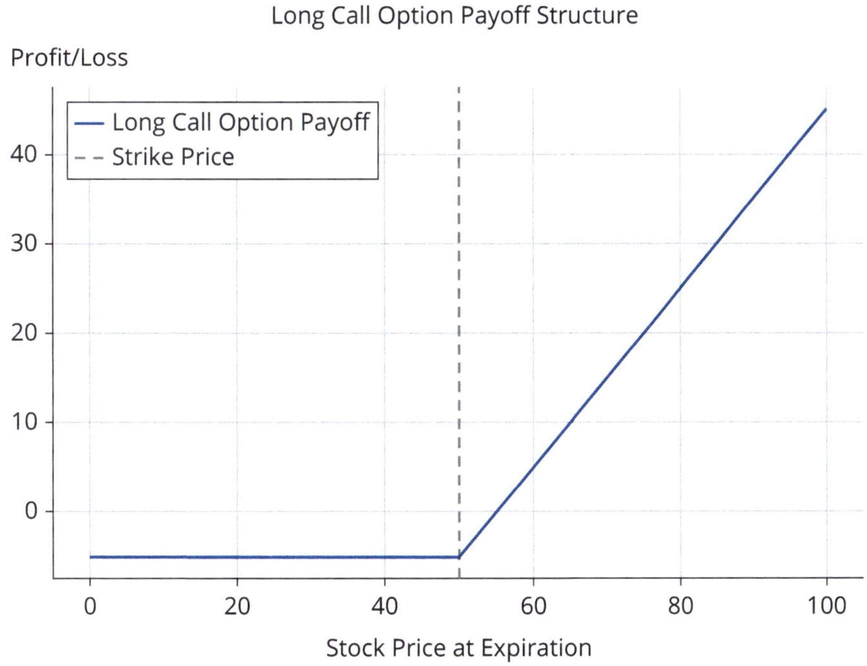

Figure 10.1 Long call option payoff structure

Source: Author

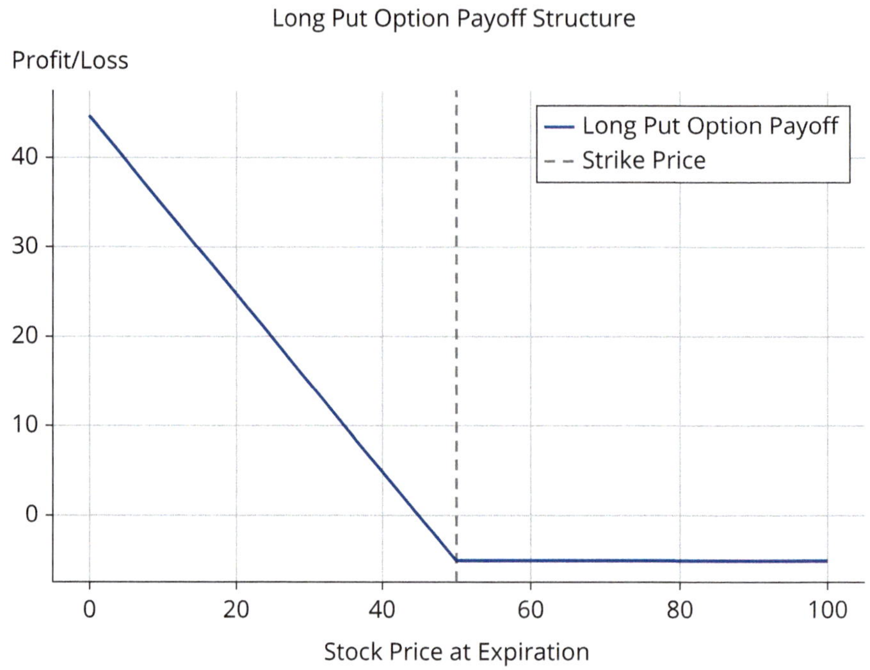

Figure 10.2 Long put payoff structure

Source: Author

Figure 10.3 Short put option payoff structure

Source: Author

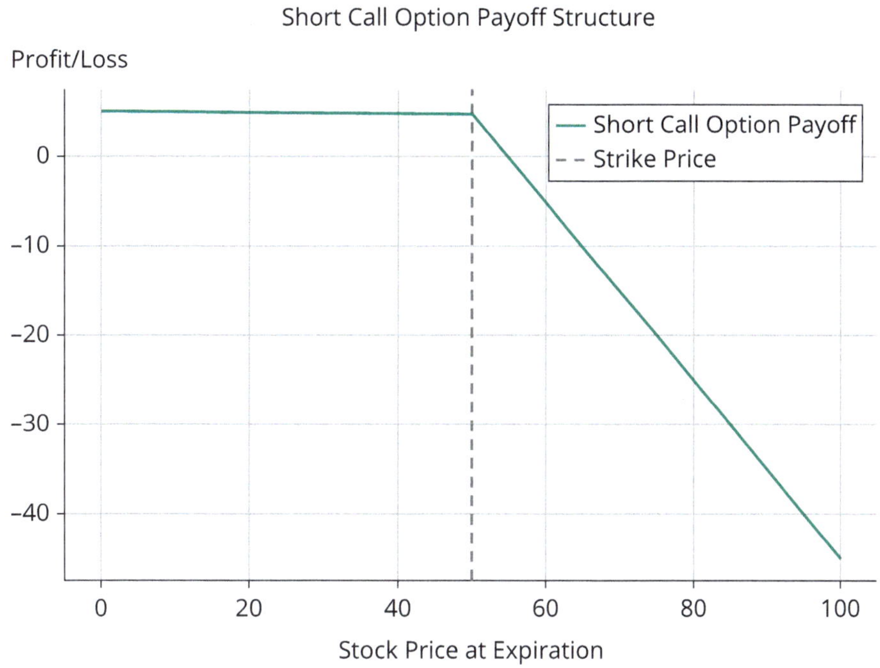

Figure 10.4 Short call option payoff structure

Source: Author

The buyer of options (long call or long put) will pay the seller of the option (short call or short put) a premium to acquire the right (but not the obligation) to buy or sell the underlying asset at a pre-determined strike price, at or before a fixed calendar date. The seller of the options (also known as the writer) will be obligated to honour the contract in case the holder elects to exercise their right (Hull, 2021). Options are traded both on exchanges, where they are standardised and regulated, and over-the-counter (OTC), where they are customised but come with higher counterparty risk. Options can be traded as American or European-style options, and the distinctions lie in their exercise terms. American options can be exercised at any time before maturity, providing greater flexibility, whereas European options can only be exercised at maturity.

Options can be based on various underlying assets, including equities, indices, interest rates, *foreign exchange* (FX), and commodities, each with active options markets. For instance, equity options are based on individual stocks, while index options are tied to broader market indices like the S&P 500 or FTSE100.

Another very popular derivative are *futures contracts*. Futures contracts are a standardised derivative agreement to buy or sell an underlying asset at a predetermined price (strike price) on a specified future date (maturity). The buyer of the contract (long position) agrees to purchase the asset, while the seller (short position) agrees to deliver it. Futures contracts are used for various underlying assets, including equities, indices, interest rates, foreign exchange (FX), and commodities like oil and gold.

Futures are similar to forward contracts but differ in that they are standardised and traded on exchanges, offering greater liquidity and reducing counterparty risk.

The payoff structure of futures contracts needs to be viewed from both long (buyer of futures contract) and short (seller of futures contract) perspectives. Figure 10.5 represents the payoff for a Long Futures position, while Figure 10.6 represents the payoff for a Short Futures position. Both charts show how the payoff varies with the price at maturity relative to the strike price K.

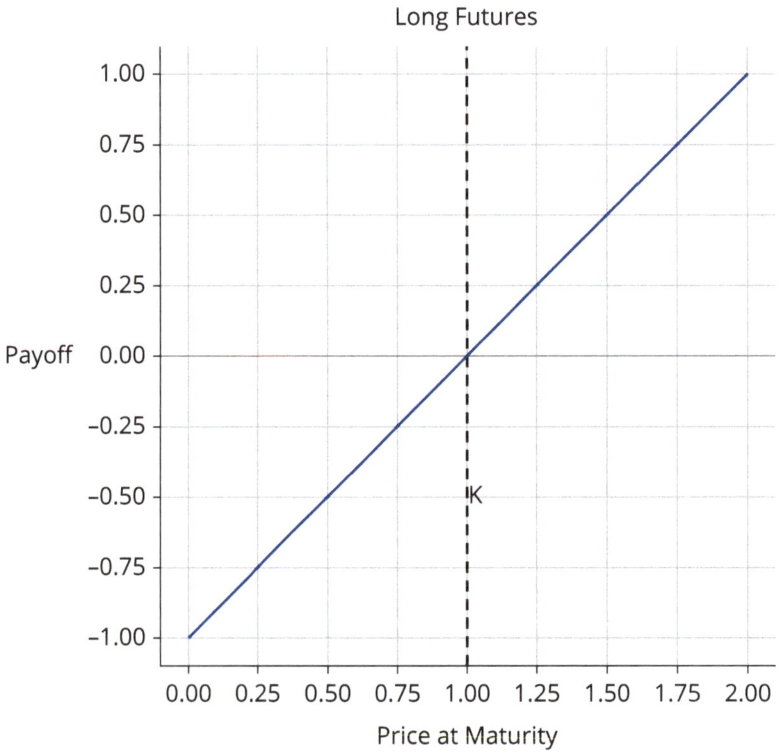

Figure 10.5 Long futures payoff structure

Source: Author

Examples of exchanges where futures trade include the Chicago Mercantile Exchange (CME) and the Intercontinental Exchange (ICE). These contracts are essential tools for hedging and speculation, allowing market participants to manage risk or capitalise on expected price movements (Hull, 2021).

To conclude, options and futures are not the only types of financial derivatives. Swaps are derivative contracts in which two parties exchange cash flows or financial instruments, often to hedge against interest rate or currency fluctuations. Common swaps include interest rate swaps and currency swaps, where parties exchange fixed for floating rates or different currencies.

Credit derivatives, such as Credit Default Swaps (CDS), provide protection against credit risk by allowing one party to transfer the risk of a borrower defaulting to another party. These instruments are crucial for managing risk in volatile markets, offering protection against unfavourable movements in underlying assets.

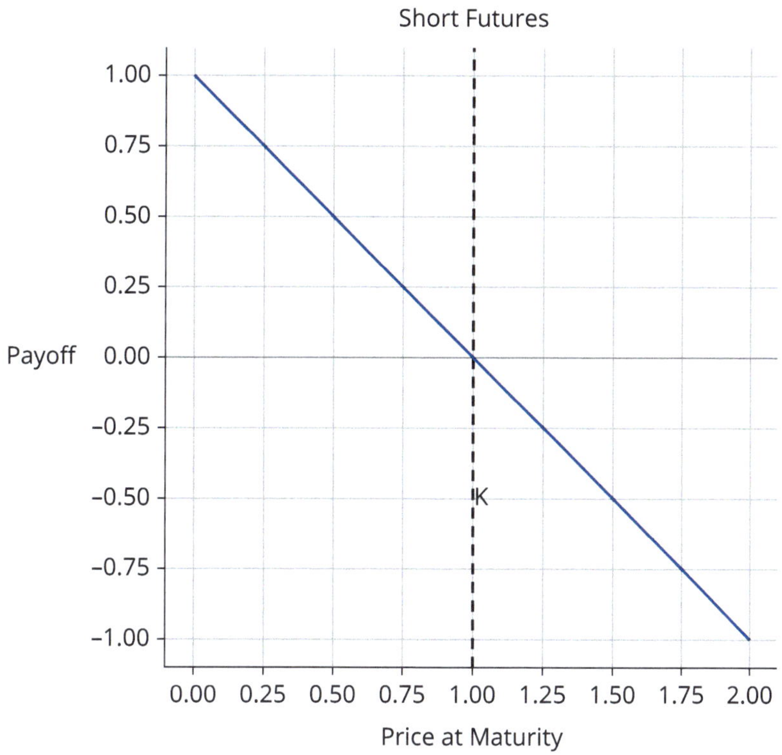

Figure 10.6 Short futures payoff structure

Source: Author

The key takeaway is that derivatives serve dual purposes: as risk management tools and as instruments for speculation. Through leverage, derivatives allow investors to control large market positions with relatively small capital outlays – for instance, controlling $100,000 worth of stocks with just $10,000 in margin. While this leveraged exposure can amplify potential gains, it also magnifies potential losses. Beyond speculation, derivatives allow asset managers to quickly pivot in the markets and adjust **asset allocations** where and when needed. Derivatives are also instrumental for creating structured products that, for example, offer investors capital guarantees.

CASE STUDY 10.2

Issuance and Trading of Carbon Credits in Global Markets

Carbon credits are financial tools granting firms the right to emit a specific amount of greenhouse gases, usually measured in metric tons of CO_2. They incentivise emission reductions by assigning a cost to pollution: firms exceeding set emission caps must

(Continued)

purchase credits from others with surplus, thus promoting investment in projects that offset emissions, such as renewable energy, reforestation, and methane capture. Regulatory bodies or independent agencies verify these projects, issuing credits based on their potential to meaningfully reduce emissions. These credits are then available for firms or third parties to trade.

Functioning within cap-and-trade frameworks, carbon credits aim to reduce emissions globally by making polluting activities financially burdensome. By setting sector-specific emission caps, regulatory bodies compel firms to adhere to quotas, turning pollution reduction into an economic necessity. This system aligns with United Nations Sustainable Development Goal (SDG) 13, Climate Action, which seeks to mitigate climate change through emission reductions, making carbon markets a critical tool in supporting climate action efforts.

Once issued, carbon credits are traded on secondary markets, including major exchanges like the European Union Emissions Trading System (EU ETS) and the Chicago Climate Exchange. These markets enable firms to manage emissions variability by buying or selling credits in response to operational needs, with prices influenced by factors such as supply, demand, and regulatory shifts. Derivatives on carbon credits, such as futures and options, further enhance market flexibility by allowing firms to hedge against credit price fluctuations. Firms anticipating increased emissions, for example, can buy carbon futures to lock in current prices, mitigating future cost risks.

Derivatives are central to carbon credit trading as they enhance liquidity and offer firms strategic tools to manage financial exposure to carbon prices. This adds a layer of adaptability to the carbon market, facilitating long-term emissions management and strategic planning. By encouraging firms to engage in sustainable practices and providing hedging mechanisms, carbon markets contribute substantially to global climate goals, reinforcing SDG 13's objectives through structured financial incentives.

Questions

1 What is the basic mechanism of carbon credits and how do they incentivise companies to reduce emissions?
2 Why would a company use carbon credit derivatives instead of buying credits directly?
3 What factors affect carbon credit prices in the secondary market?

Answers

1 Carbon credits work through a 'cap and trade' system where companies are given emission limits. If they exceed these limits, they must buy credits from companies that emit less than their cap. This creates a financial incentive to reduce emissions in two ways: companies can avoid costs by staying under their cap, and can even profit by reducing emissions further and selling excess credits. For example, a factory might invest in energy-efficient machinery to reduce emissions and sell their surplus credits.

2 Companies use derivatives like futures and options to manage risk and plan ahead. For instance, if a manufacturer knows they will need carbon credits in six months, they can buy futures now to lock in the current price, protecting against potential price increases. This helps with budgeting and provides certainty for financial planning, rather than being exposed to potentially higher spot prices in the future.

3 Carbon credit prices are influenced by:

- Supply and demand: The number of credits available versus the needs of companies
- Regulatory changes: New emission caps or rules can affect market dynamics
- Economic conditions: Industrial output levels affect emission levels and thus credit demand
- Market sentiment: Expectations about future environmental regulations
- Project verification: Success or failure of carbon reduction projects can affect credit supply

INVESTMENT MANAGEMENT

Investment management is about making decisions on where and how to allocate funds to achieve specific financial objectives. In the process, the relationship between risk and return is a fundamental concept.

- **Risk** is the possibility that the actual returns on an investment differ from the expected returns, which could lead to losses.
- **Return** is the profit or loss generated by an investment over a period of time.

The trade-off between risk and return suggests investors must be willing to accept higher levels of risk if they want to achieve higher potential returns. Conversely, lower-risk investments offer lower potential returns. As noted previously, Portfolio theory, introduced by Harry Markowitz, provides a framework on how investors can construct portfolios that maximise returns for a given level of risk by combining different assets. The theory emphasises the trade-off between risk and return. It seeks to optimise this trade-off by constructing portfolios that maximise returns for a given level of risk. The efficient frontier, which consists of a set of optimal portfolios, serves as a valuable reference for investors when making investment decisions. If two portfolios carry the same level of risk, the portfolio positioned on the efficient frontier will provide a higher return than one positioned below it. Portfolio theory also focuses on *correlation* and *covariance* between assets. Correlation measures how two assets move in relation to each other whereas covariance measures the joint variability of two assets. By combining assets with low or negative correlations, investors can minimise unsystematic risk and reduce overall portfolio risk. For instance, airline stock prices go down due to a rise in fuel prices and a decline in travelling. By diversifying into other sectors such as healthcare that has a low correlation with the airline industry, an investor can reduce the risk of a sharp decline in the portfolio value as losses in one sector may be offset by gains in another.

The Efficient Market Hypothesis (EMH) is a foundational idea in finance, firstly proposed by Louis Bachelier and further developed by Eugene Fama. It suggests that all available information is reflected in asset prices. Hence, the market is efficient. If EMH holds, it implies that no one can beat the market and get abnormal returns. Fama (1970) categorises **market efficiency** into three forms based on the availability of three types of information (past, public and private information).

- **Weak form efficiency** suggests the asset price reflects all the past information. This means technical analysis that is based on the analysis of past price movements cannot yield superior returns.
- **Second-strong form efficiency** suggests all public information (e.g. financial reports, company news) is reflected in prices. This means fundamental analysis that uses financial statements as the main source cannot consistently generate abnormal returns.
- The **strong form efficiency** suggests the asset price has all information including private information. In such a market form, no one, even insiders, can consistently outperform the market. EMH has faced challenges over the years, especially during financial crises and periods of market bubbles, where prices deviated from fundamental values. For instance, in the dot-com bubble in the late 1990s, the overvaluation of internet companies caused a stock market crash.

Behavioural finance became popular as it studies psychological biases such as herding and overconfidence, which cause the deviation of the asset prices from their fundamental value. EMH encourages investors to focus on passive investment rather than trying to beat the market through active trading. Diverse investment teams consistently demonstrate enhanced decision-making capabilities. Studies show that investment firms with greater gender and ethnic diversity achieve higher returns and better risk management outcomes. This performance advantage stems from broader perspectives in market analysis and reduced groupthink in investment decisions.

Mutual funds and hedge funds offer different pathways for investing, depending on an investor's goals, risk tolerance and access to capital. *Mutual funds* pool the funds from individuals and institutions to invest in a diversified portfolio of assets. An **index fund** is a type of mutual fund or exchange-traded fund (ETF) designed to replicate the performance of a market index. The fund is passively managed, so it is cost effective for investors with lower fees and expenses. One example of an index fund is the Vanguard 500 Index Fund which is the industry's first index fund for individual investors. The fund is designed to track the performance of the S&P 500 Index. Index funds are appealing to investors who believe in the efficient market hypothesis. Hedge funds are actively managed with the use of a wide range of strategies to generate returns. Hedge funds have the potential to earn higher returns, but they come with higher risk and fees. Moreover, hedge funds are not regulated as strictly as mutual funds, and their complex strategies and opaque disclosure can also lead to significant losses. An example of this was the collapse of Long-Term Capital Management that demonstrated excessive leverage and exposure to volatile market conditions.

In summary, investment management involves a combination of theories and strategies to balance risk and return while achieving financial goals. Risk and return are central to investment decisions. Portfolio theory provides a framework to construct diversified portfolios that maximise returns for a given level of risk. Portfolio management increasingly aligns with SDG 12 (Responsible Consumption and Production) as investors seek companies demonstrating sustainable business practices. Research shows companies with strong **ESG** practices often deliver competitive returns while supporting sustainable development goals. The efficient market hypothesis suggests that a passive, diversified approach is the best as the market reflects all the information. Index funds are strong advocates for the EMH as they passively track the performance of a market index, reflecting the belief that markets are efficient. In contrast, hedge funds pursue a wide range of strategies to generate high returns.

ACTIVITY 10.3

Using a real company's financial data:

1. Apply key financial ratios
2. Interpret the results
3. Make recommendations based on your analysis

Answers for Activity

Sample analysis using Apple Inc.:

1. Key financial ratios:
   - Current Ratio = 1.2
   - Debt-to-Equity = 1.5
   - Return on Equity = 25%
2. Interpretation:
   - Good short-term liquidity
   - Moderate leverage
   - Strong profitability
3. Recommendations:
   - Continue strong cash management
   - Monitor debt levels
   - Maintain revenue growth

OTHER FINANCIAL ASSETS

As previously noted, stocks and bonds are often the most discussed financial assets, but there are several other important categories of assets that play crucial roles in the global financial system. This section provides an overview of some of these alternative asset classes, including cash and money market instruments, foreign exchange (FX), real estate, commodities, and **cryptocurrencies**.

Cash and Money Market Instruments

Cash and money market instruments are considered the most liquid and low-risk assets in the financial world. They serve as a foundation for financial transactions and short-term investments. To understand this term, we must first determine what is meant by these two elements; cash refers to physical currency (coins and banknotes) and immediately available funds in bank accounts. It is the most liquid form of asset, providing immediate purchasing power and serving as a medium of exchange in everyday transactions.

Money market instruments are short-term debt securities with high liquidity and low risk. They typically mature within one year and are issued by governments, financial institutions, and large corporations. Common money market instruments include:

- Treasury Bills: Short-term debt obligations issued by national governments, typically with maturities of 4, 13, 26, or 52 weeks.
- Commercial Paper: Unsecured, short-term debt instruments issued by corporations to finance short-term liabilities.
- Certificates of Deposit (CDs): Time deposits offered by banks, usually with fixed interest rates and maturities ranging from a few weeks to several years.
- Repurchase Agreements (Repos): Short-term loans where one party sells securities to another with an agreement to repurchase them at a slightly higher price on a specified date.

These instruments are essential to a company for several reasons: the liquidity of the assets mean a company can meet their short-term financial obligations, or handle unexpected expenses; they often carry a lower risk compared to other options; and they enable sufficient working capital.

Foreign Exchange (FX)

The foreign exchange market, also known as the forex or FX market, is where currencies are traded. It is the largest and most liquid financial market in the world, with an average daily trading volume exceeding $9.6 trillion (Bank for International Settlements, 2025).

Key characteristics of the foreign exchange market include:

- **Decentralisation:** Unlike stock exchanges, which are traded through organised platforms between a buyer and a seller, the FX market operates through a global network of banks, brokers, and financial institutions.

- **Continuous operation:** The Financial Exchange market operates 24 hours a day, five days a week, across major financial centres worldwide. The International Monetary Fund classes major financial centres into categories as follows. The most commonly discussed are the International Financial Centres of New York, London and Tokyo. The latter appears 22nd on the Global Financial Centres Index, behind some of the more significant Regional and Offshore Financial centres, including Singapore, San Francisco, Seoul, Paris and Sydney (Wardle and Mainelli, 2025).
- **Currency pairs:** Currencies are always traded in pairs because a currency's value can only be expressed relative to another currency – it is inherently a measure of exchange rate between two economies. Commonly traded pairs include EUR/USD, USD/JPY, and GBP/USD. These pairs are often used to determine the value or strength of a currency, being able to reflect if it is strong or weak against its counterpart.
- **Volatility:** Exchange rates can be influenced by various factors, including economic indicators, political events, and market sentiment.

Real Estate

Real estate refers to property consisting of land and the buildings on it, along with its natural resources. It is a tangible asset class that can provide both income (through rent) and capital appreciation. There are many types of real estate investments available. The main four to come across are:

- **Residential:** Single-family homes, apartments, houses.
- **Commercial:** Office buildings, retail spaces, and warehouses.
- **Industrial:** Factories, power plants, and storage facilities.
- **Land:** Undeveloped property, agricultural land, and plots for development.

Real estate investment can be direct (for example purchasing and managing properties) or indirect (through *Real Estate Investment Trusts (REITs)*). REITs are companies that own, operate, or finance income-producing real estate and offer a way for individual investors to financially benefit from real estate investments without having to buy, manage, or finance properties themselves.

Commodities

Commodities are raw materials or primary agricultural products that can be bought and sold. They play a crucial role in the global economy and can serve to offset some risk against inflation. Major categories of commodities include:

- **Energy:** Crude oil, natural gas, gasoline, and heating oil.
- **Metals:** Gold, silver, copper, and platinum.
- **Agricultural products:** Wheat, corn, sugarcane, and coffee.
- **Livestock and meat:** Live cattle, feeder cattle, and sheep.

Investors can gain exposure to commodities through a range of investment opportunities, including futures contracts (an agreement to buy or sell a specific product at a pre-determined price on a specified date in the future), exchange-traded funds (in this instance, securities that track a **commodity** that can be bought or sold on a stock exchange the same way ordinary stocks can), or by investing in companies involved in commodity production.

Cryptocurrencies

Cryptocurrencies are digital or virtual currencies that use cryptography for security. They operate on decentralised systems based on **blockchain** technology, a distributed ledger enforced by a network of computers. Key features of cryptocurrencies include:

- **Decentralisation:** They operate without a central authority, such as a government or bank, which appeals to many.
- **Limited supply:** Many cryptocurrencies have a fixed maximum supply, which can make them deflationary, often leading to retention of value of the currency.
- **Pseudonymity:** While not completely anonymous, cryptocurrency transactions provide a degree of privacy.
- **Volatility:** Cryptocurrency prices can be highly volatile, presenting both opportunities and risks for investors.

Other Alternative Assets and Investment Vehicles

With such a diverse range of alternative assets available, there are several other alternative asset classes or investment vehicles worth mentioning as opportunities that are more bespoke or individual:

- **Venture Capital:** Funding provided to early-stage, high-potential startup companies.
- **Hedge Funds:** Investment funds that use pooled funds and employ various strategies to earn active returns for their investors.
- **Collectables:** Tangible assets such as art, vintage cars, rare wines, or stamps that can appreciate in value over time.
- **Intellectual Property:** Patents, copyrights, and trademarks that can generate revenue through licensing or direct use.

Understanding these various asset classes is crucial for developing a comprehensive view of the financial landscape. Each asset class has its own risk-return profile, liquidity characteristics, and role in a diversified portfolio. As financial markets continue to evolve, new asset classes may emerge, and the characteristics of existing ones may change, much like for cryptocurrencies with the introduction of Bitcoin in 2009 (Ashmore, 2024).

Sustainable Finance

In finance, the term 'sustainable finance' is topical and used a lot by public policy makers, politicians, bankers and large corporations. But what does it exactly mean? The European

Commission defines sustainable finance as follows: 'Sustainable finance refers to the process of taking *environmental, social and governance (ESG) considerations* into account when making investment decisions in the financial sector, leading to more long-term investments in sustainable economic activities and projects' (European Commission, n.d.). Sustainable finance is particularly crucial for achieving SDG 7 (Affordable and Clean Energy) by mobilising capital for renewable energy projects and clean technology development. Through **green bonds** and **sustainable investment** products, financial institutions help scale up renewable energy infrastructure while providing investors with opportunities to support the transition to clean energy.

ESG comprises three components:

- **Environmental (E)**, which covers a company's energy use, waste, and impact on the environment;
- **Social (S)**, which focuses on relationships, labour relations, and diversity; and
- **Governance (G)**, which includes the company's internal practices, decision-making processes, and compliance with laws (Henisz et al., 2019).

The overarching goal of sustainable finance is for finance to enable and support economic growth by financing activities that contribute to achieving climate and environmental objectives set out by policy makers.

So, we can see that finance can play a critical role in supporting ESG goals set by companies, governments and international policy makers. Sustainable finance plays a crucial role in promoting a greener economy by directing capital towards environmentally responsible projects and companies and thus encouraging investments that support long-term sustainability (Thompson, 2023).

One key financial product in this realm is green bonds, which are specifically designed to fund projects that have positive environmental impacts, such as renewable energy, energy efficiency, and sustainable agriculture. By issuing green bonds, governments and firms can raise capital to achieve their ESG targets, thereby contributing to the global effort to combat climate change.

Green bonds also offer investors a way to support sustainable development while potentially benefiting from the financial returns associated with environmentally friendly projects. These bonds have gained traction as governments and corporations increasingly recognise the need to align financial practices with environmental goals. Moreover, green bonds can enhance a firm's reputation by demonstrating its commitment to sustainability, which can attract socially conscious investors and consumers. Ultimately, sustainable finance is integral to fostering a greener economy and achieving the environmental targets necessary for a sustainable future.

From an investment management perspective (for example selecting mutual funds' investments), sustainable finance integrates ESG factors into the investment process by guiding investment managers to select assets that align with ethical and environmental standards. Investment managers assess potential investments through ESG screening, ensuring that companies demonstrate strong environmental practices, social responsibility, and sound governance. This process also adheres to the ethical considerations of investors, particularly those in investment funds focused on sustainability.

For example, an ESG-focused investment portfolio could exclude 'sin stocks,' such as those in gambling, weapons, alcohol, and tobacco industries. By excluding these sectors, the portfolio aligns with the values of investors seeking to avoid supporting activities that harm society or the environment. Such portfolios are increasingly popular as they offer the potential for financial returns while promoting ethical and sustainable business practices (Blitz and Swinkels, 2023).

Sustainable finance directly supports the United Nations' Sustainable Development Goals (SDGs) by channelling capital into projects that advance these global objectives. Social bonds and SDG bonds are key instruments in this effort, financing initiatives that address social challenges and promote equality. For example, social bonds can fund affordable housing projects or educational programmes, directly contributing to SDG10 and SDG4, which aims to reduce inequalities. By aligning investment strategies with the SDGs, sustainable finance helps bridge the gap between financial markets and sustainable development goals (Schoenmaker and Schramade, 2019). Another great example is how in 2023, the World Bank disbursed billions of USD to help member countries make progress towards national priorities and SDGs (World Bank, 2023). We can clearly see how finance can help to facilitate cash flows and investment decisions that will benefit overarching goals (like the SDGs).

CASE STUDY 10.3

Green Bonds in Africa

In 2023, the African Development Bank (AfDB) launched a groundbreaking $2 billion green bond programme focused on climate resilience projects across the continent. The initiative targeted investments in sustainable agriculture, renewable energy, and water management systems in multiple African nations.

The programme's innovative structure allowed for smaller minimum investment amounts ($100,000 compared to the typical $200,000), making it more accessible to regional investors. The bonds offered a 4.5% annual return, with proceeds specifically earmarked for projects that would help communities adapt to climate change while generating sustainable returns.

One notable project funded through this programme was a $300 million solar-powered irrigation system in Kenya's arid regions, benefiting over 50,000 small-scale farmers. The project not only promised financial returns through improved agricultural productivity but also addressed critical issues of food security and climate resilience.

Questions

1 How does this green bond programme balance financial returns with social impact?
2 What risks should investors consider when evaluating these green bonds?
3 How might this initiative influence the development of sustainable finance in Africa?

Answers

1 How does this green bond programme balance financial returns with social impact?

The programme balances returns through its 4.5% yield while funding critical climate resilience projects. The Kenya irrigation project demonstrates this by generating agricultural productivity gains while addressing food security and environmental challenges. The reduced minimum investment of $100,000 makes these social **impact investments** more accessible while maintaining competitive returns.

Key considerations:

- Evaluate both financial metrics and social outcomes
- Consider short-term and long-term benefits

2 What risks should investors consider when evaluating these green bonds?

Investors must consider multiple risk layers including political risks (regional stability, policy changes), project implementation challenges (technical issues, delays), and market risks (currency fluctuations, liquidity). Environmental risks are particularly crucial given the climate-focused nature of projects and their vulnerability to changing weather patterns.

Key considerations:

- Examine both macro and micro risk factors
- Consider the interconnected nature of risks

3 How might this initiative influence the development of sustainable finance in Africa?

This initiative creates a blueprint for sustainable finance in Africa by demonstrating the viability of green bonds at scale while building market infrastructure and expertise. The lower investment threshold and successful implementation encourage broader market participation and could inspire similar programmes across the continent.

Key considerations:

- Look at **market development** impacts
- Consider influence on various **stakeholders**

Sources

African Development Bank Group (2022) Annual Report 2022. African Development Bank Group. https://www.afdb.org/en/documents/annual-report-2022 (accessed September 17, 2025).

FSD Africa (2020) Africa Green Bond Toolkit. FSD Africa. https://fsdafrica.org/publication/africa-green-bonds-toolkit/ (accessed September 17, 2025).

International Finance Corporation (2024) Green and Social Bond Impact Report. World Bank Group. www.ifc.org/content/dam/ifc/doc/2024/ifc-green-and-social-bond-impact-report-fy-23.pdf (accessed September 17, 2025).

ACTIVITY 10.4

Research a company's ESG initiatives:

1. Evaluate their sustainable finance practices
2. Assess the impact on company management
3. Compare with industry standards

REFLECTIVE ACTIVITY 10.4

1. How do these findings align with your prior expectations of the company?
2. What strengths and weaknesses did you identify in their approach?
3. What one recommendation would you make to improve their ESG strategy?
4. How has this analysis changed your perspective on sustainable business practices?

FINANCIAL TECHNOLOGY (FINTECH)

Columbia University defines fintech (financial technology) simply as 'a catch-all term referring to software, mobile applications, and other technologies created to improve and automate traditional forms of finance for businesses and consumers alike' (Columbia University, n.d.). Fintech innovations are critical for achieving SDG 1 (No Poverty) by providing financial services to underserved populations. Mobile banking, digital payments, and automated lending platforms reduce barriers to financial access, helping lift people out of poverty through increased economic participation. For example, *digital banking* platforms in developing countries have enabled millions of previously unbanked individuals to access savings accounts, loans, and payment services. Examples include mobile banking, peer-to-peer payment services, crowdfunding, automated portfolio managers, or trading platforms. Cryptocurrencies also fall in the realm of what is understood by fintech. Fintech firms primarily rely on technology to conduct fundamental functions provided by financial services, affecting how users store, save, borrow, invest, move, pay, and protect money.

Banks and financial institutions will have to increasingly engage with **artificial intelligence** (AI) to develop their suite of product offerings. In addition, financial services firms will have to focus on hyper automation software (deep-learning/event-based software) to improve decision-making. **Cloud computing** will help to lower costs and increase efficiency. Open-source software and No-and-Low code development platforms will democratise access to the development and advancement of fintech (McKinsey & Company, 2024). For over a decade, fintech has helped to create more accuracy and efficiency in several areas in finance like investment management, risk assessment, fraud detection and customer services (chatbots for example). AI and deep learning can help investment managers to analyse patterns and feed data into predictive analytics. AI can also be used to analyse large datasets to analyse patterns that could lead to loans default and/or help with assessing credit risk of borrowers (Han et al., 2023).

Fintech has the potential to significantly advance the United Nations' Sustainable Development Goals (SDGs) by enhancing financial inclusion, particularly in regions like Africa where many people remain unbanked. By leveraging mobile technology, fintech can provide banking services to populations without access to traditional financial institutions, thereby supporting SDG 1 (No Poverty), SDG 8 (Decent Work and Economic Growth), and SDG 10 (Reduced Inequalities).

MINI CASE STUDY 10.1

M-Pesa

One prominent example is M-Pesa, a mobile banking service launched in Kenya. M-Pesa allows users to perform financial transactions such as money transfers, bill payments, and micro-loans through mobile phones, even in areas without bank branches. This service has revolutionised financial access in Kenya, where a significant portion of the population previously lacked banking services. By enabling secure and affordable financial transactions, M-Pesa has helped millions of people enter the financial ecosystem, fostering economic growth and reducing poverty (Ndung'u, 2017).

The advantages of bringing unbanked populations into the financial system are numerous. Access to banking services enables individuals to save money securely, access credit, and invest in their education or businesses. It also facilitates remittances, which are crucial for many families in Africa. Furthermore, financial inclusion through fintech can reduce income inequality by providing low-income individuals with opportunities to improve their financial situation.

So, fintech is not just capitalising on advancements in technology and creating efficiencies in the financial system for developed nations. Fintech is also instrumental to elevating access to finance in emerging markets and facilitating micro-businesses and individuals with loans and/or credit facilities. As we saw, fintech can make a positive impact to achieving several of the UN's SDGs.

REFLECTIVE ACTIVITY 10.5

Analyse how fintech is changing financial management:

1 What traditional practices are being disrupted?
2 How are managers adapting to these changes?
3 What are the implications for future management?

LOOKING FORWARD

The financial sector is uniquely positioned to advance multiple Sustainable Development Goals simultaneously. Through sustainable finance initiatives, financial institutions support clean energy projects (SDG 7), build resilient infrastructure (SDG 9), and promote climate action (SDG 13). Financial inclusion efforts through innovative products and technologies help reduce poverty (SDG 1) and create economic opportunities (SDG 8). The integration of ESG factors into investment decisions encourages responsible business practices (SDG 12) while supporting sustainable communities (SDG 11).

Importantly, the finance sector increasingly recognises that diversity and inclusion drive better outcomes – from more effective risk management to enhanced investment returns. Research shows that diverse teams make better financial decisions, while inclusive financial products and services help create a more equitable economy. This alignment between finance, sustainability, and inclusion demonstrates how financial decisions can generate both economic returns and positive social impact.

The evolution of financial markets through technological innovation and sustainable practices creates new opportunities and challenges. Understanding these fundamental concepts, from traditional financial instruments to modern fintech solutions, provides the foundation for navigating the increasingly complex financial landscape. As we look ahead, the integration of sustainable practices, technological innovation, and traditional financial principles will continue to shape the future of finance.

CHAPTER SUMMARY

- Finance is fundamentally about managing money and resources over time, encompassing personal decisions, business operations, and economic development.
- The time value of money is the cornerstone principle of finance – money today is worth more than the same amount in the future due to its earning potential and inflation.
- Financial markets offer various instruments (equities, bonds, derivatives) that serve different purposes for raising capital, managing risk, and generating returns.
- Risk and return are inherently linked – higher potential returns require accepting greater risk, but this can be managed through diversification and proper portfolio construction.
- Sustainable finance is transforming the industry by incorporating environmental, social, and governance (ESG) factors into financial decisions and creating new investment opportunities like green bonds.
- Financial technology (fintech) is revolutionising how financial services are delivered, improving accessibility and efficiency while creating new opportunities for financial inclusion.
- Investment management requires balancing multiple factors including risk tolerance, time horizon, and increasingly, sustainability considerations.
- Alternative assets (real estate, commodities, cryptocurrencies) provide diversification opportunities beyond traditional stocks and bonds.

- Risk assessment and management are crucial skills in finance, involving both quantitative measures and qualitative judgment.
- Finance plays a vital role in achieving sustainable development goals by directing capital toward environmentally and socially beneficial projects.

STUDENTS LIKE YOU CHANGE THE WORLD

From Apprentice to Banking Vice-President

Growing up in an economically disadvantaged area, traditional university seemed financially out of reach for some students. The prospect of overwhelming student debt made higher education feel like an impossible dream. Then came the game-changer: a degree apprenticeship with a Tier 1 investment bank through their social outreach programme. This opportunity offered the chance to earn a finance degree while gaining real-world experience - all without student loans.

For four years, they balanced studying for a BSc in Finance with hands-on work at a prestigious financial institution. While peers were learning theory, they were applying knowledge in real time, making connections, and building professional skills.

The results were transformative. They graduated with:

- A First-Class BSc in Finance
- CFA Level 1 qualification
- Four years of professional experience
- Zero student debt

Their career accelerated rapidly. Promotions followed, including an international posting and eventually advancing to Vice-President in the Markets Division. A substantial performance bonus enabled them to secure an apartment, purchase a car, and boost their pension - financial milestones many peers couldn't imagine at that stage.

This journey isn't just personal success - it demonstrates how alternative education pathways drive social mobility. By choosing an apprenticeship, they overcame barriers that might have prevented access to a career in finance.

The message is powerful: Your background doesn't define your future. With determination and the right opportunities, you can forge your own path - and in doing so, change the world by breaking barriers for those who follow.

Students like you don't just adapt to the world - you transform it.

CHAPTER EXERCISES

Time Value of Money

1. Calculate the future value of £1,000 invested for:
   - 3 years at 5% annual interest rate, compounded annually
   - 5 years at 3% annual interest rate, compounded annually
   - 2 years at 4% annual interest rate, compounded quarterly

2 Multiple Choice: What best describes the time value of money principle?

   a Money today is worth less than the same amount in the future
   b Money today is worth more than the same amount in the future
   c Money has the same value regardless of time
   d Money only has value when invested

Equities and Bond Pricing

Bond Valuation: Calculate the present value of:

- A 3-year bond paying annual coupons of £50 with £1,000 face value at 4% market interest rate
- A 5-year zero-coupon bond with £2,000 face value at 3% market interest rate

Risk Assessment

Calculate risk measures for the following annual stock returns: 12%, -3%, 8%, 15%, -2%

- Average return
- Standard deviation

Derivatives

Options Strategy: Design a hedging strategy using:

- Call options
- Put options
- Identify break-even points

Investment Management

Portfolio Construction: Create a diversified portfolio with £100,000, considering:

- Risk tolerance
- Investment horizon
- Asset allocation
- ESG factors

Sustainable Finance

Green Bond Analysis: Review a green bond prospectus and identify:

- Use of proceeds
- Environmental impact metrics
- Risk factors
- Reporting requirements

REFLECTIVE ACTIVITIES

Understanding Financial Concepts

Personal Finance Journal:

- How do you currently apply time value of money concepts?
- What role does risk assessment play in your decisions?
- How might you incorporate sustainable investing?

Market Analysis

Weekly Market Observation (4 weeks): Record and reflect on:

- Major market movements
- Global event impacts
- Sustainability initiatives
- Fintech developments

Professional Development

Career Integration:

- Identify key financial concepts in your intended career
- Research how sustainability is integrated
- Analyse potential technological disruption
- Create a skills development plan

Sustainable Finance

ESG Investment Analysis:

- Review a company's ESG report
- Analyse environmental initiatives
- Evaluate social responsibility programmes
- Assess governance structure

Technology and Finance

Reflect on:

- How fintech changes traditional banking
- Personal experience with financial technology
- Future of financial services

Final Integration

Synthesis Journal:

- Connect concepts across chapter sections
- Identify practical applications
- Note areas for further study
- Set personal learning goals

ANSWERS FOR CHAPTER EXERCISES ACTIVITIES

Time Value of Money

1 Future Value Calculations:

- £1,000 for 3 years at 5% annually: $FV = £1,000 \times (1 + 0.05)^3 = £1,157.63$
- £1,000 for 5 years at 3% annually: $FV = £1,000 \times (1 + 0.03)^5 = £1,159.27$
- £1,000 for 2 years at 4% quarterly: $FV = £1,000 \times (1 + 0.04/4)^8 = £1,082.86$

2 Multiple Choice Answer: B: Money today is worth more than the same amount in the future due to earning potential, inflation impact and immediate availability.

Equities and Bond Pricing

Bond Valuation:

- 3-year bond with £50 annual coupons, £1,000 face value, 4% rate: $PV = £50/(1.04) + £50/(1.04)^2 + £1,050/(1.04)^3 = £1,027.75$
- 5-year zero-coupon bond, £2,000 face value, 3% rate: $PV = £2,000/(1.03)^5 = £1,725.22$

Risk Assessment

For returns: 12%, -3%, 8%, 15%, -2%

1 Average Return = (12 - 3 + 8 + 15 - 2)/5 = 6%

2 Standard Deviation:

- Mean = 6%
- Deviations squared = $(12-6)^2 + (-3-6)^2 + (8-6)^2 + (15-6)^2 + (-2-6)^2$
- Variance = 66.5
- Standard Deviation = $\sqrt{66.5}$ = 8.15%

Investment Management

Portfolio Construction Example (£100,000):

- Large-cap Equities: 40% (£40,000)
- Government Bonds: 30% (£30,000)

- Corporate Bonds: 15% (£15,000)
- Cash: 10% (£10,000)
- **Sustainable Investments**: 5% (£5,000)

Sustainable Finance

Green Bond Analysis Key Points:

1. Use of proceeds should be:
    - Clearly defined
    - Environmentally beneficial
    - Measurable impact
    - Independently verified
2. Impact metrics should include:
    - Carbon emissions reduced
    - Energy saved
    - Waste reduced
    - Resources conserved

END OF CHAPTER REFLECTION

Have a look at the skills you should have developed in this unit (find more details in the Key Skills Table in the Appendix on pp. 504-5).

1. Which of the skills listed do you think you have developed the most?
2. Can you give two examples on why you feel you have now developed these skills/developed them further?
3. How will you use these new/refined skills in the future (give two examples of the impact of your development on your future behaviour)?

FURTHER READING

Madura, J. (2024) *Personal Finance* (8th edition). Pearson. Chapters 3-4.

These chapters provide a simple explanation of the Time Value of Money.

Berk, J., and DeMarzo, P. (2023) *Corporate Finance* (5th edition). Pearson. Chapters 3-5.

These chapters provide a deeper explanation of the Time Value of Money.

Jordan, B., Miller, T., and Dolvin, S. (2024) *Fundamentals of Investments*. McGraw-Hill. Chapters 8-9.

These chapters provide a simple explanation of Risk.

Hull, J.C. (2023) *Risk Management and Financial Institutions* (6th edition). Wiley. Chapters 1-4.

These chapters provide a deeper explanation of Risk.

Tyson, E. (2024) *Investing for Dummies* (9th edition). For Dummies. Chapters 5-8.

These chapters provide a simple explanation of Investment Management.

Bodie, Z., Kane, A., and Marcus, A. (2023) *Investments* (12th edition). McGraw-Hill. Chapters 5-7.

These chapters provide a deeper explanation of Investment Management.

Chandler, D. (2024) *Strategic Corporate Social Responsibility* (6th edition). Sage. Chapters 3-4.

These chapters provide a simple explanation of Sustainable Finance.

Schoenmaker, D., and Schramade, W. (2023) *Principles of Sustainable Finance* (2nd edition). Oxford University Press. Chapters 1-3.

These chapters provide a deeper explanation of Sustainable Finance.

King, B. (2024) *Bank 4.0: Banking Everywhere, Never at a Bank.* Wiley. Chapters 1-3.

These chapters provide a simple explanation of fintech.

Chishti, S., and Barberis, J. (2023) *The FINTECH Book* (2nd edition). Wiley. Chapters 2-5.

These chapters provide a more in-depth explanation of fintech.

Madura, J. (2024) *Personal Finance* (13th edition). Pearson.

This text is perfect for beginners wanting to understand basic financial concepts, with clear explanations of budgeting, investing, and financial planning. This text includes practical examples and real-world applications, with a particular usefulness for covering the Time Value of Money and Investment sections.

Berk, J. and DeMarzo, P. (2023) *Corporate Finance* (5th edition). Pearson.

This is a more advanced text with coverage of financial concepts. It is excellent for understanding corporate financial decision-making, with a strong mathematical and theoretical foundation. Recommended for deeper understanding of bonds, equities, and risk assessment.

Bodie, Z., Kane, A., and Marcus, A. (2023) *Investments* (12th edition). McGraw-Hill.

This text provides comprehensive coverage of investment principles, with a detailed exploration of portfolio theory and market behaviour. It has a strong focus on practical investment strategies, which is valuable for understanding risk management and portfolio construction.

Housel, M. (2020) *The Psychology of Money: Timeless Lessons on Wealth, Greed, and Happiness.* Harriman House.

This text provides an accessible exploration of behavioural finance, explaining how psychology affects financial decisions. It uses storytelling to illustrate complex concepts and so is excellent for complementing technical financial knowledge.

Schoenmaker, D. and Schramade, W. (2023) *Principles of Sustainable Finance*. Oxford University Press.

This is a leading text on sustainable finance and ESG investing. It links finance with environmental and social goals, and provides current examples and case studies – essential for understanding modern financial markets.

REFERENCES

Ashmore, D. (2024). 'Bitcoin price history 2009 to 2022', *Forbes.com*, April 16. https://www.forbes.com/advisor/investing/cryptocurrency/bitcoin-price-history/ (accessed September 17, 2025).

Bank for International Settlements (2025). 'Global FX trading hits $9.6 trillion per day in April 2025 and OTC interest rate derivatives surge to $7.9 trillion: Triennial Survey', *BIS*, September 30. https://www.bis.org/press/p250930.htm (accessed November 11, 2025).

Blitz, D. and Swinkels, L. (2023) 'Does excluding sin stocks cost performance?', *Journal of Sustainable Finance and Investment*, 13 (4). http://10.1080/20430795.2021.1972789

Bodie, Z., Kane, A., and Marcus, A. J. (2023) *Investments* (13th edition). McGraw Hill Education.

Columbia University (n.d.) 'What is financial technology (fintech)? A beginner's guide for 2023', Columbia *Engineering Boot Camps*. https://web.archive.org/web/20240228214211/https://bootcamp.cvn.columbia.edu/blog/what-is-fintech/ (accessed September 17, 2025).

Damodaran, A. (2012) *Investment Valuation: Tools and Techniques for Determining the Value of Any Asset* (3rd edition). John Wiley & Sons.

European Commission (n.d.) 'Overview of sustainable finance', *European Commission*. https://finance.ec.europa.eu/sustainable-finance/overview-sustainable-finance_en (accessed September 17, 2025).

Fama, E. F. (1970) 'Efficient capital markets: A review of theory and empirical work', *Journal of Finance*, 25 (2): 383–417.

Gordon, M.J. (1959) 'Dividends, earnings, and stock prices', *The Review of Economics and Statistics*, 41 (2): 99–105. http://10.2307/1927792

Han, Y., Chen, J., Dou, M., Wang, J., and Feng, K. (2023) 'The impact of artificial intelligence on the financial services industry', *Academic Journal of Management and Social Sciences*, 2 (3). http://10.54097/ajmss.v2i3.8741

Henisz, W., Koller, T. and Nuttall, R. (2019) *Five Ways That ESG Creates Value*. McKinsey Quarterly (November). https://www.mckinsey.com/~/media/McKinsey/Business%20Functions/Strategy%20and%20Corporate%20Finance/Our%20Insights/Five%20ways%20that%20ESG%20creates%20value/Five-ways-that-ESG-creates-value.ashx (accessed September 17, 2025).

Hull, J. (2021) *Futures, Options and Other Derivatives* (11th edition). Pearson.

Jorion, P. (2007) *Value at Risk – The New Benchmark for Managing Financial Risk* (3rd edition). McGraw-Hill.

Markowitz, H. (1952) 'Portfolio selection: Efficient diversification of investments', *Journal of Finance*, 7: 77–91.

McKinsey & Company (2024) 'What is fintech (financial technology)?', *McKinsey & Company*, January 16. https://www.mckinsey.com/featured-insights/mckinsey-explainers/what-is-fintech (accessed September 17, 2025).

Morgan, J.P. (1996) *RiskMetrics Technical Document* (4th edition). J.P. Morgan.

Ndung'u, N. (2017) *M-Pesa – a Success Story of Digital Financial Inclusion*. Blavatnik School of Government, University of Oxford. https://www.bsg.ox.ac.uk/sites/default/files/2018-06/2017-07-M-Pesa-Practitioners-Insight.pdf (accessed September 17, 2025).

Pagano, M., Panetta, F., and Zingales, L. (1998) 'Why do companies go public? An empirical analysis', *Journal of Finance*, 53 (1): 27–64. http://10.1111/0022-1082.25448

Ritter, J.R., and Welch, I. (2002) 'A review of IPO activity, pricing, and allocations', *Journal of Finance*, 57 (4): 1795–828. http://10.1111/1540-6261.00478

Ross, S.A., Westerfield, R.W., and Jordan, B.D. (2022) *Fundamentals of Corporate Finance* (13th edition). McGraw Hill.

Schoenmaker, D. and Schramade, W. (2019) *Principles of Sustainable Finance*. Oxford University Press.

Sharpe, W.F. (1964) 'Capital asset prices: A theory of market equilibrium under conditions of risk', *Journal of Finance*, 19 (3): 425–42.

Thompson, S. (2023) *Green and Sustainable Finance: Principles and Practice in Banking, Investment and Insurance* (2nd edition). Kogan Page.

Treynor, J.L. (1962) 'Toward a theory of the market value of risky assets' [Unpublished manuscript]. SSRN. https://ssrn.com/abstract=628187 (accessed December 19, 2025).

Wardle, M. and Mainelli, M. (2025) *The Global Financial Centres Index 37*. Z/Yen. https://www.zyen.com/publications/professional-articles/the-global-financial-centres-index-37/ (accessed September 15, 2025).

World Bank (2023) *Sustainable Development Bonds & Green Bonds: Impact Report 2023*. World Bank Treasury. https://thedocs.worldbank.org/en/doc/667f95939700497452d00a1544ba2d01-0340022024/original/World-Bank-IBRD-FY23-IMPACT-REPORT.pdf (accessed September 15, 2025).

11
ECONOMICS

Shaun Grimshaw and Olha Matviiets

INTENDED LEARNING OUTCOMES

After reading this chapter, you should be able to:

- Demonstrate an understanding of foundational economic concepts, including scarcity, opportunity cost, and marginal analysis.
- Evaluate the impact of economic factors such as inflation, market structures, and demand elasticity on business decision-making processes.
- Integrate economic theories into practical business scenarios, emphasising strategic decision-making within market contexts.

SUSTAINABLE DEVELOPMENT GOALS

In this chapter, the following SDGs will be addressed:

- SDG 1: No Poverty – Analysing economic policies that aim to reduce poverty and promote economic inclusion, evaluating the impact of social welfare programmes on poverty alleviation, and studying the economic effects of microfinance and financial inclusion initiatives.
- SDG 3: Good Health and Well-being – The economic analysis of markets that contain negative externalities, such as the production of unhealthy foods, may suggest a role for governments regulating or taxing such industries.
- SDG 9: Industry, Innovation, and Infrastructure – Tackling markets that lack competitive pressures that may also lack incentives for innovation and be inefficient and wasteful.
- SDG 10: Reduced Inequalities – Examining economic policies that address income inequality and promote social equity, analysing the impact of taxation and redistribution policies on reducing disparities, and studying the economic effects of inclusive growth strategies and social protection measures.
- SDG 12: Responsible Consumption and Production – Addressing market failures like negative externalities, ensuring that firms and consumers account for environmental and social costs in production and consumption decisions.

INTRODUCTION

This chapter will introduce you to some of the key ideas for businesses found in economics. The chapter starts with some fundamental principles of economics and then uses those to develop further ideas. This will include how we can consider a market in terms of the choices of consumers – the **demand** in the market – and of the choices of the producers, the **supply**. After that, the chapter will discuss one of the key insights of economics, that markets that are structured to be competitive can benefit society. Finally, we will focus on more realistic markets, looking at the opportunities this brings for businesses, and the wider implications for society.

What Is Economics?

Economics is a way of thinking about the decisions we see in the world around us. Every day, every person in the world interacts with economics in some way, regardless of their age, religion, social position, or employment status. Whether making decisions about purchasing goods, evaluating job opportunities, considering investments, or whether to hire or fire staff, we can use economics as a way of thinking about these choices.

Learning economics involves developing a set of **skills** that allow us to analyse decision-making in a consistent manner. Economics gives us an approach to think about decisions, such as whether to go to work for an extra day's pay or to spend the day having fun, say at the beach, so that we can begin to understand the impact of these decisions.

Why Is Economics Important?

Economics impacts every society and, in turn, every individual, including you and me. Learning about economics helps us understand constantly evolving factors such as taxation, inflation, and interest rates, all of which affect our daily lives (Samuelson and Nordhaus, 2009).

Economics offers insights into a range of health, social, and political issues that influence communities. Understanding how economics works allows us to identify patterns and trends, learn from past mistakes, and work toward creating a better society for the future (Krugman and Wells, 2018).

Understanding economics is essential for making informed business decisions. It helps managers anticipate market trends, understand competitive dynamics, and evaluate the potential impact of government policies (Case et al., 2012).

REFLECTIVE ACTIVITY 11.1

Think about an everyday decision - should you buy your next coffee from a shop or make it yourself? What factors influence such a decision?

REFLECTIVE RESPONSE 11.1

This decision involves evaluating opportunity cost, convenience and personal preferences. If you buy coffee from a shop, the opportunity cost is the money spent and potentially the time involved in going to the shop. Making coffee at home may save money but requires effort and resources. Other factors include taste preferences, the quality of the coffee, time constraints and the social experience of visiting a café.

Key Economic Principles

In a broader sense, economics is the study of how governments, businesses, and individuals decide to allocate resources to meet their needs and desires. It covers a wide range of topics, including the production, distribution, and consumption of goods and services.

Economics can be divided into two main branches: microeconomics and macroeconomics.

- **Microeconomics** focuses on the behaviour of individual consumers and businesses, exploring how they make decisions and interact in markets.
- **Macroeconomics,** on the other hand, examines the overall functioning of an economy, addressing issues such as inflation, unemployment, and economic growth.

Opportunity Cost

One of the cornerstone concepts in economics is *opportunity cost*, defined as the value of the next best alternative foregone when a decision is made. Every decision involves trade-offs, where choosing one option means sacrificing another. For example, a business investing in new equipment foregoes the opportunity to allocate those funds towards hiring additional staff or expanding **marketing** efforts (Mankiw, 2023). Recognising opportunity cost enables businesses to prioritise effectively and allocate resources in ways that maximise returns and strategic goals.

EXAMPLE 11.1

Let's take the example of Aisha, a student who regularly buys coffee at her local coffee shop. Aisha has £15 to spend on coffee each week, and her favourite coffee costs £3 per cup. So, with her budget, she can buy 5 coffees, one for each weekday.

This week, the local coffee shop offers a special deal where she can buy 6 coffees for £16 instead of her usual 5 for £15. While this deal gives her one extra coffee, it also costs £1 more than her usual budget.

(Continued)

Here's where opportunity cost comes in: if Aisha spends the extra £1 to get the deal, she won't have that £1 to spend on something else, like a snack or a small treat. The opportunity cost of choosing the coffee deal is the other things she could have done with that extra £1.

In simple terms, opportunity cost is what you give up when you make a choice. For Aisha, it's the snack or treat she could have bought if she didn't spend the extra money on coffee.

Marginal Analysis

Marginal analysis plays a critical role in decision-making by evaluating the incremental benefits and costs of an action. Businesses use marginal analysis to assess the additional benefits gained from each unit of input, such as labour or **capital**, compared to the additional costs incurred (McConnell et al., 2018). For instance, when deciding whether to increase how much of a good it makes, a **firm** will weigh the marginal revenue generated against the marginal cost of production of the additional output. This analytical approach helps businesses optimise their operations and achieve greater efficiency in resource allocation.

EXAMPLE 11.2

Going back to the example with Aisha, let's imagine she arrives at the local coffee shop with the intention of buying one £3 coffee. However, she finds she has a £5 note in her wallet and considers buying a pastry that costs exactly £2. The marginal benefit of purchasing the pastry is the enjoyment she will get from eating it alongside her coffee. The marginal cost is the additional money spent and the possibility of feeling too full afterward. Aisha conducts a marginal analysis to decide whether the added pleasure of the pastry is worth the increased cost.

Consumer Surplus

Consumer surplus represents the difference between what consumers are willing to pay for a good or service and what they actually pay. This measure provides insight into the economic benefits that consumers receive from market transactions. It is a useful tool for assessing the efficiency of markets and the welfare impact of various policies. For instance, when a new technology reduces production costs, the resulting lower prices can increase consumer surplus, indicating a welfare gain for consumers. According to Mankiw (2023), consumer surplus is crucial for understanding the gains from trade and the effects of price changes on consumer welfare.

Additionally, Varian (2014) explains that consumer surplus can also highlight the impact of taxes, subsidies, and price controls on overall **market efficiency**. By analysing consumer surplus, economists can better understand the benefits that consumers derive from market participation and make more informed decisions about policy interventions.

EXAMPLE 11.3

To understand consumer surplus from an everyday perspective, imagine Aisha arrives at her local coffee shop and finds that her typically £3 coffee is on offer for £2.50. The difference between what Aisha was willing to pay (£3) and the price she actually pays (£2.50) is £0.50. This £0.50 represents consumer surplus. It captures the extra benefit Aisha feels from paying less than what she was prepared to spend.

REFLECTIVE ACTIVITY 11.2

You are considering getting a take-away pizza and would be willing to pay £20.

- You see on the app that the price is £15, how do you feel?
- If, however, the price is £25, does how you feel change?

REFLECTIVE RESPONSE 11.2

- If you feel pleased to find the price was lower than you were expecting, that would reflect consumer surplus.
- If the price was higher than expected, you would need to consider that you would no longer be able to buy the pizza because it is an additional £5; that is the opportunity cost of the purchase.

COMPETITIVE MARKETS

This section will use the concepts set out in the previous section to develop the key **model** of *supply and demand* for a good or service. It will do so by assuming that the market for the good or service that we are considering is *competitive*. That is, it is assumed there is no one party, be they a buyer or a seller, who has influence over the market and whose choices will directly affect the price of the good or service. A simple example would be a large physical market for fresh produce with many suppliers. The market for a given good, say apples, may be competitive where there are lots of buyers and sellers.

In many actual markets, the assumption that the market is competitive is not realistic. There are often a limited number of sellers, and we will look at the effect of this later in the chapter. The assumption of a **competitive market** does, however, give us some key insights into what such a market can achieve.

Within an actual market, we would expect to see a price for the good being sold and a quantity in terms of the number of units of the good being exchanged, given the price, between buyers and sellers. For example, a local coffee shop may sell a quantity of 250 coffees in a day at a price of £3. The model of supply and demand considers the two sides of the market separately, with consumers forming the demand side of the market and producers forming the supply side.

Demand

The *demand* for a good or service is the quantities of the product that consumers would be willing to buy at various prices. Many goods have a specific advertised price, and a firm may know the quantity it can sell at that price. However, within the model, we think about demand in a more abstract manner, in the sense of the quantity that consumers would buy at a given price measured at a whole range of prices. Not all goods have a specific advertised price, indeed it may be beneficial to some businesses not to advertise a single price. Furthermore, only knowing how much a firm can sell at the current price does not really help guide the firm as to whether the current price is the most appropriate price for, say, maximising the firm's profits.

The concept of demand is based on a series of hypothetical questions, such as what quantity of the good would be bought at different prices. Consider a market stall that sells T-shirts. It would be useful information for the owner of the stall to know how many T-shirts they could sell, in the sense of how many would consumers buy, at different prices.

The concept of demand asks hypothetical questions of the form: How many T-shirts would customers buy if the price is £1? How many would they buy if the price is £2? Or if it is £3, and so on.

Frustratingly, to mathematicians and scientists, who like to draw graphs where the outcome is on the vertical axis and the input on the horizontal axis, economists like to draw their graphs the other way round. Economists plot price, which is what our hypothetical question is varying, on the vertical axis and quantity, the associated predicted outcome in the market, on the horizontal axis.

Before looking at a graph of demand, think about how it might look. As the hypothetical price falls and you move down the vertical axis, should the quantity rise? That is, do you expect people will buy more of a good when it is cheaper, and the plot of demand to slope downwards? Or, as the price falls, should the quantity fall? That is do you expect people will buy less of a good when it is cheaper, and the plot of demand to slope upwards?

Hopefully, you predicted that as the good gets cheaper, people will buy more, and that the **demand curve** slopes downwards. This is typically the case, and is sometimes called the **law of demand**, in that, as the price of a good or service falls, the quantity demanded increases. The plot of quantities of the good or service that would be bought at different prices is called the demand curve. The downward sloping nature of the demand curve reflects the larger opportunity cost associated with a higher price.

Figure 11.1 illustrates the demand curve for T-shirts from a market stall. The figure shows that at Point 1, if the price is £1, customers will buy 5,000 T-shirts, but at Point 2, if the price is £5, the customers will only buy 1,000 T-shirts.

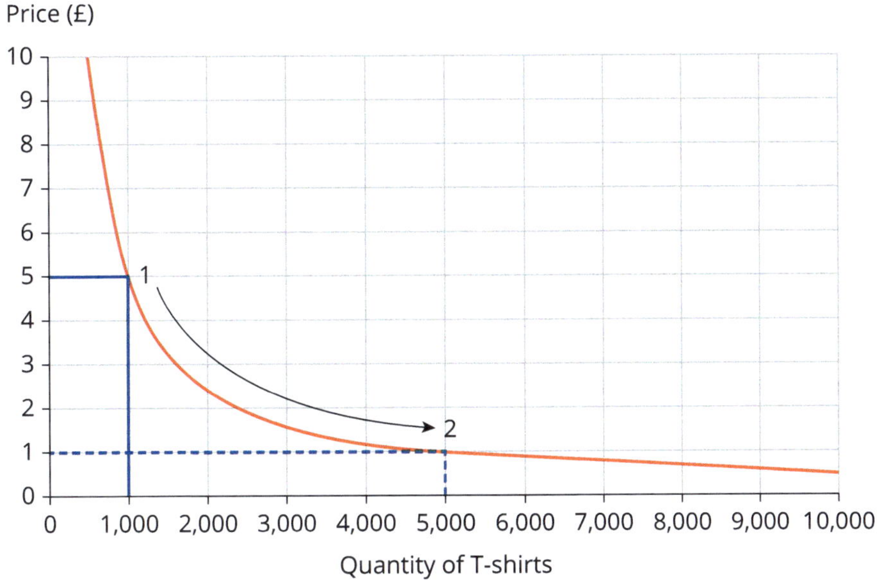

Figure 11.1 Illustration of demand curve in market for T-shirts

Elasticity of Demand

Imagine Aisha owns that small T-shirt stall at a busy market we talked about above, and she is trying to figure out how changes in price will affect her sales. This is where the concept of **elasticity** comes into play.

Elasticity is crucial for predicting how markets (demand) will respond to changes in prices and other factors. It measures how sensitive demand is to these changes. If a business increases its prices and sees a significant drop in sales, we say that demand is elastic – customers are very responsive to price changes. On the other hand, if the price increase has little effect on sales, demand is considered inelastic, meaning customers continue buying even at higher prices.

For businesses, understanding elasticity helps in setting effective pricing strategies. Knowing whether demand for their product is elastic or inelastic allows businesses to predict how price changes will impact their revenue. It also helps them adapt to competition by adjusting prices in a way that maximises profits while retaining customers.

To calculate the **price elasticity of demand** (e), we use the following formula:

$$e = \frac{\%\ \text{change in quantity demanded}}{\%\ \text{change in price}}$$

- If $|e|$ *(the absolute value of e) is greater than 1*, demand is elastic (customers are highly responsive to price changes).
- If $|e|$ *is less than 1*, demand is inelastic (customers are less responsive to price changes).
- If $|e|$ *is equal to 1*, demand is unitary elastic, meaning the percentage change in quantity demanded is exactly equal to the percentage change in price.

Continuing with the T-shirt example, we can explore elasticity. Figure 11.1 shows that when the price is £1, customers will buy 5,000 T-shirts, but when the price rises to £5, only 1,000 T-shirts are sold. This significant drop in demand when prices increase indicates that the demand for T-shirts is elastic – customers are highly sensitive to price changes. A small increase in price leads to a large decrease in the quantity demanded, meaning the business must carefully consider how much it can raise prices without losing too many sales.

Supply

The *supply* of a good or service is the quantities that producers are willing to produce and sell at a given price. We are now asking a hypothetical question of firms as to what quantity the firm would produce given it could sell the output for a particular price. In principle, a firm may be willing to supply a given quantity of a good or service so long as the price it can sell that quantity for covers the costs of production.

EXAMPLE 11.4

Let's consider Aisha, the owner of the T-shirt market stall. She plans her business week by week and last week she printed 2,000 T-shirts at an average cost of £2.00, that is the total cost of printing the 2,000 T-shirts was £4,000 and found that she was able to sell all of the T-shirts at a price of £2.50, producing a revenue of £5,000 and profits of £1,000. In planning for the forthcoming week, she wonders if she should print more T-shirts.

A naive approach would be for Aisha to simply consider the average cost of production (£2.00), and decide that as she can sell the T-shirts at £2.50, she should print more. This may, however, lead to poor decision-making by Aisha as it does not reflect marginal analysis. She should consider whether the additional cost of printing another T-shirt is more or less than the additional revenue she would receive in selling that T-shirt, not the average cost. If the additional cost of printing a T-shirt is more than the price she will sell the T-shirt for, £2.50, printing and selling the additional T-shirt will reduce her profits.

As an example, if the cost of printing the additional T-shirt is £3, the total cost of production would then be £4,003. Selling the extra T-shirt will increase revenue to £5,002.50, however, the total profit, the difference between total revenue and cost, would then be £999.50, which is less than if she had stuck to printing only 2,000 T-shirts.

A firm's costs of production are made up of two key elements.

- A firm's **variable costs** are the costs that change with changes in the level of output: producing one more T-shirt requires an additional blank T-shirt to print on.
- A firm's **fixed costs,** however, do not change with the level of output, for instance, the cost of hiring a printing press for the week will not vary with the number of T-shirts printed.

Marginal thinking focuses on the variable costs when making decisions about the level of output. A firm will be willing to output, that is to supply, an additional unit of output so long as the price of that unit is at least the associated marginal cost of production of that unit. In a competitive market, where a firm is a **price taker**, the firm's profits will be maximised where it chooses to produce at a level where the marginal cost is equal to the price it can sell the good for. The way in which the marginal cost of the firm varies with the amount of product it produces will therefore determine the quantity the firm will supply at different prices.

As before when we considered demand, think about how you might predict a graph of a firm's supply to look. As the hypothetical price increases and you move up the vertical axis, should the quantity rise? That is, do you expect firms will supply more of a good as the price rises, and the plot of supply to slope upwards? Or, as the price increases, should the quantity fall? That is, do you expect firms will produce more of a good when it is cheaper, and the plot of supply to slope upwards?

Hopefully, you predicted that as the good gets more expensive, firms will produce more, and that the **supply curve** slopes upwards. This is typically the case, and is sometimes called the law of supply, which is that as the price of a good or service rises, the quantity supplied increases. The plot of quantities of the good or service that a firm will produce at different prices is called the *supply curve*.

Figure 11.2 illustrates the supply curve for T-shirts from a market stall. The figure shows at point 1, that if the price is £2.50, producers will supply 2,000 T-shirts, but at point 2, if the price is £5, suppliers will produce 4,000 T-shirts.

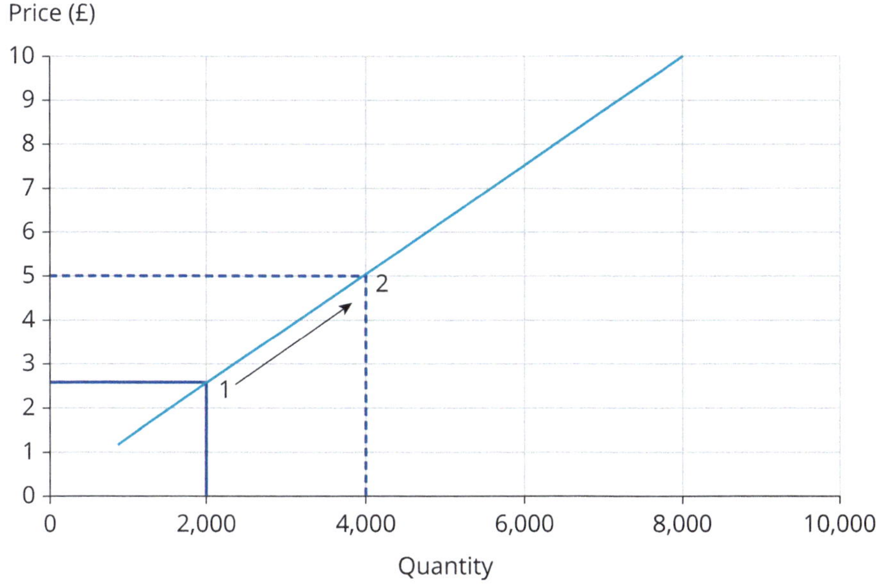

Figure 11.2 Illustration of supply curve in market for T-shirts

Market Equilibrium

Market equilibrium is the point where the quantity demanded by consumers matches the quantity supplied by producers, resulting in a stable equilibrium price and quantity. This concept is visually represented by the intersection of the supply and demand curves. At this intersection, there is no inherent tendency for the price to change unless there is a shift in supply or demand (Mankiw, 2023). Understanding market equilibrium is essential for comprehending how prices are determined in a market economy and how market dynamics function.

Let's examine market equilibrium in relation to the supply and demand of T-shirts discussed in the previous sections. Suppose there is a market for T-shirts where the demand and supply curves intersect at a specific point. This intersection represents the equilibrium where the market clears, meaning there is no excess supply (surplus) or excess demand (shortage). For instance, if the equilibrium is achieved at a point where 2,000 T-shirts are traded at a price of £2.50, this price and quantity reflect the balance between what consumers are willing to pay and what producers are willing to supply. The market equilibrium is illustrated as Point 1 in Figure 11.3.

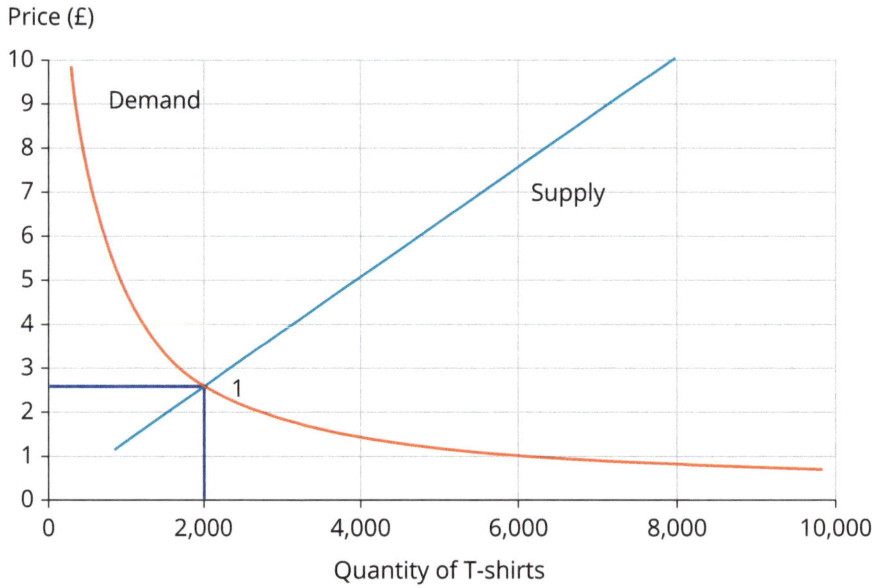

Figure 11.3 Illustration of equilibrium between supply and demand in a market for T-shirts

In our T-shirt market example, if the price were higher than £2.50, say £3.00, the quantity supplied would exceed the quantity demanded, leading to a surplus. Producers would then lower prices to clear the excess stock, moving the market back towards equilibrium. Conversely, if the price were lower than £2.50, say £2.00, the quantity demanded would exceed the quantity supplied, resulting in a shortage. Producers would raise prices in response to the high demand, again moving the market towards equilibrium.

Comparative Advantage

Comparative advantage is a fundamental concept in international trade theory, introduced by David Ricardo in the early 19th century. It states that even if one party is less efficient in producing all goods compared to another party, there can still be mutual benefits from trade. This is because comparative advantage considers opportunity cost – the cost of foregoing the next best alternative. When entities specialise in the production of goods and services where they have the lowest opportunity cost and trade with others, overall efficiency and welfare increase (Krugman et al., 2022).

EXAMPLE 11.5

Let's apply the concept of comparative advantage to Aisha, and her small T-shirt stall. Aisha is highly efficient at printing T-shirts but not as skilled at designing logos for them. Meanwhile, her friend runs a design studio and excels at creating unique logos but isn't as efficient at printing T-shirts. Although Aisha could try to manage both the printing and the design work herself, comparative advantage suggests that both Aisha and her friend would benefit more by specialising in what they do best.

Aisha should focus on printing T-shirts, where she is more efficient, while her friend should specialise in designing logos. By collaborating and trading - Aisha providing the printed T-shirts and her friend offering the designs - both will benefit. Aisha can sell better-designed T-shirts, potentially at higher prices, and her friend can focus on their design work without worrying about production.

Just as in international trade, by concentrating on the areas where each has the lowest opportunity cost, Aisha and her friend maximise their efficiency and profits. This leads to better business outcomes for both, demonstrating how the principle of comparative advantage works in real-world business decisions.

In the broader economy, comparative advantage drives trade between businesses, regions, or even countries, allowing them to specialise in what they are best at while benefiting from the goods or services others produce more efficiently. Just like Aisha's T-shirt business benefits from partnering with a design expert, countries benefit from trading with each other based on their unique strengths.

REFLECTIVE ACTIVITY 11.3

Imagine you are planning to increase spending on an online advertising strategy and must choose between one of two platforms. Your market research team tells you the average cost per customer that makes a purchase on each of the platforms.

- Why should you ask them for the marginal cost instead?

REFLECTIVE RESPONSE 11.3

You should ask for the marginal cost because it reflects the additional cost of acquiring each new (additional) customer as you increase spending. The average cost includes fixed costs spread across all customers, which doesn't show how costs change with more investment. Marginal cost helps you assess whether additional spending remains efficient and profitable.

MICROECONOMICS IN BUSINESS

Microeconomics plays a vital role in shaping the day-to-day decisions businesses make. It focuses on the behaviour of individual consumers, firms, and industries, examining how they allocate resources, set prices, and respond to market changes. In business, understanding microeconomic principles is crucial for effective decision-making.

This section will explore how businesses can use microeconomic tools to analyse their markets, set competitive prices, and optimise production strategies. Whether determining how much of a product to produce or identifying the best pricing strategy, microeconomics provides a framework for businesses to maximise profits while responding to competitive pressures and consumer needs. By applying these principles, companies can better position themselves to succeed in various market conditions.

Market Structures

Understanding **market structures** helps businesses make strategic decisions about pricing, marketing, and product differentiation. By recognising the structure of the market they are in, companies can tailor their approaches to stay competitive and meet their goals effectively.

Imagine you are opening a coffee shop in your neighbourhood. As you consider your business, two big questions arise: who are your competitors, and what kind of market are you entering? The structure of the market you are stepping into will influence everything from your pricing decisions to how you differentiate your coffee shop from others. Economists use the term *market structure* to describe the different competitive environments in which businesses operate.

Market structure plays a critical role in shaping business strategies because it determines the level of competition and the **market power** of each business. As introduced in the previous section, **perfect competition** is a market structure with many sellers and buyers, each offering similar products. However, most markets deviate from this ideal in significant ways, resulting in other types of structures, each affecting business strategies differently.

In a **monopoly**, one company has exclusive control over a product or service, often due to unique resources, patents, or government support. Imagine you are the only supplier of fresh water in a remote town. Since there are no alternatives, you can set prices without worrying about competition. However, monopolies are often regulated by governments to prevent excessively high prices and ensure the needs of society are met. Utilities, such as electricity or water suppliers, are common examples of regulated monopolies in many areas.

An **oligopoly** exists when a small number of large firms dominate a market, often seen in industries like airlines, mobile networks, or car manufacturing. In these markets, each company's actions can significantly impact its competitors. For example, if one airline drastically lowers its ticket prices, others may follow suit to avoid losing customers. In an oligopoly, businesses have substantial control over prices, but they must be strategic since competitors can quickly respond to any changes, leading to pricing wars or alliances.

Most small businesses, such as restaurants, operate within a **monopolistic competition** structure. In this type of market, many businesses offer similar but slightly differentiated products, giving them some control over pricing. For instance, your restaurant may be one of many in town, yet you can still draw in customers by creating a unique experience – perhaps by serving a signature dish, providing a stylish dining atmosphere, or offering exceptional service. Although there's competition, each restaurant can distinguish itself through its brand and customer experience, helping to build a loyal customer base even if its prices are slightly higher than nearby alternatives.

Market Power

In earlier sections, we discussed market equilibrium where firms act as 'price takers'. In such markets, businesses see the price of a good or service set by the market and adjust their supply based on that price. These firms have no influence over the market price, meaning they cannot adjust prices to increase profits or capture more market share – they simply accept the prevailing market price.

While this framework is useful for understanding simple, highly competitive markets, it does not apply to all businesses. In markets where firms have *market power*, the dynamics change. For instance, companies like Apple, which produces highly sought-after technology products, have significant market power due to strong consumer loyalty. Apple can influence prices because customers value the brand and are willing to pay a premium for its products. This ability to set prices gives them more control over revenues and profits.

For a firm with no market power – one that is a price taker – the revenue from a price increase is straightforward. If a firm sells 100 T-shirts at £10 each and the market price rises to £11, the firm earns an additional £100 in revenue simply from the price increase, assuming the quantity sold remains unchanged.

However, the situation becomes more complex when a firm has market power. In this case, the quantity sold depends on the price set by the firm. According to the law of demand, as prices rise, the quantity demanded typically falls. For example, if Aisha, who owns the T-shirt stall, raises her price from £10 to £11, she might sell fewer T-shirts – let's say the quantity sold drops from 100 to 98. In this case, the additional revenue from the price increase would only be £98, not the full £100, because the higher price reduced the quantity sold.

This provides an example of the use of marginal analysis in setting prices. Firms with market power must carefully consider whether a price increase will actually lead to higher profits. If the additional revenue generated by a price increase is greater than the additional costs, raising prices can improve profitability. However, if the revenue increase is offset by a larger reduction in sales, profits could fall.

For firms with market power, understanding how consumers react to price changes is essential. Strategic pricing, based on how sensitive customers are to price fluctuations, allows these firms to maximise their revenue and maintain a competitive edge. We will explore the role of consumer behaviour in pricing decisions in greater detail in the upcoming sections.

STRATEGY

In business, strategy revolves around planning and decision-making. **Leaders** must decide which markets to enter, which to exit, and how to respond to competitors. For example, Nokia held over 50% of the global mobile phone market in 2007, but due to strategic missteps and competitors like Apple and Samsung, its share dropped below 4% in just six years (Bouwman et al., 2014).

This scenario highlights that many markets are imperfectly competitive. Decisions made by one firm often influence those of others – a dynamic particularly relevant in markets where firms have power to set prices. To analyse these strategic interactions, economists use **game theory**, which studies interactions where the choices of one player affect the outcomes of others. The goal is often to discover the *Nash equilibrium*, where no player can improve their outcome by changing only their own strategy. Understanding and applying this theory can help businesses make optimal decisions in competitive contexts like pricing, advertising, and market entry (Tadelis, 2013).

Within game theory, two main categories of games are distinguished: *simultaneous games* and **sequential games**. In simultaneous games, players make decisions at the same time without knowledge of the other players' choices. These games are represented by a payoff matrix, which shows the payoffs for each combination of strategies chosen by the players.

Simultaneous Games

A classic example of a simultaneous game is two competing companies deciding whether to cut prices. Each company can choose to lower prices to attract more customers or keep prices steady to maintain higher profit margins. If both companies decide to cut prices, they may attract more customers overall but at lower profits, leading to a less favourable outcome for both. However, if both maintain their prices, they keep higher profits, benefiting collectively. This scenario illustrates the difficulty of achieving cooperation in competitive markets, as each company is tempted to lower prices to gain an advantage, even though mutual cooperation would lead to a better overall outcome. Another example is firms setting prices in an oligopoly. Suppose two firms must decide on pricing their products simultaneously. Each firm's profit depends on the price it sets and the price set by the competitor. If both firms set high prices, they achieve moderate profits. If one sets a high price while the other sets a low price, the firm with the low price captures a larger market share, gaining higher profits while the other incurs losses. If both set low prices, they achieve lower profits due to intense competition.

Sequential Games

Sequential games differ from simultaneous games in that players make decisions one after another, with later players having some **knowledge** of the earlier actions. These games are represented using decision trees, which map out the choices and possible outcomes at each stage. An example of a sequential game is a market entry decision. Suppose a new company is considering entering a market dominated by an incumbent firm. The incumbent can choose to either accommodate the entrant, leading to shared market profits, or engage in a price war to deter the entrant. The new company must consider the incumbent's likely response when deciding whether to enter the market. This sequential decision-making process illustrates the importance of anticipating competitor actions and planning strategies accordingly.

CASE STUDY 11.1

Game Theory in Action During the COVID-19 Vaccine Distribution

The COVID-19 pandemic presented an extraordinary test of global strategic decision-making, with governments, pharmaceutical companies, and individuals engaging in complex, interdependent actions. Through game theory, we can analyse the coordination, competition, and cooperation that shaped vaccine development, allocation, and acceptance.

During the early stages of the pandemic, pharmaceutical companies faced a simultaneous game in the race to develop vaccines. Decisions to invest heavily in research and development (R&D) were made independently, with significant stakes in financial gains, market dominance, and public health contributions. The dominant strategy for most firms was to prioritise R&D investment, as first-mover advantages could secure both substantial profits and a global health impact. This race resulted in rapid vaccine development and approval, exemplified by mRNA technology breakthroughs (Sachs et al., 2020).

Simultaneously, nations competed for limited vaccine supplies, reflecting another simultaneous game. Wealthier countries pre-purchased large quantities of doses, ensuring rapid access but creating inequities for lower-income nations. This dominant strategy of securing maximum doses highlighted the tension between national self-interest and global equity. It exposed disparities that hindered universal vaccine availability, emphasising the competitive dynamics in simultaneous games (Usher, 2021).

The rollout of vaccines involved sequential games, where governments and individuals made decisions influenced by the observed actions of others. Initially, governments prioritised high-risk groups, such as healthcare workers and the elderly, to maximise public health benefits. Countries monitored the success of early rollouts elsewhere and adopted similar strategies, learning from precedents to optimise their plans (Mathieu et al., 2021).

(Continued)

Public acceptance mirrored sequential games as well. Early adopters' willingness to get vaccinated shaped societal perceptions, reducing hesitancy among those initially sceptical. This cascading effect was pivotal in achieving higher vaccination rates, demonstrating how early moves in sequential games can influence broader behavioural trends and public health outcomes (Dror et al., 2020).

The COVID-19 vaccine distribution exemplifies the applicability of game theory to real-world crises. Simultaneous and sequential games underscored the interconnected nature of decisions made by pharmaceutical companies, governments, and individuals. These dynamics reveal the challenges of aligning individual incentives with collective outcomes in high-stakes scenarios.

Understanding these strategic interactions is vital for addressing global challenges, enabling better coordination, equitable resource allocation, and effective responses to crises. Game theory proves not just theoretical but essential in navigating complex societal issues.

Questions

1. How did the dynamics of simultaneous and sequential games influence global equity in vaccine distribution, and what strategies could have been implemented to achieve a more balanced outcome?
2. In the context of vaccine rollout and public acceptance, how can governments and public health organisations leverage insights from sequential games to combat vaccine hesitancy in future public health crises?
3. What role do incentives and first-mover advantages play in the strategic decisions of pharmaceutical companies, and how might these influence **innovation** and accessibility in global health emergencies?

Source

Sachs, J., Horton, R., Bagenal, J., Ben Amor, Y., Karadag, O., and Lafortune, G. (2020) 'Lancet COVID-19 Commission Statement on the occasion of the 75th session of the UN General Assembly', *The Lancet*, 396 (10257): 1102–24.

Product Differentiation

It is possible to think about markets in different ways. We could talk about the market for soft drinks, or the market for colas or the markets for specific types of colas, such as Coke or Pepsi. Focusing on the different types of colas, it is interesting to consider the economic approach to the differentiation of types of a product.

To economists, this is a story of the substitutability of different products. For the case of Coke and Pepsi, this represents to what degree consumers will switch their consumption of Coke to Pepsi if the price of Coke increases. If the two types of product are perfectly substitutable, that is consumers do not have a preference for one type of product compared to the other, then the consumer will only purchase the cheaper of the two. If the price of Coke rises above that of Pepsi, consumers will only buy Pepsi. However, if the two goods are not completely substitutable, then a price increase of one good will have an impact, lowering the quantity purchased for that good and increasing it for the other, but not result in a complete switch. When the different types of product are less substitutable, that is they are more differentiated, the impact of any switching from substitution of one good for the other will be reduced.

Price Discrimination

Earlier in this chapter, we noted that not all goods and services have a specific advertised price. You might have given some thought as to what types of goods and services this might apply to. Take a moment now to reconsider that and, importantly, question why firms might want to act in such a way? A simple case to consider might be a garage mechanic. Might they consider quoting the owner of a Skoda a different price to that of the owner of an Audi for the same repair?

If you think back to our description of the demand curve, it gives us information about what a consumer would be willing to pay for a good or service. In a market with a single price, consumers who have **willingness to pay** greater than the market price receive a degree of consumer surplus. A different version of the last question is to ask how might a firm transform consumer surplus into its profits; that is how could it act to get consumers, with a higher willingness to pay, pay a higher price? Methods to transfer consumer surplus into a firm's profits is known as **price discrimination**, and there are several different forms.

For firms, an ideal outcome would be where they could set a separate price for each individual according to that consumer's willingness to pay. This is clearly very difficult; consumers are often not satisfied when other people get a good for a lower price and would be reluctant to actually tell the firm the true value they would pay. The owner of an Audi may well be more willing to pay for a repair than the owner of a Skoda, but they may not be happy if they find out that was what happened.

However, in certain luxury markets, it may be possible. Take, as an example, luxury, bespoke, tailored holiday experiences. A given consumer may be prepared to accept a price for their willingness to pay for a seemingly unique product. This would allow the firm to transfer the consumer surplus that would arise from a market price to its own profits.

As noted before, such a form of price discrimination is typically very difficult. A more common approach is to segment different parts of the market that have different elasticities of demand. Common examples of this form of price discrimination would be cut-price offers on food to students on certain days of the week, or discounts to pensioners for holidays. Price discrimination of this form identifies a group with a more elastic demand for a product that can be separated from the rest of the market – e.g. with a student ID card or a pensioner's bus pass. The firm can then apply the mark up function to the different groups with different elasticates, producing different prices, that will increase profits relative to using the standard market elasticity.

A third form of price discrimination involves the use of menus. Not the type you get in a restaurant listing food, but rather a set of offers that bundle desirable features of a particular good or service with an associated price. One example is the vast array of different forms of mobile phone contract offered by any given vendor. Any particular contract will offer features such as a model of phone, an amount of **data**, an upfront versus monthly cost and a contract length. Such menus are designed to try and entice consumers with a higher willingness to pay to take up a more expensive, super bundle, offer. However, the contract design must be done in such a way that recognises if the basic offer designed for consumers with a low willingness to pay represents better value to consumers with a high willingness to pay than the alternative super bundle, they will take up the basic offer rather than the intended offer.

REFLECTIVE ACTIVITY 11.4

Some gyms offer different memberships with different levels of service (think gold or platinum service offerings with access to facilities such as a swimming pool included or not) that cost different amounts of money alongside basic pay per visit tariffs.

- How does this pattern relate to the concept of price discrimination?

REFLECTIVE RESPONSE 11.4

Gyms use price discrimination by offering different membership levels (e.g., gold or platinum) that cater to customers with varying willingness to pay. High-tier memberships with premium features target customers who value additional services and are willing to pay more. Basic pay-per-visit tariffs appeal to price-sensitive customers who might not otherwise join the gym.

By segmenting the market based on demand elasticity, gyms can maximise their revenue. Customers with inelastic demand for premium features pay higher prices, while those with elastic demand are still included in the customer base through lower-priced options. This strategy transforms potential consumer surplus into additional revenue for the business.

ECONOMICS FOR SOCIETY

Economics is not only about how businesses and consumers make decisions; it also plays a crucial role in society by influencing policies, resource allocation, and overall well-being. Economic activities, like production and trade, often have impacts that go beyond the people directly involved. These broader impacts can lead to both positive and negative outcomes for society as a whole.

Sometimes, markets do not allocate resources in a way that benefits everyone. For instance, a factory may produce goods efficiently, but if it pollutes the air, it creates problems for people living nearby. These unintended effects, or 'spillover effects,' are often called externalities. When these effects are ignored by the market, they can lead to market failures – situations where resources are not used in a way that maximises societal benefits.

Another issue that can lead to market failure is asymmetric information. This occurs when one party in a transaction has more or better information than the other. For example, if a car dealer knows about a hidden defect in a car but the buyer does not, the buyer may end up paying more than the car is worth. These information gaps can result in unfair or inefficient outcomes.

This section will focus on exploring why effective resource allocation in markets is essential for the overall well-being of society, how the unintended side effects of economic activities can create positive or negative impacts on communities, and how imbalances in information access can lead to market failures and unfair outcomes. Through examining these concepts, we'll see why understanding economics is essential not only for business success but also for promoting a fair and efficient society.

Efficiency

A central theory in economics is that competitive markets can produce outcomes that maximise societal welfare, typically termed *market efficiency*. One way to think about market efficiency is in terms of trade. Where market participants can come to a mutual agreement on the exchange of goods, we say that there is a gain from the trade, otherwise one or more of the parties would refuse to trade. An economy is efficient when prices reflect consumers' wants and producers' capabilities in such a way that the goods produced are all consumed in a way that means that there no further gains from trade. That is, there are no ways that any exchange of goods or changes in production could improve the situation of someone in the economy without making someone else worse off.

The real world, however, presents several challenges to this theory, as it is based on a model that simplifies many of the conditions and interactions that we typically observe in actual markets. For instance, firms having market power, as discussed above, can be seen as barriers to efficiency, as they will underproduce goods relative to the levels that would be seen in a competitive market. The firm does this as it can use market power to generate additional profits, however this may come at a wider cost to society. Governments often set up agencies, such as the Competition and Markets Authority, which are tasked with maintaining competitiveness in markets.

A further problem with the concept of market efficiency is that it says nothing about equity or fairness. Outcomes that are market efficient can be highly inequitable and such inequity may not actually be what a society would choose if it were able to. Questions that seek to consider what a government ought to do, such as to address issues of inequity in society and what the impact of such interventions would be, form a branch of economics known as **normative economics** that underpins studies of public **finance** and public policy (Gruber, 2022).

Externalities

Interactions between consumers and businesses, between different consumers and between different businesses characterise markets. The majority of such interactions work through prices; if a good becomes more fashionable or desirable, people will be willing to pay more for it. This will lead to more production of that good and less of a now relatively less desirable good and a reallocation within the economy. Such a shift can be viewed as markets performing their role in producing efficient outcomes.

Some interactions, however, sit outside markets and the price mechanism, forming an **externality**. An example of a negative externality, in that the activity places a cost on a third party outside of the price mechanism is pollution: in manufacturing a good a firm may produce pollutants that harm nearby residents and traffic congestion, and people commuting in cars do not consider the impact their car use has on other commuters. We can also consider positive externalities, where the interaction places a benefit on others, such as vaccinations or education. Vaccinated people help others by reducing the risk of a disease spreading; highly educated individuals may increase the productivity of people who work with them.

An important insight from the study of externalities is that goods that incur negative externalities will be over-produced relative to the socially desirable level, whereas goods with positive externalities will be under-produced. The presence of externalities can serve as an argument for government intervention in markets, as outcomes for society can be improved. Using the model of supply and demand, we can show that taxes can be used to increase the price of a good that creates pollution and thereby reduce the level of production. The tax revenue raised can be used to offset some of the damage caused by the pollution (Mankiw, 2023). A similar analysis can be used to show that subsidies can reduce the price and therefore promote further engagement with education, which is desirable given the presence of positive externalities that would not be accounted for under a market solution.

CASE STUDY 11.2

Soft Drinks Industry Levy: Sugar Taxes in the UK

It has recently been estimated that obesity costs the NHS £6.5 billion per year (Bell and Deyes, 2022). The consumption of various high calorie foodstuffs, notably soft drinks with a high sugar content, forms a major contributing factor to the rising prevalence of obesity in the UK.

We can view this as an externality in that the medical costs of people who go on to have health complications that require medical treatment relating to their consumption of sugary drinks are shared with other people who do not consume sugary drinks in the same way (Allcott et al., 2019).

The Soft Drinks Industry Levy, introduced in April 2018, aimed to reduce the consumption of high sugar drinks by raising the price of them relative to other, low sugar alternatives and to promote the reformulation of products with lower sugar content by manufacturers.

Evidence suggests that policy has achieved some of its aims, both in terms of reducing the quantity of sugary drinks purchased and consumed per household (Cobaic et al., 2024) and in leading to the reformulation of products with lower sugar content (Scarborough et al., 2020). An important additional feature, though, is that the increased price of drinks with a high sugar content better reflects the social damage the consumption of such products creates at market prices that do not account for the presence of the externality.

There are potentially other benefits from such a measure, in relation to improved productivity, lower social care costs and improved quality of life (Allcott et al., 2019). There is a potential further argument for action by government to prevent its citizens from the self-harm induced by the consumption of sugary drinks, though libertarian thinkers would strongly reject such an argument.

Questions

1. How effective do you think the Soft Drinks Industry Levy has been in addressing the negative externalities associated with high sugar consumption, and what additional measures might strengthen its impact?
2. To what extent should governments intervene in personal consumption habits, such as sugary drink consumption, to protect public health, and how can such interventions balance public welfare with individual freedoms?

Sources

Allcott, H. Lockwood, B.B., and Taubinsky, D. (2019) 'Should we tax sugar-sweetened beverages? An overview of the theory and evidence', *Journal of Economic Perspectives*, 33 (3): 202-27.

Bell, M. and Deyes, K. (2022) 'Estimating the full costs of obesity: A report for Novo Nordisk', *Frontier Economics Report*, 26 January. https://www.frontier-economics.com/uk/en/news-and-articles/articles/article-i9130-the-annual-social-cost-ofobesity-in-the-uk (accessed September 18, 2025).

Asymmetric Information

In the world of economics, information asymmetry plays a crucial role in shaping market dynamics (Akerlof, 1970). This concept arises when one party in a transaction possesses more or superior information than the other. Such disparities can lead to *adverse selection,* a situation where one party withholds vital information that could significantly influence the transaction outcome.

Consider the market for used cars. Here, sellers often have a more comprehensive understanding of their vehicles' history and potential issues than prospective buyers. This knowledge gap can create a scenario where buyers assume that all used cars are of low quality. Consequently, they tend to offer only low prices, deterring sellers of high-quality vehicles from participating in the market. As a result, a market that should thrive on a variety of options may become saturated with low-quality goods, as sellers with better vehicles withdraw from the competition.

This situation exemplifies how information asymmetry can lead to inefficiencies in the market, including the phenomenon of **moral hazard**. Moral hazard occurs when one party takes on greater risks because they do not bear the full consequences of those risks. A common example is insurance. Suppose you buy car insurance that covers all damages regardless of fault. Feeling protected, you might drive less carefully, knowing the insurer will pay for any accidents. The risk increases for the insurer because your behaviour changes after the transaction. Moral hazard can also appear in businesses where employees might misuse company resources because they don't own the business and don't feel the full impact of their actions.

A related concept that stems from information asymmetry is the **principal-agent problem**, which is particularly relevant for management students. This dilemma arises from the conflict of interest and the imbalance of information between the principal – who delegates authority – and the agent, who acts on behalf of the principal.

In corporate settings, shareholders (the principals) hire managers (the agents) to operate the company. However, these managers may prioritise personal goals, such as enjoying perks or maximising short-term bonuses, over the long-term interests of shareholders. This misalignment can lead to decisions that are detrimental to the company's health and the shareholders' investments.

To address the principal-agent problem, businesses often implement strategies such as performance-based incentives, monitoring systems, and alignment mechanisms like **stock** options or profit-sharing schemes. However, these solutions can introduce their own challenges and costs.

CASE STUDY 11.3

Principal-Agent Problem in the 1MDB Scandal

The 1Malaysia Development Berhad (1MDB) scandal highlights the principal-agent problem, where misaligned incentives between agents (government officials and executives) and principals (Malaysian citizens) led to massive fraud and corruption. The scandal exposed how weak governance and lack of oversight allowed agents to misappropriate billions of dollars (Jones, 2020). 1MDB, founded in 2009 by Prime Minister Najib Razak, was intended to foster economic development through global investments. However, key figures siphoned off large sums, leading to allegations of embezzlement and money laundering, and culminating in a global scandal.

Principal-Agent Dynamics

Government Officials and Citizens (Principals): The Malaysian government and its people trusted 1MDB to invest the country's wealth in strategic projects for long-term economic benefit.

Najib Razak and 1MDB Executives (Agents): The agents, including Najib Razak, former 1MDB executives, and business associates, had incentives to misappropriate the funds for personal enrichment, diverting billions of dollars into various schemes including luxury goods, real estate, and bribes.

Through complex financial dealings, the executives and their associates misled auditors, investors, and the Malaysian public, hiding the true nature of the transactions. They falsely represented 1MDB's financial position and used the fund to finance lavish lifestyles, including the purchase of artwork, real estate, and even funding for the production of the Hollywood film *The Wolf of Wall Street*.

The misappropriation of funds was initially hidden through a combination of false accounting, fake investments, and fraudulent loans. The scandal was uncovered in 2015 when a series of investigative reports and leaks exposed the theft. The fallout included investigations from international regulators, a significant loss of public trust in the Malaysian government, and a major international money-laundering case.

Consequences

Financial Impact: The scandal caused massive financial losses, with billions of dollars stolen. The crisis also strained Malaysia's financial reputation on the international stage, leading to audits, investigations, and the eventual arrest and conviction of several key figures involved in the scandal, including Najib Razak (Teichmann and Falker, 2021).

Political Fallout: The scandal led to widespread protests, a shift in political power in Malaysia, and the eventual removal of Najib Razak from office. His successor, Mahathir Mohamad, who had previously served as Malaysia's Prime Minister, promised to bring those responsible for the scandal to justice (Jones, 2020).

Questions

1. How can governments and other principal **stakeholders** ensure that executives and agents act in their best interests when managing public funds?
2. What role do transparency and monitoring mechanisms play in preventing large-scale financial scandals in state-owned enterprises?

Sources

Jones, D.S. (2020) '1MDB corruption scandal in Malaysia: A study of failings in control and accountability', *Public Administration and Policy*, 23 (1): 59–72.

Teichmann, F.M.J. and Falker, M.-C. (2021) 'The 1MDB case and the Swiss banking sector', *Journal of Money Laundering Control*, 24 (2): 278–90. doi.org/10.1108/JMLC-04-2020-0037

REFLECTIVE ACTIVITY 11.5

Climate change represents one of the largest challenges facing the world today.

- How might you frame the debate around climate change in relation to the concept of externalities?
- How does this link to the idea of a carbon pricing?

REFLECTIVE RESPONSE 11.5

Climate change is a result of negative externalities, where the production and consumption of goods (e.g., burning fossil fuels) impose costs on third parties (e.g., health issues, environmental degradation). These costs are not reflected in the market prices, leading to overproduction of harmful goods and underproduction of sustainable alternatives.

Carbon pricing, such as carbon taxes or cap-and-trade systems, internalises these externalities by attaching a cost to carbon emissions. By increasing the price of carbon-intensive goods, producers and consumers are incentivised to reduce emissions, promoting sustainable practices.

This approach aligns market outcomes with societal goals, aiming to achieve a socially optimal level of carbon emissions. It also generates revenue that can be reinvested in green technologies or used to mitigate the impact on affected communities.

CHAPTER SUMMARY

- The chapter introduces key principles like opportunity cost, marginal analysis, and consumer surplus, providing a framework for understanding economic decision-making at individual and business levels.
- Microeconomics examines resource allocation, market behaviour, and pricing strategies for businesses, using tools like supply and demand, market structures, and elasticity to optimise decision-making.
- Market structures such as perfect competition, monopoly, oligopoly, and monopolistic competition shape business strategies, pricing, and differentiation.
- Pricing strategies like market power, price discrimination, and marginal analysis help businesses maximise profits while adapting to consumer behaviour.
- Externalities, both positive and negative, impact resource allocation and highlight the need for government intervention.
- Game theory helps businesses analyse competitive interactions and strategic decision-making.
- Macroeconomic factors such as inflation, unemployment, and **globalisation** influence long-term business strategies and economic growth.

- Asymmetric information leads to issues like adverse selection, moral hazard, and the principal-agent problem, with strategies to mitigate these problems.
- Sustainability in economics aligns with the Sustainable Development Goals, focusing on responsible production, decent work, and infrastructure innovation.
- Economics plays a key role in policymaking, addressing inequities, externalities, and inefficiencies to create a fair and sustainable economy.

STUDENTS LIKE YOU CHANGE THE WORLD

Sanmarie Grobler and Tom Trow - Bazoo

Figure 11.4 Sanmarie Grobler and Tom Trow - Bazoo

Sanmarie Grobler (BA Liberal Arts) and Tom Trow (BSc Business Economics) are the innovative co-founders behind Bazoo, innovating responsibly and providing a sustainable alternative to regular toilet paper and other household products. They set out to create an environmentally-friendly product that would make a positive impact on the planet, and the brand is now loved by over 28,000 customers.

The University of Exeter's Student Startup programme provided resources, guidance and grant funding to turn their ambitious idea into a thriving business. Bazoo were also joint winners in the Environmentally Conscious category at the 2021 Student Startup Awards.

Today, Bazoo is making waves in the eco-friendly market with its bamboo toilet paper, which is 100% FSC-certified, and packaged in plastic-free, recyclable packaging. The company also protect 100m^2 of endangered habitats for every box sold, by partnering with Rainforest Trust UK, and so far have helped protect over 1,000,000,000m^2 of endangered habitat, an area equivalent to more than 3,952 tennis courts.

Sanmarie and Tom's commitment to sustainability and innovation exemplifies how young entrepreneurs can make a significant positive impact on the environment and inspire others to follow suit.

Sources

Blunt, E. (2021) 'Exeter graduates launch world's first carbon-negative loo roll company', *SETsquared*. https://www.setsquared.co.uk/exeter-graduates-launch-worlds-first-carbon-negative-loo-roll-company/ (accessed October 27, 2025).

University of Exeter (2025) 'Success stories: For Good – Bazoo', *University of Exeter*. https://www.exeter.ac.uk/research/centres/entrepreneurship/studentstartups/successstories/ (accessed October 27, 2025).

END OF CHAPTER REFLECTION

Have a look at the skills you should have developed in this unit (find more details in the Key Skills Table in the Appendix on p. 505).

1 Which of the skills listed do you think you have developed the most?
2 Can you give two examples on why you feel you have now developed these skills/developed them further?
3 How will you use these new/refined skills in the future (give two examples of the impact of your development on your future behaviour)?

FURTHER READING

Froeb, L.M., McCann, B.T., Shor, M., and Ward, M.R. (2023). *Managerial Economics: A Problem Solving Approach* (6th edition). Cengage Learning.

This book offers an excellent extension of the key principles presented in this chapter, with a particular emphasis on applications in business and management. It presents economic concepts through a practical, problem-solving approach relevant to managerial decision-making.

Conway, E. (2022) *50 Economics Ideas You Really Need To Know*. Quercus.

A clear and engaging introduction to key concepts in economics, ideal for readers seeking accessible explanations of fundamental ideas.

Samuelson, P.A. and Nordhaus, W.D. (2009) *Microeconomics* (19th edition). McGraw-Hill.

A classic and authoritative textbook that develops the fundamental ideas of economics in depth. It explores core principles such as supply and demand, market equilibrium, and the behaviour of consumers and firms.

Krugman P.A. and Wells, R. (2018) *Economics* (5th edition). Worth.

This comprehensive textbook offers a modern overview of economic theory and practice. It connects core principles with contemporary economic challenges and real-world policy applications.

Tadelis, S. (2013) *Game Theory: An Introduction*. Princeton University Press.

This book is an excellent introductory guide to the application of strategy through the use of game theory.

REFERENCES

Akerlof, G. (1970) 'The market for lemons: Quality uncertainty and the market mechanism', *Quarterly Journal of Economics*, 84 (3): 488–500.

Bouwman, H., Carlsson, C., Carlsson, J.P., Nikou, S., Sell, S., and Walden, P. (2014) 'How Nokia failed to nail the Smartphone market', 25th European Regional Conference of the International Telecommunications Society (ITS): 'Disruptive Innovation in the ICT Industries: Challenges for European Policy and Business', Brussels, Belgium, June 22nd–25th 2014, International Telecommunications Society (ITS), Calgary.

Case, K.E., Fair, R.C. and Oster S.M. (2012) *Principles of Economics* (10th Edition). Prentice Hall.

Cobaic, L.J., Rogers, N.T., Adams, J., Cummins, S., Smith, R., Mytton, O., White, M., and Scarborough, P. (2024) 'Impact of the UK soft drinks industry levy on health and health inequalities in children and adolescents in England: An interrupted time series analysis and population health modelling study', *PLoS Medicine*, 28: article #e1004371. doi.org/10.1371/journal.pmed.1004371

Dror, A.A., Eisenbach, N., Taiber, S., Morozov, N.G., Mizrachi, M., Zigron, A., Srouji, S., and Sela, E. (2020) 'Vaccine hesitancy: The next challenge in the fight against COVID-19', *European Journal of Epidemiology*, 35 (8): 775–9.

Gruber, J. (2022) *Public Finance and Public Policy* (7th edition). Worth.

Krugman P.A. and Wells, R. (2018). *Economics* (5th edition). Worth.

Krugman, P.A., Obstfeld, M., and Melitz, M.J. (2022) *International Economics: Theory and Policy.* (12th edition). Pearson Education.

Mankiw, N.G. (2023) *Principles of Economics* South-Western College Publishing.

Mathieu, E., Ritchie, H., Ortiz-Ospina, E., Roser, M., Hasell, J., Appel, C., Giattino, C., and Rodés-Guirao, L. (2021) 'A global database of COVID-19 vaccinations', *Nature Human Behaviour*, 5, 947–53. doi.org/10.1038/s41562-021-01122-8

McConnell, C.R., Brue, S.L., and Flynn, S.M. (2018) *Economics: Principles, Problems, and Policies*. McGraw-Hill Education.

Samuelson, P.A. and Nordhaus, W.D. (2009) *Microeconomics* (19th edition). McGraw-Hill.

Scarborough, P., Adhikari, V., Harrington R.A., Elhussein, A., Briggs, A., Rayner, M. [...] and White, M. (2020) 'Impact of the announcement and implementation of the UK Soft Drinks Industry Levy on sugar content, price, product size and number of available soft drinks in the UK, 2015–19: A controlled interrupted time series analysis', *PLoS Medicine*, 17 (2): article #e1003025.

Tadelis, S. (2013) *Game Theory: An Introduction*. Princeton University Press.

Usher, A.D. (2021) 'A beautiful idea: How COVAX has fallen short', *The Lancet*, 397 (10292): 2322–5. doi.org/10.1016/S0140-6736(21)01367-2

Varian (2014) *Intermediate Microeconomics: A Modern Approach* (9th edition). W.W. Norton.

World Health Organization (WHO) (2021) 'COVAX: Working for global equitable access to COVID-19 vaccines', *WHO*. https://www.who.int/initiatives/act-accelerator/covax (accessed September 18, 2025).

12
AI, DIGITAL TECHNOLOGY, AND TRANSFORMATION

Shirley Atkinson, Beth Kewell, and David Walker

INTENDED LEARNING OUTCOMES

After reading this chapter you should be able to:

1. Understand and appreciate data and the different types of data sources encountered in daily life.
2. Explain the significance of data, its role in the digital economy and impact upon modern life.
3. Assess the benefits and risks associated with AI augmented technologies considering their impact on data privacy, economic growth and societal well-being.

SUSTAINABLE DEVELOPMENT GOALS

In this chapter, we address the following SDGs:

- SDG 2: Zero Hunger – By collecting data on food consumption, production and supply chains, better decisions can be made to optimise food systems.
- SDG 3: Good Health and Well-being – Tracking health metrics and making personalised recommendations can empower individuals to take control of their well-being to lead healthier lives.
- SDG 4: Quality Education – AI and data help personalise education while skills covered in this chapter go beyond education into key employability skills.
- SDG 9: Industry, Innovation and Infrastructure – Data is a driver of innovation and economic growth.
- SDG 11: Sustainable Cities and Communities – Data and AI help transform community experiences.

- SDG 12: Responsible Consumption and Production - Understanding the use of data, analytics and AI resource use can be optimised, waste in supply chains reduced and transparency in production and consumption patterns can be improved.
- SDG 13: Climate Action - There is a need to mitigate the environmental impact of data-intensive technologies and this chapter emphasises the need for sustainable practices.

INTRODUCTION

This chapter provides you with the **knowledge** and **skills** to appreciate what is involved in **data creation**, as well as what can happen when data is deployed in real-world situations, where human and organisational dynamics come into play. In this chapter, we look at the science and application of data, as the foundational '**commodity**' of the 21st century and the basis for its ever-growing **Digital Economy** (The Economist, 2017). The chapter will explain why it is important that everyone gains an education in data – including learning how to work with it in a technical way to write code, and how to store and safeguard data effectively while aiming to put this information to use, productively and ethically. This chapter will introduce you to data and why it matters before looking at our reliance on data. We take you through concepts of concern, why we should be careful about our data before looking at how it fuels economic growth. From these foundations we look at analytics, the role of statistics and coding before considering storage of data in databases, linked and **open data** before finally considering the impact of AI in our decision-making, creation of content and application to working life.

Digital World

In engaging with previous chapters of the book, you will have already developed a familiarisation with the increasingly interrelated topics of **Artificial Intelligence (AI)**, **Digital Technology** and **Digital Transformation**.

You may have noted that the evolution of AI is part of a wider story, following in the footsteps of other digital **innovations** born of the '**4th Industrial Revolution**', for example, robotics, 3-D printing and scanning, smart manufacturing, 5G, and **blockchain**. Notably, each of these examples is reliant in one way or another on vast data sets accrued within computer mainframes, cloud storage facilities, and **edge devices** (peripherals capable of processing data).

The AI systems currently grabbing so much public attention are but the latest incarnation of a 'data-driven' digital technology revolution, which uses massive amounts of information gathered and stored electronically as fuel for performing information processing tasks at high speed (The Economist, 2017).

Everything in the digital world relies on digital data. Much of your education at university will involve learning about data – how it is created and put to use in industry, the economy and society; how it is quantified and qualified; what we need to know about its calibration and deployment; as well as the potential opportunities and hazards it represents and how it continues to change the world!

We could not do justice to this multiplicity in a single chapter. Our intention is instead to offer you a guide to two modes of learning that you will encounter whilst studying for a university degree:

1 Learning through **data creation:** as seen in computer engineering and data science. The whys and wherefores of data, how to collect it, prepare it and analyse it effectively; and increasingly design and program computers to do much of this work for us, at scale.
2 Learning about **deployment-in-the-wild**: this covers what we do with data once it is ready for use 'in-the-wild' by which we mean how it is put to use in people's homes, work environments, the cities we live in, and society at large.

Digital data is especially significant to business, providing managers with the information they need to keep processes moving and make changes where necessary. It is in this context that data can be deployed in ways that transform what businesses do – and how they do it – leading to an outcome known as '**business model** transformation.'

What Is Data and Why Does It Matter?

Data is everywhere, and everyone leaves a data trail whether they like it or not! Data is in constant use everywhere you look, in all the devices we rely on, from the things we wear to the mobile phones and tablets we carry. Our cars and home energy systems help make life more liveable, and transport systems, smart cities and communications infrastructures keep us on the move and in contact with one another. It is a small wonder that we sometimes forget that our 'digital world' is dependent on tiny packets of data, organised in a binary fashion (i.e. as zeros and ones) and transmitted between machines.

At a finite level data is a single byte (a tiny unit of memory that stores information and therefore value). During the 21st century, we have learned to do some truly wonderous – and terrifying – things by combining millions of these tiny data points into a flow of computerised energy. A 'fuel' that some have described as the 'new oil,' which generates and feeds our appetites for new knowledge, new innovations and new forms of wealth creation (The Economist, 2017). In founding the digital culture we are part of, data has also become embroiled in some notable ethical debacles and cautionary tales. Our discussion includes learning from these events and understanding how we deal with the ethical challenges of handling data.

Data is the collection and storage of facts and numbers about things that you care about that can be kept on file and used for analytical purposes later on. These facts and numbers can be words, numerals or even images.

Stored data keeps a record of the activities we have created and the events we have experienced. Consider for a moment the last meal you ate. If you were trying to manage your health, you might want to record some facts about that meal. Maybe you want to know how many calories it contained, or the different elements of nutrition, or maybe you are watching your budget and need to know the cost of it. All of these facts are data.

Data is a collection of recordable observations. By the time we arrived at the mid-2010s the ability to save, store and process huge amounts of data meant we had recorded so much that the era has been referred to as a 'Data Age'. Our modern life is fuelled by data agreements, certainly if you consider Clay Shirky's assertion that the internet is 'just a set of agreements about how to move data between two points' (Shirky, 2010: 10).

Data allows us to see what works and does not. We can use it to make better informed decisions about our own health or care for the planet. For example, we can create data to benefit improved health outcomes. The UN Sustainable Development Goals (SDGs) look towards ending hunger, enabling food security and promoting sustainable agriculture. Collecting data about what we eat, how it is produced, where the raw ingredients are obtained from, shipped and stored will help us move towards achieving those goals. We can use the data to make better choices, help people lead healthier lives and adjust the **supply** and production of food to meet those SDGs.

To work effectively, data must keep flowing. Indeed, much of modern life relies on continuous data flows to keep systems up to date and prevent bottlenecks from hampering the delivery of goods and services, for example, where food outlets rely on deliveries of raw ingredients.

CASE STUDY 12.1

Kentucky Fried Chicken

Consider when 800 of 870 Kentucky Fried Chicken (KFC) stores in the UK ran out of chicken. The data from the KFC ordering system failed to synchronise with their new logistic provider's software, meaning that chicken was not properly ordered and the supply chain collapsed, providing an interesting case example of what can go wrong when data is deployed in-the-wild (Young and Bhattacharyya, 2024).

> This critical incident describes a situation faced by Meghan Farren, Chief Marketing Officer for KFC in the UK. When she learned of missed chicken deliveries to several restaurant locations, it surfaced as a delay from a traffic backup involving two accidents. On that same morning, DHL launched its new delivery service, becoming KFC's sole logistics provider for UK and Ireland. The accidents had masked what was about to come. DHL had failed to deliver chicken as promised. Approximately 800 KFC locations closed their doors having run out of chicken. For Farren, the crisis could cripple the chain and damage the relationship with its franchisees. While KFC looked to DHL to fix the supply problem, Farren was primarily concerned about the franchisees. Students are asked to recommend actions Farren can take to mitigate the ongoing damage to the franchisees and assist them in welcoming customers back to stores when reopened.

Questions

1. What are the potential risks and challenges associated with combining and synchronising data from different systems held by different organisations?
2. How might these risks be mitigated to prevent supply chain disruption?
3. What approaches could help identify potential solutions?

Source

Young, J. and Bhattacharyya, K. (2024) 'No chicken at KFC: A logistics debacle?', in Sage Business Cases. Sage. https://doi.org/10.4135/9781071945285.

Data has driven much of the innovation we see around us. Many of us use apps and software to navigate our way through daily life. Recommendations are given based on our previous usage of that software. More 'intelligence' is incorporated into the software; we now have artificial intelligence (AI) affecting much of what we do. AI needs data to work and can't work without it.

Data Trails

The ability to store large quantities of data whilst allowing easy access has changed the way we can work.

REFLECTIVE ACTIVITY 12.1

Reflect for a moment on the many and varied data sources in modern life, and consider the data trail that you might have created this morning.

- Did you check your social media accounts earlier today? Any posts, likes or shares would have been recorded and attributed to your profile.
- You may have walked past some sensors recording the temperature, humidity, or even number of people in a room or on a street.
- Increasingly CCTV cameras have facial recognition abilities and images and video are saved to remote servers.
- Perhaps you took a photo on your smartphone to send to someone you know or upload to your social media.
- You might have made a purchase that would have created transactional data and added it to knowledge about your purchasing habits as well as how much money you have in your account.
- All of this is likely to be logged on a server somewhere. Many of the apps you use on your smartphone log activity, connect via the cellular network and upload their data for further processing.

Big Data

This is the rise of Big Data. Data is 'big' if it is high volume, has a variety of formats or data types, and if it varies regularly. It is frequently used to analyse consumer behaviour and identify **marketing** trends. Increasingly wearable technologies allow us to record our heart rate, identify the best way to exercise, nudge us when we may have been sitting down for too long. Aggregation of data, especially in the financial arena, allows for better fraud identification. Is there a pattern of spending on your bank card that seems odd? This could allow the bank to stop any authorisation on further spending.

Cloud Computing

Corporations are increasingly turning to **cloud computing** to store their data and manage their IT infrastructure. They have moved away from investing in people and on-premises hardware instead to outsourcing the work to companies with data storage and management expertise. At the time of writing there are four major companies controlling two-thirds of the global cloud data market: Amazon, Google, Microsoft and Alibaba Cloud.

Aggregating a large amount of something provides for new **behaviours**. New communications in the early 2010s aggregated the individual's ability to create and share. Following quickly on, cloud data storage has enabled corporate data to be widely shared and processed by a global audience.

The cloud storage provider handles scalability – the ability of the technology to handle millions of connections without failing. As a company engages with a worldwide audience, they no longer have to worry about whether their data can be accessed by everybody – that is handled by those with the knowledge and ability. This is good example of data being used, in-the-wild, to make changes to the way we live and work, sometimes upending existing conventions about the way things are done, in a process known as **digital disruption**.

REFLECTIVE ACTIVITY 12.2

When digital technologies are introduced, they can cause people to think differently about the way things are organised.

At present, AI is a major 'disruptor' in our world. The widespread uptake of ChatGPT has, for instance, rapidly changed how universities teach and assess students.

- Do you think that students should be allowed to use AI assistants in their studies?
- Should universities step in and regulate their use?

Sometimes digital disruption can prove to be transformative, as in the case of remote working that became a reality after the introduction of cloud storage systems that all authorised employees could access – taking away that sinking feeling that an important piece of data is held on a machine back at the office and inaccessible – unless of course of you forgot to upload it to the cloud service.

Companies can link different offices globally, allowing their global teams to properly collaborate across the world in a way that means data is more secure and robust. Data can be processed in real time – no lengthy delays in obtaining it.

A further implication of easier access to data has meant a wider range of software tools to analyse the data came into play. Better views of the data that are more relevant to the people who need it can be provided.

INFORMED TRUST: CRITICAL APPROACHES TO DATA

As we have seen so far, there are enormous benefits to be gained from harvesting large quantities of data and storing them digitally in the cloud environment. However, as with everything we do, the acts of creating and deploying data come with significant risks. How do you know whether to trust some data or information? **Critical thinking** skills are crucial in a world where data can be presented in so many ways.

Disinformation

Creating content for people to see online is easily done with social media – for example short video clips can be uploaded easily to social media sites such as TikTok, YouTube, Instagram or Facebook. This ease of uploading for all to see can help promote **disinformation**. There are those who would act maliciously, plant deceitful comments and seek others to spread those comments further to create disinformation. Dias Ruiz and Nilsson (2023) provide a definition of disinformation:

> An adversarial campaign that weaponizes multiple rhetorical strategies and forms of knowing.

Beyond active spreading of disinformation we must also consider how data is collected, stored and analysed because mistakes can easily be magnified and in turn cause **misinformation** (see later in this chapter). Makin and Orban de Xivry (2019) provide a list of ten common mistakes made when publishing scientific data that lead to wrong assumptions. These include the absence of a proper control group, misinterpreting comparisons between effects without direct comparisons, using inflated units of analysis, spurious correlations, small sample sizes, circular analysis, flexibility of analysis (p-hacking), failing to correct for multiple comparisons, over-interpreting non-significant results, and confusion between correlation and causation.

This is why data has always been a factor in assessing risk; providing the inputs needed to reduce uncertainty, clarify ambiguities, plug knowledge gaps, improve prediction **modelling**, and generate more accurate forecasts, so that we may represent the world around us as effectively as possible.

Good Quality Data

To do this well, we need to identify the right kinds of good-quality data, from the sources of insight around us. Up until the invention of home PCs and the internet (mid-1980s to mid-1990s), scientists acquired all of the data needed for risk modelling from natural sources and human observations in the physical world, often referred to as 'In Real Life' or **IRL**. In the current era, our sources of data include everything IRL plus a vast realm of generated and synthesised information generated from online sources.

Some years before the first 'hello world' email was sent, the French philosopher Baudrillard argued that there would be a blurring of boundaries between physical reality (the IRL) and the virtual realm (Baudrillard, 1994). His argument was that '**Hyperreality**', as he termed it, was a place where simulations or representations of reality replaced the original experience of reality to become more real. We might consider this in relation to the rise of **generative AI**:

- Artificial worlds, generated art, deep fake videos can create simulations that will mimic human creativity, thought, and interaction.
- Blurring of boundaries between creation and authorship. When algorithms blend with human input we can see a challenge to traditional notions of authorship.
- AI systems can present a version of reality in a convincing way leading to situations where truth cannot be determined from illusion. Ethical concerns therefore arise.

This fusion of simulation and reality is a data-driven phenomenon. For emails to be sent, posts shared, and avatars created, binary data packets must be processed and exchanged. Each click or movement of a mouse or screen pointer generates a data trail that serves various purposes, extending well beyond monitoring and maintenance. Many of these purposes are tied to monetisation strategies and behavioural tracking. (See Chapter 6.)

Hyperreality, as described above, does have an effect on the way we perceive risk and uncertainty, sometimes making it difficult to discern reliable information from hyperbole. It is important to reflect further on how representations in the media (social or otherwise) shape people's view of risk and uncertainty, for example dangerous risks encountered in daily life and any tolerance for them (Dragin et al., 2022; Haidt and Schmidt, 2023).

REFLECTIVE ACTIVITY 12.3

- How do you get your information about the world?
- How are risks portrayed in the media you consume?

Prior to the mass consumption of computing power in terms of personal computers and digital devices, life was viewed through single viewpoints. Everyday existence frequently was filtered either by television, newspapers, radio, books or film. The information resided in 'silos' where people could hop between them. This was the traditional media. It was, and still is, governed by strict editorial policies providing what could be perceived as 'authoritative voices' to aid understanding of the risks that society faced. This was referred to by Bell back in 1980 as the 'analogue' instantiation of the Information Society (Bell, 1980).

The growth of digital media has exponentially increased the number of available viewpoints while also making it more difficult to check their validity. Navigating the messaging we see under hyper-real conditions therefore requires a much greater level of **digital literacy** than during the analogue phase of the Information Society. There were clear boundaries that allowed us to accept or reject, ignore or question these voices of authority, depending on the evidence, expertise, or opinions being presented. Beck's 1992 landmark thesis *The Risk Society* presents the idea of 'reflexive modernity' – a situation where traditional values and structures are questioned. For example, *behavioural economics* is the discipline of understanding why we make the decisions we do (Heukelom, 2007) including an analysis of why we do dangerous things, despite knowing they are bad for us (Lupton, 1999; Lupton, 2018). Instead of simply accepting statements of risk and uncertainty, people critically reflect and react accordingly. Without these boundaries, it has become far more difficult to tell whether a viewpoint is factually correct. It is also far more difficult to tell whether a comment or finding is based on 'good' or 'bad' data, unless we have very high levels of digital literacy, such as those you will acquire when studying data science and **data analytics** at degree level or when taking a social science, humanities or business studies module designed to make you more aware of misinformation and its consequences for understanding the biases behind racism, sexism, religious prejudice, social exclusion or belief in conspiracy theories.

Accepting that something was deemed risky and harmful relied on the quality of the data collected combined with our ability to interpret the data for ourselves, allowing positive changes in society and better viewpoints of behaviour (Beck et al., 1994).

This critical thinking has become ever more important in our own time such that we have come to rely increasingly on **data-driven** techniques to establish the validity and reliability of data, for example, in Behavioural Economics, which uses behavioural data to better understand why we make the decisions we do (Heukelom, 2007) or Design Science, where **machine learning** techniques are used to identify potential faults in consumer goods, such as car seats and running shoes.

Risk Analysis

Risk Analysis is the systematic process of identifying, assessing and predicting problems based on data to inform decision-making and to manage uncertainty. Risk Analysis is crucial for ensuring that the business continues to operate and that anything that is of importance to the business is protected. Figure 12.1 illustrates how this has changed over time.

Traditionally, this process would be carried out using structured and verified data to estimate the likelihood of adverse events. In addition, data could be tested using principles such as Karl Popper's principle of falsifiability (Popper, 2005 [1959]), where it must be possible to prove a hypothesis false to be scientifically valid. For example, a financial institution would use historical, traceable data to model and quantify risks such as market volatility, project failures or natural disasters.

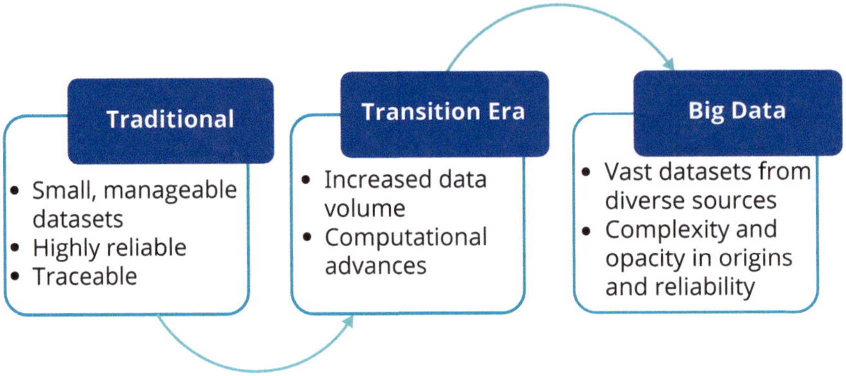

Figure 12.1 Timeline for risk analysis

Source: Author

The growth of Big Data, from circa 2012, provided the ability to use huge, diverse and less structured datasets. Figure 12.1 alludes to this time as the transitional era. Analysts could use vast pools of data to refine their predictive models and identify patterns across many more elements (Hacking, 1990). Advanced statistical models, algorithms and machine learning could be used across these datasets, which we discuss later in this chapter. However, whilst the impact of Big Data can be beneficial in improving predictions, it does also introduce complexities around the reliability and transparency of data because it can be hard to trace back to the source.

The iPhone was introduced in 2007 with social media platforms starting to be available on smartphones later that year, and by 2012 social media platforms had become ingrained in everyday life. This combination led to exponential increases in socially and economically valuable data. Home based internet activity such as online shopping and remote work added to the pool of personal data being collected giving rise to privacy concerns (Madden et al., 2013; Blank et al., 2014; Shozi and Mtsweni, 2017). Additionally, the advent of the front-facing camera in 2010, combined with social media and the concept of monitoring the self (Lupton, 2016) brought with it a detrimental impact on adolescent mental health (Haidt, 2024).

The Big Data era with vast datasets from diverse sources has provided scientific opportunity to study risk behaviour. Major advances in risk psychology and neuropsychology have been made, fundamentally changing how we understand motivation (Song et al., 2020; Fabrègue and Bogoni, 2023).

MINI CASE STUDY 12.1

The Internet of Things (IoT)

The ability to judge risk is now impacted by the seamless integration of the physical and the virtual through the use of sensors, software and connectivity. An example of this is the

Internet of Things (IoT) where everyday objects are connected. Your washing machine can now be linked via your home network to an app on your phone. Whilst away on holiday you too can be alerted to the fact the rest of your family are now getting on with the normal household chores such as doing the washing. This example illustrates how the increasingly sophisticated deployment of data-in-the-wild has changed what some people expect items of kitchen equipment, such as a washing machine, to do on their behalf. At one time, this just meant washing clothes quickly and effectively. Now washing machines gather data, which they communicate to their users; expanding their 'mental construct' of a washing machine to include this new feature. Once these expectations change, so do people's behaviours, leading to consequences for how humans interact with machines.

ACTIVITY 12.4

- How much of your home environment is internet enabled? Your washing machine? Your home thermostat? Your cat flap?
- What might be the data being created here?

IoT devices combine into an infrastructure with phones, computers, watches, printers, and cars that are constantly gathering data about your interaction with them. This data can be processed using machine learning and other AI tools.

When we consider the approach to risk analysis combined with whether we trust the data or not, we note that from the potential for huge information overload, we become selective in the information we receive and how we might form opinions. Problems can arise if this filtering is done by bots rather than experts (Cho, 2007; Kudugunta and Ferrara, 2018; Orabi et al., 2020).

Misinformation

Earlier in this chapter we alluded to misinformation noting that the difference was predominantly around intent. The vast quantities of data and selective interpretation of these lead to a pervasive issue where adversaries can denounce each other with cries of 'Fake News' (Miró-Llinares and Aguerri, 2021) and information found can contradict authoritative sources (Southwell et al., 2022).

The prevalence of misinformation makes it much harder for us to identify what is true and what is a risk. There is an imperative therefore that we should learn as much as we can about how information is presented to us to become critically aware and literate in a world of data-driven activity. Remember that data can be manipulated, bias introduced, adaptations made in such ways that will impact, and alter, the risk perceptions of potentially millions of people. The need for governance is addressed through the EU AI Act whereby guidelines are set and manipulative AI practices prohibited (Edward, 2021; Laux et al, 2024).

REFLECTIVE ACTIVITY 12.4

- How do you recognise and critically evaluate risks?
- How do you know who to trust in terms of judgement about what is a risk?
- How much insight do you use from the physical world and how much is driven by algorithms in the media you consume?

ECONOMIC GROWTH

It is important to consider how the flows of data in our connected world influence the things we want to buy, and the services we want to access. Economic growth looks at an increase in the quality and quantity of these things.

As the digital environment around us has changed and evolved over time, so too have the economic drivers. If we consider what Park et al. (2023) view as the web evolution (illustrated in Figure 12.2) we see how we have moved from 'bricks and mortar' **commerce** with the web being used as a placeholder for a catalogue, through the dynamic content driven time categorised as Web 2.0 (Allen, 2013) to a more distributed and decentralised approach where data is not held centrally but in a widely distributed system.

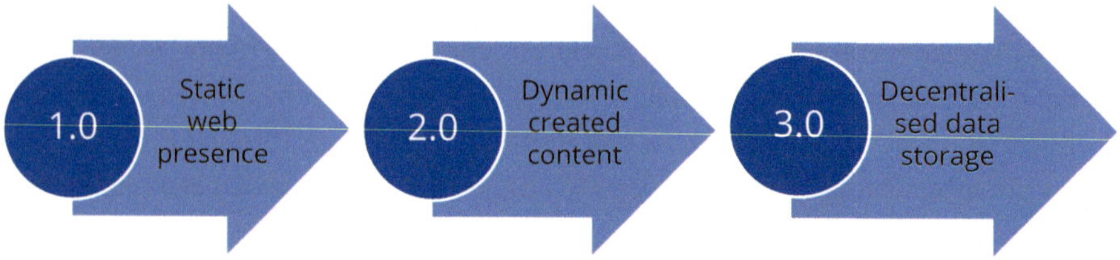

Figure 12.2 Web evolution

Source: Author

Web 1.0

Web 1.0 consumption was driven by real life choices. Static pages offered products for sale that were the same good you would find in the stores but now you could purchase from your home office, dining table, sofa – anywhere you had an internet connection that could cope with downloading the data quickly enough. People would often be connected using dial-up, which used a physical phone line and a device called a modem to access the pages. Purchasing activity could be very slow and because of this, high resolution images were very rarely used.

REFLECTIVE ACTIVITY 12.5

- Have you recently bought something online?
- How long did it take?
- Imagine for a moment needing to wait for an image to take 3-5 minutes to appear on your screen. Would you still wait to make your purchase?

Web 2.0

The web developed into a more social and interactive space with Web 2.0. Personalised marketing, convenience and rewards for loyalty became many of the economic drivers. Wireless connections became the norm, effectively removing geographical constraints on markets. Consumers and merchants, buyers and sellers could engage in trade without boundaries. No longer did you need to be at home to shop, you could shop on the move.

The personalised marketplace is created by:

- mining **data trails**,
- applying machine learning, and
- semantic modelling to recommend goods and services.

These processes take advantage of our attention span and aim to deliver accurate matches to what we think we might want.

Platform businesses such as Amazon, eBay or Airbnb provide services to both sides of the e-commerce spectrum. They support both sellers and buyers providing payment services along with support with dispute management where needed.

Platform Economics became key to economic activity during the COVID-19 pandemic of the early 2020s but came with three key hazards:

1. **Environment** – substantial increase in air and transport mileage.
2. **Fraud** – substantial increase in fraudulent goods and services.
3. **Personal data** – exploitation of personal data collected from interactions to be reused and repurposed for financial gain.

Web 3.0

The concepts of Web 3.0 are now being considered in the realm of distributed computing combined with the use of **cryptocurrencies** and **Non-Fungible Tokens (NFTs)** (Park et al, 2023; Investopedia Team et al., 2025). Key to this concept is the blockchain. Blockchain stores blocks of data, linked together in a chain across a peer to peer network. Each block has a unique identifier and contains a hash and the data. All of this is encrypted with no changes being allowed without any other party to the data being notified (Nofer et al., 2017).

MINI CASE STUDY 12.2

Blockchain Technology

Blockchain technology enables data to move across computer networks, without risk to data integrity, providing unique forms of time-stamping and data encryption, the latter of which is exceptionally difficult to code-break.

Monetary transactions may also take place safely within blockchains. In fact, blockchain was first put to use as the technology behind virtual cryptocurrencies such as Bitcoin and Ethereum.

In recent years, many new applications have been found for blockchain technology, including the fulfilment of some important SDG goals, for example those related to supporting displaced peoples, by providing refugees from war and natural disasters with blockchain credentials that can be substituted for lost identity documents.

In so doing, blockchain credentialling can provide refugees with access to vital governmental services, while also allowing displaced individuals to buy basic commodities such as food.

Worldwide charities such as Oxfam have been at the forefront in trialling these forms of 'blockchain for good,' to assist economically vulnerable communities threated by conflict, climate change, such as on the Island of Vanaatu in the Pacific, or where the livelihood of farmers is threatened by **sustainability** challenges such as soil erosion.

Blockchain has offered real-world solutions for pooling resources that help people build their way out of resource poverty and/or reclaim their lives following emergency situations.

Energy deprivation (i.e. going without or having no access to power for substantial periods of time) is a significant form of resource poverty. Blockchain projects in Africa have supported solar power microgrids (shared between households) to generate community-owned electricity, with the option to sell surplus power back to the grid, yielding a potential additional income stream for local residents. This is a good example of how blockchain technology can be used to ensure the supply of essential services while also providing people on the ground with the economic incentives they need to remain motivated prosumers.

Digital Divide

Data-driven economic growth however may not benefit all. Some people may well have better lives than others as a consequence, leading to a situation known as the Digital Divide (Myovella et al., 2020; Subramanian et al., 2020). Millions across the world remain excluded from the services we take for granted, many existing without phones, bank accounts and access to digital resources. 5.4% of EU school age children were classed as digitally-deprived, having no personal computers and/or families not being able to afford an internet connection for personal use (Ayllón et al., 2023). Advocates for Web3.0, however, argue that deploying technologies such as blockchain can connect digitally disenfranchised individuals and communities to an emerging 'Internet of Everything' (Langley et al., 2017; Cengiz, 2023; Lee et al., 2023).

Data Privacy

Buying online originally raised concerns around the safety of our transactions. We needed to be reassured with the padlock in the browser that we were safe, safe to buy, safe from fraud. As the technology advances, society reacts, especially when it comes to privacy and surveillance. Deborah Lupton (2014) describes how people become wary of the emerging risks as technology advances, in turn leading to resistance and social movements against the risks.

REFLECTIVE ACTIVITY 12.6

Reflect for a moment - when you walk to the shop:

- How many CCTV cameras are on your route?
- How do you feel about them being there?
- Do you have a mobile phone?
- Do you have location data enabled?
- How do you use that information?

Information about our shopping and financial habits are lucrative data generated by our actions online. Combine this with tracking data, visual images of us going about our daily lives and any comments we make on social media and we become commodities. Our data, sold, monetised through targeted advertising and making billions for the platforms that we create content for (Scholz, 2013). Tim Berners-Lee, the founder of the world wide web, considers that more should be done where we take back ownership of our own data (Solanki, 2021; see also Zhao et al., 2023). His SOLID (Social Linked Data) project proposes a fundamental restructuring of how data is stored on the web; personal data would be stored in 'Pods' allowing individuals to control their own data and manage who can access it.

The Hub of all Things (or HAT; https://www.hubofallthings.com/) was funded by the Engineering and Physical Sciences Research Council (EPSRC) to find the technical means for each of us to store our personal data trails in one place, with the aim of allowing people to decide for themselves how it might be reused and even make a small profit by selling this information to companies for a fee.

REFLECTIVE ACTIVITY 12.7

- What information would you sell about yourself?
- How much would you charge for its use?
- To whom would you sell it?
- Is it ethical for people to profit from selling information about themselves?
- Is it ever ethically correct to sell information that you may hold on other people?

A partially hidden cost of this driver of economic growth is that all this data is stored in data centres which are expensive to run, partly down to their security depending on complex cryptography taking time and computing power. Data storage is known to vastly increase electricity usage, with consequences for atmospheric carbon levels (Wiboonrat, 2020). There are, therefore, climate consequences as data reshapes the economy around the large platforms.

There is now widespread recognition that each of us contributes more to the digital economy than we may receive in return in terms of economic **dividends** or income into the tax system. Many digital corporations receive tax breaks but those at the forefront of the **Gig Economy** struggle to make ends meet – the taxi driver using the Uber platform, the student delivering food on their bike.

Generative AI

As mentioned before, data fuels the AI tools we see proliferating online which makes privacy issues more complex. Generative AI which creates new content relies on huge, varied datasets to create that new content. This is raising some complicated legal challenges in the areas of **intellectual property** rights and ethical considerations.

At the time of writing industry and other areas are exploring the perceived benefits of Generative AI tools, aiming to perform routine jobs more effectively and efficiently, on the basis of learning from previously collected datasets holding information about past interactions (Brynjolfsson, 2024). Add human creativity and you have a new direction for new types of employment where the tools enhance content creation.

As a student of the data-driven world, you will need to know what data is and what it does, including some of the far-reaching economic effects we have discussed in this section of the chapter. You will be confronted by data privacy issues at every turn, whether studying or working for a digital business. As the next section of the chapter makes clear, you will also need to know how to devise, apply and interpret the *data analytics* tools that **firms** and governmental institutions use when turning the vast quantities of data produced by humans and machines into viable products and services.

WHAT'S THIS THING CALLED ANALYTICS?

A dictionary definition of **analytics** describes it as a systematic way of looking at data to look for patterns and meaningful insights. Whilst in the past, analytics was quite a manual process, in our modern age of interconnected computing, we can apply statistics, create appropriate models for understanding and also use coding to get to these meaningful insights.

Whether we are considering analytics, business analytics, data science, decision support or business intelligence, we are carrying out predominantly the same processes. We are using collected data to help us make meaningful decisions. Our world is data rich and we need to make meaning from the relevant data – picking through the disinformation highlighted earlier.

Making decisions is becoming more and more challenging with the amount of data collected.

REFLECTIVE ACTIVITY 12.8

Consider this - when watching television:

- How do you choose what you want to watch?
- How many options do you have for what to watch? Do you subscribe to a streaming service? Do you have catch-up television services? What about the Freeview options? Ask your relatives who are older? How did they choose what to watch in the past? You may well find that the less choice there was, the easier it was to make a decision.

Whilst making decisions in the home can be fairly low risk, making decisions within a business setting is a very different matter. Modern business needs to be agile, to grab opportunities and markets as they arise. The decision makers within a business need timely and relevant data to make decisions effectively. Analytics is there to support those decision makers.

Data is not only growing exponentially but also in complexity and so we need individuals with expertise in being able to manipulate and understand the data, create and communicate the models for understanding, and expertise in carrying out the analytics process.

Analytics can be referred to in a number of ways; it may be considered data science for business, business intelligence or leading into operations research and management science.

Analytics needs to collect the data from different sources and then organise it to make it useful. The next section considers the processes and the environment that is needed.

Statistics, Context, and Coding

The previous section introduced analytics as a systematic way of looking at data. That systematic approach requires an understanding of statistics, being able to use numerical approaches and computer models to make sense of data. The application of that systematic approach allows better decisions to be made.

Mathematics, statistics, predictive modelling, and machine learning are all essential techniques when extracting meaningful patterns from the wealth of data held. The focus for business analytics is on applying the understanding developed from mining the data into predicting what might happen in the future and then aligning business decisions accordingly.

REFLECTIVE ACTIVITY 12.9

Consider one of our initial examples, your last meal. Looking ahead, maybe you want to prioritise the environmental impact of what you eat. Reflect for a moment on what data you would need to collect, what is the context? Are you in an area that has a good amount of food production? In the South West of England there are many farms and a number of food producers who will sell from the farm gate. If you live in a highly urbanised environment having access to this type of food is much more problematic. Thus, the context needs to be factored into your model.

As technology has developed, software has evolved to provide support not just for handling the saving and storing of data but also to support problem solving. Consider the predictive text now enabled on most smartphones. This may have created some unintentional responses when on a mobile device, but on the whole it has enabling quicker, more convenient responses.

Given that data is facts and numbers collected and stored, we need to ensure there is a context alongside to allow for information to be understood from that data. We have connected sensors for the Internet of Things (IoT), but raw data is not helpful on its own.

MINI CASE STUDY 12.3

Light Sensors

Consider a light sensor in a smart home system. It may give you a reading of 1,500 lux. Without knowing the time of day or the location of the sensor, this data is not helpful. If, though, you knew that the time of day was about 1pm and that the sensor was situated near a window you could work out that there was plenty of natural light. If the time, however, was 1am in the morning then you might be asking questions about who was awake at that time or if the light had been left on.

When confronted with large amounts of data, coding repetitive actions to process that data is crucial. Artificial intelligence and machine learning are key in being able to pull out patterns and trends in large datasets that might be missed by the human eye.

Where Is the Data? Introducing Databases

Data needs to be stored so that we access it easily. Many businesses will have legacy software systems and may be faced with needing to access their data in certain ways. In the 1970s and 80s relational database systems met the need for business data to be accessed easily. Relational databases were very much driven by the theories of E.F. Codd who outlined a model based on set theory (collections of objects) and predicate logic (a way of expressing a statement to find values). This allowed for a method of manipulating data that worked well and was sound. The adoption of Codd's model by large players such as IBM and Oracle bought about usable Relational Database Management Systems (RDBMS) software that businesses could make use of.

To work with RDBMS there is a need to understand how to create the database, how to design it, use the language and implement it. To first design the database, there needs to be an understanding of how you put collections of data together and about data structures.

Going back to our example of storing information about what we eat, an ingredient has a name, it has nutritional value and we would need to know how much of it goes into our recipe:

Cheese; dairy; 50g

In this example we can see that 'cheese' is a word. Therefore, we would need to store it as a string of letters, as text. However, the measurement of the amount used is a number. We could store the number in one place and the unit of measure somewhere else.

Codd's relational model used tables to represent the data. These were created by considering the 'things' of importance in the domain being analysed – in our example of what we eat a thing of importance is an ingredient or food item that occurs in a recipe. These 'things' of importance are our entities and the entities become our tables. Tables needed to relate to one another and so the relationships between these entities are important to understand, hence the relational model.

When designing a database the developer of that database needs to go through a process of modelling, first conceptually and then logically. Initially they create a high level conceptual model and then refine that model to get to the database description, or **schema**, that works for them.

Entity Relationship (ERD) Modelling is a technique for describing data in a very structured way. This is referred to as a conceptual view. By modelling, we can abstract out the complexity and manage handling the data without really needing to know the details of how it is stored. The start of the process for ERD Modelling is considering basic elements of a system to build it up. What it is *not* is a flow of data through a system.

At the core of the ERD is the 'thing' – the entity (ingredient or recipe). The ERD also shows how the 'things' are related (an ingredient appears in a recipe) and in some cases will show what the 'things' contain, known as attributes or properties (an ingredient has a name). When planning to create a database or even when adapting an existing one to suit new needs, the first step is to identify what the entities are. One way of doing this is to look at the process or procedure you are trying to model, look for nouns, phrases and verbs and create a diagram to represent them.

The ERD shown in Figure 12.3 illustrates the relationships between the entities of person, ingredient and recipe. In this model a person can create one or more recipes, each of which can contain many ingredients. Ingredients can be found in multiple recipes which indicates a many-to-many relationship between recipes and ingredients. The diagram uses crows feet notation to depict how many instances of one entity can relate to another. This is particularly

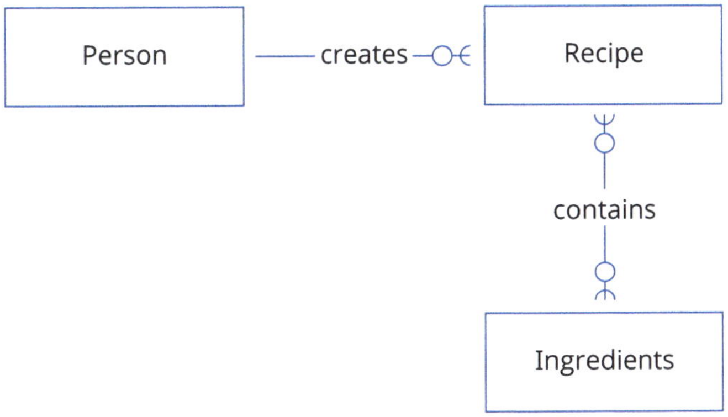

Figure 12.3 ERD for part of a recipe database

Source: Author

important for database implementation as it highlights the need for a linker table to manage this many-to-many relationship. This linker table will store pairs of IDs from the recipes and the ingredients tables allowing for proper association between the entities.

Database design has three stages:

- the conceptual,
- the logical, and
- the physical.

The ERD modelling is the conceptual design phase. The logical design phase looks at the data items within the entities making sure that they are logically stored and organised without needing to consider the physical storage. Here any constraints are considered, for example the age of a person must be represented as a number, cannot be a negative one and possibly should not be greater than 150. Moving on from the logical phase is the physical design and this is where a specialist dialect is used, Structured Query Language.

Structured Query Language (SQL) is the standard way to interact with any RDBMS. Users can write SQL to access and modify data without needing to know how the data is stored.

While RDBMS have been fundamental to database management, they are only one part of the overall story for databases. The rapid growth of social media and e-commerce has meant more challenges particularly around meeting increasing **demands**, the growth in connections and need for access to the data as well as adjustments for changing data structures. The solution to the limitations of scalability and flexibility was the NoSQL database.

Primarily open source and free, NoSQL databases were offered as a solution to scalability concerns. Unlike the RDBMS, NoSQL does not rely on a fixed table structure, which provides a greater flexibility. They are designed to operate across a cluster of servers, offering greater availability which makes them well suited to the demands of modern, always on environments.

Linked Data

Storing data with the ability to be able to access it via any networked device brings with it a number of questions to be answered around how we understand the context of the data and who is allowed to have access.

In the early 2000s Tim Berners-Lee (2009) proposed new ways of structuring data so that it can be easily linked with other data online, evolving his original ideas around hyperlinks which of course formed the basis of the World Wide Web we know today. Having data structures conform to open standards allows for others to be able to access and use the data meaningfully.

Linked data requires a few key rules:

1. It has to be structured using an open standard, the one proposed by the W3C is the **Resource Description Framework (RDF)**.
2. It has to have a unique identifier and uses the **Uniform Resource Identifier (URI)** to identify it.

3 The **URI** should be accessible over the internet, specifically via an **HTTP (Hypertext Transfer Protocol)** network.
4 Data should be linked to other **URIs** to provide the context.

Increasingly governmental data is published in this linked data format; both US and UK governmental data uses **RDF** and other linked data standards.

Who Can Access Data

Making data more accessible and connected raises the important question about who can access it. Businesses have their own corporate data, but there are more benefits as more of the data is shared. In the early 2000s, RESTful APIs (Application Programming Interfaces), provided a standardised way for machines to communicate by following a simple set of rules, which in turn significantly streamlined and simplified the process of sharing data between systems. Businesses could choose what data they wished to share and with whom. For example, artisans can share data about their products for sale in an ecommerce system and by using APIs from established shipping companies and payment gateways they can ensure payment and handle deliveries without having to create the software themselves. These are not part of the same company but partnered and enabled via APIs.

Open Data

APIs not only facilitate the technical processes of data sharing between systems but also play a crucial role in the broader concept of open data. **Open data** refers to data that is freely available for anyone to access, use and share without restrictions. This openness encourages transparency, innovation and collaboration as datasets from different sources can be combined to generate new insights and solutions.

The principle of open data has substantial societal and economic benefits. For example, businesses and developers can use open datasets to create new products or services, improve decision-making, or enhance efficiency. Societally, open data supports transparency in governance, enables better public services and empowers communities by providing access to information.

In 2020 the European Data Portal highlighted the tangible impacts of open data, noting that easy access to open data sets not only saved time but also saved lives and reduced energy consumption (Huyer, 2020). For instance, during emergencies like natural disasters or public health crises, open data can provide critical information that helps coordinate response efforts more effectively, ensuring resources are allocated to where they are needed the most. During the COVID-19 pandemic, publicly accessible infection and hospital-capacity data enabled governments and health services to track outbreaks in real time and deploy medical resources more efficiently.

Increasingly economic value as well as societal value can be derived from having open access to data, but there is a balance to be had with ensuring privacy and security. Ursula von der Leyen summarises this very well in her agenda for Europe (von der Leyen, 2019: 13):

> Data and AI are the ingredients for innovation that can help us to find solutions to societal challenges, from health to farming, from security to manufacturing. In order to release that potential we have to find our European way, balancing the flow and wide use of data while preserving high privacy, security, safety and ethical standards.

Data-Driven Decision-Making

We have already established the importance of good data for use in AI systems. Common tools are becoming augmented with 'AI' which can mean any number of things. Your search engine quite possibly will not only return a number of links but may also provide you with an 'AI Overview'. An important consideration here is the quality of these summaries, given that users are used to believing what they are told by search engines.

If you use a mobile phone, you will have been exposed to AI tools such as virtual assistants. Newer operating systems are being augmented with AI tools with the aim of making handsets easier and quicker to use. However, this will increase battery and data usage.

Whilst chatbots and virtual assistants have been with us for a while, since 2022 there has been a phenomenal growth in software tools that can create content – Generative AI or 'GenAI'. These tools are trained on vast amounts of data, and they use that data to create new content based on queries ('prompts') posed by the users. ChatGPT and DALL-E were early releases of advanced AI models to the general public demonstrating capabilities of large-scale AI in transforming how humans interact with computers and the ability to create content.

More and more, we encounter software embedded in everyday objects that aims to perform tasks quickly and efficiently – tasks once handled by people. Machines historically lacked contextual awareness, but now AI enables them to incorporate historical nuances in context. For example, an AI might interpret a mention of a cat differently depending on whether a family loves their cat, doesn't own a cat, or someone is allergic to cats. Each situation would require a different response. AI is advancing to enable machines to interpret and act based on analysis of sentiment.

Machine Learning

AI refers to an overarching concept where software appears to behave in what appears to be an intelligent manner. **Machine Learning (ML)** is a subset of AI that focuses on how machines make sense of data. It focuses on the creation of algorithms and statistical models that allow computers to learn from data and support decision-making and predictions without being specifically trained on that data. Common challenges in ML are computer vision, recommendation predictions, and natural language understanding. You will have encountered solutions to these challenges in everyday life, with applications including predictive text on your mobile phone, personalised recommendations on an e-commerce website, face recognition in modern cameras, route finding in digital map tools, and many others.

Analytics increasingly needs ML to work across large collections of data to provide insights and offer predictions or suggestions. Data on how successful those insights and suggestions have been are fed back into the ML algorithm so it can do better next time – thus 'learning' from the experience.

ML is reliant on data, and it is therefore essential that the data can be considered complete and representative. This is frequently not the case, giving rise to the potential for bias, inaccuracy, and unfair outcomes if the data is flawed in any way. ML models are only as good as the data they are trained on. For example, ML in a medical context needs to account for a diversity of human beings. Having something that will only recognise one colour of skin or one gender for example results in a tool that in the best-case scenario is less useful than it could be and, in the worse case scenario, is dangerous. The potential for AI to speed up and reduce the cost of decision-making makes it an attractive option for organisations and groups looking at the bottom line, however the risks of making the wrong decision based on AI in the healthcare or, for example, the criminal justice systems, has the potential to cause irreparable damage to individuals' lives. AI-based tools are being used in both sectors.

Finally, if ML is heavily integrated into a decision-making process, and that decision-making process affects the lives of humans, then ethical implications must be front and centre. Consider for a moment how societal inequalities might be reinforced if this ethical consideration is not made. One approach to guarding against such problems is to use a 'human-in-the-loop' process, whereby decisions are made by humans based on information analysed by AI tools. Consider the difference between AI-based 'decision-making' and 'decision support'.

Automation is touted in many cases as 'enabling customer choice'. The full automation of airports with self-service bag drops, check-in online and automated entry gates is dominant in the UK (AiQ, 2022), but this does not allow for those who wish not to have their lives online or to use a smartphone. Getting caught up in a computer error in this situation leads to a stressful experience.

There is potential that the excessive over-use of technology and the widespread inclusion of AI in all walks of life will lead to a reality where human beings lose the ability to influence their circumstances because it has become too automated. Weizenbaum foresaw this in the 1970s and Gerdes (2025) revisits the concepts outlined by Weizenbaum of technical solutions being automatically preferred over human judgement and points out how the marginalised are still not included.

CHAPTER SUMMARY

- This chapter has introduced you to the concept of data and its importance in the world, noting that data is not just a collection of recordable observations but useful as the basis for informed decisions.
- The internet is fuelled by data agreements, allowing for better decision-making around health and care for the planet and providing new approaches for content creation.

- Understanding the economic impacts of data and privacy issues are important skills in the modern workforce.
- Effective use of data requires technical knowledge, problem solving abilities and ethical consideration.

STUDENTS LIKE YOU CHANGE THE WORLD

Knowledge and skills regarding AI and data have the power to transform our society. Whether it is improving healthcare, enhancing education, or addressing global challenges, your contributions make a significant impact.

The case of a very famous student who changed the world is that of Bill Gates. While a student at Harvard University, in late 1974, Gates and his high-school friend Paul Allen saw the January 1975 issue of Popular Electronics, which featured the Altair 8800 microcomputer. They decided to develop a BASIC interpreter for it - a project realised in a Harvard lab using a PDP-10 mainframe. What began as a student side-project later evolved into Microsoft - the company that would revolutionise personal computing, shaping digital transformation globally. Microsoft's software, especially the Windows operating system and Office suite, made computing accessible and practical for millions worldwide, fundamentally changing how people work, communicate, and manage information. His early innovations as a student and entrepreneur helped drive the digital revolution and shaped the modern tech-driven economy.

This highlights the importance of embracing curiosity and innovation. The field of AI and Data is constantly evolving. Stay curious, explore new ideas and do not be afraid to challenge the status quo. Innovation often comes from those who dare to think differently.

As you work with AI and data, always consider the ethical implications of your actions. Strive to use your skills responsibly, ensuring that your work benefits society and respects the rights and dignity of all individuals.

END OF CHAPTER REFLECTION

Have a look at the skills you should have developed in this unit (find more details in the Key Skills Table in the Appendix on p. 506).

1. Which of the skills listed do you think you have developed the most?
2. Can you give two examples on why you feel you have now developed these skills/developed them further?
3. How will you use these new/refined skills in the future (give two examples of the impact of your development on your future behaviour)?

FURTHER READING

Bernstein, P.L. (1996) *Against the Gods: The Remarkable Story of Risk*. Wiley.

This book provides a comprehensive history of risk management, offering valuable insights into how understanding and managing risk has shaped human progress and decision-making.

Christensen, C.M. (2006) 'The ongoing process of building a theory of disruption', *Journal of Product Innovation Management*, *23* (1): 39–55.

Christensen's work on disruption theory is essential for understanding how innovative technologies and business models can transform industries and create new market leaders.

Kewell, B., Adams, R. and Parry, G. (2017) 'Blockchain for good?', *Strategic Change*, 26: 429–37. http://doi.org/10.1002/jsc.2143

This article explores the potential of blockchain technology to drive positive social change, making it a must-read for those interested in the intersection between technology and social impact.

Mansell, R. and Steinmueller, W.E. (2020) *Advanced Introduction to Platform Economics*. Edward Elgar.

This book offers a clear and concise introduction to the economics of digital platforms, which is crucial for understanding the dynamics of modern digital markets.

McQuade, B. (2024) *Attack from Within: How Disinformation Is Sabotaging America*. Seven Stories.

McQuade delves into the impact of disinformation on society, providing an important context for studying the effects of digital media on public opinion and democracy.

Oliver, H. (2015) *The Automagic Box of Beauty: A Prototypical Smart Device as Use Case Example for User-Centered Decision Support via the Hub-of-all-Things*. https://api.repository.cam.ac.uk/server/api/core/bitstreams/a26d0209-e90a-4cdf-9aa9-147f93c92b90/content

A case study on smart devices and user-centred decision support, offering practical insights into the development and implementation of IoT technologies.

Truby, J. (2018) 'Decarbonizing Bitcoin: Law and policy choices for reducing the energy consumption of Blockchain technologies and digital currencies', *Energy Research & Social Science*, *44*: 399–410.

Truby considers the environmental impact of blockchain technologies, highlighting the importance of sustainable practice in the development of digital currencies.

Oxfam (n.d.) 'UnBlocked Cash Project: Using blockchain technology to revolutionize humanitarian aid', *Oxfam International*. https://www.oxfam.org/en/unblocked-cash-project-using-blockchain-technology-revolutionize-humanitarian-aid

A project showing the innovative use of blockchain in humanitarian aid, showcasing how technology can enhance transparency and efficiency in aid distribution.

REFERENCES

AiQ (2022) 'Airport Automation - building airport capacity beyond 2022 - Part 2', *AiQ Consulting,* October 25. https://www.aiqconsulting.com/aiq-news/airport-automation-building-airport-capacity-beyond-2022-part-2/ (accessed September 19, 2025).

Allen, M. (2013) 'What was Web 2.0? Versions as the dominant mode of internet history', *New Media & Society,* 15 (2): 260–75.

Ayllón, S., Holmarsdottir, H., and Lado, S. (2023) 'Digitally deprived children in Europe', *Child Indicators Research*, 16 (3): 1315–39.

Baudrillard, J. (1994) *Simulacra and Simulation* (S. Glaser, trans.). University of Michigan Press.

Beck, U. (1992) *Risk Society: Towards a New Modernity*. Sage.

Beck, U., Giddens, A., and Lash, S. (1994) *Reflexive Modernization: Politics, Tradition and Eesthetics in the Modern Social Order.* Stanford University Press.

Bell, D. (1980) 'The social framework of the information society', in T. Forester (ed.), *The Microelectronics Revolution*. Blackwell. pp. 500–49.

Berners-Lee, T. (2009) 'Linked data', w3.org, June 18. https://www.w3.org/DesignIssues/LinkedData (accessed September 19, 2025).

Blank, G., Bolsover, G., and Dubois, E. (2014) 'A new privacy paradox: Young people and privacy on social network sites', *Prepared for the Annual Meeting of the American Sociological Association* (Vol. 17). http://doi.org/10.2139/ssrn.2479938

Brynjolfsson, E., Jin, W., and Steffen, S. (2024) *Do IT Capabilities Still Drive Productivity and Innovation in the Digital Age?* https://siepr.stanford.edu/publications/working-paper/do-it-capabilities-still-drive-productivity-and-innovation-digital-age (accessed September 19, 2025).

Cengiz, F. (2023) 'Blockchain governance and governance via blockchain: Decentralized utopia or centralized dystopia?', *Policy Design and Practice*, 6 (4): 446–64.

Cho, J., Kwon, K., and Park, Y. (2007) 'Collaborative filtering using dual information sources', *IEEE Intelligent Systems*, 22: 30–8. http://doi.org/10.1109/MIS.2007.48

Dias Ruiz, C. and Nilsson, T. (2023) 'Disinformation and echo chambers: How disinformation circulates on social media through identify-driven controversies', *Journal of Public Policy & Marketing*, 42 (1): 18–35. http://doi.org/10.1177/07439156221103852

Dragin, A.S., Majstorović, N., Janičić, B., Mijatov, M.B., and Stojanović, V. (2022) 'Clusters of Generation Z and travel risks perception: Constraining vs. push-pull factors', in P. Mohanty, A. Sharma, J. Kennell and A. Hassan (eds), *The Emerald Handbook of Destination Recovery in Tourism and Hospitality*. Emerald. pp. 375–95.

The Economist (2017) 'The world's most valuable resource is no longer oil, but data', *The Economist Leaders*, May 6. https://www.economist.com/leaders/2017/05/06/the-worlds-most-valuable-resource-is-no-longer-oil-but-data (accessed September 19, 2025).

Edwards, L. (2021) 'The EU AI Act: A summary of its significance and scope', *Ada Lovelace Institute.* https://www.adalovelaceinstitute.org/resource/eu-ai-act-explainer/ (accessed September 19, 2025).

Fabrègue, B.F., and Bogoni, A. (2023) 'Nudging: A double-edged sword in the era of Big Data', 2023 8th International Conference on Smart and Sustainable Technologies (SpliTech): pp. 1–4. http://doi.org/10.23919/SpliTech58164.2023.10192971 (accessed December 17, 2025).

Gerdes, A. (2025) 'Weizenbaum's legacy in the era of public interest AI', in H. Asghari and T. Züger (eds), *PI-AI 2024 Workshop on Public Interest AI 2024*. Pre-print:

https://www.hiig.de/wp-content/uploads/2024/09/Gerdes2024-WeizenbaumsLegacy-1.pdf (accessed September 19, 2025).

Hacking, I. (1990) *The Taming of Chance*. Cambridge University Press.

Haidt, J. (2024) *The Anxious Generation: How The Great Rewiring of Childhood is Causing an Epidemic of Mental Illness*. Random House.

Haidt, J. and Schmidt, E. (2023) 'AI is about to make social media (much) more toxic', *The Atlantic*, May 23. https://www.theatlantic.com/technology/archive/2023/05/generative-ai-social-media-integration-dangers-disinformation-addiction/673940 (accessed September 19, 2025).

Heukelom, F. (2007) *Kahneman and Tversky and the origin of behavioral economics*. Tinbergen Institute Discussion Paper, No. 07-003/1, Tinbergen Institute. https://www.econstor.eu/bitstream/10419/86560/1/07-003.pdf (accessed September 19, 2025).

Huyer, E., (2020) *The Economic Impact of Open Data: Opportunities for Value Creation in Europe*. European Comission. https://data.europa.eu/sites/default/files/the-economic-impact-of-open-data.pdf (accessed September 19, 2025).

Investopedia Team, James, M., and Li, T. (2025) 'Web 3.0 *explained, plus the history* of Web 1.0 and 2.0', *Investopiedia*, May 25. https://www.investopedia.com/web-20-web-30-5208698 (accessed September 19, 2025).

Kudugunta, S. and Ferrara, E. (2018) 'Deep neural networks for bot detection', *Information Sciiences*, 467: 312–22. http://doi.org/10.1016/j.ins.2018.08.019

Langley, D.J., van Doorn, J., Ng, I.C., Stieglitz, S., Lazovik, A., and Boonstra, A. (2021) 'The Internet of Everything: Smart things and their impact on business models', *Journal of Business Research*, 122: 853–63.

Laux, J., Wachter, S. and Mittelstadt, B. (2024) 'Trustworthy artificial intelligence and the European Union AI act: On the conflation of trustworthiness and acceptability of risk', *Regulation & Governance*, 18 (1): 3–32. http://doi.org/10.1111/rego.12512

Lee, D.K.C., Low, L., Lim, J., and Shih, C.C.M. (2023) *Inclusive Disruption: Digital Capitalism, Deep Technology and Trade Disputes*. World Scientific.

Lupton, D. (ed.) (1999) *Risk and Sociocultural Theory: New Directions and Perspectives*. Cambridge University Press.

Lupton, D. (2014) *Digital Sociology*. Routledge.

Lupton, D. (2016) *The Quantified Self*. John Wiley & Sons.

Lupton, D. (2018) 'How do data come to matter? Living and becoming with personal data', *Big Data & Society*, 5 (2). http://doi.org/10.1177/2053951718786314

Madden, M., Lenhart, A., Cortesi, S., Gasser, U., Duggan, M., Smith, A., and Beaton, M. (2013) *Teens, Social Media, and Privacy*. Pew Research Center https://www.pewresearch.org/internet/2013/05/21/teens-social-media-and-privacy/ (accessed September 19, 2025).

Makin, T.R. and Orban de Xivry, J.J. (2019) 'Ten common statistical mistakes to watch out for when writing or reviewing a manuscript', *eLife*, 8: article #e48175. http://doi.org/10.7554/eLife.48175

Miró-Llinares, F. and Aguerri, J. (2021) 'Misinformation about fake news: A systematic critical review of empirical studies on the phenomenon and its status as a "threat"', *European Journal of Criminology*, 20: 356–74. http://doi.org/10.1177/1477370821994059

Myovella, G., Karacuka, M., and Haucap, J. (2020) 'Digitalization and economic growth: A comparative analysis of Sub-Saharan Africa and OECD economies', *Telecommunications Policy*, 44: article #101856. http://doi.org/10.1016/j.telpol.2019.101856

Nofer, M., Gomber, P., Hinz, O. and Schiereck, D. (2017) 'Blockchain', *Business & information Systems Engineering*, 59: 183–7.

Oliver, H. (2015) *The Automagic Box of Beauty: A Prototypical Smart Device as Use Case Example for User-Centered Decision Support via the Hub-of-all-Things*. https://api.repository.cam.ac.uk/server/api/core/bitstreams/a26d0209-e90a-4cdf-9aa9-147f93c92b90/content (accessed September 19, 2025).

Orabi, M., Mouheb, D., Aghbari, Z., and Kamel, I. (2020) 'Detection of bots in social media: A systematic review', *Information Processing and Management*, 57 (4): article #102250. http://doi.org/10.1016/j.ipm.2020.102250

Park, A., Wilson, M., Robson, K., Demetis, D., and Kietzmann, J. (2023) 'Interoperability: Our exciting and terrifying Web3 future', *Business Horizons*, 66 (4): 529–41.

Popper, K. (2005 [1959]) *The lLogic of Scientific Discovery.* Routledge.

Scholz, T. (ed.). (2012) *Digital Labor: The Internet as Playground and Factory*. Routledge.

Schwab, K. (2017) *The Fourth Industrial Revolution*. Crown Currency.

Shirky, C. (2010) *Cognitive Surplus: Creativity and Generosity in a Connected Age*. Penguin Press.

Shozi, N. and Mtsweni, J. (2017) 'Big data privacy in social media sites', *2017 IST-Africa Week Conference (IST-Africa)*, 1-6. http://doi.org/10.23919/ISTAFRICA.2017.8102311

Solanki, M.R. (2021) 'Solid: A web system to restore the control of users' personal data', in *ICT Systems and Sustainability: Proceedings of ICT4SD 2020, Volume 1*. Springer Singapore. pp. 257–67.

Song, J., Han, Y., Kim, K., and Song, T.M. (2020) 'Social big data analysis of future signals for bullying in South Korea: Application of general strain theory', *Telematics and Informatics*, 54: article #101472.

Southwell, B., Brennen, J., Paquin, R., Boudewyns, V., and Zeng, J. (2022) 'Defining and measuring scientific misinformation', *The ANNALS of the American Academy of Political and Social Science*, 700: 98–111. http://doi.org/10.1177/00027162221084709

Subramaniam, Y., Masron, T., Hadiyan, N., and Hassan, S. (2020) 'The digital divide in developing countries', *International Organisations Research Journal*, 15 (4): 115–39. http://doi.org/10.17323/1996-7845-2020-04-06

Von der Leyen, U. (2019) *A Union that strives for more. My agenda for Europe. Political guidelines for the next European Commission, 2024*–2019 https://commission.europa.eu/document/download/063d44e9-04ed-4033-acf9-639ecb187e87_en?filename=political-guidelines-next-commission_en.pdf (accessed September 19, 2025).

Wiboonrat, M. (2020) 'Energy management in data centers from design to operations and maintenance', in *2020 International Conference and Utility Exhibition on Energy, Environment and Climate Change (ICUE)*. IEEE, October. pp. 1-7

Young, J. and Bhattacharyya, K., (2024) 'No chicken at KFC: A logistics debacle?', in Sage Business Cases. Sage. http://doi.org/10.4135/9781071945285

Zhao, R., Goel, N., Agrawal, N., Zhao, J., Stein, J., Verborgh, R. Binns, R., Berners-Lee, T. and Shadbolt, N. (2023) 'Libertas: Privacy-preserving computation for decentralised personal data stores', *arXiv preprint*. https://arxiv.org/pdf/2309.16365 (accessed September 19. 2025).

13
ACADEMIC SKILLS

Jude Fleming, Emma Sweeney, Lee Snook,
Martin Darling, and John Shanahan

INTENDED LEARNING OUTCOMES

After reading this chapter, you should be able to:

1. Recognise key academic skills
2. Demonstrate an understanding of and apply effective business communication skills
3. Create effective search strategies
4. Identify, evaluate, and reference a variety of different information sources

SUSTAINABLE DEVELOPMENT GOALS

In this chapter, we address the following SDGs:

- SDG 4: Quality Education - Developing skills that can be taken beyond the educational sector into the world of work.
- SDG 8: Decent Work and Economic Growth - Building transferrable skills for the workplace.
- SDG 10: Reduced Inequalities - Promoting intercultural awareness and collaborative working.

INTRODUCTION

This chapter begins by exploring what is meant by academic English for business and also considers the role of **culture** and cultural differences. It is organised to move through a lifecycle of academic skills starting with lectures, seminars, groupwork, tutorials and **critical thinking**. It then moves through the library and research skills and the techniques required for academic writing and written assessments. The final section covers academic integrity and referencing. The organisation is intended to reflect the way in which you will use academic skills in order to succeed in your studies.

What Are Academic Skills and Why Are They Important?

Academic skills are the strategies and **behaviours** that help students excel in their studies and future careers. You may be coming to university from school or college, either in the UK or abroad, or you may be studying as a mature student alongside your employment. Whatever your route or reason for studying, you will need to develop effective academic skills in order to produce academic work of a high standard, which is well-researched, critically evaluated and clearly presented and communicated. This chapter addresses these key academic skills.

In common with most professions, groups and communities, information in the study of business and management is shared through different forms of communication, some of which will be familiar to you and some of which may be new. These forms of communication have their own style, format and jargon, which you will have to learn. In addition, the study of business and management attracts a diverse range of participants.

Academic English for Business

English is widely used in trade, international business and education (including in many countries where English is not the first language). Beneath the umbrella of English come various varieties of English for specific purposes, including specific disciplines. In this chapter we are particularly interested in how the English language is used in academia, and specifically for the study of business and management within higher education.

Academic English includes both written (essays, reports, and other written assignments) and spoken English (lectures, seminar discussion and presentations) and supports the communication of facts, ideas and arguments to facilitate learning and understanding. Academic English for Business can be described as a hybrid variety of English that encompasses academic tasks and professional communication activities.

The approach in this chapter is to help you understand the purpose of different forms of academic communication and the skills and strategies that you can use to make the most of these forms.

You may have limited experience in using academic English for business, and you won't be alone. However, there are ways in which you can boost your familiarity with the genre and prepare yourself to use it.

- **Learn from experienced users:** As you read, make a note of how texts are organised and how paragraphs and sentences are structured. The more you read, the more familiar you will become with the appropriate style. Listen to lectures and presentations given in an academic or business style and pay attention to how speakers organise and deliver their messages. There are many online platforms that host a range of different presentations on topical issues.
- **Keep a log of useful technical language from your discipline:** Record the words with a definition and practical usage; if English is not your first language, you may also like to add a translation.

- **Become your own best editor and proof-reader:** You should always review your writing after you finish. You may even like to read it aloud to yourself, as this can help you to spot errors or sections that are unclear. You can also record yourself presenting and listen to it with a critical ear to evaluate whether you are communicating clearly.
- Above all **be patient and remember that good communicators are made, not born.** These are skills that develop with practice and experience.

LEARNING ACTIVITIES

A range of different types of learning activity take place at university. You will typically encounter large group sessions such as lectures and smaller group activities such as seminars, workshops and tutorials. The traditional approach is to begin with the lecture and follow up with deeper learning through small groups activities. However, you may also encounter the 'flipped classroom' approach, where students engage with learning materials before the formal teaching activities commence. This section provides guidance on getting the most out of these activities.

Lectures

Lectures are a vehicle for communicating a lot of complex information in a compressed way and are a gateway into a topic with the lecturer introducing students to key topics and areas of research. The lecture is only ever a starting point for the student's own exploration and research, a doorway through which you enter and begin to explore the subject.

The usual lecture format is a large lecture theatre and a large audience. Because of these features, lectures do not normally lend themselves to much interaction between the lecturer and the audience, which means that it is important to prepare to get the most out of your lectures. You can prepare for the lecture by reading around the lecture topic. Where presentation slides are available ahead of the lecture, download these and make them the basis of your notes; attempting to transcribe a lecture is a relatively passive activity that can lead you to focus on the words being said rather than their meaning and significance. Annotating the lecture notes allows you to follow the structure of the lecture and fill in gaps for yourself. This kind of note-making invites you to play a much more active role and to be a more active listener, to think about how the lecturer is presenting information, and what their points of emphasis are.

To add to the existing lecture notes, you may also need to 'translate' what the lecturer is saying into terms that make sense to you as quite complex terminology may be used. This processing and reforming of information is an important element of the learning process and a key academic skill, namely the ability to summarise an idea and synthesise it with the ideas gained from other scholars as well as your own thoughts on the topic, which takes you into the territory of critical thinking.

As you can see, getting the most from lectures requires more than simply listening and taking notes. You will need to exercise active listening skills, synthesise the lecture content with other material you might have studied previously and exercise critical thinking!

Live lectures may also be recorded so that you can use them as learning materials throughout your course. You can watch them at your own pace to revisit key learning points, to make study notes and revision materials. Watching the recording however is not a substitute for attending in person!

You also need to think about the best way of capturing your own thoughts on the lecture topics. How we make notes can be a very individual thing; first, do you like to make your notes on paper or in digital form? Handwriting notes has been argued to have its own particular benefits (Van der Weel and Van der Meer, 2024). However, it has also been argued that such benefits have been overstated, and that handwritten and digital notes share more similarities than significant differences (Pinet and Longcamp, 2025). Digital notes offer significant benefits in that they can be organised, saved, searched and retrieved much more easily. Perhaps a hybrid system of both suits you? Software solutions such as OneNote, Evernote or similar offer note-making functionality. Whatever your preference, it's worth paying some attention to which kind of system suits you from the outset if your notes are to be useful at a later date.

Note-Making Techniques

- What do you need to capture? Where slides or notes are provided by lecturers, do you really need to rewrite them? Your attention is better focused on annotating, clarifying and contextualising these notes for your own benefit.
- What techniques could you use? The important principle is to match the technique to what you want to capture. For instance, if you are trying to capture key points then bullet points or a series of sub-headings might do this succinctly. A process, technique or series of events might be quickly captured using a flow chart. Sometimes a lot of complex information can quickly be captured in a table, pie chart, graph or similar illustration. Tables can also be used to compare ideas or processes with, for instance, advantages and disadvantages as column headings, or points of similarity and difference. Diagrams can be effective ways of identifying and labelling constituent parts.
- How can you capture more complex forms of information? Spider diagrams or mind maps can present complex information such as a range of opinions on a subject, contributing factors to an event – or key arguments within a debate.

Since there is a range of ways of capturing some forms of information quickly, economically and in ways we can readily understand later, you shouldn't think of note-making as adopting only one of the approaches outlined. It is usually more effective to use a combination of techniques.

REFLECTIVE ACTIVITY 13.1

- How does your note-making compare to the strategies set out above?
- Have you been satisfied with your notes as a resource you have been able to consult later?

- Have your notes helped you think things through, process, and rephrase ideas in ways that make sense to you and help you create links with other topics or areas you have been studying?
- Take some time to think about how you have used notes in the past and how you can adapt your note-making to make it more effective for you.

Smaller Group Sessions

Whereas the lecture is a format that is focused on the lecturer's delivery and is often one where interaction with individual students is difficult due to large class numbers, smaller group sessions offer opportunity for student engagement and discussion of the topics that may have been introduced at the lecture.

There are a variety of different models of small group learning such as:

- **Seminars** – group 'classroom' teaching usually to support the lecture topics.
- **Workshops** – group task-based activities, for example, in computer labs.
- **Tutorials** – one-to-one or group discussion meetings between tutor and student/s.

Seminars or workshops may be led by the lecturer, a guest presenter or the students themselves. For example, common activities include tasking a student with researching and presenting a topic for discussion with the rest of the student group and students working in small groups on a problem-based task.

REFLECTIVE ACTIVITY 13.2

Before a small group session, think about what your areas of interest are and why, as this will prompt you when formulating questions.

- Can you think of any examples where working in a setting like a seminar helped you to learn from others?
- How did learning in this way differ from learning from reading, or attending lectures?
- Also think about the groupwork format, what transferable skills will it help you develop?

Groupwork and Intercultural Competencies

Groupwork can be something that causes a lot of anxiety among students for several reasons; it can mean a student's grade for an assignment, or part of it, is reliant upon the performance of the group as a whole; it can give rise to anxiety about working with other people who you may not know, and it can be particularly demanding if you have not had any previous experience of studying in this way. The student cohort on business related courses tend to be very diverse, and differing cultural backgrounds can present a challenge when working together. However, that is to think of groupwork as a barrier or something to be overcome, when it is far more valuable to embrace the format as an opportunity to develop transferable skills that are crucial for the workplace. Alongside the key skills of working as a team, students can develop an understanding of other cultures and business practices that will be invaluable to their ability to develop effective international business practices.

Alongside the research-related skills normally needed for an assignment, you will need to develop good organisational skills. Once you know who is in your group, you'll need to meet, either in person or virtually, to establish group rules and to decide roles. Establishing group rules is an opportunity to consider values and etiquette that are acceptable to all and include all members of the group. This is an early opportunity to consider any cultural issues that need to be considered and how the group will communicate. Communication can, of course, take many forms, but how often and when should it take place?

Once basic communications are agreed, the group would need to consider team roles. Here you might agree to draw on the kinds of expertise within the team. Does the group want a leader? Is one member good at leading and organising? If not, in what other ways will agreement be negotiated? What other skills within the team could be put to most effective use? Editing skills, social media posts, proofreading, designing presentations and local **knowledge** might all be areas where an individual's skills can be put to good use. Of course, you might decide that you want to take the opportunity to learn some new skills such as communication, **leadership** and negotiating, and this too is something that could be negotiated early in the task.

Once roles and agreed rules and values are established, the team will need to agree deadlines for the different phases of the task that take into consideration team members' other commitments. The team will also need to agree processes for saving outputs such as shared folders, SharePoint or OneDrive.

Another key transferable skill developed through groupwork is that of problem solving. Within even the most organised teams, things go wrong, and events intervene; if a team member falls ill at a crucial point, or a planned activity does not deliver the anticipated outcomes, how does the team react? Are there contingency plans in place, or how can tasks be reallocated to ensure a crucial task is completed?

Let's return to the idea of groupwork giving rise to anxieties amongst students, particularly grade anxiety. Many of these can be addressed through the groupwork process; if the group works well together and allows everybody to contribute to the best of their ability, the chances of a successful outcome increase, so it is in everyone's interest that each member of the group feels included and able to contribute in ways they are comfortable with and confident about. Anything less than this is not conducive to good groupwork, likely to reflect negatively on the team and, therefore, is unlikely to lead to a successful assignment.

Viewing groupwork tasks as an opportunity to develop new experience, knowledge and skills amongst the group members is, in many ways, the point of a groupwork task. The opportunity to draw on the cultural backgrounds of the group members is a way of gaining understanding of potential international markets and ways of working, and this makes groupwork a particularly valuable method of learning for business students.

The Part Culture and Cultural Background May Play in Groupwork

As you read this section, remember that cultures don't communicate, people do, and that as they communicate, their behaviour may be influenced by a range of factors including personality, culture, and the environments in which they grow up, are educated, or work.

When people communicate, they do so by encoding their messages using verbal and non-verbal communication strategies. The strategies that they use will be influenced by a variety of factors that include personality and past experiences, as well as cultural factors. These same factors are also likely to influence the way that they interpret the messages communicated by other people. Figure 13.1 below draws on Shannon and Weaver's (1949) Linear Model of Communication to illustrate this.

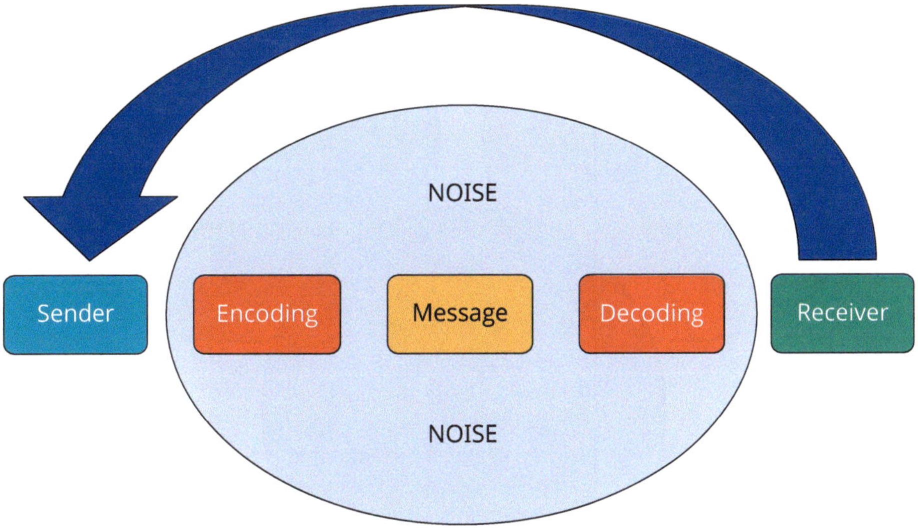

Figure 13.1 Communication model

Source: Author

In this diagram, the sender encodes a message, using their accumulated knowledge of effective and appropriate communication, and the receiver decodes the message, also using their accumulated knowledge of effective and appropriate communication. The receiver then provides feedback, usually in the form of a response or reaction. If the encoding and decoding criteria are different, then the potential is there for a communication breakdown, and this potential may be increased by any noise.

Noise is something additional that may interfere with successful communication. For instance, it could be a noisy environment that makes it difficult to hear the message, or a poor connection that impedes online communication. It can also come from the internal impact of stress or external pressures such as managing a heavy workload and tight deadlines.

Similarly, it may come from the additional cognitive load of working in a second language or understanding unfamiliar accents. In addition, it could be the attitudes and pre-conceptions that we bring into a communicative situation, for example, nervousness, insecurity, overconfidence, frustration or other emotions.

The Impact of Cultural Differences

Because of the way in which cultural factors can influence our communication and understanding of the way in which we do things, cultural differences can create barriers to studying and working in diverse groups. A greater awareness of differences that may occur can help to overcome the barriers and improve ways of working together. Some of the differences are summarised in Figure 13.2 below.

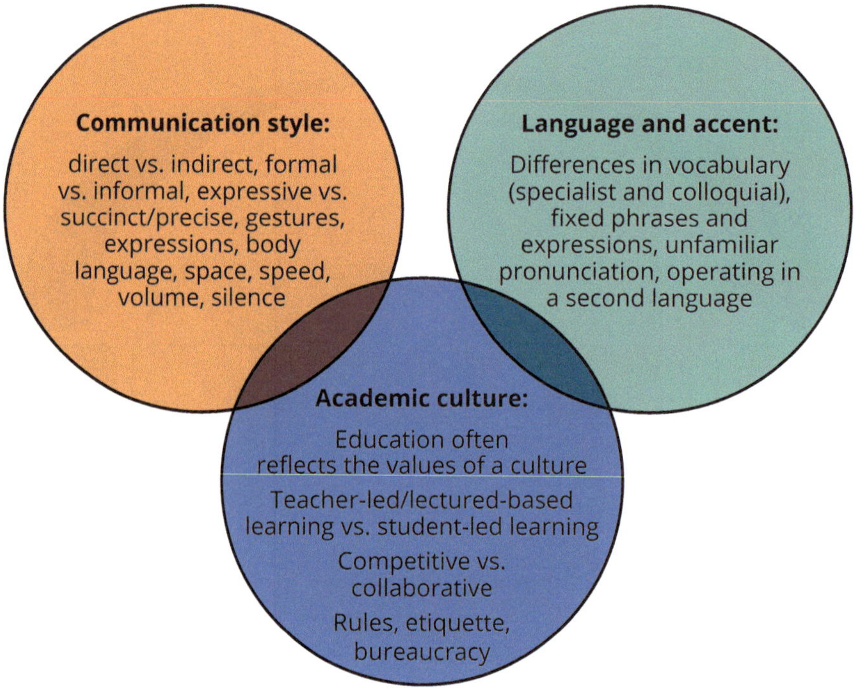

Figure 13.2 Cultural differences

Source: Author

When people say things in a way we don't expect, or things happen in a way that we don't expect, this may create a situation in which meaning becomes unclear. However, the issues that most frequently emerge are about what is considered effective and appropriate communication and behaviour in one cultural context but not in another. For example, people who are accustomed to using indirect messages where explicit meaning is softened with hints or cautious language may consider very direct (explicit) messages to be impolite or confrontational.

Being able to navigate different approaches to communication is useful for making the most out of your university experience. It can not only help you to perform better in your studies but will also enable you to develop a vital skill for future employability. Table 13.1 below provides useful question prompts to help you activate strategies for better cultural awareness.

Table 13.1 Strategies for developing your cultural awareness

Strategy	Question prompts
Self-awareness	How do you prefer to communicate? What does polite and appropriate mean to you? What are your expectations of academic culture? Are these influenced by your experiences?
Open-mindedness	Before you react to something, think about what other interpretation might be possible: Could this be a cultural difference? Could there be other factors that you have not considered?
Curiosity	What is important to people from other cultures? What are important etiquettes that I can learn? How can I make others feel more comfortable in this setting?
Flexibility	How can I adapt my strategies to be more effective?
Resilience	What can I learn from my mistakes?

REFLECTIVE ACTIVITY 13.3

- What kinds of things might you learn from a fellow student from another country or cultural background?
- What kinds of things would you want them to know about your cultural background and why?

Taking a Critical Approach

You may come across different terms such as *critical thinking, criticality, critical analysis, critical appraisal* or *critical reflection*. This means that you compare ideas and theories, and analyse the evidence used to support arguments. You will need to take a critical approach every day when you are studying; when you are reading, writing, listening and discussing.

This is a concept that many students struggle with, and it is often the difference between a good grade and a very good grade. The term 'critical' often leads students to assume that it involves some kind of negative commentary on the work of established authors and researchers, allied with a need for the student to come up with their own original ideas, a task for which they often feel unprepared and lack confidence about. But this is only part of what thinking critically means; to think critically broadly means not to take things at face value, but rather, to ask questions about something, to recognise when something is good, but also to be able to say what makes it good, as well as recognise the significance of that for the subject as a whole – is it a game changer that takes the subject in a new direction, or offers a different way of seeing or doing things?

Thinking critically also means taking into account the negative aspect too; what are the weaknesses in a particular study? How could it be improved? Is there any element of bias? Can the findings easily be applied in different circumstances with similar results? Is the research confirmed by other studies or is it something that sits uneasily alongside other studies, and why might that be?

By adopting this critical approach to research, the student moves beyond simply demonstrating understanding of something, to showing they are aware of the implications of the research for the subject as a whole. They also show they are aware where it sits within the field of research, and, where there is debate, which research the student finds most convincing and why.

LIBRARY AND RESEARCH SKILLS

As a university student it is important to draw on a wide range of resources to support your academic work as this will enable you to develop your arguments and produce better-informed assignments. Academic staff will appreciate reading a well-researched piece of work, and assessment grading criteria reflect evidence of the range, use and quality of sources used.

Independent Research, Breadth of Sources and Going Beyond Your Reading List

Most modules have a reading list provided by the module leader. These will be made available via the module handbook or **Virtual Learning Environment (VLE)**, and these represent a *starting place* for your academic reading. Evidence suggests that students who undertake independent reading and research tend to achieve better grades than their peers who do not. For example, research found that students who used academic library services and resources at least once during the academic year had higher GPA (grade point average) and retention on average than their peers who did not use library services (Soria et al., 2014).

Using the right reading strategy can help you to save time and be more productive. You do not need to read every article you come across. You can scan an article and read the abstract or executive summary of a document to identify if it is relevant to your studies and worth reading in full. Similarly, you will not often need to read a book in full, but should identify key chapters or sections using indexes, tables of contents or a search function.

Research material can be drawn from a wide range of different research resources. As well as using traditional sources such as books and journal articles, you may want to use news items, government reports, statistical or audiovisual material. The exact combination will depend on the nature of your academic work.

Before you start searching for sources, think about your topic and start building a list of the different types of information that could be useful. This will help you when it comes to tracking down information later. For example, if you want to include news coverage you can focus on the news databases. If you need company information and statistics, you can target the specialist business or company databases.

It is likely that you will use a combination of a library catalogue / search service, academic databases, and internet searching via services like Google and Google Scholar to track down all the information you require. Whichever database or search service you use, there are effective searching techniques that you can use to optimise your online searching and ensure you find relevant information.

Effective Searching Techniques

To get the best results from online search services you need to input effective searches.

Whilst it is tempting to jump in and start searching for information on a topic, it really pays off to spend a bit of time planning out a search strategy. It helps to think of this as a three-stage process as illustrated in Figure 13.3.

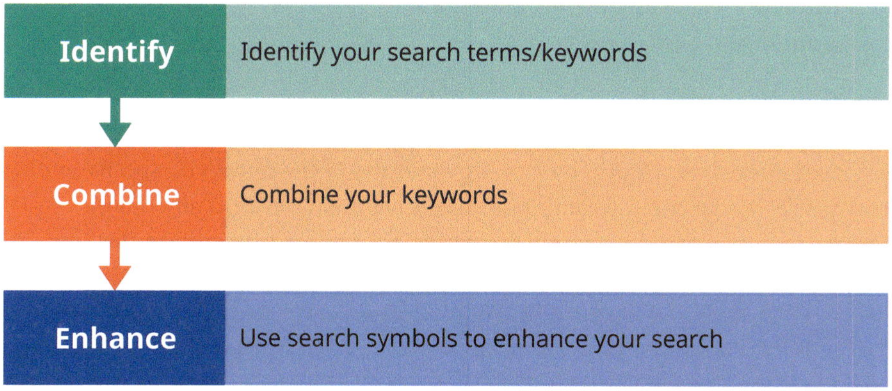

Figure 13.3 Search strategy process

Source: Author

Step 1 – Identify Keywords

Online search services do not understand your search topic. They produce results based on the presence or absence of the search terms / keywords that you enter. This means that these keywords really are KEY! As choosing the right keywords is so fundamental to online searching, spend some time generating lists of possible keywords before you start searching.

Think about the information you need and do some brainstorming to produce a list of keywords/phrases and synonyms (alternative words that have a similar meaning) that you can use when searching. For example, if you were interested in the topic of corporate social responsibility, you might consider search terms such as:

- **Corporate Social Responsibility** or CSR
- Ethical business
- Total Societal Impact or TSI
- Human rights and business
- Sustainable business
- ESG or Environmental, Social and Governance

Step 2 – Combine Keywords with Link Words

It is possible to use link words to combine different search concepts and keywords. These link words define the relationship between your keywords, support focused searching and enhance the relevance of your search results. The three most widely used operators, known as **Boolean operators,** are *AND, OR, NOT* and these can be used in all online search services.

AND

- Narrows down a search and works by looking for both terms you specify (in any order).
- This narrows a search as all terms must appear.
- e.g. business *AND* sustainability

OR

- Broadens a search and works by looking for either of the terms you specify and will find articles where either term or both terms are mentioned (in any order).
- This broadens a search as is useful for retrieving synonyms or variant spellings.
- e.g. ethical *OR* moral

NOT

- Excludes terms from your search.
- Use with care as you may exclude useful articles that cover a range of topics of relevance to you.
- Useful if you are finding large numbers of results and you want to exclude some irrelevant content that is being captured in your search.
- e.g. advertising *NOT* television

Step 3 - Enhance Your Keywords with Search Symbols

You can use search symbols to increase, reduce or improve the relevancy of your search results, making it easier to access the right materials. There are a wide variety of different symbols in use, and checking on the Help pages of the search service you are using will indicate which symbols are supported in each service. The two most common symbols are the truncation and phrase symbols.

Truncation: Asterisk Symbol *

- Broadens your search to include various word endings and spellings.
- Enter the root of a word and put the truncation symbol at the end.
- Will find results that include any ending of that root word.
- Use it with care to avoid finding too many alternatives.
- e.g. *entrepreneur** finds *entrepreneur, entrepreneurs, entrepreneurship, entrepreneurial, entrepreneurialism,* etc.
- The asterisk * symbol is most commonly used for truncation. However, check out the database help screens as !, ?, or # may also be used.

Phrase Searching: "Quotation Marks"

- Narrows your search as it is used to specify that your terms must appear next to each other, and in the exact order you specify.
- Phrase searching is commonly achieved by surrounding your phrase with "quotation marks".
- Always check the Database Help screens, as some databases may use different symbols.
- e.g. "influencer marketing"

MINI CASE STUDY 13.1

Example Search Strategy

Your search strategy is a combination of your keywords, link words and search symbols. It might look something like this:

(business or compan*) AND (CSR OR "corporate social responsibility") AND (benefit* OR advantage* OR reward*)*

In this example:

- **OR** is used to find the alternative words used to describe a concept or idea.
- **Brackets/parentheses** are used to group the *OR* words together so they are processed together.
- **AND** is used to link the search concepts together and find material that contains all aspects of your question.
- *** truncation symbol** is used for variant word endings.
- **" " quotation marks** are used for phrase searching.

If you are entering your search in one search box it is important that you use AND, OR and brackets in combination so that the search is processed correctly.

Alternatively, use the Advanced Search options that are available in many search services to separate out your search terms (entering each concept's keywords in a separate search box), this saves you having to add the brackets (see Figure 13.4).

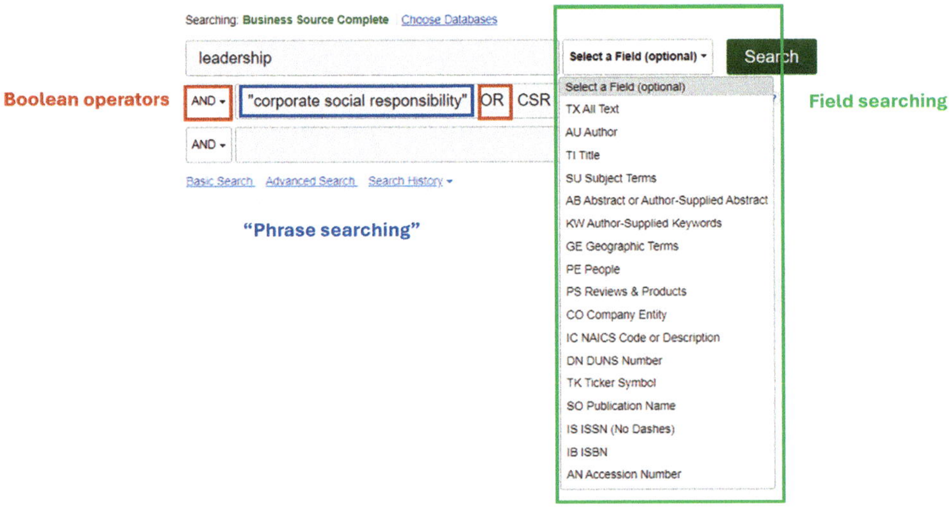

Figure 13.4 Advanced search

Source: Business Source Complete

Try out your search strategy to see how well it works. Often you will need to try lots of different search term combinations to see what works best. If the results you retrieve are not as relevant as you hoped, try changing up your search terms and check you have used appropriate link words and search symbols. Think of this as a 're-search' process. The final search strategy that you settle on may go through numerous iterations before you decide on one that delivers the best results. You are likely to discover search terms you had not originally thought of as you begin finding and reading sources and those can be incorporated to build and enhance your search strategy.

Library Catalogues and Search Services

A Library Catalogue / Search service is a good place to try out a search strategy before you run more in-depth searching in academic databases later. This enables a broad search across all kinds of different sources such as books, journals, articles, audio visual material and more on your chosen topic. All libraries have their own library catalogue search services that you can use to discover the print and electronic resources that are available via that library. You can also use WorldCat (https://search.worldcat.org/) which is the world's largest library catalogue website enabling you to search across multiple library collections.

Once you have settled on a search strategy that is producing useful results you can follow up with a more focused database search if you require additional information to support your research. Library catalogues / search services are great as research starting points as they draw on a wide range of sources across many disciplines but for more complex and comprehensive searching you will need to use the academic journal databases.

Google and Google Scholar

In our information rich society, a vast amount of information is published and disseminated online, and Google is great for general searches for information on the web. It can be a very effective way to find material such as grey literature, which is information not published through commercial publishing platforms or included in online research databases. For business students the type of information you may search the internet for includes company **data** within corporate websites, or information about non-commercial organisations such as a government department, international organisation, or a charity.

Google has an Advanced Search function and you can use the same search techniques you use with the online databases for your internet searching, such as phrase searching and truncation. Using these techniques will help improve your search results.

You can also narrow your results using filters to help with the information overload that can arise when searching the web. For example, you can limit by language, region, date and site/domain. A search for *"energy security" site:parliament.uk* would retrieve just results with that phrase that are hosted on the UK Parliament webpages and you can browse these results for information added in the past day, week, month, year etc. However, the quality of sources found on the web will always be an important consideration. Always evaluate the information you source via Google or any other search engine.

Whereas Google searches public web content, Google Scholar is different. It searches the same kinds of books and journal articles that you would find when using library catalogues and databases. You can think of it as an online, freely accessible search engine for locating scholarly literature. From one place, you can search across many disciplines and sources: articles, theses, books, abstracts and court opinions, from academic publishers, professional societies, online repositories, universities and other websites.

When retrieving results Google Scholar aims to rank documents the way researchers do, weighing the full text of each document, where it was published, who it was written by, as well as how often and how recently it has been cited in other scholarly literature. The cited by feature is a quick way to explore related works and see how topics have been discussed and developed across academic communities.

It can be a great time saver when it comes to finding scholarly content, but you should be aware of its limitations when compared to using academic research databases. Content is harvested automatically from the web so that Google Scholar is not a curated and controlled database. Also, whilst it is a very convenient way to access scholarly literature, it will not contain everything you would find via your library's research databases, nor does it have some of the advanced search functionality that the databases offer. It also may not always include the full text of the article or request you to pay for it (which you don't want to do!). It is best to think of it as a convenient starting point for scholarly research rather than a comprehensive approach to finding sources.

You can link Google Scholar to your university library's collections. This means when you are viewing results you can jump quickly to your university's subscribed content. Use the Google Scholar settings to link with a library.

Use of Generative Artificial Intelligence (GenAI)

GenAI tools can help with academic research and writing in a number of ways, for example:

- Brainstorming ideas
- Assisting with research or gathering information
- Understanding key theories and concepts
- Identifying trends and themes as part of data analysis
- Suggesting a plan or structure for an assessment
- Obtaining feedback on a draft
- Generating images or figures
- Proof-reading and grammar correction
- Generating citations or references

There are many GenAI models with different capabilities. You may be familiar with ChatGPT, DALL-E, Gemini and Copilot for example, but there are many more and new examples are being developed all the time. It is important that they are used with integrity – in an ethical, appropriate, responsible and transparent way – and that any generated content is critically evaluated. GenAI tools are not actually 'thinking' when they generate content, rather they are using a dataset they have been trained on to produce responses to inputs. While it can produce highly coherent and informative text, it also has its limitations and can sometimes generate false or unreliable information. Always check your assignment briefs for information on permitted use of AI and ensure you declare and reference your use of GenAI tools and outputs. This is a rapidly changing environment so it is important that you keep up to date with the current guidance and policies for your assignments at your institution. They may produce guidance, such as https://libguides.exeter.ac.uk/AI, or support materials to guide you in using AI as part of your research process, for example https://libguides.glos.ac.uk/c.php?g=711836&p=5244165. For further advice speak to the library service at your institution.

Academic Journals / Database Searching

Journals are key sources to use when carrying out research as they provide information on the latest scholarly research and cutting-edge knowledge in a subject. They are published at regular intervals throughout the year and are sometimes called periodicals. Each issue contains a number of articles that cover areas of current interest or address specialist topics in much greater detail and are more up to date than is usually possible in books. Articles are often *peer reviewed*. Usually, journals contain a mix of research articles, reviews and communications.

Research articles are the formal publication of a research project, written by those who carried out the research. Research articles are usually published in peer-reviewed journals and will document the aims, methodology, outcomes, data and conclusions reached as a result of the research project. The peer review process means that articles may be published a considerable time after the research was carried out. However, increasingly articles may be fast-tracked for publication and appear in the electronic version of the journal before publication in print. This 'online first' facility is an important means of providing faster access to cutting edge research.

Review articles critically examine the current state of research in a particular field, including key advances and discoveries, current debates, and ideas about the future direction of research. Their reference lists can be very important sources of information about the key works in a field. Some journals specialise in review articles, but many journals contain both research articles and reviews.

Research/academic journal databases enable you to see what has been published in the area you are researching. They are a valuable way of searching for published scholarly research across a wide number of sources and subject areas, and contain detailed records of thousands of journal articles, book references and conference proceedings. These records usually include the article's title, authors, abstract (a brief summary), keywords (to enable your search to find it) and more.

It's important to note that:

- Some databases are primarily indexes or bibliographic databases, and although they provide information about the content of a journal article, they may not provide full-text access to the actual article itself.
- Some databases are a mixture of full-text and indexed/bibliographic access.
- In most cases, it is possible to access the full text by following the links provided.

Academic journal databases may be cross-disciplinary or subject-specific. For example, Scopus and Web of Science are key cross-disciplinary indexed/bibliographic databases covering scholarly literature in many fields, supporting comprehensive literature searches. Not all results will provide the full-text content. Some examples of business-specific journal databases are Business Source Complete, ProQuest One Business and EconLit, which provide access to a wide variety of full text business and management information sources, for example business news, company information and current affairs research.

All of these databases allow you to build complex searches ensuring that the results are likely to be highly relevant to your needs. For example, you can use search techniques, such as Boolean operators, phrase searching and field searching. If you choose for your keywords to be included in the title or abstract, the results will be more relevant than if the words are found anywhere in the full text of the document. If you don't select a field, it will search the default option, which is often all fields of the record.

Search results can be filtered further by using the refine options (usually presented on the left-hand side), for example, by publication date (crucial if you require very current information) and by publication type, publisher, language, full text, peer-reviewed, etc. (see Figure 13.5).

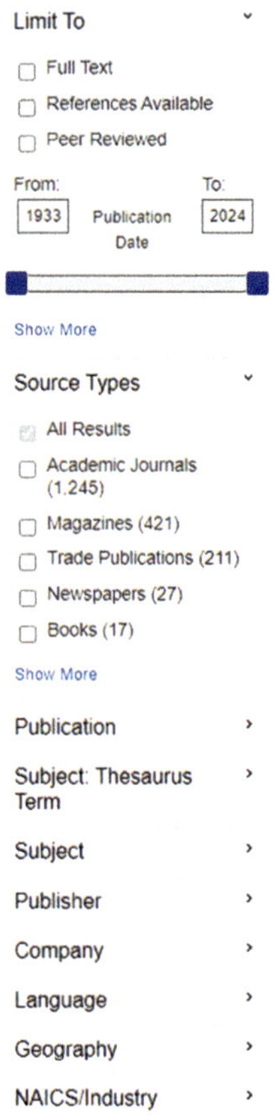

Figure 13.5 Refine results

Source: Business Source Complete

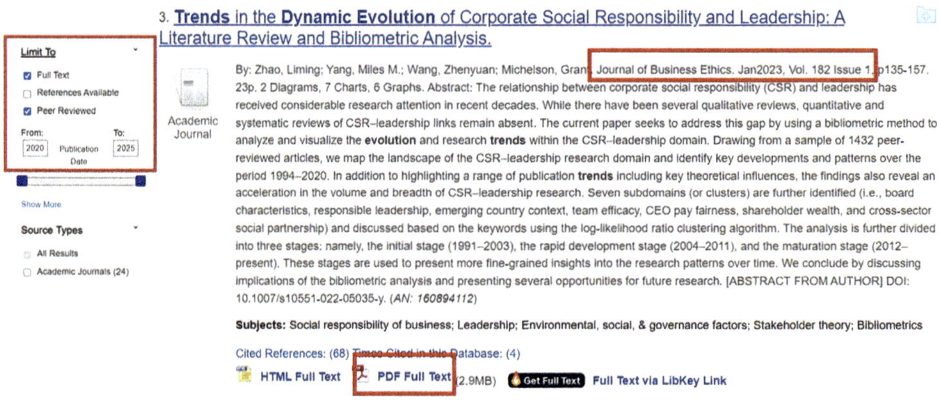

Figure 13.6 Search results

Source: Business Source Complete

Your results list (see Figure 13.6) will display key information such as author, publication title, date and issue number, and description or abstract. You can scan this information to see if it looks relevant before reading the full text. The results will also show if the full text is available.

You can add relevant articles to your folder within the database, ready to export into reference management software.

Specialist Business Databases

Many Business Schools and university libraries subscribe to specialist business databases, which can include company, financial and industry information. Orbis is an example of a company database providing around ten years of firmographic, financial and ownership information for millions of global companies. You can search for a company by name, registered number, or build a list of companies based on certain criteria, such as industry or activity, location, size, key financials, year of incorporation and many other variables. All data can be exported into an Excel spreadsheet. Industry databases provide two main types of market research information: industry research and information on the broader business and economic environment.

Resources specialising in industry research will usually provide profiles with data and analysis on individual sectors. Profiles will often focus on industries within the context of a specific country. They may include market size/drivers, forecasts, leading companies and market share, keys trends, consumer behaviour and SWOT/PESTLE analyses. Resources that include information on the wider business and economic environment will also present their information in the form of 'economic profiles', usually focusing on international regions, countries or cities. Most resources will provide a mix of statistics, analysis and economic,

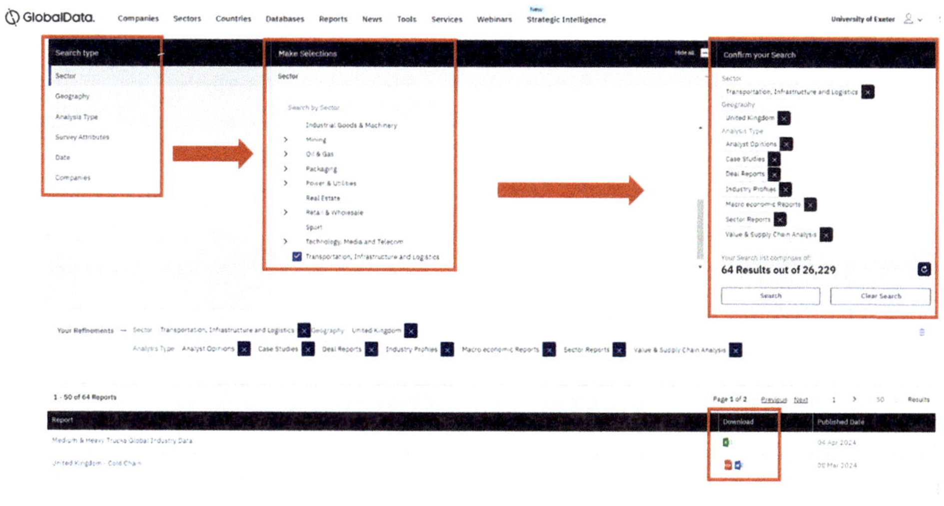

Figure 13.7 Building a search

Source: GlobalData Explorer

macroeconomic, business and consumer trends, demographic information, and SWOT/PESTLE analyses. Key industry databases that many universities and Business Schools subscribe to include Mintel, IBISWorld, Statista and GlobalData Explorer. You can simply search via keyword or build more complex searches by introducing variables such as geography and report type as illustrated in Figure 13.7. Most reports can be downloaded as PDFs and data can be exported into Excel.

Evaluating Sources

Evaluate all the sources you are considering using for your research. It is important to be critical: not all information will be of equal quality. It is also important to be selective: choose the sources that best meet your needs.

Some materials such as scholarly books and journals go through a rigorous 'peer review' process where they are analysed by experts in the field for reliability and quality before publication. Others, such as content uploaded to the web, may have no quality control process applied either for accuracy, objectivity or expertise of the author. There are many ways to evaluate sources, but the CRAAP Test is a useful and widely used test, invented by Sarah Blakeslee (2004) at the Meriam Library California State University, Chico. It guides you to ask a series of questions about a resource to help you ensure you are using credible and reliable resources that are the most appropriate choice for your research project (Meriam Library, 2010). Different criteria will be more or less important depending on your situation or need. Authority is always important as it encourages an assessment of the qualifications or expertise of the writer.

The five key criteria that form the CRAAP test for evaluating sources are:

1 **C**urrency: Timeliness of the information; e.g. Check the publication or revision date to ensure the information is up-to-date.
2 **R**elevance: Importance of the information for your needs; e.g. Determine if the source directly addresses your research topic and is suitable for your audience.
3 **A**uthority: Source of the information; e.g. Assess the author's credentials and expertise on the subject matter.
4 **A**ccuracy: Reliability, truthfulness and correctness of the information; e.g. Verify the source's claims with other reliable information and look for potential errors.
5 **P**urpose: Reason the information exists; e.g. Identify why the information exists (to inform, persuade, sell, etc.) and be aware of bias.

Research Methods

As well as referring to published research generated by others, your coursework may require you to conduct and generate your own research through the completion of an individual or group research project. Research methods are techniques and processes you can use to guide the collection and analysis of data to answer a business research question.

There are a wide range of different techniques and processes that can be used when doing research. These are typically characterised as:

- **Quantitative Research Methods:** gathering numerical data for statistical analysis to identify trends and make inferences, e.g. a feedback form measuring satisfaction ranked on a scale of 1–5. Useful for objective measurement and comparisons.
- **Qualitative Research Methods:** gathering data on experiences and behaviours for thematic or content analysis, e.g. observing student behaviour in study spaces.
- **Mixed Methods:** combining aspects of both qualitative and quantitative techniques in order to carry out a multi-faceted analysis of your topic.

The choice of methods depends on the nature of your research project. For research questions about experiences that cannot be measured numerically, a qualitative approach would be most appropriate. Examples of qualitative methods include:

- Focus groups
- Interviews
- Observations

Quantitative methods are most effective for collecting and analysing large amounts of numerical data to examine for correlations or to test hypotheses. Examples of quantitative methods include:

- Surveys or questionnaires
- Computational manipulation of gathered data
- Experiments

Your university may also have access to a resource such as Sage Research Methods, which is a large research methods database providing guidance and support on conducting all aspects of the research generation process.

Ask Your Librarian

Most universities have a subject librarian or academic liaison librarian allocated to specific disciplines. They are specialists in information retrieval and are always happy to help students with improving their search techniques, evaluation skills and advising them on selecting the most appropriate sources of information for their specific needs. Just ask! Go and look up the details of your librarian so you can get in touch for support when you need it.

TYPES OF ASSESSMENT

Business Schools use a variety of methods to assess students throughout their course. These can include authentic assessments which require student to apply their learning to real-life situations, for example, producing a business report, preparing a presentation to a board or completing a Capstone Project (conducting research to address a real-world problem). These methods help students develop and apply the skills and knowledge needed for the world of business.

There may be a whole range of different assessment methods used throughout the course; examples include:

- Case study analysis
- Company audits
- Consultancy reports
- Debates and discussions
- Essays
- Exams
- Individual and group projects
- Learner journals and reflective logs
- Presentations
- Quizzes and online tests

Finally, academic writing is directed to a task: an essay question or a research project (Alexander et al., 2008: 182).

Whatever the form of assessment, one of the most common concerns of lecturers is that students do not answer the assessment question (Mounsey, 2013: 104).

Note that:

1. The first rule of assessment is: Answer the question.
2. The second rule of assessment is: *Answer the question!*
3. The third rule of assessment is: Answer the question *in the way it was asked!*

Academic Presentations

Students are often required to give individual or group presentations. Assessment will be made of the content, the quality of the presentation and the sources on which the presentation is based. For group presentations marks may be awarded in relation to teamwork and transition between presenters. This is an authentic form of assessment as delivering presentations is a common task in the workplace.

Exams and Revision

The purpose of an exam is to not only test what the students know, but also what they understand (Hamilton, 2011). Students should ensure they always read the exam questions carefully to fully understand what is required and in what timeframe.

It is important for students to revise the course content and practice exam techniques. Past exam papers can be used to practise answering typical questions. Revision requires effective note-making. Notes should be taken of key points and clearly organised. After this, make a summary to reinforce memory and strengthen understanding. Points could be put on cards, sticky notes, or virtual sticky notes on the computer.

Written Assignments

At university a range of written assessment types are used. Examples include essays, reports, and dissertations and they all follow recognised structures. Business students are often asked to write reports. The typical structure for all these types of assessment is as follows:

- Introduction
- Main body (the discussion)
- Conclusion

(Bailey, 2011: 4; Prinz and Arnbjornsdottir, 2021: 25)

Reports tend to use sub-headings for the different sections and may have shorter paragraphs. In contrast, essays typically do not have any sub-headings and paragraphs are often longer. Essays, in the main, focus on arguing theory qualitatively, whereas assignments and reports tend to concentrate more on quantitative, measurable topics. However, these are guidelines and there is some overlap between the two. Always check the assignment instructions which will clarify the structure required.

In the UK, dissertations are longer research projects. They follow a similar structure but often have extra sections that, for example, relate how data was collected (the methodology). This is typically followed by an outline of the most significant results. After this there is some discussion of the results.

The purpose of a report in business is to recommend the best course of action to a client; this might be advice in relation to making investments or adopting a new training programme. Consequently, reports at university have the same purpose and a similar structure to those in the world of business. A report often includes an executive summary at the beginning which will outline the content of the report.

ACADEMIC WRITING

The majority of assessment at university involves writing in some form. Academic writing may be defined as any writing that is done at university by both students and lecturers. The primary characteristic of academic writing is clarity (Alexander et al., 2008: 179). If the writing is unclear then the message will be lost and the grade will inevitably be lower. The reader must be able to understand and follow the discussion. This requires following an accepted structure for whatever type of writing the student is doing, whether it is an essay, an exam, a report or a dissertation. Unless the task asks for a personal or reflective response, academic writing is usually based on reading prior published research. The writer then builds their opinions based on what they have read (Mounsey, 2013: 45; Strongman, 2013: 2).

The academic process in the UK is typically in this order:

1 Pre-course reading from the reading list (students take notes)
2 Lectures (directing student to reading, more note-making)
3 Reading (note-making)
4 Seminars (other ideas are mentioned)
5 Reading (note-making)
6 Independent research and/or data collection
7 Planning (putting notes from reading into a structure)
8 Writing

The Structure of Academic Writing

As stated above, the typical structure for all academic writing includes an introduction, main body and conclusion.

Introduction

The purpose of the introduction is to give the reader (the tutor) a context for the discussion: to outline the situation and to relate what happened that led to the current circumstances. Following this, there is a brief mention the problem, or disagreement. Next the writer states their position, or stance, in relation to the problem in the form of a thesis statement: 'This essay will argue that…' (Bailey, 2011: 80; Mounsey, 2013: 42). Noticeably, the position the writer adopts is *usually* given at the beginning in the introduction. The purpose of this is to help guide the reader through the discussion (Hamilton, 2011: 95; Mounsey, 2013: 41). An essay is not a murder mystery story where the killer/the position is revealed at the end. Finally, to also guide the reader, there is an outline of how the discussion will be structured during the essay.

The Main Body

This is the section where the writer discusses the various positions of the topic. In the UK, the opposing position with which the writer does *not* agree is usually given first and then in following paragraphs, the writer 'rebuts' (argues against) this by offering their differing point of view that they have developed from their reading (Bailey, 2022: 107–109; Mounsey, 2013: 45).

Conclusion

Here the writer gives a summary of the discussion to remind the reader and then re-states their position. Depending on the essay, they might also add areas for future research (Bailey, 2011: 83). No new information is added in the conclusion.

Writing with Clarity

The writer should move from point to point logically within a paragraph. Typically, paragraphs begin with a topic sentence that informs the reader of the theme or point being discussed. However, do *not* write, 'The paragraph will discuss...' This is unnecessary. Instead mention the topic during the first sentence. After the topic sentence, further sentences should both support and give extra detail in relation to the topic (Hamilton, 2011: 104). The writer should use sources to support their discussion and the points made (Zemach and Rumisek, 2005: 5; Bailey, 2011: 74; Prinz and Arnbjornsdottir, 2021: 90), and it often helps to give an example so that the reader may more effectively follow the discussion. To further guide the reader, make use of cohesive devices (linking words), for example, 'however', 'additionally', and 'consequently'. Equally, good academic style is achieved by avoiding repetition. In this example 'this' is used to avoid repeating an expression; 'To maintain productivity, teambuilding is essential. Managers who ignore this [teambuilding] do so at their peril.' At the end of a paragraph, use a concluding sentence that reinforces the point being made.

Tone and Formality

Authority in academic writing is achieved through the use of evidence (the research of others) to convince the reader of the writer's position (Hamilton, 2011: 58). Hedging language, such as 'may', 'could' and 'a number of' is typically used (Bailey, 2022: 197–8), and terms such as 'always' or 'never' are usually avoided. Given this, a writer should not 'preach' or adopt a tone in their writing that comes across as arrogant. They must show using evidence, not tell.

The writer should also avoid becoming chatty and using informal language. Terms such as 'lots', or 'massive' should not be used and 'much', 'many', or 'a great deal' utilised instead. Two-word verbs (phrasal verbs) tend to be avoided where possible. Rather than 'find out', the writer should use 'discover'. Likewise, emotional language, for example 'terrible', should not be used. Similarly, personal pronouns, for example, 'me', 'you', 'your', 'we', and 'us' are also considered informal as academic writing is characterised by being impersonal (Prinz and Arnbjornsdottir, 2021: 9). An exception is made when the task asks for a personal response and then 'I' may be used. Contractions, such as 'don't' and 'can't', should also be avoided.

Reflective Writing

Reflection is the process of examining what has happened in order to learn from the experience. Students may be asked to use reflective writing in relation to tasks they have done. These might be examining the interactions, or personal performance in a group task, or a written discussion in relation to a presentation that they had delivered. Reflection is always personal and, as stated above, usually the writer will be required to use 'I' in their reflective writing (Bailey, 2022: 142–4). The reflection can take many forms, such as a journal, a learning diary, a personal blog, vlog or podcast.

While reflective writing represents the thoughts of the writer, reference will still be made to academic sources to support the analysis of the observations that the writer makes. The primary challenge of reflective writing is frequently the ability of the writer to judge themselves. Human beings often find it difficult to see themselves honestly and this will be even more difficult if the writer has little experience of reflection. In spite of this, reflection is a common part of many courses and often a part of assessment. Reflective writing enhances the benefit that students gain from learning activities on their academic course. It requires students to assess their experience, think about positive and negative aspects, and draw conclusions to inform future performance (Bailey, 2022: 142).

Time Management

It is important not to leave everything to the last minute. Instead make a schedule for both completing assignments and preparing for exams (Mounsey, 2013). Engage with some tried and tested time management techniques to support you with this important skill; you will need it not just in your studies but also in the world of work. See further reading for recommendations.

A popular time management technique is the Pomodoro Technique. Typically, there are six steps:

1. Decide on what is to be done.
2. Set a timer for 25 minutes.
3. Work on whatever the task is.
4. When the timer rings, stop and take a short break of about 5 to 10 minutes.
5. Repeat Step 2 until you have gone through the process four times. After going through the process four times, take a longer break of about 20 to 30 minutes.
6. After your long break return to Step 2 again (Nöteberg, 2010).

ACADEMIC HONESTY AND REFERENCING

Academic honesty means never falsifying the results of any work and always giving full credit for other people's contributions to our own achievements. Passing off someone else's work as your own would constitute plagiarism.

Examples of plagiarism include:

- **Direct copying of text, or illustrations, from a book, article, fellow student's essay, or other source (including AI) without proper acknowledgement.** This is the most basic form of plagiarism, whereby an individual directly copies a piece of text or an idea belonging to another into their own work, without proper acknowledgement. This means that the person marking the student's work could assume that these words belong to the student, when in fact they do not. All responsible academics acknowledge where they are using the work of others to support and inform their own writing and research. By acknowledgement we mean a correct reference in line with the stated policy of the student's discipline.

- **Claiming individual ideas derived from a book, article etc. as one's own, and incorporating them into one's work without acknowledging the source of those ideas.** This is where an individual takes an idea that may have been expressed for example by an academic within a journal article, which is then paraphrased and placed within the individual's own work without any form of acknowledgement. This leads the person reading the student's work to assume this idea is from the individual student, when in fact this idea originates from someone else.
- **Resubmitting a piece of work that has been previously submitted either at the university or another academic institution.** Students are expected to produce an individual piece of work for each assessment. It is an offence of self-plagiarism to resubmit a piece of work that has previously received a mark. This should not prevent a student from developing an idea from one of their essays. For example, you may state an argument in a paragraph of a single essay and then develop this argument over the course of a dissertation.

Plagiarism can be either intentional, i.e. where the individual means to take and use the work of another, or it can be unintentional where the individual has not referenced materials used. Students are expected to familiarise themselves with the guidance on plagiarism, and on the referencing conventions within their discipline.

Referencing

Referencing is a key element of academic writing demonstrating that you have acknowledged and built upon the work of others. It shows that you can identify and use information appropriately without plagiarising the work of others.

There are many different styles of referencing. Your university will have comprehensive guidance on the style(s) you should use. For example, APA belongs to the 'Harvard' family of citation styles. It is an author-date in-text citation system as opposed to a numeric system which uses footnotes (for example Chicago and Vancouver). In an in-text citation style, the author(s)' surname and publication date (and page number(s) if appropriate) are included within the body of the text, for example after a quote or paraphrase, with the full details of the source provided in a reference list at the end of the document, which is presented alphabetically by author(s)' surname. There are subtle differences between individual styles; for example, most Harvard styles require the *place of publication* as well as the publisher in the reference list, whereas APA does not.

References can be managed manually, or you can use reference management software. Many academic information sources have a citation option, where you can select your reference style and copy and paste the reference into your list. Cite Them Right is an online tool provided by many universities that provides referencing examples for numerous different sources in various styles. There are also many books which give advice on referencing styles, and websites focusing on a particular style, e.g. APA: https://apastyle.apa.org/ and Chicago: https://www.chicagomanualofstyle.org/home.html

Here are examples of references for different types of sources:

E-BookTip!

Citation order:

- Author/editor (surname followed by initials)
- Year of publication (in round brackets)
- Title (*in italics*)
- Publisher
- URL or DOI (Digital Identifier of an Object, see https://doi.org/) if available

Reference list format:

Collings, D., Wood, G., & Caligiuri, P. M. (2015). *The Routledge companion to human resource management*. Routledge.

Journal Article

Citation order:

- Author (surname followed by initials)
- Year of publication (in round brackets)
- Title of article
- Title of journal (*in italics*)
- Volume number (*in italics*)
- Issue number (in round brackets)
- Page numbers or article number
- URL (including access date) or DOI

Reference list format:

Meyer, E. (2024). Build a corporate culture that works. *Harvard Business Review, 102*(4), 66–75. https://hbr.org/2024/07/build-a-corporate-culture-that-works (accessed September 22, 2025).

Market Research Report from Online Database

Citation order:

- Author or name of group
- Year of publication (in round brackets)
- Title (*in italics*)
- URL or DOI

Reference list format:

Mintel. (2024). *Social Media: Engaging with Brands UK 2024*. http://academic.mintel.com

Web Page

Citation order:

- Author (surname followed by initials)
- Date the web page was published/last updated (in round brackets, include month and day if known)
- Title of web page (*in italics*)
- Website name (if applicable and different to the author)
- URL (include an access date and consider creating a web.archive.org capture to ensure future readers can access the resource in the same state)

Reference list format:

Gavin, M. (2019, May 23). *10 important business skills every professional needs*. Harvard Business School Online. https://online.hbs.edu/blog/post/business-skills-every-professional-needs (accessed September 22, 2025).

Reference Management Software

There are different types of reference management software that you can use to help you manage your references. Free to download examples include Mendeley and Zotero. The online version of EndNote can also be downloaded free of charge but the desktop version, which has more advanced features and output styles, requires a subscription – check if your institution provides this.

Reference management software helps you to keep and organise your references all in one place and the add-in in Microsoft Word enables you to create in-text citations in your document and build your reference list as you write. However, it is worth considering the time you will need to invest in learning how to use it effectively versus the time taken to create and manage your references manually.

CHAPTER SUMMARY

In this chapter you have been introduced to the academic skills that you can use throughout your university experience and beyond into further studies and employment. This is a learning journey and your competence and confidence in developing and utilising these academic skills will increase as you progress through your studies.

STUDENTS LIKE YOU CHANGE THE WORLD

Yan is a student from China studying international business in the UK. She shared her thoughts on adapting to a very different academic culture:

> When I first came to the UK, I found the most challenging for me [was] the language. I [also] had some difficulty in academic life, and I found that the reality is quite different from my expectation.

One of the things that Yan found difficult was comparing herself to other students and feeling that their experiences were more valuable and that she was just not as good as they were. What she did to overcome these feelings was to be as authentic as possible, and always to be honest about how she was feeling. She adopted a positive outlook, maintaining confidence and self-belief and taking note of the progress that she made. She sought help, asked questions and learnt new strategies through observation. According to Yan, the key to overcoming cultural barriers is openness and sharing.

> Be frank and be [...] openminded to let them know what you are thinking, what you are experiencing [...] regardless of whether it is right or wrong.

END OF CHAPTER REFLECTION

Have a look at the skills you should have developed in this unit (find more details in the Key Skills Table in the Appendix on pp. 506–7).

1 Which of the skills listed do you think you have developed the most?
2 Can you give two examples on why you feel you have now developed these skills/developed them further?
3 How will you use these new/refined skills in the future (give two examples of the impact of your development on your future behaviour)?

FURTHER READING

Mounsey, C. (2013) *How to Write: Successful Essays, Dissertations, and Exams.* Oxford University Press.

This book provides students of all levels with essential and easy-to-follow guidance on how to plan, research, and write essays, dissertations, and exams.

Cottrell, S. (2019) *The Study Skills Handbook* (5th edition). Red Globe Press.

This title introduces higher-level study skills and allows students to develop a deeper understanding of the learning process itself, encouraging a reflective and well-informed approach to study.

Cottrell, S. (2023) *Critical Thinking Skills: Effective Analysis, Argument and Reflection* (4th edition). Bloomsbury Academic.

This book will help students to develop the ability to locate and recognise arguments in texts with greater speed, engage in dialogue with the arguments and produce better critical, analytical writing for assignments.

Bell, E., Bryman, A., and Harley, B. (2022) *Business Research Methods* (6th edition). Oxford University Press.

Developed specifically with business and management students in mind, this textbook explores the nature and purpose of business research and the issues it entails, while also providing students with practical advice through 'tips and skills' boxes.

Tracy, B. and Leinberger, A. (2020) *Eat That Frog! For Students: 22 Ways to Stop Procrastinating and Excel in School*. Berrett-Koehler.

Students at all levels can struggle with managing their time and juggling university and social/work/home life. This book provides methods, techniques and strategies that are practical, proven and fast acting in tackling procrastination or poor time management.

Baldwin, J.R., Means Coleman, R.R., Gonzalez, A., and Shenoy-Packer, S. (2014) *Intercultural Communication for Everyday Life*. Wiley Blackwell.

This book provides a comprehensive and accessible introduction to theoretical frameworks as well as practical considerations. It is an excellent starting point for students who have not studied intercultural communication before.

Chan, C.K.Y., and Colloton, T. (2024) *Generative AI in Higher Education: The ChatGPT Effect*. Routledge. doi.org/10.4324/9781003459026

This book provides a comprehensive examination of the use and impact of ChatGPT and Generative AI in Higher Education.

Pears, R. and Shields, G.J. (2022) *Cite Them Right: The Essential Referencing Guide* (12th edition). Bloomsbury Academic.

This book is renowned as the most comprehensive yet easy-to-use guide to referencing text available to students and authors. The advice guides students in the skills of identifying and referencing a wide range of information sources and avoiding plagiarism.

REFERENCES

Alexander, O., Argent, S. and Spencer, J. (2008) *EAP Essentials: A Teacher's Guide to Practice and Principles*. Garnet.

Bailey, S. (2011). *Academic Writing for International Students of Business*. Routledge.

Bailey, S. (2022) *Academic Writing for University Students*. Routledge.

Blakeslee, S. (2004) 'The CRAAP Test', *LOEX Quarterly*, 31 (3): 6-7. https://commons.emich.edu/cgi/viewcontent.cgi?article=1009&context=loexquarterly

Hamilton, C. (2011) *Anthem Guide to Essay Writing*. Anthem.

Meriam Library, California State University, Chico. (2010) *Evaluating information: Applying the CRAAP Test*. https://library.csuchico.edu/sites/default/files/craap-test.pdf(accessed September 21, 2025).

Mounsey, C. (2013) *How to Write Successful Essays, Dissertations and Exams*. Oxford University Press.

Nöteberg, S. (2010). *Pomodoro Technique Illustrated*. Pragmatic Bookshelf.

Pinet, S. and Longcamp, M. (2025) 'Commentary: Handwriting but not typewriting leads to widespread brain connectivity: a high-density EEG study with implications for the classroom', *Frontiers in Psychology*, 15, article #1517235. doi: 10.3389/fpsyg.2024.1517235.

Prinz, P. and Arnbjornsdottor, B. (2021) *The Art and Architecture of Academic Writing*. John Benjamins.

Shannon, C.E. and Weaver, W. (1949) *The Mathematical Theory of Communication*. University of Illinois Press.

Soria, K.M., Fransen, J., and Nackerud, S. (2014) 'Stacks, serials, search engines, and students' success: First-year undergraduate students' library use, academic achievement, and retention', *The Journal of Academic Librarianship*, 40 (1): 84-91. doi.org/10.1016/j.acalib.2013.12.002

Strongman, L. (2013) *Academic Writing*. Cambridge Scholars Publishing.

Van der Weel, F.R.R. and Van der Meer, A.L.H. (2023) 'Handwriting but not typewriting leads to widespread brain connectivity: A high-density EEG study with implications for the classroom', *Frontiers in Psychology*, 14: article #1219945. doi.org/10.3389/fpsyg.2023.1219945

Zemach, D.E. and Rumisek, L.A. (2003) *Academic Writing from Paragraph to Essay*. MacMillan.

GLOSSARY

Active failures The things workers do that are unsafe, which directly and immediately cause an accident.

Actual performance The observed or measured performance of the activity in practice.

Asset An asset is defined as a present economic resource (a right that has the potential to produce economic benefits), controlled by the entity as a result of past events.

Asset allocation Process of dividing investments among different asset categories.

Artificial Intelligence (AI) Computer systems designed to mimic human intelligence by performing tasks that typically require human cognition, such as pattern recognition, learning from experience, and decision-making.

Behaviours The actions, reactions, or conduct of an individual or group in response to internal stimuli or external circumstances. In business and management, behaviour often refers to how people act in professional settings, including decision-making, communication, and interaction with others.

Beta (in finance) Measure of a stock's volatility relative to the market.

Big Data Extremely large and complex datasets that are generated at high speed from various sources, such as social media, sensors, transactions, and digital interactions. In HRM, big data is used to uncover patterns, trends, and insights to support decision-making in areas like recruitment, employee engagement, and workforce planning.

Blockchain Distributed ledger technology underlying cryptocurrencies.

Boolean operators Logical connectors used in search engines, databases, and programming to refine and combine search terms or conditions. The primary Boolean operators are AND, OR, and NOT, which help narrow, broaden, or exclude results based on specified criteria.

Brand equity The value a brand adds to a product or service beyond its functional benefits. It is built on customer perceptions, experiences, and associations with the brand.

Branding The process of creating a unique identity, image, and perception in the minds of a company's customers. In many ways, it can be considered as the process to create the story of a company, its vision and how it wants to be seen by its audience.

Business model The term has become a way of describing several aspects of a firm's activities and outlook at once. It is a term that combines an understanding of what a firm does with what it aspires to do and how it intends to make a profit (see Ovans, 2015).

Call option Contract giving the buyer the right, but not the obligation, to buy an asset at a specified price within a set time period.

Capital Financial resources available for investment or business operations.

Capitalism An economic system where private individuals or businesses own and control property, industries, and trade with the goal of generating profit, guided by market competition and minimal government intervention.

Career capital The product of skills, behaviours, experiences, and interpersonal connections that enhance an individual's professional value and employability.

Cash The term normally refers to coins and paper banknotes which are legal tender, used for everyday transactions and physically exchanged in hand. However, in financial/accounting, cash is referred to as the most liquid form of assets, including physical currency, demand deposits and other funds immediately available for use in day-to-day operations, and sometimes short-term equivalents that are readily convertible to currency.

Cloud computing A model of delivering computing services – such as storage, processing power, and software – over the internet ('the cloud'). It allows users to access and use resources on demand without needing to own or manage physical infrastructure.

Commerce A subset of business and pertains more to the distribution side of a business.

Commodity Raw material or primary agricultural product.

Community-based enterprises (CBEs) 'a community acting corporately as both entrepreneur and enterprise in pursuit of the common good [...it is] the result of a process in which the community acts entrepreneurially to create and operate a new enterprise embedded in its existing social structure' (Peredo and Chrisman, 2006: 310).

Community resilience The ability of a community to use local resources, entrepreneurship, and collective action to withstand shocks, adapt to change, and create sustainable economic and social outcomes.

Comparative advantage The ability to produce goods and services at a lower opportunity cost, not necessarily at a greater volume or quality.

Competitive market A market structure where many buyers and sellers exchange similar or identical goods or services, with no single participant able to influence the price.

Complex Adaptive Systems (CAS) Systems which comprise many interacting, independent agents. The network of interaction gives rise to emergent patterns of behaviour. The systems cannot be understood by looking at the individual parts and the whole becomes greater than the sum of the parts. These patterns of interactions allow the systems to adapt to environmental changes.

Complex systems Complex systems are systems with many components interacting in a disorderly way. The differ from complicated systems (like a car engine) because they are not predictable and they do not follow the rules of cause and effect.

Compound interest Interest earned on both the initial principal and accumulated interest.

Consumer surplus The difference between what consumers are willing to pay for a good or service and what they actually pay.

Content marketing A strategic approach to engaging customers by creating and sharing valuable, relevant, and consistent content.

Corporate Social Responsibility (CSR) A company's commitment to manage its operations in an ethical and sustainable way, considering its social, environmental, and economic impacts, and engaging with stakeholders to contribute positively to society.

Corporate social responsibility A business model where companies integrate social and environmental issues in their business operations.

Corporation A large company or group of companies designed as a legal entity giving a number of advantages, including that of limiting liability.

Counter-productive work behaviours Behaviours which can harm, or negatively impact, either the organisation or other employees. This can include behaviours such as gossiping, taking long breaks, and even more extreme behaviours such as stealing and embezzlement (Dalal, 2005).

Coupon rate Interest rate paid by a bond.

Credit derivatives Financial instruments whose value is derived from the creditworthiness of other entities, used to transfer credit risk between parties.

Credit risk Risk of default on debt obligations.

Critical thinking, criticality, critical analysis, critical appraisal, critical reflection These terms refer to adopting a questioning approach. This means that you compare ideas and theories, and analyse the evidence used to support arguments.

Cryptocurrency Digital or virtual currency using cryptography. Cryptocurrency works on a computer network, it is not controlled by a central authority and has any transactions recorded in a decentralised system using cryptography.

Culture A fuzzy set of basic assumptions and values, orientations to life, beliefs, policies, procedures and behavioural conventions that are shared by a group of people, and that influence (but do not determine) each member's behaviour and his/her interpretations of other people's behaviour (Spencer-Oatey, 2008: 3).

Customer retention The ability of organisations to keep their customers over time. Positive customer retention means that customers return to the organisation, continue to buy their products and build a positive ongoing relationship with them.

Customer value The customer's perception of the benefit that an organisation's product or service gives them, in comparison to its cost.

Dark side of leadership Based on leadership characteristics which are normally seen as a strength but when leaders do not exercise self-control, these characteristics have negative effects. This most often happens under stress.

Data A collection of recordable observations.

Data analytics The systematic process of examining data to uncover patterns, draw conclusions, and support decision-making. It involves using statistical and computational techniques to analyse data and gain insights that can help improve business operations, strategies and outcomes.

Data creation The process of generating new data through various means such as manual input, automated systems, sensors, or software tools. In HRM, this can include creating employee records, feedback forms, recruitment entries, or performance metrics.

Data-driven Refers to Large Language Models (LLMs) that churn their way through billions of data points at a time, looking for pattern matches that answer text-based Boolean queries, set by operators (that's us, typing words into a search box on either Google, Amazon, eBay or similar). Increasingly, data-driven means to work with AI based enquiry agents that produce sophisticated, sentient-looking outputs, mirroring human judgement but where they are in point of fact, just exceptional simulations of prose, brought together in the form of ventriloquism.

Data trails The digital records or traces left behind by individuals or systems as they interact with digital technologies. These can include logins, clicks, location data, communications, and other behavioural or transactional information collected over time.

Decolonisation Originally referring to countries under the rule of colonial powers gaining independence, this term has come to include 'identifying colonial systems, structures and relationships, and working to challenge those systems' (Library and Cultural Services, 2025).

Demand Refers to the quantity of a good or service that consumers are both willing and able to purchase at various prices over a given period of time.

Demand curve A graphical representation showing the relationship between the price of a good or service and the quantity demanded by consumers.

Deployment-in-the-wild The implementation of a digital system, model, or algorithm in real-world environments outside controlled testing conditions. It involves exposing the technology to real users, unpredictable data, and operational complexities, providing critical insights into performance, reliability, and adaptability.

Derivative (in finance) Financial instrument whose value depends on underlying assets.

Digital data Data that is produced by computers and/or 'electronic technology that generates, stores and processes data in terms of positive and nonpositive states. Positive is expressed or represented by the number 1 and nonpositive by the number 0. Thus, data transmitted or stored with digital technology is expressed as a string of 0s and 1s. Each of these state digits is referred to as a bit; a string of bits that a computer can address individually as a group is a byte' (see: Yasar, 2023).

Digital disruption A transformation caused by emerging digital technologies that significantly alter or replace traditional business models, processes, or industries. It often leads to shifts in customer expectations, competitive landscapes, and operational strategies.

Digital economy An economy that is based on digital technologies, including digital communication networks, computers, software, and other related technologies. It encompasses all economic activities driven by digital tools, platforms, and data, including e-commerce, digital services, online platforms, and the use of Big Data and AI in business operations.

Digital literacy Encompasses a range of skills required to work with information systems and computer technology, ranging from the ability to use a phone keypad to being able to recognise misinformation online. (For an overview of key concepts in digital literacy, see Loewus, 2016.)

Digital technology Electronic tools, systems, devices, and resources that generate, store, or process data. These include computers, smartphones, software applications, cloud computing, artificial intelligence, and the internet – all of which enable digital communication, automation, and data-driven decision-making.

Digital transformation A comprehensive process through which organisations integrate digital technologies into all areas of operation, fundamentally changing how they deliver value to customers and stakeholders. It involves a cultural, organisational, and operational shift that leverages digital tools, data analytics, and emerging technologies to enhance performance, improve customer experiences, and foster innovation. Digital transformation extends beyond mere technological adoption to include strategic rethinking of business models and practices in the digital age.

Discount rate Rate used to calculate the present value of future cash flows.

Disinformation Deliberately spreading something that is false with the intention to deceive. 'An adversarial campaign that weaponizes multiple rhetorical strategies and forms of knowing' (Dias Ruiz and Nisson, 2023).

Diversification (in finance) Strategy of spreading investments across different assets.

Dividend Distribution of company profits to shareholders.

Dividend yield Annual dividend payment divided by stock price.

Duality A fundamental accounting concept stating that every financial transaction has two equal and opposite effects. It ensures that the total assets of a business entity are always equal to the sum of its liabilities and equity, forming the basis of the accounting equation: Assets = Liabilities + Equity.

Edge device usually at the periphery of a cloud computing network. Phones, printers, smart watches, and wearables are all examples of edge devices with which we are highly familiar. As home appliances and vehicles have become 'smarter', they too have been added to a growing list of edge devices, many of which are linked to information system hubs via a 5G enabled 'Internet of Things' (see IBM, n.d. a). Edge devices are capable of processing data locally without having to send it to a server first.

EDI (sometimes referred to as DEI) stands for Equality, Diversity, and Inclusion An important set of ideas and practices which aim to ensure a fair and equitable environment in workplaces and other contexts, including places of study.

Elasticity of demand Measures how responsive the quantity demanded of a good is to changes in one of its determinants, such as price, income, or the price of related goods.

Emergence Describes the patterns and behaviours that arise from the interaction of agents within a complex system. These patterns are not easily explained through an understanding of the system's component parts in isolation. Examples from the natural world include the amazing patterns formed by murmuration of starlings. The patterns 'emerge' from the interaction of thousands of birds following simple rules: 1. Align direction and speed with your neighbours; 2. Keep a constant distance from your neighbours; 3. Avoid collisions. Human systems often show this type of emergence. This has been studied in crowd behaviour and in the stock market.

EMH Theory stating that market prices reflect all available information, making it difficult to consistently outperform the market through analysis.

Emotional Intelligence (EI) is the ability to recognize, understand, and manage one's own emotions, and to recognize, understand, and influence the emotions of others.

Employer branding Employer branding involves managing your reputation as an employer in employment markets using techniques that are similar to those used when marketing products and services to consumers.

Engagement The full investment of yourself into your work or job role (Rich et al., 2017).

Entity concept The entity concept requires the separation of the business from the owner for accounting purposes.

Entrepreneurship The capacity to take decisive action, transforming innovative ideas into viable new economic activities.

Equity (in business) Ownership interest in a company, typically in the form of shares.

Equity (in EDI) The principle and practice of ensuring fair treatment, access, opportunity, and advancement for all individuals, while striving to identify and eliminate barriers that have historically led to unequal outcomes. Unlike equality, which gives everyone the same resources, equity recognises that people have different circumstances and allocates the specific resources and support needed to achieve fair and just outcomes.

Ergonomic change refers to the physical environment in which work is carried out. It may involve reorganising office space, for example, or relocating workers to new locations.

ESG Environmental, Social, and Governance factors.

Externality a consequence of an economic activity that affects third parties who did not choose to be involved in that activity.

Extrinsic motivation A type of motivation driven by external rewards or pressures rather than inherent interest or enjoyment. According to self-determination theory, extrinsic motivation can vary in the degree of autonomy, ranging from external regulation (e.g., rewards or punishments) to integrated regulation (e.g., aligning external goals with personal values).

Face value Amount paid to bondholder at maturity.

Finance Management of money, investments, and resources over time.

Financial markets Organised systems where financial instruments are traded.

Financial reports Formal statements prepared by an organisation's management that summarise its financial position, performance, and cash flows over a specific period, providing information primarily for external users such as investors, lenders, regulators, and other stakeholders.

Fintech Technology and innovation that aims to compete with traditional financial methods.

Firm A 'firm' is any organisation that provides a professional service. The firm can operate under a specific structure – such as a company/partnership/community interest company. In economic terms, a firm is a profit making business.

Fixed-income instruments Financial instruments that pay a fixed amount of interest at regular intervals, such as government and corporate bonds.

Fixed costs Expenses that remain constant regardless of a company's production or sales volume.

Fourth (4th) Industrial Revolution (referred to colloquially as the 4IR) This has been taking place all around us since the early 2010s. Primarily, the 4IR relates to information technology innovations that rely on 'Big Data.' The Founder and Executive Chairman of the World Economic Forum, Klaus Schwab (2016) published a seminal report, which defined the 4IR concept and is still in use today.

Fragile and conflict-affected systems (FCAS) These are often a focus of international aid projects. An estimated 23% of the world's population currently live in fragile situations and this includes low and middle income countries. Fragility is defined by the OECD as 'the combination of exposure to risk and insufficient coping capacity of the state, system and/or communities to manage, absorb or mitigate those risks. It occurs in a spectrum of intensity across six dimensions: economic, environmental, human, political, security and societal' (OECD, 2022).

Furlough A furlough scheme operated in the UK, as in many countries, during the COVID-19 pandemic. Government funds were used to provide a proportion of employees' incomes while they were unable to go out to work during lockdown periods.

Future (in finance) Agreement to buy/sell asset at predetermined future price.

Future Value (FV) Value of a current asset at a specified date in the future.

Futures contract Standardized agreement to buy or sell a specific asset at a predetermined future date and price.

Game theory A branch of applied mathematics that helps analyse situations where multiple parties, or players, make interdependent decisions.

Generative AI (GenAI) Artificial intelligence systems designed to create new content such as text, images, audio, or code by learning patterns from existing data. Examples include tools like ChatGPT, DALL·E, and other models that generate human-like or creative outputs.

Gig economy An economic model characterised by short-term, flexible, and freelance work arrangements, often facilitated through digital platforms. Workers in the gig economy typically engage in temporary jobs or 'gigs' instead of traditional, long-term employment contracts.

Gilts Fixed-income securities issued by the British government, considered low-risk investments due to their backing by the UK Treasury.

Globalisation Globalisation in business means companies aren't just thinking about selling and buying within a single country, like the UK. They're operating across the globe – selling products in Asia, sourcing materials from South America, and maybe having their customer support in India. When goods or services are imported from other countries, governments can impose extra fees known as tariffs. These tariffs can have a negative impact by increasing the costs faced by businesses and the prices paid by consumers.

Graduate premium The difference in real-term median salaries of graduates compared to non-graduates.

Green bond Bond specifically earmarked for climate/environmental projects.

Headhunting agencies Headhunters are recruitment agents who make a living by matching people who are looking for work with employers who have job vacancies they are looking to fill.

Hedge funds Funds that use pooled funds and employ various strategies to earn active returns for their investors.

High Reliability Organisations (HRO) Operate in situations with the potential for large scale harm. The culture in HROs is orientated towards achieving error-free performance as the consequence of an error could be catastrophic.

Hypertext Transfer Protocol (HTTP) A protocol used for transmitting and receiving information on the World Wide Web. HTTP defines how messages are formatted and exchanged between web browsers and servers, enabling users to access websites and web-based resources.

Hyperreality A place where simulations or representations of reality replaced the original experience of reality to become more real.

Impact investments Investing with the intention to generate measurable social/environmental impact.

Imperialist perspective An imperialist perspective is seeing the world mainly from the viewpoint of a powerful country wanting to control weaker ones for its own benefit. It often overlooks the negative impact on those controlled.

In Real Life (IRL) The physical reality.

Index fund Investment fund tracking a market index.

Initial Public Offering (IPO) First sale of stock by a private company to the public.

Innovation The successful exploitation of new ideas.

Intellectual property Patents, copyrights, and trademarks that can generate revenue through licensing or direct use.

Internet of Things (IoT) A network of physical devices – such as sensors, appliances, vehicles, and wearables – connected to the internet, enabling them to collect, exchange, and act on data. IoT enables real-time monitoring, automation, and smarter decision-making across various sectors.

Intersectionality A framework for understanding how different aspects of a person's identity – such as race, gender, class, sexuality, and disability – interact and overlap, creating unique experiences of discrimination or privilege. It highlights how social inequalities are interconnected and cannot be examined separately. This term was coined by Kimberlé Crenshaw in 1989.

Intrapreneurship Refers to the process by which employees within an existing organisation take initiative to develop new products, services, or processes, acting with the creativity and autonomy of entrepreneurs while using the organisation's resources to drive innovation from within.

Intrinsic motivation A form of motivation where an individual engages in an activity for its inherent satisfaction, interest, or enjoyment, rather than for some separable consequence. It is considered the most autonomous form of motivation within self-determination theory and is associated with greater engagement, creativity, and persistence.

Knowledge The theoretical understanding of a subject you develop through your educational experiences, the facts, information, and principles you will acquire.

Law of demand The law of demand states that, all else being equal, the quantity of a good or service demanded by consumers will fall as the price rises.

Latent errors Pre-existing conditions in an organisation such as systems, poor equipment design, job distractions, fatigue, stress, working hours and culture which may be dormant for many years. These don't directly cause accidents, but they make the active failures more likely.

Leader An individual who influences, guides, or directs a group toward the achievement of goals. In organisational and social contexts, a leader is characterised by the ability to inspire, motivate, and facilitate others to contribute effectively to the success of a team or organisation.

Liability A present obligation of the entity, to transfer an economic resource as a result of past events.

Machine Learning (ML) A subset of AI 'focused on algorithms that can "learn" the patterns of training data and, subsequently, make accurate inferences about new data. This pattern recognition ability enables machine learning models to make decisions or predictions without explicit, hard-coded instructions' (IBM, n.d. b).

Marginal analysis Examines the additional benefits and costs of a decision when considering a small incremental change, such as producing or consuming one more unit of a good.

Market development Involves entering new markets with existing items.

Market efficiency Refers to the extent to which market prices reflect all available information about an asset, good, or service.

Market equilibrium The point where the quantity demanded by consumers matches the quantity supplied by producers, resulting in a stable equilibrium price and quantity.

Market penetration Aims to boost sales of existing products or services in the current market. This can be achieved through aggressive marketing efforts, promotional offers, increased product visibility, and better distribution networks.

Market power The ability of a company or entity to influence or control the price of a product or service in the market.

Market research Essentially gathering and evaluating data – an essential tool for analysing market dynamics, customer behaviour, and competitive forces. In a business environment where data is often plentiful, understanding whether data is useful can be the first and often most significant challenge.

Market structure An economic term that describes how a market is organised and how firms and buyers behave within it.

Marketing 'is the activity, set of institutions, and processes for creating, communicating, delivering, and exchanging offerings that have value for customers, clients, partners, and society at large' (American Marketing Association, 2017).

Marketing communications mix The techniques and medium often used as part of a communications campaign, such as social media, advertising and public relations.

Marketing mix, also known as the four Ps (Product/Price/Place/Promotion) This term was first established in the 1940s by Professor Neil Borden (Borden, 1964) but remains a key principle, even today. Though constantly reinvented and adapted, this framework highlights how, by carefully considering each of the Ps, organisations are better positioned to match customer needs, differentiate themselves from competition, and increase sales.

Metacognition The awareness and regulation of one's own thinking and learning processes. It encompasses two key components: *metacognitive knowledge* (understanding of strategies, tasks, and one's own cognitive abilities) and *metacognitive regulation* (planning, monitoring, and evaluating one's learning activities). Metacognition plays a critical role in effective problem-solving, self-directed learning, and academic achievement, as it enables individuals to adapt their strategies based on task demands and performance outcomes.

Microeconomics The social science that studies the implications of incentives and decisions and how they affect the utilization and distribution of resources on an individual level.

Misinformation False information shared without the intent to deceive.

Model (in economic terms) A simplified representation of reality used to explain, predict, or analyse economic behaviours and outcomes.

Monopolistic competition A market structure where many companies offer similar but differentiated products, and compete for customers.

Monopoly A market structure with a single seller or producer that assumes a dominant position in an industry or a sector.

Moral hazard Occurs when one party may choose an action that negatively impacts another, given misaligned incentives.

Mutual fund Investment vehicle pooling money from multiple investors.

New world management New world thinking sees organisations as messy, like a garden. Cause and effect are not easily determined and managers act as gardeners, creating conditions for plants to grow and the garden to develop in the way they would like it to.

Non-Fungible Tokens (NFTs) A unique digital asset where ownership can be proven, as it represents ownership or proof of authenticity of a specific item—such as art, music, or virtual goods—using blockchain technology. Unlike cryptocurrencies, NFTs are not interchangeable because each has distinct value and characteristics.

Normative economics Deals with questions as to what ought to be rather than what is.

Old world management Old world thinking sees organisations as machines in which control can be exercised rationally. Cause and effect are linear so we can predict the effect changes will have. Managers act as mechanics, altering the inputs into systems to get the outputs they require.

Oligopoly A market structure wherein a small number of producers work to restrict output or fix prices so they can achieve above-normal market returns.

Open data Refers to data that is freely available for anyone to access, use and share without restrictions.

Open systems These interact with their environment so include most organisations, countries, societies etc.

Option (in finance) Contract giving right but not obligation to buy/sell at set price.

Organisation chart A visual representation of the structure showing the chain of command and reporting systems.

Organisational citizenship behaviours Behaviours which have a positive impact on the organisation or other individuals within the work context, which are outside of a specified job role. For example, this could be related to helping a colleague out, volunteering for unpaid responsibilities, or taking informal leadership roles (Dalal, 2005).

Organisational silos Self-contained groups within a department that operate independently. These group members often prioritise their own objectives over the broader organisational goals. This can lead to reduced effective communication and collaboration, and may often lead to conflicts.

Paris Accord (or Paris Agreement) An international treaty adopted in 2015 to combat climate change by limiting global warming to well below 2°C, with efforts to limit it to 1.5°C, through nationally determined contributions from participating countries.

Perfect competition An economic theory that describes a theoretical market where all suppliers are equal and there is no competitive advantage among firms.

Permit to Work A management system to ensure work is carried out safely and correctly. It is a formal system specifying exactly what work is to be done, when the work needs to be done and which parts of the system are safe.

POLC cycle (Planning, Organising, Leading, and Controlling) A management framework outlining the four key functions—planning, organising, leading, and controlling—used to achieve organisational goals effectively and efficiently.

Present Value (PV) Current worth of a future sum of money at a specified rate of return.

Price discrimination The action of selling the same product at different prices to different buyers, in order to maximize sales and profits.

Price elasticity of demand Measures the responsiveness of demand after a change in a product's own price.

Price taker A company or individual who has no control over the market price of a product or service.

Price-to-Earnings (P/E) ratio Share price divided by earnings per share.

Principal-agent problem This happens when the principal (owner) delegates control of an asset to an agent, but the agent's actions may not align with the principal's best interests.

Product development Involves businesses reviewing their products regularly, to ensure that they are developing new products that meet changing customer needs.

Put option Contract giving the buyer the right, but not the obligation, to sell an asset at a specified price within a set time period.

Relationship marketing A strategy focused on building and maintaining long-term relationships with customers to enhance loyalty, satisfaction, and repeat business, rather than just focusing on individual transactions.

Repatriation Refers to the process at the end of an expatriate assignment when people who have been working overseas return to work in their home countries and parent organisation. Rather than a simple relocation, this process entails a complex re-entry transition involving: re-integration into a role that effectively utilises the global competencies gained abroad; managing reverse culture shock, as the individual and their family readjust to home-country norms and environments; knowledge transfer and retention management.

Resource Description Framework (RDF) A W3C standard for describing and linking data on the web using simple statements (subject–predicate–object) that enable information to be shared, connected, and understood across different systems.

Risk (in finance) Potential for unplanned loss or underperformance.

Risk analysis The systematic process of identifying, assessing, and predicting risks based on data to inform decision-making and to manage uncertainty. Risk analysis is crucial for ensuring that the business continues to operate and that anything that is of importance to the business is protected.

Sample variance A statistical measure that indicates how much the values in a sample differ from the sample mean, calculated as the average of the squared deviations from the mean. It reflects the dispersion or spread of data within a sample.

Scenario planning A way of developing plausible scenarios describing how we think things may work out in the future. They ask 'what if?' and explore how the future could unfold. Shell have used scenario planning for many years and each year publish their scenarios for the future. See, e.g., Shell (n.d.).

Schema A logical blueprint of how data is organised.

Skills Represent your ability to perform tasks and apply knowledge effectively. They encompass both technical skills, such as essay writing or data manipulation in Excel, and interpersonal skills like communication, critical thinking, and teamwork. You can expect to develop skills throughout your programme by engaging in activities and gaining new experiences, both within your academic studies and through extracurricular involvement (Andrews and Higson, 2010).

Social capital The networks, relationships, and norms of trust and reciprocity that facilitate cooperation and collective action within a society or group.

Social Contract Theory This refers to the implicit agreement between a business and its customers, where the company is expected to act ethically and responsibly in exchange for consumer trust and loyalty. This includes fair practices, transparency, and social responsibility.

Stakeholders Stakeholder groups include everyone who has a legitimate interest in the success of an organisation. They include owners and investors, but also employees, suppliers, contractors and customers.

Standard deviation (in finance) Measure of investment volatility/risk.

Standards of performance Set and agreed by experts in the field. They can be set internally or, more often, are agreed international standards. They describe the best way of doing something and often set the minimum acceptable level of performance.

Stock Security representing ownership in a corporation.

Structured Query Language (SQL) A standardized programming language used to manage and manipulate relational databases. SQL is used for tasks such as querying data, updating records, creating and modifying database structures, and controlling access to data.

Strike price Price at which derivative contract can be exercised.

Supply Supply of a good or service refers to the quantity that producers are willing and able to offer for sale at various prices.

Supply curve A graphical representation showing the relationship between the price of a good or service and the quantity produced by suppliers.

Sustainability The practice of meeting present needs without compromising the ability of future generations to meet their own. It involves balancing environmental, social, and economic considerations to ensure long-term ecological health, social equity, and economic viability.

Sustainable investment Investment approach considering ESG factors.

Swap (in finance) Agreement to exchange cash flows or financial instruments.

Systematic risk Market-wide risk that cannot be diversified away.

Tail risk The probability of extreme events occurring at either end of a normal distribution curve, representing rare but potentially catastrophic losses that exceed standard risk measures.

Uniform Resource Identifier (URI) A standardised string of characters used to uniquely identify a resource on the internet or within a data system (such as a web page, file, or concept).

Upskilling involves increasing the level and variety of skills that people are able to deploy at work to a high degree of competence.

Unsystematic risk Company or industry-specific risk that can be diversified.

Values-based strategy Values-based recruitment involves looking to hire people whose approach to their work matches that expected by the organisation. It goes beyond hiring based purely on skills and experience.

Value creation Creating value is the purpose of innovation and entrepreneurship. It can be analysed in financial terms, employment or growth, environmental sustainability, or improving social welfare outcomes.

Value proposition The benefit offered by an organisation's products or services.

Variable costs Expenses that fluctuate in direct proportion to production or sales volume.

Virtual Learning Environment (VLE) A digital space providing online access to educational materials.

VUCA (Volatile, Uncertain, Complex, and Ambiguous) An acronym used to describe situations or environments characterised by rapid change, unclear information, interconnected challenges, and ambiguous outcomes.

Willingness to pay The maximum amount a consumer is willing to spend on a particular good or service.

Yield to Maturity (YTM) Total return anticipated on a bond held to maturity.

Zero-coupon bond Bond that doesn't pay periodic interest.

REFERENCES

American Marketing Association (2017) 'Definitions of marketing'. https://www.ama.org/the-definition-of-marketing-what-is-marketing/ (accessed September 28, 2025).

Andrews, J. and Higson, H. (2010) 'Graduate employability, "soft skills" versus "hard" business knowledge: A European study', *Higher Education in Europe*, 33. http:/doi.org/10.1080/03797720802522627

Borden, N.H. (1964) 'The concept of the marketing mix', *Journal of Advertising Research*, 4: 2–7.

Dalal, R.S. (2005) 'A meta-analysis of the relationship between organizational citizenship behavior and counterproductive work behavior', *Journal of Applied Psychology*, 90 (6): 1241–55. https://doi.org/10.1037/0021-9010.90.6.1241

Dias Ruiz, C. and Nilsson, T. (2023) 'Disinformation and echo chambers: How disinformation circulates on social media through identify-driven controversies', *Journal of Public Policy & Marketing*, 42 (1): 18–35. https://doi.org/10.1177/07439156221103852

IBM (n.d. a) 'What is edge computing?', *IBM Think*. https://www.ibm.com/think/topics/edge-computing (accessed September 28, 2025).

IBM (n.d. b) *IBM Think*. https://www.ibm.com/think/topics/machine-learning (accessed September 28, 2025).

Library and Cultural Services (2025) 'Decolonising the library', *University of Essex Library*. https://library.essex.ac.uk/edi/whatisdecolonisation (accessed September 28, 2025).

Loewus, L. (2016) 'What is digital literacy? Digital literacy: An evolving definition', *Education Week*, 36 (12): 5–6. https://www.edweek.org/teaching-learning/what-is-digital-literacy/2016/11 (accessed September 28, 2025).

OECD (2022) 'What is fragility', *OECD*, September 9. https://www.oecd.org/en/blogs/2022/09/what-is-fragility.html (accessed September 28, 2025).

Ovans, A. (2015) 'What is a business model?', *Harvard Business Review*, January 23. https://hbr.org/2015/01/what-is-a-business-model (accessed September 28, 2025).

Peredo, A.M., and Chrisman, J.J. (2006) 'Toward a theory of community-based enterprise', *Academy of Management Review*, 31 (2): 309–28.

Rich, B.L., Lepine, J.A., and Crawford, E.R. (2017) 'Job engagement: Antecedents and effects on job performance', *Academy of Management Journal*, 53 (3). https://doi.org/10.5465/amj.2010.51468988

Schwab, K. (2016) 'The Fourth Industrial Revolution: What it means, how to respond', World Economic Forum. https://www.weforum.org/stories/2016/01/the-fourth-industrial-revolution-what-it-means-and-how-to-respond/ (accessed September 28, 2025).

Shell (n.d.) 'What are the previous Shell Scenarios', *shell.com*. https://www.shell.com/news-and-insights/scenarios/what-are-the-previous-shell-scenarios.html (accessed September 28, 2025).

Spencer-Oatey, H. (2008) *Culturally Speaking: Culture, Communication and Politeness Theory* (2nd edition). Continuum.

Yasar, K. (2023) 'What is digital?', *Tech Target What Is*, November 1. https://www.techtarget.com/whatis/definition/digital (accessed September 28, 2025).

APPENDIX

KEY SKILLS, SDG, AND EDI TABLES

KEY SKILLS TABLES

Chapter 1 – The World of Business

Table A.1 Chapter 1 – The World of Business

Relevant Key Skills	Applications in the World of Business
Innovative Problem-solver	• Adapt to rapid changes and develop creative solutions for ambiguous challenges, especially in a VUCA world. • Appreciate how legislation and case law can support, or hinder, ethical and sustainable decision-making.
Pro-active Collaborator	• Build agile teams capable of working flexibly and effectively in dynamic situations. • Foster a sense of belonging within diverse teams. • Collaborate across sectors to achieve shared goals, such as the UN's Sustainable Development Goals (SDGs).
Digitally Fluent	• Keep up with emerging technologies and digital tools to stay competitive and adapt to rapid industry changes. • Digital research skills to be able to locate relevant laws and legislation.
Resilient Self-advocate	• Embrace change, maintaining a positive outlook, and building personal and team resilience. • Promote sustainable and ethical practices, even when faced with pressures to the contrary. • Manage multiple and conflicting demands from employees and a range of stakeholders. • Efficiently manage time and tasks to prioritise responsibilities and meet deadlines.
Critical Thinker	• Assess the long-term implications of operational decisions on people, planet and profit, balancing profit with responsibility. • Utilise analysis techniques such as PESTLE and SWOT to make informed strategic decisions. • Question traditional paradigms and recognise systemic biases.
Confident Communicator	• Bridge cultural gaps with effective and sensitive communication. • Explain or justify a decision clearly and accessibly to someone without technical knowledge.

(Continued)

Table A.1 (Continued)

Relevant Key Skills	Applications in the World of Business
Globally Engaged	• Consider the interconnectedness of global events and their impact on business decisions. • Incorporate global challenges like poverty or climate change into decision-making. • Consider the impact global differences in legal structure can have on how economic, social and commercial decisions are made. • Support strategies to meet the **EDI** (Equality, Diversity and Inclusion) needs of all individuals, especially with international teams.

Traits that will help you to succeed in the world of business include: *Empathetic analytical, quick-thinking, resilient, objective* and *evidence-based.*

Chapter 2 - Strategic Management

Table A.2 Chapter 2 - Strategic Management

Relevant Key Skills	Applications in Strategic Management
Innovative Problem-solver	• Take responsibility to make decisions when faced with uncertainty and incomplete data.
Pro-active Collaborator	• Understand the importance of trust in building relationships and managing others. • Awareness of your own management style and the impact it might have on others.
Digitally Fluent	• Navigate remote work environments and engaging teams by leveraging online platforms and collaborative tools.
Resilient Self-advocate	• Reflect on personal experiences to understand the impact others have had on yourself.
Critical Thinker	• Find robust business data sources to substantiate management decisions.
Confident Communicator	• Adapt communication style to contexts and circumstances to help manage an effective result. • Confidently express your opinion with supporting evidence.
Globally Engaged	• Appreciate how managers take responsibility for ethical and sustainable decision-making. • Embrace opportunities to work with others from around the world to understand how culture and background impacts management style.

The traits of a strong manager are: *engaged, curious, healthily sceptical, resourceful* and *pro-active.*

Chapter 3 - Organisational Behaviour

Table A.3 Chapter 3 - Organisational Behaviour

Relevant Key Skills	Applications in Organisational Behaviour
Innovative Problem-solver	• Adopt a person-centred approach that considers micro, meso, and macro levels to effectively tackle organisation and workplace problems. • Utilise frameworks, processes and options to enable individuals to make informed decisions within an organisation. • Use organisational behaviour theories to identify the root causes of issues and develop practical strategies to address them.
Pro-active Collaborator	• Form effective relationships between individuals, recognising the different and unique skillsets that each person brings to the group. • Empower teams to work efficiently and navigate challenges, particularly by understanding the stages of group development and the distinct roles individuals can contribute to teamwork.
Digitally Fluent	• Utilise key technological advancements in flexible work arrangements and virtual teams, AI, automation, and data analytics, and recognise their impact on workplace dynamics. • Introduce novel digital approaches to team collaboration, such as using gamification or psychometrics to solve group challenges.
Resilient Self-advocate	• Explore your own values and self-identity, reflecting on how they align or conflict within groups and teams. • Identify your own strengths and weaknesses and consider how they impact the workplace.
Critical Thinker	• Build an awareness of the causes and potential impact of biases as well as approaches to mitigate these within an organisation. • Recognise the risks of groupthink in decision-making and implement strategies to avoid it.
Confident Communicator	• Be aware of the barriers that can arise in group communication that prevent smooth exchange of information. • Differentiate between the range of formal, informal and digital group communication channels to work effectively in groups.
Globally Engaged	• Advocate the importance of protective characteristics with equality, diversity, and inclusion (EDI) as central pillars in organisations and 'fair' workplaces. • Support workforces to recognise the inevitability of change, especially when organisations expand globally and navigate diverse cultural dynamics, while minimising employees' resistance to it. • Unite individuals within an organisation to work effectively towards sustainability development goals (SDGs).

Approaching organisational behaviour with an *open mind* and *holistic* perspective, together with being *conscientious, diligent,* and *respectful,* will equip you to succeed in an organisation.

Chapter 4 - Leadership

Table A.4 Chapter 4 - Leadership

Relevant Key Skills	Applications in Leadership
Innovative Problem-solver	• Navigate change and overcome challenges to lead with authenticity. • Balance the financial, ethical and social responsibilities you hold as a leader for the betterment of your team and organisation.
Pro-active Collaborator	• Consider characteristics and skills of a team and adapt leadership approach to best support and inspire them towards success. • Mentor less experienced, qualified, or confident colleagues to add value to the organisation in different ways.
Digitally Fluent	• Audit and recognise relevant digital advancements and lead selection or implementation of these where it is deemed advantageous and feasible.
Resilient Self-advocate	• Implement metacognitive learning habits to ensure continuous improvement, effective reflection and self-development. • Develop resilience strategies, such as calm communication, embracing mistakes, remaining positive in the face of challenges and set-backs.
Critical Thinker	• Consider VUCA environments and gather intelligence to ensure leadership approach reflects all the demands and pressures in the internal and external environment.
Confident Communicator	• Communicate with stakeholders in a way which ensures messages and values are clear and authentic to yourself as a leader and to the organisation you represent. • Lead teams and projects with clear confidence which ensures that the goals and roles are clearly defined and supported.
Globally Engaged	• Read and research to ensure a high level of cultural awareness and recognition of differences in communicating with and leading diverse teams. • Engage with and motivate colleagues from diverse backgrounds.

The following are often behaviour traits of strong leadership: *responsible, inclusive, agile* and *professional*.

Chapter 5 - Human Resource Management

Table A.5 Chapter 5 - Human Resource Management

Relevant Key Skills	Applications in Human Resource Management
Innovative Problem-solver	• Make decisions in situations where there are no clear right and wrong answers and where the stakes can be very high for individuals and groups of people.
Pro-active Collaborator	• Work effectively in teams and with a wide variety of stakeholders on the development of organisational policies and rules that are sufficiently flexible but also compliant with the law and principles of good people management practice.

Relevant Key Skills	Applications in Human Resource Management
Digitally Fluent	• Lead the development of projects aimed at harnessing digital technologies which have the potential to render HR work more efficient, while improving the quality of decision-making across the field of people management.
Resilient Self-advocate	• Develop both the soft and hard management skills needed to thrive in HR work. Understanding the need to be emotionally intelligent, detail-focused and tough-minded, all at the same time.
Critical Thinker	• Appreciate the importance of combining evidence-based management decision-making in the field of people management (i.e., robust published research findings) with personal judgement based on experience and observation of developing situations.
Confident Communicator	• Develop the skills required to communicate effectively both verbally and in writing, formally and informally, publicly and confidentially, with people employed at all levels in organisations.
Globally Engaged	• The capacity to work thoughtfully, ethically and effectively with individuals and teams from a wide variety of cultures and countries.

The important traits in the field of human resource management are *resilience, empathy, conscientiousness, detail-orientation* and a natural ability to *negotiate* effectively.

Chapter 6 - Marketing

Table A.6 Chapter 6 - Marketing

Relevant Key Skills	Applications in Marketing
Innovative Problem-solver	• Bring fresh and creative thinking to finding and engaging new customers. • Design bespoke programmes to secure long-term customer loyalty.
Pro-active Collaborator	• Work with colleagues across the organisation to fully understand current and future marketing needs.
Digitally Fluent	• Use digital marketing metrics to design marketing plans for business and communities. • Devise techniques to effectively utilise AI tools to optimise marketing practices. • Keep informed about the evolution of digital technology and the impact on consumer behaviour.
Resilient Self-advocate	• Reflect on your own personal branding and effectively communicate your value to organisations, communities and networks.
Critical Thinker	• Use market research, competitor performance, and customer feedback to identify and evaluate marketing opportunities.
Confident Communicator	• Create compelling stories and value propositions. • Articulate ideas and concepts clearly and confidently to diverse audiences.
Globally Engaged	• Reflect on your own consumption behaviours to better appreciate ethical and sustainable marketing practices.

Traits that are important in marketing include being: *dynamic, responsible, leading, a team-player, efficient* and *influential*.

Chapter 7 - Operations and Supply Chain Management

Table A.7 Chapter 7 - Operations and Supply Chain Management

Relevant Key Skills	Applications in Operations and Supply Chain Management
Innovative Problem-solver	• Create innovative solutions to improve supply chain operational performance, adapt to changes and challenges in different operating contexts. This can also be achieved by using simulations to understand the phenomenon in a virtual world. • Develop creative and efficient approaches to achieve project objectives and manage scope. • Make evidence-based decisions by analysing intricate operations and supply chain data to identify trends.
Pro-active Collaborator	• Coordinate with various supply chain stakeholders and teams to manage large-scale projects or integrate multiple departments to solve operational issues collaboratively.
Digitally Fluent	• Examine how AI, Machine Learning, the Internet of Things, Blockchain, and Big Data Analytics can enhance efficiency, accuracy, and agility in O&SCM. • Devise innovative solutions for projects with high complexity or novel technology and apply these to streamline operations and improve decision making.
Resilient Self-advocate	• Flexibility to be able to adapt quickly to shifting demands or unexpected disruptions in supply chain networks. • Harness internships, any networking events, and leadership opportunities to build resilience and the confidence to advocate your ideas to others.
Critical Thinker	• Engage in process analysis and supply chain optimisation projects, breaking down complex problems, analysing data, and proposing actionable solutions. • Use qualitative and quantitative forecasting techniques to predict future outcomes and demand planning. • Analyse different performance measures and their internal/external effectiveness.
Confident Communicator	• Present findings in a range of format deliveries essential for working across departments and with external partners. • Articulate ideas clearly and effectively in different contexts, perhaps by delivering 'pitches' to industry experts, or participating in debates.
Globally Engaged	• Evaluate performance measures in diverse international contexts, supporting sustainable development goals and adapting strategies to global standards and practices. • Take a holistic approach to social responsibility, encompassing sustainable practices like reducing carbon emissions, supporting societal welfare, ensuring ethical conduct, and promoting fair trade and local businesses. • Make decisions that balance business goals with ethical considerations and sustainability.

Approaching operations and supply chain management with *curiousity* and an enthusiasm to continuously *learn,* together with being *analytical, adaptable* and *collaborative* will enable you to cope with the fast-changing environment.

Chapter 8 - Entrepreneurship and Innovation

Table A.8 Chapter 8 - Entrepreneurship and Innovation

Relevant Key Skills	Applications in Entrepreneurship and Innovation
Innovative Problem-solver	• Identify problems as future opportunities. • Create solutions to address and solve real problems or fulfil a need. • Consider how communities can build resilience through entrepreneurship.
Pro-active Collaborator	• Engage management and leadership to support a culture of intrapreneurship. • Harness the opportunity to work with people who are different from you, to create or develop ideas. • Empathy to understand customer and team requirements. • Listen and learn from others to identify their needs and to facilitate collaboration.
Digitally Fluent	• Use a range of digital platforms to project manage the innovation process.
Resilient Self-advocate	• Recognise how a failure-tolerant culture supports the processes for innovation, intra- and entrepreneurship. • Apply a growth mindset to problem-solving.
Critical Thinker	• Acknowledge any unintended consequences of entrepreneurial and innovative practices. • Critically reflect to learn from experiences.
Confident Communicator	• Communicate effectively with stakeholders and teams in different contexts. • Effectively articulate ideas to potential investors, customers, or stakeholders.
Globally Engaged	• Appreciate the value of bringing diverse perspectives to consultation processes. • Be conscious of adopting responsible, inclusive and sustainable practices.

Entrepreneurial and innovative traits include being *empathetic, conscientious,* and *holistic* as well as *perseverance.*

Chapter 9 - Accounting

Table A.9 Chapter 9 - Accounting

Relevant Key Skills	Applications in Accounting
Innovative Problem-solver	• Interpret financial data to create solutions that improve business processes and support strategic decision-making. • Apply accounting principles, such as budgeting, forecasting, and resource allocation, to solve management challenges.
Pro-active Collaborator	• Collaborate across disciplines to ensure financial data is integrated into wider business planning and operations. • Work with teams across an organisation to collect information to support informed decision-making.

(Continued)

Table A.9 (Continued)

Relevant Key Skills	Applications in Accounting
Digitally Fluent	• Use Excel to support data analysis and information management. • Leverage AI and data analytics for enhanced decision-making.
Resilient Self-advocate	• Maintain focus, manage time effectively and meet deadlines, without compromising accuracy. • Stay informed and adjust quickly to new tax laws, compliance regulations, or accounting standards.
Critical Thinker	• Analyse financial statements and business metrics to identify risks, inefficiencies, and growth opportunities. • Evaluate financial and non-financial data to provide managers with evidence-based recommendations.
Confident Communicator	• Present financial insights and relevant recommendations in a clear and persuasive manner, tailored appropriately to the audience needs.
Globally Engaged	• Appreciate the implications of global financial regulations. • Recognise the importance of both EDI and sustainability reporting requirements and their influence on business decision-making.

Someone who is strong in accounting will be *accurate, analytical* and *trustworthy.*

Chapter 10 – Finance

Table A.10 Chapter 10 - Finance

Relevant Key Skills	Applications in Finance
Innovative Problem-solver	• Understand the nuances of the financial market to be able to select and adjust (tweak) relevant formulas. • Translate accounting information by using mathematical formulas to create new information. • Keep up to date with the news to inform financial decision-making.
Pro-active Collaborator	• Work with non-financial experts to aid and support their financial business development. • Draw on the knowledge and expertise of experts in other fields: law, accounting, and sustainability.
Digitally Fluent	• Keep skills updated to adapt to new financial tools, technologies, or methodologies.
Resilient Self-advocate	• Remain calm and methodical when analysing complex financial data, resolving discrepancies, or tackling unexpected financial challenges.
Critical Thinker	• Combine finance and economics knowledge to make informed decisions. • Develop a wide understanding of the factors that impact financial decisions.

Relevant Key Skills	Applications in Finance
Confident Communicator	• Utilise language and communication to translate information from one format into another (e.g. quantitative to qualitative). • Articulate and simplify complex financial information as appropriate to the context of the audience.
Globally Engaged	• Integrate environmental, social, and governance (ESG) principles into financial decision-making. • Utilise finance skills and knowledge to understand the significance of current global financial market trends.

Key traits for finance acumen include a *desire for learning, interest in finance* and being *analytical, data-driven,* and *questioning.*

Chapter 11 – Economics

Table A.11 Chapter 11 – Economics

Relevant Key Skills	Applications in Economics
Innovative Problem-solver	• Feed economic theory into strategic decision-making. • Consider the impact a decision will have on others, how others will react and the potential consequences on a sequence of events. • Adapt and be creative in order to address challenges beyond the traditional boundaries of competitive market frameworks.
Pro-active Collaborator	• Actively bring economic insights and concepts into group decision-making processes.
Digitally Fluent	• Utilise digital skills (such as Excel) to support calculations and analysis. • Use simulation tools to test the potential impacts of managerial decisions.
Resilient Self-advocate	• Make decisions when faced with incomplete information. Facilitate informed decisions, accepting the risks of uncertainty, and learning from outcomes to improve future approaches. • Navigate changes such as recessions, inflation, or supply chain disruptions by staying informed, recalibrating strategies, and maintaining focus on long-term goals, despite uncertainty.
Critical Thinker	• Recognise the importance of marginal thinking by assessing the potential outcome of incremental actions in order to estimate the net value added by business decisions. • Focus on the key details that matter and adopt a fundamental approach to identify and interpret patterns.
Confident Communicator	• Discern what is relevant and explain complex economic theories to non-technical audiences in a clear, compelling, and appropriate way.
Globally Engaged	• Acknowledge the difficulties in identifying and quantifying externalities, like climate change, and analyse approaches to minimise their negative and often sensitive effects.

The traits that are important from an economic lens include: *Patience, adaptability, perseverance* and *focus.*

Chapter 12 – AI, Digital Technology, and Transformation

Table A.12 Chapter 12 – AI, Digital Technology, and Transformation

Relevant Key Skills	Applications in AI, Digital Technology, and Transformation
Innovative Problem-solver	• Recognise where and how data can be utilised to solve problems and assess its appropriateness for a given situation. • Utilise machine learning algorithms and tools in unique ways to solve complex problems.
Pro-active Collaborator	• Appreciate the relevant behaviours and tools to use in a collaborative, digital, and global world of work.
Digitally Fluent	• Apply appropriate mathematical and computer models to understand and process data. • Recognise the range of current technological tools available and critically select the appropriate tool to apply to a specific problem.
Resilient Self-advocate	• Reflect on how your choice and use of data impacts others. • Consider the value of your own personal data and the responsibilities you have. • Develop emotional intelligence to manage the blend between the online and offline world. • Know what to do when encountering problematic online material and be aware how to preserve your own sense of self.
Critical Thinker	• Understand how to design, implement, and interpret data analytics tools commonly used in personal applications, organisational settings, and governmental institutions. • Question and challenge the validity of open-source data. • Collect data from a variety of sources and organise it to make it useful. • Develop the ability to identify misinformation and how to minimise its risks and impact.
Confident Communicator	• Provide visualisation and interpretation of data in clear, concise language that non-specialists can understand. • Tailor communication style to suit the audience's level of technical expertise.
Globally Engaged	• Consider the risk of data having bias and the impact this could have on decision outcomes. • Integrate the environmental impact of data usage and the effects of technological redundancy into decision-making processes.

The important traits when managing technology and data are: *Tenacity, lateral-thinking, creativity.*

Chapter 13 – Academic Skills

Table A.13 Chapter 13 – Academic Skills

Relevant Key Skills	Applications in Academic Skills
Innovative Problem-solver	• Create effective search strategies to address research questions.
Pro-active Collaborator	• Identify the specific skills needed to be an effective group member.

Relevant Key Skills	Applications in Academic Skills
Digitally Fluent	• Efficiently use online search tools and databases to source information.
Resilient Self-advocate	• Take responsibility to identify your own skills gaps and to seek development opportunities. • Identify the cause of any academic stress or anxiety, and personally seek out support and solutions. • Develop strategies to effectively manage your own time and to optimise study techniques. • Utilise reflective writing techniques to gain insights from your personal experiences.
Critical Thinker	• Recognise how to identify, distinguish, and appropriately reference reliable information from a variety of sources. • Understand how to appropriately use AI and to build the relevant skills needed.
Confident Communicator	• Appreciate the subtleties of language and communication styles to be able to adapt it to different academic, business and management contexts. • Be aware of different writing structure for presentations, essays, reports and blogs.
Globally Engaged	• Embrace the opportunity to work with students from across the world to develop your own understanding of other cultures and business practices. • Engage with literature from a wide variety of countries, cultures, and perspectives.

Traits that support academic success include: *Questioning, attention to detail, structured, methodical* and *self-direction*

SDG TABLES

For SDGs, see https://www.un.org/sustainabledevelopment/sustainable-development-goals/ (accessed September 29, 2025).

Table A.14 Chapter 1 – World of Business

Relevant UN SDGs	Applications in the World of Business
SDG 1: No Poverty	• Ethical business practices and fair wages help lift people out of poverty.
SDG 2: Zero Hunger	• Sustainable businesses could improve food security (e.g., **Corporate Social Responsibility [CSR]** programs funding regenerative farming).
SDG 4: Quality Education	• Companies investing in employee training and community education contribute to lifelong learning.

(Continued)

Table A.14 (Continued)

Relevant UN SDGs	Applications in the World of Business
SDG 5: Gender Equality	• Implementing policies to ensure equal pay and opportunities for all genders. • Promoting women in leadership roles within business organisations. • Creating inclusive workplace environments that support diversity and gender equality.
SDG 7: Affordable and Clean Energy	• Businesses investing in renewable energy support access to sustainable power (e.g., solar energy startups in rural communities).
SDG 8: Decent Work and Economic Growth	• Developing sustainable business practices that create jobs and boost economic growth. • Investing in employee training and development programmes. • Supporting fair trade and ethical labour practices.
SDG 9: Industry, Innovation and Infrastructure	• Investing in research and development to drive innovation. • Building resilient infrastructure to support business operations. • Collaborating with other organisations to foster technological advancements.
SDG 12: Responsible Consumption and Production	• Implementing sustainable supply chain practices. • Reducing waste and promoting recycling within business operations. • Encouraging responsible consumer behaviour through education and awareness campaigns.
SDG 13: Climate Action	• Adopting eco-friendly practices to reduce carbon footprint. • Investing in renewable energy sources for business operations. • Supporting initiatives to combat climate change and its impacts.
SDG 16: Peace, Justice, and Strong Institutions	• Ethical governance and anti-corruption measures build fairer economies.
SDG 17: Partnerships for the Goals	• Forming strategic partnerships to achieve sustainable development goals. • Collaborating with governments, NGOs, and other businesses to drive positive change. • Sharing knowledge and resources to support global sustainability efforts.

Table A.15 Chapter 2 – Strategic Management

Relevant UN SDGs	Applications in Strategic Management
SDG 1: No Poverty	• Providing economic benefits to countries to help address poverty.
SDG 4: Quality Education	• Investing in education and training to build a skilled workforce.
SDG 5: Gender Equality	• Reducing inequality by fostering inclusive policies and practices.
SDG 8: Decent Work and Economic Growth	• Developing strategies to create sustainable business models. • Implementing workforce planning and talent management. • Integrating ethical labour practices to ensure fair treatment of employees.

Relevant UN SDGs	Applications in Strategic Management
SDG 9: Industry, Innovation and Infrastructure	• Formulating innovation strategies to stay competitive and drive business growth. • Investing in infrastructure development. • Collaborating with industry partners.
SDG 10: Reduced Inequalities	• Promoting social and economic inclusion through fair policies.
SDG 12: Responsible Consumption and Production	• Sustainable supply chain strategies to minimise environmental impact. • Implementing waste reduction and recycling initiatives. • Educating stakeholders on responsible consumption.
SDG 13: Climate Action	• Integrating climate action into corporate strategy. • Investing in renewable energy solutions as part of strategic initiatives. • Developing risk management strategies to address climate change impacts.
SDG 16: Peace, Justice, and Strong Institutions	• Promoting ethical management and leadership through transparent governance and social justice.
SDG 17: Partnerships for the Goals	• Forming strategic alliances. • Collaborating with governments, NGOs, and other businesses. • Sharing knowledge and resources.

Table A.16 Chapter 3 - Organisational Behaviour

Relevant UN SDGs	Applications in Organisational Behaviour
SDG 3: Good Health and Well-being	• Promoting employee well-being through health and wellness programmes, including mental health support. • Encouraging work-life balance.
SDG 5: Gender Equality	• Developing policies to ensure gender equality and prevent discrimination. • Promoting diversity and inclusion in leadership roles. • Creating a supportive environment through training and awareness programmes.
SDG 8: Decent Work and Economic Growth	• Fostering an organisational culture that supports employee growth and development. • Implementing fair labour practices. • Encouraging continuous learning and professional development opportunities.
SDG 9: Industry, Innovation and Infrastructure	• Encouraging a culture of innovation and creativity. • Supporting infrastructure improvements that enhance workplace efficiency. • Encouraging collaboration and knowledge sharing to drive innovation.
SDG 10: Reduced Inequalities	• Implementing policies to promote equality within the workplace. • Fostering an inclusive organisational culture. • Providing equal opportunities for all employees.
SDG 16: Peace, Justice and Strong Institutions	• Promoting ethical behaviour and integrity. • Implementing conflict resolution programmes. • Ensuring transparency and accountability.

Table A.17 Chapter 4 - Leadership

Relevant UN SDGs	Applications in Leadership
SDG 4: Quality Education	• Promoting a culture of lifelong learning within the organisation. • Supporting educational programmes and partnerships to enhance skills and knowledge.
SDG 5: Gender Equality	• Championing gender equality and diversity in leadership roles. • Implementing policies to ensure equal opportunities for all genders. • Leading by example.
SDG 8: Decent Work and Economic Growth	• Driving strategies that promote sustainable economic growth and job creation. • Leading efforts to ensure fair and decent working conditions. • Encouraging innovation and entrepreneurship within the organisation.
SDG 10: Reduced Inequalities	• Advocating for policies that reduce inequalities and promote inclusion at all levels of the organisation. • Ensuring equitable treatment and opportunities for all employees.
SDG 12: Responsible Consumption and Production	• Responsible organisational practices that consider environmental and social impacts. • Promoting responsible consumption and production within the organisation. • Encouraging employees to adopt environmentally friendly practices.
SDG 16: Peace, Justice and Strong Institutions	• Upholding ethical standards and promoting integrity in leadership and decision-making. • Ensure transparency and accountability within the organisation. • Promoting a culture of peace and conflict resolution.
SDG 17: Partnerships for the Goals	• Building strategic partnerships to achieve shared sustainability goals. • Collaborative efforts with other organisations, governments and NGOs to showcase best practice in leadership. • Sharing knowledge and resources to support global leadership initiatives.

Table A.18 Chapter 5 - Human Resource Management

Relevant UN SDGs	Applications in Human Resource Management
SDG 3: Good Health and Well-being	• Modern HRM functions implementing comprehensive health and wellness programmes for employees, including mental health support and resources. • Promoting work-life balance through flexible working arrangements.
SDG 4: Quality Education	• Offering continuous learning and development opportunities for employees. • Supporting educational initiatives and training programmes. • Encouraging a culture of lifelong learning.

Relevant UN SDGs	Applications in Human Resource Management
SDG 5: Gender Equality	• Ensuring equal opportunities and pay for all genders through HRM policies in recruitment, promotion and compensation practices. • Promoting diversity and inclusion in recruitment. • Creating a supportive environment through training and awareness programmes.
SDG 8: Decent Work and Economic Growth	• Developing fair labour practices and ensuring decent working conditions. • Implementing workforce planning and talent management strategies. • Encouraging innovation and entrepreneurship.
SDG 10: Reduced Inequalities	• Implementing policies to promote equality and reduce disparities within the workplace. • Fostering an inclusive organisational culture that provides equal opportunities for all employees.
SDG 16: Peace, Justice and Strong Institutions	• Promoting ethical behaviour and integrity. • Implementing conflict resolution and mediation programmes. • Ensuring transparency and accountability in HRM practices.

Table A.19 Chapter 6 – Marketing

Relevant UN SDGs	Applications in Marketing
SDG 3: Good Health and Well-being	• Promoting health and wellness products and creating awareness about mental health in marketing messages. • Promoting responsible advertising, e.g. in industries like healthcare and food. • Partnering with health organisations to support community wellness initiatives.
SDG 4: Quality Education	• Supporting educational initiatives through marketing sponsorships and partnerships. • Collaborating with educational institutions.
SDG 5: Gender Equality	• Challenging gender stereotypes and highlighting diversity in marketing campaigns. • Promoting products and services that empower women. • Ensuring inclusive representation in marketing materials and advertisements.
SDG 8: Decent Work and Economic Growth	• Marketing products and services that contribute to economic growth and job creation. • Promoting fair trade and ethical business practices. • Campaigns that highlight the company's commitment to decent work conditions.
SDG 9: Industry, Innovation and Infrastructure	• Showcasing digital and innovative products and services in marketing campaigns. • Promoting the company's investment in infrastructure and technological advancements. • Collaborating with industry partners to enhance marketing efforts and reach.

(Continued)

Table A.19 (Continued)

Relevant UN SDGs	Applications in Marketing
SDG 10: Reduced Inequalities	• Promoting products and services that support social inclusion and reduce inequalities. • Highlighting the company's efforts to reduce disparities in marketing messages. • Ensuring diverse and inclusive representation in all marketing materials.

Table A.20 Chapter 7 - Operations and Supply Chain Management

Relevant UN SDGs	Applications in Operations and Supply Chain Management
SDG 8: Decent Work and Economic Growth	• Ensuring fair labour practices and decent working conditions throughout the supply chain. • Implementing efficient operations to support sustainable economic growth. • Investing in employee training and development.
SDG 9: Industry, Innovation and Infrastructure	• Adopting innovative technologies and new manufacturing procedures to improve operational efficiency and encourage reuse of resources where possible. • Developing resilient infrastructure to support robust supply chain operations. • Collaborating with industry partners to drive innovation in supply chain management.
SDG 11: Sustainable Cities and Communities	• Optimising logistics and transportation to reduce environmental impact in urban areas. • Supporting local suppliers and businesses to strengthen community economies. • Implementing sustainable practices in operations to contribute to the development of sustainable cities.
SDG 12: Responsible Consumption and Production	• Designing sustainable supply chain strategies to minimise waste and environmental impact. • Implementing circular economy principles in production and operations. • Promoting responsible consumption through transparent and ethical supply chain practices.
SDG 13: Climate Action	• Reducing carbon footprint in operations and supply chain activities. • Investing in renewable energy sources for production and logistics. • Developing strategies to mitigate the impact of climate change on supply chain resilience.
SDG 17: Partnerships for the Goals	• Forming strategic partnerships to enhance supply chain effectiveness. • Collaborating with governments, NGOs, and other businesses to achieve shared sustainability goals. • Sharing best practices and resources.

Table A.21 Chapter 8 - Entrepreneurship and Innovation

Relevant UN SDGs	Applications in Entrepreneurship and Innovation
SDG 5: Gender Equality	• Promoting gender equality in entrepreneurial ventures and leadership roles. • Supporting women entrepreneurs through mentorship and funding opportunities. • Creating inclusive business environments.
SDG 7: Affordable and Clean Energy	• Developing innovative solutions for affordable and clean energy. • Investing in renewable energy startups and technologies. • Promoting sustainable energy practices in entrepreneurial ventures.
SDG 8: Decent Work and Economic Growth	• Creating job opportunities and sustainable economic growth through innovative business models. • Encouraging fair labour practices and decent working conditions in new ventures.
SDG 11: Sustainable Cities and Communities	• Developing innovative solutions to address urban challenges. • Supporting local businesses and startups that contribute to sustainable communities. • Promoting sustainable practices in urban development and entrepreneurship, including in housing, mobility and infrastructure.
SDG 12: Responsible Consumption and Production	• Innovating sustainable products and services that minimise environmental impact and promote responsible consumption. • Implementing circular economy principles in entrepreneurial ventures.
SDG 17: Partnerships for the Goals	• Forming strategic partnerships to drive innovation and sustainability. • Collaborating with other entrepreneurs, businesses, and organisations to achieve shared goals. • Sharing knowledge and resources to support global sustainability initiatives.

Table A.22 Chapter 9 - Accounting

Relevant UN SDGs	Applications in Accounting
SDG 4: Quality Education	• Providing continuous professional development and training for accountants. • Supporting educational initiatives and scholarships in the field of accounting. • Promoting financial literacy and education within the community.
SDG 5: Gender Equality	• Ensuring equal opportunities and pay within accounting firms. • Promoting diversity and inclusion in hiring and career advancement. • Implementing policies to prevent discrimination in the workplace.

(Continued)

Table A.22 (Continued)

Relevant UN SDGs	Applications in Accounting
SDG 8: Decent Work and Economic Growth	• Supporting fair labour practices and decent working conditions in accounting firms. • Contributing to economic growth through accurate financial reporting and advisory services. • Encouraging ethical practices and integrity in financial management.
SDG 9: Industry, Innovation and Infrastructure	• Adopting innovative accounting technologies and practices. • Supporting infrastructure development through accurate financial planning and reporting. • Collaborating with industry partners to drive innovation in accounting practices.
SDG 12: Responsible Consumption and Production	• Implementing sustainable accounting practices to minimise environmental impact. • Promoting transparency and accountability in financial reporting. • Encouraging responsible consumption through financial advisory services.
SDG 13: Climate Action	• Integrating climate-related financial disclosures into accounting practices. • Supporting businesses in measuring and reporting their carbon footprint. • Advising clients on sustainable financial practices to mitigate climate change impacts.
SDG 16: Peace, Justice and Strong Institutions	• Promoting ethical behaviour and integrity in accounting practices. • Ensuring transparency and accountability in financial reporting. • Supporting strong institutions through accurate and reliable financial management.

Table A.23 Chapter 10 - Finance

Relevant UN SDGs	Applications in Finance
SDG 1: No Poverty	• Developing financial products and services that support poverty alleviation. • Providing microfinance and loans to underserved communities. • Supporting initiatives that promote economic inclusion and financial literacy.
SDG 4: Quality Education	• Investing in educational programmes and scholarships. • Promoting financial literacy and education within the community. • Supporting continuous professional development for finance professionals.
SDG 7: Affordable and Clean Energy	• Financing renewable energy projects and technologies. • Developing sustainable investment products. • Supporting businesses in transitioning to clean energy solutions.
SDG 8: Decent Work and Economic Growth	• Promoting sustainable economic growth through responsible investment. • Supporting inclusion, job creation and fair labour practices through financial services. • Encouraging ethical practices and integrity in financial management.

Relevant UN SDGs	Applications in Finance
SDG 9: Industry, Innovation and Infrastructure	• Investing in infrastructure development and innovation projects and supporting technological advancements. • Collaborating with industry partners to drive innovation in financial services.
SDG 10: Reduced Inequalities	• Developing financial products that promote social inclusion and reduce inequalities. • Ensuring equitable access to financial services for all communities. • Supporting policies and initiatives that address economic disparities.
SDG 11: Sustainable Cities and Communities	• Financing urban development projects that promote sustainability and developing products, such as municipal bonds, to fund public infrastructure. • Supporting local businesses and community initiatives through investment. • Promoting sustainable practices in urban planning and development.
SDG 12: Responsible Consumption and Production	• Developing sustainable investment strategies that minimise environmental impact. • Promoting transparency and accountability in financial reporting. • Encouraging responsible consumption through financial advisory services.
SDG 13: Climate Action	• Integrating climate-related risk and financial disclosures into investment practices. • Supporting businesses in measuring and reporting their carbon footprint. • Advising clients on sustainable financial practices to mitigate climate change impacts.

Table A.24 Chapter 11 – Economics

Relevant UN SDGs	Applications in Economics
SDG 1: No Poverty	• Analysing economic policies that aim to reduce poverty and promote economic inclusion. • Evaluating the impact of social welfare programmes on poverty alleviation. • Studying the economic effects of microfinance and financial inclusion initiatives.
SDG 3: Good Health and Well-being	• Assessing the economic impact of healthcare policies and programmes. • Analysing the relationship between economic growth and public health outcomes. • Evaluating the cost-effectiveness of health interventions and their economic benefits, including markets that contain negative externalities (e.g. unhealthy foods).
SDG 9: Industry, Innovation and Infrastructure	• Studying the role of innovation and infrastructure development in economic growth, and how these can be applied in markets lacking competitive pressures. • Analysing the economic impact of technological advancements and industrial policies. • Evaluating the effectiveness of public and private investments in infrastructure.

(Continued)

Table A.24 (Continued)

Relevant UN SDGs	Applications in Economics
SDG 10: Reduced Inequalities	• Examining economic policies that address income inequality and promote social equity. • Analysing the impact of taxation and redistribution policies on reducing disparities. • Studying the economic effects of inclusive growth strategies and social protection measures.
SDG 12: Responsible Consumption and Production	• Evaluating the economic implications of sustainable consumption and production practices, accounting for environmental and social costs. • Analysing the impact of environmental regulations on economic performance. • Studying the economic benefits of adopting circular economy principles.

Table A.25 Chapter 12 - AI, Digital Technology, and Transformation

Relevant UN SDGs	Applications in AI, Digital Technology, and Transformation
SDG 2: Zero Hunger	• Optimising agricultural production and reducing food waste by collecting data on food consumption, production, and supply chains. • Using digital technology to improve supply chain management in the food industry. • Implementing data analytics to enhance food security and distribution.
SDG 3: Good Health and Well-being	• Utilising AI for predictive analytics in healthcare to improve patient outcomes. • Implementing personalised digital health solutions to enhance access to medical services and empowerment of individuals. • Using technology to monitor and promote public health initiatives.
SDG 4: Quality Education	• Leveraging AI and digital tools to personalise learning experiences. • Implementing online education platforms to increase access to quality education. • Using technology to support continuous learning and professional development.
SDG 9: Industry, Innovation and Infrastructure	• Driving innovation through AI and digital transformation in various industries. • Developing smart infrastructure solutions using digital technology. • Collaborating with industry partners to advance technological innovation.
SDG 11: Sustainable Cities and Communities	• Implementing smart city solutions to improve urban living conditions. • Using AI and digital technology to optimise urban planning and development. • Enhancing community resilience through digital transformation initiatives.

Relevant UN SDGs	Applications in AI, Digital Technology, and Transformation
SDG 12: Responsible Consumption and Production	• Using AI to optimise resource utilisation and reduce waste in production processes. • Implementing digital solutions to promote sustainable consumption patterns. • Leveraging technology to enhance transparency and accountability in supply chains, but also in the supply and storage of data and computing services.
SDG 13: Climate Action	• Mitigating environmental impact of data-intensive technologies. • Using digital technology to support renewable energy initiatives and to mitigate climate change impacts. • Implementing data analytics to enhance climate resilience and adaptation strategies.

Table A.26 Chapter 13 - Academic Skills

Relevant UN SDGs	Applications for Academic Skills
SDG 4: Quality Education	• Enhancing skills that can be taken beyond the educational sector into the world of work. • Encouraging a consideration of the cultural aspects and benefits of learning together. • Using high quality, reliable academic sources to inform writing and present critical analyses.
SDG 8: Decent Work and Economic Growth	• Building transferrable skills for the workplace. • Supporting employability through understanding team and group dynamics. • Developing effective business communication skills.
SDG 10: Reduced Inequalities	• Developing cultural awareness. • Promoting intercultural collaboration. • Engaging with literature from global perspectives.

EDI TABLES

Table A.27 Chapter 1 - World of Business

Relevant EDI Values	Applications in the World of Business
Discovery	Exploring how business plays a role in shaping equitable and inclusive societies.
Respect	Encouraging ethical business leadership and fair trade practices.
Excellence	Promoting leaders with diverse backgrounds and innovative business models.
Inclusion	Ensuring equal opportunities for diverse entrepreneurs and employees.
Community	Recognising business as contributors to economic and social well-being and flourishment.

Table A.28 Chapter 2 - Strategic Management

Relevant EDI Values	Applications in Strategic Management
Discovery	Identifying strategic approaches to fostering inclusive organisations.
Respect	Embedding fairness and ethical leadership policies and practices in corporate strategy.
Excellence	Adopting diverse perspectives to ensure business decision-making is competitive and inclusive, and is endorsed by key stakeholders.
Inclusion	Developing inclusive strategies for leadership and talent retention and progression.
Community	Creating strategies that align with societal values and community growth.

Table A.29 Chapter 3 - Organisational Behaviour

Relevant EDI Values	Applications in Organisational Behaviour
Discovery	Understanding how inclusive workplaces drive organisational success.
Respect	Promoting respect and dignity within workplace interactions.
Excellence	Encouraging high-performance cultures that value diversity.
Inclusion	Removing barriers to inclusiveness in workplace strategy and activities.
Community	Fostering a culture of respect, belonging, and support within organisations.

Table A.30 Chapter 4 - Leadership

Relevant EDI Values	Applications in Leadership
Discovery	Encouraging diverse leadership styles and approaches.
Respect	Ensuring fairness and ethical responsibility in leadership practices.
Excellence	Promoting diverse leadership teams to improve decision-making facilitating productivity and sustainable growth.
Inclusion	Providing pathways for underrepresented groups in leadership.
Community	Strengthening organisational cultures that champion inclusivity.

Table A.31 Chapter 5 - Human Resource Management

Relevant EDI Values	Applications in HRM
Discovery	Exploring HR's role in developing equitable workplaces.
Respect	Implementing fair and unbiased hiring and promotion policies.
Excellence	Ensuring diverse talent pipelines and leadership development.
Inclusion	Creating opportunities for employees of all backgrounds.
Community	Building collaborative and inclusive work environments in which every individual can flourish.

Table A.32 Chapter 6 - Marketing

Relevant EDI Values	Applications in Marketing
Discovery	Challenging stereotypes through inclusive marketing strategies.
Respect	Ensuring ethical marketing practices and consumer representation.
Excellence	Encouraging development of marketing campaigns that celebrate diversity.
Inclusion	Ensuring fair representation across media and advertising.
Community	Using marketing to promote positive social values and inclusion.

Table A.33 Chapter 7 - Operations and Supply Chain Management

Relevant EDI Values	Applications in Operations and Supply Chain Management
Discovery	Recognising the role of ethical supply chains in global business.
Respect	Ensuring fair treatment of workers throughout supply networks.
Excellence	Promoting sustainable and inclusive sourcing practices for business competitiveness and growth.
Inclusion	Encouraging and rewarding supplier diversity and ethical labour practices.
Community	Strengthening global partnerships through societal and stakeholder engagement.

Table A.34 Chapter 8 - Entrepreneurship and Innovation

Relevant EDI Values	Applications in Entrepreneurship and Innovation
Discovery	Encouraging diverse entrepreneurial initiatives and ecosystems.
Respect	Supporting inclusive innovation and business models.
Excellence	Promoting equitable access to business funding and mentorship for startups for growth and flourishment.
Inclusion	Expanding opportunities for entrepreneurs from underrepresented and underprivileged backgrounds.
Community	Encouraging and supporting social enterprises that drive positive change.

Table A.35 Chapter 9 - Accounting

Relevant EDI Values	Applications in Accounting
Discovery	Ensuring transparency and equity in financial reporting.
Respect	Promoting fairness and ethical decision-making in accounting practices.
Excellence	Addressing economic disparities through emphasis on integrated reporting practices.
Inclusion	Encouraging financial accessibility and equity by addressing distribution gaps in financial decisions.
Community	Supporting equitable resource allocation across sectors.

Table A.36 Chapter 10 - Finance

Relevant EDI Values	Applications in Finance
Discovery	Recognising finance as a tool for inclusion and social change.
Respect	Ensuring fair access to financial products and services.
Excellence	Promoting responsible and inclusive investment strategies.
Inclusion	Reducing financial barriers for disadvantaged communities.
Community	Supporting economic mobility through financial literacy.

Table A.37 Chapter 11 - Economics

Relevant EDI Values	Applications in Economics
Discovery	Understanding the impact of economic policies on social equity.
Respect	Addressing income inequality through inclusive economic models.
Excellence	Promoting fair and diverse economic participation.
Inclusion	Ensuring equitable access to economic opportunities.
Community	Strengthening policies that support economic fairness.

Table A.38 Chapter 12 - AI, Digital Technology, and Transformation

Relevant EDI Values	Applications in AI, Digital Technology, and Transformation
Discovery	Exploring the role of AI in creating inclusive opportunities.
Respect	Addressing bias towards and ethical concerns in information and technology.
Excellence	Ensuring digital transformation addresses diversity and inclusion in its policy scope.
Inclusion	Mitigating bias in AI and algorithmic decision-making.
Community	Expanding digital and information accessibility to all communities.

Table A.39 Chapter 13 - Academic Skills

Relevant EDI Values	Applications in Academic Skills
Discovery	Discovering high quality resources from globally and culturally diverse sources through the application of effective search strategies.
Respect	Recognising and respecting the cultural diversity of others.
Excellence	Developing strategies, behaviours and professional skills to excel in academic study and future careers.
Inclusion	Working collaboratively with people from different nationalities and backgrounds.
Community	Building effective communication strategies to support effective groupwork activities and disseminate information to and within diverse audiences.

INDEX

Page numbers followed by 'f' indicate figures; those followed by 't' indicate tables.